The Welfare State

since 1945

Related titles from Palgrave Macmillan

Derek Fraser, *The Evolution of the British Welfare State*, 3rd edition
David Gladstone, *The Twentieth-Century Welfare State*
Bernard Harris, *The Origins of the British Welfare State: Society, State and Social Welfare in England and Wales, 1800–1945*
Robert Page and Richard Silburn (eds), *British Social Welfare in the Twentieth Century*

The Welfare State in Britain since 1945

Third Edition

RODNEY LOWE

First published 2005 by
PALGRAVE MACMILLAN
Houndmills, Basingstoke, Hampshire RG21 6XS and
175 Fifth Avenue, New York, N.Y. 10010
Companies and representatives throughout the world

PALGRAVE MACMILLAN is the global academic imprint of the Palgrave
Macmillan division of St. Martin's Press, LLC and of Palgrave Macmillan Ltd. Macmillan®
is a registered trademark in the United States, United Kingdom and other countries.
Palgrave is a registered trademark in the European Union and other countries.

ISBN–13: 978–14039–1192–6 hardback
ISBN–10: 14039–1192–4 hardback
ISBN–13: 978–14039–1193–3 paperback
ISBN–10: 14039–1193–2 paperback

This book is printed on paper suitable for recycling and made from fully
managed and sustained forest sources.

A catalogue record for this book is available from the British Library.

A catalog record for this book is available from the Library of Congress.

Library of Congress catalogue CardNumber – 2004051336

10   9   8   7   6   5   4   3   2
14   13   12   11   10   09   08   07   06

Printed in China

Contents

Illustrations, Figures and Tables

Preface to the Third Edition

The first edition of this book was published in 1993 to coincide with the fiftieth anniversary of what many regard to be the 'blueprint' for the British welfare state, the Beveridge Report. It was the first full history of the postwar welfare state. There are now many others, of which two are exceptional. Howard Glennerster's *British Social Policy since 1945* demonstrates the power of a social scientist to reduce complex issues to simple, but far from simplistic, analysis. Nicholas Timmins's *The Five Giants* represents journalist skill and flair at its very best, particularly in relation to the period after the election of Mrs Thatcher in 1979. In the past, consumers of welfare were reputedly denied effective choice and an objective of recent reform has been to empower them through the provision of a range of competing services. Readers and students of welfare history used to find themselves in a similar situation but now have a 'market' opportunity of which – so publishers, authors and not least their bank managers hope – they will take full advantage.

The second edition coincided with the fiftieth anniversary of the creation of the welfare state itself as represented by the 'Appointed Day' of 5 July 1948, when four major services including the National Health Service, National Insurance and National Assistance were implemented. Its principal purpose was to acknowledge regional variations within the United Kingdom, which had inexcusably been overlooked in earlier analyses, and to strengthen international comparisons. The United Kingdom, particularly in relation to social policy, has always been more of a federal than a 'unitary' state, as conventionally depicted. The election of a separate Scottish Parliament and Welsh Assembly in 1999 underlined this point, and the exercise of their devolved powers has led to further variations particularly in relation to education and long-term care for the elderly. Comparative research is also essential to appreciate the common pressures which all welfare states have experienced and the unique response of each. Those who know only one country, as it has rightly been said, know none. In 1990 such research entered a particularly exciting and constructive phase with the publication of Gosta Esping-Andersen's *The Three Worlds of Welfare Capitalism*. It has since provided a common framework for a wide range of pioneering work, with even its acknowledged flaws helping to identify and clarify new issues. Somewhat ironically, this greater sensitivity to the variety of welfare states has coincided with 'globalization', with its perceived pressure on all countries to achieve greater uniformity at an ever lower level of welfare provision – a 'race to the bottom'.

This third edition can take stock of these debates, written as it is some 25 years after the election of Mrs Thatcher's first government and towards the end of New Labour's second term in office. Has there been a 'race to the bottom' or has the welfare state survived first the oil shocks of the 1970s and now the pressures of globalization? If it has survived, has it fundamentally changed? Is New Labour's record, given its unprecedented parliamentary majority and thus freedom to legislate, evidence that a new Thatcherite consensus has replaced the old social democratic one? Is this an experience unique to Britain and, if not, did Britain pioneer the change or has it merely followed an international trend – pioneered, as in so many other areas, by the USA? Sufficient time has now elapsed since the original crises of the 1970s that analyses have been written not just by participants but by those who can provide a more dispassionate overview. It was, after all, not just the welfare state but the welfare state industry – all those experts and academics who write and advise on policy – which have suffered a series of crises. The fundamental assumptions upon which they worked have been challenged. In the British context, one of the most positive responses of an academic discipline in crisis has been the publication of the various editions of *The Student's Companion to Social Policy*, edited by P. Alcock, A. Erskine and M. May, under the sponsorship of the Social Policy Association. Here readers may find brief introductions to all the topics with which welfare policy is now concerned, written by leading experts in their field.

This book, aimed at both historians and social scientists (and hopefully not falling between two stools), is not designed to compete with, but to complement such overviews. Academic analysis of welfare policy tends to be a modern tower of Babel in which each policy area, let alone the major disciplines of history, economic and social history, politics, social policy and economics, has not only its own assumptions but also its own language. Interdisciplinary study, however, is essential. Historians can but benefit from the insights of those focused on current welfare policy. A superb example of such interdisciplinary work, and international cooperation, is the examination by scholars in the five Scandinavian countries of Denmark, Finland, Iceland, Norway and Sweden of the 'Nordic model' of welfare, published in the *Scandinavian Journal of History* (26) 2001. True to their professional principles (and some social scientists might unfairly argue pedantry) each concluded that it was a 'model with five exceptions'; but the exercise identified what was common to and unique in each country, thereby enriching an understanding of the history of far more than just welfare policy in each country. Similarly, social scientists are acknowledging that a fuller knowledge of the evolution of each welfare state is crucial to an understanding of its unique nature and likely development – even if their bibliographies sometimes bear testimony to the successful containment of their curiosity. Exaggerated claims for Britain's 'classic' welfare state made by those involved in contemporary controversies, for example, are not the best grounds for identifying discontinuities in policy and the replacement of one consensus by another.

Between editions, I have sought to make some contribution to the narrowing of interdisciplinary divisions. There are now four guides to official records held at the National Archives (formerly known as the Public Record Office) on economic and social policy in Britain between the Second World War and 1964. The one on which a deepening understanding of the classic welfare state can best be based is arguably the volume prepared with Jane Lewis and co-authored with Paul Bridgen: *Welfare Policy under the Conservatives, 1951–1964* (PRO Publications, 1998). With Margaret Jones I have also co-edited a documentary history of the welfare state, which provides a natural companion to this book: *From Beveridge to Blair: the first fifty years of Britain's welfare state, 1948–98* (Manchester University Press, 2002). In undertaking this and other related work, I have received generous financial assistance from the Arts and Humanities Research Board, the British Academy, the Economic and Social Research Council, the Leverhulme Trust and the University of Bristol. I am also extremely grateful for the hospitality extended to me by the Universities of Oslo and Stockholm, the Urban Research Programme at the Australian National University and St John's College, Oxford. I am equally grateful to Martin Powell and John Stewart for sharing their respective expertise on New Labour and devolution. Finally, I should like to acknowledge the help in the selection of illustrations of the Centre for the Study of Cartoons and Caricature at the University of Kent at Canterbury. Its incomparable database can be accessed at URL: http://library.ukc.ac.uk/cartoons/

Less happily, I have since the last edition come to know the British health and hospice service rather more fully than I would have liked owing to the terminal illness of my partner, Rebecca Rutherford. During this time, I was greatly helped by the understanding of my colleagues at the Cabinet Office (where, no doubt to the relief of many, I work solely as a historian – although I should add all the views expressed in this book are strictly my own and do not benefit from access to any privileged information). I have also benefited greatly from the support of my family, in particular Gini (now in the front-line of the NHS herself as a midwife) and Alex, as well as the intellectual stimulus and companionship provided by Margaret Jones, Hugh Pemberton, Peter King, Jane Lewis, John Jenkins and Heather Grant. They will fully understand why this book is dedicated to Rebecca, with all my love.

Rodney Lowe

Introduction

The welfare state in crisis: 1975–76

In the mid-1970s the welfare state in Britain was, or at least was widely considered to be, in crisis. With unemployment standing at just under one million, the Labour government in its budget of April 1975 chose not to reflate the economy. It thus became the first postwar government, other than during a temporary balance of payments or sterling crisis, to abandon the goal of 'full' employment. The reasons for this decision were made explicit in the following year, after a serious sterling crisis had obliged the government to seek a loan from the International Monetary Fund (IMF). As Prime Minister James Callaghan told his Party conference in September 1976:

> We used to think that you could just spend your way out of a recession and increase employment by cutting taxes and boosting government spending. I tell you in all candour, that option no longer exists, and that in so far as it ever did exist, it worked by injecting inflation into the economy. And each time that happened the average level of unemployment has risen. Higher inflation was followed by higher unemployment. That is the history of the last twenty years.[1]

One of the original props of the welfare state – the confidence of Keynesian economists that governments could *and should* guarantee a high level of employment – was thereby kicked away.

This revolution in economic thinking and policy had an immediate impact on social policy. Cash limits were imposed in all areas of public expenditure and a projected expansion of the social services was thereby checked. More fundamentally, it led to the abandonment of one of the major assumptions underlying the 1942 Beveridge Report, which has been conventionally regarded as the principal blueprint of the welfare state. Beveridge's proposed system of social security was dependent on the maintenance of a high level of employment. Administratively, how else could traditional fears about the consequences of state welfare, such as the undermining of the will to work, be laid to rest if claimants could not be offered jobs to test their sincerity? Socially, was security of income alone – without the positive benefits of productive employment – an 'adequate provision for human happiness'? Economically, would not the cost of social security become 'insupportable' were mass unemployment simultaneously to increase expenditure on unemployment benefit and (by lowering economic activity) reduce government revenue?[2] Increased unemployment, in short, threw into jeopardy the whole nature and practicality of Beveridge's proposals.

The mid-1970s saw the destruction of a further prop of the welfare state which had been made explicit in another of its blueprints, the 1944 *Employment Policy* white paper. This paper had argued that the maintenance of employment was ultimately dependent not on government action alone but on the 'understanding and support of the community as a whole – and especially on the efforts of employers and workers in industry'.[3] The understanding and support of employers, given their conflicting interests and organization, had admittedly remained ambivalent but amongst trade unionists and the public it grew strong. This began to change with the apparent inability of government to manage the economy and thus satisfy increasing expectations of welfare. In 1973 the Conservative government had been branded as managerially incompetent following its clash with the miners and the resulting three-day week. Largely in consequence, the Labour Party won two elections in 1974 on the ground that it could maintain industrial cooperation. Its main weapon was the 'social contract', whereby trade unions agreed not to use the market power they derived from full employment (which by increasing wages and hence costs might eventually undermine Britain's international competitiveness and thereby create unemployment) on condition that an equivalent distribution of wealth and income would be provided by government through the social services and taxation. However, the imposition of cash limits on the social services combined with an (albeit voluntary) prices and incomes policy convinced the trade unionists, particularly in the public sector, that the contract was unlikely to be honoured. Consequently they used their market power to demand wage increases of up to 35 per cent. The resulting 'winter of discontent' of 1978–9, in which rubbish piled up high in the streets and in certain instances the dead could not be buried, led to a public backlash. This was the direct prelude to the election of a Conservative government in May 1979. The public sector unions, as one incensed insider noted, effectively elected Margaret Thatcher.[4]

Margaret Thatcher had become the leader of the Conservative Party in February 1975, just before Labour's tacit abandonment of 'full' employment, and represented a major break in postwar political assumptions and attitudes. As she readily admitted, she felt none of the 'bourgeois guilt' for the mass unemployment of the interwar years, which had so coloured the planning and implementation of the welfare state during and after the Second World War.[5] Instead her philosophy and policies were shaped by her perception of Britain's declining economy and rising ungovernability since 1945. In her view, and that of the increasing section of the electorate to whom she appealed, the policies of *full employment, expanding social services* and *corporatism* which underlay the postwar welfare state had failed. They, and the attitudes which validated them, urgently needed to be replaced. As she informed *The Times* on 19 January 1984, she wanted her government to be remembered as the one 'which decisively broke with the debilitating consensus of a paternalistic government and a dependent people; which rejected the notion that the State is all powerful and the citizen is merely its beneficiary; which shattered the illusion that Government could somehow substitute for individual performance'.

This crisis in the welfare state was not unique to Britain but was experienced, to varying degrees of intensity, in all Western industrialized countries. The world recession, exacerbated by the quadrupling of the price of oil in 1973–4, checked the economic growth which each country had enjoyed since 1945 and upon which each had depended for the increased revenue necessary to finance the expanding welfare services its electorate demanded. With projected revenue falling short of projected expenditure a 'fiscal crisis' occurred. This led commentators of diametrically opposed political views to reach equally apocalyptic conclusions. On the right, the conviction was that liberal democracies had become ungovernable. As one highly respected financial journalist wrote in a serious academic journal, they were 'likely to pass away within the lifetime of people now adult'.[6] On the left, a rejuvenated body of Marxist analysts heralded the final and inevitable crisis of capitalism. This had last been spotted in 1931 but then, in their opinion, temporarily postponed by war and the implementation of Keynesian economics. Rather more mundanely, the popularity of all social democratic parties was eroded. Even in Sweden, where the SDP had been in government since 1932, it lost power in 1976. Everywhere Keynesian economics and welfare programmes, or at least projected increases in welfare programmes, were either being abandoned or modified.

Crisis? What crisis?[7]

When the dust settled in the 1980s, however, one remarkable fact was as true for Britain as for all other welfare states. Not only had liberal democracy and capitalism survived but social spending in absolute terms, rather than decreasing, had actually continued to rise. This was partly due to technical factors: the changing age structure of the population (with an increasing number of elderly people, in particular, requiring greater expenditure on pensions and institutional care); the increasing burden of unemployment benefits (as predicted by Beveridge); and increases in the relative cost of labour-intensive welfare services which could not match the savings achieved by increased industrial productivity (in the fashionable jargon of the day, 'the relative price effect'). It was also due, however, to the continuing popularity of welfare policy amongst the electorate. Public opinion, so far as it could be divined, may have wanted cuts in public expenditure, but not at the expense of those welfare services from which the majority would benefit directly.[8] Governments, therefore, dared not make significant cuts but confined themselves to eliminating the more obvious cases of waste and checking the projected rise in expenditure.

What did this all signify? Despite the survival of both liberal democracy and capitalism, should the mid-1970s still been seen in Britain, as elsewhere, as a fundamental watershed in the history of postwar welfare provision?

- Had the policy reappraisal, forced on politicians and public alike by the oil shock, fatally exposed the inherent weaknesses of centralized and frequently monopolistic state services? Had the legitimacy of state intervention thereby been destroyed?
- More broadly, had the increasing globalization of the world economy destroyed the essential preconditions for national welfare states? Had national governments any longer the authority or capacity independently to manage their economies and finance social programmes? In particular, given the threatened migration of jobs to countries (particularly in Asia) where different cultural values and alternative forms of welfare resulted in significantly lower social and labour costs, were all developed welfare states engaged in a headlong 'race to the bottom'?
- In short, should the postwar welfare state be seen in Britain – if not necessarily elsewhere – as an aberration? Through a combination of internal and external pressures, had the 1970s heralded a reversion to a balance within the 'mixed economy of welfare' more in keeping with national tradition and culture? Had the dominance of, and thus individual dependence upon, government been halted, with individual well-being being increasingly provided through the market and voluntary organizations?

Alternatively had political rhetoric and academic analysis grossly exaggerated the depth of the crisis facing not only democracy and capitalism but also the welfare state in particular?

- Politically, in the jargon of the time, was 'the right-wing reaction . . . only half successful' with the repudiation of Keynes but not of Beveridge?[9]
- In social policy, was the real crisis only an intellectual one? For traditional adherents of state welfare – both political and academic – fundamental assumptions had been exploded such as the permanence of economic growth, continuing electoral support for income redistribution, and the assured success of programmes aimed at the structural causes of poverty. How were they to be replaced, particularly once news of the death of capitalism had been shown to be somewhat exaggerated?
- Was the welfare state simply to make good market weaknesses – acting as a 'piggy bank' efficiently redistributing an individual's income over their lifetime rather than, like Robin Hood, redistributing it to someone else?[10] Was it more actively to forge a new accommodation between the needs of individuals and the market by providing new skills and ending social exclusion? Alternatively, was the opportunity to be taken to meet minority needs and concerns which had previously been neglected?

- Rather than being dismantled, in other words, was the welfare state restructured and modernized after 1976? Did 1976 represent not a crisis, but the start of a period of necessary, constructive adaptation to changing domestic and international pressures? And, to the extent that it was in the vanguard, can Britain draw as much credit from this adaptation as it did from the initial development of the welfare state in the 1940s?

The structure of the book

The purpose of this book is to answer such questions by examining in depth the period from the establishment of the welfare state in the mid-1940s to its perceived crisis in the mid-1970s and then separately the years since 1976. It is divided into three parts.

Part I.   Unusually perhaps for such a history, Part I provides a brief guide to the competing theories of both the state and of the policy-making process which have been fashionable at various times since 1945. Its purpose is to introduce readers to a wide range of ideas from the disciplines of economics, political science, sociology and policy studies, and thereby to enable them to reach their own independent conclusions. At the same time, it is designed to make explicit the assumptions on which the book itself is based.

The use of theory by historians places them in an unresolvable dilemma. The time spent mastering the intricacies of one theory, let alone a set of theories, is time forfeited in the study of empirical evidence which must be their prime concern. Over the full range of their interests, therefore, no historian can afford to become an expert theorist.[11] Theoretical awareness is, nevertheless, indispensable. By identifying implicit, and often confused, assumptions it can expedite research by clarifying how an argument should be structured and what sort of evidence should be sought. By helping to counterbalance the bias of contemporaries and of extant records, it can help in the task of both empathizing with the past and assessing it critically. By opening horizons and suggesting new relationships, it can give meaning to evidence which might otherwise be overlooked. It can also, in supra-national developments such as the evolution of welfare states, provide the means by which international comparisons can be made.

Part I, therefore, addresses such questions as:

- Why did welfare states develop simultaneously in a wide range of countries after the Second World War and then experience a simultaneous crisis in the mid-1970s?
- Beneath the surface, how similar is each welfare state?
- Why are welfare issues conceptualized in a particular way at a certain time and why are certain policy options politically acceptable at certain times but wholly ignored at others?
- Why does there appear to be so great a gap between the intentions of policy-makers and the actual impact of policy?

Part II. As in earlier editions, albeit to a lesser extent, the heart of the book remains Part II. This provides a historical analysis of the 'classic' welfare state judged not just in hindsight but in the light of contemporary aspirations and constraints.[12] Such an emphasis is important to historians and social scientists alike. For historians, the 'classic' welfare state needs to be analysed both in its own right and, equally importantly, as a means for the better understanding of postwar British politics and society as a whole. For social scientists and policy makers, it retains some power as a model and one to which resort may be had should current policies fail. Moreover, as a recent text has agreed: 'it is important to examine the debates in terms of the understandings of contemporary actors rather than modern interpretations with excessive hindsight. Analyses through a modern lens have sometimes resulted in "whiggish" interpretations that have both overemphasised and underemphasised the significance of the classic welfare state'.[13]

Part II addresses such questions as:

- What exactly did the term 'welfare state' mean when it came into common usage in the 1940s?
- What were its original objectives?
- How did they change over time?
- To what extent were they achieved?
- To what extent was any failure – if failure there was – the result of a lack of political will (individual or collective), unavoidable constraints (of an economic or international nature) or faulty logic and unrealistic assumptions?

The major chapters concentrate on the six traditional areas of welfare policy – employment policy, social security, health, education, housing and the personal social services. They are prefaced by an examination of the economic, social and political context in which policy was formulated and implemented, and succeeded by another analysing the combined impact (if any) of all policies on the distribution of power, income and wealth.

Part III. The final part concentrates on welfare policy after 1976. It follows a similar pattern to Part II although, in order to distinguish the political contribution of the Conservative Party and New Labour to the restructuring of the welfare state, the analysis is divided chronologically. The major questions it addresses are:

- Has the meaning of the term 'welfare state' changed?
- If so, has the classic welfare state in practice been dismantled or just restructured?
- To what extent has any change been an international phenomenon or unique to Britain?
- Is it possible to talk of a new welfare consensus? If so, should it be termed 'Thatcherite' (driven domestically by New Right ideology) or 'Washington' (driven globally by supra-national bodies such as the IMF and the World

Bank)? Given that the postwar 'social democratic' consensus was continually contested, are there similar tensions which shape but do not negate this new consensus?

- If there is no new consensus, what are the major points of ideological and party political dispute?

A feature of each chapter will be the liberal use of 'boxed' material. Boxes contain illustrative material of two types. First, as in Part I, specific examples of welfare policy are used to illustrate – and make less arid – the assumptions and assertions of competing theories. To aid comparison, all the examples are taken from the National Health Service. Then, in later chapters, the boxes provide detailed information about each policy area to support and justify the overview of development presented in the text. Peter Baldwin, amongst others, has demonstrated how the significance of policy often lies in its 'nuts and bolts'.[14] Understanding cannot be achieved without detail, yet detail can also obscure the broader picture and hence understanding. The separation of general analysis from detailed examples is designed to assist a better appreciation of both the broad sweep and the profound richness of welfare policy.

Part

I

Theoretical Perspectives

2

The Nature of the Welfare State

CONTENTS

The purpose of this chapter is to examine the competing definitions and theoretical interpretations of the welfare state before making explicit the assumptions on which this book is based – and thus its unavoidable bias. Such a theoretical approach can become very arid, so to minimize that danger the subject will be approached in two ways. First the welfare state will be defined and the four broad political strategies which have influenced its development in Britain will be examined. Then the more general theories, on which these assumptions and those of the more academic commentators have been based, will be analysed. Each of the latter will be related to the early history of the National Health Service (NHS) to illustrate how, from different theoretical assumptions, totally different and yet equally logical conclusions can be drawn from the same 'facts'.

> The NHS has been chosen to illustrate broader themes for a number of reasons. It has always been one of the most popular services within the British welfare state and the two institutions have often been regarded by the public as synonymous. The political battle which it immediately provoked (over whether charges should be made for dental and ophthalmic care) epitomized the hard managerial and political decisions
>
> →

inseparable from the determination of priorities which, given the scarcity of resources in the real world, have to be made in all areas of welfare. It was also the occasion for a long-term split in the Labour Party which was to have serious consequences for the way in which the British welfare state was to develop. In the 1980s, moreover, the NHS became the key focus for the ideological battle over the privatization of welfare and, in an attempt to improve the efficiency of service delivery, administrative experiments such as the creation of 'internal markets'. Under New Labour it has remained the testing ground for administrative experiment as well as the government's commitment to the public services.

2.1 THE DEFINITION OF THE WELFARE STATE

There is no agreement amongst historians and social scientists over when the first welfare states were established or what the term actually means. Some historians have even described the Elizabethan poor law as a 'welfare state in miniature'. More seriously, others have identified their establishment in nine-teenth-century Europe particularly after 1880, whilst others have located it exclusively in the period after the Second World War. Some, inevitably, have done both. Thereafter, there is general agreement that there was 'a golden age' or 'classic welfare state' between the Second World War and the mid-1970s, but then the term again becomes problematic. For Britain, for example, it has been argued that there was a distinctive 'restructured welfare state' until 1997 followed by a 'modern welfare state', while yet others have argued that indus-trialized countries are moving 'beyond the welfare state'. New Labour itself, in announcing its 1998 reform programme *A New Contract for Welfare*, some-what muddied the water by describing 'four ages of welfare' of dubious historical validity, with the fourth age targeted to commence in 2020.[1]

Analytically, many social scientists (and politicians) have used the term broadly to describe the full range of powers exercised by government or indeed a whole society. Others have used it more narrowly as a synonym for a discrete range of social services. This may be restricted, largely under the influence of the USA, to cash benefits or include services in kind such as the NHS. *A New Contract for Welfare* again illustrates the confusion. In it, the Prime Minister referred to 'those of us who believe the welfare state is not just about cash benefits' and the text itself starts: 'The welfare state was born 50 years ago. At its birth, the vision was broad and encompassed all welfare services, such as education and health as well as social security benefits.'[2] The programme then concentrates almost exclusively on social security.

Terminological confusion has frequently led to despair. For example, one pre-eminent commentator on postwar welfare, Richard Titmuss, concluded somewhat lamely after a lifetime of study: 'I am no more enamoured of the indefinable abstraction the "welfare state" than I was some twenty years ago . . . Generalized slogans rarely induce concentration of thought: more often they prevent us from asking significant questions about reality.' More recently, John Veit-Wilson has argued more vehemently that the term 'has become emptied of all meaning and is used as a synonym for modern indus-trialised states, all of which provide welfare for some of their inhabitants'. He then tellingly begs the question of why 'the converse of the term (what modern industrialised state is not a welfare state?) is rarely if ever addressed'. The continuing use of the term, he suggests, has even been deliberately used by some politicians to disguise and legitimize 'political oppression'.[3]

The origin of the species

One way to cut through this confusion and establish a working definition, for Britain at least, is to determine the time at which the term first became widely used and the reason for its public acceptance. Changes in language suggest the recognition of a new phenomenon which no existing expression can adequately describe.

The term was coined in the 1930s. It was used first in Germany as a term of abuse (*Wohlfahrstaat*) against the Weimar Republic, whose constitution was seen to have burdened the state with so many social responsibilities that it had undermined the country's political and economic viability.[4] With the subsequent rise of totalitarianism, the term was developed in Britain as an antonym for the 'warfare' or power state. A welfare state was conceived to be an organ of the community whose role was to serve the welfare of its citizens and respect international law, as opposed to the tyrannical 'warfare' state which imposed its will on both its citizens and its international neighbours. Such usage reached its apogee in a book, *Citizen and Churchman*, written in 1941 by the Archbishop of Canterbury, William Temple, but Temple did warn that the power assumed by a benevolent state to advance its citizens' welfare could lead to totalitarianism. Consequently he recommended that as many responsibilities as possible should be delegated to non-state agencies.

In the late 1940s, however, the term came to be used to describe just such a growth in the power of the state under the Labour government; and it was in this sense that it rapidly won international acceptance. British politicians were initially reluctant to use the phrase since in the United States, as in Germany in the 1930s, it was still a term of abuse and Britain was dependent at that time on American aid (not least to finance its welfare services); but by 1949 it was in regular use in both academic and political circles. In 1950 the Labour prime minister, Attlee, felt sufficiently confident to commend to his Party's by-election candidates the government's achievement in laying the 'foundations of the Welfare State' and in 1952 *The Times* felt equally confident to inaugurate the first of many debates on 'The Crisis in the Welfare State'.[5]

Rapid international acceptance of the term signified the way in which the British welfare state reflected popular aspirations which had accompanied the growth of industrialization and political democracy not just in Britain but in all Western countries. These aspirations were more specifically expressed in another term which came into popular usage during the war, 'social security'.

This meant the freedom (or security) of all citizens from the fear of poverty; and it was by providing the means by which such security could be attained that the British welfare state, and more particularly the 1942 Beveridge Report, gained its international reputation. The Report enjoyed a somewhat unusual fate for a government white paper. At home, it attracted on its day of publication a queue of purchasers one-quarter of a mile long. Abroad, it was parachuted into occupied territories as an expression of the ideals for which the Allies were fighting. Thus it both attracted immense popularity and was seen, politically, to give substance to the vague aspirations of the Allies' first statement of war aims: the 1941 Atlantic Charter (into which Churchill had been obliged, by Labour ministers in his coalition, to insert the term 'social security').[6] It consequently found ready endorsement in many national reconstruction plans, such as the *Chartre de la Résistance* in France, as well as in many international conventions, culminating with the 1948 Universal Declaration of Human Rights by the United Nations. One American historian has even gone so far as to describe the publication of the Report and the subsequent expansion of state welfare as 'an historic event equivalent in importance and stature to the French and Russian Revolutions'.[7]

International tensions

However, the worldwide adoption of the term 'welfare state' threatens to confuse rather than to clarify its meaning because, in both their practices and objectives, welfare states have diverged as well as converged. In each country, postwar reforms had to be welded on to existing services which had over many years acquired distinctive national peculiarities. They had also to be introduced in a variety of economic and political circumstances. Hence it is hardly surprising that individual services, such as the health service, continued to vary between countries both in their coverage and in their methods of finance and administration.

The ultimate objectives of welfare states have also varied because each reflects (or is 'embedded' in) different cultures and political accommodations with powerful interest groups. Three 'worlds of welfare' have been identified by Esping-Andersen. In the social democratic model, to which Scandinavian welfare states approximate, the state relieves its citizens of traditional market and family pressures by providing high earnings-related benefits (which guarantee accustomed living standards during absence from work) and extensive state services for the old and young. The corporatist model, reflected in the German and French welfare systems, is more conservative. High benefits are administered by a variety of occupationally based funds which maintain the difference in status between their members. There are also fewer services to relieve women in particular of their caring role. In both these worlds, however, government actively seeks to ensure the right to employment and security by brokering deals with both sides of industry which ensure that such rights are matched by responsibilities (such as the commitment to retrain or to modify wage claims). In the third liberal world, to which

Esping-Andersen controversially consigned Britain as well as the USA, there is no such brokerage and the state provides only a minimum of services. Individuals seeking to maintain accustomed living standards or to free themselves from family responsibilities have to resort to the market, although they are frequently subsidized to do so. Australian social scientists have added a fourth variant, the wage earners' welfare state, in which government obviates the need for extensive services by ensuring, through arbitration awards, that workers have wages sufficient to meet their welfare needs.[8] Other variants have also been identified such as the 'Southern European' and the 'East Asian' model. All these 'worlds of welfare' represent very different concepts of the proper relationship between government and the individual; and inevitably after the 1970s each world of welfare begat, in Paul Pierson's phrase, different 'worlds of welfare reform'.[9]

Domestic tensions

Such differences in practice and objectives also exist within individual countries because, as with all policy, welfare policy evolves as a result of changing circumstances and is constantly contested. Britain after 1945 was no exception. The war left a curious legacy. Widely varying standards in nationally financed services (as revealed by evacuation), the perceived economic efficiency of the wartime state (as compared to the perceived inefficiency of the market in the 1930s) and the common need of all classes in the blitz to rely on the social services each paved the way for a degree of state intervention and a centralization of welfare services strikingly at variance with the national tradition of individual freedom and decentralization. This tradition stemmed from the seventeenth-century concept of the 'freeborn Englishman', which dissenters significantly took with them when emigrating to the American colonies. Its relevance to welfare policy has been best summarized by José Harris, who has written:

> In contradistinction to much continental political thought, it saw 'civil society' . . . as the highest sphere of human existence . . . The 'state', by contrast, was an institution of secondary importance . . . The corporate life of society was seen as expressed through voluntary associations and the local community, rather than though the persona of the state . . . More extensive government was widely viewed as not merely undesirable but unnecessary, in the sense that most of the functions performed by government in other societies were in Britain performed by coteries of citizens governing themselves.

As a result the mid-1940s constituted a 'profound break with some of the major conventions of the previous hundred years' and there was an 'elusive but important change in perceptions of the mutual relationship between society and the state'.[10]

As will be shown more fully in the next section, traditional liberal values did not start fully reasserting themselves until after 1975. However, even within the broad collectivist consensus, there was an underlying conflict of purpose. On the one hand, there were the 'reluctant collectivists'. After the economic dislocation and poverty of the 1930s they were willing to accept increased state intervention as a 'mechanism for making good the failure of the market to control avoidable ills', but they did not wish to use it overtly as an 'instrument for economic change'.[11] On the other hand, there were others who wished to use welfare policy to engineer a new type of society in which income, wealth and power would be more equally distributed. Political influence oscillated between the adherents of these two strategies and so the ultimate purpose of state intervention was contested. This helps to explain why the British welfare state evolved more slowly than in countries where centralist traditions were more deeply embedded and why eventually the crisis of the 1970s had a more profound impact.

A pragmatic definition

Despite the international adoption of the term 'welfare state' therefore, and despite also the widespread belief in the 1950s that a combination of social security and the mixed economy marked the final stage of the development of industrial society ('the end of ideology'), there has never in reality been unanimity, within or between nations, over the nature and ultimate purpose of a welfare state. This does not mean, however, that the term is meaningless; and even if certain commentators are tempted to abandon it, it is a term in common usage and so demands a definition. Accordingly a welfare state, as pragmatically defined in this book, will be seen to have three immutable characteristics.

- The term refers not simply to a discrete range of social services but to a society in which government actively accepts responsibility for the welfare (broadly defined) of all its citizens.
- Welfare states were the creation of the 1940s.
- They have an inalienable core of universal services.

The last two require further explanation.

A creation of the 1940s

Chronologically, welfare states were the unique creation of the 1940s – as indeed the origins of the term suggest. This is because it was in the 1940s that, across the range of industrialized countries, evolutionary changes in government policy reached a critical mass at which – consciously or unconsciously – they transformed the fundamental nature of the relationship between the state and its citizens. This revolution was reflected by, and acknowledged within, the Beveridge Report.[12] The Report's individual proposals may have been mere rationalizations or developments of past practice. Cumulatively, however, they had a totally different significance epitomized by the two ideals of universalism and comprehensiveness. For the first time in history *all* citizens were to be insured 'from the cradle to the grave' against *every* eventuality which might lead to the inadvertent loss of their income. At a stroke, therefore, they were released by the state from the fear of poverty – hitherto a predominant and constraining influence on their lives – and given a freedom which previously had been the exclusive privilege of the rich. This was, by any historic standard, a revolution and one that did much to repair the reputation of Western democracy, tarnished in the 1930s by unemployment and descent into totalitarianism. It was duly acknowledged in Britain by, amongst others, T. H. Marshall. Events, he concluded, transformed an 'evolutionary process' into a revolutionary change. 'We adopted the term "Welfare State" to denote this new entity composed of old elements.'[13]

Core functions

What, however, were the core functions of this 'new entity'? In 1961 Asa Briggs produced what many at the time considered to be the classic definition of the welfare state. He wrote:

> A 'Welfare State' is a state in which organized power is deliberately used (through politics and administration) in an effort to modify the play of market forces in at least three directions – first, by guaranteeing individuals and families a minimum income irrespective of the market value of their work or property; second, by narrowing the extent of insecurity by enabling individuals and families to meet certain social contingencies (for example, sickness, old age and unemployment) which lead otherwise to individual and family crises; and third, by ensuring that all citizens without distinction of status or class are offered the best standards available in relation to a certain agreed range of social services.[14]

The first two objectives, he admitted, were little different from those of inter-war social policy - although, in practice, the former could ultimately only be delivered through the Poor Law (which, owing to its stigma, people shunned) and the latter was selective. It was the third, which embraced the concept of universalism and 'optimum' standards, which was the really distinctive characteristic of a welfare state.

This definition reflects the values of the 1960s. It understates the importance to individual welfare of the state's modification of market forces in the *provision* of work (which ironically declined over time) as opposed to the redistribution of income. The terms 'minimum income' and 'best standards available' are also open to many interpretations. As will be seen later, there has been a fierce battle over whether 'minimum income' should equate to a minimum *subsistence* income (adequate to meet a given set of needs) or a minimum *participatory* income (a higher amount designed to combat social exclusion by allowing the recipient fully to participate in society). The finite resources of government compared to the infinite possibilities of modern technology also means that many policies have to be curtailed well below what is technically available.

Nevertheless the definition can still be satisfactorily modified to the effect that a welfare state is a society in which government is expected to ensure the provision for all its citizens of not only social security but also a range of other services – including health, education and housing – at a standard well above the barest minimum. In so doing it consumes resources (through expenditure on goods and the employment of manpower) on such a scale that it cannot but affect the working of the economy. For this reason, and in order both to finance its own expenditure and to minimize political dissatisfaction or unrest, it is concerned with the underlying health of the economy. Thus it plays a more active role in the economy than the mere fatalistic assurance that conditions are conducive for the working of a self-regulating market.

The history of the NHS illustrates, in a British context, the foregoing characteristics of a welfare state. To an extent its creation was in Beveridge's words a 'natural development from the past'. There had long been concern over the financial viability of the hospital system and embarrassment that the most vulnerable members of poor families (children, the majority of mothers and the retired) were not covered by the state's health insurance scheme. On the other hand, it also exemplified the revolutionary impact of the Second World War. Bombs did not discriminate, and rich and poor alike required immediate access to free and uniform medical care. Hence the wartime Emergency Medical Service set the precedent for a new universal service. Moreover, the right to free healthcare transformed the lives of many which had previously been overshadowed by fear of sudden illness and of excessive medical bills.

As will be shown later, universalism had certain detrimental effects. It had, however, the unquestionable advantage of making politically acceptable the state's provision of healthcare above a minimum standard, be it for altruistic reasons (a general willingness to pool resources so that everyone was entitled to the best possible treatment) or more cynical ones (the articulate middle classes wished to ensure the best possible standards for a service in which they were now participants). However, the best was never the 'optimum' because, as was explicitly acknowledged as early as 1956, public expectation and the possibilities of medical science were boundless whereas the economic resources of government were not.[15] The level at which healthcare was to be provided, therefore, was a political not a professional decision and inevitably fell below the technical optimum.

Is Britain still a welfare state?

By this pragmatic definition, did welfare states internationally survive the 'crisis' of the 1970s? More particularly, has Britain remained a welfare state? As has been seen, there was increasing evidence in the 1970s that postwar welfare policy and in particular the management of the economy and anti-poverty programmes were failing. Arguably they were making worse the very problems they were supposed to resolve. As one American commentator, for example, later described the dilemma surrounding anti-poverty programmes:

We want to offer financial support to those with low incomes, but if we do we reduce the pressure on them and their incentive to work. We want to help people who are not able to help themselves but then worry that people will not bother to help themselves. We recognize the insecurity of single-parent families but, in helping them, we appear to be promoting and supporting their formation. We want to target our money to the most needy but, in so doing, we often isolate and stigmatize them.[16]

The orthodoxies surrounding Keynesian economics and structural explanations of poverty tended to deny the magnitude, or even the existence, of such dilemmas. They also inhibited, or even prohibited, debate. Nevertheless, the electorate sensed the problem and there consequently occurred the 'sea change' of opinion which Callaghan, as the Labour prime minister defeated by Mrs Thatcher, admitted he was powerless to combat.[17]

This 'sea change' coincided with a genuine fiscal crisis in industrialized countries. There is some dispute over whether this was caused by globalization or 'post–industrialism': an autonomous switch from a manufacturing to a service economy, which led to a slowing in the rate of economic growth. In any case, the consequent reduction in government revenue coincided with an urgent need for more money to meet the cost of the maturing of earlier promises, the ageing of the population, and changes in household structure (which meant less 'free' family care and support). Hence, in Paul Pierson's phrase, the arrival of a 'new era of austerity' in which, because of a tax-payers' revolt, cost containment became a political as well as a financial imperative. However, this did not lead automatically to an assault on welfare policy. This was because 'the irresistible forces of post-industrialism' met the 'immovable object of the welfare state' or more particularly, and somewhat contradictorily given the tax-payers' revolt, its 'enduring popularity'. Welfare states (defined by Pierson as 'an umbrella term covering a range of government activities') were, therefore, not dismantled. Rather, they were restructured or 'recalibrated' – modernized both to improve their delivery of existing goals ('rationalization') and to enhance their capacity to meet new ones ('up-dating').

Welfare states, in summary, proved resilient because:

- They had the 'intense' support of up to half the electorate which was employed in, benefited from or (particularly in relation to pensions and healthcare) anticipated benefiting from welfare policy. Support was 'intense' because the threat to a specific service concentrated minds. In contrast, the benefits of - and so support for - tax cuts were more diffuse.
- Welfare policy was embedded in national culture. Institutions such as the NHS were seen as an embodiment of national virtue, as well as the guarantor of individual rights and a source of social stability.
- Welfare policy was also embedded politically in the organization of both outside interests and government agencies. Over time they had been shaped by, and incurred considerable costs in adapting to, the development of welfare policy. Their willingness, let alone ability, to change was therefore strictly limited. So too was the way they *could* change. (This is what political scientists have termed 'path dependency'.)

• Welfare states generally came to be seen less as a 'protective reaction' against capitalism, as portrayed by social democrats, and more as a 'fundamental part of modern capitalism', designed to make it more efficient to the potential benefit of all.

As a result, Pierson concluded, there was little sign in most countries that 'the basic commitments to a mixed economy of welfare face[d] a fundamental political challenge'. Nor was there 'much evidence of a convergence towards neo-liberal orthodoxy'.[18]

Was Britain, however, an exception? At the very least, was there a radical change in the balance of its mixed economy of welfare after the mid-1970s? Britain had the potential to be an exception. Despite being the pioneer of the classic welfare state, it has conventionally been classified in Esping-Andersen's three worlds of welfare as a liberal welfare state. Partially as a legacy of the concept of the 'freeborn Englishman', welfare taxes, spending and employment have been *relatively* low. Employers and trade unionists, with their instinctive faith in free collective bargaining, have also been *relatively* uninvolved in the corporatist deals that have shaped welfare policy in other worlds of welfare. Consequently both electoral and institutional support for the welfare state is more conditional than elsewhere. Moreover, within liberal regimes, central government in Britain enjoys an exceptional power. The freedom to act of the president of the USA, for example, can be constrained by Congress, the judiciary or individual states. Individual states can also constrain the power of other federal governments, such as Canada and Australia. Once British prime ministers have secured a working majority in the House of Commons, however, their powers are relatively unlimited. The first-past-the-post electoral system historically has obviated the need, as elsewhere, for compromise within coalitions. Local government (and even devolved government in Scotland, Wales and Northern Ireland) is fiscally weak and so poses no real challenge. The central civil service is also powerful. British governments, in short, are confronted by few 'veto points'. Prime ministers such as Mrs Thatcher and Tony Blair can act decisively and by so doing have established international reputations as reformers.

Has the welfare state been dismantled by their reforms? *Economically*, the abandonment of Keynesian demand management in 1976, its replacement by the Conservatives with monetarism in 1979 and the entrusting by New Labour of monetary policy to an independent Bank of England in 1997, unquestionably reduced the power of government actively to guarantee full employment. The latter action was particularly surprising given Labour's analysis of the causes of global depression in the 1930s and its consequent nationalization of the Bank of England in 1946. Why, the chancellor was asked, having been out of power for 18 years, had New Labour immediately surrendered it? Given the absence of an economic recession since 1997, it remains uncertain what proactive initiatives government can take other than to encourage, as in the interwar years, a 'private enterprise' recovery.[19]

The sense of community on which the postwar welfare state was built was also challenged by an increasing emphasis on the satisfaction of individual consumer needs (or greed) and, in particular, by Mrs Thatcher's reported conviction that 'there was no such thing as society'. The full statement from which this extract was taken, however, merely elucidated her belief that the community was best expressed through voluntary groups and neighbourhoods rather than the state.[20] This, as has been seen, was common in the Victorian and even interwar period. In other words she was merely expressing a preference for a return to the earlier balance within the mixed economy of welfare. A similar ambition, as will be seen, is harboured by communitarians within New Labour. Such an ambition, however, is illusory. As José Harris argued, there was after the 1940s an important change in the 'mutual relationship between society and the state'. The state became, and has remained, predominant. If it does not itself provide welfare services, then it subsidizes and regulates them. Both local government (largely financed and audited by the centre) and voluntary associations (bidding competitively for and regulated by government contracts) are no longer an equal or superior partner to central government. They are also far less an independent expression of community but rather a mere alternative means of service delivery.[21]

More positively, *the range of services* provided or financed by government has also been little diminished. This, as will be seen, is demonstrated by the size of social expenditure and the tax take as a percentage of gross domestic product (GDP). There has been no serious erosion of universal social security, even if there have been cuts at the margin and benefits have not met the minimum participatory level as defined by some. Services in kind have similarly remained universal and well above minimum prewar standards. Where the perceived needs of the market, the individual and social justice (and particularly the reduction of 'social exclusion') have coincided, there has even been some positive 'recalibration' (such as improved counselling and working families tax credits).

Whatever its unique character, therefore, the British welfare state has proved resilient. The reason for this is similar to that in other countries: it is historically embedded in national culture and institutions. The classic welfare state was as much the creation of long-term political, economic and social forces as of either temporary forces unleashed by the Second World War or of particular ambitions harboured by postwar social engineers. Between the wars successive governments had come to realize that, following the introduction of universal adult suffrage in 1918 and 1928, they would be under constant electoral pressure both to match equal political status with a more equal distribution of economic resources. At the same time, the structural needs of an advanced industrial economy, working within a highly competitive international economy, obliged them first to intervene in and then to accept some responsibility for the economy.[22] The balance of responsibility within the existing mixed economy of welfare, it was realized, was increasingly inappropriate. Out of a pragmatic recognition of changing political and economic reality, therefore, and not out of moral weakness or political venality (as asserted by critics of the welfare state), the responsibilities and functions of government changed. Later attempts to 'roll back the state' have been unable to reverse this change in its functional role. Indeed they have typically been aimed against the additional objectives to which postwar social engineers sought to direct state intervention. In the meantime, welfare policy has been recalibrated in the sense of both rationalization and up-dating.

In short, Britain continues *to have* a welfare state, which should not be equated solely with the social security system but to the broader 'joined-up' vision of Beveridge. It also *is*, or at least (given the contested definition) aspires to be, a welfare state. This is because the assumption that the state should ensure to all a comprehensive range of services at a standard well above the barest minimum is embedded in national culture and institutions even if, on occasion, a government not fully committed to such values is in power.

The NHS might be regarded as an institution representative more of a social democratic than a liberal 'world of welfare' because it is financed mainly by taxation and is available to all, free at the point of access. Since the 1970s, however, its development has epitomized that of the welfare state as a whole. In 1981 and 1987, the Conservatives gave serious consideration to placing it on a contributory insurance basis, be that social insurance (as in corporatist welfare states) or private insurance (as in the USA). Such considerations came to nothing but competitive 'market' disciplines were introduced *within* the NHS, particularly by the introduction of 'internal markets'. This included the allocation of budgets to 'fund-holding' GPs who were then free, on the patient's behalf, to purchase services (such as hospital care) from either the pubic or private sector. Internal markets were maintained by New Labour, despite commitments to the contrary in its 1997 manifesto. They were even extended through Primary Care Trusts (the combination of all, not just selected, GPs in larger fund-holding bodies). Other links with the market were also maintained, such as the Private Finance Initiative whereby most major new buildings were constructed, financed and owned by private companies. So too was competition within the service through the controversial introduction of Foundation Hospitals.

Such hospitals were not to enjoy, however, the freedom of voluntary hospitals under the interwar 'mixed economy of welfare'. The power of government, in regard to both regulation and finance, has been transformed. For instance, New Labour has issued innumerable targets to regulate performance; founded the National Institute of Clinical Excellence (NICE) to issue clinical guidelines for all medical conditions; and established the Commission for Health Improvements to inspect hospital regularly to ensure these and other guidelines are followed. At the same time, two official reports by a financier (the Wanless reports of 2001 and 2002) dismissed the possibility of alternative sources of finance. Subsequently, New Labour committed itself to an unprecedented increase in public funding of 43 per cent over six years in an attempt to bring health expenditure up to the European average.

→

Rather than being dismantled, therefore, the NHS was eventually recalibrated: modernized both to achieve traditional goals better and to meet, in the words of Wanless, 'the technological, democratic and medical trends' of the next 20 years. Its resilience was due in part to its relative efficiency and path dependency. As Wanless reported, there was 'no evidence that any alternative financing method to the UK's would deliver a given quantity of healthcare at a lower cost to the economy'. In part this was because there was no alternative means of delivery. For example, the 'approved' societies which had distributed funds before 1940s, unlike social insurance funds in continental Europe, had not survived the war. Professional organizations, medical suppliers and political institutions had adapted their behaviour to the continuing existence of the NHS. Even more importantly it had become embedded in national culture. As Wanless reported, 80 per cent of people considered that the NHS was 'critical to British society and must be retained'.[23]

2.2 THE FOUR PRAGMATIC APPROACHES TO WELFARE IN BRITAIN

Allusion has already been made to the four broad political strategies which have directly influenced the development of the British welfare state: reluctant collectivism, democratic socialism, the New Right and the Third Way.

- Reluctant collectivism is broadly synonymous with the policy of the moderate wing of the Conservative Party which, following the modernization of Conservative policy by R. A. Butler in the 1940s, dominated the party until Margaret Thatcher's election as leader in 1975.
- Democratic socialism was developed by the reformist wing of the Labour Party which reached its intellectual peak in the 1950s and early 1960s with the publication of Crosland's *The Future of Socialism* (1956) and the work, at the London School of Economics, of a group of social scientists led by R. M. Titmuss.
- The New Right steadily gained support within the Conservative Party throughout the 1960s and has been the inspiration behind Thatcherism.
- The Third Way, first developed as the political strategy of the Democratic Party in the USA under Clinton and underpinned by the writings of the sociologist Anthony Giddens, has provided the organizational framework for New Labour policy after 1997.

These strategies, while having much in common, differ fundamentally on the three critical issues of political freedom, economic efficiency and social justice.

2.2.1 Reluctant Collectivism

Pre-eminent amongst the reluctant collectivists were the two intellectual founders of the British welfare state, Keynes and Beveridge. Both were essentially liberals, personally committed to the free market because, in their opinion, the minimization of state intervention maximized the freedom of the individual and hence political freedom, economic efficiency and social variety. On reading Hayek's *The Road to Serfdom* (1944), the right-wing polemic which attacked the wartime consensus about the beneficence of state intervention upon which both the welfare state and Butler's 'new conservatism' were based, Keynes even acknowledged himself to be 'morally and philosophically . . . not only in agreement . . . but in deeply moved agreement'.[24] In practice, however, reluctant collectivists such as he realized that, for a variety of economic and political reasons, the market was no longer working in the ideal way assumed by classical economic theorists. It had after all been responsible in interwar Britain for an unacceptable level of economic waste and social distress. On technocratic and humanitarian grounds, therefore, they accepted the need for greater state regulation. Politically too they realized that such intervention was essential. Beveridge, for example, argued that freedom had to be positive and not just negative – freedom not simply from 'the arbitrary power of government' but also from 'economic servitude to want and squalor'.[25] The state alone could guarantee this freedom for everyone. Moreover, he acknowledged, were governments to permit economic waste and social inequality to continue, parliamentary democracy might be discredited and political stability threatened.

Beveridge.   Beveridge's specific recommendations regarding the extent of state intervention varied greatly over time. In *Full Employment in a Free Society* (1944) he proposed the continuation of wartime planning and controls over many years in order to remedy the structural weakness of the British economy, which the market had appeared incapable of correcting in the interwar period. However, one of the three guiding principles of the Beveridge Report – despite later charges levelled against the social security system – was that 'the State in organising security should not stifle incentive, opportunity, responsibility'.[26] Consequently, in both the social insurance and assistance schemes, the state's role was to be strictly limited to guaranteeing each citizen a subsistence income. Individual living standards above that minimum should be determined not by the state but by personal effort and voluntary contributions to private insurance.

Keynes.   Keynes envisaged a similarly limited role for the state. Like the classical economists, he sought to restrict its role to the provision of the conditions under which the free market could work efficiently. Where he disagreed with his predecessors was in his judgement of what those conditions were. It was his conviction that the market was no longer self-regulating and that state intervention was required to ensure that there was neither deficient nor excess demand in the economy; but once the state had performed that task, the market should be left to function freely. Consequently, the rate of economic growth (and thereby living standards) should remain the ultimate responsibility of industry, just as the nature of the goods produced should continue to be determined by consumer choice.

Reluctant collectivism was, and is, therefore, grounded on firm philosophical premises. The market is conceived as the best practical mechanism for ensuring individual initiative and hence political freedom, economic efficiency and social justice; but its flaws are recognized and thus the need for a judicious degree of state intervention. The critical question is just how much intervention is required. The answer depends, at any given time, on a fine judgement about the market's relative strengths and weaknesses. Such pragmatism identifies reluctant collectivism closely with the traditional Conservative philosophy of conserving what is best in the old while adapting constantly to the new; and indeed, under the initial inspiration of Butler, it did provide the philosophical justification for the Conservative Party's defence of the welfare state after its return to power in 1951.[27]

Continual pragmatism, however, lays open the political exponents of reluctant collectivism to the charge of unprincipled opportunism; and this provided a double handicap for the Conservative Party in the 1950s and 1960s. On the one hand, by seeming merely to react to weaknesses in the existing system and then to lament the moral consequences of state intervention, it ceded the intellectual initiative to the democratic socialists, who championed a more positive role for the state. On the other hand, the inherent tension between the reluctant collectivists' recognition of the fundamental virtues of the market and yet the need for its pragmatic reform led to considerable hesitation in both the implementation of Butler's 'new conservatism' and the deployment, let alone acceptance, of a new practical political programme.[28] After January 1958, when the battle was temporarily resolved in favour of the moderates – as symbolized by the resignation of Thorneycroft as chancellor of the exchequer – policy drifted even further from the market with the commitment of Harold Macmillan to economic planning and of Edward Heath to corporate bargaining. This made it the more vulnerable to attack from the ideologues of the New Right.

2.2.2 Democratic Socialism

Despite the predominant influence of Beveridge and Keynes in the early postwar years, it was the ideals of the democratic socialists which gave the British welfare state its unique international reputation. At home these ideals also infused the welfare legislation of the 1945–51 Labour governments and provided the logic for further advances which Conservative ministers struggled to refute. To the social democrats, state intervention was not a mere corrective for market failings but the means of engineering a more equal and fair society. Like the reluctant collectivists, they condemned the unregulated market as economically inefficient. They attacked it also as undemocratic (because it concentrated economic, and thus effective political, power in a few hands), socially unjust (because it failed to reward people according to need) and unethical (because it encouraged self-interest and greed). They conse-quently sought to transform, by democratic means, the existing capitalist soci-ety into a socialist one in which production, through the utilization of all available resources for the common good, would be efficient; in which the government, through the equalization of economic power, would ensure political freedom for all; and in which social justice would be guaranteed by a predominant altruism.

The leading postwar social democratic thinkers were:

- T. H. Marshall (Professor of Sociology, London School of Economics, 1954–6).
- Richard Titmuss (Professor of Social Administration, London School of Economics, 1950–73).
- Anthony Crosland (a revisionist Labour MP and cabinet minister in the 1960s and 1970s, most notably as secretary of state for education between 1965 and 1967).

Marshall.   Marshall in 1948 developed a whig theory of history, whereby British citizens gained their civil rights between 1650 and 1832, their political rights between 1832 and 1918 and their social rights thereafter. The latter entailed the right to social services which, by increasing both the recipient's real income and services that could be universally enjoyed (such as the health service), effectively minimized the inequality of living standards and 'legiti-mate expectations' which would otherwise have resulted from differences in money income. Thereby all citizens, despite their unequal money income, enjoyed equal status and an 'equal social worth'. The welfare state, by insti-tutionalizing these social rights, Marshall argued, raised society on to a higher plane where the sense of community, which had been fleetingly experienced in the war, might become permanent. It also provided a temporary resolution to the fundamental conflict between the capitalist need for incentive (and hence unequal money incomes) and the democratic need for egalitarianism (and hence equal status). 'The conflict of principles', wrote Marshall, 'springs from the very roots of social order in the present phase of the development of democratic citizenship. Apparent inconsistencies are in fact a source of stabil-ity, achieved through a compromise which is not dictated by logic. This phase will not continue indefinitely.' Thus, the welfare state was a hybrid but a workable hybrid. It was a pragmatic and constructive compromise between capitalism and socialism, from which a more socialist society would eventu-ally emerge.[29]

Titmuss.   Titmuss and his colleagues at the London School of Economics provided both a continuing critique of individual policies within the welfare state and a grand vision of its essential purpose. Their successes included the early dispelling of the myth that expenditure on the NHS was out of control and consuming a rapidly increasing proportion of gross national product (GNP); the development of the concept of the 'social division of welfare', by which the existing welfare state could be exposed as surreptitiously transferring substantial resources not to the poor but to the rich by means of fiscal welfare (tax relief) and the subsidizing of occupational welfare (management's fringe benefits, such as private health insurance); and the rediscovery, through redefinition, of poverty in the 1960s. Titmuss's concern with the real-world impact of policy was reflected by his tenure of the deputy chairmanship of the Supplementary Benefit Commission, the agency responsible for ensuring that no-one's income fell below the official poverty line. He was also alive to the practical economic and political value of universal welfare services. Selectivity, he argued, wasted resources by demoralizing the poor and lowering each service's standard. The potentially positive contribution that social expenditure could make to economic growth was thereby restricted. Selectivity also fostered political unrest by depriving society of a sense of fairness and unity. 'While means-testing seems to save money in the short-term by narrowing eligibility', one of Titmuss's colleagues has since argued, 'over the long-run it may add to the political and social costs of a . . . divided society'.[30] Such costs, of course, go unrecognized in the conventional cost–benefit analyses applied to social expenditure by economists.

Titmuss's overriding mission, however, was to emphasize the moral purpose of the welfare state – as was revealed by his ever-willingness to confront the frequent assertion, especially from the New Right, that economic growth would reduce poverty and inequality and thereby allow the welfare state to wither away. Not only could such an analysis be disproved empirically, he argued, but the purpose of welfare went far beyond the relief of a hard core of deprivation. Its purpose was to provide social justice, by providing compensation for the increasing social costs of economic change (such as illness arising from environmental pollution or unemployment arising from technological redundancy) which fell disproportionately on the poor and which traditionally went uncorrected by the market. It was also to elevate society by institutionalizing a deeper sense of community and mutual care. Hence his singling out of the blood donor service (by which one citizen voluntarily gave a life-saving resource to another) as the epitome of the welfare state.

Crosland.   Crosland's *The Future of Socialism*, which was designed to redefine democratic socialism as the practical basis for Labour Party policy, built upon the work of academic social scientists such as Marshall and Titmuss. Crosland's ideal was to create a 'classless society' in which greater equality and fraternity would prove their economic worth – in contrast to the 'material inefficiency of capitalism' – by minimizing both the waste of talent and the social antagonism which lay behind Britain's poor growth record and bad industrial relations (on which, incidentally, Crosland's main rival within the Party, Aneurin Bevan, was deemed to capitalize).[31] Crosland's particular target was the Marxist underpinnings of current Labour Party policy. Marxism, he argued, had 'little or nothing to offer the contemporary socialist either in respect of practical policy or of the correct analysis of our society, even of the right conceptual tools and framework'. Its predictions about the immiseration of the poor and capitalism's impending collapse had been constantly confounded, whereas its obsession with the economic power of the capitalist class had obscured the fact that political power, and hence effective economic power, had been transferred to the state. Capitalism, he maintained, had been peacefully transformed. Universal adult suffrage and full employment had given the workforce effective political and social power; and the welfare state had bestowed upon everyone a security and a range of services that had previously been the privilege of the rich. Simultaneously the transfer of power within industry from the owners to the managers had had a profound psychological impact which had made industry more socially responsible. In response to such changes, and armed with the new Keynesian techniques of demand management, 'the passive state has given way to the active, or at least the ultimately responsible state; the political authority has emerged as the final arbiter of economic life; the brief, and historically exceptional, era of unfettered market relations is over'. It was incumbent on social democrats in general, and the Labour Party in particular, to use this enhanced power of the state to further economic growth and social justice. The means to those ends were not traditional policies, such as nationalization, but a direct assault on the major remaining sources of inequality and waste, in particular the education system and inherited wealth.

Despite the defeat of the Labour Party in the elections of 1951, 1955, 1959 and 1970, it was these social democratic ideals which underpinned popular support for the welfare state. The basic assumptions underlining this consensus have been vividly summarized by David Donnison:

1. The growth of the economy and the population would continue. That, by itself, would not solve any problems; but it provided an optimistic setting for debate. The pursuit of social justice could be carried forward by engines of economic growth which would produce the resources to create a fairer society without anyone suffering on the way.
2. Although inequalities in incomes would persist, their harsher effects could be gradually softened by a 'social wage' (consisting of social services distributed with greater concern for human needs) and by the growing burden of progressive taxes, taking more from the rich than the poor, which were required to finance the social services.
3. Despite fierce conflicts about important issues (comprehensive schools, pensions, rent controls and so on) the people with middling skills and incomes – 'middle England' you might call them – would eventually support equalizing social policies and programmes of this kind. Trade unions and the Labour movement would usually provide the political cutting edge for reform; and the Conservative governments which followed them would accept most of its results.
4. Therefore government and its social services, accountable to this central consensus, were the natural vehicles of progress. Among their generally trusted

instruments were the doctors, teachers, town planners, nurses, social workers and other public service professions. The pretensions and powers of these professions should be critically watched, but progressive governments were expected to recruit more of these people . . . .

5. Although economic crises, political accidents and sheer ineptitude would often compel governments temporarily to abandon these aims, over the longer run they would all try to increase industrial investment and improve Britain's lagging productivity, to secure some broad agreement about the distribution of incomes, to get unemployed people back into jobs, to free poorer people from means tests by giving them adequate benefits as of right, to give children a better start in life and more equal opportunities for the future, and to provide better care and support for the most vulnerable people and for families living on low or modest incomes. 'Middle England', we assumed, would not tolerate any radical departure from those aims. A government which allowed – let alone encouraged – a return to the high unemployment, the social conflicts and means tests of the 1930s could not survive.[32]

The social democratic consensus, therefore, assumed economic growth and, whilst recognizing the danger of bureaucracy, regarded the growth of state intervention as both natural and beneficent. It even admitted the ratchet effect of party politics, later denounced by the New Right. On succeeding Labour, Conservative governments did not return policy to the 'common ground', upon which all parties were agreed in principle, but (because of the essential pragmatism of the reluctant collectivists) to an indeterminate 'middle ground' halfway between conservatism and socialism. Thus the 'middle ground' moved relentlessly further from the market. Social democracy, at least until the mid-1970s, had history on its side.

2.2.3 The New Right

While this consensus was at its height the old liberal values, which were later to be termed the New Right and which had last found expression in Hayek's *The Road to Serfdom* (1944), were exiled to an 'intellectual Siberia'.[33] In 1955 the Institute of Economic Affairs (IEA) was tentatively established to propagate these values which, with encouragement from the USA, gathered support to such effect throughout the 1960s that they temporarily influenced Conservative government policy between 1970 and 1972. Only after 1975, however, were they reintegrated into the main stream of political thought. By then the failure of Keynesian demand management, not only to sustain economic growth but also to resolve the combination (previously considered impossible) of high inflation and mass unemployment, had obliged both the Labour and Conservative Parties to reconsider their economic policy. Their common conclusion was that they should no longer actively manipulate demand but, more fatalistically, exercise a greater control over money supply. The market was thus to be given greater freedom to determine the country's fate.

This revival of faith in the market was sustained more naturally within the Conservative Party which, under Mrs Thatcher's leadership, argued with increasing conviction – and in direct defiance of reluctant collectivism and democratic socialism – that it was not the state but the market that was the best long-term guarantor of economic efficiency, social justice and political freedom. With regard to economic efficiency, Sir Keith Joseph argued that 'the blind, unplanned, uncoordinated wisdom of the market . . . is overwhelmingly superior to the well-researched, rational, systematic, well-meaning, cooperative, science-based, forward looking, statistically respectable plans of government'.[34] This was because individual producers, in order to maximize their profits in a competitive environment, had to satisfy speedily the ever-changing needs of individual consumers with goods of the highest possible quality at the lowest possible price. Consequently, the market was the most efficient mechanism for the synchronization of individual needs. The state might in the short term be able to correct the market's temporary failings but, however expert and benevolent, it could never in the longer term collect sufficient information to act efficiently – be efficiency defined either as the most economical use of resources or the speedy satisfaction of individual clients. Moreover, in the real world, the state could never achieve the disinterest and the altruism which both the reluctant collectivists and the democratic socialists naively believed to be possible. It would be subject to many insidious pressures, not least of which might be politicians' desire for short-term electoral advantage and bureaucrats' desire to extend their empires in order to enhance their own pay and career prospects. As the IEA concluded in 1965:

> Political priorities are established in response to such irrelevant pressures as the personalities of rival ministers, administrative convenience, the unequal power of organized lobbies, or simply short-term electoral calculations. Who will assert that the outcome of such crude, capricious pressures must necessarily prove superior to the dispersed preferences of consumers who know what they want and increasingly have money to pay their way?[35]

Such fallibility brings into question the paternalistic assumption that the state should define and thereafter engineer social justice. Even if there can be, at any given time, one incontrovertible definition of social justice, by what criteria are politicians and civil servants in the real world qualified to make it? Equally serious is the threat of state intervention to political freedom because if the democratic socialists sought through economic planning to impose a common morality on society they would run the risk of becoming, like their predecessors in the German Weimar Republic, 'the cultivated parents of a barbarous offspring'.[36] As Hayek argued in 1944, economic planning would set democracy on the road to serfdom because 'individual freedom cannot be reconciled with the supremacy of one single purpose to which the whole society must be entirely and permanently subordinated'. However much the electorate might request the rational planning of society, therefore, the temptation should be resisted. If it were acceded to, Parliament (faithfully reflecting the diversity of individual beliefs) would eventually find itself unable to draft a satisfactory, unitary plan and democracy would fall into disrepute (as it indeed had done in the 1930s through unfavourable comparison with the 'efficiency' of fascism and communism). Responsibility would consequently be transferred to technical experts or else to economic dictators, and Parliament would be unable to challenge any part of the ensuing plan for fear of jeopardizing the whole. 'The democratic statesman', concluded Hayek, 'who sets out to plan economic life will soon be confronted with the alternative of either assuming dictatorial powers or abandoning his plans.' This was indeed the experience of the Labour government in the 1940s. Democratic socialism, in other words, was a chimera.

The New Right consequently maintains that it is the market and not the state that is the best guarantor of political stability and freedom. Negatively, it prevents a drift into dictatorship. Positively, by catering for minority interests and enabling mistakes to be speedily remedied, it ensures that there are no permanently frustrated minorities resentful of, and therefore unwilling to obey, coercive laws. More especially it permits people to act spontaneously, to determine their own morality and to be responsible for the satisfaction of their own objectives. This is, in Hayek's phrase, 'the freedom in economic affairs without which personal and political freedom have never existed'. Economic inequality, it is admitted, can deny individuals political freedom if it confines them below the subsistence level; but such inequality is essentially the consequence of scarce resources which the market, through encouraging economic efficiency, is best able to remedy. State planning not only constricts economic growth and thereby the opportunity for greater economic self-sufficiency, but also denies the freedom of choice which such self-sufficiency should bestow. By the same logic, the political power of the capitalist should be feared far less than that of the state for it is fragmented and flexible, whilst that of the state is centralized and rigid.

The New Right, except on its extreme libertarian wing, does not wholly reject state intervention. The government should be strong in order to set and enforce the rules by which the market can function freely – unimpeded, for example, by monopolies and cartels. With regard to welfare, Hayek in the 1940s acknowledged that Britain had accumulated sufficient wealth to permit a certain collectivism without 'endangering general freedom'. This included state action to guarantee a minimum of physical efficiency (national assistance/income support), to overcome common hazards (social insurance) and, rather surprisingly, to combat general fluctuations in economic activity.[37] The ideal, however, was to minimize state intervention by subjecting it to constant reappraisal and, where state welfare was unavoidable, to provide it not directly but in the form of subsidies (or vouchers) to enable the recipient to choose freely in the market. This policy is deemed to be both efficient and potentially popular. For example the IEA, in a series of surveys of public attitudes towards welfare in the 1960s, discovered – like other pollsters – that 80 per cent of those questioned appeared to support the NHS; but such a response, it concluded, was biased by a 'widespread civic illiteracy' about the true costs of the service.[38] Once that cost had been explained and the possibility raised of vouchers, which might be exchanged for whatever mix of healthcare the individual wanted and topped up (if desired) by private payments, the popularity of the NHS dramatically declined.

2.2.4 The Third Way

The Third Way has a far shorter pedigree than the other strategies and has had far less time to develop. The broad concept was initially developed in the USA by the Democratic Party under Clinton after 1991 and in Britain by Giddens' *Beyond Left and Right* published in 1994. The precise term was adopted, after a high-powered seminar hosted by Hillary Clinton and Blair, with the simultaneous publication in 1998 of Blair's pamphlet *The Third Way: new politics for a new century* and Giddens' *The Third Way: the renewal of social democracy*. So great was the impact that the Third Way was named 'European of the year' by *Newsweek*, a wide-ranging internet discussion was launched and a series of seminars held for leading European statesmen. As the subtitle of Giddens' pamphlet suggested, the intended purpose was similar to that of Crosland: to adapt social democracy to changed circumstances. The globalization of finance and communications, so it was argued, had reduced the capacity of national governments to take independent action. Simultaneously, increasing individualism and lifestyle diversity had reduced their ability centrally to impose standardized policies. The Third Way was thus a 'popular name for a theory of social justice and individualism in the context of the global economy'.[39] The outcome, as suggested by Giddens in 1994, might even transcend the materialist concerns of both conventional social democracy and the New Right to address 'life politics' (or issues concerning the quality of life in a 'post-scarcity' age, such as those raised by feminists and environmentalists concerning the 'democratic family' or sustainable growth).

The most fundamental revision sought to social democracy concerned economic efficiency. There was, Giddens asserted, 'no alternative to capitalism' because, having proved their ability to anticipate and supply consumer needs, markets were the key to 'productive efficiency'.[40] Consequently, the government's role was not to plan or even manage the economy but to ensure, on the supply side, that autonomous markets could and would work optimally. This required investment in both human capital (ensuring people had both the skills and the will to work) and social capital (strong institutions, such as families and communities, within 'civil society' which would generate the stability and trust needed by markets). Hence, in the terminology of the Labour Party's 1994 Commission on Social Justice, the government should create an Investor's Britain. It should, for example, invest heavily in education over an individual's working life (so that they could respond flexibly to changing technology) and ensure that the terms on which welfare benefits were paid did not discourage work (or create a 'dependency culture'). This vision was contrasted with that of a Leveller's Britain, as favoured by traditional social democrats. Here a policy of high taxation and high public spending, adopted in a laudable attempt to achieve greater equality, typically had the perverse consequence of slowing economic growth and creating a dependency culture. It was contrasted also with a Deregulator's Britain, as favoured by the New Right, in which a denial of any social responsibility – again perversely – ultimately undermined the conditions for market efficiency and social justice.

The Third Way also challenged traditional social democratic values of social justice and political freedom. It explicitly jettisoned the concept of 'equality of outcome' in favour of 'equality of opportunity', as favoured by reluctant collectivists. This was alternatively called 'asset-based egalitarianism' or, more commonly, social inclusion. It was recognized in Britain, if not in the USA, that there could be structural causes of poverty (that is, causes beyond an individual's control). The speed of technical change also enhanced the risk to everyone's livelihood. Should anyone be so disadvantaged they should, as Titmuss had insisted, be compensated. In contrast to Titmuss, however, this compensation need not be in cash but could also take the form of 'assets' (such as the opportunity to retrain) which would ensure full participation in society (or, in other words, prevent 'social exclusion'). Even more important, compensation was not unconditional. Beneficiaries had responsibilities as well as rights – benefits could be withdrawn if, for example, work or training was refused.[41] This new definition of social justice might appear restricted and harsh. In fact it was the opposite. Everyone in society, including employers and taxpayers, had to acknowledge their respective responsibilities as well as rights. 'The revival of civic culture', as Giddens asserted, was 'a basic ambition of third way politics' and so individuals became 'embedded in social relationships which gave structure and meaning to their lives'. This had political consequences for both individual freedom and the role of government. As 'responsible risk-takers' individuals were empowered, the more so since political decisions were to be taken at a more local level (according to their diverse needs) rather than at the centre (according to prescriptions of experts). At the same time, the New Right critique of government was largely accepted. As Giddens concluded: 'the welfare state, seen by most as the core of social democratic politics, today creates almost as many problems as it resolves.' Government had to provide a more proactive or preventive service - providing, in a slogan of the time, 'a hand up rather than a hand out'. It had also to play a less dominant role, supporting other institutions and thereby 'deepening and widening democracy'.

Many have been dismissive of the Third Way. Some have portrayed it as a surrender to New Right ideology, and in particular to the power of global capitalism. Others have accused it of 'fundamental hollowness'.[42] This was a view enhanced by its much trumpeted eclecticism in its choice of instruments to implement policy – 'what works is what counts'. Others, perhaps even

THE THIRD WAY...

1   *The Third Way*
The Third Way was widely seen as a capitulation to Conservative ideology. *Marxism Today* depicted Tony Blair as 'Mrs Thatcher in trousers'. The verdict of *The Times* was equally graphic.
Source: © Peter Brooks, *The Times*, 30 April 1998.

more humiliatingly, have accused it of being anything but new. New Liberalism before the First World War, Macmillan's 'middle way', One-Nation Conservatism and even Crosland's 'classless society' thereafter had, for example, sought a similar accommodation between capitalism and social-ism. Scandinavia, so it was argued, had long practised a form of 'modified capitalism' and so the Third Way was a novelty only to liberal welfare states. Its proponents nevertheless have maintained that it is seeking to end the arti-ficial and damaging polarities, as for example between 'wealth creation' and 'social justice' or between 'the market' and 'community', promoted by adver-sarial right-wing and left-wing politics. As Blair has written:

> The Third Way stands for a modernized social democracy, passionate in its commitment to social justice . . . but flexible, innovative and forward-looking in the means to achieve them . . . . It moves decisively beyond an old left preoccupied by state control, high taxation and producer interests, and a new right treating

public investment, and often the very notions of 'society' and collective endeavour, as evils to be undone . . . . It is about traditional values in a changed world.

In this view the Third Way creates a virtuous circle. Stable growth at a macro-economic level and market efficiency at a micro level together provide individual opportunity (and thus the preconditions for social justice and political freedom) which ensures the social cohesion that feeds back into economic growth.

2.2.5   The Political Divide

Each of the four strategies which have shaped the development of the British welfare state, therefore, shares a common belief in the need for the state to define and enforce the conditions under which the market can operate efficiently. The major difference between the reluctant collectivists, the New Right and the Third Way is in their pragmatic judgement about how extensive state intervention should be. The reluctant collectivists and the Third Way assume that, as society grows more complex and the world economy more open, intervention must increase at either a macro-economic or micro-economic level. In contrast the New Right seeks, by constant reappraisal, to minimize it. The fundamental ideological divide, however, is between the New Right and the democratic socialists. The New Right asserts that the market maximizes efficiency in both the use of resources and the satisfaction of individual need, whereas democratic socialists maintain that the market wastes talent and resources and that economic efficiency is dependent on national planning. Such planning the New Right identifies as a major threat to political freedom since it deprives all citizens of choice. Political freedom, retort the social democrats, can be provided only by the state because it alone can guarantee that no-one is condemned to exist at so low a standard of living that free choice ceases to be a reality. The state alone can create an altruistic society and thereby ensure social justice. The New Right questions the meaning of such a term, especially if it is to be defined and imposed by one agency, and sees the essence of a just society in the freedom of everyone to make – and accept the consequences of – their own choices.

Many issues remain unresolved in this confrontation. The New Right is still vulnerable to the charge that the market is imperfect (tending towards monopoly, which will stifle competition, and unable to identify and thereby compensate the social cost of economic change). This can undoubtedly alienate people and generate political conflict. Democratic socialists, in their turn, have yet to confront the real-world fallibility of the state and the danger that a centralisation of power will result not in an altruistic society but in economic stagnation, bureaucratic inefficiency and alienation. This is the circle which the Third Way has sought to square by embedding a free market and an 'enabling' state in an active civil society which constantly reaffirms both social justice and political freedom.

2.3 GENERAL THEORIES OF SOCIAL WELFARE

2.3.1 Pluralism, Elitism and Corporatism

The political theory which has underpinned these four approaches to welfare, and which has generally informed popular and academic reaction to them, is pluralism. *Pluralism* assumes that society is essentially stable and that power is widely diffused so that no-one is completely powerless and no group (or class) dominant. The role of the state is to mediate between the various interest groups in society in order to reconcile their differences. Certain objections can be raised to this theory. For example, as the New Right has argued, the politicians and civil servants who constitute 'the state' may not be neutral arbiters but interested parties in their own right. The nature of the compromise they negotiate may, therefore, maximize their own interests rather than those of the public. Moreover, as *elite theorists* have argued, certain groups with special contacts, expertise and knowledge may command unequal access to government and thereby permanently enjoy an unequal share of power which they can turn to their own selfish advantage. Pluralists and elitists can reach very different conclusions about the nature of the welfare state, as the history of the NHS demonstrates.

Pluralists assume that through the NHS, the state mediates between the consumers of healthcare (the public) and its producers (the various branches of the medical profession). Consequently, the ultimate nature of the service represents the most acceptable compromise between their competing interests. In contrast elitists maintain that, since its stormy inception under Bevan, the NHS has been dominated by the medical profession with its specialist expertise and knowledge. The result has been the development of a 'medical model' of healthcare. This has concentrated attention on the biological causes of illness in individual patients and thus directs a disproportionate amount of resources to hospitals and specialist surgery. Other models of healthcare, which lay equal stress on individual life-styles or the quality of the environment, have been relatively ignored with the consequence that health education (such as anti-smoking campaigns) and preventive medicine (such as stricter anti-pollution controls), which arguably offer better value for money, have been denied adequate resources. As in most Western countries, the reason for the predominance of the 'medical model' of healthcare in Britain is that it serves best the prejudices and the interests of the established medical profession. The public (as both patient and tax-payer) lacks the information and expertise to challenge its authority, which will continue to predominate until effectively challenged by another elite (such as health planners within government).[43]

A third deviation from pluralism is the theory of *corporatism*, which aroused particular interest in Britain in the late 1970s. Its essential premise is that, in

advanced capitalist societies, pluralism declines and power is shared –
usually covertly – between the state and several powerful interest groups to
the exclusion of all others. As with most political theories there are many
competing – and often conflicting – variations of corporatism. Its purpose can
be either economic (to support technologically advanced and increasingly
monopolistic industries) or political (to maintain stability). Corporatist institutions may be the creation of the state (as in fascist Germany and Italy where
national organizations of employers and workers were created specifically to
regiment their constituents) or spontaneous developments (as in Britain
where employers' organizations and trade unions existed well before the
major extension of state intervention).

One variation of corporatism, 'corporate bias', has been specifically applied
to postwar Britain by Keith Middlemas.[44] He has argued that, particularly as
a result of the two world wars, successive governments have increasingly
shared power with institutions such as the Confederation of British Industry
(CBI) and the Trades Union Congress (TUC), which have thereby been transformed from ordinary pressure groups (as in a pluralistic society) to 'governing institutions'. In return for this exceptional power they have undertaken to
control their own members and thereby minimize public unrest. The consequences have been an increase in the power of the civil service, which is
instrumental in negotiating the covert deals; a decrease in the power of
Parliament, which is powerless to overturn them; and an ineffectual policy of
mere 'crisis avoidance', because any radical attempt to remedy Britain's
underlying weaknesses – such as its bad industrial structure or industrial relations – would challenge the interests of the 'governing institutions', destroy
the covert deals and thereby lift the constraints on public unrest. In the 1970s
the New Right was especially aware, and critical, of corporatist trends within
the welfare state. Rising unemployment, inflation and the seeming ungovernability of Britain were, for it, proof of the corruption of government that
inevitably accompanies the release of the state from the discipline of both the
market and freely expressed political opinion.

2.3.2 Marxism

Marxism has had little direct impact on the development of welfare policy in
Britain and, indeed, was rejected as obsolete by Crosland.[45] It has, however,
underpinned both the 'fundamentalist' beliefs of the left wing of the Labour
Party, with which Crosland was embattled, and many academic critiques of
the welfare state. It is the complete antithesis of pluralism. It assumes that
society is in fundamental conflict, with the pace of change being determined
by a continual battle between those who own the means of production (the
ruling class or the 'bourgeoisie') and those who do not (the working class).
Any outburst of unrest is not regarded as wasteful and unnecessary, as it is by
pluralists, but as 'creative' because it propels capitalism further along the road
to the inevitable goal of socialism and communism. A welfare state which
contains such unrest is therefore generally regarded by Marxists as neither a

new form of society nor a half-way house between capitalism and socialism (as democratic socialists maintain), but an advanced stage of capitalism and, as Bismarck had intended all state welfare to be, a bulwark against socialism.

There are three major variants of Marxism, each of which has been as vigorously attacked by the others as they have been by non-Marxists. The classical *instrumentalist* variant assumes that a coherent, class-conscious ruling class personally controls the extended 'state', which includes not just the government and the civil service but also other agencies of 'repression' such as the judiciary, army and police force. The state is thus the instrument for the furthering of the interests of the ruling class and the NHS, for instance, acts in this way because the leaders of the medical profession are bound by close personal and cultural ties to that ruling class. This interpretation has been applied most fully to Britain by Ralph Miliband and has been attacked on the empirical grounds that – despite some obvious personal interrelationships – the constant battles within and between each agency of the 'extended state' provide little evidence of a coherent ruling class.[46]

In contrast, the *structuralists* argue that members of the 'extended' state do not usually have close personal ties with the ruling class but that the state is obliged to act in its long-term interests because of certain structural constraints. The state is therefore only 'relatively autonomous'.[47] One such constraint is the state's dependence for its revenue on continuing economic growth and hence on the profitability of industry, which prevents it from attempting anything that might permanently undermine the confidence of businessmen and financiers either at home or abroad. This reticence has not only affected welfare policy in times of emergency, such as in the 1940s when Britain was dependent on US aid or in the 1970s when an IMF loan was being sought, but throughout the whole postwar period when the successful management of the economy was dependent on the willingness of both business to invest and financiers to support sterling. The perceived weakness of this theory is that the state is depicted as being simultaneously strong and weak. On the one hand, it is sufficiently strong to implement reforms essential to the long-term stability of capitalism (such as the NHS which helps to ensure a healthy workforce) despite the well-documented objections of capitalists to their short-term cost. On the other hand, despite the ability to surmount such opposition, it is incapable of acting against capitalism's long-term interest. No logical explanation has been provided for this seeming contradiction and structuralists have consequently been condemned for excessive 'functionalism'. Their theory, it is claimed, rests on the crude assumption that because capitalism has survived, despite Marx's predictions, the function of the state must have been to support it.

The third *neo-Marxist* variation is inspired by the writings of the Italian Marxist, Gramsci.[48] This explains the continuing dominance of capitalist values, despite conflicts within the ruling elite and the relative autonomy of the state, by admitting that the ruling class is fragmented (between for instance industrialists and financiers); and by arguing that capitalist 'hegemony' is maintained by a series of alliances forged – through the agency of the state – between the dominant 'fraction' of the elite and the other groups in society. By this means the short-sighted resistance to reform of certain fractions within the ruling class, which might eventually provoke unrest, can be overcome while capitalism's long-term interests are secured. Thus the creation of the welfare state can be represented as a 'passive revolution' whereby the most far-sighted fraction of the elite conceded, through the agency of the Labour Party, a series of reforms which in effect strengthened capitalism economically (by generating the demand for goods which had been lacking in the 1930s) and politically (by reconciling a majority of the electorate to capitalist values, as illustrated by successive Conservative victories between 1951 and 1959). As soon as the welfare state started to conflict with capitalism's long- term interest, as it did in the 1970s, it could be revoked and another series of alliances (as represented by Mrs Thatcher's populism) negotiated. Both the strength and the weakness of this theory lie in the concept of hegemony, the process by which capitalist values become so dominant – through, for example, formal education, the media and the social services' inculcation of the 'work ethic' – that other classes 'internalize' them and mistakenly believe them to serve their own interests. This self-delusion cannot, by its very nature, be empirically proven and its existence depends on the highly dangerous assumption that, for any given historical period, theorists are better able to judge than contemporary individuals or groups the nature of their true interests. Hard evidence of the state's negotiation of the necessary alliances is also, as yet, lacking.

From these general theories a specific critique of the welfare state has emerged from O'Connor in the USA and Gough in Britain.[49] They classify welfare expenditure in capitalist societies as either social capital or social expenses. Social capital assists industrial profitability ('the process of capital accumulation') by providing services which will either increase productivity (for example improvements to the infrastructure, such as roads) or reduce the costs to industry of securing a healthy, well-educated workforce. All these services the market is itself incapable of providing profitably. Social expenses make politically acceptable ('legitimize') capitalism by eradicating the worst abuses which might provoke unrest and by creating a general impression of social justice.

The NHS, by both helping to create and maintain a healthy workforce and by providing a free service according to need, is an example of social capital and social expenses. Moreover it demonstrates that neither serves the true interest of the working class. That class has paid its full share of the cost of the 'free' health service through direct and indirect taxation, and yet its vulnerable 'non-productive' members (such as pensioners and the mentally handicapped) receive a disproportionately low share of available resources. In contrast the careers of hospital doctors and the profits of drug companies, which had been threatened by the impending bankruptcy of

→

the voluntary hospital system in the 1930s, have revived; and, through the 'medical model' of healthcare, industry has been able to disguise its responsibility – and thereby evade the payment of compensation – for ill health arising from its pollution of the environment. The 'medical model', therefore, serves not simply the interests of the medical profession (as maintained by elite theorists) but also, more significantly, the interests of the ruling class.

There is, continue O'Connor and Gough, an inherent contradiction in this dual role of capitalist welfare. There inevitably comes a time, as during the fiscal crisis of the 1970s, when the cost of social expenses starts to undermine, through rising taxation and inflation, the process of capital accumulation. To reduce it, however, is impossible because it risks the exposure of capitalist exploitation and thus social unrest. As Claus Offe has remarked: 'the contradiction is that while capitalism cannot coexist *with* the Welfare State, neither can it exist *without* the Welfare State'.[50]

Such a contradiction is welcome because it heralds capitalism's impending collapse. However there is also – as critics have been quick to point out – a parallel contradiction in the Marxists' own critique. Social reform is seen both as a concession from above consolidating capitalism (as in the concept of the 'passive revolution') and as the result of coercion from below forcing capitalism further towards a socialist society (resulting, for instance, from a 'creative' confrontation between the working class and the ruling elite, be it at an election or during a period of overt social unrest). If welfare cuts are threatened, as in the 1970s, should Marxists therefore welcome them as a relaxation of social control, which will increase the likelihood of confrontation, or should they oppose them as an attack on working-class living standards, painfully acquired? They cannot do both. The usual conclusion is that, despite their constant condemnation of welfare reform as a means of social control, they ultimately acknowledge – in conformity with the democratic socialists and indeed Marx's own interpretation of the nineteenth-century Factories Acts – that welfare reform presents a fundamental challenge to capitalism. 'The Welfare State', as Dearlove and Saunders have concluded, 'represents a "Trojan horse" within the citadels of capitalism in that it rests firmly on a set of values which are fundamentally opposed to those of capitalism.'[51] This inherent contradiction has been seen to weaken Marxism as a practical political philosophy, if not as a powerful critique of welfare policy in capitalist society.

2.3.3 Feminism

A further critique of the welfare state which has been gathering strength since the late 1960s arises from feminism. It too has many variants. Liberal feminists accept that social policy will inevitably reflect prevailing imbalances in gender relations, but trust that either directly (through, for instance, child benefits paid to mothers or equal opportunity legislation) or indirectly (through full employment or access to higher education) these imbalances will be eroded. Marxist and radical feminists, on the other hand, believe that inequality is the inevitable consequence of capitalism or patriarchy (the biologically determined or socially constructed dominance of men over women).

The history of welfare policy before 1945 has gradually been recast. Most early legislation, it is agreed, was 'paternalist' in that it was designed to make good interruptions to the earnings of the male breadwinner so that, even when unemployed or sick, he could maintain economic dominance over his family. Nevertheless, championed by women in government and in the 'shadow welfare state' of voluntary provision, there was a simultaneous 'maternalist' strand of policy providing services solely to women, such as maternity benefits and health clinics. Such legislation raises a fundamental question. Was it *'pro-family'* or *'women friendly'*? In other words, was its essential purpose to help women in their own right or simply as mothers – with the ulterior motive of ensuring the quantity and quality of children as future workers and soldiers? Such a question can only be resolved by the precise detail and scope of legislation. Did cash payments, for example, simply reflect the additional costs of parenthood or were they paid direct to mothers at the level of a 'living wage', thereby giving women a genuine measure of 'economic autonomy'? Did health services only assist fertility or did they give women control over their own bodies (including the right to abortion)? A similar question can be asked of postwar legislation, overtly designed to ensure equal citizenship for men and women. It can also be extended. *Formal equality*, it is argued, can only be translated into *actual equality* by a revolution in social, economic and political practice – what Giddens meant in his definition of the Third Way by the creation of a 'democratic family'. In other words, actual equality in the 'public sphere' of work and politics is unattainable unless responsibilities in the 'private sphere' of housework and child-rearing are genuinely shared between men and women, and more flexible work practices introduced to accommodate such responsibilities. Even advanced social democracies such as Sweden are held to be deficient in this respect.[52] Sweden's requirement that all lone mothers should speedily return to work also denies the essential variety of women's interests.

Historical analysis has yet to address these issues fully but the pervasive assumption is that the postwar British welfare state has been more coercive than emancipatory for women. This is particularly true of the social security system. Thus the Beveridge report has been generally perceived not as a blueprint for beneficent reform, but as 'one of the most crudely ideological documents of its kind ever written'. The explicit assumption underlying its proposals was that the majority of women who married should enter into a 'partnership' with their husbands and remain economically dependent upon them whilst, in the national interest, they bred and reared children. In one particularly notorious passage, for instance, it is noted that Beveridge asserts:

the attitude of the housewife to gainful employment outside the home is not and should not be the same as that of a single woman. She has other duties.'[53]

It is initially difficult, with historical perspective, to accept that the welfare state has been coercive rather than emancipatory. It has generally been acknowledged that in the interwar years it was women's diet and health which suffered most severely from the loss of family income occasioned by unemployment and, when unemployed themselves, women had no free access to medical care. In contrast the welfare state has provided the psychological and material advantages of a guaranteed income and free access to healthcare, as well as a foremost demand of interwar feminists – family allowances. In addition the maintenance of full employment has offered married women the opportunity of work and thus an independent income, not least in the expanded social services. It has even consolidated some of women's advantages over men. For example, as Titmuss argued in 1955, the average woman derives considerably more benefit than the average man from the state pension because of her earlier age of retirement (60 not 65) and her greater longevity.[54]

Such benefits were acknowledged and welcomed by women during and after the war.[55] For instance, the reaction of one ordinary, instinctively feminist housewife to the Beveridge Report was: 'His scheme will appeal more even to women than to men, for it is they who bear the real burden of unemployment, sickness, child-bearing and rearing and the ones who, up to now, have come off worse.' A survey of women's opinions on 'family needs and the social services' in the mid-1950s discovered general enthusiasm for the social services, especially the NHS. The impact of the welfare state on income, housing and health (together with other changes such as reduced working hours and reduced family size – again in defiance of Beveridge) was also seen by the mid-1950s to have altered fundamentally traditional relationships. As an early survey in the East End of London reported: 'In place of the old comes a new kind of companionship between man and woman, reflecting the rise in status of the young wife and children which is one of the great transformations of our time. There is now a nearer approach to equality between the sexes and, although each has a peculiar role, its boundaries are no longer so rigidly defined nor is it performed without consultation.'

However, the achievement of feminist analysis is that it can now be seen that these undeniable advances were achieved at a certain cost.[56] Marxist feminists have argued that the welfare state has served only to reinforce women's traditional role in capitalist society: to reproduce an adequate, healthy and contented workforce through the unpaid care of children and husbands. In addition, some have argued that women are a 'reserve army' of cheap labour to be welcomed into employment in periods of labour shortage (and often into part-time jobs specifically tailored to deny them social rights) only to be dismissed first in a recession. Other feminists have questioned the 'liberation' experienced by married women from increased job opportunities owing both to the 'dual role' they have to play as wage-earners and housewives and to the sexual stereotyping to which they are subjected at work. The social services themselves have also reinforced, overtly and covertly, the inferior position of women. The right to insurance benefit, for example, has traditionally been established through contributions paid whilst in employment and because women on average are paid less and have more interrupted careers (owing in particular to childbirth and rearing) their rights are considerably less. The rights of non-working mothers have also been established by their husbands' contributions, so that the increasing number of divorcees and unmarried mothers are placed in a vulnerable position where their needs can only be met by means-tested supplementary benefit, with all the disadvantages that that entails. Other supposedly progressive policies (such as family allowances and community care) can similarly be seen as being essentially designed not to help individual women as mothers and patients, but to encourage women in general to continue their traditional biological and unpaid caring role in order both to ensure the nation's future and to cut the escalating costs of institutional medicine.

The NHS, as an employer and provider of healthcare, can be seen as a prime example of exploitation. It reinforces the sexual division of labour, as dominant positions (such as doctors and managers) are normally held by men and subordinate positions (such as nurses and ancillary workers) by women. By placing women's health and most personal needs under the control of predominantly male doctors, male standards of emotional and physical health are regarded as the norm and specifically female problems minimized. Reproduction is also regarded as central to women's personality, so that infertility is treated with far greater sympathy than abortion and family planning. Above all childbirth has been removed from the home, where it was the concern of female relatives and midwives, and (in the perceived medical interest of mother and child) removed to hospitals, where the greater use of impersonal machinery adds to the status of the doctor if not to the actual comfort of the mother.[57] In short, free access to the NHS has, like all welfare reform, reinforced male domination over women.

2.3.4 The Anti-Racist Critique

Another critique of the welfare state, which owes much to feminist theories, is the anti-racist critique. Gathering strength since the 1970s, it first addressed issues of racial inequality and then the even more fundamental problems of multiculturalism – how to design and deliver universal welfare services when, in an increasingly multi-ethnic society, there are fewer common 'core' values. This critique has yet to have a major impact on policy, let alone the history of welfare policy.[58] Nevertheless it addresses issues which, as demonstrated by current controversies over immigration and 'asylum seekers', are of great political importance throughout Western Europe. Moreover, it has the potential to challenge conventional analyses of welfare policy both by broadening its definition (to include areas such as race relations) and by questioning its underlying rationale.

Before the 1970s, it had long been recognized that the delivery of welfare was frequently besmirched by individual instances of overt racism, such as the signs in rented accommodation in the 1950s proclaiming 'no Irish, no blacks, no dogs'. The new contention, which the anti-racist critique initially advanced, was that the depth and persistence of more generalized deprivation was caused by covert institutional racism. In a 'male-breadwinner state', as has been seen, women can be doubly disadvantaged by their lower socio-economic status which welfare policy then reinforces. Similarly in a 'white' welfare state, black immigrants and their descendants typically enjoy lower wages and life-styles than their white counterparts. These disadvantages are then reinforced by welfare policy through, for example, lower earnings related benefits or the 'right to buy' only the lower quality housing, to which they were initially allocated. Black women may even be triply disadvantaged since they either typically rely on relatively disadvantaged men or are disproportionately the head of single-parent families. Moreover, disadvantage can be reproduced across generations as children's low expectations feed into educational underachievement and thus into low-paid employment. In short, even after *formal* racial equality has been established through various Race Relations Acts, *actual* equality may not exist.

Since the 1980s, the welfare state has also become a central focus of a heated debate over multiculturalism. Multiculturalism, as identified by a major report in 2000, *The Future of Multi-Ethnic Britain*, poses some fundamental questions. In particular:

> How should disputes and incompatible values between different communities be handled? How is a balance to be struck between the need to treat people equally, the need to treat people differently, and the need to maintain shared values and social cohesion? [59]

The need for some difference of treatment, such as the provision of information in a range of different languages and sensitivity to the beliefs of different faiths, is widely accepted. However it has been equally widely argued that, if social cohesion (which, as has been seen in Section 2.1 above, is crucial to any definition of a welfare state) and above all the willingness of the majority of tax-payers to fund welfare is to be maintained, entitlement to services should be conditional on the acceptance of some core values. Possibly, it has been argued, there should be a two-tier welfare state with one providing for permanent citizens (who have formally accepted such values and have a full tax record) and the other for temporary residents (such as asylum seekers and economic migrants). Neither group of beneficiaries should, or need, be ethnically defined. This, the anti-racists retort, is exactly what would happen. Moreover such a solution does not address the issue of permanent citizens who reject core values as defined by the dominant white majority. Rather, everyone in Britain should simultaneously be treated as equal *and* different. If

Christian schools are to be state funded, for instance, then so too should be Muslim schools – even if they may reflect and reinforce gender attitudes which offend, amongst others, feminists.

The 'anti-racist' critique can itself be insensitive. In the past it has over-looked differences between and within ethnic groupings (with some groups of Asians, for example, as opposed to Afro-Caribbean children outperforming their white counterparts). Similarly it has disguised the fact that, just as women can be the worst exploiters of women, so some members of ethnic groups can equally exploit other members of that group (as the history of housing after the 1957 Rent Act demonstrates). In addition it can lack balance. Racial discrimination, after all, is also not an exclusively postwar problem or one restricted to skin colour (as earlier racist treatment of the Jews and Irish, let alone the Scots and Welsh, testifies). Within Britain, moreover, 'race' has not yet had so profound an impact on welfare policy as in the USA and immigrants have enjoyed fuller rights than, for example, Turkish 'guest-workers' in Germany.[60] Nevertheless, like feminism, the anti-racist critique has identified within the values and the practices of welfare policy the potential for the disadvantaging of a discrete set of citizens. As such it is essential to any serious conceptualization of, or effective attack upon, social exclusion.

As an employer and provider of healthcare the NHS can be portrayed as exploiting ethnic minorities, just as it does women. Their low socio-economic status is typically reinforced by employment at the lowest levels (although the educational 'overachievement' of some Asian students is reflected by their disproportionate attainment of medical qualifications). Conventional medicine also tends to pay insufficient attention to illnesses peculiar to black people (such as sickle-cell anaemia amongst Afro-Caribbeans), causes doctors to act discriminatorily (as with the disproportionate diagnosis and acute treatment of psychosis amongst Afro-Caribbeans) and disregard distinctive cultural needs. In other words, in the words of the Parekh report on multi-ethnicity, the NHS harbours a 'striking paradox'. It 'depends, and for several decades has depended, on the contributions of Asian, black and Irish doctors, nurses, managers and ancillary staff. At the same time, levels of mortality and morbidity are higher in Asian, black and Irish communities than in the population as a whole, and there is much insensitivity in the NHS to the distinctive experiences, situations and requirements of these communities'.[61] Increased immigration has exacerbated the potential of the NHS to reflect and reinforce racist assumptions. As a result of the 1993 and 1996 Asylum and Immigration Acts, for instance, it has been increasingly possible to question the right of free access to healthcare of anyone who, particularly through the colour of their skin, appears 'foreign'.

2.3.5 The Green Critique

The green, like the anti-racist, critique of the welfare state has developed since

1970s when a perceived 'ecological crisis' led to the foundation of two influential pressure groups, the Friends of the Earth and Greenpeace. It too has had little direct influence on policy, let alone the history of welfare policy, although it addresses issues of fundamental importance such as global warming and the quality of modern life.

The 'green' critique is both general and fundamental. Its basic premise is that economic growth is unsustainable (because of finite resources and the environmental damage caused by pollution) and undesirable (because it does not add to human well-being spiritually or materially given, for instance, rising inequality and crime).[62] To achieve a higher quality of life an alternative 'mixed moral economy of well-being' is therefore sought which includes a better balance between work and leisure as well as an enrichment of both the community and the environment. The resultant strategy has been described as 'think global, act local'. Power should be decentralized and an emphasis placed on self-provision. At its most ideal, a basic income should be provided for everyone which, as well as recognizing everyone's equal worth, would address the traditional discrepancies in rewards between paid, unpaid and voluntary work. Alternatively, to strengthen communities, there could be local employment transfer schemes where individuals trade skills and time.

More practical policies pursued when Green politicians have achieved political power (as in Germany) or influenced political agendas (as in Britain) have been nature conservancy measures, anti-pollution taxes and improvements to the local environment (such as the provision of better, and better maintained, parks for children). Such initiatives, as will be confirmed in Chapter 9, build on a tradition of environmental issues which welfare policy has traditionally addressed, such as urban sprawl (with a succession of Town and Country Planning Acts), conservation (with the 1949 National Parks Act) and air pollution (with the highly successful 1956 Clean Air Act).

The NHS, as currently conceived, is a principal target of the Greens. They are particularly critical of the 'medical model' of healthcare favoured, as has been seen, by the medical profession and drug companies. To them it epitomizes the inability of centrally controlled increases in expenditure to achieve either material or spiritual gains. Rather health outcomes and expenditure should be optimized by a concentrating on prevention (such as anti-pollution measures to halt the explosion in childhood asthma) and the empowering of individuals (through, for instance, the choice of different therapies including complementary medicine and more sympathetic personal care, such as midwife-assisted home births).

2.4 CONCLUSION

Each of the preceding theories, as indeed each of the four political approaches to welfare in postwar Britain, is persuasive when judged on its own assumptions. Each also appears somewhat fallible when judged against hard historical evidence. This fallibility has tempted many historians, initially sympathetic to the application of theory to historical analysis, to fall back on their profession's traditional assumption that each society in each age is unique. There can, they feel, be no general theory which can satisfactorily explain the simultaneous international development of welfare states after the Second World War by encompassing all their similarities and dissimilarities.

However, as argued in Chapter 1, no historical analysis can be atheoretical and so each should, as far as possible, admit its underlying bias. The assumptions upon which the structure of this book and its selection of evidence are based are essentially those of *pluralism* and *reluctant collectivism*. The traditional imperfections of pluralist analysis are admitted. In contrast to the bold Marxist theory of class conflict, it tends to ascribe historical change unheroically to 'broad, amorphous, evolutionary trends', whilst political analysis can descend into a myopic study of the 'immediate manoeuvrings of interest groups' which obscure the wider struggle for power which these manoeuvres represent.[63] There is also a tendency to underestimate the divergent strengths of the various competing interest groups, not least of whom are the politicians and administrators (who are far from neutral). However, pluralism represents the values that were most prevalent in postwar Britain and, on that count alone, has considerable historical validity as an explanation of contemporary decisions. With hindsight it would also appear to accord most satisfactorily with the evidence.

Marxism is rejected not just for the technical reasons identified already, but because of its fundamental assumption that historical change is determined by the conflict between two economically determined classes. The central feminist assumption, that the main purpose of the welfare state is to reinforce patriarchy, is also adjudged too extreme. To succeed in a democratic society any policy must reflect the general values of the time, and the initial values which the welfare state reflected appear to have been as acceptable to women as to men. By institutionalizing these values the welfare state inevitably tended to reinforce them. That, as the New Right would emphasize, is the inherent danger of centralization. However, by remedying the deprivation from which women suffered in the interwar years, the welfare state has given women (and society as a whole) the strength to recognize these covert controls and to proceed to dismantle them. Parallel reservations can be held about the still underdeveloped anti-racist critique.

With regard to 'corporate bias', the accuracy of the evidence used to support its alleged evolution has been challenged elsewhere, and the conclusion appears inescapable that the most significant fact about corporatism in Britain is not that it has been attempted but that it has consistently failed.[64] Elitism seems eminently reconcilable with pluralism, once it is acknowledged that each elite is essentially transient, vulnerable at times to outside pressures and limited in power to particular areas of policy. Finally, the 'green' critique is as yet insufficiently developed and too abstract. These brief and perhaps over-simplistic conclusions are not to deny that each rejected theory has invaluable insights to offer, but merely to argue that a pluralistic perspective would appear to provide the most satisfactory premise on which to analyse the postwar British welfare state.

Reluctant collectivism similarly appears to be the most realistic of the postwar welfare strategies. The idealistic objective of the democratic socialists to create an altruistic society is instantly attractive, but it *is* idealistic. It overlooks the real-world limitations of 'the state'. In its expressed wish to re-create the social solidarity and efficient central planning of the Second World War it would also seem to overlook the evidence of Titmuss himself. His account of wartime evacuation, for example, records – as do other commentaries – not social solidarity but frequent antagonism between the evacuees and their hosts. It also reveals the dislike of both for central planning, with large numbers of evacuees spontaneously returning home both in 1940 and at the end of the war. Titmuss concluded 'that people behaved in an unexpected way. By their behaviour they made planning difficult: they made a good plan look, in the end, like a bad plan.'[65] Such a conclusion hardly inspires faith in the practicality of social engineering.

Likewise the New Right provides some acute criticisms of the many failings of the welfare state, but its strength lies essentially in its powers of criticism. Its own positive championing of the market, for both economic and political reasons, ignores the long-standing market failures which resulted in the depression of the interwar years. It turns a blind eye also to the fact that the market is inefficient in many technical ways, not least because imperfect knowledge results in a misallocation of resources and a degree of social inequality which is both economically disadvantageous and politically dangerous. In contrast reluctant collectivism, by endorsing the economic and political strength of the market while seeking simultaneously to correct its acknowledged weaknesses, offers an effective compromise. Between 1945 and 1975 this strategy may have revealed many of the conventional weaknesses of compromise but, as Marshall argued, there is no reason why such a compromise should not combine the strength of the two opposing ideologies and become a viable, principled philosophy. With greater private determination and public education it can, in other words, provide a positive programme for conviction politics. The same might well be said in the near future of the still untested, but in many aspects the remarkably similar, Third Way.

2.5 FURTHER READING

As suggested in the preface, the natural starting point for further examination of issues raised in this chapter is P. Alcock, A. Erskine and M. May (eds), *The Student's Companion to Social Policy* (Oxford, 2nd edn, 2003). This may be supplemented by M. Powell and M. Hewitt, *Welfare State and Welfare Change* (Buckingham, 2002) with its wide if slightly indigestible review of the relevant literature. The same sweep of history and theory is covered from a neo-marxist perspective by C. Pierson, *Beyond the Welfare State?* (Cambridge, 2nd edn, 1998). Two good collections of readings are C. Pierson and F. G. Castles, *The Welfare State Reader* (Cambridge, 2000) and, from an historian's perspective, M. Jones and R. Lowe, *From Beveridge to Blair* (Manchester, 2002).

The classic comparative works on the rise and restructuring of welfare states are G. Esping-Andersen, *The Three Worlds of Welfare Capitalism* (Cambridge, 1990) and P. Pierson (ed), *The New Politics of the Welfare State* (Oxford, 2001). The fullest historical treatment up to the crisis of the 1970s is P. Baldwin, *The Politics of Social Solidarity* (Cambridge, 1990). A clear and stimulating account of the parallel development since the 1970s of welfare thought in Britain and the USA, together with the moral choices thereby exposed, is A. Deacon, *Perspectives on Welfare* (Buckingham, 2002).

Excellent introductions to competing concepts of welfare applied to post-war British experience are V. George and P. Wilding, *Ideology and Welfare* (1994) and R. Mishra, *Society and Social Policy* (1981). They may be supplemented by the more uneven V. George and R. Page (eds), *Modern Thinkers on Welfare* (1995) which includes chapters on race and the environment. These perspectives are further developed in F. Williams, *Social Policy: a critical introduction* (Cambridge, 1989); and applied empirically in N. Ellison and C. Pierson (eds), *Developments in British Social Policy* (Basingstoke, 1998).

A general introduction sympathetic to Marxist analysis is J. Dearlove and P. Saunders, *Introduction to British Politics* (Cambridge, 1991). A good feminist reader is C. Ungerson and M. Kember (eds), *Women and Social Policy* (1996) whilst a challenging basis for further empirical and theoretical analysis is provided by J. Lewis, *Women in Britain since 1945* (Oxford, 1992) and A. Orloff, 'Gender and the social rights of citizenship', in *American Sociological Review*, 58 (1993) 303–28. D. S. King, *The New Right* (1987) is a stimulating introduction contrasting the early experience of Britain and the USA, whilst the most noted historical 'New Right' attack on the welfare state is C. Barnett, *The Audit of War* (1986). Its strengths and weaknesses are appraised by J. Harris in 'Enterprise and Welfare States: a comparative perspective', *Transactions of the Royal Historical Society*, 40 (1990) 175–95; and the same author has lamented the lack, in practice, of any philosophical underpinning of postwar state intervention in 'Political thought and the state' published in S. J. D. Green and R. C. Whiting (ed.), *The Boundaries of the State in Modern Britain* (Cambridge, 1996). The NHS is analysed in the light of competing theories by C. Ham, *Health Policy in Britain* (1992) and comparatively in M. Moran, *Governing the Healthcare State* (Manchester, 1999).

On the developing political strategies, there is really no substitute for the views of their original proponents: *The Collected Writings of John Maynard Keynes*, esp. vols 21–6 (1979–82); the Beveridge Report (Cmd 6404); T. H. Marshall, *Citizenship and Social Class and other Essays* (1950); P. Alcock et al. (eds), *Welfare and Wellbeing: Titmuss' contribution to social policy* (Bristol, 2001); C. A. R. Crosland, *The Future of Socialism* (1956); F. A. Hayek, *The Road to Serfdom* (1944); and A. Giddens, *The Third Way* (Cambridge, 1998). These works may be supplemented for reluctant collectivism by J. Harris, *William Beveridge* (Oxford, 1997) and R. Shepherd, *Iain Macleod* (1994); for social democracy by N. Ellison, *Egalitarian Thought and Labour Politics* (1994); and for the New Right, by R. Harris and A. Seldon, *Overruled on Welfare* (1979).

chapter 3

The Nature of Policy-Making

CONTENTS

The historical analysis of the welfare state benefits from theoretical insights into the distribution of power in society and the ultimate objectives of state intervention. It can also benefit from similar insights into the formulation of policy and the criteria for its effectiveness. This requires a change of focus from the general theories to the more technical aspects of political science and economics which are concerned with how political decisions are taken and implemented, and how policy objectives (once determined) can best be achieved. For instance:

- Does state intervention, as its early proponents (such as Keynes and Beveridge) seemed to assume but as its opponents (the New Right) would dispute, really entail the taking of decisions by disinterested experts in command of the full range of relevant information?
- Are these decisions then automatically implemented in such a way that all citizens benefit, and only benefit, from them in the manner intended?
- In a specific policy area, what are the criteria for determining whether the use of scarce resources will be maximized, in general, by state intervention or the market and, in particular, by a given policy?

Such theoretical questions as these have spawned a vast empirical literature, from which examples will again be largely selected from the history of the NHS.

3.1 THE POLITICAL SCIENCE PERSPECTIVE

3.1.1 The Three Faces of Power

One subject which political science has done much to illuminate is the nature of power. Three types (or 'faces') have been identified. The *first*, which is the easiest to recognize, is the power exercised by one individual or group over another in face-to-face confrontation. The *second* is the power to keep certain policy options off the political agenda and thereby stifle an unwelcome policy before an overt decision has to be taken ('the theory of non-decision making'). Policy debate is thereby constrained by the 'anticipated reaction' of powerful professional and bureaucratic interests. The consolidation of policy-making departments at the core of wider 'policy networks' has also resulted, so it has been recently contended, in their becoming the 'focus for a closed relationship which has a substantial impact on policy outcomes through its ability to exclude particular groups and issues from the policy agenda'.[1] The *third* face of power is the power so to shape people's ideas that they never conceive, let alone articulate, certain policy options which are in their interests. This type of power is synonymous with the neo-Marxist concept of hegemony. It is therefore the hardest to identify.

This distinction between the three faces of power has obvious implications for an understanding of policy-making and consequently for the identification and analysis of historical evidence. Policy-making must be defined by the historian not only as visible decisions between well-defined options, but also as the covert avoidance of other options and even the mere maintenance of the *status quo*. The history of welfare policy has therefore to recognize and explain not only what has happened in the past but also what has not. This is a dangerous task made all the more difficult because evidence for non-decision making and hegemony is, by its very nature, sparse.

As the history of the NHS demonstrates, however, there is the evidence on which to make such judgements and it is sufficient to raise doubts about the reputation of the 'classic' welfare state for rationality, reasonableness and pragmatism. The disdain accorded to the IEA and women's medical needs, for instance, suggests that it was extremely intolerant of any idea which threatened the consensus on which it was based. It was not only in the 1980s that policy makers had to be 'one of us'.

An obvious example of the *first* face of power within the NHS is the conflict in 1951 between Bevan and Gaitskell over the introduction of dental and ophthalmic charges. Gaitskell won the battle within Cabinet, the Labour government introduced charges and Bevan resigned.

The *second* is represented by the respective success of the medical profession and the Treasury in resisting the extension of local authority health centres and community care in the 1950s. The former were wanted by the

→

Labour Party as a local focus for all the health services provided by central and local government. The latter was recommended by the 1956 Guillebaud Report as a humane and cheap alternative to the institutional care of the old. Neither was actively championed, however, because of the known hostility of the medical profession towards local authorities and of the Treasury towards any increase in local grants which it could not directly control.[2]

The exercise of the *third* face of power was exposed by the rise of feminism, which revealed the power of male doctors in the 1950s – under the guise of 'scientific' medical expertise – to shape women's definition of their own needs. Similarly the IEA in the 1960s argued that the high degree of popular satisfaction with the NHS was maintained largely because politicians and civil servants, for their own ends, deliberately fostered 'civic illiteracy' over its true cost and limitations.[3] Only when that 'tacit conspiracy' was broken, so the IEA argued, would the public be able to identify its interests and consequently 'think the unthinkable'.

3.1.2 Bureaucracy and the Formulation of Policy

One institution which in all industrial countries has been involved in the exercise of all three faces of power, and which has accordingly been subject to extensive scrutiny, is the civil service (or 'bureaucracy', to use that term in its neutral sense).[4] Opinion became so divided over its beneficial or deleterious effect on policy that in Britain, as elsewhere, its postwar development – and its academic analysis – experienced a major discontinuity.

In Britain the key event in this hiatus was the implementation in 1988 of the *Next Steps* programme, which eventually divided a previously unified civil service into a number of executive agencies (employing ten years later some 80 per cent of officials under differing terms and conditions) headed by a small core of policy advisers. The implementation of this programme reflected a triumph for the principles of 'new public management'. Based on private sector practice in the USA, this had the self-proclaimed mission of introducing market discipline into government and thereby transforming 'unresponsive, paternalistic and leaden bureaucracies' into 'customer-driven, flexible, quality-orientated and responsive organizations'.[5] This administrative revolution was matched by an equally fundamental political change from the concept and, arguably, practice of 'government' (where effective power is held at, and exercised from, the centre) to 'governance' (where there is a more pluralistic spread of power throughout society and, in the favoured jargon of the time, government does not row but steers). Because of this discontinuity, analysis must be divided chronologically.

Bureaucracy and the classic welfare state

Bureaucracy's foremost theoretical champion is Max Weber, the German sociologist who helped to draft the constitution of the Weimar Republic after the First World War. His ideas underpinned – if only unconsciously – the growth of the British civil service in the first three-quarters of the twentieth century. *Weber* argued that bureaucracy was the only rational means by which modern society could be organized. This was because of its efficiency (ensured by such organizational characteristics as a clear hierarchy and its adherence to rules). It was also due to its broad societal role (rising above sectional interest to define and act in the national interest). He was sufficiently realistic to acknowledge that there was an inherent tension between bureaucracy and democracy. Officials might develop a specialist expertise against which ministers would appear as 'dilettantes'. To avoid criticism they might favour secrecy and thus 'a poorly informed, and hence powerless parliament – at least insofar as ignorance is compatible with bureaucracy's own interest'. Officials' own interests might also intrude into and therefore bias their working definition of the 'by no means ambiguous' concept of the national interest.[6] Weber maintained, however, that an enlarged state bureaucracy was indispensable to good government; and he trusted that in each country its potential dangers would be checked by such countervailing forces as strong ministers, informed public opinion and industry's own bureaucracy.

Weber's theoretical assumptions were attacked by both Marxists and the New Right. Given their fundamental belief in class conflict, *Marxists* (as has been seen) denied that there could be a single 'national interest' within capitalist society. Their basic assumption was, therefore, that bureaucracy could but serve the interest of the ruling class. In contrast the *New Right* denied the efficiency of bureaucracy in the allocation of scarce resources. This was in part because of bureaucratic self-interest. The nature of democratic politics (the need to win votes) biased politicians towards greater state expenditure, it was argued, and officials exploited this bias to maximize their budgets and hence their own salaries, power and prestige. However, even the most disinterested and public-spirited of bureaucrats could be guilty of serious economic misallocation. Because of their imperfect knowledge, for example, zealous social reformers could concentrate resources on one particular reform at the expense of others, which might well have better served the public interest. Similarly, committed administrative reformers, in their determination to eliminate waste and promote honesty, could undermine good government. This was by both removing competition between rival departments (which had previously kept them responsive to changing public needs) and displacing efficiency with honesty as the main criterion of official performance.[7] In short, the New Right argued, bureaucracy inherently discouraged the very values which were needed to ensure a speedy response to conflicting and changing need. The more zealous and public-spirited the officials the greater the economic damage they could unwittingly cause.

Weber's assumptions were also challenged empirically. In Britain the civil service's lack of specialist and managerial skills was constantly condemned not least by the Fulton Committee on the Civil Service (1966–8). Likewise there was a torrent of attacks on its political power following the publication of Richard Crossman's diaries in 1975.[8] *Crossman* himself, as minister of housing, complained that he felt himself placed in a 'padded cell' where officials could insulate him from any information or pressure group that might challenge the 'departmental view'. A further 'key to the control by the civil service over politicians', he was convinced, were official interdepartmental committees. They, under the guise of coordinating government policy, could be used by officials either to frustrate initiatives (which they might even have promised ministers to implement) or to construct complex packages of policies (which could only be dismantled and reassembled by a determined and united cabinet). Increasing emphasis on the planning of public expenditure after 1960 also placed ministers firmly within a straitjacket of policies largely devised by officials.[9]

Crossman's particular *bête noire*, as for most other critics of the British civil service, was nevertheless the Treasury. Its power, which was exceptional for any Western ministry of finance, sprang from its three main responsibilities:

- economic policy, which determined the resources available for all other policies
- the control of public expenditure, which made its prior sanction necessary for all policy changes
- the management of the civil service, which tied the loyalty of civil servants, bent on promotion, to the Treasury rather than to their departmental minister.

Such power, so it was argued, had been exercised with neither noticeable expertise nor disinterest by its officials. Their lack of specialist economic and managerial skills was the source of constant criticism. Moreover, they were perceived consistently to have imposed their vested interests or 'departmental view' throughout the civil service, to the particular detriment of welfare policy. They had, for instance, been reluctant to dispense with annual budgeting because of the strict control it permitted over public expenditure. This was despite the fact that efficient economic management and welfare expenditure required a longer perspective. Their dependence on financial markets, both at home and abroad, to raise loans to fund the national debt and to maintain the value of sterling, also gave them a vested interest in minimizing public, and especially welfare, expenditure. Consequently, in both their routine work and in major crises (such as that over the 1976 IMF loan) they appeared to resort to every possible device to attack welfare expenditure. This fostered the conviction – especially amongst democratic socialists – that the civil service had regularly frustrated the wishes of ministers, parliament and the electorate.

The power of the civil service, however, could be – and was – greatly exaggerated; and the history of welfare policy is replete with examples of success for Weber's three countervailing forces. For instance, Harold Macmillan (as minister of housing and local government between 1951 and 1954) provided a classic example of a strong spending minister imposing his will upon officials.[10] The Cabinet's acceptance of the Beveridge Report in 1943 was an equally classic illustration of the power of public opinion. Treasury officials had strenuously opposed the Report on philosophical, economic and administrative grounds.[11]

However the popular reception of the Report, and a backbench revolt in Parliament against Churchill's Coalition government, made such objections politically untenable. The Report's main principles were therefore immediately incorporated into postwar reconstruction plans. Finally the ability of the CBI and TUC to frustrate successive prices and incomes policies demonstrates the ability of pressure groups to defeat policies favoured by the civil service, as does the influence of the British Medical Association (BMA) on the establishment and development of the NHS.

Given such a catalogue of bureaucratic 'defeats', serious doubts must be harboured about the real 'political' power of the postwar civil service and even the Treasury. The civil service was not, after all, a homogeneous body, and battles both between and within departments could be easily exploited. Strong ministers who sought to reject or refine 'the departmental view', for example, could usually depend upon the expertise and zeal of junior officials. When ministers were defeated, therefore, it was often not the result of any bureaucratic conspiracy. It was because they lacked either the prime minister's support, a clearly defined party policy or the agreement of powerful vested interests. Moreover, a 'departmental view' might not simply be a sign of bureaucratic power. It might embody officials' desire to develop a non-partisan policy which, for the convenience of the public as well as the administrator, would ensure the continuity and practicality of policy whichever party was in power. Indeed the considered opinion of two highly respected ministers of education in the 1960s was that, although it inevitably had considerable influence over policy, the civil service did not seriously constrain ministers. The major constraints lay elsewhere: in the power of pressure groups, the need to respect local autonomy, the legacy of the past (such as inadequate and unevenly distributed school buildings) and the general economic climate.[12]

Examples abound within the history of the NHS of the inherent administrative and political failings of bureaucracy, as popularly perceived. Inefficiency was exemplified by the serious underestimation of the demand for healthcare by Ministry of Health officials at the end of the war. This led to massive supplementary estimates in 1948 and 1949, which long tarred the NHS with a reputation for financial extravagance and mismanagement. A powerful 'departmental view' also allegedly confronted Barbara Castle, as secretary of state for social services between 1974 and 1976, when her senior officials opposed her wish to phase out pay beds in NHS hospitals in 1975. Finally, the Treasury's own departmental interests lay behind its repeated opposition, as cited above in Section 3.1.1, to preventive healthcare and planned capital expenditure.

On the other hand, the NHS provides plentiful evidence of the limited power of bureaucracy. Its establishment, for instance, was shaped as much by Bevan's ministerial determination and the BMA's lobbying power as by official planning. Officials thereafter repeatedly deferred to professional

→

expertise. Moreover, the departmental view on pay beds (which Barbara Castle admitted was confined largely to senior staff) was arguably based not on officials' self-interest but their concern over the BMA's anticipated reaction and the future willingness of doctors to work within the NHS.[13]

New public management and the 'hollowed-out' state

By the mid-1970s a combination of this weight of criticism and the drive to 'roll back the state' (be that the result of New Right ideology or globalization) fundamentally affected the role of the civil service. The application of new public management theories, by introducing market discipline, destroyed the clarity of both the hierarchy of power within departments (as responsibility for achieving specific goals was 'hived off' into 'accountable' management units, such as executive agencies) and the authority with which the public were dealt. Simultaneously, the privatization of specific services reduced the range of officials' direct responsibilities.

So great was the resultant change in the conceptualization, and arguably the practice, of government that new life was breathed by political scientists into the old term 'governance'.[14] Government, so it was argued, no longer could – or indeed should – exercise political power unilaterally. Rather power should be diffuse, with policy-making becoming a shared process of exchange and negotiation between government and a wide range of outside bodies or interests. Through such 'policy networks' mutually agreeable decisions could be reached not least over the extent to which civil society should be 'self-steering'. Government thus became but one actor in the policy-making process and dependent upon the expertise and goodwill of others to achieve its goals ('power dependent').

This moderation of power could be regarded as either benign or malign. On the one hand, it represented a belated recognition – after all the panic in the 1970s over governmental 'overload' – of the constraints within which government had always worked. For example the attainment of such a fundamental welfare goal as full employment, as will be seen, had always been dependent on the underlying health of the world economy. Likewise, the delivery of the personal social services had been reliant upon the voluntary and informal sectors. It also promised flexibility in meeting the increased variety of individual need (for which Giddens called) as well as a strengthening of civil society (for which both the New Right and the Third Way called). On the other hand, government could be portrayed as increasingly impotent and therefore irrelevant. In Michael Freeden's vision, for example:

> the state is reduced to the status of one actor among many, both internationally and domestically, appearing as pathetically subservient to global economic forces, and unwilling to generate policies through its bureaucracies because it no longer believes in the power of politics as a central force for change. Societies have simply become too complex for wielders of political power and authority to manage.[15]

According to this version, the state was 'hollowed out' with effective power being translated from Whitehall and Westminster upwards to multinational corporations or international bodies (such as the European Union), outwards to semi-autonomous agencies (such as, in the health service, the NHS Management Executive) and downwards to special purpose bodies (such as hospital trusts). The consequence was that society became 'centreless' and policy-making both fragmented and dysfunctional. In the model of professional and hierarchical government (the 'Westminster model'), to which Beveridge and Keynes subscribed at the start of the classic welfare state, order and continuity were promised. The 'hollowed out' state offered an alternative vision of disorder, discontinuity and thus policy disasters.

Academic analysis never fully accorded with the impression of strong government under Mrs Thatcher, despite the occasional policy disaster such as the poll tax. Consequently, just as in the light of empirical evidence the concept of 'dismantling' was superseded by that of the 'restructuring' of the welfare state, so the concept of 'hollowing out' has been challenged by a belief in the 'reconstitution' of the state. Central government may have lost some of its direct powers, but this has been more than compensated for by increased powers of regulation. Even if power has become more diffuse within policy networks, therefore, government remains the predominant partner in those networks. Government, in short, has not capitulated but adapted.

Within the 'reconstituted' state, however, the role of the civil service has unquestionably changed. The 'political' influence, for which it had earlier been attacked, has decreased. In part, this is because ministers have become more proactive. This is due, amongst other things, to a greater ideological commitment, bolstered by the availability of alternative advice from special advisers or 'think tanks', and the increased number of 'bilateral' meetings with the prime minister. 'Political' influence has also declined because senior officials have become more involved in management and policy implementation, concentrating on giving 'ministers what they said they wanted, rather than functioning as . . . "quasi-academics" who tried to show politicians the full consequences, adverse as well as positive, of their policy proposals'.[16] This greater concentration on management also corrected another of the alleged failings for which senior officials were traditionally pilloried.

One traditional demand of reformers, however, has not been met. The power of the Treasury, rather than being tamed, has increased. This is a consequence of the increased departmentalism caused by the greater diffusion of power and the taking of policy decisions not by the 'core executive' but within policy networks, of which the relevant ministry is a member. To counter this fragmentation of policy-making, the Treasury somewhat ironically has been entrusted with greater powers of coordination. Hence, under New Labour, the introduction of the Comprehensive Spending Review, the signing of 'public service agreements' by ministers with the Chancellor, and the lead the Treasury has taken on such key welfare policies as labour market reform.

There have been other attempts to attain 'joined up government'. For example, coordination units reporting direct to the Prime Minister (such as the Performance and Innovation Unit) have been established. So too have 'task forces' (such as the cancer task force established in 2000). They embody the concept of 'governance' since, in addition to ministers and officials, they typically include representatives of the private and voluntary sectors. Improved coordination, it might be argued, could be attained – with the achievement of clearer lines of accountability – by a reversion to the fuller use of Cabinet and of the interdepartmental committees (so maligned by Crossman). Even were that to occur, however, any analysis of welfare would have to acknowledge an unquestionable change in the civil service's policy role since the 1970s. The state may not have been hollowed out, but the civil service definitely has been. From the traditional policy-making core, power has been translated upwards to ministers, outward to task forces or agencies, and downward to contractors.

The managerial revolution in Whitehall was typified by the 'hiving off' in 1990 of full day-to-day running of the NHS to the NHS Executive and the subsequent contracting out of service delivery to, amongst others, GP fundholders and hospital trusts. Power was further diffused by the introduction in 1992 of the Private Finance Initiative whereby private companies (rather than government) finance, construct and own hospitals (which are then leased to the NHS).

In reaction, however, the Department of Health countered any potential loss of control by increasing its regulatory powers. Typical of such powers were performance targets and, under New Labour, the establishment of the Commission on Health Improvement (to inspect all hospitals) and national service frameworks (to standardize the path which each medical treatment should follow). Such regulation could be imposed because the NHS remained almost exclusively tax-financed (hardly the characteristic of a 'centreless' society). Significantly, the renewal of the commitment to tax finance in 2002 came most emphatically from the Treasury, following its commissioning of the Wanless Reports. The Treasury also opposed the Department of Health's plans to diffuse power further in 2003 to Foundation hospitals.

Three other variants of policy-making advanced by political scientists may be illustrated by attempts to modernise the NHS in the 1980s.

• The conspiratorial 'bureaucratic coordination' model (attacked by Crossman). This appeared to be validated when, for example, officials within the Department of Health and Social Security successfully emasculated political attempts to devolve power to an autonomous NHS Management Board between 1983 and 1988.
• The 'prime ministerial clique' model, whereby a power network is constructed via an inner cabinet or prime minister's department with its own clear agenda. Mrs Thatcher's unilateral imposition of the radical 1983 Griffiths and the 1988 ministerial reviews, not to mention later coordination units, apparently confirm this interpretation.

➜

• The 'ministerial' model, whereby strong ministers can circumvent collective responsibility by such stratagems as bilateral agreements. Such a concept gained strength when, for instance, Kenneth Clarke as minister of health drove through the implementation of the 1988 review despite Mrs Thatcher's cold feet and fierce opposition from the BMA.[17]

The validity of such models, it would seem, depends on individual personalities and circumstance.

3.1.3 The Implementation of Policy

The greater sophistication of policy analysis has led to a renewed emphasis on the implementation as opposed to the formulation of policy. This reflects a conviction that policy should not just be judged on its actual impact (rather than its intention) but that it is actually *made* in the course of implementation. Implementation theory originally challenged the traditional 'top-down' model of policy-making by which, in the Weberian ideal, unambiguous central decisions are faithfully translated into action by well-disciplined officials untroubled by either economic constraints or social resistance. In its place there was substituted the more dynamic (and riskily entitled) 'bottom-up' approach. This views policy as the constantly evolving interpretation of legislation, which has often been deliberately left ambiguous at the centre, by local officials ('street-level bureaucrats') who are heavily influenced by economic constraints, prevailing social prejudice and the actions of other actors. Policy in this perspective is not what Cabinets, senior officials or even heads of executive agencies plan but what lower paid officials do. With administrative devolution, such theories have become all the more pertinent.

Historical analysis has traditionally accorded some importance to policy implementation. Problems encountered at a local level have been seen to feed back in to the centre and be used to refine policy. It has also been recognized that Parliament and ministers have sufficient time only to debate the principles behind new legislation. The authority to draft, and later to interpret and refine, policy has therefore conventionally been delegated to officials. Indeed the increased resort to 'delegated legislation' was regarded by critics of the interwar British civil service as irrefutable evidence of the country's slide into bureaucracy.[18] Such traditional analysis, however, is essentially in accord with the 'top-down' model. In contrast the new 'bottom-up' approach begs three major new questions about the nature, and thus the analysis, of policy.

First, what is the true nature of policy when – as in the case of the 1970 Chronically Sick and Disabled Persons Act – central government deliberately frustrates the specified objectives of a given item of legislation by apportioning to it insufficient finance? Should government policy be judged by the declared objectives of its legislation or by its subsequent administrative action?

Second, what is the true nature of national policy when, to permit adjustment according to local circumstances or professional judgement, discretion is specifically drafted into legislation that is to be implemented by local authorities or professional bodies? As a consequence of such discretion 'national' policy can vary considerably not only from area to area but also from the intentions of central policy makers. Local government, for example, became particularly notorious in the 1980s for its ability to use its discretion (and such political and financial independence as it derives from local elections and rate finance) directly to frustrate central government policy.

Finally, 'bottom-up' theorists have argued that policy is often effectively made by local officials, even when they are employed directly by central government. In the Weberian model this would be impossible because local officials working in a hierarchical institution and governed by clear rules would automatically implement the well-defined wishes of the legislators. However, this model is deemed never to have been true for areas of policy such as national assistance (the forerunner of the present system of income support). Here, as Michael Hill has argued, the intention of the original 1948 National Assistance Act – to eradicate the stigma of the Poor Law and thus the low take-up of benefit – was never realized.[19] A major reason for this was that sufficient funds were never allocated to the service. Consequently, in the absence of any clear criteria by which to ration benefit, local officials fell back on the traditional – but highly arbitrary and unscientific – distinction between the 'deserving' and 'undeserving' poor. Most of the 'special cases', where claimants' circumstances did not conform neatly to the rules and qualification for benefit therefore remained at the discretion of officials, were duly classified as 'undeserving'. Administrative discretion thus came to be used – and was seen to be used – illiberally.

There were many reasons for officials acting in this way. Such illiberality generally accorded with their own prejudices and those of a particularly articulate section of the public about 'scrounging'. It was a means not only of rationing scarce resources but also of simplifying the complex human problems with which they were faced. Moreover it helped some to secure acceptance, and possible promotion, in a system which openly professed its intention to eradicate not only stigma but also fraud and abuse. Whatever the reasons for the action of individual officials, however, the history of national assistance makes it patently clear that local officials – when faced with conflicting signals from central policy makers – can play a major role in determining what the actual impact of policy should be on individual clients. Thus the success of New Labour's welfare-to-work programme lies as much in the hands of personal consultants, who advise individual claimants on how to shed their 'dependency culture', as of senior policy advisers in Whitehall.

The history of the NHS provides many example of local power. During the classic welfare state, for instance, regional and local health authorities frequently used their professional expertise to diverge from central government policy. Thus the Leeds Regional Hospital Board in the 1960s actually developed its own mental health strategy in direct opposition to government guidelines.[20] Moreover, the ultimate example of 'street-level' power is the 'clinical freedom' traditionally enjoyed by doctors. This is because the size and structure of the NHS budget is ultimately determined by professional judgement, on such issues as the rate of admissions to hospitals and the prescription of drugs, rather than by any centralized plan. Significantly, it is this freedom which New Labour has attempted to qualify by the standardization of clinical guidelines by new agencies (such as NICE) and new regulations (such as national service frameworks).

3.1.4 Incrementalism

The political science perspective thus reveals the full complexity of analysing welfare policy. Policy is revealed as never having been – even during the classic welfare state – a series of clear-cut decisions taken by ministers on the advice of disinterested civil servants, sanctioned by Parliament and automatically implemented. Rather it is a complex web of decisions and actions, resulting in both change and the avoidance of change, taken at every level within the government machine and often negotiated at length with outside pressure groups. Different parts of the state may act in a contradictory fashion at any one time. The purpose of policy is always shifting and its actual impact may often be very different to that originally intended. Temporary expedients may become entrenched as established principles.

Faced by such a bewildering array of potential evidence, historians may be tempted to assume – as does this book – that the only realistic approach to welfare policy is an incrementalist approach. Policy, in those areas where government enjoys effective power, should be seen not as the outcome of some far-seeing rational plan. Rather, it is typically a series of small adjustments, often governed by expedience and limited objectives which have unforeseen consequences.

Incrementalism does not deny that there may, at any given time, be some common assumptions shared by the majority of policy-makers. Nor does it deny that, at certain critical points in history, far-seeing rational decisions may have the major effect on policy. Indeed the creation of the welfare state in Britain in the 1940s might be depicted as just such a time – although the gradual, uncertain evolution of the phrase would suggest that (for all the wartime planning) the overall consequences of reconstruction policy were not consciously predetermined. Rather, incrementalism stresses, over time and at all levels, the complex mixture of rationality and realism, short-term expediency and planned development that determines policy. The resulting tension has been most vividly summarized by an early adherent of planning, Karl Mannheim, who wrote in 1951:

> The last bitter decades have taught us that one can neither conceive of a Good Society without reference to the actual state of affairs nor reconstruct a whole social order by piecemeal administrative reforms . . . . In times of slow change one can proceed more or less by intuition without constantly consulting principles. But in a post-war social landslide, when greater upheaval takes place in a month than in normal decades, awareness of the social significance of events is a prerequisite to survival.[21]

These comments, as Part III will demonstrate, are as relevant to the so-called period of 'governance' as they were to the classic welfare state.

3.2 THE ECONOMIC PERSPECTIVE

Since 1945 economics has become pre-eminent amongst the social sciences. In relation to more recently developed disciplines (such as sociology) it is seen to provide a more rigorous logic with which to analyse complex problems.[22] Alternatively, in relation to equally well-established sciences (such as philosophy) it is seen to be of more immediate relevance. Hence economists have been called upon not just to provide the theoretical criteria by which to judge the performance of the welfare state, but actually to participate in the formulation and implementation of policy. Their participation, moreover, has not been confined solely to the management of the economy. It has also included the allocation of scarce resources to and within social policy.

Practical weaknesses

The record of economists within government has not been particularly distinguished. Their advice has often been contradictory, as was particularly apparent in the late 1970s with the open warfare between Keynesians and monetarists. It has also frequently appeared ineffectual or positively harmful. It even became fashionable in the 1960s, for example, to chart the decline of the British economy in direct relation to the number of economists employed in Whitehall. On one level such criticism was unjustified. Economists themselves rarely took major policy decisions and could justifiably argue that those who did either ignored or misused their advice. On another level, however, professional economic advice has increasingly revealed certain shortcomings which have raised questions about both the applicability of economic theory to the real world and the very assumptions upon which that theory is based.

In macroeconomic policy, such failings are well illustrated by the record of the Keynesian theory of demand management between 1945 and 1975 – although the record of monetary policy after 1979 is equally instructive.[23]

Keynesianism had been opposed long before its implementation on practical as much as on theoretical grounds, and such objections (as will be seen in Section 5.1) coloured the Treasury's contribution to the famous 1944 *Employment Policy* white paper. Subsequent events appear to have justified the Treasury's misgivings. Problems constantly reoccurred, for example, over the prompt collection of reliable data, the forecasting of future economic trends and the devising of remedial action which would have its desired (and full) effect within the requisite time span. This convinced many commentators that – regardless of any 'unanticipated' behaviour by the public – the economic techniques simply did not exist to enable even the most disinterested chancellor of the exchequer successfully to 'fine-tune' the economy. Indeed, as the authoritative Plowden Committee argued as early as 1961, demand management as a 'remedy' for fluctuations within the economy could 'be even worse than the disease'.[24] It could both destabilize the economy at the macro level, and at the micro level militate against the achievement of 'value for money' in public investment. This was because investment (such as the building and staffing of a hospital) could not be accelerated or retarded simply to counteract forecasted bouts of unemployment or inflation. The practical failure of economists, in other words, lay not just in the misuse of their advice by others but in the very nature of that advice.

Theoretical weaknesses

At a theoretical level, reservations have been voiced about the objectivity of conventional economic theory and its technical limitations, particularly in relation to social policy. Microeconomic analysis, for example, concentrates on the attainment of the maximum 'output' of welfare from a limited amount of resources (which cannot satisfy all need). On the demand side, it takes as its implicit standard the behaviour of 'economically rational' man making isolated decisions in a market where the price of each good is clearly signalled. Thus 'marginal analysis' assumes that people will always make choices that maximize their individual well-being (utility). When they are forced to make choices because of limited resources, they will choose to purchase an object up to a point where the extra pleasure it brings (its marginal utility) is equal to the pleasure that has to be forgone through the non-purchase of an alternative object (its marginal opportunity cost). The price placed against each object facilitates choice.

Such a standard is held by many, particularly democratic socialists, to be inherently flawed – if only because it replicates the values of the market which, in their opinion, has over time proved itself incapable of maximizing welfare. There are three main objections.

First, marginal analysis simultaneously underestimates and overestimates human nature. People do not always seek to maximize their own material welfare but often choose, as Titmuss's blood donors illustrate, to act altruistically. Conversely, for reasons of either finance or personality, people have different abilities to express and satisfy their needs. Consequently, their totality will not be accurately represented by the market. Moreover, individual purchasers are generally unaware of the consequences to others of their choices (externalities). Therefore collective decisions, although smacking of paternalism, can maximize the *sum* of individual welfare more efficiently than individual decisions within a free market.

Second, marginal analysis would appear to condone the existing distribution of resources within society, however unequal it might be. The economist's classic definition of maximum welfare, or of the most efficient use of scarce resources, is the concept of *Pareto optimality*: the allocation of scarce resources in such a way that no one individual can be made better off without simultaneously making at least one other person worse off. The serious limitations of such a definition are well exposed by a commentator's subsequent remark that 'a socially efficient use of resources in the economist's sense of the term could . . . be one in which there was a great deal of poverty and hardship – providing the preferences of people with money to express themselves through the market were being met as fully as was possible'.[25] Consequently Pareto optimality is frequently contrasted unfavourably with *Rawls's* theory of social justice. This argues, *inter alia*, that social and economic inequality can be condoned only insofar as they benefit the least advantaged. In other words, there should be no reallocation of resources unless it is to the advantage of the least well-off.[26] Hence high salaries for hospital consultants, and further pay awards for them, are justified only so long as they serve to provide better medical treatment for (amongst others) the poorest members of society.

Finally, there is the question of quantification. Some aspects of welfare, such as the quality of life, are simply unamenable to pricing. Therefore, in its costings, marginal analysis has either to ignore them or to use surrogate measures. Both strategies can seriously bias its conclusions.

The problem of quantification can be illustrated within the health service by the calculation of the relative cost of institutional and community care. The costs of the former can be calculated with relative ease. Those of the latter cannot so far as it depends on 'unpaid' relatives or carers. Relative costs can therefore be seriously misrepresented. One convention is to price the cost of the unpaid carers by the income forgone in the jobs they might otherwise have undertaken. This, however, ignores the possible decline in their quality of life (and therefore their welfare) resulting from the loss of their freedom to choose an alternative job and to have an independent income. Problems of quantification are raised even more acutely by the 'price' of human life in relation to the terminally ill. In seeking to maximize the 'output' of welfare from scarce resources, marginal analysis clearly focuses attention on relievable need. Logically this would deny treatment to the terminally ill, unless some price can be put on the value of the dying person's life and the peace of mind of both doctors and relatives ('vicarious' welfare).

Costs and benefits

It is when such calculations of life and death, identified in the preceding box, come to be made that charges and countercharges of callousness and sentimentality between economists and non-economists become most virulent. Such confrontations, however, are largely unproductive. The better economists recognize the limitations of their science. In macroeconomic policy they accept that the successful management of the economy depends as much on political judgement and luck as on 'pure technique'.[27] In welfare policy they equally recognize that they are no more (and no less) qualified than anyone else to advise on the ideological and moral issues behind the allocation of scarce resources. Once a decision has been taken on these issues, however, they can offer a set of techniques backed by a body of theory which is better developed than those of most other social sciences. It is not, after all, amoral to attempt to identify the economic cost of 'social justice'. Nor should such attempts be discouraged. Rather it is amoral to pretend that the humane treatment of a dying person has no cost and that (given scarce resources) certain other needs, which could have been relieved, will as a consequence be relieved less quickly. Within its acknowledged limitations, the strength of economics is that it has the means to confront such hard issues. As such it has much of value to say about the economic efficiency of both state intervention in general and of individual welfare policies in particular.

3.2.1 The Economics of State Intervention

State intervention in relation to welfare policy has traditionally been defended on ethical grounds. It has been argued, for instance, that all citizens should have certain social rights (such as freedom from poverty) which the market cannot automatically guarantee. On the grounds of social justice, there should also be a more equitable distribution of income and wealth. Such ideals are not without their economic benefits. For example, more equitable income distribution has, as Keynesians recognized, consequences for consumer demand and hence production. It can also legitimize society and thereby contribute to political stability and social cohesion. They in turn can facilitate economic growth. State intervention can, however, be defended on purely economic criteria, regardless of any ethical arguments. As one recent text has concluded: 'it does things which private markets for technical reasons either would not do at all, or would do inefficiently. We need a welfare state of some sort for efficiency reasons, and would continue to do so even if all distributional problems had been solved.'[28] What are these technical reasons? What sort of welfare state do they justify?

The rationale of state intervention

Four main reasons are usually advanced to justify state intervention. The first two are concerned with the absence in the real world of the theoretical preconditions for market efficiency:

- *Imperfect knowledge..*   One of the preconditions for market efficiency is that everyone should be able to recognize both their own needs and the most efficient way of meeting them (perfect knowledge). Clearly this can rarely be the case. Consequently, so it is argued, independent consumer choice will always be inefficient. If welfare is to be maximized, therefore, there is a *prima-facie* case for state intervention.

- *Imperfect competition.*   This occurs when one – or a few – producers have cornered the market for a given product. Although concentration of production can reduce costs ('economies of scale'), there is also the danger that it will lead to the charging of unnecessarily high prices (which will deny people the resources to buy other goods) or incur unnecessarily high costs (X-inefficiency). Both would waste resources.

Imperfect knowledge is inherent amongst consumers of healthcare. It would, for example, *diminish* people's welfare if they spent most of their leisure time amassing sufficient knowledge about the range and price of treatment for all possible illnesses so that, when the due moment finally arrived (and assuming of course that they were conscious) they could make a rational choice. Moreover, medical science is so complex that, however much leisure time they forfeited, most people would be unable to acquire sufficient knowledge to act rationally.

   Imperfect competition is also endemic. Elements of monopolistic behaviour are most apparent in the multinational drug companies. There is also a tendency in a free market for doctors to exploit their privileged position to oversupply certain types of treatment. This is especially true when – as typically in the USA but not in the NHS – doctors are paid for each transaction or when an insurance policy disguises from the patient the actual cost of treatment.

The final two theoretical justifications for state intervention are concerned with weaknesses inherent in the market:

- *Externalities.*   This is the technical term for the consequences to others, either beneficial or adverse, of actions by an individual or firm for which no direct reward or compensation is paid. Most actions have consequences for others. Consequently, if welfare is to be maximized, the benefits accruing both to those who take the decisions and to those indirectly affected (its private and its 'external' benefits) must outweigh private and 'external' costs. Education, for example, produces beneficial externalities because an individual's education can benefit not just that individual but also others, in terms of his or her increased socialization or productivity. Conversely the drift of industry to the south-east of England, for the quite legitimate reason of maximizing private profit, can involve adverse externalities. It necessitates the replacement of facilities such as schools and hospitals, which have been abandoned elsewhere. Consequently, industrial relocation consumes resources that could have been used more advantageously. The market, because it reflects largely individual (or private) costs and benefits, will inevitably tend to oversupply goods with adverse externalities. Equally, it will tend to undersupply those with beneficial externalities. Hence there is a *prima-facie* case for arguing that collective decisions, which can take into account all private and external costs and benefits, are more efficient in maximizing welfare than individual market decisions.

- *Public goods.* These are services, such as defence and public health, which are in everyone's interest but for which a market price cannot easily be charged. How, for example, could a private producer of defence or public health exclude a non-payer from enjoying those services? Because of people's reluctance to pay for goods they can enjoy at the expense of others, the market will tend to undersupply them. Consequently, if welfare is to be maximized and the 'responsible' citizen protected from the irresponsibilities of others (in relation, for example, to contagious diseases), state coercion is needed.

> It was because of the joint issue of externalities and public goods that economists, even in the heyday of nineteenth-century *laissez-faire*, were willing to advocate public expenditure on defence, education and, eventually, public health.

The means of state intervention

There are some sound theoretical justifications for state intervention. However, they do not automatically determine *how* the state should provide welfare or indeed whether, in the real world, state provision will be any more efficient than the market. There are in fact four main methods of state intervention:

- cash benefits
- regulation
- finance, including taxation and subsidies
- public production.

Each entails a different degree of interference with the market. Cash benefits entail the least. They seek only to correct the market's weakness on the demand side, by distributing resources to those who would otherwise lack the ability to purchase a necessary minimum of goods. At the other extreme, public production largely supersedes the market.

Each method of intervention is employed in healthcare. *Cash benefits*, such as old-age pensions, minimize calls upon the NHS. For instance, they provide potential clients with an income which enables them either to maintain their own health or to be supported by relatives in their own homes. *Regulations*, such as those concerning food hygiene, minimize disease by protecting consumers from the consequences of their imperfect knowledge. *Taxation* increases the price of goods which can damage health (such as cigarettes) whilst *subsidies* reduce the price of those which are beneficial (such as medicine). Finally, through the NHS, health is *publicly produced*. Everyone in Britain is protected from the danger of their own imperfect knowledge by the provision, free at the point of access, of a full range of treatment by specialists. They are paid by the state and consequently have no direct pecuniary (or private) interest in the choice of treatment they prescribe.

The choice between the alternative means of intervention is controversial. Economists of the New Right, who acknowledge the need for the state to correct the imperfections of the market, clearly advocate the least interference. They assert in particular that, in the real world, the state suffers from failings identical to those of the market. For instance, officials lack the technical ability to measure over time the full social costs and benefits of individual actions (imperfect knowledge). Consequently, the state is no more able than the market to resolve the problem of externalities. Indeed, because of its monopoly position, the state is not even under competitive pressure to keep consumers informed of the full range of opportunities open to them. Nor is it under pressure to produce goods at the minimum possible cost. Thus the inherent danger of public production is, they conclude, the production of goods that satisfy the self-interest of politicians, bureaucrats or experts rather than maximize welfare.

In response, other economists stress the inherent real-world inefficiency of the market. The market solution to such inefficiency is insurance, but voluntary insurance itself has acknowledged imperfections. The three principal ones, which could to some extent be corrected by state regulation of the insurance market, are the problems of:

- the free rider
- adverse selection
- moral hazard.

The example economists use to illustrate the imperfections of insurance is healthcare, as in the following box.

The uncertain but potentially enormous cost of medical treatment to any one individual can be met (as it still largely is in countries such as the USA) by voluntary insurance. Many people may choose not to insure themselves. If they then fall ill this imposes externalities on others – such as the spread of contagious disease or the need ultimately for others to pay for their medical treatment. This is the problem of the *free rider*. Alternatively many people who are prepared to insure themselves, such as the chronically ill or those suffering from HIV, may find it impossible to find cover – at least at a cost which they can afford. This may be because they are adjudged too great a risk, so the insurance company could not make a profit. Alternatively it may be because the insurance company fears that relevant information about the degree of risk may not be disclosed. This is the problem of *adverse selection*. Moreover certain contingencies, such as visits to the doctor or pregnancy, will usually not be covered since they are not random but within the power of the insured person to control. This is one of the facets of the problem of *moral hazard*. Another type of moral hazard is the possible collusion between patient and doctor over the prescription of an unnecessarily expensive form of treatment since it is not they who will be paying (in increased charges or reduced profits) but the insurance company. Such collusion will nevertheless have high social costs because it will result in the unnecessary consumption of scarce resources.

Many of these imperfections can be corrected by state regulation. For example, the state could make health insurance compulsory (and indeed most European states today operate such a system of social insurance). Alternatively, it could require all insurance companies to take their fair share of high-risk applicants and provide an inspectorate to monitor collusion. Such regulation is, however, expensive and would increase the already considerable administrative costs involved in private companies estimating individual risks, issuing individual policies and paying individual claims. A far cheaper alternative (as is shown by the lower administrative costs of the NHS in relation to insurance-based schemes in both the USA and Europe) is for the principle of insurance to be superseded altogether by state finance and state production. Scarce resources can thereby be released for more constructive purposes.[29]

Internal markets

There are, then, sound economic reasons for judging the market to be an inefficient mechanism for maximizing welfare and for concluding that state intervention is functionally desirable. What form that intervention should take, however, raises as many controversial economic questions as it does philosophical ones (see Section 2.2). Those New Right economists who acknowledge the real-world failure of the market seek the minimum of remedial state intervention (such as health vouchers to ensure everyone has the power to purchase an agreed level of healthcare). To them the market alone has the potential to maximize welfare. This is because it alone can provide the mechanism through which individuals can freely express their wishes and be made aware of the consequences (the marginal opportunity costs) of their choices. In contrast their opponents assert that, in advanced industrial countries, the state offers a potentially better mechanism both for providing public goods and for minimizing the dangers arising from imperfect knowledge, imperfect competition and externalities. They admit that in the real world state intervention can itself be far from perfect. They therefore acknowledge that it is incumbent upon them to develop the microeconomic concepts and techniques which will enable the state, in practice as well as in theory, to allocate resources efficiently. One way to achieve a practical compromise between these views is to develop 'internal' or 'quasi' markets. This was the favoured solution of the 1990s. The role of government as both the paymaster and the monopolistic provider of welfare is divided. The actual delivery of services is contracted out to competing outside bodies. Consumers are thereby given the opportunity to express their preferences and generate competition (and greater efficiency) amongst the producers of welfare

An internal market was introduced to the NHS in 1990 and has since been retained. The health budget was allocated to District Health Authorities and 'fund-holding' GPs (later renamed Primary Care Trusts). They were then free to purchase services on behalf of their patients from a competing range of hospitals, be they public or private and inside or outside their region. 'The intention' so its supporters have written, 'is to reap the efficiency gains of the introduction of competition – lower costs and greater responsiveness to patients – without sacrificing the equity goals met through tax provided finance.'[30]

3.2.2 The Economics of Individual Welfare Policies

The real-world failure of the state which microeconomists have particularly sought to rectify is the misallocation of scarce resources by incrementalism, by elites and by misguided humanitarianism. Three particular problems have been identified. *First*, given the political and administrative complexity of policy formulation and implementation (summarized in the first half of this chapter), state intervention tends to permit only the marginal adjustment of resources over time between policies. Consequently objective overviews of the total allocation of resources, in order to determine whether the overall mix of policies is correct, are infrequent. *Second*, where the allocation of resources is entrusted to elites, there tends (as argued in Section 2.3.1) to be misallocation because of either that elite's self-interest or its inability to appreciate the full external costs of its actions. *Finally*, state intervention shields voters from the direct consequences of their choices. This tends to encourage demand for expenditure which, however laudable in humanitarian terms, may actually reduce the eventual sum of individual welfare. After all, given scarce resources, money spent on causes (however good) cannot then be spent on other policies which might have benefited more people over time. Money spent on short-term famine relief is, for instance, money denied to projects to ensure that famine will not recur in those areas.

Measuring cost-effectiveness

The microeconomist's partial remedy for such government failure is the concept of cost-effectiveness: the evaluation of the total private and external costs over time of a specific policy in relation to each 'unit' of welfare produced. This provides an immediate challenge to the 'common sense' of bureaucratic managers or professional elites who are concerned either with short-term considerations or with the expenditure of resources within a given budget.

> Doctors are encouraged by their professional training to concentrate on the choice of treatment (however expensive) that will totally cure their patient. The logic of cost-effectiveness requires them, on the other hand, to consider whether the sum of individual welfare would not be increased if a similar amount of money were spent on a larger number of people, even if they were less seriously ill or if total cures could not be effected.

Two of the major aids to the measurement of cost-effectiveness are:

- marginal analysis
- cost–benefit analysis.

Marginal analysis again challenges conventional 'common sense' by requiring the reallocation of resources to be based on marginal rather than average costs. For example, in the debate over community or institutional care for the elderly, community care would appear the cheaper option because the average cost of maintaining an individual at a given level of well-being in the community is less than the average institutional cost. However, the patients who will be affected (in other words those who would either leave institutional care or would not now enter it) are not average patients. They are generally less infirm than the average patient in institutional care (and therefore their cost should be less than average). Conversely, they are more infirm than the average patient in the community (and therefore the cost of their community care should be higher than average). Reallocation of resources, therefore, should depend on whether the 'above-average' cost of marginal patients in the community remains less than their 'below-average' cost in institutional care. This need not always be the case. The apparently 'cheaper' option may in certain circumstances be the more expensive.

> In the 1970s and 1980s marginal analysis was incorporated into the Resource Allocation Working Party formula to the enhancement of the allocation of resources between regional health authorities.[31]

Cost–benefit analysis is an even more sophisticated and complex attempt, particularly in relation to new policy initiatives, to quantify the full costs and benefits over time of a given policy. Its major benefit is that it places the immediate cost of a policy (which might appear prohibitive) in the context of future savings. Thus decisions can be made on criteria which are broader and more long term than is usual. It must, however, be admitted that its record in the real world – for instance over the location of London's third airport in the 1970s – has been far from encouraging.

Costs and benefits

A major reason for the general inability of such microeconomic techniques to provide more than a partial remedy for real-world government failure is their vulnerability to the weaknesses identified earlier in relation to marginal analysis. The problem of quantifying the unquantifiable is particularly acute when, to aid comparison between different policies, all individual well-being has to be reduced to a common 'unit' of welfare. How is the prolongation of the life of one individual to be weighed against the increased self-sufficiency of another? Moreover, even in the simpler tasks of quantification, such as the construction of the 'points' system by which individual housing need is measured prior to the allocation of council housing, in-built prejudices and values are betrayed by the relative weighting given to different needs. Finally, cost–benefit analysis, like Pareto optimality, is coldly technocratic in that it is not concerned with the distribution of costs and benefits. All the costs might accrue to one group of people and all the benefits to another.

It might be argued that attempts to measure cost-effectiveness, however imperfect, are better than nothing. This is not necessarily true. By placing undue weight, however unintentionally, on variables that can be quantified, these variables can be given a spurious importance which may seriously prejudice subsequent analysis. Nevertheless it is reasonable to argue that – handled with due care – the rationality of microeconomic analysis can provide an effective challenge to the assumptions underlying the decisions, or non-decisions, of existing policy-makers and thereby clear the ground for better policy-making.

3.2.3 Economic Rationality

Economics, as is illustrated by the battle between Keynesians and monetarists over the fundamental nature of economic relationships, is a far from precise science. Nevertheless it does provide a reasonably rigorous set, or sets, of analytical criteria by which to judge the relative efficiency of the welfare state in general and individual policies in particular. Economists of the New Right assign to the state only the provision of public goods and a minimum of manipulation and regulation to counteract the acknowledged real-world failures of the market. This would so limit the role of government that, by the definition provided earlier (in Section 2.1), the welfare state would no longer exist.

However, other economists argue that, given the problems of imperfect knowledge, imperfect competition and externalities, the state should adopt a more interventionist role in the interests of functional economic efficiency, let alone social justice. It is admitted that in the real world there are as many potential government failures as market failures, but internal markets can be developed and microeconomic techniques refined in order to minimize them. Above all microeconomic analysis – by concentrating attention both on the unavoidable scarcity of resources and the 'output' of welfare – provides a rational approach to the maximization of welfare, which is itself a major factor in the maximization of social justice. To this extent economists can not only provide a functional justification for the welfare state but also prove themselves to be not the rivals but the allies of those who seek social justice.

3.3 FURTHER READING

Many of the books cited for further reading at the end of Chapter 2 are relevant also to this chapter. An additional compact introduction to political science theory is M. Hill, *The Policy Process in the Modern State* (Hemel Hempstead, 1997) with its accompanying *The Policy Process: a reader* (Hemel Hempstead, 1997). General theory has been applied more simply to welfare policy in M. Hill, *Understanding Social Policy* (Oxford, 2003); and to the NHS in C. Ham, *Health Policy in Britain* (1999).

The classic work on bureaucracy is M. Albrow, *Bureaucracy* (1970); whilst traditional criticisms of the civil service are summarized in P. Kellner and Lord Crowther-Hunt, *The Civil Servants* (1980), and, considerably more wittily, in G. Kaufman, *How to be a Minister* (1980). They can be matched against the standard histories of the civil service which are P. Hennessy, *Whitehall* (2001) and K. Theakston, *The Civil Service since 1945* (Oxford, 1995). The Treasury in the early postwar years is best analysed in S. Brittan, *Steering the Economy* (Harmondsworth, 1971); and, more conversationally, in H. Young and A. Sloman, *But Chancellor* (1984). A laudable attempt to apply recent theories to the reality of public administration is D. Richards and M. J. Smith, *Governance and Public Policy in the UK* (Oxford, 2002) although its treatment of history and welfare policy would have benefited from a closer acquaintance with the work of historians and social policy (particularly comparative) experts. Lively but rather less accessible is R. A. W. Rhodes, *Understanding Governance* (Buckingham, 1997).

The standard works on the economics of welfare policy are J. Le Grand, C.

Propper and R. Robinson, *The Economics of Social Problems* (1992); and N. Barr, *The Economics of the Welfare State* (Oxford, 1998). The latter contains valuable non-technical summaries to the theoretical chapters. It can now be supplemented by N. Barr, *The Welfare State as Piggy Bank* (Oxford, 2001). R. Middleton provides an encyclopaedic yet accessible coverage of the theoretical issues and empirical evidence relevant to the growth of public expenditure in Britain between 1890 and 1979 in *Government versus the Market* (Cheltenham, 1996).

Part II

The Classic Welfare State, 1945–1975

chapter

4

The Historical Context

The empirical analysis of welfare policy, as argued in Part I, needs to be informed by competing theoretical interpretations of the nature of both the welfare state and policy-making. It also needs to be placed in historical context. It is all too tempting to consider the overall development of policy – or to judge the relative success or failure of an individual policy – in isolation and according to some internal logic. Indeed, a belief in incrementalism encourages this. However, it must be recognized that welfare policy was subject to external forces to which successive governments, distracted by other problems, responded within the constraints of what was deemed to be administratively and politically possible. The purpose of this chapter is to identify these various constraints and influences.

- What was the economic context in which welfare policy developed ?
- To what demographic pressure was it subject?
- Who held political power and how did this affect the priority accorded to welfare policy?
- How did the machinery of government at a central, regional and local level adapt to the more positive welfare role which the state had assumed?
- How receptive was public opinion, as represented by vested interests and the electorate, to the duties as well as the rights imposed by state welfare?

The evolution of the NHS underlines the importance of such questions. The crisis which resulted in Bevan's resignation from the Labour Cabinet in 1951 was triggered not just by its own unexpectedly high costs but also by the *economic* restrictions placed on welfare expenditure by inflation and the trebling of defence expenditure occasioned by the outbreak of the Korean War in June 1950. The incoming Conservative government accorded the NHS a lower *political* priority, with the result that the minister of health did not sit in Cabinet for the rest of the 1950s. Its longer term needs were not given serious consideration until the early 1960s when, in a new mood of planning, there was the coincidence of a new minister, a new permanent secretary to the ministry and a new chief medical officer. These needs revolved around the *demographic* problem of an ageing population but the most cost-effective response – community rather than institutional care – was rejected. This was in part because of the *vested interest* of hospital consultants, but also because of the perceived *administrative* weakness of local government. It was this same perceived weakness which, as much as socialist ideology, had lain behind the original decision in 1948 to nationalize the hospital service. To understand fully, therefore, the nature and pace of change within the NHS, the historian must be alive to the economic, political, administrative and social contexts in which it developed.

4.1 THE ECONOMIC CONTEXT

The performance of the economy is clearly a major influence on both the development and the ultimate nature of welfare policy. A high level of *employment*, as Beveridge recognized, is the best guarantor of individual welfare. Also, by reducing the demand for cash benefits and simultaneously generating increased wealth, it provides the resources which can enable welfare policy to expand and diversify. *Unemployment*, conversely, by concentrating an increased proportion of diminishing resources on basic income support, inhibits the development of other policies. Equally essential to the expansion and diversification of policy is *economic growth*. Financially it keeps government revenue buoyant as taxable income and profits increase. Politically it enables high levels of taxation to be levied with relative ease, because taxation is more likely to be resisted – and hence the financing of welfare policy jeopardized – when it threatens an anticipated rise, or even an absolute fall, in income. This was well recognized by the democratic socialists, one of whose basic assumptions (as summarized by Donnison) was that 'the pursuit of social justice' was dependent on the 'engines of economic growth which would produce the resources to create a fairer society without anyone suffering on the way'.[1]

Employment and economic growth

The expansion of welfare policy was therefore greatly assisted by the unprecedented and consistently high levels of employment and economic growth throughout the period 1945–75. A definition of 'full employment' has never been universally agreed. In the 1940s Keynes suggested an ideal of 5 per cent unemployment whilst, between 1942 and 1944, Beveridge reduced his target from 8.5 per cent to 3 per cent. The latter figure alone was exceeded as an annual average, and then only marginally, on four occasions before 1975: in 1947, 1971–2 and 1975 when the highest figure (4.1 per cent) was recorded. By contrast the comparable figure for the interwar years had been 10.9 per cent with annual averages ranging from 7.4 to 17 per cent of the total workforce.[2] Equally impressive was the record of economic growth, with GDP doubling in real terms between 1948 and 1973 at an average annual rate of 2.8 per cent. The corresponding average for the 40 years before the First World War had been below 2 per cent and that for the years between 1924 and 1937 only 2.2 per cent. The detailed record was: 1950–5, 2.9 per cent; 1955–60, 2.5 per cent; 1960–4, 3.1 per cent; 1964–9, 2.5 per cent; 1969–73, 3.0 per cent. These figures reveal that growth was at its fastest in the first half of each decade.[3]

Such major achievements did not mean, however, that welfare policy was unaffected by economic constraints of both a regular and a random nature. The aggregate figures cited above concealed certain disturbing trends. National figures for unemployment hide higher regional averages. Throughout the 1950s, for instance, unemployment averaged 7.7 per cent in Northern Ireland. Average economic growth was also half that of the EEC and so British governments had relatively fewer – and increasingly fewer – resources to devote to welfare policy. Of more immediate short-term importance were random shocks to the economy, such as the outbreak of the Korean War in June 1950 and the quadrupling of oil prices between 1972 and 1974. Both fuelled inflation and required a reordering of expenditure priorities, with the result that ceilings had to be placed on public expenditure – such as that imposed on the NHS in 1951. There were also five major economic cycles between 1951 and 1972, during which governments sought to expand or contract public expenditure (in 'go' and 'stop' phases) in order to boost economic activity or to control it. Welfare expenditure was by no means the only component of public expenditure, and private consumption and investment were also constantly varied by budget changes to taxes and allowances; but welfare policy and, in particular, capital expenditure were frequently affected. The timing of the peaks and troughs in these respective economic cycles is therefore important to a full understanding of welfare policy and they are summarized in Table 4.1. There were, as can be seen, expansionary budgets in 1953, 1959, 1963 and 1972, the last two stimulating periods of economic growth known respectively as the Maudling and Barber booms, after the then Conservative chancellors.

Table 4.1   Postwar economic cycles, 1951–73

Peak	Trough
1951 (i)	1952 (iii)
1955 (iv)	1958 (iii)
1960 (iii)	1963 (i)
1965 (i)	1967 (iii)
1969 (i)	1972 (i)
1973 (ii)	

Note: Roman numerals identify the relevant quarter of the year.
Source: S. Pollard, *The Development of the British Economy* (1983) p. 422.

Balance of payments and sterling crises

There was no equivalent budget in 1968 but rather a severe deflationary package which included, amongst other things, the reintroduction of prescription charges (which the Labour government had withdrawn on its return to office in 1964). Retrenchment was necessitated by the devaluation of the pound in November 1967. This underlines another constant check on welfare policy throughout this period – a series of interrelated balance of payments and sterling crises of which the devaluation of 1967 was merely an extreme example. Each crisis required government action to reduce domestic demand and thereby to discourage imports, encourage exports and reassure foreign bankers. Before 1964, as Table 4.2 illustrates, there had been isolated packages of economic cuts such as the September measures of 1957 and the Little Budget of 1961. What the table particularly highlights, however, are the annual crises which so constrained the Labour governments in the 1960s.

Inflation

The final major economic constraint on welfare expenditure was inflation. Before 1972, inflation was not particularly severe, although contemporary expectation – especially in the 1950s – was that there should be no price increases at all. During the Korean War, admittedly, it was severe, with prices rising by 20 per cent between 1949 and 1951; but between 1945 and 1963 prices rose on average by only 3.7 per cent per annum, and between 1964 and 1972 by only 5.4 per cent. Then inflation took off as the following price rises indicate: 1973–4, 16.1 per cent; 1974–5, 23.1 per cent; 1975–6, 16.3 per cent. Economists have identified many causes of inflation and prominent amongst them is welfare policy. The maintenance of full employment both strengthens the bargaining position of trade unions for increased wages and creates excess demand in the economy (cost-push and demand-pull inflation). Social security benefits provide an ever higher floor from which unions can start their

Table 4.2   Major stimuli to economic expansion and contraction, 1947–74

	'Stop'	*'Go'*
1947 Aug.	Convertibility crisis	
1948–50		Marshall Aid
1949 Sept.	Devaluation	
1950 June	Korean War (to 1952)	
1953 April		Budget +£100–150m
1955 April		Budget +£156m
1955 Oct.	Autumn budget – £113m	
1956 Dec.	Suez	
1957 Sept.	Sterling crisis: September measures	
1959 April		Budget +£360m
1960 June	Balance of payments crisis	
1961 July	Sterling crisis: Little budget	
1962 Feb.	IMF loan	NEDC announces 4% growth target
1963 April		Budget +£450m: Maudling boom
1964 Nov.	Balance of payments crisis: IMF loan	
1965 June	Sterling crisis	
1965 Sept.		National Plan published
1966 July	Sterling crisis: July measures	
1967 Nov.	Devaluation	
1968 March	Budget – £923m	
1969 April	Budget – £340m	
1971 March		Budget +£256m
1972 April		Budget +£1,211m Barber boom
1972 July		£ floated
1973 Dec.	OPEC oil price rises Public expenditure cuts	
1974 Feb.		
1974 March	Healey budget	Social Contract

Notes: Unbroken lines denote change of government, dotted lines peaks of the economic cycle. Figures for the budget specify the extent to which *The Economist* estimated it expanded or contracted the economy.

negotiations. Finally, government borrowing to finance public expenditure can increase money supply. Before 1975, therefore, cuts in (or at least a slowing down in the rise of) public expenditure were recommended as an antidote to inflation, most significantly by Thorneycroft before his unprecedented resignation as chancellor in January 1958 and by Healey in his 1975 budget.

The Golden Age

So sustained was economic growth throughout the Western world between 1945 to 1975 that the period has been called the 'golden age' and the classic welfare state has been commonly regarded as coterminous with it. Undoubtedly, the broad economic climate was highly favourable to the expansion and diversification of welfare expenditure, but in Britain in particular there were short-term constraints imposed by cyclical downturns in the economy, balance-of-payments crises and inflation. Because of the political difficulties that might be incurred, current expenditure on, for example, cash benefits was rarely cut, although its increase in line with either public expectations or inflation might be delayed. Capital expenditure (such as the building and equipment of hospitals) was more permanently affected because its contraction raised fewer immediate protests and its expansion took longer to plan and execute. Certainly short-term fluctuations may be seen to have hampered the stable development of welfare policy which the continuation of full employment and economic growth might have been expected to – and elsewhere in Europe did – facilitate.

4.2 THE DEMOGRAPHIC CONTEXT

If the performance of the economy ultimately determines the level of resources available to welfare policy, demographic change has a major influence on the level of demand – regardless of any improvements in the standard of service. For instance:

- All periods are 'victims' of the birth rate of some 20 and 60 years before, as those generations reach child-bearing and retirement age.
- Any variation in birth rates within a given period will affect successively the cost of family support and of education, the demand for housing, the nature of the labour market and, ultimately, the cost of pensions and hospital care.
- The demand for all services will also be progressively affected by improvements in the death rate.

Consistency of trends of demographic change is therefore clearly desirable both to prevent fluctuations in demand for services with fixed costs, such as education, and to provide an even balance between those within the workforce (generating wealth) and those outside (consuming it). There was no such consistency between 1945 and 1975.

The birth rate

Given the consistently falling birth rate during the interwar period, an unexpected source of postwar instability was the annual variation in the number of births – and in particular the baby booms of 1942–7 and 1955–65 (see Figure 4.1). Many explanations have been advanced for these baby booms. Falls in the number of women never marrying, in the average age at marriage and in the mother's average age at the birth of her first child were common to both periods, and were especially important after 1955 to counteract the impact of the low interwar birth rate which had decreased the number of potential parents. In the 1940s parenthood was also encouraged by greater confidence in the future and a decrease in the economic disincentives to having children (such as rationing and tax changes which diverted resources to families). Between 1955 and 1965 increasing affluence again enabled couples to have children without seriously reducing their living standards. However, by the later 1960s slower economic growth was starting to disappoint people's increasing expectations. Childbirth also meant loss of income for women, who were becoming increasingly accustomed to working for relatively high wages. The economic disincentives of childbirth were therefore returning, and they helped to increase both the average age at marriage and (with the help of the newly introduced contraceptive pill) the age at which mothers had their first child. This trend did not necessarily indicate the desire for smaller families, merely their later conception; but in the short term it led to a dramatic fall in the annual birth rate.

A falling birth rate had been one of the great fears of the 1940s. Beveridge, for example, had advocated state support for children by such means as family allowances – and such policies had become politically acceptable –

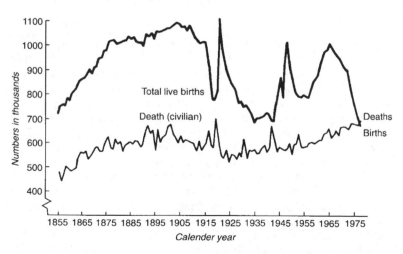

Figure 4.1   Birth and death rates, 1855–1975
Source: J. F. Ermish, *The Political Economy of Demographic Change* (1983) p. 6.

because it was projected that the population would go into absolute decline by the late 1960s. This danger was obviously averted. The population of Great Britain rose from 48.9 million to 54 million between the censuses of 1951 and 1971, with the number of children under 15 rising to 12.9 million or 23.7 per cent of the population rather than Beveridge's estimate of 7.6 million or 16.5 per cent of the population.

> The unsettling consequences of a fluctuating birth rate are best illustrated by their impact on education. As the postwar baby boom worked its way through the system, there was a sudden increase in demand for primary education in 1947, for secondary education in 1952 and for higher education in the late 1950s. Demand then fell away successively until the cycle was restarted in the 1960s, only to be halted once again in the early 1970s. More teachers and buildings were required to meet the expansion. They then became redundant.

The death rate

The second main fear of the 1940s was the ageing of the population through a decrease in the death rate. This did occur and came to dominate policy. A significantly greater number of people were not living into *advanced* old age, but fewer people were dying at a younger age. Life expectancy at birth for men rose from 66.5 years to 70 years between 1930 and 1977, for instance, but life expectancy at 65 remained almost constant at 77.[4] This ageing of the population put an ever-increasing strain on the hospital and welfare services, for which the elderly (and in particular those over 75) were the major clients.[5] Most political concern, however, was concentrated upon pensions.

> Pension policy was particularly affected by demographic change because the practice in Britain – as elsewhere – was that payments after the mid-1950s were financed not from a fund into which pensioners had paid throughout their lifetimes but directly from the contributions of those in work (pay as you go). The relative size of the labour force, however, was declining. This was because the large number of people born when the birth rate was high between 1890 and 1915 were retiring from employment. They were being replaced by the smaller number born in the interwar period. Thus there was a demographic shrinkage of the workforce. This clearly had serious implications, one of which was the abandonment of Beveridge's principle of flat-rate pensions and the introduction of earnings-related pensions in the late 1950s. This was politically (and financially) desirable as higher earnings-related contributions could immediately be collected from those in work, whilst earnings-related pensions would not have to be paid in full for a further 20 years. By this time, of course, the workforce would again be expanding as a result of the postwar baby booms.

The dependency ratio

The problem of pensions highlights one of the major ways in which demographic change affects welfare policy as well as economic growth: the variation in the number of 'non-productive' young and elderly people who are dependent on the wealth created by those of working age. The changing age structure of postwar Britain is summarized in Table 4.3, with the 'dependency ratio' expressed as a percentage both of those of working age (column 4) and, more significantly, of those actually working (column 5). Figures for 1911 have also been included to show that, although the postwar dependency ratio was 'deteriorating', it was only reverting to that prevailing at the turn of the century. However, there was a dramatic change in the causes of dependency, with a relative decline in the number of children and a relative increase in those aged over 65. In 1911, for instance, there were 12.3 people of working age to support each person over 65; by 1971 there were only 3.6 (column 6). Such changes in the dependency ratio were clearly a major factor behind the increased need for welfare expenditure after 1945, although their potentially damaging consequences for economic growth could be countered by improvements both in the productivity of the workforce and in the employment ratio of those of working age. A major reservoir of untapped labour was indeed found in married women, whose participation in the labour market (often on a part-time basis only) rose from 10 per cent to 43 per cent between 1931 and 1971.

Household structure

A further demographic factor which can have a significant impact on policy is changing household structure. A rise in the number of people living alone, especially amongst the elderly, is likely to increase demand for health and welfare services (although neighbours or nearby relations may be able to provide support when needed). Similarly a rise in the number of one-parent families is likely to increase demand for transfer payments. Both trends developed after 1945.[6] The proportion of people living alone rose from 1.8 per cent to 6.3 per cent of the population between 1931 and 1971. Meanwhile the number of divorces accelerated from an annual average of 7335 in 1936–40 to 32,168 in 1951–5 and 121,772 in 1971–5. This, in part, resulted from the introduction of legal aid in 1948 and the Divorce Act of 1969, which respectively made divorce more financially and legally practicable. Rates of remarriage remained high, but by 1976 it was nevertheless estimated that 1.25 million (or 9 per cent) of all dependent children were living in one-parent families. A further important change in household structure was a reduction in household size, from 4.1 in 1931 to 2.7 by 1971, as younger people sought – and were able to finance – a home of their own. To facilitate this change, the housing stock had to expand faster than the population.

Table 4.3 Demographic change, 1911–71

	Age structure (%)			Dependency ratios		
	(1) *0–14*	*(2)* *15–64*	*(3)* *65 +*	*(4)* *% of* *population* *of working age*	*(5)* *% of* *working* *population*	*(6)* *ratio of population* *of working age to* *pensioner*
1911	30.6	64.2	5.2	55.8	60.2	12.3
1951	22.1	66.8	11.0	49.6	56.1	4.7
1961	23.0	65.1	11.9	53.6	60.9	4.2
1971	23.7	62.9	13.3	58.8	66.6	3.6

Notes: Figures in columns 1–4 and 6 are for England and Wales only; column 5 refers to Britain as a whole.
Sources: A. H. Halsey (ed.), *British Social Trends* (1988) pp. 106, 127; J. Ermisch, *The Political Economy of Demographic Change* (1983) p. 14.

Migration

Migration can also generate demand for welfare expenditure. The continuation of the interwar drift of the population to the south of England and the Midlands and then, from the 1960s, an accelerating exodus from urban areas made social services redundant in certain regions, whilst requiring their replacement elsewhere. Such movement had, for example, a greater impact than population change on the increase in house-building in the South and, by reducing the number of children in inner-city areas, forced the closure of schools.

International migration was of less significance nationally, although of considerable political and local importance. Immigration from the West Indies peaked in the early 1960s and from the Indian subcontinent in 1968. Thereafter it was constrained by the Commonwealth Immigrants Acts of 1962, 1968 and 1971. Throughout the period it led to an increase in the aggregate population only in the late 1950s; and the net impact of emigration and immigration appears to have had little effect on either the gender or occupational balance of the population as a whole.[7] Increased black immigration did, however, necessitate the introduction of race relations legislation in the 1960s, and in certain localities the concentration of immigrants with different languages and cultural values (such as the acceptance of large and one-parent families, respectively, amongst Asian and West Indian communities) created particular problems. The increased concentration of resources on the personal social services and on inner-city areas by the Labour governments between 1964 and 1970 was one of the considered policy responses.

4.3 THE POLITICAL CONTEXT

The ultimate responsibility for the development of welfare policy in the face of such economic and demographic pressure fell not to disinterested experts (as Beveridge and Keynes appeared sometimes to assume) but to party politicians. The ideological differences between the Labour and Conservative Parties, which shared power after 1945, have already been discussed in Section 2.2. Welfare policy, however, was also shaped by:

- personal and ideological tensions within both parties
- short-term electoral calculations
- competition, for both attention and scarce resources, from other policies.

The Labour Party

Six of the first ten postwar elections were won by the Labour Party, which was consequently in power for 13 years between 1945 and 1975 (see Table 4.4). There was, as noted in Section 2.2.2, an underlying popular sympathy throughout the period with democratic socialist ideals concerning the welfare

state, but this was not fully capitalized upon by successive Labour governments. To some extent this was due to sheer bad luck. Each of Labour's periods in office coincided with economic crises (not solely of the government's
making) that were so severe that the pound had to be devalued in 1949 and
1968, and a loan sought from the IMF in 1976. Circumstances were therefore
not favourable to the expansion of welfare expenditure. Moreover, in 1960
and 1963 there occurred the premature deaths of the Party's deputy leader
and leader, Bevan and Gaitskell. Both were passionately committed to the
achievement of a more egalitarian society and had respectively the charisma
and the technocratic expertise to consolidate, in the wake of the 'economic
miracles' abroad, public acceptance for greater state intervention and to
implement it successfully.

Earlier, however, both Bevan and Gaitskell had compounded Labour's
misfortunes by exacerbating the ideological differences within the Party,
which compromised its electoral image in the 1950s and were to do so again
after 1970. The essence of the dispute was the speed and ultimate objective of
socialist policy. Was socialism an ethical 'crusade' to ensure that those in
power within a mixed economy acted with 'social responsibility' and thereby

Table 4.4   Election results, 1945–74

	Labour		Conservatives		Others	
	Seats	% vote	Seats	% vote	Seats	Elected prime minister
1945 July	393	47.8	213	39.8	34	Attlee
1950 Feb.	315	46.1	299	43.5	11	Attlee
1951 Oct.	295	48.8	321	48.0	9	Churchill
1955 May	277	46.4	345	49.7	8	Eden
1959 Oct.	258	43.8	365	49.4	7	Macmillan
1964 Oct.	317	44.1	304	43.4	9	Wilson
1966 Mar.	363	47.9	253	41.9	14	Wilson
1970 June	288	43.0	330	46.4	12	Heath
1974 Feb.	301	37.1	297	37.9	37	Wilson
1974 Oct.	319	39.2	277	35.8	39	Wilson

Notes: The dividing lines denote changes of government. The number of seats
was reduced from 640 to 625 in 1950, but was increased by five in 1955
and 1974.

Source: D. and G. Butler, *British Political Facts, 1900–1985* (1986) pp. 226–7.

gradually achieved a more equal society; or was its objective the more direct and immediate transfer of economic, and hence political, power from the market to the state?

The key policy issue was nationalization. The Attlee government between 1945 and 1951 had nationalized some 20 per cent of the economy; but neither the economic performance nor the managerial efficiency of the relevant industries had been noticeably improved and public opinion polls showed nationalization to be electorally unpopular. The 'consolidationists' within the Party accordingly sought to postpone any further nationalization. Then, after the publication in 1956 of Crosland's *The Future of Socialism*, the revisionists argued that nationalization was only a means to an end and that the objective of egalitarianism could be better achieved by other means, such as educational reform. Such views were anathema to the 'fundamentalists' under Bevan and then to the various splinter groups of the New Left after 1957. On broad Marxist lines, they argued that without a direct transfer of economic power to the state there could be – in the words of the official 1973 *Labour Programme* – no 'fundamental shift in the balance of power and wealth to working people and their families'.

The dispute had serious consequences for the Labour Party. It totally disrupted, through the 13 years the Party spent in opposition between 1951 and 1964, the serious planning of, and agreement with the trade unions on, a programme for the modernization of Britain, for which the electorate was calling by the early 1960s. It also publicly discredited the Party at the very time it needed to reinforce the core of its 'working-class' support, which was being eroded by increasing affluence and the consequent shift, for example, from manual work and council tenancy to white-collar work and owner-occupancy. A disciplined programme of reform, extending state intervention over the economy and the distribution of wealth, could have won and retained new members. Instead, there was the spectacle of the bitter battles between Gaitskell and both the Party's National Executive Committee (NEC) and Conference over the repeal of Clause 4 of the Party's constitution (the commitment to the 'common ownership of the means of production, distribution and exchange') and unilateral nuclear disarmament.[8] These battles revealed another key feature of the Labour Party: the deliberate location of the power to determine policy in the annual conference and, between conferences, in the NEC. Since the trade unions controlled, with their block votes, five-sixths of the votes at Conference and two-thirds of the seats on the NEC, this gave the public impression that the party leader was controlled by a powerful interest group – which appeared simultaneously to oppose economic growth and greater equality through its defence of 'restrictive practices' and the wage differentials of skilled workers.

It was factors such as these that prevented the Party from becoming, as many anticipated, the 'natural party of government' with the opportunity to develop the welfare state along social democratic – and possibly Swedish – lines. Indeed four of its election victories (in 1950, 1964 and twice in 1974) were so narrow that it was only between 1945 and 1950 and between 1966 and 1970 that Labour governments had a sufficiently comfortable parliamentary majority to pass controversial legislation. Nevertheless the welfare state bears the hallmarks of those two governments, especially the Attlee government of 1945–50. This government has been criticized, with some justice, for being conservative and backward looking. For instance, in his national broadcast on the Appointed Day of 5 July 1948 (the 'official birthday' of the welfare state, when both the NHS and the national insurance scheme came into operation) Attlee chose not to herald the dawn of a new egalitarian age, but to describe the reforms uncontroversially as:

> the culmination of effort made by all the people of this country over forty years or more to build together a social structure of mutual provision for contingencies, which if they were all left to face them alone, would overwhelm some and leave the confidence of others a prey to anxiety and fear.[9]

Nevertheless his government's incontrovertible achievement was to ensure the integrity of democratic institutions (when they came under genuine threat) and to pass an unprecedented range of economic and social legislation in the face of mounting economic crises and discouraging advice. Similar crises and advice had led in 1921 to the Geddes Axe and the abandonment of many reconstruction promises made during the First World War. With a different government that experience might well have been repeated. Instead the Attlee administration honoured the trust it felt it owed its prewar supporters and the 1945 electors; and it established, in the words of Kenneth Morgan, 'the essential basis for future advance'.[10]

The 1966–70 Wilson government (which many expected to secure this advance) is widely considered, in contrast, to have betrayed the trust placed upon it to manage the economy more efficiently and to effect a greater measure of social equality. It inherited, as has been seen, an economic crisis and relentless demographic pressure on both the education system and pensions. It was also undermined by bitter personal rivalries, fomented in the 1950s, which the pragmatism – or short-term expediency – favoured by an increasingly paranoid Prime Minister did little to resolve. By taking the wrong strategic decisions (such as the unsuccessful three-year battle to avert devaluation) and, above all, by failing to ensure that increases in public expenditure achieved commensurate results, the government undoubtedly did much to discredit the efficacy of state intervention. Nevertheless it was essentially a humane government which passed much liberal legislation (on, for example, family planning, divorce and equal pay) and directed extra resources to the underprivileged (through increased expenditure on the personal social services and better publicized cash benefits). It was only an increase in the number of the underprivileged, largely for demographic reasons, and the exaggerated hopes of its supporters that have obscured this latter achievement.

The Wilson governments of 1974–6 were potentially even more important, with the formal agreement by the trade unions of a social contract in which increases in welfare benefits ('the social wage') were accepted as a *quid pro quo* for lower rises in industrial wages. Here indeed was the opportunity to forge an alliance on Swedish lines. However, the political stalemate arising from the inconclusive election of February 1974, and then from the Cabinet's unprecedented 'agreement to disagree' during the referendum on Britain's continuing membership of the EEC in 1975, paralysed the policy's implementation whilst inflation escalated.

The Conservative Party

The Conservative Party won only four elections before 1975 but each of its victories secured a working majority in relatively favourable economic circumstances. Consequently, its 17 years in office (1951–64 and 1970–4) provided it with a major opportunity to influence welfare policy; but this influence was somewhat ambivalent because, as noted in Section 2.2.1, there was an inherent tension within the Party between a fundamental belief in the

2 *Demolishing the classic welfare state?*
The Conservatives have consistently been depicted as hostile to state welfare. This was true even in the early 1960s. Here the supposed vandals are Selwyn Lloyd and Powell. They actually promoted economic planning and the ten-year Hospital Plan.
Source: © Vicky, *Evening Standard*, 9 February 1961.

virtues of the market and an awareness of its past failings. This tension was a source of internal political divisions which, although they did not match in either public or personal bitterness those within the Labour Party (at least until the mid-1970s), led to the unprecedented resignation of the chancellor of the exchequer in 1958 on the issue of 'excessive' welfare expenditure.

The essence of this dispute was the balance to be struck between the free market and state intervention. Most Conservatives sought to reduce taxation in order to maximize personal incentive and choice; but reduced taxation required reduced public expenditure and this, the moderates feared, would jeopardize both the Party's electoral support and the cooperation of the trade unions, which was essential for the achievement of higher production. The 'economic liberals' (who were increasingly in the 1960s to swell the ranks of the New Right) dismissed such arguments as unprincipled expediency but, in their own determination to restore market forces, they were in turn accused of acting on narrow class lines and of being politically naïve.[11] A balance was maintained between these opposing views until the mid-1950s, when the creation of the IEA in 1955 and the chancellor's resignation in 1958 signified the economic liberals' defeat.

Thorneycroft's resignation well illustrated the crux of the dispute. In order to reassure foreign bankers and to control inflation, he wished to place a strict ceiling on public expenditure regardless of the political and social cost. His proposals included a £76 million package of cuts in welfare expenditure including, critically, the withdrawal of family allowance from the second child. This the Cabinet ultimately rejected on both political and practical grounds. Politically, as Macmillan argued, government 'in modern society' had an 'inescapable obligation to large sections of the community, the evasion of which would be both inequitable and unacceptable to public opinion'. In practice the proposals would be counter-productive – fuelling rather than reducing inflation because, in the real world of full employment, trade unions were likely to demand and secure compensatory wage increases. In 1949 all sections of the Party had combined to repudiate 'any suggestion that the deliberate creation of unemployment was necessary to maintain high production and industrial discipline'. This was the Achilles' heel of the economic liberals.[12]

The corresponding weakness of the moderates' policy, which was to remain predominant until the mid-1970s, was its inability to establish an incontrovertible link between state intervention and economic efficiency, which could both reassure the supporters and distinguish Conservative policy from that of Labour. There was no explicit statement of Conservative welfare policy after 1945. During the modernization of policy under Butler in the late 1940s there was, for instance, no social services charter, only the famous *Industrial Charter* which committed the Party to both full employment and a code of good industrial practice in order to reinforce the security of industrial workers.

Despite Butler's later pre-eminence, however, not even the *Industrial Charter* was implemented speedily. Little progress was made in either the voluntary or statutory implementation of its code until the early 1960s, when measures such as the Contracts of Employment Act (1963) and the Redundancy Payments Act (1965) were either enacted or planned.

The unofficial backbench One Nation group did seek to fill the void.[13] 'Economic and social policies must be so balanced', it argued, 'that they reinforce one another. The creation of more wealth must lead to better social conditions, and better social conditions to greater production.' More specifically, social security benefits were not condemned as demoralizing but rather welcomed as providing a guaranteed minimum income and thereby enlarging freedom and security: 'such freedom and such security are the basis of a responsible society – and not its enemy'. Housing and education policy were also highlighted as particularly beneficial to economic growth through their potential to create a mobile and trained workforce. However, on its own admission the group never succeeded in fully squaring the circle of market economics and state welfare. This dilemma was nowhere more apparent than in the proposals of two of its original members, Macleod and Powell, to reduce and more effectively target social expenditure by abandoning universal benefits in favour of selectivity. Such a policy, both acknowledged, would require the extension of the means test which in the real world was both electorally unpopular and administratively inefficient.

Similar problems were encountered by another of the original members when, as party leader in the late 1960s and prime minister in the early 1970s, Heath sought to plan and implement a policy which could reconcile a return to 'market forces' with interventionist social policies. Consequently, just as the Labour Party had failed to take the hard decisions which had enabled the Swedish SDP to reach an accommodation with the unions on the creation of a more egalitarian society, so the Conservative Party failed – unlike the Christian Democrats in West Germany – to identify the means by which welfare policy could constructively support the market economy.

The Conservatives' terms in office can be divided into three phases. Following their traumatic defeat in 1945 and their failure to win any by-elections from Labour before 1951, the Party was convinced of – if not wholly converted to – the need to guarantee full employment and maintain the broad structure of the welfare state, as established by the Attlee government. The administrations headed by Churchill (1951 to April 1955) and Eden (1955 to January 1957) were largely content to confound the Labour Party's prediction that they would create mass unemployment, abandon the welfare state and antagonize the trade unions. Any distinctive innovations were the result not of a coherent strategy but of the initiative of individual ministers such as Macmillan and Eden who sought, respectively, to honour the election pledge to build 300,000 houses per annum and to expand technical education.

With a paramount need to rebuild party morale after the Suez debacle, Macmillan did not revert to market forces (as Thorneycroft's resignation testifies) but sought to develop an 'opportunity' as opposed to a 'welfare' state – in which state intervention encouraged individual responsibility and effort by such means as tax incentives for house ownership and earnings-related benefits. The realization of Britain's relative decline also precipitated greater economic planning with, most notably, the creation of the National Economic Development Council (NEDC) at which government could meet with the two sides of industry to discuss the future rate of economic growth (and, by implication, the future boundaries of public expenditure). These attempts to revitalize Britain ended in disillusion and disarray. The 1960 balance of payments crisis tarnished the government's reputation for managerial efficiency, while France's rejection of Britain's application to join the EEC in 1963 halted the momentum of modernization. Politically, Macmillan's dismissal of one-third of the Cabinet in July 1962 betrayed panic; and the scramble for the leadership after his resignation in 1963, amid various sex and spy scandals, was uncharacteristically undignified. His eventual replacement by the fourteenth Earl of Home, under whom Macleod and Powell refused to serve, also did little to further the image of a 'modern' party. Therefore, while many of the reforms inaugurated by Macmillan were highly appropriate for the 'developmental' state which – in the wake of the economic miracles abroad – he was trying to establish, their implementation ultimately lacked cohesion and conviction.

This was a weakness which Heath deliberately set out to remedy through the creation, while he was leader of the opposition between 1965 and 1970, of over 30 policy committees. As a result his government was one of the best prepared of all postwar governments; but the philosophy underlying its proposals had been neglected in favour of technocratic reform and no fall-back position had been prepared should unforeseen difficulties arise – as they certainly did with the rise in unemployment to over one million, the intransigence of the trade unions, and finally the quadrupling of oil prices in October 1973. Consequently, the government was characterized by spectacu-lar 'U-turns' in policy and ended with the miners' strike and the three-day week. Having sought to modernize every area of British society, from the reform of industrial relations to the restructuring of the health service and local government, it left possibly 'the fewest policy legacies of any post-war government'.[14]

The political cycle

Apart from the unresolved disputes and the shifting balance of power within each of the governing parties, welfare policy was also fashioned by short-term electoral calculation. During this period a 'political' cycle was perceived to develop as a result of the manipulation of the economy to provide a climate favourable to the government during the run-up to a general elec-tion. The Labour government to their credit – but also to their cost – declined to act in such a way in 1950 and 1970; but during the Conservatives' terms of office there were expansionary budgets in 1955 and 1959, and a delay to deflation in 1964, which many consider to have been not wholly justified by conventional economic indicators. Welfare policy, in addition, could be paralysed by inconclusive elections, such as those of 1974, and stimulated by by-elections or, more regularly, local government elections.

Political priorities

A final political influence on welfare policy was its need to compete, for both the Cabinet's attention and scarce resources, with other areas of policy. This was especially true of foreign affairs and defence where, apart from the outbreak of actual hostilities such as the Korean War (1950–2) and the Suez campaign (November to December 1956), there were four predominant issues: the Cold War, decolonization, entry into the EEC and Northern Ireland. The problem of Northern Ireland seriously distracted the Heath administration, whilst entry into the EEC created major divisions within both parties after 1960 and helped to paralyse the Wilson government in 1975. Over a longer period, the largely successful retreat from Empire (principally from the Indian subcontinent in the 1940s and from Africa and the Caribbean after 1960) also exhausted ministers and created particular problems for the Macmillan government when it had to seek support for its modernization programme from irate backbenchers.

Throughout the whole period, however, the most serious demands on the Cabinet's time and on resources came from the escalation of the Cold War (from the Berlin blockade of 1948–9 to Russia's invasion of Czechoslovakia in 1968) and of the arms race. They diverted the attention of successive prime ministers, without whose involvement and encouragement no radical innovation in welfare policy could succeed. Attlee, for example, was involved in the creation of NATO, whilst Macmillan pioneered the concept of 'summit' meetings to reduce the threat of nuclear war. They also consumed scarce manpower and financial resources. To contain communism, as well as to protect essential supplies such as oil, Britain maintained sizeable forces in the Middle and Far East, as well as in Europe, until the withdrawal from East of Suez in 1968. It also developed its own independent nuclear deterrent. This was portrayed in the mid-1950s as a cheap alternative to conventional weapons; but it diverted highly skilled manpower from civilian production, became increasingly expensive with the greater sophistication of weaponry, and was unable in practice to replace conventional weapons in regionalized conflicts. It is true that defence expenditure (although higher than that of trading rivals such as Germany and Japan) did decline considerably as a percentage of GDP throughout the period, thus releasing resources for welfare policy. Individual policies such as social security and education came indeed to exceed defence in overall cost (see Appendix, Table A.3).[15] The continuing competition for resources between defence and welfare policy, however, is a salutary reminder that, to achieve a full understanding, welfare policy should never be studied in isolation.

Political consensus

The period from 1945 to 1975 has been conventionally portrayed as one of political consensus. This is justified in relation to the basic framework of welfare policy, where there was a continuing all-party commitment to the mixed economy, the maintenance of full employment and a minimum standard of social security. However, there was bitter animosity between the two major parties (perhaps because their policies appeared so similar) as well as fundamental differences in their underlying philosophies even when, as in 1962, they appeared to be converging on a policy of modernization.[16] Labour's priority was to engineer a more equal society through greater state intervention and, if necessary, higher taxation. The Conservatives were willing only to accept that degree of intervention and taxation which was compatible with market efficiency and personal initiative. Neither strategy, however, was developed to its logical conclusion – as in Sweden or West Germany. This was in part because of both parties' serious internal divisions and other distractions; but it was also, as will be seen, the result of advice emanating from the civil service and of the perceived wishes of the electorate.

4.4 THE ADMINISTRATIVE CONTEXT

Both political parties were dependent for the successful formulation and implementation of policy upon the administrative capability of the civil service and 'sub-central' government. As has been seen in Section 3.1, there are many ways in which bureaucracy can influence – and even determine – policy; and so it was of major significance for welfare policy that, in the early 1960s, both the traditional ethos of the civil service and the structure of 'sub-central' government were widely regarded as obsolete. This was, in particular, the view of two exhaustive enquiries appointed at the height of the campaign to 'modernize' Britain: the Fulton Committee on the Civil Service (1966–8) and the Redcliffe-Maud Royal Commission on Local Government in England (1966–9). It was also the fundamental reason behind increasing dissatisfaction with the nature of devolved government in Northern Ireland and Scotland.

The civil service

The conviction of the Fulton Committee was that the civil service had singularly failed to adapt to the transfer of the state's responsibilities from the 'passive and regulatory' to the 'active and positive'. As it argued:

> To meet these new tasks of government the modern Civil Service must be able to handle the social, economic, scientific and technical problems of our time, in an international setting. Because the solutions to complex problems need long preparation, the Service must be far-sighted; from its accumulated knowledge and experience, it must show initiative in working out what are the needs of the future and

how they might be met. A special responsibility now rests upon the Civil Service because one Parliament or even one Government often cannot see the process through.[17]

Instead, the civil service was an introverted, poorly managed, badly structured and essentially amateur institution which was unable efficiently to discharge its existing responsibilities – let alone plan and execute new ones. In particular, officials lacked the essential economic, statistical and accountancy skills to manage efficiently the economy or major spending programmes such as the NHS. They lacked also the training and the vision, instilled into French civil servants by the Ecole Nationale d'Administration, to plan and implement bold initiatives. They sought rather to maintain political consensus by preserving the *status quo*.

The administrative failings identified by Fulton were all the more culpable because, as a result of the reforms forced upon it during the Second World War, the postwar civil service potentially had the skill and dynamism to respond immediately to the state's adoption of a more positive role. There was an effective blend of regular and irregular civil servants. Specialists had become accustomed to reporting directly to ministers. Management skills had been encouraged. A new generation of talented officials, who considered 'everything was achievable', was also vying for permanent appointment. 'Postwar Whitehall', as Hennessy has remarked, 'was *the* place to be for the young and clever with a high personal charge of public duty.'[18] However, by the early 1950s the irregulars had either left or lost their independence; specialists had been made subordinate to generalists; and the new generation was being trained, as policy advisers, in the art of crisis avoidance rather than, as executive managers, in risk-taking.

All the perceived failings of the civil service, as noted in Section 3.1.2, were characterized by the Treasury which had overall responsibility for the management of the service and thus for the lost opportunity for postwar reform. Until the 1960s it employed few economists or statisticians. Its strategic vision was limited by the demands of an annual budget. It preferred to advise others rather than take any direct responsibility for the implementation of policy – ultimately welcoming demand management, for instance, because it required officials only to manipulate (as Marquand has observed) 'the controls on the economic dashboard' and not to 'lift the bonnet and dirty their hands in the engine'.[19] Finally, its characteristic response to new economic initiatives – from the implementation of demand management in the 1940s to the programme analysis review in the 1970s – was to give responsibility to officials who were sceptical of, rather than committed to, their success.

The failings of the postwar civil service admittedly may not have been as comprehensive as its detractors averred. Ironically the appointment of the

Fulton Committee itself delayed reforms that were already being implemented by the Treasury as the result of the more restrained yet equally radical recommendations of the 1961 Plowden Report.[20] Nor were any failings the sole responsibility of the civil service. Just as its successive heads paid insufficient attention to the machinery of government, so too did successive Cabinets – which was particularly surprising in the case of Labour Cabinets, which looked to the state and its officials, rather than to the market, for economic and social advance. There was also the genuine constitutional obstacle of ministerial responsibility, which demoralized officials by discouraging them from taking initiatives whilst adding to ministerial 'overload' and thus led, inevitably, to hasty and ill-considered decisions. The Fulton Committee was noticeably reticent about the consequences for parliamentary democracy of officials' responsibility for policies which would take 'more than one Parliament or even one Government' to implement fully.

Nevertheless the consequence for welfare policy was that the civil service lacked the expertise and the vision to resolve those critical issues which both political parties failed to confront in opposition – whereas officials in Italy and France during the 1950s made good even more serious failings in national politics.[21] It also lacked the management expertise and drive to establish beyond doubt the efficacy of state intervention even in those areas where the market had demonstrably failed in the 1930s. An attempt was made to correct these failings in the early 1970s. In the wake of the Fulton Report, both business and personnel management within Whitehall were gradually improved. Heath also introduced such reforms as programme analysis review and the Central Policy Review Staff in order to keep the effectiveness of individual policies under continuous review and to fix the Cabinet's attention on broad strategic objectives. Under the pressure of external events, however, the Heath government became, ironically, the postwar government most characterized by 'U-turns' in policy and by ministerial 'overload'.

Local government

The period from 1945 to 1975 has also been portrayed as one of decline for local government in England and Wales. In the late 1940s the Attlee government deprived it of many traditional responsibilities (such as gas and electricity) as well as newer ones (such as national assistance and hospitals). In the 1970s it also lost its residual health services and responsibility for water. Its financial dependence on Whitehall grew as the percentage of its income coming from central government grants rose from 30 per cent to 45 per cent. Its administrative dependence was well illustrated by the need after 1970 to seek approval from the Department of Health and Social Security for all appointments to the post of director of social services.

Conversely, the period has also been described as 'the years of greatest affluence for local government'.[22] Its aggregate expenditure trebled in real terms and consumed an ever greater percentage of GDP (see Appendix, Table A.1). Its formal dependence on Whitehall may have grown but there remained, as argued in Section 3.1.3, considerable scope for independent action in the implementation of major spending programmes such as education and housing. Some legislation was even designed to encourage local variation; and in 1958 the major change in central government finance from specific to general grants, whilst placing a ceiling on Treasury commitments, reduced detailed supervision of expenditure. Moreover, as has been seen, Whitehall departments preferred to advise rather than to direct. The 1944 Education Act, for example, gave the Ministry of Education the constitutional power to 'control and direct' local education authorities, and yet there was the well-documented case of the Ministry's acquiescence in the refusal by Cardiff in the 1940s to fulfil its statutory obligation to abolish all-age schools.[23] Finally, during this period local government acquired many new responsibilities, especially in the area of the personal social services. It could therefore be argued that it was only in the mid-1970s, with the greater politicization of local government and the perceived need to combat inflation through greater control of public expenditure, that the independence of local government came seriously under attack.

Wherever the real power lay, the quality of many welfare services still depended on the administrative capacity of local government; and this, at the time, was widely agreed to be defective. On the one hand, there were serious doubts about the quality of administrative staff and councillors, internal management systems and the coordination of policy. There was a series of enquiries in the 1960s which led to later, and by no means wholly successful, experiments in corporate planning. Most significant for welfare policy was the report of the Seebohm Committee on Local Authority and Allied Personal Social Services (1965–8) which dismissed the existing specialist services of local authorities as 'irrelevant to people's problems' because they prevented all the problems facing one individual or family from being tackled collectively.[24] Hence the Report's recommendation, and the achievement in 1970, of a single social services department in each local authority. On the other hand, there was the question of local government structure. The historical legacy of some 1500 authorities had resulted in an irrational system in which many authorities were too small for efficient administration. Moreover, the confusion of responsibilities between various highly antagonistic types of authority was demoralizing to administrators and the public alike.[25] County councils, for instance, were responsible for the personal social services in their areas (including the problem of homelessness) but they had no authority over the building or allocation of housing, which was the responsibility of the smaller district councils.

The nettle of local government reform was finally grasped in 1966 by the Redcliffe–Maud Royal Commission, and it provided as damning an indictment of the existing system as the Fulton Committee. It argued that:

> Each local authority should be responsible for a continuous area that makes, so far as practicable, a coherent social and economic whole, matching the way of life of a mobile society and giving the authority the space it needs to assess and tackle its

problems. . . . Whether an authority is resolving people's housing problems, settling the pattern of schools and colleges, or providing personal services for families and individuals in need of care or help, it is more likely to meet people's requirements and make most effective use of resources if its responsibility extends over the whole area that includes people's homes, the offices and factories they work in, the schools where their children are taught, the shops they buy their goods from and the places they go to for entertainment and recreation.[26]

Consequently, it recommended the creation of 58 'unitary' authorities, containing no less than one-quarter of a million people and with sole responsibility for all the services in their area. Only in Manchester, Liverpool and Birmingham were these services, as in London, to be divided between two tiers of government. The Commission, however, fell victim to party politics. It had been commissioned by the Wilson government and had recommended, in essence, the extension throughout the country of the existing county boroughs (where the Labour Party was politically strong). This was rejected by the incoming Heath government because it would have effectively destroyed all the existing county councils (where the Conservative Party was strong). Heath's own Local Government Act, implemented in 1974, duly reduced the number and increased the size of existing local authorities on the ground of efficiency; but, largely for political reasons, it retained county councils and thus the two-tier system. This perpetuated the old administrative antagonisms and the damaging divisions between interrelated services. In the 47 non-metropolitan counties of England and Wales, for example, responsibility for the personal social services and housing continued to be divided between the county and its districts.

The distinctiveness of Northern Ireland and Scotland

The quality and structure of local government in Scotland came under similar attack in the 1960s. Indeed it had been the Scottish Office's frustration with the inability of local government to provide a focus for economic planning that started the reform process in Whitehall; and it culminated with the creation of nine new regions and 53 districts supplemented by three island areas as well as major policy changes (such as, to the surprise of all, the establishment of unified social work departments well in advance of the rest of Britain). Such divergences underline the fact that although Britain enjoys a reputation for being a centralized 'unitary' state, it had – and still has – many features in common with federal governments such as the USA and Germany.[27] Northern Ireland and Scotland (and to a lesser extent Wales) have histories and cultures which are very different from England's – and from each other's – and those differences are reflected and reinforced by distinctive institutions and laws, which in turn have had a major impact on both the formulation and implementation of their welfare policies. This is particularly true of housing policy which accordingly will be highlighted.

Northern Ireland was the more distinctive because of the extent of its devolved powers from the partition of Ireland in 1920 to the reimposition of 'direct rule' in 1972. The 1920 Government of Ireland Act devolved legislative and administrative responsibility for welfare policy to a separately elected parliament (Stormont). However, effective independence was constrained by a lack of tax-raising powers, the economic slump into which the province immediately plunged and the political desire to maintain parity of welfare services with the mainland, both as a symbol of union with Britain and as a means of distancing itself from Eire. Complex negotiations between Stormont and Westminster were held from 1936 (when parity of cash benefits was assured) to 1954 (when further subsidies were agreed in order to raise other services to British standards and to offset higher levels of unemployment and need).

Despite formal devolution, therefore, postwar social security and health provision were broadly comparable with that in the rest of the UK. In contrast, prewar legacies and religious antagonism ensured significant differences in education policy. As a result of strictly unconstitutional action in the 1920s, Protestant and Catholic schools remained separate; and although government increasingly subsidized the latter (paying all salaries and the bulk of capital and current costs) they remained, unlike Protestant schools, in the voluntary sector. In all areas of policy there were also significant time lags. The English Education Act of 1944, for example, was not replicated until 1947 and the school leaving age was not raised to 15 until 1957. Moreover there were subtle differences in the small print of legislation. Social security laws as late as 1966, for instance, included residential qualifications designed to deny workers from Eire rights to which they were entitled on the mainland. Despite being forced by financial and political pressures broadly to shadow Westminster legislation, therefore, there were sufficient divergences in both the implementation and detail of policy to label Northern Ireland more accurately as a 'selective imitator' and 'an associate member of the British welfare state'.[28]

In 1945 a major housing-building programme was launched to remedy prewar neglect. Unlike in England and Wales, however, half of the new state housing was built (in a portent of the Thatcherite 1980s) not by local authorities but by an executive agency – the Northern Ireland Housing Trust. Local government was perceived to be too inefficient, corrupt and partisan to be entrusted with the whole task. The prime objective of Unionist and Nationalist councils alike in the building and allocation of housing was not to relieve need but to maintain the political balance of their area and to reward supporters. Indeed it was the reallocation of a house to a single Protestant woman from a family of Catholic squatters in North Tyrone which provided the immediate pretext for the outbreak of civil unrest in 1968. In short, housing like educational policy did not foster greater harmony (as Titmuss, amongst others, had hoped) but rather served to reinforce cultural and political differences in the province.[29]

Scotland did not enjoy so formal a devolution of power but its welfare policy was equally distinctive. Instead of a separate parliament, a special minister had represented Scotland's interests in Cabinet since 1885; and in 1939 statutory responsibility was invested in this minister (now the Secretary of State for Scotland) for the implementation of policy by the Scottish Office in Edinburgh. For cash benefits the responsibility amounted to little more than the administration of British legislation. In other areas, however, there was ample scope for Scotland 'to experiment and go its own way as long as general standards were maintained'.[30] This was due largely to the continuing existence of separate systems of local government, law and education, guaranteed by the 1707 Act of Union, and the distinctive professional worlds and cultural values which developed as a result. The Scottish Office brokered pluralistic bargaining within these worlds and thereby ensured that not only was British legislation adapted to Scottish needs but also that, as in Northern Ireland, education and housing policy remained distinct.

The education system was almost wholly separate with, for example, the Scottish Office controlling within secondary schools the curriculum, different sets of examinations and teacher training. In higher education there were no polytechnics. Organizational differences also characterized the NHS and the personal social services which, as with the creation of executive agencies in Northern Ireland, often anticipated later reforms in England. Teaching hospitals, for example, were never administratively separate from other hospitals as they were in England and Wales until 1974 and the extra tier of administration introduced then (but withdrawn in 1982) never applied to Scotland. The establishment of unified social work departments in 1969 and of children's hearings in 1971 (which located the remedy for child neglect *and* juvenile delinquency within the family) also projected Scottish practice from one of the more backward to the most advanced in Europe (see Section 10.1). Despite the lack of formal political autonomy enjoyed by Northern Ireland, therefore, the conventions of 'parallel administration' or 'technocratic autonomy' gave Scotland an equal – or even greater – freedom to develop a distinctive welfare policy.[31]

Scotland's exceptional housing needs had already led, during the First World War, to the national adoption of rent control and subsidies for public building which distinguished Britain from the rest of Western Europe. After 1945 there was a renewed housing drive, which led to the building of a million houses by the late 1970s. This reinforced differences within Britain. Partly due to higher subsidies, four-fifths of Scottish – as opposed to a half of English – building was in the public sector with the result that the balance of Scotland's housing stock by 1978 (33 per cent owner-occupied and 56 per cent publicly owned) was almost a mirror image of England's. In certain areas of Glasgow, moreover, up to 99 per cent of houses were publicly owned. This reflected a class polarization of society and a use of

→

housing to consolidate and reward political support totally foreign to the experience of even equally depressed, Labour-controlled areas in England. Council rents were also on aggregate only two-thirds those in England, so that when the attempt was made in 1972 to make tenants pay a full 'economic' rent (see Section 9.3) special legislation had to be passed for Scotland to stagger what would otherwise have been a precipitous rise.

By the 1960s, however, both systems of devolved government had fallen into disrepute. This was not because they had failed, in any material sense, to serve their regions well. Because of the lower cost of living in Northern Ireland and Scotland, for example, parity of cash benefits gave claimants a higher real income than in England. Previous areas of disadvantage, especially housing, were largely made good. In education and health provision (as judged by crude indicators such as attendance at university and beds per population) standards were ever higher. This relative improvement was reflected by an increasing shift of resources from England, as illustrated by Table 4.5.

Nationalist opinion, however, was growing restless in Northern Ireland with the discrimination inherent in welfare policy and in Scotland with the frustration of regional economic needs by the wider problems of the UK economy. As the major reorganization of local government in the early 1970s demonstrated, central government was also increasingly concerned with the quality of service delivery. This was at its worst in housing where it was not just the dominance of Unionists in Northern Ireland but also of the Labour Party in Glasgow that led to gross inefficiency and corruption. Indeed housing in Scotland in the early 1970s has been condemned as 'overwhelmingly public, monolithic and monotonous in structure, inadequately managed and maintained and providing precious little reward for decades of consumer loyalty'.[32] The remedy was seen to lie in totally opposite directions. In Northern Ireland, Stormont was suspended and 'direct rule' from

Table 4.5 Identifiable public expenditure per head in the UK, 1959–82

	1959/60	1964/5	1969/70	1982/3
England	100	100	100	100
Scotland	105	116	131	127
Wales	95	117	116	111
Northern Ireland	88	109	118	147

Source: T. Wilson, *Ulster: conflict and consensus* (Oxford, 1989) p. 84.

Westminster imposed. Welfare policy was largely entrusted to appointees on the Housing Executive, four 'health and social services' and five 'education and library' boards. In Scotland, by contrast, the demand for a devolved parliament grew and was only narrowly and controversially rejected by a referendum in 1978.

An administrative audit

The quality of administration in central, regional and local government was not entirely without merit. At the centre there remained by international standards an exceptional degree of integrity. At a central and local level there was also much successful improvisation and innumerable individual examples of effective management. The sweeping criticisms of Fulton and Redcliffe–Maud should be counterbalanced by their own admitted weaknesses. Both ignored commissioned evidence when it contradicted their prior assumptions and, in the drive for technocratic efficiency, disregarded the political dimension of policy-making. Both reports, therefore, not only provided a vivid picture of the administrative weaknesses of both central and local government, which seriously hampered welfare policy at this time, but also reflected the continuing inability to resolve them.[33] In Northern Ireland and Scotland, and particularly in the latter, there was also an effective adaptation of policy to regional need. Moreover, where obvious deficiencies were identified, remedies were devised – such as the Northern Ireland Housing Trust and the devolution of responsibility to Housing Action Areas in Glasgow in the 1970s – which paved the way for future reform in Britain as a whole.

4.5 THE CULTURAL CONTEXT

A final determinant of welfare policy is the prevailing cultural values of society, to which policy-makers not only respond but of which they themselves are also an integral part. The formulation and implementation of policy is obviously influenced by:

- Public opinion (particularly as expressed at elections) and political perceptions of what is publicly acceptable (especially in relation to taxation).
- Public willingness to accept the consequences of desired objectives. For instance the 1944 *Employment Policy* white paper emphasized that the attainment of a high and stable level of employment depended ultimately not on government but on 'the understanding and support of the country as a whole'.[34]
- The values of leading vested interests or 'governing institutions' if corporatist assumptions (as summarized in Section 2.3.1) are accepted.
- A wider set of cultural values, expressed alternatively in changing patterns of consumption, life-styles and artistic achievement.

Public opinion

The postwar period is the first for which detailed evidence of public opinion exists, following the establishment in the late 1930s of such organisations as the Gallup Poll and Mass-Observation. There remain, however, many problems of interpretation. As Addison has warned, 'judgements about the "movement" of public opinion have always to be tempered by the knowledge that many people never change their opinion, while some never have any to change'.[35] In the late 1940s it also became generally accepted that, in relation to welfare policy, one-third of the population was either 'chronically ignorant or apathetic'. Such a conclusion would seem to be confirmed by later polls. In 1956, for instance, 49 per cent of mothers polled neither recognized nor could define the term 'welfare state', and in 1964 there was discovered a 'widespread civic illiteracy' over the cost of the social services.[36] Public opinion is, therefore, an elusive concept and is best divided (for analytical purposes) into three interrelated categories: general and uninformed opinion (such as the 'latent' opinions which in 1943 obliged the Coalition government against its better judgement to adopt the Beveridge Report); special and informed opinion (such as pressure groups and the 'Middle England' on which, according to Donnison, the democratic socialists relied); and public opinion as perceived by politicians.[37]

Public opinion, both expressed and perceived, strongly supported welfare policy between 1945 and 1975 and, as the most authoritative study of electoral behaviour in the 1960s has concluded, 'the rise and endurance of the welfare state was directly related to this fact'.[38] Certainly Conservative Party policy was strongly influenced by it in the 1940s and continued to be so in the 1950s, as the resignation of Thorneycroft testified. However, public opinion was also contradictory and restrictive, and this severely constrained the positive role that the welfare state could play in the resolution of Britain's underlying structural economic and social problems. The contradictions can best be illustrated by the findings of two surveys. In 1963 and 1970, 97 per cent and 92 per cent respectively of those polled by Butler and Stokes wanted expenditure on pensions and the social services either to increase or remain stable. Yet simultaneously 52 per cent and 65 per cent wanted tax cuts as opposed to increased welfare expenditure. Similarly in October 1974, 84 per cent of those polled by Sarlvik and Crewe felt that it was 'very' or 'fairly important' that expenditure on the NHS and anti-poverty programmes should increase, whilst 70 per cent wanted expenditure on the social services to be either cut back or stabilized.[39]

Such contradictions might be interpreted as simply reflecting the incompatibility of views held by the respondents. However, as has been persuasively argued, it is more likely that they reflected a support for the welfare state that was both selective and selfish. People were willing to accept higher taxation so long as it financed services (such as the NHS or pensions) which did – or would – directly benefit themselves. They were far less sanguine about expenditure that helped minorities, such as the unemployed and one-parent families (who might be deemed responsible for their own problems) and, more surprisingly, children. There was little evidence here of the community spirit, the altruism or the desire for greater equality which Titmuss and the Labour Party in particular hoped the welfare state could either build upon or foster.

This lack of altruism was matched by a popular reluctance to accept the duties, as opposed to the rights, implied by welfare policy. This reluctance was most pronounced in the field of industrial relations where, in defiance of the hopes expressed in the 1944 *Employment Policy* white paper, resistance to technological change continued and calls for wage restraint were spurned. In the older industries, where attitudes and institutions had been forged by the permanent threat of unemployment, such behaviour was perhaps under-standable in the short term; but it was common also in the newer industries which were even more reliant for their international competitiveness on adaptation to changing demand and production methods.

The reasons for the reluctance to accept responsibilities as well as rights were analysed in a classic study of the 'affluent worker' in the 1960s.[40] Following Labour's third election defeat, it discovered that manual workers were being neither drawn into the middle class nor alienated by increasing affluence. Rather, they were developing a more private and materialistic life-style. Hence increasing membership of trade unions represented not so much workers' greater sense of communal or class solidarity, but a calculated desire to belong to a 'service organisation of advantage to them in defending and furthering their personal economic interests'. Just as only 8 per cent of those polled were actively seeking to realize their material ambitions through self-advancement or promotion, so only a minority were concerned with the broader social objectives of the trade unions and the Labour Party. On the other hand, 83 per cent participated in the election of shop-stewards because it was at the factory, as opposed to the national, level that the power to secure improvements in pay and working conditions was believed to lie. Accordingly there was an escalation in unofficial strikes led by shop-stewards which came to be widely identified abroad as a major cause of Britain's relative economic decline.[41] Such short-term materialism, however, was not restricted to the affluent worker. It was endemic through-out society. As one pragmatic justification of Macmillan's 'you've never had it so good' election of 1959, for example, has concluded: 'the generation which came to maturity in the 1950s had been born in the Great War, schooled during the slump, conscripted in the Second World War and rationed for years afterwards. It had no inclination to forgo the security and comforts now within its grasp in the hope of long-term economic growth.'[42]

The prime responsibility for changing such attitudes, so that they not only reflected the new reality of full employment and social security but could also ensure their continuance, was the government's. In the interwar period liberal opinion had become increasingly reconciled to state intervention by the concept of 'active citizenship'. By relieving basic need, welfare expenditure was seen not as a rival to philanthropy and self-help, but as a means of freeing charities to concentrate on other challenges and of providing the poor with a basic independence. In the 1940s the Labour government strove to ensure that the cost and availability of the social services demoralized neither the tax-payer nor the recipient. On the Appointed Day in July 1948, for instance, it launched a campaign to remind the recipient that the social services were not 'free', but had to be earned through higher productivity; and to stress to the tax-payer that state welfare was more cost-effective, and therefore represented better value for money, than private insurance.[43] However, the campaign was attacked in Parliament and in the press both as party propaganda and as unnecessarily expensive and, when the Conservatives returned to power, all such attempts at 'public education' were largely abandoned.

Another campaign, prepared by Gaitskell, to nurture those attitudes which the 1944 white paper had identified as essential for the attainment of high and stable employment was also suspended and only bore fruit (too little and too late) with the publication of the 1956 white paper *The Economic Implications of Full Employment* (Cmd 9725). Thereafter, throughout the corporatist attempts to plan the economy, successive governments increasingly limited their ambition to mere 'mechanical' change: the superficial manipulation of public opinion rather than an active attempt to win people's minds.

Vested interests

The values of the corporatist elite also were – and remained – essentially antipathetic to any sustained, collective attempt to resolve Britain's long-standing weaknesses. Financiers remained more concerned with short-term pressure on sterling than with the underlying health of the economy. Their conversion to Keynesianism, and in particular deficit finance as a remedy for unemployment, has been widely questioned and their acceptance of increased welfare expenditure was largely expedient. As one international banker remarked in response to the chancellor's resignation in 1958: 'I would like to see the Government cutting every penny of expenditure, but if it is a matter of political judgement I would prefer to trust Macmillan rather than Thorneycroft.'[44] The TUC sought to act 'responsibly' with the successful attempt to contain wages between 1948 and 1950, its membership of the NEDC after 1961 and the 'social contract' of 1974. It remained, however, a prisoner of its own history, trying to reconcile the competing interests of its member unions without the necessary central resources or authority. Moreover, to retain authority over their increasingly militant shop-stewards, union leaders had to respond to the short-term materialistic demands of their members – with few tangible concessions from government, which would have enabled them to argue that increases in the 'social wage' justified restraint over the industrial wage. Rather, during the 1950s the TUC regarded Conservative attempts to revive the economy through tax cuts 'not as an industrial dynamic but as class politics, likelier to increase middle-class consumption than general production', and their suspicions were intensified by repeated later attempts to introduce prices and incomes policies.[45] In other words the TUC, unlike the LO in Sweden, was in no position to agree with government on – let alone implement – any long-term commitment concerning the future development of the welfare state.

Finally, there were the employers, to whom both Crosland and Butler looked with confidence for the exercise of greater social responsibility – 'private enterprise in the public interest'. Certainly by 1960 they were so disillusioned with 'stop–go' economic policies that they were willing to enter into tripartite talks on the planning of the economy. As a whole, however, they demonstrated neither the readiness nor the hard-headed competence to take the long-term investment decisions which modern industry required, to break down the class barriers between management and the shop-floor, or to implement the code of good industrial practice that would have minimized the need for state intervention. Even more than the TUC they lacked a sense of unity – the CBI only being formed in 1965 through the merger of three rival national associations of employers. Certainly they lacked the necessary collective will to agree and implement long-term decisions that might have conflicted with their members' short-term interests. The individualism and suspicion of government, validated by Britain's industrial dominance in the nineteenth century, was still all-pervasive. 'The commonsense of nearly 200 years ago', as Marquand has argued, 'was the chief obstacle to successful economic and social adjustment.'[46] What was needed after 1945 to counteract the legacy of the industrial revolution was an equally dramatic cultural revolution.

Cultural values

A cultural revolution did indeed occur after 1945, but it was one which intensified rather than reduced individualism.[47] Pioneered in the USA, driven on by advertising (especially after the inauguration of commercial television in 1955) and increasingly financed by hire purchase (especially after 1958), there was a consumer boom which transformed the austerity of the rationed 1940s into the affluence of the 'swinging sixties'. In 1950, for instance, there were only 350,000 televisions and 2.3 million cars whilst only 8 per cent of households had fridges. By 1971, 91 per cent of households had television, 69 per cent had fridges and there were 11.8 million cars. This was the context of the increasingly private, domestic life-style of the affluent worker and the abandonment of the wartime acceptance of 'fair shares'. Accompanying the incipient consumer boom in the mid-1950s there was also a questioning of established values. 'Angry young men' such as Kingsley Amis and John Osborne – the authors, respectively, of *Lucky Jim* (1954) and *Look Back in Anger* (1956) – attacked the superficiality and snobbery of existing society and were accorded a reception more usually associated with French novelists and playwrights. Even the monarchy came under considerable attack. This was the start of the general questioning of established institutions, which culminated in the Fulton and Redcliffe–Maud reports. It was also the start of the satirical movement, which spawned *Private Eye* and such television programmes as *That Was The Week That Was*.

Attempts to plan the economy and to engineer a more equal society 'from the top down' were not aided by such widespread irreverence for politicians and political institutions. They also appeared inconsistent with the remarkable spectacle, after the opening of Mary Quant's first boutique in 1955 and the arrival of rock 'n' roll in 1956, of the old and the rich following the lead of the young and the relatively poor. There were those who argued that such consequences of affluence represented a lowering of class barriers and a popular vitality which provided the opportunity not just for radical anti-establishment movements but also for government, through the welfare state, to achieve a major redistribution of political and economic power. As has been seen, however, this was a challenge to which successive governments were extremely reluctant to rise.

4.6 CONCLUSION

Welfare policy is heavily influenced by, and is itself an influence upon, the broad economic, social and political development of society. Between 1945 and 1975, in the highly favourable climate of economic growth and political consensus, its steady evolution was interrupted and shaped by short-term economic crises, an unstable birthrate, an ageing population, the general inflexibility of the political and administrative system and, above all, by an ingrained cultural resistance – despite the common sacrifices of the Second World War – to collective action. All the major problems posed to the maintenance of full employment and rising living standards by an outdated economic structure and class system were, as later chapters will show, successfully recognized. This did not mean, however, that each could be successfully resolved.

4.7 FURTHER READING

There are innumerable books on individual aspects of postwar Britain, but few good comprehensive surveys. The best are P. Clarke, *Hope and Glory* (1996) and K. O. Morgan, *The People's Peace: British history, 1945–1989* (Oxford, 2001). They may be supplemented by K. Burk (ed.), *The British Isles since 1945* (Oxford, 2003) which contains two particularly strong chapters on culture as well as a useful chronology and bibliography. Two good sets of essays for the periods 1945–51 and 1951–64, respectively, are M. Sissons and P. French (eds), *Age of Austerity* (1963) and V. Bogdanor and R. Skidelsky (eds), *The Age of Affluence* (1970). The latter has been consciously updated by L. Black and H. Pemberton (eds), *An Affluent Society? Britain's post-war 'golden age' revisited* (Aldershot, 2004).

On the economy the latest research is summarized in R. Floud and P. Johnson (eds), *The Economic History of Britain since 1700*, vol. 3 (Cambridge, 2004) and R. Middleton, *Government versus the Market* (Cheltenham, 1996). Simpler introductions to the period and to the framework within which it is best studied are R. Middleton, *The British Economy since 1945* (Basingstoke, 2000) and J. Tomlinson, *The Politics of Decline* (Harlow, 2000). The Labour Party's record is also well covered in J. Tomlinson, *Democratic Socialism and Economic Policy: the Attlee years, 1945–51* (Cambridge, 1997) and *The Labour Governments, 1964–70: economic policy*, vol. 3 (Manchester, 2004). On demography the pre-eminent books are A. H. Halsey (ed.), *British Social Trends since 1900* (1988) and J. F. Ermisch, *The Political Economy of Demographic Change* (1983).

Of the many political histories, the most lively – if now dated – is arguably P. Hennessy and A. Seldon (eds), *Ruling Performance* (Oxford, 1987) which has detailed chronologies and bibliographies for each postwar government. It can be best supplemented by D. Childs, *Britain since 1945: a political history* (2000). The journals *Twentieth Century British History* and *Contemporary British History* provide the most direct introduction to more recent research, as does the website of the Centre for Contemporary British History (http:// icbh.ac.uk/welcome.html). The peculiarities of Scotland and their relevance to welfare policy are well analysed in J. G. Kellas, *The Scottish Political System* (Cambridge, 1975) and L. Paterson, *The Autonomy of Scotland* (Edinburgh, 1994). A similar service for Northern Ireland, from suitably conflicting perspectives, is provided by D. Birrell and A. Murie, *Policy and Government in Northern Ireland* (Dublin, 1980) and T. Wilson, *Ulster: conflict and consent* (Oxford, 1989). Authoritative introductions to administrative history are P. Hennessy, *Whitehall* (2001) and K. Theakston, *The Civil Service since 1945* (Oxford, 1995), whilst the record of the Treasury is covered in G. C. Peden, *The Treasury and British Public Policy, 1906–1959* (Oxford, 2000) and S. Brittan, *Steering the Economy* (Harmondsworth, 1971).

Succinct historical introductions to local government are K. Young and N. Rao, *Local Government since 1945* (Oxford, 1997) and A. Alexander, *The Politics of Local Government in the United Kingdom* (1982), whilst M. Loughlin, M. D. Gelfand and K. Young (eds), *Half a Century of Municipal Decline* (1985) provides a more analytical and pessimistic view. K. Middlemas has produced the boldest, but not always an accurate and clear, summary of the views of the 'governing institutions' in *Power, Competition and the State* (3 vols, 1986 and 1990). It may be supplemented by R. Taylor, *The Trade Union Question in British Politics* (Oxford, 1993).

M. Shanks, *The Stagnant Society* (1961) and C. Booker, *The Neophiliacs* (1969) are stimulating contemporary accounts of the 1950s and 1960s. They can be put into context by P. Lewis, *The Fifties* (1978) and, more generally, by A. Marwick, *British Society since 1945* (Harmondsworth, 1990). Marwick has also written the introductory *Culture in Britain since 1945* (Oxford,

1991) which can be profitably expanded through A. Sinfield, *Literature, Politics and Culture in Postwar Britain* (1989). The standard work on the press and broadcasting is J. Curran and J. Seaton, *Power without Responsibility* (1991).

chapter

5

Employment Policy

1944	*Employment Policy* white paper (Cmd 6527). Beveridge's *Full Employment in a Free Society*	1958	Resignation of Thorneycroft as chancellor over 'excessive' public expenditure
1947	*Annus Horribilis* – Labour government's abandonment of physical planning and tacit acceptance of Keynesian demand management	1961	Plowden Committee on Control of Public Expenditure (Cmnd 1432): establishment of Public Expenditure Spending Committee (PESC)
1948	Monopolies Commission established	1962	'Keynesian plus' era heralds more planning: establishment of the National Economic Development Council (NEDC) and Office (NEDO); tax regulator; comitment to 4 per cent growth target
1949	Devaluation. 'Bonfire' of controls		
1950	'Full' employment defined at UN as 3 per cent		
1952	'Robot' scheme rejected – Conservative government's tacit acknowledgement of commitment to full employment	1963	First white paper on public expenditure (Cmnd 2235)
		1964	Department of Economic Affairs and Ministry of Technology established by new ➔

	Labour government to enhance planning and productivity		first time since 1945. Policy U-turn: Industry Act, statutory
1965	National Plan		prices and incomes policy,
1968	Devaluation and deflation; Industrial Expansion Act and creation of Industrial Reorganization Corporation (IRC)	1973	sterling floated Entry into EEC. OPEC oil price rises
		1974	National Enterprise Board established by new Labour
1970	Conservative government promises less planning: IRC abolished	1976	government Sterling crisis: Callaghan's speech to Labour Party
1972	Unemployment above 1m for		abandoning Keynesianism

The maintenance of a high and stable level of employment was one of the fundamental assumptions of the Beveridge Report and an objective to which all governments were positively committed after 1944. Its achievement was seen as a direct way to enhance individual welfare as well as to stimulate all other areas of welfare policy. If the workforce were fully employed, economic growth was more likely to be achieved and revenue sufficiently buoyant to finance expanding services. Moreover, if Keynesian techniques of demand management were used, there would be a positive economic reason (the maintenance of aggregate demand) to justify increased social expenditure when it was most needed, in a depression. Economic and social policy would, in theory, be once again in harmony rather than in direct conflict, as they had been in the interwar years (when classical economic theory had required cuts in public expenditure during a depression in order to reduce costs and thereby encourage investment) and as they were to become again in the 1980s.

As shown in Section 4.1, employment was maintained at an historically high level between 1945 and 1975; but whether this achievement was the result of government intervention in general or of Keynesian demand management in particular is a matter of continuing dispute. At the time, but more especially after the renunciation of the commitment to full employment by both the Labour and Conservative Parties in 1976, critics argued that high employment was the consequence not of government action but of buoyant market conditions, arising from a backlog of technological innovation and rising world trade. In the short term demand management, rather than being helpful, actually destabilised the economy. In the long term it increased unemployment by discouraging investment through its stop–go cycles and by fuelling inflation. Callaghan's denunciation of Keynesian economics in 1976, quoted on the first page of the Introduction to this book, was the first official endorsement of such an historic undercurrent of criticism. Moreover, the advantages of Keynesianism to social policy have also been questioned. If increased public expenditure were the remedy for periods of deficient demand, then in periods of excess demand (which predominated after 1945) the corollary was that expenditure should be cut – regardless of administrative logic or social need. Was it logical to leave a hospital half-built or, once built, unequipped and unstaffed? Further, if Titmuss's argument is accepted that the social costs of economic change fall disproportionately on the poor (see Section 2.2.2), would the need for social expenditure automatically fall in an inverse relationship to economic growth? In practice, therefore, Keynesianism provided no simple elixir for either economic or social policy.

The purpose of this chapter is to examine this dispute.

- To what extent was government responsible for the achievement of full employment?
- What part did social policy play in economic strategy?

To answer such questions, the two halves of that strategy, macroeconomic demand management and microeconomic industrial intervention, must be examined in the light of both the original commitment to a high level of employment and its later renunciation.

5.1 THE COMMITMENT TO FULL EMPLOYMENT

The 1944 *Employment Policy* white paper is conventionally regarded as the genesis of postwar economic consensus, by which all three major parties positively committed themselves to the maintenance of a high level of employment and the Keynesian method of its achievement. Such a view has its justification in the first and third sentences of the paper's foreword:

> The Government accept as one of their primary aims and responsibilities the maintenance of a high and stable level of employment after the war. . . . A country will not suffer from mass unemployment so long as the total demand for its goods and services is maintained at a high level.[1]

The rest of the paper was, however, both contradictory and vague.

Chapters 4 and 5, admittedly, did advance a Keynesian analysis of the causes of unemployment and its possible cures. A depression, it was argued, could result from a shortfall in one or more of the five components of demand in the economy (private consumption and investment, the government's current and capital expenditure, and foreign trade), and it was the government's responsibility to counteract immediately such a shortfall. This responsibility, it was acknowledged:

> involves a new approach and a new responsibility for the State. It was at one time believed that every trade depression would automatically bring its own corrective, since prices and wages would fall, the fall in prices would bring about an increase in demand, and employment would thus be restored. Experience has shown, however, that under modern conditions this process of self-recovery, if effective at all, is likely to be extremely prolonged and to be accompanied by widespread distress, particularly in a complex industrial society like our own.

Monetary policy would not be enough to effect a speedy recovery. A five-year programme of public investment needed to be prepared for immediate implementation should private investment falter. Similarly the government should be prepared to vary taxation, social security contributions and its own bulk purchases to compensate for shortfalls in private consumption. 'The Government believe', it was concluded, 'that in the past the power of public expenditure, skilfully applied, to check the onset of a depression has been underestimated.'

However, the optimism of these two chapters, which were initially drafted by academic economists within the Economic Section of the War Cabinet, was qualified by the more pessimistic or 'realistic' joint authors of the report on which the white paper was based – experienced administrators within the Treasury. They disagreed with the Economic Section on both the predominant cause of unemployment and the practicability of the proposed remedies. Their concern (in line with classical economic theory) was not with cyclical unemployment, caused by a temporary shortfall in demand, but with the structural – and in particular regional – unemployment which had predominated in the interwar years. Its only permanent remedy lay in a revival of world trade and in greater industrial investment to restructure and re-equip industry and thereby restore its international competitiveness; and these remedies were dependent, respectively, on the actions of foreign governments and on the initiative and self-restraint of the two sides of industry (in relation, for example, to long-term capital investment, restrictive practices and wage restraint). There was little the British government itself could do other than provide such microeconomic measures as retraining programmes and the provision of grants or tax concessions to encourage both investment and a 'balanced' geographical distribution of industry. Macroeconomic demand management could at best merely provide the general market conditions under which such structural adjustment might be encouraged.

Treasury officials, furthermore, doubted the ability of government in the real world directly to influence the level of employment. First, how would it know the precise moment at which to intervene? The available statistical information would never be sufficiently up to date or accurate. Second, how could unemployment in an export industry be suddenly relieved by an increase in domestic consumption? The transfer of labour between one abstract category of demand and another was in practice impossible. Third, how speedy and effective could remedial action be? Keynes claimed that a planned programme of public works could vary demand by £150 million over two years, but Treasury officials were convinced by their interwar experience that such a figure was wildly optimistic. Finally, there was the question of probity. A balanced budget in the past had automatically imposed a discipline on politicians and civil servants who might attempt to respond to a short-term crisis with financial concessions which, rather than solving the underlying problem, would more likely fuel future demands for concessions and thus inflation. How was public expenditure to be controlled once the precedent had been set that, in order to balance demand within the economy, government expenditure could exceed its revenue?[2] Given these basic theoretical, administrative and political disagreements, it was hardly surprising that the white paper contained many thinly disguised contradictions and was, on specific issues, extremely vague.

Two of the most blatant contradictions concerned budget deficits and labour mobility. In Paragraph 74, for example, it was clearly stated that 'none of the main proposals contained in this Paper involves deliberate planning for a deficit in the National Budget'. Yet in Paragraph 77 it was argued that government action should not be restricted by 'a rigid policy of balancing the Budget each year . . . . Such a policy is not required by statute nor is it part of our tradition.' Similarly, in Paragraph 29 it was stated that 'where a large industrial population is involved, the Government are not prepared either to compel its transfer to another area or to leave it to prolonged unemployment and demoralisation'. Conversely, it was argued in Paragraph 56 that 'if an expansion of total expenditure were applied to cure unemployment of a type due . . . to the failure of workers to move to places and occupations where they were needed, the policy of the Government would be frustrated'.[3] Amongst the issues shrouded in uncertainty were the means by which the government should intervene and its precise objective. The white paper contained few detailed proposals to guide future policy – the one major exception being the proposal to vary social insurance contributions, which ironically was never implemented.[4] The commitment to 'full employment' was also modified to a guarantee of a 'high and stable level of employment'. What percentage of unemployment did that actually mean? The appendix hinted at a figure of 8 per cent which – as has been shown in Section 4.1 – was a target considerably less ambitious than the one Keynes and Beveridge were championing at the time.

Beveridge was, in fact, the reason why the Coalition government permitted such a contradictory and vague white paper to be produced. It was the assumption of the 'maintenance of employment' in his 1942 Report that had started an urgent debate within government on postwar economic policy; and Beveridge himself had mounted a simultaneous enquiry. The government had been seriously embarrassed by the popular acclaim which had greeted the 1942 Report and was determined not to be embarrassed again. All official assistance was denied Beveridge's new enquiry and, when it was learnt in the spring of 1944 that its report was complete, the government was determined to act quickly in order to steal his thunder.[5] It was as well that it did, for Beveridge (despite his early insistence on a minimum of state intervention) produced a radical report which recommended a 20-year programme of industrial planning, under a national investment board, both to modernize the country's economic infrastructure and to ensure the defeat of the five giant evils of Want, Disease, Ignorance, Squalor and Idleness. Only then was the market to be given the freedom to determine the pace and nature of economic change.

The whole thrust of Beveridge's second report (which he significantly called *Full Employment in a Free Society*) was that 'while employment policy *per se* does not require the socialisation of industry, it does require the effective subordination of private investment to public policy'.[6] He expressed shock at the relative timidity of the white paper which, he argued, appeared to treat 'British industry as if it were a sovereign independent State, to be persuaded, influenced, appealed to and bargained with by the British State'. Its priorities were misconceived. 'The Government in the White Paper are conscious of the need for giving confidence to businessmen', he concluded, but 'they appear to be unconscious of the still greater need of giving confidence to the men and women of the country that there will be continuing demand for their services.'

Judged by its actual contents, therefore, the 1944 white paper was far from an impressive document. Nevertheless, like the Beveridge Report before it, it did have an immense political impact because it aroused within the electorate an expectation which politicians subsequently felt unable to disappoint. The Labour Party committed itself in the 1945 election to the maintenance of full employment. The Conservatives, under the combined influence of the Treasury and Hayek's *The Road to Serfdom,* temporarily played down their commitment (to their obvious cost); and there undoubtedly remained an undercurrent of feeling within the Party that the threat, or even the reality, of unemployment was necessary to ensure industrial discipline and wage restraint. After 1951, however, their decisions in government (such as the rejection of the Robot proposal to float the pound in 1952, the enforced resignation of Thorneycroft in 1958, the modernization programme of 1962–4 and Heath's dramatic 'U-turn' away from the policy of 'disengagement' in 1972) proved beyond doubt that they had by then accepted the maintenance of full employment as an electoral and a moral, if not an economic, necessity.[7] *Full* employment, moreover, by the 1950s was the correct phrase since, in a statement to the United Nations, Gaitskell had committed the British government to a level of 3 per cent unemployment; and thereafter reflationary measures always appeared to be taken when unemployment approached 2.5 per cent. The fundamental objective of economic policy had, therefore, been politically resolved. What remained unresolved was the means by which it could be attained. This was a continuing dilemma which Britain – unlike other European countries – appeared unable to resolve.

5.2 THE MANAGEMENT OF THE ECONOMY

The Attlee government did not immediately seek to clarify and implement the 1944 white paper. More direct interventionist measures, such as nationalization and economic planning, were its chosen weapons to combat unemployment. However, in the absence of any perceived alternative to moderate inflation, the budget was unbalanced in 1947 to reduce aggregate demand,

and thereafter demand management became the principal economic tool of government (supplemented increasingly by monetary policy after 1951, and by economic planning and direct industrial intervention after 1961– the so-called 'Keynesian plus' experiment[8]).

- Did the continuing low level of unemployment belie the Treasury's conviction that demand management was impractical?
- What were the consequences for social expenditure of its use as an economic regulator?

Technical difficulties

The overwhelming consensus is that Treasury officials had been correct both to challenge the practicability of demand management (at least insofar as very precise and ambitious policy objectives were sought) and to predict its destabilizing impact on the economy. The key to demand management was the annual spring budget. The previous autumn statistics were collected for each major indicator (such as employment, the balance of payments and consumer spending) and a forecast made of likely trends over the next 12 to 18 months. If it was predicted that there would be insufficient demand in the economy fully to employ all the country's productive resources (the 'deflationary gap') or conversely if excessive demand were predicted (the 'inflationary gap'), then remedial action was proposed in the budget and, after lengthy parliamentary debate, implemented. The potential pitfalls in such a procedure were many.

First, as Treasury officials had forewarned, the statistics used were likely to be outdated and inaccurate – especially when the burden and cost of their collection fell on non-government bodies. In the 1960s, for instance, quarterly statistics for the balance of payments took ten weeks to collect and those for employment nine months. These statistics then had to be assimilated into an economic model which (given the imprecision of economics, as suggested in Section 3.2.1) was unable to identify all the constantly evolving interrelationships between the various indices. Finally, the appropriate remedial measures had to be decided by a chancellor of the exchequer fully alive to their political as well as their economic consequences. Given such fallible statistics, the imprecision of economic modelling and the political interest of the chancellor, it was unlikely that – in economic terms – the correct remedial action would be agreed. Moreover, even if it were (and it remained uncompromised by sudden crises, such as Suez) it was by no means axiomatic that it would have the desired effect. The time lag between the ratification of policy changes by Parliament and their full impact upon the economy was typically two years. The period between the trough and the peak of postwar economic cycles was approximately two and a half years (see Section 4.1). There was, therefore, the very real danger that any 'remedial' action, rather than assisting natural market adjustments within the economy, would actually counteract them.

Examples of incorrect economic statistics, forecasts and policy decisions during this period are legion. Statistics for private consumption were particularly unreliable. It has been calculated, for example, that for only three of the years between 1955 and 1969 was the retrospective revision of the statistics for a particular year less than the consequences (the 'full-year revenue effect') of the tax changes in that year's budget. Export statistics, as the Treasury had predicted, were also notoriously unreliable and directly responsible for major forecasting errors. In 1962, for example, a neutral budget was agreed on the basis of a forecasted 4 per cent growth in exports. Exports did not increase and by the autumn unemployment was rising because of deficient demand. The consequence was the dismissal of Selwyn Lloyd as chancellor in the 'night of the long knives' which so discredited the Macmillan government (see Section 4.3). Similarly in 1967 a 4 per cent growth in exports was forecast whereas the actual out-turn (aggravated by a dock strike and a slump in world trade) was a 7 per cent decrease. This seriously affected the timing of devaluation.[9]

Equally serious were the budget errors of 1959 and 1963 which, it is now generally agreed, resulted in the excessive reflation of the economy. These errors, as recently released government documents make plain, were caused only in part by the chancellor's concern about an impending general election. They also arose out of the Treasury's continuing inability to estimate correctly the full effects of tax cuts on demand. Given economists' relative ignorance about changing consumption patterns this is hardly surprising; but it also reflected a genuine technical dilemma – how to devise a budget strategy which would have the required short-term impact without any unwanted long-term effects. This dilemma was all the more difficult to resolve because the immediate impact of tax cuts was *reduced* by unavoidable administrative delays (such as the reworking of tax codes) and the government's clawback of purchasing power (through taxes on expenditure). Conversely the long-term impact was increased by the 'secondary' effects of any such cuts. Immediate purchases would give employment to others, who would spend their increased income ('the multiplier') and thereby encourage manufacturers to expedite investment ('the accelerator'). Indeed, in the 1960s it was estimated that only 66 per cent of the *total* impact of income tax cuts (and only 80 per cent of the *direct* impact) would be felt in the first year. The Treasury traditionally overcompensated for the immediate shortfall. In 1961 a major innovation was designed to alleviate this problem. Changes in indirect taxation were believed to have a less complex and more immediate impact and so the 'regulator' was introduced, whereby purchase tax and excise duty (on such goods as cigarettes and alcohol) might be altered between budgets by up to 10 per cent of their existing rate.[10] 'Fine-tuning' however remained an extremely hazardous art.

Policy conflicts and constraints

Demand management was therefore bedevilled by technical difficulties. It was bedevilled also by confusion over policy instruments, principal amongst which was the frequent incompatibility of fiscal policy (the variation of taxes or public expenditure) and monetary policy (the variation, in particular, of interest rates and the money supply). This confusion reflected in part the differing needs of the domestic economy and of sterling as an international reserve currency. The war had massively increased Britain's international indebtedness ('sterling balances') as a result both of military expenditure abroad and the imbalance in trade resulting from the restriction of exports. In 1939 sterling balances and the country's gold and dollar reserves had virtually been in balance, but by 1945 the former stood at £3567 million and the latter at only £610 million. In the 1950s and 1960s, moreover, the gold and dollar reserves were sufficient to cover only two months' imports, whereas in most other European countries they covered six months'.[11] Both these factors made sterling vulnerable to speculators, and it was frequently deemed necessary after 1950 to have a high bank rate in order to maintain confidence in sterling and attract funds to the City of London. High bank rate, however, increased interest payments on borrowing in general and on the national debt in particular, thus contradicting two of the Treasury's other traditional objectives – industrial investment and low public expenditure.

This conflict was but one of the dilemmas thrown up by the attempt simultaneously to achieve four potentially incompatible objectives through demand management: full employment, balance of payments equilibrium, price stability and economic growth. Full employment (defined as 3 per cent unemployment) in particular conflicted with the other objectives. It conflicted with economic growth because the constant modernization of industry required a reserve of labour which was both geographically and industrially mobile. It conflicted with price stability (especially in the eyes of monetarists) because, *inter alia*, it strengthened the power of trade unions to demand high wages and the ability of employers to finance them by passing on – in the short term at least – the increased cost to consumers in higher prices. However, as shown in Section 4.1, its main conflict was with the balance of payments, the consequences of which were the 'stop–go' cycles of the 1950s and 1960s. When unemployment threatened, demand was expanded. This increased imports and diverted potential exports into the home market, which in turn created a balance of payments deficit. Demand was then decreased and unemployment again started to mount.

The underlying problem, which the incompatibility of the policy objectives of full employment and balance of payments equilibrium revealed, was the uncompetitiveness of British industry. To an extent this was not a new problem. From the time records began until 1939 Britain had had a deficit in visible trade in all but four years, but the net income from investments overseas had been sufficient to cover half the cost of imports in 1914 and a quarter in 1939.[12] The wartime sale of assets reduced the figure to 15 per cent; and simultaneously the price of imports in relation to exports (the 'terms of trade') rose so sharply, owing to world shortages, that by 1950 it required a 75 per cent increase in the 1938 volume of exports to balance imports running at only 70 per cent of their 1938 volume. The immediate challenge was met under the Labour government; and then fortuitously the terms of trade changed dramatically in Britain's favour so that in the 1950s, on average, an extra £100 million worth of imports could be financed each year by the same volume of exports. Oil in particular, which rose from supplying 10 to 50 per cent of Britain's energy needs, became relatively cheap.

In the 1960s however the terms of trade stopped improving and after the quadrupling of oil prices in 1972–4 (combined with a world boom and the consequent rise in the cost of other scarce resources) they deteriorated dramatically. This exposed the true vulnerability of the British economy, no longer shielded by the windfall profits derived from its nineteenth-century world monopoly. Radical measures were duly taken. The withdrawal of troops stationed abroad, especially after 1968, was designed to improve the balance of payments by reducing government expenditure abroad; and also in 1968, sterling ceased to be an international reserve currency. In 1967 the pound was devalued and in 1972 allowed to 'float' so that the market could determine its value. The effectiveness of such measures, however, was lessened by their being, in essence, reactions to immediate crises rather than an integral part of a sustained modernization programme.

In addition to the technical complexities and the policy conflicts of demand management, there was also substance in the Treasury's forewarning that the government lacked the political freedom to determine the level of economic activity. The oil price rises which helped to double the total cost of imports between 1972 and 1974 were a prime example of Britain's vulnerability to international pressures. Moreover, as was shown in Section 4.5, financiers and employers collectively failed to identify and implement the long-term investment decisions needed to maintain the competitiveness of British industry; the workforce as a whole displayed neither the adaptability nor the self-restraint for which the 1944 white paper had called; and the electorate was perceived to demand from government short-term benefits regardless of their long-term costs. In vain, it would appear, had Treasury officials inserted into the foreword of the 1944 white paper the warning that 'employment cannot be created by Act of Parliament or by Government action alone' – although (with the possible exception of the early 1960s) they were as guilty as anyone of resisting the necessary changes to attitudes and institutions.

Demand management: the record

Despite all this evidence it would nevertheless be wrong to conclude – as have the monetarists – that demand management was wholly deleterious, or that government was in no way responsible for the full employment which lay at the root of the exceptional improvements in economic and social welfare before 1975. Full employment may well have resulted from an increase in world trade and private investment, but such 'spontaneous' developments were unquestionably assisted by international agreements to reduce trade barriers (such as the General Agreement on Tariffs and Trade) and the known commitment of government to increase demand in order to prevent a repetition of the great depression of the 1930s. Stop–go policies may, at the margin, have discouraged long-term investment, but overall there had never been – as Britain's trading rivals recognized – a more rational time at which to undertake such investment. If British industry did not respond, there may well have been a case – as Beveridge had argued– for more, rather than less, government intervention.

Social expenditure as an economic regulator

The potential conflicts in demand management were nowhere more evident that in the field of social expenditure. As already shown in Section 4.1, the level of social expenditure could be affected by cyclical fluctuations in the economy regardless of the amount of social need. Variations in taxation, designed to regulate such fluctuations, could also have a social impact. An increase in indirect taxation, for example, could disproportionately affect the low-paid and (in particular) pensioners, whilst a decrease in income tax could disproportionately favour the rich. Consequently, tax changes made for economic reasons could jeopardize the effectiveness of other policies designed to reduce poverty or to achieve a greater equality of income through progressive taxation (see Chapter 11). Even more seriously, however, constant variations in the level of social expenditure could demoralize those responsible for its administration and thereby jeopardize all attempts to achieve maximum cost-effectiveness. This was certainly the conclusion of the Plowden Committee on the Control of Public Expenditure, appointed in 1959 as concern in government and Parliament grew over its escalating cost.

The Plowden Report directly refuted the assertion of the 1944 white paper that 'in the past the power of public expenditure . . . to check the onset of a depression has been underestimated'. Rather it argued that, after a decade of practical experience, the Treasury's earlier pessimism had been duly confirmed. As it concluded:

> The Government are required by public opinion to seek to manage the national economy with only small variations in the level of employment. It is natural, therefore, to explore the possibilities of using variations in public expenditure to help in this task. Experience shows, however, that Government current expenditure cannot be varied effectively for this purpose. Attempts, at moments of inflationary pressure, to impose short-term 'economies' (or to make increases at moments when 'reflation' is called for) are rarely successful and sometimes damaging, and we think that these attempts should be avoided. There has been a tendency in the past to overestimate the possibilities of useful short-term action in public investment, and to under-estimate the indirect losses caused by sudden changes. Experience shows that . . . the effect of the action taken may well appear at the very moment when the economy is already on the turn. The remedy may, therefore, be worse than the disease.[13]

The Committee's recommendations were, accordingly, that the use of current and capital social expenditure to regulate the economy should be minimised, and that its cost-effectiveness should be increased by the strengthening of both the civil service's technical and administrative expertise and the Cabinet's sense of collective responsibility. In particular a five-year survey of public expenditure should be prepared annually to relate future spending plans to the anticipated rate of economic growth. This was the genesis of the Public Expenditure Survey Committee (PESC) – a committee which since 1961 has collated all departmental spending plans in preparation for the government's autumn public expenditure white paper (first published in 1963 to demonstrate the 'modernity' of the Conservative government, and then published regularly after 1969).

Before 1975 PESC was not an unqualified success. The government continued to vary social expenditure contracyclically, and neither the civil service nor the Cabinet displayed the committed responsibility for which the Plowden Committee had called. An over-optimistic estimate of economic growth, for example, was immediately adopted which reduced the need to take hard decisions about the priority to be accorded different policies. It was not until the introduction of Programme Analysis and Review in the early 1970s that a sustained critical look was taken at the cost-effectiveness of existing, as opposed to new, proposals. Forward planning in terms of volume (services to be provided regardless of their eventual cost) rather than cash also fuelled any inflationary tendencies within the economy.[14] Ultimately therefore the Plowden Committee was more significant for what it failed to, rather than for what it did, achieve. It provided a belated opportunity for the necessary political and administrative adjustment to the demands of the positive new responsibilities which government had assumed since 1945. It also offered a chance to reconcile the competing demands of economic and social policy, which demand management had done much – but clearly not enough – to minimize. Both opportunities were not fully seized, to the particular disadvantage of long-term investment in the social services.

A Keynesian revolution?

Two broader questions arise from the history of postwar demand management. The first is whether there was a 'Keynesian revolution' in policy-making. Keynesian economic assumptions undoubtedly became predominant after the war in the economics profession and in Whitehall – especially after the retirement of the 'interwar' generation of civil servants by the mid-1950s. There were also institutional innovations which favoured the adoption of Keynesianism. The establishment of the Central Statistical Office (CSO), for example, in 1940 led to the collection of aggregate statistics needed for national income accounting, and their approach to economic analysis was insinuated into the budgetary process in the late 1940s. In 1941 for the first time the object of the budget was not just to balance the government's books but to secure the optimum allocation of resources within the economy; and, as has been seen, it was deliberately unbalanced in 1947 to counteract inflation. For many, however, the crucial test of a full 'Keynesian revolution' is a government's willingness to use a budget deficit deliberately to combat depression. Until 1975 there was always excess demand in the economy, and so the role of demand management was necessarily limited to the variation of the amount by which the budget was in surplus. There was no need for a deficit budget until the mass unemployment of 1975 – and then, as has been seen, the challenge was declined. Would it have been so declined had a depression occurred earlier when the wartime commitment to avoid the wastage of interwar unemployment was still burnt into political and public consciousness?

Such evidence as exists suggests that the challenge might well have been refused. In 1954, for example, Butler (as chancellor) was faced with an anticipated depression in the USA which would have reduced British exports, but despite the explicit commitment in the *Industrial Charter* he refused to contemplate a deficit budget. His explanation was, essentially, that it would undermine foreign confidence.[15] In the event the depression was not sufficiently severe to affect the British economy and so Butler's resolution remained untested. The critical point remains however. Given the postwar weakness of both Britain's reserves and balance of payments, governments were dependent on foreign bankers to support sterling and to finance the national debt. They certainly were not converts to Keynesianism. Had a serious depression occurred earlier, therefore, would the needs of the unemployed or the interests of bankers have triumphed? The question must remain an open one.

Butskellism

Butler's hesitation in 1954 begs a second broad question: what is the historical value of the term 'Butskellism', coined by *The Economist* to describe the coincidence between Butler's instincts and those of the former Labour chancellor, Gaitskell? Both sought to moderate the extreme demands of their backbenchers (respectively for a return to the free market and an extension of nationalization) and to use Keynesian techniques temporarily to manage aggregate demand. *The Economist* itself, however, cast doubt on whether this coincidence of instincts could have withstood a harsher economic climate than that prevailing in the 1950s. Certainly Butler himself, whilst admitting he spoke the same 'language of Keynesianism', denied he shared any of Gaitskell's political convictions; and Gaitskell, prior to the Labour government's defeat in 1951, had been preparing a new employment white paper to give real teeth to its 'tentative and speculative' predecessor. The philosophy behind the paper was summarized at the time as:

> Always keep demand just above supply, in order to hold full employment, and rely on *physical* controls – especially on total imports, capital exports, building location and essential material – even when no longer 'in short supply' – to hold inflation. . . . Always have a bit of inflationary pressure, but use physical controls to prevent it breaking through.[16]

Such a permanent commitment to physical controls would have been anathema to Butler. Beneath the superficial similarity of their policies there remained, therefore, fundamental ideological differences. Essentially Butler, as a reluctant collectivist, relied upon the rationality of the market whilst Gaitskell, as a democratic socialist, relied upon the rationality of government planning (see Sections 2.2.1 and 2.2.2). This fundamental ideological difference between the two Parties was to become more explicit when it was commonly agreed, in the early 1960s, that macroeconomic management needed to be supplemented by microeconomic industrial intervention.

5.3 DIRECT INDUSTRIAL INTERVENTION

After 1945 four alternatives, or supplements, to demand management were advanced and – with varying degrees of commitment and success – implemented. They were:

- the Treasury's suggestions for microeconomic intervention, put forward in the 1944 white paper
- the Labour Party's long-term commitment to nationalization and economic planning (which many continued to equate with industrial efficiency, especially after the Soviet Union's triumph over the USA in 1957 with its launching of the first space satellite)
- 'indicative' planning, which became the fashionable explanation in the early 1960s for Europe's high growth rate, and
- direct discriminatory industrial intervention.

Microeconomic intervention

Not surprisingly it was the Treasury's proposals, based largely on prewar precedent, which were the most consistently applied. Hence, to remove restrictive practices, the Monopolies Commission was established in 1948, a Restrictive Trade Practices Court in 1956 and the Office of Fair Trading in 1973.[17] An attempt to create a more skilled workforce was made not just through the expansion of the education system but also by such legislation as the 1964 Industrial Training Act, which enabled government to establish supervisory training boards with the novel power to raise a compulsory levy on all firms within their respective industries. Industrial investment was also encouraged by a wide range of tax allowances (by which the initial cost and depreciation of capital equipment could be set against tax) and, between 1966 and 1970, cash grants (to assist those industries which were insufficiently profitable to qualify for the full tax concessions). These allowances and grants were especially generous in areas where unemployment was relatively high. 'Regional' policy, in accordance with Chapter 3 of the 1944 white paper, was more explicitly pursued in the 1940s with the building of new towns, a ban on investment in overcrowded regions, and grants to encourage the transfer of

key workers and equipment from those areas. In the 1960s, in the absence of
– and as a stimulant to – local government reform, regional planning councils
were also set up to coordinate local economic and social development; and
between 1967 and 1970 a regional employment premium was paid for each
employee in areas of high unemployment which amounted effectively to an 8
per cent subsidy on wages. All these measures were additional to the normal
range of government activity – from taxation and prices and incomes policy
to factory legislation – which had both intended and unintended consequences for industrial development.[18]

Regional policy has frequently been attacked for confusing economic and
social policy, to the benefit of neither. Private profitability is not always the
best guarantor of the public interest (see Section 3.2.1), and before 1939 the
government had slowly come to recognize that the migration of workers to
jobs had economic disadvantages such as the increased congestion of the
Midlands and the south-east of England and the need to supply there, at the
tax-payer's expense, the social infrastructure (such as housing and schools)
abandoned elsewhere. However political influence on regional policy – especially on prestige projects such as the building of a new car plant at Linwood
near Glasgow – resulted in many investment decisions which were never able
to gain long-term commercial viability. Regional policy has therefore always
promised more than it has actually delivered.

Nationalization and economic planning

Similar problems dogged nationalization. In the 1940s nationalization was
seen by many within the Labour Party as the means by which the state could
control and develop the economy in the public interest; and this belief was
vigorously renewed in the early 1970s when the Labour Party became committed, in opposition, to the nationalization of the leading 25 companies. In the
1950s, however, the practical experience of those essential but loss-making
industries which had been nationalized (such as coal and the railways) was
widely considered to show that improvements in industrial relations and efficiency could not be realized – although a symbolic battle was fought over the
essential *and* profitable steel industry which was nationalized, denationalized
and subsequently renationalized. A major cause of the weakness of the nationalized industries was the continuing uncertainty over whether they should be
run on strictly commercial lines or, alternatively, assist 'full employment'
policy by providing both abundant jobs and subsidized services for other
industries. In 1961 the first serious attempt was made to resolve this dilemma.
The white paper *Financial and Economic Obligations of the Nationalised Industries*
specified that 'although the industries have obligations of a national and non-
economic kind, they are not, and ought not, to be regarded as social services
absolved from economic and commercial justification'.[19] Specific commercial
criteria were established for determining both investment and pricing.
Continuing political pressure meant, however, that these criteria – difficult
enough to meet in the industrial world – were inevitably compromised.

When the deficiencies of demand management became increasingly apparent in the early 1960s, therefore, the microeconomic policy of successive governments took the form not of further state ownership but of state intervention in private industry. The first attempts at such intervention had been made by the Labour government after the war, when innumerable controls existed to allocate scarce materials throughout industry. Any attempt in peacetime to institute direct economic planning along Soviet lines (whereby government *replaced* the market by determining the output targets for each industry) was rapidly acknowledged to be undesirable. Although the terminology of 'economic planning' was retained, it was admitted that:

> Economic planning in the United Kingdom is based upon three fundamental facts: the economic fact that the United Kingdom economy must be heavily dependent on international trade; the political fact that it is, and intends to remain, a democratic nation with a high degree of individual liberty; and the administrative fact that no economic planning body can be aware (or indeed could ever be aware) of more than the very general trends of future economic development.[20]

Consequently, what the Labour government sought to implement was 'indicative' planning. In its economic surveys it set broad targets for the economy over the following year; and it then strove to ensure that industry acted in accordance with such targets, largely by persuasion.

Indicative planning

These experiments in indicative planning provided the initial inspiration for successful French planning in the 1950s to which ironically Britain turned in the early 1960s for a cure for her relatively low growth rate.[21] Even more ironically, planning was resurrected by a Conservative government (under Macmillan) with the active encouragement of the Federation of British Industry (which had become disillusioned with the impact on investment of stop–go policies) and of Keynesian economists (who, in an open economy committed to free collective bargaining, had become convinced of the need for import and wage controls). There were three major institutional innovations: the National Economic Development Council, at which government discussed particular economic problems and planned growth with the two sides of industry; its secretariat, the National Economic Development Office; and the establishment of individual Economic Development Councils to identify the problems and needs of specific industries.

In opposition, the Labour Party cast doubt over the Conservatives' commitment to planning, suggesting that it was essentially a political stratagem both to reconcile trade unions to wage restraint and to project a failing party in a 'modern' light. In government it sought to prove its own commitment by creating, uniquely for Britain in peacetime, a specialist planning ministry – the Department of Economic Affairs. The Department hastily produced a National Plan to expand the economy annually by 4 per cent over five years.

Equally hastily, however, the plan was undermined by the deflationary measures designed to correct the severe balance of payments crisis.

Direct industrial intervention

Direct intervention in industry nevertheless accelerated. A Ministry of Technology was established in 1964 to take responsibility for the government's sponsorship of research and development, and it expanded thereafter as the active, sponsoring department of a wide range of well-established industries (such as aerospace) and new industries (such as computers). Its path was smoothed by the Industrial Expansion Act of 1968, which gave government the power to finance individual investment decisions without recourse to further legislation; and it was assisted by the newly created Industrial Reorganisation Corporation which (in potential conflict with monopoly policy) was charged with the encouragement of industrial mergers – to particular effect in the electronics and car industries, where GEC and British Leyland were formed. Through the Ministry of Technology and the IRC, British government started slowly to shed its traditional, neutral role and to move towards the European practice whereby, in key strategic decisions, the judgement of officials replaced the judgement of the market.[22]

Such a development naturally concerned the Conservative Party which had in opposition, as Labour had predicted, renounced its support for economic planning. On its return to office in 1970 a policy of 'disengagement' was implemented with, for instance, the abolition of the IRC and many of Labour's regional initiatives. However, the bankruptcy in 1971 of Rolls-Royce (a key defence contractor) and rising unemployment in 1972 changed the government's conception of what was electorally, if perhaps not economically, necessary; and its 1972 Industry Act restored, and even expanded, the interventionist powers which the Ministry of Technology and the IRC had enjoyed. Indeed so great was its interventionist potential that the incoming Labour government of 1974 could with little controversy establish a National Enterprise Board – not to nationalize the leading 25 companies but, with a budget of £1000 million, to stimulate the modernization of British industry in general and of the nationalized industries in particular.

These successive attempts at direct, discretionary intervention failed to match the success of parallel developments abroad. Why was this? The widely accepted reason is the lack of the necessary administrative, political and cultural support to sustain, over a sufficiently long period, a consistent policy. The British civil service as a whole, as noted in Section 4.4, lacked the specialist expertise either to use public investment or to intervene decisively to accelerate industrial modernization. Its instinct was also to act as a referee not as a participant in such a process. Moreover, even when it painstakingly acquired specialist knowledge and a readiness to act, these virtues were precipitately dissipated by political action – such as the abolition of the IRC in 1970. Both political parties, indeed, conspired to create the worst of all possible worlds. In government, both (with the possible exception of the

Conservatives between 1970 and 1972) had a common policy of 'state-supported capitalism'. In practice, however, both frustrated it. This was not just because, in opposition, they reverted to the adversarial policies of 'disengagement' and 'nationalization' when they should have been planning practical policies. It was also because, in office, they sought to achieve consensus through tripartite bodies such as the NEDC which, despite the work of NEDO, lacked the capacity to forge a constructive accommodation between the short-term instincts of both the City and the workforce and the long-term investment needs of industry. They were also discouraged by such bodies – unlike corporate bargainers in Sweden or planners in France – from working with the most dynamic industrial leaders, who were by definition both atypical and mistrusted by their colleagues. Instead they were tied to the 'canker of the average firm' and the very industrialists and trade unionists who were most sensitive to the fears aroused by ideological rhetoric.[23] Consequently industrial policies were far from exhibiting 'the celebrated realism' which continental observers had come to expect of Britain. Rather, in the words of one permanent secretary to the Ministry of Technology, there was a 'virtually unique (amongst advanced countries) lack of understanding or even hostility between government and industry'. What was desperately lacking was 'the will and creative power to make an effective relationship and community of interest between government and industry'.[24]

Policy failure

The failure of indicative planning and industrial intervention was critical to the long-term future of the welfare state because it undermined governments' ability to honour their guarantee of a high and stable level of employment. Experience had shown that demand management was not enough and that Keynes's faith was ill-founded that the market, given an adequate level of aggregate demand, could restructure the economy and ensure both the requisite quantity and quality of investment. Not only did government require an industrial strategy because it was itself directly responsible for approximately two-fifths of capital investment. It required one also because, in an advanced technological society, international competitiveness depended on long-term investment decisions which could conflict with the short-term requirements of private profitability. Government was thus required to anticipate the needs of the community and – where necessary – to override the logic of the market. There might be valid ideological objections to such intervention, but abstention was no longer feasible because, as the first report of the National Enterprise Board argued:

> It is a feature of the western world that governments of almost every major manufacturing country respond to public pressures and try to stimulate the pace and direction of industrial development. If we stand aside in this country and allow market forces alone to operate we shall be overtaken and displaced by those of our competitors who have learned the skills of forcing the pace of development and

seizing the market opportunity by reinforcing commercial drive with the impetus of public financial support.[25]

During this period private industry (despite its own declared preferences) required, but did not receive, consistent government support. Consequently, demand management was also denied what it (despite the claims of its original advocates) most required, the underpinning of an effective industrial policy.

5.4 CONCLUSION

The maintenance of full employment was both a direct contribution to individual welfare and an essential support for other welfare services because it simultaneously maximized revenue and minimized demand for them. Informed opinion at the time accorded much of the credit for the maintenance of full employment to government and, despite Treasury forebodings, it would appear that government policy (whatever its technical shortcomings and mystifying complexity) did help to create the conditions in which the spontaneous buoyancy of world markets could be exploited. Government policy, however, had its drawbacks. The stop–go cycles in demand management, which led to sudden cuts in investment being succeeded by equally sudden bursts in demand, was debilitating.[26] Similarly stop–go cycles in industrial policy discouraged the development of the administrative expertise necessary to identify and implement the hard investment decisions which are functionally required of government in an advanced industrial society.

This chronic instability of macro- and microeconomic policy was all the more surprising because, in government, both the Labour and Conservative Parties appeared to accept the need for 'state-supported capitalism'. Beneath the surface, however, there lay a fundamental ideological conflict over whether power should lie ultimately in the market or with the state; and herein perhaps lay the initial and continuing attraction of Keynesian demand management. It allowed this conflict to remain unresolved because, although the day-to-day power to determine the speed and nature of economic change was clearly left with the market, democratic socialists (such as Crosland) could believe that ultimate power lay with the state, should it choose to act. The ultimate attraction of Keynesianism, in other words, was essentially a negative and not a positive one.

The direct effect of economic policy on social expenditure was similarly ambivalent. Keynesian policy promised a constructive role for welfare policy in a depression, but Beveridge had warned that 'keeping communal investment on tap to fill gaps in private investment' was not only unacceptable but also impracticable.[27] After a decade of practical experience, the Plowden Committee confirmed his judgement by demonstrating that current and, above all, capital welfare expenditure had suffered from its use as an economic regulator. On the other hand, continuing economic growth ensured an increase in the absolute (and relative) amount of resources allocated to welfare expenditure – as the tables in Appendix 1 demonstrate. Also it permitted a consolidation of the changed attitudes to welfare initiated in the 1940s. However tenacious the traditional aims of economic policy (including the defence of sterling and heavy military expenditure overseas) the traditional means of financing them in times of perceived crisis (cuts in social expenditure) were, at least after Thorneycroft's resignation in 1958, no longer accepted.[28] Economically, welfare expenditure had come of age. However, just as the future of demand management was threatened by the continuing absence of an effective industrial policy, so this new-found legitimacy of welfare expenditure was threatened by the continuing rise in unemployment. This was the spectre overshadowing 1975.

5.5 FURTHER READING

The best introductory texts have already been cited in the further reading for Chapter 4. They can be usefully supplemented by P. A. Hall, *Governing the Economy: the politics of state intervention in Britain and France* (Cambridge, 1986). Amongst the other, fuller political economies of the period the outstanding ones are A. Cairncross, *Years of Recovery: British economic policy, 1945–51* (1985); J. C. R. Dow, *The Management of the British Economy, 1945–60* (Cambridge, 1970); and S. Brittan, *Steering the Economy* (Harmondsworth, 1971). Complementary texts include A. Shonfield, *British Economic Policy since the War* (1959); W. Beckerman (ed.), *The Labour Government's Economic Record, 1964–70* (1972); and F. T. Blackaby (ed.), *British Economic Policy, 1960–74* (Cambridge, 1978). A. Shonfield, *Modern Capitalism* (1969) is illuminating on foreign comparisons.

Two good introductions to economic planning are A. Budd, *The Politics of Economic Planning* (1978) and the more detailed J. Leruez, *Economic Planning and Politics in Britain* (Oxford, 1975). S. Young and A. V. Lowe, *Intervention in the Mixed Economy* (1974) provides an introduction to industrial policy between 1964 and 1972, whilst N.F. R. Crafts and N. W. C. Woodward (eds), *The British Economy since 1945* (Oxford, 1991) contains valuable summaries of specific topics such as regional policy. An overview and the latest research on a long-neglected topic is provided respectively in D. Edgerton, *Science, Technology and British Industrial Decline* (Cambridge, 1996) and J. Tomlinson and N. Tiratsoo, *Thirteen Wasted Years? The Conservatives and industrial efficiency, 1951–1984* (1998). J. Tomlinson, *Government and Enterprise* (Oxford, 1994) is also of value.

There has been a lengthy debate in the *Economic History Review* on the character and significance of the 1944 *Employment Policy* white paper, details of which are provided in G. C. Peden, *Keynes, the Treasury and British Economic Policy* (1988). Two other important contributions are S. Glynn and A. Booth, *The Road to Full Employment* (1987), which provides a good introduction to its origins, and N. Rollings, 'British budgetary policy, 1945–54: a '"Keynesian revolution"?', *Economic History Review*, 41 (1988) 283–98, which provides a review of its early fate. Nothing is more stimulating, however, than the original texts themselves: *Employment Policy* (Cmd 6527) and Sir W. Beveridge, *Full Employment in a Free Society* (1944).

Finally A. Ringe, N. Rollings and R. Middleton, *Economic Policy under the Conservatives, 1951–64: a guide to documents in the National Archives of the UK* (2004) not only provides a guide but a comprehensive introduction to all aspects of economic policy at the time.

Social Security

CONTENTS

1942 Beveridge Report, *Social Insurance and Allied Services* (Cmd 6404)	explicit. National Insurance Act – all short-term benefits earnings-related. Rating Act – rate rebates become statutory
1945 Family Allowance Act	
1946 National Insurance Act	
1948 National Assistance Act. The 'Appointed Day' (5 July)	**1968** Family allowances uprated in real terms for the only time
1955 Pre-election uprating of insurance benefits by 22 per cent	**1970** Family Income Supplement introduced – selectivity introduced into child support
1959 National Insurance Act – introduction of earnings-related benefits	**1972** Housing Finance Act – rent rebates statutory
1963 Institute of Economic Affairs, *Choice in Welfare*	**1973** Keith Joseph's 'cycle of deprivation' speech
1965 *The Poor and the Poorest* published – the 'rediscovery' of poverty; foundation of the Child Poverty Action Group (CPAG)	**1975** Employment Protection Act – maternity benefit statutory. Child Benefit Act. Social Security Act – introduction of State Earnings-Related Pensions Scheme (SERPS)
1966 Supplementary Benefit Act – legal right to benefit made	**1976** Wage stop abolished

Together with the maintenance of full employment, the provision of social security was the principal objective of both the Beveridge Report and the postwar Labour government. The concept of social security was novel to Britain in the 1940s, having been first formally acknowledged in the 1941 Atlantic Charter. It means, in essence, the guarantee by government to all its citizens of an income sufficient to ensure an agreed minimum standard of living. In the 1940s the realization of this guarantee depended largely on the expansion of various interwar insurance schemes. However, as argued in Section 2.1, the nature of these schemes was fundamentally changed by their being extended to the whole population, to cover all risks to an individual's income and to provide – in theory at least – subsistence-level benefits.

The adoption of these three principles of *universalism, comprehensiveness* and *adequacy* meant that the government's social services were no longer 'reserved for the poor' and therefore, almost inevitably, poor services. Society became, in essence, more egalitarian and humane through the involvement of everyone, including the rich, in a programme of mutual insurance (the creation of a 'common risk pool') which, for the first time in history, freed everyone from the threat of absolute poverty. Moreover the guarantee of subsistence by government came to be widely accepted as a precondition of, rather than a threat to, personal responsibility. It was this revolution in values and in the role of government which led to the coining, and the public acceptance, of the term 'welfare state'.

From the start, the cost of social security dominated postwar welfare expenditure. The size of the social security budget exceeded that of defence by the mid-1960s and remained thereafter the most expensive single item of government policy (see Appendix, Tables A.3 and A.4). Its share of *public* expenditure rose from 12.1 per cent in 1951 to 17.8 per cent in 1971 before declining slightly. It also accounted for one-third of all *social* expenditure and was conventionally 50 per cent more costly than the next most expensive item, education. These figures, however, can be misleading. On the one hand, they exaggerate the importance of social security expenditure because the money involved was only being transferred from one individual to another ('transfer payments'). Except for the cost of administration, it was not being consumed by government ('exhaustive' expenditure) – as it was for example in education or defence policy, where government employed trained staff, constructed and maintained buildings, and purchased equipment. Consequently the government's role was limited to the determination of who should spend money rather than how it should be spent and this limited its economic, if not its political, significance (see Appendix 1.2). On the other hand, the figures underestimate social security expenditure because they excluded most expenditure in kind – such as the right to free healthcare – which is as essential to an individual's peace of mind as cash benefits.

The enormous sums of money within the social security budget were, as demonstrated by Table 6.1, dispensed in three ways.

• The vast bulk, varying over time from 59 to 73 per cent, was paid out in national insurance benefits, for which recipients qualified through the payment of insurance contributions (see lines 1–7 of Table 6.1).

- Between 10 and 14 per cent was dispensed through means-tested benefits, financed out of general taxation (lines 10–13, 15).
- A percentage, rapidly declining from 24 to 7 per cent, was paid through tax-financed benefits, such as family allowances/child benefits, to which all qualified people were automatically entitled (lines 8, 9 and 17).

The beneficiaries were overwhelmingly and increasingly the elderly, who never received less than half of the total expenditure (lines 1, 9, 10, 14). Expenditure on the unemployed also expanded from 3 to 10 per cent as the economy faltered (lines 6–11). In contrast the relative value of benefits for children declined, whilst that for other groups, such as the sick, remained largely static.

Despite its seminal importance to the concept of a 'welfare state', its initial popularity and its potential electoral significance (arising from both its overall cost and its direct relevance to all voters), social security policy attracted little popular or political enthusiasm after 1945. Initially it aroused little open controversy. Beveridge was somewhat over-sanguine when he claimed 'reconstruction of social insurance . . . to ensure security of income from all risks . . . raises no issue of political principle or of party', but even Hayek admitted that 'there is no reason why in a society that has reached the general level of wealth which ours has attained, the first kind of security [the certainty of a given minimum of sustenance] should not be guaranteed to all without endangering general freedom'.[1] All political parties were soon agreed upon a universal, comprehensive scheme financed in the main through contributory insurance. Moreover, as shown in Section 3.2.1, many economists still regard compulsory state insurance as technically superior to private insurance.

By the mid-1950s, however, doubts were beginning to grow about the long-term cost and viability of existing policy, and in the mid-1960s the 'rediscovery' of poverty raised serious doubts about the government's ability to resolve existing problems. Two interrelated controversies arose.

- Technically, how could an increasingly bureaucratic and complex system be simplified? How, in addition, could those in need be targeted more cost effectively?
- Politically, what was the fundamental purpose of social security policy? Was it essentially to support the capitalist economy by compensating its victims, whilst simultaneously reinforcing its values? Alternatively, was it to engineer a more equal society through the modification, or even supersession, of market criteria for the allocation and distribution of resources?

Disputes over the respective merits of 'universalism' and 'selectivity' and the erosion of the work ethic by guaranteed subsistence benefits, last voiced in the 1930s, were revived.

The purpose of this chapter is to analyse the development of policy, both in general and in relation to the needs of particular social groups, in the

Table 6.1 Social security: government expenditure, 1951–77

	1951–2		1956–7		1961–2		1966–7		1971–2		1976–7	
	£m	%	£m	%	£m	%	£m	%	£m	%	£m	%
National Insurance		59.2		63.1		70.3		73.2		68.9		69.6
1. Retirement pensions	281	40.0	455	42.7	800	47.8	1290	48.8	2091	45.7	5,573	48.3
2. Widows' benefit and guardians' allowances	25	3.5	40	3.7	83	5.0	146	5.5	203	4.4	439	3.8
3. Sickness benefits	66	9.4	101	9.5	161	9.6	271	10.3	434	9.5	1,091	9.5
4. Maternity benefits	9	1.3	15	1.4	25	1.5	38	1.4	44	1.0	72	0.6
5. Death grants	3	0.4	3	0.3	6	0.4	8	0.3	14	0.3	15	0.1
6. Unemployment benefits	16	2.3	24	2.3	41	2.4	85	3.2	250	5.5	578	5.0
7. Industrial injuries benefits	16	2.3	35	3.3	60	3.6	95	3.6	117	2.5	250	2.2
8. War pensions	77	10.9	91	8.5	103	6.1	118	4.5	136	3.0	290	2.5
9. Non-contributory o.a.p	25	3.5	17	1.6	10	0.6	3	0.1	–	–	–	–
Supplementary Benefits		10.6		10.3		10.0		11.5		14.5		14.0
10. Old	34	4.8	61	5.7	89	5.3	167	6.3	286	6.2	489	4.2
11. Unemployed	6	0.9	9	0.8	22	1.3	32	1.2	155	3.4	601	5.2
12. Sick	18	2.6	23	2.2	32	1.9	54	2.0	84	1.8 }	518	4.5
13. Other	16	2.3	17	1.6	25	1.5	52	2.0	140	3.1		
14. Old person's pension	–		–		–		–		24	0.5	38	0.3
15. Family income supplement	–		–		–		–		5	0.1	20	0.2
16. Attendance allowance	–		–		–		–		6	0.1	144	1.2
17. Family allowances	66	9.4	119	11.2	140	8.4	156	5.9	359	7.9	564	4.9
18. Administration	45	6.4	56	5.3	78	4.6	116	4.4	230	5.0	845	7.3
Total public expenditure on social security benefit	703	100.0	1,066	100.0	1,675	100.0	2,642	100.0	4,578	100.0	11,527	100.0

Sources: Social Trends (1970, 1977); *Annual Abstract of Statistics* (1964).

context of such controversies. First, however, it is necessary to establish the objectives of – and the objections to – the Beveridge Report, upon which the postwar social security system was largely based, and the nature of the 'redis-covery' of poverty.

6.1 THE BEVERIDGE REPORT AND ITS CRITICS

Despite its somewhat unglamorous title (and author), the Beveridge Report on *Social Insurance and Allied Services* immediately acquired immense popu-larity, both at home and abroad, as a practical programme for the elimination of poverty, and it has subsequently come to be regarded by many as a 'blue-print' for the welfare state (see Section 2.1). The government's intention had not been to produce so popular a report. Indeed Beveridge's assignment to what was originally intended to be a secret and highly technical exercise to minimize the overlapping responsibilities of the existing social services had been an attempt to remove him from a central wartime role. However, through a combination of Beveridge's own skill (both as a propagandist and as a synthesizer of other people's ideas) and luck (the coincidence of the Report's publication in November 1942 with a burst of national optimism following Britain's first major victory at El Alamein), the Report revolution-ized perceptions in Whitehall and Westminster of what was politically possi-ble – and necessary. The urgent search for a postwar economic policy, which culminated in the 1944 *Employment Policy* white paper, is a measure of its success.

Beveridge rightly saw social security as something more than the provision of a minimum cash income. He acknowledged, in his own distinctive language, that apart from 'want' four other 'giants on the road to reconstruc-tion' had to be slain: disease, ignorance, squalor and idleness.[2] However, the bulk of the Report's 299 pages was devoted to the eradication of want.

- What were the Report's major principles?
- Why did it initially arouse such opposition within government?
- How appropriate a solution to postwar poverty did it offer?

Principles

The Report itself summarized 'the main feature of the Plan for Social Security' as:

> A scheme of social insurance against interruption and destruction of earning power and for special expenditure arising at birth, marriage or death. The scheme embod-ies six fundamental principles: flat rate of subsistence benefit; flat rate of contribu-tion; unification of administrative responsibility; adequacy of benefit; comprehensiveness; and classification. . . . Based on them, and in combination with national assistance and voluntary insurance as subsidiary methods, the aim of the Plan for Social Security is to make want under any circumstances unnecessary.[3]

Its whole logic was, therefore, based on the far from revolutionary decision to maintain the prewar system of contributory insurance, based on the weekly payments of employees, employers and the state. No other system (such as one financed solely from taxation – long advocated by the Labour Party) was seriously considered on the ground that it would be a 'departure from existing practice, for which there is neither need nor justification and which conflicts with the wishes and feelings of the British democracy'.[4]

Insurance, according to Beveridge, suited the interests of government, employers and the public alike. *Government*, faced with increasing demands for public expenditure, required an acceptable form of taxation. Contributory insurance was, moreover, cheap to administer, automatically established a claimant's right to benefit and could moderate demands for greater expenditure by fixing in the electorate's mind the need to match higher benefits with higher contributions. *Employers* might complain of a tax on employment, but a healthy 'secure' workforce would be a productive one. Thus for business, as well as humanitarian reasons, employers should be directly involved in its administration. Above all, contributory insurance was what the British *public* – through the increasing popularity before 1939 of statutory and voluntary insurance – had shown that they wanted. As the Report maintained: 'the capacity and the desire of the British people to contribute for security are among the most certain and most impressive social facts of today'. One reason for this was a desire for independence. People wanted 'security not as charity but as a right'. Another, less propitious for the future of the welfare state, was a residual dislike and distrust of government. Insurance implied a contractual obligation on which, it was felt, government could not renege.

Many issues were left unresolved by the decision to retain the principle of insurance:

- What should the premium be?
- Who should be included ?
- To what benefits should contributors be entitled?

The Report proposed that, in the main, premiums and benefits should be flat rate but that, unlike interwar practice, cover should be universal. Each of these recommendations, as will be seen, aroused considerable controversy.

An obvious disadvantage to flat-rate premiums, tied to what the poorest paid contributor could afford, was that it limited the scheme's income. This was partly counteracted by the three *assumptions* upon which the Report was based: the provision by government of universal family allowances and a comprehensive health service (both financed by taxation) and the maintenance of a high level of employment.[5] The first two assumptions relieved the insurance scheme of two of the most expensive prerequisites of social security. The latter maximized the number of active contributors whilst minimizing the number of claimants.

(2) An equally obvious problem for a universal scheme, based on insurance contributions made at work, was how to cater for the variety of people's work experience, and indeed for those who had no paid employment. To counteract this problem the Report classified the population into six groups, each with their own different level of contributions. The groups were: (1) employees; (2) the self-employed; (3) housewives; (4) others of working age, not gainfully employed; (5) those below working age; and (6) the retired above working age. The most difficult groups to cover were groups (3) and (4). With regard to the former, it was recommended that all married women should qualify for a wide range of benefits 'by virtue of their husbands' contribution'.[6] If they worked, they might in addition opt to pay a lower contribution to qualify for the full range of benefits, albeit below the standard rate. With regard to the latter, there was no option – for claimants such as non-working single women who were unable to make contributions – but to provide relief through the tax-financed, but means-tested, national assistance scheme. National assistance was, nevertheless, expected to be a subsidiary scheme covering a very small and ever-decreasing number of people.

In relation to benefits, it was recommended that they should not only be flat-rate but also comprehensive and adequate. In consequence, all insured persons – whatever the reason for the loss or interruption of their income – should normally receive an identical cash benefit which was adequate to provide an agreed minimum standard of living and would last as long as required. Inevitably there was some variation in the availability, value and duration of benefits to meet the wide variety of individual circumstances and need. For example, those in classes (2) to (4) would not qualify for unemployment benefit. For class (3) Beveridge also designed an exclusive 'housewives' charter' which included a furnishing grant upon marriage, free domestic help when ill, and a separation allowance on the breakdown of marriage. Several benefits were also paid above the flat-rate subsistence level, either to encourage 'desirable' behaviour or to maintain an individual's customary (as opposed to subsistence) standard of living. The former included a supplement to the standard pension for those who continued to work after the official retirement age. The latter included industrial injury benefit which, after 13 weeks, was related to previous earnings. Finally, the duration of benefit for widows of working age without dependants was limited to 13 weeks and the continued payment of unemployment benefit could become dependent on retraining.[7] Despite such anomalies, however, the principle was largely maintained – at least within each class – of flat-rate contributions and benefits.

Beveridge's sixth and final principle was the unification of administrative responsibility. Through the consolidation of payments into one insurance stamp and the establishment of one responsible ministry, he hoped, both government and claimants would become the beneficiaries of greater 'co-ordination, simplicity and economy'.[8]

The flat-rate principle, as the Report acknowledged, set Britain apart from the normal practice in other countries, which was that both contributions and benefits should be earnings-related. Beveridge was determined that Britain should remain different in order to enhance the self-reliance that the popularity of insurance had earlier demonstrated. 'To give by compulsory insurance', he argued, 'more than is needed for subsistence is an unnecessary interference with individual responsibilities.'[9] If people wanted to insure themselves against a fall in their customary standard of living, then they should insure themselves privately. Indeed Beveridge wanted to involve trade unions and other non-profit-making friendly societies (of which there were over 19,000 in 1939) in the administration of state benefits, not just to humanize the state system and to prevent possible abuse but also to make private insurance readily available. Such a hope was to prove forlorn, however, as was demonstrated by the need for government to fall into line with international practice and introduce earnings-related benefits in the 1960s.

Contemporary criticisms

On publication, the report provoked widespread criticism, particularly within the Conservative Party and the higher civil service. Why? Objections were based largely on personal, political and logical grounds.

Personally, Beveridge was disliked for his awkward, autocratic manner. More pertinently, this dislike was intensified by both the unerring accuracy with which he exposed administrative shortcomings and the success with which he forced the pace of political change against even Churchill's wishes.

Politically, the concept of social security was attacked as excessively expensive. The Treasury in 1943 calculated that postwar governments would have at best a surplus revenue of £925 million, of which all but £100 million would be required for defence, the repayment of the national debt and the remission of taxes.[10] It would therefore be impossible to spend, as Beveridge wanted, £86 million on social security, especially as (within the social services) priority should be accorded to housing and education policy. These policies would at least assist the economy by helping to create a mobile and trained workforce, whereas to spend money on social security would, in the Chancellor of the Exchequer's words, be simply to 'throw it down the sink'.[11] Even worse, by guaranteeing workers subsistence benefits and demanding higher payments from employers and tax-payers, the Beveridge proposals might even be counterproductive by discouraging hard work and entrepreneurial risk-taking. The dangers of non-compliance and hostility from the USA were two further objections. The poor, the employers and the rich (who had no need for insurance benefits) might refuse to pay insurance contributions on the grounds that they either could not or should not pay such high premiums. Likewise American loans – on which postwar Britain would inevitably rely – might not be forthcoming if their purpose was seen to subsidize such an unproductive project.

Beveridge had been alerted to these objections during the Treasury's lengthy perusal of his draft proposals and he was thus able either to revise his plans or to answer his critics directly in the final report. In relation to the overall costs, he contemptuously dismissed the Treasury's traditional pessimism. 'There are no easy care-free times in early prospect', he admitted, 'but to suppose the difficulties cannot be overcome . . . is defeatism without reason and against reason.' He did, nevertheless, make some major concessions (and thereby partly jeopardized the Report's principles) in an attempt to cut costs. He proposed, for instance, delaying for 20 years the payment of pensions at the full subsistence rate 'in view of the vital need of conserving resources in the immediate aftermath of war'; and in order to save a further £100 million per annum, he decided that no family allowance should be paid for the first child.[12] This meant that many elderly people and large families on low incomes might not have their subsistence needs met automatically and that, consequently, they would have to resort to means-tested national assistance. Such concessions, however, did reduce the overall cost of his proposals to little more than the sum to which government was already committed, given inflation and various wartime promises. 'The Chancellor of the Exchequer', concluded Keynes, 'should thank his stars that he has got off so cheap.'

On the intrinsic value of social security, Beveridge rebutted each of the Treasury's objections with equal vigour. Social security, he argued, would encourage not discourage economic growth because the elimination of poverty would improve workers' physical and mental well-being and thereby increase productivity. Claimants would not be demoralized because, as has been seen, the whole purpose of the Report was to encourage self-sufficiency. Indeed, as one recent commentary noted, 'the crucial consideration' for Beveridge appeared to be 'not the provision of adequate subsistence benefits but the maximizing of personal responsibility and the maintenance of the conditions of social independence'. Neither workers nor employers would refuse to pay their contributions because, on average, the former were being asked to contribute less than they were already paying in voluntary and statutory premiums, whilst employers were to pay no more than their European counterparts.[13] Finally, in relation to the American reaction, Beveridge effectively called the politicians' bluff. His proposals, he explained, were merely a practical demonstration of how to 'cover ground which must be covered, in one way or another, in translating the Atlantic Charter into deeds'. Surely Churchill was not intending to renege on wartime promises?

Far more ominous for the Report's future success were two *logical inconsistencies* identified by its critics in relation to the principles of universalism and adequacy. If Beveridge's objective really was to eliminate 'want', they argued, why was relief not targeted on those in need? Universalism would involve a 'vast and essentially purposeless' bureaucratic exercise to collect contributions from and distribute benefits to those who did not need state support. It would then (given the ultimate resource constraints on the social security budget) fail effectively to relieve those in genuine need because benefits would have to be distributed too widely. Family allowances were singled out as a particularly expensive universal benefit which, despite their aggregate cost, would lack the necessary finance to attain their foremost objectives of relieving child poverty and encouraging larger families.[14] If the major reason for universalism was a desire to eliminate the means test, then this again was illogical because such a test was to be retained for many pensioners, those with high rents and – above all – in the assessment of the income of tax-payers, who were expected to help finance social security. In the 1960s, as the cost of the welfare state escalated, such arguments in favour of 'selectivity' were to be revived.

The principle of adequacy proved to be the Report's Achilles' heel. Beveridge admitted that 'any estimate of subsistence income' could not be scientific but had to be 'to some extent a matter of judgement'. He justified his basic flat-rate benefit of £2 per week for a couple in terms of Rowntree's 'absolute' poverty, which was based on an estimate of an average house-hold's expenditure on food, rent, clothing and sundries – although the latest research would suggest that (in his determination to maintain the work ethic) he actually calculated the lowest normal manual worker's income and then fixed his subsistence level just below it.[15] Whatever the basis of the calculation, the fundamental anomaly remained that Beveridge was attempting to provide a subsistence-level payment through a flat-rate bene-fit, when in practice the price of 'necessities' varied considerably between seasons and, above all, between regions. Rowntree himself recognized this in relation to one of the more volatile items in the working-class budget – rent – and suggested that both the insurance and the assistance schemes should provide a nominal subsistence benefit plus the claimant's actual rent. Beveridge rejected this suggestion, as he also rejected the objection of civil servants that it was illogical to provide a full subsistence benefit when it was known that most claimants had some income either in kind (such as help from relatives) or in cash (such as savings). His objection in both cases was that a means test would be required.

However, given the essential artificiality of the concept of subsistence and the variety of benefit levels which (as has been seen) the Report already envisaged, it was inevitable that cost-conscious governments would ulti-mately reject the principle of adequacy. Just as the commitment to 'full' employment had been watered down by 1944 to the 'maintenance of a high and stable level of employment', so social security was modified first to 'social' and then to 'national' insurance. Both parties within the Coalition government agreed that the rate of benefit should only be one which provided 'a *reasonable* insurance against want'.[16] The effect of this compro-mise was to destroy the whole logic of the Report because the payment of insurance contributions would no longer automatically guarantee freedom from poverty. If claimants had no other source of income, they would have to apply for means-tested national assistance in order to supplement their inadequate insurance benefits.

Retrospective criticisms

With the passage of time, the Beveridge Report was exposed as a flawed blueprint for the eradication of poverty. Both practical and conceptual flaws were revealed.

The major *practical* limitation was the attempt to base an extremely expensive system of relief (universal benefits) on a very restricted source of income (flat-rate contributions tied to what the poorest worker could afford). This meant that there would never be sufficient resources to respond flexibly to inflation or to changes in either social need or social demands. The assumption of full employment inevitably raised the spectre of inflation, but there could be no resources set aside to fund increases in benefit above the level warranted by the original, actuarially based contributions. Such increases would have to be provided on a 'pay as you go' basis from the current workforce, which undermined the whole principle of insurance.

The Report also assumed that most risks to income were 'insurable', whereas demographic change in particular swelled the ranks of those who were unable to make insurance contributions. The needs of the increasing number of one-parent families, for instance, had to be met – in the absence of any contingency fund – by means-tested benefit. This in turn meant that the role of national assistance, rather than diminishing as predicted by the Report, became increasingly important. Most seriously of all, however, lack of resources jeopardized the acceptance of the principle of 'adequacy' not only in the 1940s, when poverty could still be defined as an 'absolute' concept to be measured in terms of a given set of subsistence needs, but more especially thereafter, when it became increasingly defined as a 'relative' concept (see Section 6.2). As the Report itself acknowledged, its proposals were based on a restricted definition of poverty; but it lacked the resources to eradicate it by this definition, let alone the later one.[17]

The Report was also exposed, in time, as having failed to anticipate the merging of the taxation and benefit systems. Given the principle of 'universalism', most people were to be provided with insurance benefits whilst, with increasing affluence, most were also to enjoy the privilege of being taxpayers. Yet two separate administrative bodies, the Inland Revenue and the Ministry of Social Security (under its various titles), continued to collect direct taxes in the form of income tax and insurance contributions and to dispense benefit in the form of tax allowances and insurance payments. In the payment of benefit, they were also joined by the National Assistance Board/Supplementary Benefits Commission and other agencies, such as local authorities responsible for rent and rate rebates. Each essentially worked in isolation, with its own administrative criteria, and thus there was none of the 'co-ordination, simplicity and economy' which the Report had envisaged.

Attempts were later made to replace the whole bureaucratic basis of Beveridge's proposals with a unified tax and benefit system, such as a negative income tax. Such a new system, whilst admittedly blurring the distinction between tax and insurance, would have had the additional advantage of confronting one part of the welfare system which Beveridge had totally overlooked: tax allowances or 'fiscal welfare'. Tax allowances were indeed used, after the war, to encourage what Beveridge had particularly wanted – private insurance – but they cost government considerable sums of money (which, it was simultaneously argued, were not available for the underwriting of the insurance scheme) and, by redistributing resources from the poor to the rich, conflicted with the essential purpose of the Report. New Labour's system of tax credits finally achieved some unity (see Section 15.1).

With regard to the Report's *conceptual* flaws, one major attack by feminists has already been noted in Section 2.3.3. These critics have sometimes overlooked Beveridge's proposal for a 'housewives' charter', which successive governments failed to implement. They have also tended to discount the genuine efforts made to meet the needs of underprivileged groups, such as non-working single women. No-one else at the time (including the feminist groups to which Beveridge appealed) was able to devise a practical means of relief within an insurance system, which was what the vast majority of the public was then demanding. There was no question, however, that an insurance system based on participation in a labour market, in which women were not equally represented or rewarded, could only disadvantage women in relation to men. They, together with other groups such as the disabled who did not have equal access to full-time work, were effectively being denied full and equal citizenship. Just as political citizenship (the right to vote) had been dependent on the ownership of property before 1918, so after 1945 – despite the rhetoric of universalism – social citizenship (the automatic right to social security) had to be 'earnt' through insurance contributions.

Another fundamental attack on the Report has been made by those who view poverty as the result not of a temporary loss or interruption of earnings but of the inequality inherent in a capitalist society. In 1943 some within the Labour Party warned that the Report offered no more than the 'co-ordination of the nation's ambulance services': true social security was dependent on full employment and high wages.[18] More radically, it was argued in the 1960s and 1970s (with the development of the concepts of 'relative poverty' and 'relative deprivation') that poverty could only be reduced by a major redistribution of economic resources and hence of political power. Beveridge did envisage some redistribution. Family allowances and the health service, for instance, were to be funded by general taxation. In *Full Employment in a Free Society*, he was also insistent (as has been seen in Section 5.1) that industrial investment should be directed by the state towards the elimination of the 'five giants'. Redistribution, however, was not to be too radical. Abolition of want, the Report argued, could not be achieved solely by increased production. There would have to be some redistribution of income, but 'correct distribution does not mean what it has been taken to mean in the past – distribution between different agents in production, between land, capital, management and labour. Better distribution of purchasing power is required among wage-earners themselves.'[19] The Report has, therefore, been seen by many as not merely technically unsuited to the relief of 'relative poverty' by the state, but as philosophically inimical to it.

Revolutionary or conservative?

The Beveridge Report was unquestionably a visionary document, so far as its principles of universalism and comprehensiveness are concerned. It has even been compared in 'importance and stature to the French or Russian Revolutions'.[20] This is because it appeared to offer a historic compromise between the competing virtues of collectivism (the communal solidarity which was the attraction of interwar totalitarianism) and individualism (for which interwar democracies had fought). In return for a weekly insurance contribution, everyone in work could join a 'common risk pool' with their fellow citizens and thereby enjoy social security without recourse to a means test. Social solidarity was attainable with the minimum loss of personal freedom. It was this prospect which, by so exciting popular imagination and breaking the fatalism of both the Coalition government and the higher civil service, transformed perceptions of what was politically possible and necessary.

As a practical blueprint for reform, however, the Report was far from a revolutionary and logical document. It was inherently conservative in its retention of the insurance principle, its effective denial to many of full social citizenship, its limitation of the state's responsibility to the provision of a subsistence-level benefit and its emphasis on voluntary insurance. Its logic, particularly in relation to the principles of universalism and adequacy, was flawed and it perceived neither the need nor the opportunity for a merger of the tax and benefit systems. Other Western countries were drawn instinctively to Beveridge's vision (which several have yet fully to realize) but then uniformly rejected his detailed proposals.[21] This was not just because they were ill-suited to existing national institutions or cultures but because they were not seen to be a practical way forward. The same, as will be seen, was true for Britain. The Beveridge Report may have offered an excellent blueprint for the relief of poverty in the interwar period, when unemployment had been high and public expectations low. It was not well-suited to a period of rising affluence.

6.2 THE 'REDISCOVERY' OF POVERTY

Throughout the 1950s there was growing concern within government about the nature of the social security system, but there was no sustained public criticism of it until Christmas Eve 1965. It was then that, for maximum effect,

Brian Abel-Smith and Peter Townsend (two of Titmuss's colleagues) published *The Poor and the Poorest,* in which they claimed that the number of people living in poverty, rather than decreasing under the welfare state, had actually increased from a minimum of 600,000 in 1953–4 to 2 million in 1964. This 'rediscovery' of poverty needs to be qualified in two ways. First, unlike the poor of late Victorian England or the 1930s, the poor of the 1960s were neither a coherent social group who attracted widespread public sympathy nor a perceived political threat. Rather, as has been remarked, poverty in post-war Britain was 'essentially a statistical concept. The poor did not make themselves visible; they were discovered at the bottom of income tables by social scientists.' Second, as Deacon and Bradshaw have stressed, 'poverty was rediscovered only after it had been redefined'.[22] By the definition adopted in the Beveridge Report, very little poverty could be said to have existed after the 1950s. Nevertheless, within policy-making circles, the 'rediscovery' had a profound effect.

- What was the new definition of poverty?
- How could it be measured?
- In what ways was it a more 'accurate' measure than previous definitions?

Defining poverty

The definition of poverty employed by the Beveridge Report was the one developed in the classic house-to-house surveys of local poverty in the first part of the century, particularly by Rowntree in York. It was in essence an 'absolute' or subsistence-level definition based on the minimum expenditure on food, rent, clothing and 'sundries' required by a family to maintain its 'physical efficiency'. It could be measured on two levels. 'Primary' poverty referred to families which simply lacked the income to meet this minimum expenditure. 'Secondary' poverty referred to a family which had sufficient income but was, in the opinion of the investigator, living in a state of *actual* poverty because part of its income was 'absorbed by other expenditure, either useful or wasteful'. The new definition of poverty was a 'relative' one. As Townsend has argued:

> Individuals, families and groups in the population can be said to be in poverty when they lack the resources to obtain the type of diet, participate in the activities or have the living standards and amenities which are customary, or at least widely encouraged or approved, in the societies to which they belong. Their resources are so seriously below those commanded by the average individual or family that they are, in effect, excluded from ordinary living patterns, customs and activities.[23]

The concept of relative poverty was not as novel as many have assumed. As Townsend himself admitted, it had a pedigree stretching back to Adam Smith in the 1770s. It had also been used, if somewhat mutedly, in the twentieth century in line with rising public expectations. For example, Rowntree himself had consistently allowed increased expenditure on 'sundries' (such as presents and holidays) so that his supposedly 'static' poverty line actually increased by 75 per cent in real terms between his surveys of York in 1899 and 1950. The measurement of secondary poverty in the surveys also depended on his investigators' judgement of whether families, despite their 'adequate' income, were in fact living in conditions below those which were 'customary or at least widely encouraged and approved' at the time. Even the Conservative government itself raised the level of national assistance in 1959 above that justified by inflation, so that claimants could have a 'share in increasing national prosperity'. At the same time a new secretary to the National Assistance Board (Sir Donald Sargeant) had instigated a wide-ranging investigation into the adequacy of benefit which acknowledged the validity of a 'minimum participatory income level'.[24] The approach of Abel-Smith and Townsend was novel only in that it attempted to break totally with a finite set of minimum needs and to base the participatory level on average national 'living standards and amenities' rather than local, working-class ones.

Underlying changes to the definition of poverty was a changed under-standing of its *causes*. In the 1950s the concept of the 'problem family' was pervasive. This was a modified version of the concept of a dangerous 'residuum' of 10 per cent of the population (which had so concerned Edwardian social commentators) and of the 'social problem group' (which, because of its members' irremediable hereditary failings, could in the view of interwar eugenicists only be countered by measures such as steriliza-tion). The 'problem family', living in domestic squalor and apparently unable to cope with modern life, was similarly seen to be the result of personal failings (typically the 'emotional immaturity' or 'fecklessness' of the mother). However, such families – so it was believed – could be assisted and even 'cured' by sympathetic case work provided by social workers, employed either by local authorities or voluntary organizations such as the Family Service Units (see Chapter 10.2).

By the early 1960s, the 'problem family' as a concept came under attack itself, as the conviction grew that poverty was caused by environmental (structural) rather than biological (individual) factors. Such an argument was advanced, for example, in a pamphlet widely accredited as a milestone in the 'rediscovery' of poverty – A. Harvey, *Casualties of the Welfare State* (1960), with its history of the Stevens 'problem' family. The policy conse-quence was that government, rather than blaming the poor for their plight, should reconsider the causes of inequality – or social exclusion – in society. It should then remove them through, for instance, educational and housing policy. This structural explanation duly became the prevailing orthodoxy. Then in the 1980s, under the influence of American commentators such as Charles Murray, the concept of an 'underclass' was disinterred. Attention once again became focused on individual behaviour and the need to 'remoralize' the poor.[25]

Measuring poverty

It is not just the definition of poverty that has traditionally provoked controversy. It is also the means by which *any* definition can be translated into a practical measure of those living in poverty. By the 1960s critics had come to condemn calculations of absolute poverty as abstract, arbitrary and subjective. They were abstract because measurement was based on 'scientific' need (the amount of food, for example, that could be bought most cheaply to provide the requisite number of calories) rather than 'observable' need (the actual spending patterns of the poor, which were based not just on nutritional but also social and psychological need). They were arbitrary in, for example, their ever-changing choice of sundries. Finally, they were subjective because the measurement of secondary poverty was dependent on the personal judgement of each investigator.

Could the measurement of relative poverty be any more 'accurate'? One option was simply to classify as being in poverty any household whose income fell below a given percentage of national average income. However the choice of the particular percentage can only be arbitrary; and, in the assessment of any 'abstract' national average, there are problems in the standardization of the difference between earnings and effective take-home pay (given, for example, variations in the incidence of personal taxation and other unavoidable expenditure such as travel expenses to work).[26] Another option, employed by Townsend in his major study of poverty in 1968–9, was to construct an index of 'relative deprivation' which measured not only income but also the ability of people to participate in normal activities (such as holidays) and to control their own lives (especially in the housing market).[27] The trouble with such an index is again its arbitrary nature. Who was to define 'normal' activities and 'effective' control? Non-participation in 'customary' activities may also result from individual choice, not from a lack of resources. Townsend's index, it could be argued, was based upon assumptions about how people *should* behave, which were just as subjective and moralistic as those made by the early poverty surveys about how people *should not* behave.

Largely by default, it was the current level of national assistance (and subsequently supplementary benefit/income support) by which relative poverty came conventionally to be measured in the 1960s. For policy analysis this approach had the additional advantage that it measured the number of people falling below the government's 'official operational definition of poverty' and thus the success of the policy at any given time.[28] However, it was by no means uncontroversial because the benefit level is itself a far from objective standard. The exact basis on which the government makes its calculations has never been publicly disclosed. It reflects not so much a standard of living which is 'widely encouraged or approved', but what government at a given time feels it can afford. Moreover it has the peculiar 'scientific' quality that, should government raise the level of benefit, more people will automatically be classified as living in poverty – whereas, should the level be allowed to fall, poverty could (without any change in actual living standards) be eradicated.

There are also major problems in determining the current level of national assistance/supplementary benefit and even income support. Benefits consist, as Rowntree recommended to Beveridge in 1942, of a cash payment plus claimants' actual housing costs. Allowances for children also vary according to their age. Any one figure for the current value of benefit has therefore to assume a rather abstract average figure for rent and children's allowances. Moreover, in the official calculation of need, certain existing income (such as small savings) is disregarded and regular additional payments or one-off lump sums can be made at the discretion of officials to meet exceptional need. For these reasons the main standard of poverty used in *The Poor and the Poorest* was 140 per cent of the basic rate of national assistance plus rent; and it was by this standard that numbers in poverty rose dramatically from 600,000 in 1953–4 (a figure consistent with Rowntree's findings) to 4 million and from 2 to 7.5 million in 1960. The choice of the figure of 140 per cent was, however, somewhat arbitrary and it was not uniformly adopted by other social scientists.

Calculations of relative poverty could be said to have been no less abstract than the findings of house-to-house surveys. Those surveys, albeit local, were at least comprehensive. Relative poverty has been calculated from government statistics which, albeit national, have other flaws – not least because they were collected for purposes other than the analysis of poverty. What series is the most suitable? The longest-running of any value is that published by the Inland Revenue on the distribution of income. Inevitably it excluded non-tax-payers or, in other words, those most likely to be in poverty. The General Household Survey commenced in 1971 but, in addition to its late start, it lacks adequate detail. The series that has most commonly been used, therefore, is the Family Expenditure Survey. It has been compiled since 1957 to determine actual patterns of household expenditure so that the correct weights can be incorporated into revisions of the retail price index. However, the use of this series tends to underestimate the incidence of poverty for a number of reasons.

- The returns are voluntary and the sample is consequently biased because the response of the elderly and the sick tends to be disproportionately low. The samples are also small, and the numbers in poverty even smaller. In the 1960 survey analysed in *The Poor and the Poorest,* for instance, there were only 3450 respondents from an original sample of 5000 and the number of those living below the national assistance level was 167.[29]
- Respondents who are temporarily without earned income (for example because of sickness or unemployment) are required to return their 'normal' income.

→

- The series also records the circumstances of whole households rather than individual 'tax' or 'benefit' units – so that, for example, pensioners who are not claiming the benefits to which they are legally entitled (and therefore, by definition, are living below the official poverty line) may not appear to be in poverty because their income is being supplemented by relations with whom they are living.

The importance of the last two factors can be vividly illustrated in relation to the 1971 Fiegehen survey. This survey recorded a poverty level of 4.9 per cent, but the figure would have risen to 6.5 per cent had 'actual' been substituted for 'normal' income and to 8.8 per cent had 'benefit units' been used rather than households.[30]

The extent of poverty

The results of the principal postwar poverty surveys are provided in Table 6.2.[31] There were only two major house-to-house surveys, by Rowntree in 1950 and Townsend in 1968–9. Rowntree's survey was the last of the classic surveys of local poverty and concluded that virtually no one in York remained in primary poverty, whilst only 1.66 per cent of the total population was in secondary poverty. Complacency about the success of the welfare state was compounded by the calculation that whereas 2.77 per cent of the working-class population were in secondary poverty, the figure would have risen to 22.18 per cent had it not been for recent welfare legislation.[32]

To generalize from such figures would, however, be dangerous. Was York a sufficiently representative town upon which to base estimates of national poverty? The survey was also based upon an idiosyncratic definition of the working class (which alone was examined) and of course on a measure of absolute poverty. Atkinson has reworked the figures to show that, had the current level of national assistance been used, 5.8 per cent of the population would have been recorded as living in poverty.[33] Townsend's figures are somewhat higher than corresponding surveys and may provide some corrective for the underestimates of poverty inherent in the use of the Family Expenditure Survey. The estimates based on the Inland Revenue Series and the General Household Survey are also high. This is mainly because the former is based on tax units rather than households and the latter on the higher long-term rates of supplementary benefits to which few claimants other than pensioners were actually entitled. The figures for Abel-Smith and Townsend, as explained earlier, represent their minimum rather than their preferred calculations.

Bearing in mind these qualifications, and the statistical anomalies identified earlier, the findings of the surveys detailed in Table 6.2 are surprisingly consistent. They suggest that in the 1960s and early 1970s there were, at minimum, between 1.3 million and 2.6 million people living in poverty representing, respectively, 2.3 per cent or 4.9 per cent of the population. Higher

Table 6.2   Estimates of poverty in the UK, 1950–75

Year	Study	Source	Unit	% of total population	Number (million)
1950	Rowntree*	Survey	Household	1.7	
	Atkinson*			5.8	
1953–4	Abel-Smith and Townsend	FES	Household	1.2	0.6
1954	Gough and Stark	IR	Tax unit	12.3	6.3
1959	Gough and Stark	IR	Tax unit	8.8	4.6
1960	Abel-Smith and Townsend	FES	Household	3.8	2.0
1963	Gough and Stark	IR	Tax unit	9.4	5.1
1967	Atkinson	FES	Household	3.5	2.0
1969	Atkinson	FES	Household	3.4	2.0
1968–9	Townsend	Survey	Household	6.4	3.8
1971	Fiegehen et al.	FES	Household	4.9	2.6
1975	Beckerman and Clark †	FES	Household	2.3	1.3
1975	Layard et al. †	GHS	Household	8.7	4.6
1975	Berthoud and Brown	GHS	Household	11.3	6.1

*York only.
† Great Britain only.
Source: Adapted from R. Hemming, *Poverty and Incentives* (Oxford, 1984) p. 53.

estimates can be justified by the use of different criteria and statistical conventions. No one figure is incontrovertible, however, because – despite all claims to the contrary – neither the concept of relative poverty nor its measurement is or can be scientifically precise.

6.3 THE ABANDONMENT OF BEVERIDGE

The Beveridge Report provided a powerful and popular set of principles upon which to develop a system of social security and they were, with a few crucial exceptions, followed by the first postwar governments. Within 20 years, however, poverty had been 'rediscovered' and the system was coming increasingly under attack. Why was this?

- Was it because successive governments had failed fully to implement Beveridge's recommendations?
- Was it because these recommendations, as suggested earlier, were impractical?
- Was it because, with rising affluence, political values and public expectations changed? If so, what alternative policies were proposed and implemented?

Four policy phases

1945–56. This was the first broad stage into which postwar policy can be divided and in general there was satisfaction that, through the implementation of the Beveridge Report (by such legislation as the 1945 Family Allowances Act, the 1946 National Insurance Act and the 1948 National Assistance Act), poverty had been virtually eliminated. Complacency was encouraged by the findings of Rowntree's 1950 survey of York, the rising surplus in the National Insurance Fund (resulting from unemployment being far lower than estimated)[34] and continuing economic growth (which, it was assumed, would mean increased living standards). The one cause for concern was the number of claimants on means-tested national assistance which, far from declining, had increased by 1954 to 1.8 million. The obvious reason for this blemish was successive governments' refusal to make flat-rate insurance benefits 'adequate' because, as seen earlier, it was adjudged both illogical and impracticable. Consequently, their value fell consistently below the 'official poverty line' of national assistance which, in particular, met claimants' *actual* housing costs and was regularly increased in line with inflation. The majority of claimants for national assistance were, therefore, those seeking to 'top-up' insurance payments; and in an exceptional attempt to resolve this anomaly, insurance benefits were raised by 22 per cent just before the 1955 election.

1957–65. This phase opened with the Conservative government, in the aftermath of Suez and confronted by a sterling crisis, seeking to build an 'opportunity' rather than a 'welfare' state. It had also, rather more prosaically, to refashion the national insurance scheme in the light of a decline in its surplus and a rise in public expectations. The core of the problem was the non-implementation of another of Beveridge's proposals. This was the more regressive suggestion that, because of the need to build a healthy surplus in the Insurance Fund to meet the long-term cost of the population's increased longevity, full subsistence pensions should not be paid for 20 years. The Attlee government, however, had found such a proposal politically unaccept-able and had authorized the immediate payment of the full pension, albeit below the subsistence level, to all those who qualified. After ten years it was to be made universal – which meant that a 55-year-old man, who had only started to contribute in 1948, would then be entitled to a pension ten times higher than his contributions actuarially warranted.[35]

The chickens thus released came home to roost in 1957, when both the Cabinet and the Treasury were already becoming concerned about the rising level of existing public expenditure. Their solution was two-fold. First, to cut government expenditure the Treasury's contribution to the Insurance Fund was capped. Its relative size subsequently declined from Beveridge's target of 33 per cent of total contributions to a mere 14 per cent by 1973–4.[36] This starved the Fund still further of resources, and explicitly transformed the national insurance system from an actuarial scheme (in which the level of contributions was determined by the anticipated cost of future liabilities) to a pay-as-you-go scheme (in which current contributions directly financed current outgoings). Second, to raise revenue, the foreign example of earnings-related contributions was adopted with regard to pensions. This initiative had other advantages. It was electorally popular; and by providing eventually an earnings-related supplement to the flat-rate pension, it could both lift many claimants off supplementary benefit and offer, in an 'opportunity' state, some reward for hard work. However, for the Conservatives it had the disadvan-tage that were it to be administered exclusively by government it would threaten voluntary insurance and private initiative. Despite Treasury protests about lost revenue, therefore, contributors were allowed to 'contract out' of the state scheme, should they so choose, into an approved tax-subsidized occupational pension. The relevant Act was passed just before the 1959 elec-tion.

1965–70.   The third phase lasted broadly from the publication of *The Poor and the Poorest* to Labour's election defeat. To raise extra revenue and to 'float' further claimants off means-tested benefit, the earnings-related principle was extended to unemployment, sickness, industrial injury and widows' benefit in 1966 (without any provision for contracting-out or matching state contribu-tions). There was also a major extension in both the range of, and the number of claimants on, means-tested benefit. For example, rate rebates (to be admin-istered by local government) were introduced in 1966, and the number depen-dent on national assistance/supplementary benefit alone rose to 7.7 per cent of the population (see Table 6.3). This growth of means-testing conflicted not only with Beveridge's proposals but also with traditional Labour Party policy. In particular it contradicted the Party's election pledge to introduce an 'income guarantee', whereby no-one would have to apply for subsistence benefit but would receive it automatically through the tax system. The realities of office, however, soon convinced the Wilson government that such a guarantee was administratively and financially impractical. Equally it was convinced by the deteriorating economic situation that no major uprating of universal benefits could be afforded. There was, therefore, no alternative to an extension of means-tested benefit.

A positive attempt was nevertheless made to make such benefits more acceptable and accessible. To minimize stigma, the administration of national insurance and national assistance was united – as Beveridge had wished – in a Ministry of Social Security; national assistance was renamed supplementary benefit; and the claimant's legal right to benefit was made explicit. To combat low take-up, greater publicity was given to the full range of benefits, application procedures were simplified, and all the discretionary payments for which pensioners in particular might qualify were consolidated into a single 'long-term additional' benefit. However, the continuing economic crisis and declining popular sympathy for the poor both restricted the resources and discouraged the changes in official attitude which were essential if such reforms were to be fully effective. Disillusion and dissatisfaction amongst the well informed and the politically committed began to escalate; and there was a consequent proliferation of expert pressure groups (such as the Child Poverty Action Group, founded in 1965 on the publication of *The Poor and The Poorest*) and militant protest groups (such as the local Claimants' Unions which started to form, especially in universities, in 1968).

1970–75. The final phase extended saw both a further, deliberate expansion of means-testing and renewed attempts to rationalize the whole social security system. The objective of means-testing was to target the poor more effectively and, in particular, to relieve child poverty and to counteract the ravages of inflation. In 1968 the only serious postwar attempt to increase the value of universal family allowances had been made, with any extra benefit accruing to the better-off being 'clawed back' through the tax system. In 1971 – in defiance of the Conservatives' election pledge – this expedient was not extended. Instead a new means-tested benefit, Family Income Supplement, was introduced, guaranteeing to the low-paid half the difference between their gross pay and the appropriate level of supplementary benefit. To combat inflation mandatory rent rebates and more generous rate rebates were introduced; and national insurance benefits were divided more distinctly into long-term and short-term benefits with the more generous long-term benefits being reserved for those (such as pensioners) unable to participate in the labour market and therefore in rising real wages. The intention behind such reforms was well-meaning, but they greatly added to the complexity of an already confused, and

Table 6.3 Claimants receiving national assistance/supplementary benefit, 1948–74 (000s)

	National assistance				Supplementary benefit	
	1948	1951	1961	1965	1970	1974
1. Retirement pensioners and national insurance widows 60 years and over	495	767	1075	1,239	1,745	1,712
2. Others over pension age	143	202	220	196	156	96
3. Unemployed with national insurance benefit	19	33	45	34	73	73
4. Unemployed without national insurance benefit	34	33	86	78	166	228
5. Sick and disabled with national insurance benefit	80	121	134	149	164	95
6. Sick and disabled without national insurance benefit	64	98	133	138	159	165
7. Women under 60 with dependent children	32	41	76	108	191	245
8. National insurance widows under 60	81	86	58	55	63	42
9. Others	63	81	17	15	20	24
10. Total persons receiving supplementary benefit	1,011	1,462	1,844	2,012	2,738	2,680
11. Total number of claimants and dependants	1,465	2,048	2,608	2,840	4,167	4,092
12. Claimants and dependants as a percentage of the total population	3.0	4.2	5.1	5.4	7.7	7.5

Note: Figures are for Great Britain only.
Source: R. Lister, *Social Security* (CPAG poverty pamphlet, no. 22, 1975) p. 9

confusing, system. Before 1970, for example, concern had been expressed about the 'unemployment trap' – the disincentive to an increasing number of supplementary benefit claimants to take low-paid work because, with the loss of means-tested benefits and an increase in both their tax liability and travel costs, their real income could actually fall. Family income supplement created a similar 'poverty trap', whereby the take-home pay of low-paid workers could actually fall after the award of a pay increase.[37]

It had been the initial intention of the Heath government to remove all such anomalies by rationalizing the tax and benefit systems through the introduction of 'tax credits'; but like the earlier income guarantee this reform was ultimately rejected as administratively and financially impractical. A more modest administrative rationalization was sought by the returning Labour government in its 1975 Social Security Act. All insurance contributions were made earnings-related. Beveridge's Class 4 contributions (made by those of working age, not gainfully employed) were abolished. So too was the working wife's right to opt out of full insurance contributions. The distinction between long-term and short-term insurance benefit was also consolidated, with the former being index-linked to earnings (thereby maintaining its relative value) and the latter to prices (thereby only maintaining its real value). The Act was, however, wholly incapable of resolving the escalating problems arising from mass unemployment and inflation, as was illustrated by the rise in the number of those within the poverty trap from 12,000 in 1975 to 63,730 in 1979.[38]

Beveridge as a flawed blueprint

The outstanding characteristic of these four periods was the fact that all Beveridge's principles were either rejected outright or surreptitiously jettisoned. 'Adequacy', as has been seen, was never accepted despite Beveridge's restricted definition. Consequently a significant, and ever-rising, number of those in need were never – as his Report had promised – automatically freed from the fear of poverty but had to claim means-tested benefit. The principle of flat-rate contributions and benefit, which Beveridge himself had qualified with his special arrangements for different insurance classes, was wholly abandoned with the introduction of earnings-related contributions and benefits and, later, with the differentiation between long-term and short-term insurance benefits. The principle of comprehensiveness was also breached, in the coverage of persons, with the contracting-out clauses in the pensions legislation. Finally, Beveridge's system of classification was eroded by the abolition of Class 4 contributions.

The abandonment of these five principles in turn affected the whole nature of the social security system. The 'subsidiary' service of national assistance did not, as predicted, wither away; and with the introduction of earnings-related benefits, voluntary insurance was no longer entrusted exclusively with the task of ensuring relative – as opposed to subsistence –

living standards. Voluntary insurance, it is true, did increase with rising affluence, but it was not the type of expansion which Beveridge had sought. The successful insurance companies were not the small, participatory friendly societies (which had so impressed him as an example of working-class self-help) but the large, impersonal profit-making companies which were better able to exploit the artificial market conditions created by tax exemptions and the contracting-out clauses in pensions legislation.

Even the very essence of the Beveridge Report – the insurance principle – was eroded. No scheme of national insurance could tailor contributions to individual circumstances as could a private policy, but since 1911 contributions had been based on an estimate of the Insurance Fund's future liabilities. Beveridge had adjudged this modified insurance contract to be to everyone's advantage; but when the cost of national insurance began to rise in the late 1950s the government's contribution was capped and any attempt to maintain an actuarial system abandoned. Contributions were continued because they provided a relatively uncontentious form of taxation and discouraged demands for higher benefits. The insurance principle was therefore a convenient political fiction. By the late 1970s, however, it was becoming an increasingly costly fiction. Not only were some 100,000 civil servants required to collect the contributions at an annual cost of £100 million, but it also obstructed the much-needed rationalization of the tax and benefit systems.[39]

The high cost of social insurance highlights the failure of Beveridge's sixth principle: the unification of administrative responsibility. Superficially unification had been achieved in 1966 with the creation of the Ministry of Social Security. 'Want', however, continued to be relieved by a wide range of means-tested benefits, administered by local government and the NHS, such as rent rebates, school meals and free prescriptions. In 1975 there were, indeed, 45 major means-tested benefits, each with its own assessment criteria. Moreover, not even the unification of national insurance and national assistance under the Ministry of Social Security achieved Beveridge's objectives of 'coordination, simplicity and economy'. Social insurance may have been expensive, but its administrative costs were, on average, only 3 pence in every pound. The cost of the expanding and more labour-intensive supplementary benefit system was over 10 pence in the pound.[40]

Far more seriously, supplementary benefit was so uncoordinated and complex that it not only discouraged personal initiative (through the creation, for example, of the unemployment and poverty traps), but it actually denied the poor their legal rights through either a lack of information or the deliberate action of officials. Despite the extensive publicity campaigns of both the Wilson and Heath governments, under 50 per cent of those entitled to claim were applying for supplementary benefit and under 40 per cent of those entitled to rate rebates and family income supplement. The single major reason for this was lack of knowledge.[41]

The growing complexity of the system demoralized officials as well as claimants. 'The book of rules', lamented the chairman of the Supplementary Benefits Commission between 1975 and 1980, 'which in 1945 every National Assistance Board officer had been able to carry around in his pocket had grown to several massive volumes, so often amended and so complicated that even the staff could not understand them'. Approximately 10,000 pages of new or amended rules were added in 1975 alone. The only way in which staff could reduce their work-load to manageable proportions (as suggested in Section 3.1.3) was actively to discourage people from making claims.[42] The social security system was, therefore, not – as Beveridge had planned – making 'want under any circumstances unnecessary'. Rather, it was making it inevitable.

Flawed alternatives

Why was a more satisfactory system not devised? Both parties, as has been seen, did try unsuccessfully to merge the tax and benefits systems. The Labour Party's income guarantee was a modified form of negative income tax (ironically championed by the right-wing IEA) which would provide, through the tax system, an automatic payment to anyone whose income fell below a given limit. Such a universal payment would have been costly, but the main objections were administrative. At a time when it was being asked to prepare a wealth tax, the Inland Revenue would have had to locate all non-tax-payers (no easy task, as the introduction of the poll tax in 1990 demonstrated), redesign all its assessment forms and institute weekly, as opposed to annual, assessments (as those in need could scarcely wait for retrospective annual payments). The Conservative Party's tax credits were a more modest attempt to replace personal tax allowances, family allowances and family income supplement. Their value would have been equivalent to these benefits and, should anyone's level of taxation have fallen below that value, the balance would have automatically been paid to them. The drawbacks were again cost and administrative duplication. If the value of the credits had been sufficiently high to 'float' most claimants off supplementary benefit (which was after all the reform's main justification), the basic tax rate would have had to be raised to approximately 45 per cent. This conflicted with the Conservatives' commitment to reduce taxation in order to restore incentives. Moreover, all but one of the 45 means-tested benefits would have survived.

Both schemes consequently suffered from the typical weaknesses of all such attempts to merge the tax and benefits systems.[43] They were superficially attractive in that, through automatic payments, they would resolve the problem of the non-take-up of means-tested benefits. They would also remove the absurdity, and the administrative expense, of government taxing the poor with one hand and paying out benefit to them with the other. However, were such schemes to be universal, they would have typically required basic tax rates higher than 45 per cent, which successive govern-

ments adjudged politically unacceptable. Were benefits to be
pound-for-pound as income increased, personal incentives would also
been undermined (as with the poverty trap). No simplified system could
moreover, be sufficiently flexible to deal with the wide variety of human
need. A residual relief agency would have had to be retained. Finally, and
most importantly, all such schemes begged major questions about the fundamental purpose of social security: was it to redistribute income simply to
relieve basic need, or significantly to reduce inequality?

Universalism versus selectivity

This basic question was the critical issue in the academic debate which broke
out over the future of social security in the 1960s, of which the 'rediscovery of
poverty' was a part. The protagonists were the 'universalists', led by Titmuss,
and the 'selectivists', of whom the IEA was the most effective representative.
The universalists favoured not a merger of the tax and benefit systems but a
'back to Beveridge' approach. Insurance benefits should be made 'adequate'
so that the majority of claimants could be 'floated' off supplementary benefit.
In addition non-means-tested benefit should be introduced for groups, such
as one-parent families, for whom Beveridge had failed to cater. The cost was
to be borne by such redistributive measures as the withdrawal from the
better-off of tax allowances, the removal of the ceiling on national insurance
contributions, and greater state contributions to the Insurance Fund (financed
in part by a wealth tax). Universal state provision by such means was justified
not only as administratively efficient but also, as seen in Section 2.2.2, on
moral and ethical grounds.

This was of course anathema to the IEA. It saw the rediscovery of poverty
as proof that Beveridge's wartime opponents within the Treasury and the
Conservative Party had been right to condemn universalism as impractical.
With rising affluence, it argued, state provision of welfare should wither
away. Everyone should buy services (including pensions, education and
health) in the open market – supported if necessary by state subsidies, to
ensure either a necessary minimum personal income or sufficient demand for
such public goods as education. Personal responsibility and initiative would
thereby be strengthened and competitive efficiency amongst the producers
increased (see Section 2.2.3). The role of state bureaucrats should be reduced
to helping directly only those in absolute poverty.

This battle of ideas was conducted at a rarefied level and had little direct
impact on policy, although the increasing provision of means-tested benefits
after 1966 did reflect the influence of the selectivists' arguments. Essentially
neither political party could accept the full logic of either side. Social scientists,
both as technocrats and as polemicists, were therefore unable to provide practical answers to the dilemmas facing politicians and, more importantly, the
poor themselves. The consensus which sanctioned the extension of means-testing, and thus of the growing confusion of supplementary benefits, was essentially a negative one based on the lack of any perceived practical alternative.

..., Crossman (secretary of state for social services) ... the universalists, and especially Townsend, with ... have been expected to agree. His argument was that the ... would not tolerate the degree of redistribution they were ... ually the Heath government rejected selectivist panaceas. ...icularly disillusioned with means-testing as a result of the ...(despite extensive publicity) of family income supplement. It ... away from the electoral repercussions of withdrawing universal ben... from the poor whilst reducing the tax burden on the better-off and of the increased inequality that any return to the market in areas such as healthcare would entail.

6.4 THE TARGETING OF NEED

How well in effect did this increasingly complex system cater for those in actual need? Unquestionably one of the major postwar achievements was the virtual elimination of absolute poverty – and, equally importantly, the fear of absolute poverty, which as late as the 1930s had been a reality for many working-class families. This achievement, however, has to be qualified in four ways.

- It was an achievement not just of the social security system but also of full employment.
- The 'absolute' level of poverty, as has been seen, was not the sole concern of the poor. Relative living standards were of equal importance. Thus although the real value of benefits approximately doubled between 1945 and 1975 (with the noticeable exception of child support), the poor felt hardly any 'better-off' since the relative value of benefits remained remarkably stable at about 20 per cent of the average wage for single people, 30 per cent for couples and 40 per cent for couples with two children (see Tables 6.4 and 6.5).
- The means test was becoming more, rather than less, prevalent.
- There were, as shown in Section 6.2, a significant and growing number of people living below the official poverty line. Supplementary benefit was failing as a safety net not just because of non-take-up but for two other reasons: it was unavailable to those in work and claimants could not receive in benefit more than they had been paid in their previous job, even if their wages had been below the poverty line. This latter restriction, the 'wage-stop', was not abolished until 1976.

Those who had to resort to means-tested benefits, and those who remained below the official poverty line, were largely drawn from the same groups of people: separated, divorced and widowed women; the sick and disabled; the unemployed; and the elderly (see Tables 6.3 and 6.6). The one major difference, which was the exceptional finding of *The Poor and the Poorest*, was the

Table 6.4 Benefits as a percentage of average male manual earnings, 1948–74

	Retirement pension		Unemployment benefit (flat-rate)		Supplementary benefit (ordinary)		Supplementary benefit (long term)	
	single	couple	couple	couple + 2 children	couple	couple + 2 children	single	couple
1948	18.9	30.5	30.4	38.1	29.0	39.9	–	–
1950	17.3	27.9	27.9	35.1	28.9	39.6	–	–
1955	17.9	29.2	29.1	38.1	28.3	39.0	–	–
1960	17.2	27.5	27.5	36.8	29.2	40.3	–	–
1965	20.4	33.2	33.2	43.8	32.0	43.5	–	–
1970	17.8	28.9	28.9	38.7	28.0	38.0	20.3	32.1
1974	20.6	32.9	28.6	38.9	28.1	37.9	21.4	33.6

Note: Supplementary benefit figures exclude rent and assume the children to be under 5 years of age.
Source: R. Lister, *Social Security* (1975) pp. 34–7.

Table 6.5 The real value of social security benefits, 1948–75 (£s, 1981 prices)

	July 1948	April 1961	September 1971	November 1975
1. Unemployment benefit	19.64	26.88	34.96	36.47
2. Retirement pension	19.64	26.88	34.96	42.96
3. Supplementary benefit	17.93	25.31	33.39	35.10
4. Child support: one child	4.87	4.36	4.27	3.67
5. Child support: three children	17.60	16.62	15.36	13.81

Note: Lines 1–3 are standard benefits for couples; line 3 excludes payment for rent; lines 4 and 5 include tax allowances.
Source: R. Hemming, *Poverty and Incentives* (Oxford, 1984) p. 29.

Table 6.6   The immediate causes of poverty, 1936–60

| | Rowntree | | Abel-Smith and Townsend* | |
| | 1936 | 1950 | 1960 | |
	%	%	%	approx. number (millions)
1. Old age	14.7	68.1	33	2.50
2. Death of chief wage earner	7.8	6.4	10	0.75
3. Sickness	4.1	21.3	10	0.75
4. Unemployment	28.6	–	7	0.50
5. Inadequate wage/large family	44.8	4.3	40	3.00

* At their preferred poverty line of 140 per cent national assistance plus rent.

large number of families with children living below the poverty line because of low wages – who were, by definition, unable to claim national assistance/supplementary benefit. They were particularly concentrated in the traditionally depressed areas, such as Northern Ireland. By 1975, 13 per cent of supplementary benefit there was wage-stopped (compared to the national average of 4 per cent) and on the introduction of Family Income Supplement (FIS), 14 per cent of claims were made in the province although it accounted for only 3 per cent of the population. The fate of each group is examined below.

Women

Beveridge, as has been seen, had been unable to find any satisfactory solution for separated, divorced and widowed women within an insurance scheme. His instinct to treat the breakdown of marriage as an 'insurance risk' foundered on the technical problem of moral hazard (see Section 3.2.1): a wife might either be responsible for or collude in the breakdown. Moreover, any special treatment might inadvertently favour the unmarried over the married (as had unemployment insurance in the 1930s) and contravene fathers' legal responsibility for maintenance. These problems remained unsolved; and one-parent families (who numbered some 276,000 by 1975) in particular had to resort to supplementary benefit, where special payments were not forthcoming until 1976. Beveridge's suggestion that the state should pay maintenance directly to deserted mothers and then pursue defaulting fathers through the courts was not adopted.[45] In contrast the treatment of widows by successive governments was more generous than Beveridge had recommended. Those over 50 were not deprived of their pension after 13 weeks, the expectation that they would return to work was relaxed in 1956, and the higher initial rate of payment (to permit adjustment to changed circumstances) was extended to six months in 1966. Pensions to those under 50 also became payable after 1970.

The disabled

Beveridge had also failed to cater adequately for those disabled other than in war or at work.[46] These 'civilian' disabled were either unable to build up an adequate insurance record or found that the level of insurance benefit was inadequate for their special needs. By the late 1960s there were about 1.1 million 'civilian' disabled, of whom 140,000 were receiving no benefit. One of the objectives of targeted legislation after 1970, such as mobility and attendance allowances, was to meet their needs and those of their carers; but although it was fairly comprehensive, both the small print of such legislation and its inadequate funding meant that those needs were not adequately met.

The unemployed

Remarkably less generous was the treatment of the unemployed. Their insurance benefit was not limitless, as Beveridge had recommended, and there were strict disqualification rules in relation to strikes. Moreover, the interwar practice of refusing payment for the first three days of unemployment ('the waiting period') was reintroduced in 1971. Once on supplementary benefit the unemployed were treated with suspicion. Disqualification could start after four weeks if (in another throw-back to the 1930s) claimants could not prove that they were 'genuinely seeking work' and the long-term unemployed were denied the enhanced benefits that were accorded to other long-term claimants after 1966. Government action reflected the popular prejudice that – despite the deteriorating economic situation in the 1960s – unemployment was the fault of the individual and should under no circumstances be condoned.[47] This permanent emphasis on the danger of scrounging (which surveys repeatedly showed to be grossly exaggerated) and the 'four week' rule were taken by left-wing critics of the social security system as proof that its priority was not the welfare of individual claimants but the maintenance of the work ethic and of the capitalist economy.

Children

By 1975 approximately 20 per cent of those dependent on supplementary benefit were children (see Table 6.3, line 11); and the actual number of children living below the poverty line because of their parents' low wages was even higher. Three practical remedies for child poverty and the related problem of low pay were readily available. A national minimum wage, by increasing labour costs, might have proved counterproductive by making certain industries uncompetitive and thereby pricing workers out of a job (although this did not actually happen in 1998 when one was introduced). Nevertheless trade boards, or wages councils, had existed since 1908 to determine realistic minimum wage levels in individual industries. Latent political opposition to such price-fixing by government had, however, been made explicit by Conservative back-bench opposition to Bevin's Catering Wages Act in 1943 – a breach of the 'party truce' to which Labour back-bench reaction to the government's handling of the Beveridge Report had been an immediate riposte. Their expansion was consequently limited. A second obvious solution was to reverse the increasing tax burden on the low-paid. By 1971, for example, it has been calculated that income tax alone – regardless of expenditure taxes, national insurance contributions and rates – was pushing the income of many of the low-paid below the official poverty line.[48]

Above all, however, the remedy lay in the raising of the real value of family allowances. The withdrawal of family allowance from the first child had been one of the economies conceded by Beveridge in his unsuccessful attempt to placate the Treasury in 1942; and in addition he had breached the principle of adequacy by making them only an aid to subsistence. To make matters worse they were never paid at the level Beveridge had suggested, on the ground that children would be receiving benefit in kind – which either never materialized (such as universal free school meals) or were withdrawn (such as universal free welfare foods). They were also rarely adjusted to inflation – before the upratings of 1968, there had in fact been no cash increase for the second child since 1952 or for other children since 1956. Consequently the value of child support, in total contrast to every other major benefit and to practice abroad, especially in France, consistently fell throughout the period (see Table 6.5, lines 4 and 5).[49] Easy remedies existed, therefore, to eradicate the problem of child poverty and the related problem of low wages. What did not exist, as illustrated by Thorneycroft's desire to remove family allowances from the second child in 1957 and the consistent hostility to family allowances identified in opinion polls, was the political and popular will to employ them.[50]

> The related problem of low wages and child poverty had long been identified as a cause of poverty. In 1936, for example, Rowntree had identified inadequate wages (that is, wages inadequate to provide for a family with three children or less) as the cause of 9.2 per cent of poverty, and 'large families' (with four or more children) of 8 per cent. By 1950 the respective percentages had fallen to 1.1 and 3.2 per cent; but, by the relative standard of Townsend and Abel-Smith, the combined figure had risen by 1960 to 40 per cent of individuals living in poverty – a figure which included 2.25 million children (see Table 6.6, line 5).[51]

The elderly

It was the elderly rather than the young who dominated the social security system from the start and created the greater political problems. Pensions and other benefits for the elderly consistently accounted for over half of social expenditure, and over half of supplementary benefit claimants were retired people (see Tables 6.1 and 6.3). Despite this, old age remained a major cause of poverty. Rowntree in 1950 found it accounted for 68 per cent of those living below his poverty line and although the figure in 1960, as recorded in *The Poor and the Poorest*, had fallen to 33 per cent, this was because of the relative increase in other causes. It still represented, at minimum, 2.5 million people (see Table 6.6). The potential cost of any pensions system that could 'float' so many off national assistance/supplementary benefit created something approaching panic in government circles.

Beveridge had been alert to the problems which could arise from increased longevity, in particular the ultimate cost of pensions. 'It is dangerous', he warned, 'to be in any way lavish to old age.'[52] He consequently recommended, despite his commitment to 'adequacy' and an end to means-testing, that full subsistence pensions should not be paid for 20 years. Both to maximize production and to minimize government expenditure, he also proposed that both men and women should be encouraged to stay at work after their respective 'official' retirement ages of 65 and 60, with insurance contributions after those ages being matched (in defiance of his principle of flat-rate benefits) by additions to pensions when they were finally drawn. Successive governments, however, rejected such harsh measures. Full pensions were paid immediately – with a delay of only ten years for those who had not contributed before 1948.

The relative 'lavishness' of successive governments towards the elderly did not eliminate distress, as the figures for those living below the poverty line demonstrate. 'Full' pensions were kept below the subsistence level. Their 'limited objective' was, in the words of one official report, to 'provide a reasonable basis of provision for old age involving supplementation in only a modest percentage of cases'.[53] By 1965, however, the 'modest' percentage of those who were entitled to national assistance/supplementary benefit had reached 47 per cent and many others remained above the poverty line only because their state pension was supplemented by private income (most noticeably occupational pensions). Inevitably many of those entitled to supplementary benefit (numbered at some 855,000) did not claim, largely because of pride or lack of information.[54]

Why were governments more generous to the elderly than to children? Such action made little economic sense. It would have been far more logical to invest in the future, rather than reward the past workforce. It could not have been solely the result of compassion because those who benefited from the ten-year rule were, by definition, not the poorest but those whose income had exceeded the maximum for the prewar scheme. In essence it was a crude political decision, reflecting the voting power of the elderly and the greater popularity of pensions over family allowances, as consistently revealed by opinion polls. In deference to the TUC and employers, successive governments also failed to match their words about late retirement with action; and even those workers who expressed a preference to stay at work soon bowed, as in other countries, to peer pressure.[55]

By the late 1950s the question of pensions was beginning to dominate social security policy; but because of fundamental political differences between the Conservative and Labour Parties little was achieved for 20 years. To contain cost, both parties were agreed upon the need for earnings-related contributions and pensions. They remained implacably opposed, however, on the extent to which any reform should be redistributive and, alternatively, on the extent to which market forces and personal initiative should be encouraged by the right of contributors to 'contract out' of the state scheme.

The original proposal, designed by Titmuss and adopted by the Labour Party in 1957, was highly redistributive. It would have guaranteed all those on average pay or below a state pension worth 50 per cent of their final salary. The Conservatives' riposte, the 1959 National Insurance Act, was wholly inadequate in terms of policy. In return for extra contributions, it offered a very low return which was not inflation-proofed. It was, however, a major political triumph. As 'reluctant collectivists', the Conservatives wanted to minimize the role of the state and the possibility of social engineering. As the then Minister of Pensions and National Insurance explained:

> The modest nature of these proposals derives from the dilemma which faces a Conservative government in extending well above subsistence level a State administered scheme of National Insurance. We all of us desire to keep any graduated scheme as small an animal as possible, both because we dislike intruding further than we must into the sphere of private enterprise and because we fear the extension of state liability, and consequently the field of political pressure, any higher up the pensions scale than is necessary.[56]

This is exactly what the Act achieved because, through its contracting-out clauses, it won time for private insurance companies to extend the coverage of occupational pensions to over half the workforce (12.2 million people by 1967). No Labour government, already under pressure from white-collar unions to permit contracting out, could in future afford to ignore so powerful a vested interest. Thereafter both parties produced major new bills reflecting their different principles. Crossman's 1969 plan for Labour was substantially redistributive in that it guaranteed an inflation-proofed state pension, worth at least half the national average wage, and permitted contracting-out only on terms which were far from favourable to private insurance companies. The 1973 Joseph Social Security Act for the Conservatives proposed a far less generous state scheme, which was not inflation-proofed and was designed to encourage the majority of contributors to opt for private occupational pensions. Both shared the same fate of being annulled by electoral defeat.

Whilst the parties bickered, the elderly suffered. They typically received a pension worth only 35 per cent of their final salary, whilst their counterparts in Germany and the USA received pensions worth 60 per cent and 56 per cent respectively. Pensions policy, therefore, provides the prime example of that lack of constructive consensus in Britain which was responsible for the gradual development of a relatively expensive but poorly targeted social security system.

Pensions policy was so technically complex and reflected so many political and administrative tensions that it has become an adventure playground for political scientists as well as historians. Civil servants not only baulked at the potential cost and practicality of political proposals but also at their principles. A senior official, for example, opened a major policy review in 1965 somewhat disdainfully: 'while we must certainly take account of proposals put forward in Labour Party documents over the last few years, the subject is one of such intricacy that a proper examination of alternatives is needed and the answers should not be pre-judged'. The major impediment to reform, however, was disagreement within as much as between parties. The TUC (unlike its counterpart in Sweden) was particularly insistent on the immediate relief of those in need rather than the construction of a complex state earnings-related scheme which would ensure 'social solidarity' in the long term – at the cost of preserving income inequality in retirement. This was particularly important in 1974 when, through the social contract, the TUC had a major influence on policy. Within the Conservative Party, those seeking greater reliance on the market were similarly frustrated by those within the industry who resisted the regulation that was essential were the state not to be left with a problem of free riders.

Above all, government freedom of action was constrained by the expectations and entitlements generated by earlier legislation. As Crossman despairingly wrote on the introduction of another abortive attempt at reform in 1968: 'if we were starting *de novo* we would design a universal state scheme covering every employed worker up to one-and-a-half times average male earnings; and we should limit private schemes to the useful purpose of providing extra cover beyond the level and on top of the benefits of the State scheme for any group of workers the firm might wish to benefit in this way'. No reform, however, could start *de novo*. The problem of path dependency, identified by Pierson as a principal impediment to welfare retrenchment also dogged welfare development.[57]

6.5 CONCLUSION

The history of postwar social security was riddled with contradictions. The promise of the Beveridge Report to realize the new ideal of social security, through a simplified system of state relief without resort to the hated means test, aroused immense popular enthusiasm and lay at the heart of the new values and perspectives upon which the welfare state was initially built. Yet within ten years the social security system was no longer popular. 'Most services', concluded one poll of public attitudes towards the welfare state in 1956, 'are felt to be helpful by those who use them. This is least likely to be the case where national insurance and national assistance are concerned.'[58] The means test did not wither away and the system started to become so complex that it became self-defeating.

The contradictions, superficially at least, went even further. In the formulation of policy, the detailed proposals of the Beveridge Report were soon revealed to be far from revolutionary and logical. The Labour Party, despite its commitment to greater egalitarianism, advocated earnings-related pensions and thus the continuation into retirement of the inequality experienced at work. The Conservative Party, in its emphasis on means-tested benefits, attacked the principle of 'universalism' from which its own supporters, in relation to pensions especially, had so benefited. More generally, it was the lower paid who were the most vehement opponents of more generous relief, particularly to the involuntary unemployed. The concepts of 'absolute' and 'relative' poverty were portrayed as being radically different, although (with the constant additions to the list of sundries in the former and the measurement of the latter in the 1950s in relation to the 'subsistence' national assistance level) each contained common elements. Moreover, scientific accuracy was often claimed for the new 'relative' definition, although it was in fact as abstract, arbitrary and subjective as the old 'absolute' measure. Finally, plans to simplify the payment of relief through a merger of the tax and benefits systems threatened not to reduce but to increase confusion.

These contradictions can in part be resolved. The Beveridge Report was revolutionary in its vision of a society freed from the historic fear of absolute poverty. Labour Party policy reflected trade unions' traditional adherence to pay differentials and was in accordance with European practice where, after a heated debate in 1959, even Swedish social democrats accepted the state's maintenance of inequality through earnings-related benefits. The Conservative Party for its part was careful not to attack those universal services which most benefited its supporters and, above all, tax exemptions. The reaction of the poor may be taken as an example of the third face of power (see Section 3.1.1). The adoption of the relative standard of poverty, however measured, was also the inevitable consequence of rising living standards – achieved by postwar economic growth – and accurately reflected both long-standing popular instinct and international practice. The one set of contradictions that could not be resolved was that inherent in the proposed merger of the tax and benefit systems. Any cost-effective policy targeted upon the poor could not but undermine incentive as benefit was withdrawn in line with rising income. Equally, any automatic system of payment – designed to overcome the problem of low take-up – inevitably lacked the necessary flexibility to deal with the full range of human need.

Such difficulties underline the fact that no ideal system of social security is ever attainable; and all criticisms of the Beveridge Report and the subsequent development of policy should acknowledge this fact. This does not mean, however, that the transparent lack of constructive consensus between 1945 and 1975 should be condoned. Hard decisions were not taken when necessary, at either a political, administrative or popular level, about the amount of resources that should be devoted to social security and how, in the national interest (however defined), those resources should be apportioned. Had such decisions been taken it would have been possible for government to encourage individuals to provide for themselves all the other services they wanted.

A residual state welfare service could then have reverted to the task it had performed well during the war and which it had initially been expected to continue in peace: the humane care of those who genuinely could not care for themselves.

6.6 FURTHER READING

There are no good, comprehensive studies of postwar social security. The best introductions are the historical chapters in general texts, in contemporary poverty surveys and in later attempts to reform the system. Amongst the first, the best are A. Deacon, 'Spending more to achieve less? Social security since 1945', in D. Gladstone (ed.), *British Social Welfare* (1995) and P. Alcock, *Poverty and State Support* (1987). The two outstanding contemporary surveys, from the full list provided in note 31 of this chapter, are A. B. Atkinson, *Poverty in Britain and the Reform of Social Security* (Cambridge, 1969) and G. C. Fiegehen, P. S. Lansley and A. D. Smith, *Poverty and Progress in Britain, 1953–73* (Cambridge, 1977). The contemporary mood is also well evoked by D. Bull (ed.), *Family Poverty* (1971) and K. G. Banting, *Poverty, Politics and Policy* (1979). Of the later books, the most rewarding are R. Berthoud and J. C. Brown, *Poverty and the Development of Anti-Poverty Policy in the United Kingdom* (1981) and A. W. Dilnot, J. Kay and C. N. Morris, *The Reform of Social Security* (Oxford, 1984).

On particular topics, the Beveridge Report is well served by a magisterial biography, J. Harris, *William Beveridge* (Oxford, 1997); the essays collected in J. Hills, J. Ditch and H. Glennister (eds), *Beveridge and Social Security* (Oxford, 1994); and K. and J. Williams, *A Beveridge Reader* (1987). There is also a shrewd review of the report's long-term impact in J. Harris, 'Enterprise and welfare states: a comparative perspective', in *Transactions of the Royal Historical Society*, 40 (1990) 175–95. Legislative changes to social insurance are covered exhaustively, in an international context and with a few telling insights, in P. A. Kohler and H. F. Zacher, *The Evolution of Social Insurance, 1881–1981* (1982). Means-tested benefit is particularly well covered by A. Deacon and J. Bradshaw, *Reserved for the Poor* (1983) and the reflections of an erstwhile chairman of the Supplementary Benefits Commission, D. Donnison, *The Politics of Poverty* (1982). The background to postwar pensions is fully, if partially, provided by J. Macnicol, *The Politics of Retirement in Britain, 1878-1948* (Cambridge, 1998); whilst their later history is covered, equally partially, by E. Shragge, *Pensions Policy in Britain: a socialist analysis* (1984). Meanwhile L. Hannah, *Inventing Retirement: the development of occupational benefits in Britain* (Cambridge, 1986) is one of those few academic books which one wishes were longer.

Contemporary poverty surveys are of course valuable in their own right. Particularly stimulating are the very short by B. S. Rowntree and G. R. Lavers, *Poverty and the Welfare State* (1951); the more technical by B. Abel-Smith and P. Townsend, *The Poor and the Poorest* (1965); the more impressionistic study of

Nottingham in 1966–7 by K. Coates and R. Silburn, *Poverty: the forgotten Englishmen* (1970); and the exhaustive 1968–9 survey by P. Townsend, *Poverty in the United Kingdom* (Harmondsworth, 1979). A detailed commentary, with an exhaustive bibliography, is provided by I. Gazeley, *Poverty in Britain, 1900-1965* (Basingstoke, 2003).

Predominant amongst contemporary texts, however, is the Beveridge Report itself (Cmd 6404, 1942). Its length and its close, if sometimes inconsistent, reasoning can be forbidding, but it provides effective summaries of its main proposals (paras 1–40), the insurance principle (272–99), its main principles (303–9) and its three assumptions (410–43). Particular problems are also summarized in relation to women (107–17, 339–48) and both rent and old age (193–264). There is a pre-emptive strike against its critics (444–61) and there is also an extremely helpful summary of international practice (Appendix F).

CONTENTS

1944   *A National Health Sevice* white paper (Cmd 6502)

1945   National Health Service Act

1948   BMA poll – 90 per cent of doctors vote against joining NHS (March). 'Appointed Day' – inauguration of NHS (July)

1949   Nurses Act – standardizes profession's pay and conditions

1951   Dental and opthalmic charges introduced by Labour

1952   Prescription charges introduced by Conservatives

1956   Guillebaud report published, *The Cost of the NHS* (Cmd 9663). Medical Research Council accepts link between smoking and cancer, although action has to await Royal College of Physicians' report in 1962

1959   Mental Health Act

1961   Patient's Association formed

1962   Hospital Plan launched. Porritt report – medical profession seeks reorganization to end tripartite structure

1965   GPs' charter introduced after threatened strike. Prescription charges dropped (reintroduced 1968)

1966   Salmon report on structure of nursing – advocates greater responsibilty for nurses

1969   Nurses' 'raise the roof campaign' – first instance of militancy. Ely Hospital report (Cmnd 3975) exposes ill-treatment of mentally ill

1972   *National Health Service Reorganisation: England* white paper (Cmnd 5055), followed by NHS Act in 1973. Briggs report on nursing (Cmnd 5115) – advocates improved training

➜

1973	MIND formed to campaign for	1974	NHS reorganized
	better mental health service. First	1975	Pay beds controversy.
	national strike by ancillary work-		Consultants and junior doctors
	ers. Hospital Plan abandoned		threaten to strike

As the initial enthusiasm for social security waned, the NHS quickly became, as it was to remain thereafter, the most popular welfare service. Within three months of its establishment it was being hailed in a Gallup poll as the greatest achievement of the Labour government; and later opinion polls rarely recorded levels of support below 80 per cent. Indeed, so dominant a position did the NHS come to command in popular perceptions of the welfare state that the two terms were commonly regarded as synonymous.[1]

The reasons for the popularity of the NHS are not hard to identify. Poor health and the inability to pay for adequate medical treatment have traditionally been amongst people's greatest fears. In the 1940s, therefore, the promise of comprehensive medical care, free to all equally in time of need, represented as revolutionary a social advance as the guarantee of social security – and one of more direct value because, whilst poverty had been alleviated by full employment since 1940, the legacy and incidence of poor health remained.

The interwar system of healthcare had also been unpopular.[2] The National Health Insurance scheme (under which most manual workers received free treatment from a panel of GPs) was widely criticized for its incomplete coverage of both treatment and people. Hospital care, for example, was excluded, as were the most vulnerable members of society – 'non-working' mothers and pre-school children. It was also actively disliked because of the unequal treatment GPs were perceived to give private and 'panel' patients, and the clear restriction by the 'approved' insurance companies of doctors' clinical freedom in order to safeguard their profits. At the same time private patients (who included most non-manual workers) were becoming increasingly concerned at the escalating cost of private insurance premiums, or of healthcare itself, at a time when their income was being more heavily taxed. Consequently there was never any serious danger of opposition, as there was in the field of social security, to the principle of universalism.

A further reason for the popularity of the NHS was the coincidence of its establishment with major medical advances. The war pioneered major advances in surgery and ancillary services, such as blood transfusions. It also greatly increased the supply of drugs, such as sulphonamides and antibiotics, which were able to effect dramatic reductions in the incidence and virulence of infectious disease. For example the four traditional killer diseases of children (scarlet fever, diphtheria, whooping cough and measles) were quickly brought under control after the war with the result that infant mortality, which had been cut in England and Wales by two-thirds between 1900 and 1940, was cut by a further two-thirds between 1940 and 1975 (from 56 deaths per 1000 live births to 16). Doctors, for one of the few times in history, appeared to have effective cures for disease and the NHS offered the means by which their expertise could be shared equally by all.

During the 1950s and 1960s, however, doubts began to grow about whether the popularity of the NHS was justified. Improvements in postwar health standards provided no real proof of its efficiency because such improvements were common to all industrial nations, whatever their system of healthcare. Moreover, they were largely dependent on medical advances attained before 1948 and on factors outside the health service, such as improvements in real income and housing. The NHS was certainly directing much-needed money into healthcare, consuming one-fifth of social expenditure (see Appendix, Table A.4); but was this money well targeted and efficiently spent? In particular an increasingly disproportionate percentage of the health budget, amounting to some 70 per cent by 1975–6, was being allocated to hospitals (see Table 7.1). Did this mean that the NHS was providing a national *sickness* rather than a national *health* service, devoting too many resources to the curing of individuals rather than to the prevention of ill-health? There were also persistent complaints from both within and without the NHS about the nature and quality of its administration. GPs had bitterly opposed its establishment in 1948 and threatened to withdraw their labour in 1965. Junior doctors and hospital consultants resorted to similar threats in 1975. Simultaneously, in the late 1960s the Labour government planned, and in 1974 the Conservative government effected, a radical administrative overhaul. Clearly all was not well.

The history of the NHS between 1943 and 1975 therefore provides an intriguing contrast between the popularity of the service as a political ideal and its increasingly criticized record as a practical deliverer of healthcare. In this respect at least its close identification with the welfare state may be justified because it represented, in microcosm, the problems inherent in any collective attempt to provide a 'just' and cost-effective service in a society characterized by inherited inequalities, self-interest and scarce resources. The NHS sought to use the 'rationality' of central planning to secure the better coordination and fairer distribution of services as well as to safeguard the interests of the less articulate (which the market had traditionally overlooked). However, it thereby placed in jeopardy two vital prerequisites of effective policy – local knowledge and professional expertise – and introduced major new administrative problems. Consequently, four fundamental challenges faced the NHS during its stormy inception and during the years of pragmatic adjustment before its radical overhaul in 1974:

- Could local initiative be encouraged without endangering the integrity of central planning and the 'responsible' expenditure of central finance?
- Could professional expertise be trusted without upsetting the delicate balance between clinical freedom and the pursuit of professional self-interest?
- As the size of the NHS grew (so that by 1975 it was employing just under

Table 7.1   The National Health Service: selected current and capital expenditure, 1951–76

	1951–2		1956–7		1961–2		1966–7		1971–2		1975–6	
	£m	%	£m	%	£m	%	£m	%	£m	%	£m	%
Current expenditure												
1. Hospital services *less* receipts from patients	268 }	52.7	377 }	57.0	538 }	57.4	797 }	54.5	1,462 }	59.1	3,943 }	70.0
	–4		–5		–6		–9		–13		–23	
2. General services *less* receipts from patients	165	31.9	202	27.3	274	25.1	387	25.3	609	22.2	1,134	18.8
of which (net cost)	–5		–24		–41		–22		–65		–85	
3. Pharmaceutical	53	10.6	–	–	78	8.4	163	11.3	224	9.1	456	8.1
4. Dental	36	7.2	–	–	52	5.6	67	4.6	96	3.9	200	3.6
5. Ophthalmic	10	2.0	–	–	10	1.1	14	1.0	14	0.6	55	1.0
6. General services	48	9.6	–	–	88	9.5	112	7.8	196	8.0	338	6.0
7. Local authority health services	39	7.8	55	8.4	81	8.7	132	9.1	151	6.1	–	–
8. Departmental administration etc	13	2.6	23	3.5	31	3.3	47	3.3	59	2.4	169	3.0
9. Total current expenditure	477	95.2	628	96.1	875	94.4	1,332	92.2	2,203	89.8	5,138	91.8
Capital expenditure												
10. Hospitals	15	3.0	20	3.1	42	4.5	98	6.7	191	7.8	355	6.4
11. Local authority	3	0.6	2	0.3	8	0.9	14	1.0	54	2.2	91	1.6
12. Other	6	1.2	3	0.5	2	0.2	2	0.1	5	0.2	12	0.2
13. Total capital expenditure	24	4.8	25	3.9	52	5.6	113	7.8	250	11.2	458	8.2
14. Total NHS expenditure	501	100.0	653	100.0	927	100.0	1,445	100.0	2,453	100.0	5,596	100.0

Notes: The statistics in lines 1, 7 and 11 were assimilated in a slightly different fashion after 1971–2, and are therefore not strictly comparable.

Sources: Social Trends (1970, 1976); *Annual Abstract of Statistics* (1984).

one million people, or one-thirtieth of the population of working age) could the traditional bureaucratic failings of inefficiency and insensitivity to changing public needs be avoided?
* Given rising public expectations and the boundless possibilities of medical science, could the technical expertise be developed to ensure the optimum allocation of scarce resources?

7.1 THE ESTABLISHMENT OF THE NHS, 1943–51

Both the planning and the early years of the NHS were overshadowed by a permanent sense of crisis. This arose initially from the complex and bitter negotiations between government and the medical profession over the nature of the service, which began in earnest once the Beveridge Report had recommended the establishment of a 'comprehensive health and rehabilitation' service. The negotiations were complex because they had not only to seek the rationalization of existing services (each with its own jealously held traditions) but also to surmount two changes of government and the mutual suspicion of the two main professional negotiating bodies, the British Medical Association (which represented mainly, but not exclusively, general practitioners) and the Royal College of Physicians (whose president, Lord Moran – Churchill's personal doctor – was considered, not least by himself, to represent hospital consultants). The resulting bitterness was epitomized by the rejection in March 1948, just three months before the Appointed Day, of the Labour government's detailed proposals for the NHS by 90 per cent of doctors voting in a BMA membership ballot.

After 1948 the sense of crisis was perpetuated by the inability of the NHS to keep within its budget. The Labour government, already beset by economic difficulties, was accordingly obliged to resort to a series of expedients, the last of which was the introduction in May 1951 of charges for dental and ophthalmic care. This breached the principle of a free health service and provoked Aneurin Bevan (who, as minister of health between 1945 and January 1951, had had prime responsibility for planning the service) to resign from the Cabinet. It was thus the financial difficulties of the NHS which occasioned the split within the Labour Party which was so to damage its chances of re-election in the 1950s, and consequently, its ability directly to shape the development of the welfare state. Might not these successive crises have been handled better to the mutual advantage of the Labour Party and the NHS?

Prewar problems

In retrospect the complexity and bitterness of the negotiations preceding the establishment of the NHS would appear to have been wholly unnecessary. Agreement was virtually universal on the basic principles of reform – the provision of a comprehensive, free and equal service which would provide the 'best possible' care for patients whilst simultaneously safeguarding doctors' clinical freedom.[3] As early as 1920 an authoritative advisory body to the Ministry of Health had established, in the famous Dawson Report, the principle of 'best possible' care. In 1926 the Royal Commission on National Health Insurance had suggested that healthcare should be financed out of general taxation. The public had long been demanding, and the government pressurizing the 'approved' societies to provide, a more comprehensive coverage of both specialist treatment and the insured's dependants. Finally, GPs and consultants alike had become increasingly frustrated by the restrictions placed upon their clinical freedom by, respectively, the commercial interests of the approved societies and the impending bankruptcy of voluntary hospitals. Indeed, with the creation of the Nuffield Provincial Hospital Trust in 1939, there had even been an autonomous move within the voluntary hospital system to confront traditional antagonisms and to pool resources. The one major breach in this consensus concerned the future *financing* of a national health service. Instead of a tax-financed system, the BMA wanted to retain contributory insurance and to restrict its coverage to 90 per cent of the population so that some income could be ensured from private practice.

> Small though it might appear, the reservation of doctors over the future funding of the NHS went to the heart of the conflict between government and the medical profession and explains much of its bitterness. This was because it raised the fundamental question of where power was ultimately to lie within the new service. The doctors feared that, should they become wholly dependent on the state for their income, both their independent status and their clinical freedom would ultimately be jeopardized. This was the explicit fear that had been exposed during the battle over the organization (as opposed to the principles) of the NHS, as it evolved from a utopian ideal in the 1920s through to the Coalition's reconstruction white paper in 1944. It dominated the negotiations thereafter.

The critical *organizational* challenge facing the NHS was the need to provide an administrative framework which could effectively coordinate the three separate services, provided respectively by individual practitioners (GPs, dentists and opticians), hospitals and the local authorities. There was, as will be seen from a review of the interwar health services, a clear and logical solution. However, this was the very one which the medical profession feared most.

During the 1930s the individual practitioner service was dominated by some 30,000 registered *GPs*. Their morale was low on account of both overwork and their perceived inability to keep abreast of rapid medical advance.[4] This was partly their own fault. In contrast to prevailing experience abroad, they mostly worked on their own rather than in group practices, where costs could be shared, rational working hours arranged and medical views exchanged. Consequently, after a lengthy and costly training, they had typically to take out a loan to purchase the goodwill of a practice for about £2000–£3000, which in turn had to be financed from an annual salary that rarely rose above £1600. Capitation fees – the fixed annual fees for panel patients – were kept low by local Insurance Committees, among which the 'approved' societies had a dominant voice; and so GPs had, out of financial necessity, to move from poor areas (where need was greatest) to richer areas (where they could generate more income from private practice). GPs, as in other countries, also feared that their generalist skills were becoming less appreciated and relevant as they were increasingly excluded from both advanced surgery in hospitals and the specialist clinics run by local authorities.

Dentists and *opticians* were equally demoralized. By international comparison there were few well-qualified dentists in Britain; and in any one year, only 7 per cent of those insured received any dental treatment.[5] In ophthalmology 75 per cent of the population had no access to free care, and there were bitter professional disputes between the dispensing opticians in the high street and those providing specialist treatment in hospitals and local authority clinics.

The *hospital service* was similarly divided. There were approximately 2000 local authority hospitals, providing 400,000 beds. Most of these had been inherited from the Poor Law, following the 1929 Local Government Act, and had yet to be fully integrated with the other hospitals run by the local authorities. Almost half the beds were accounted for by 300 large mental hospitals. In contrast there were 1000 voluntary hospitals, most of which were very small, providing some 100,000 beds. A quarter had fewer than 30 beds and only 75 had more than 200. These larger hospitals included the prestigious teaching hospitals where most medical advance was pioneered and where consultants offered their services free – their income coming from private practice elsewhere. In the smaller 'cottage' hospitals GPs undertook minor surgery, often to a very low standard.

The majority of voluntary hospitals were facing severe financial problems in the 1930s. The London teaching hospitals, for example, derived only 34 per cent of their income from their major traditional source of finance, voluntary donations, despite the increasing number of 'flag days' on which medical staff openly solicited money from the public. Government provided only 8 per cent of income, and so the vast bulk had to be raised from the patients themselves either directly (23 per cent) or through subscription schemes (16 per cent).[6] This meant that voluntary hospitals had to turn from their original purpose, the free treatment of the poor, to the care of those who could afford to pay for their treatment. As a consequence the poor, and especially the chronically ill, were obliged to apply for admission to local authority hospitals – which were themselves bedevilled by financial difficulties and acrimonious disputes (especially over financial liability when, for example, a patient's last place of residence fell outside the receiving hospital's catchment area). So complex had the system become by 1939 that a 62-page booklet had to be issued to cover all the eventualities that might arise should wartime evacuees require hospital treatment.

The logical solution to this chaotic and highly inefficient situation, and one favoured at the time by both officials within the Ministry of Health and the Labour Party, was a concentration of responsibility on the third provider of healthcare – *the local authorities*. In the nineteenth century local government had pioneered advances in public health (such as the provision of drainage and supplies of pure water); and after 1900 it had taken the initiative in health education and the curing of disease through the School Medical Service (1906), TB sanatoria (1911), welfare clinics for mothers and children (especially after 1918) and cancer clinics (1939), in addition to the inherited Poor Law hospitals (1929). The gradual concentration of responsibility on local government, therefore, appeared the most natural way to construct a coordinated national health service, which would be both under democratic control and – as with the education service – have an assured source of finance through a combination of local rates and national taxation.

> This concentration of all health provision under local authorities was actively promoted before 1939 by certain progressive Labour local councils, such as the London County Council (LCC). Their ideal was that each neighbourhood should have a 'health centre' to coordinate the 'primary care' provided by individual practitioners, clinics and the public health service; and that from these centres patients requiring more specialist treatment should be referred to the 'secondary' level of district hospitals.

Wartime planning

The principle of concentarting healthcare under local authorities was broadly endorsed by the Coalition government in its 1944 white paper. It proposed that, under the supervision of the Ministry of Health, there should be some 30 to 35 joint regional boards (consisting of councillors coopted from local authorities in the relevant area) to plan both primary and secondary care.[7] They would themselves directly administer the hospitals, whilst individual local authorities would employ under contract the majority of GPs (who would increasingly work in health centres) and discharge their traditional public health functions. Overall coordination of policy would be ensured by the relevant councillors' membership of the joint board. The importance of professional autonomy was also not overlooked. Each tier of government was to have a professional advisory committee. In addition a central medical board, consisting mainly of doctors, would act as the ultimate 'employer' of GPs, overseeing their contracts with local authorities, their geographical distribution and, above all, professional discipline.

The fatal flaw in this otherwise logical plan was that it was perceived, in the short term at least, to be administratively and politically impractical. *Administratively* medical officers of health (the senior doctors employed by local authorities) had, despite their pioneering role in the nineteenth century, become increasingly conservative and there were serious doubts about their ability to provide the requisite local leadership.[8] There were also serious objections to the proposed regional boards. The ideal local authorities, it was agreed, were the county councils, provided they were able to incorporate the independent county boroughs within their boundaries. However, this was impossible because the two types of authority, the one traditionally Conservative and the other increasingly Labour, had a long history of territorial rivalry (see Section 4.4). Joint boards were no effective substitute because they lacked the authority of a directly elected body and would have deprived existing local authorities of control over their existing hospitals – which they were determined to keep. Even more important were the political objections. Doctors were appalled at the prospect of becoming the employees of local government. Consultants had traditionally shunned local authority hospitals with their lack of 'glamorous' responsibilities. GPs throughout the interwar period had been fighting a guerrilla war with local authority clinics over the specialist treatment of patients. Both despised the medical officers of health and were fearful of bureaucratic and political encroachment upon their clinical freedom.[9] The Coalition government was, therefore, forced to retreat hastily from its 1944 proposals.

A final solution?

After Labour's election victory in 1945 it was the prejudices of the medical profession (rather than those of local government) which dominated the negotiations that led eventually to the National Health Service Act of May 1946 and the inauguration of the service in July 1948. To the surprise and dismay of many (including the leaders of the progressive interwar Labour councils) the conclusion of these negotiations was that interwar trends were reversed and local government deprived of all responsibility for hospitals.[10] In its place, 14 regional hospital boards (RHBs), consisting solely of persons appointed by the minister of health, were charged with the planning of the service in England and Wales and the supervision of 380 hospital management committees (HMCs, likewise appointed by the minister of health), which were to be responsible for the day-to-day running of each hospital or group of hospitals. Moreover, the ideal of administrative unity was not attained. RHBs could not fully coordinate hospital policy because, although each region was designed to include at least one major teaching hospital, these hospitals were to remain independent under a separate board of governors. Nor could they coordinate healthcare as a whole. GPs, dentists and opticians remained independent under their executive councils, whilst local authorities retained control over a miscellaneous 'rump' of responsibilities, including vaccination, ambulances and the public health services. Broadly similar structures were agreed for Scotland and Northern Ireland, although some areas of potential conflict were avoided. The five RHBs in Scotland and the Northern Ireland Hospital Authority, for example, were given responsibility from the start for both the teaching hospitals and ambulance services in their area.

This administrative settlement was far from ideal. As later events were to prove, the tripartite division between hospitals, executive committees and local authorities discouraged rather than encouraged coordination; and in the first two services there was the danger that professional self-interest might predominate over democratic accountability. 'Effective decisions in policy', the 1944 white paper had insisted, 'must lie entirely with elected representatives answerable to the people for the decisions they take', but the initial constitution of the NHS was anything but democratic – with the one exception that ultimate power lay with an elected minister.[11] Undue power was also conceded to doctors, especially hospital consultants, and this unbalanced structure had major policy implications. Not only might scarce resources be allocated to those who had power (in particular, hospitals) at the expense of others (such as the preventive health services administered by local government), but other inequalities also became entrenched. Within publicly funded hospitals for instance, private practice or 'pay beds' were permitted (to increase consultants' salaries) and provided a continuing source of political dispute. Despite financial constraints, consultants were also allowed to award themselves permanent merit awards, which in many cases doubled their effective salary. In relation to general practice, the power of the Central Medical Board to direct GPs to under-doctored areas, as recommended in the 1944 white paper, was greatly modified.

The fate of health centres exemplified the imbalance of power between the consumers and producers of healthcare (the 'democratic deficit') within the new organizational structure. Rather than becoming the common focus of all primary care in a given region, they were reduced to an infrequent experiment; and indeed only 18 were built before they became more fashionable in 1964. In other words, patients were expected to seek out professional care. Doctors were not expected to make themselves readily available to patients. [12]

Bevan: hero or villain?

The original administrative structure, therefore, was the genesis of the conflicting reputations of the NHS as a political ideal and as a practical deliverer of healthcare. Yet it is this structure for which the Labour government in general and Bevan in particular were accorded at the time – and have been accorded since – considerable praise. Was, and is, such praise justified?

Neither the challenges facing Bevan nor his undoubted achievement should be minimized. The interwar health services were inefficient and inequitable; and interwar politicians had abjectly failed to reform the structure of local government which otherwise would have provided a natural administrative framework for a democratically controlled national health service. The prestige of the medical profession worldwide was such that it was not only in Britain that there was an undue concentration of power in the hands of hospital consultants. All other countries experienced a similar and usually worse misallocation of resources to the hospital sector be their health services financed essentially by the tax-payer (as in Sweden), by social insurance (as in France and Germany) or by private insurance (as in the USA). Public opinion in Britain also tended to support the doctors in their battle for 'independence' against the government and, perhaps as a consequence of imperfect knowledge, little resentment was expressed at the inconvenience resulting from the tripartite division of healthcare.[13] Despite such pressures, however, Bevan succeeded in removing two of the commercial intrusions into healthcare which had been most resented in the interwar period: the approved societies and the sale of GPs' practices.[14] Uniquely he also abolished the system of contributory health insurance which (despite the acknowledged fact that it was less cost-effective than state provision, see Section 3.2.1) was retained by every other Western country with the partial exception of Sweden. Thereby the *political* ideal of a free and equal service for all was secured.

These undoubted achievements should not, however obscure the fact that Bevan was not the most skilled of negotiators and that he actively promoted some of the key decisions which lay at the root of the NHS's later problems. The negotiations with the medical profession required a considerable degree of tact and self-control. Tact, however, was not one of Bevan's greatest strengths. Having raised hackles, Bevan then often appeared over-ready to make concessions. For instance hospital consultants (the elite within the profession whom the Labour Party might have been expected to favour least) completed the negotiations not only with considerable advances in their income (through assured salaries, merit awards and pay beds) but also greatly increased power (through their appointment to RHBs and HMCs, as well as the independent status of teaching hospitals). Even a militant conservative member of the BMA was amazed, recalling of the early days:

> We assembled at the first meeting expecting that our beautiful profession was to be hung, drawn and quartered. Instead we were reprieved . . . . On one point after another . . . the Minister had accepted what we were demanding before we had the opportunity to ask him for it. We were jubilant and stunned.[15]

Given the well-known divisions within the profession (which might have been better exploited), its interwar financial difficulties and its wartime flirtation with the idea of salaries and health centres (both of which were to become perfectly acceptable in the 1960s), might not a harder bargain have been struck? After all, in the 1940s the medical profession was as much in need of state finance as the NHS was in need of its expertise.

Examples of Bevan's diplomatic lapses are legion. For example, when he finally dropped his initial insistence on a salaried medical profession, he confided publicly that 'there is all the difference in the world between pluck-ing fruit when it is ripe and plucking it when it is green'.[16] This did little to reassure GPs about the future intentions of Labour governments. Similarly, as part of the embattled middle class, doctors were somewhat less than enthusiastic about his description of the Conservative Party, two days before the Appointed Day, as 'lower than vermin'.

In the determination of the NHS's administrative structure, Bevan's lack of previous ministerial and administrative experience would also appear to have been a handicap. It was very much his personal decision that hospitals should be 'nationalized' and their running entrustrusted to doctors. As has been seen, however, such objectives carried with them the dangers that curative might predominate over preventive medicine, and professional self-interest over democratic accountability. Were such dangers to be avoided, a greater specialist expertise and a ready willingness to intervene had to be instilled into officials in the Ministry of Health, who were the ultimate guarantors of democratic control. There is no evidence, however, that Bevan recognized the need for, let alone encouraged, such an initiative. Indeed, in his handling of administrative matters, he appeared to be 'radical in everybody else's ministry except his own'.[17]

Bevan's raw instincts, therefore, may have been invaluable in sustaining the political ideals behind the NHS where more worldly ministers might have compromised, but his lack of administrative – and ultimately political – insight prevented the establishment of an administrative structure through which those ideals could be realized. In a long-term perspective – embracing the growing interwar consensus for a national health service, the spur to greater regionalization and rationalization provided by the wartime Emergency Medical Service (EMS), and the need for a radical administrative overhaul as early as 1974 – it would appear that the 1940s represent an oppor-tunity missed, not seized.[18]

Bevan's strong personal convictions had been forged in South Wales, where the relative absence of well-equipped modern hospitals had denied ordinary people the benefits of rapid medical advance and where commer-cial intrusions into healthcare had been particularly resented. His natural instinct was, therefore, to give priority to the better national distribution of hospitals and the appointment of doctors to positions of administrative importance. 'Doctors', he declared on one notable occasion, 'deserved to participate fully in the administration of their own profession.'[19]

The crisis over charges

The NHS's reputation for efficiency – and with it Bevan's reputation as an administrator – was further tarnished by the battles within Cabinet between 1948 and 1951 over the escalating cost of healthcare. In its first two years the NHS exceeded its budget by almost 40 per cent (see Table 7.2); and thereafter, although expenditure was kept within the estimates, its net overall cost was three times higher than that forecast in the 1946 National Health Service Act. It was, moreover, only contained at this high level by two extreme expedients: the appointment of a senior Cabinet committee in May 1950 to monitor the monthly expenditure of the NHS (a humiliating experience for Bevan as the 'responsible' minister) and the introduction of charges a year later.[20]

The initial high cost of the NHS was to an extent justified. It was caused principally by the need to relieve the backlog of interwar ill-health and to make good the chronic underfunding of the health services. Thus by 1953 26.1 million pairs of glasses and six million sets of false teeth had had to be provided. In addition a series of independent review boards had awarded pay rises well above the rate of inflation.[21] Such expenditure was exceptional and unlikely to recur. A steep rise in the cost of medicine posed a more permanent problem but, given the increased efficacy of drugs, this too could be justified.

What could not be justified was the Ministry of Health's inability to predict (despite much outside advice) the cost of exceptional short-term need and to devise a sound financial and administrative structure for future expenditure decisions. The declared policy of 'universalizing the best' provided no effective criteria for the allocation of scarce resources (given that the possibilities of medical science and public expectations were boundless). Similarly the effective devolution of power over expenditure to doctors (either in GPs' surgeries, through the prescription of drugs and referral to hospitals, or on RHBs) was inherently dangerous since it defied the first principle of public finance, that those who benefit from spending tax-payers' money should also share the unpopularity of raising it.

Various solutions to these problems were considered by the Cabinet committee on the NHS. In order to restore fiscal responsibility, for example, it was suggested that RHBs should be abolished (with the Ministry of Health assuming their planning and supervisory role) and that those responsible for maintaining financial discipline on the HMCs should be given 'protected' status so that they could be dismissed only with the express approval of the minister. More direct economies were also suggested, such as the compilation of a list of proscribed drugs, the moderation of consultants' merit awards and, above all, the introduction of charges. To each of these suggestions Bevan at times appeared to give his support. He admitted for instance that the RHBs (which he had just established) were an administrative anomaly in that 'it was inherently impossible to ensure a proper implementation of national policy at the periphery when that policy is mediated by fourteen separate regional bodies, all naturally watchful of their prestige and their independence'. Most surprisingly he accepted in 1949 the need for prescription charges, not so

Table 7.2 Parliamentary estimates for the NHS, 1948–52 (£m)

| | 1948/9 (9 months) | | | 1949–50 | | | 1950–1 | | 1951–2 | |
	Original	Final	Excess	Original	Final	Excess	Original	Final	Original	Final
Gross total	198.4	275.9	77.5	352.3	449.2	96.9	464.5	465.0	469.1	470.6
Appropriation in aid	48.7	67.6	–	92.6	90.7	–	71.6	72.1	71.0	71.0
Net total	149.7	208.3	58.6	259.7	358.5	98.8	392.9	392.9	398.1	399.5

Note: Figures for Great Britain.
Source: C. Webster, *The Health Services since the War*, vol. 1 (1988) p. 136.

much to raise revenue but to prevent abuse – to moderate, in his words, the 'ceaseless cascades of medicine pouring down people's throats'.[22]

Such apparent concessions, however, he later dismissed as tactical manoeuvres to offset more immediate threats to health expenditure; and once these threats had diminished, he reverted to a robust defence both of the principle of a free service and professional autonomy. Indeed he even went further, actively justifying high spending as a sign of the success and popularity of the NHS. 'The cost of the health service', he argued in 1950, 'not only will, but ought to increase'; and rather than welcoming the eventual containment of expenditure within its cash limit, he demanded that any surplus should be spent immediately.[23] Such bravura might have won him the admiration of his civil servants, who were impressed by the resources he acquired for the NHS, but it only served to exasperate his Cabinet colleagues who, in deference to the principle of collective responsibility, continued to contain their own expenditure within agreed budgets.

The final break between Bevan and the Cabinet occurred over the decision in the April 1951 budget to introduce charges for dental and ophthalmic care. The principles behind the dispute were clear-cut. Gaitskell had been frustrated by a series of defeats at the Cabinet committee on the NHS for proposals to limit health expenditure and thereby release money for other areas of welfare policy, such as retirement pensions, which he regarded as of equal importance. Charges for ophthalmic and dental care, he argued, were politically acceptable because they would reduce demand only in 'non-essential' areas of healthcare and would not lay the government open to the accusation (as would prescription charges) of removing a free service which had been available to the poor since 1911. They would also raise some revenue for the NHS. Above all they would symbolize the ability of Cabinet to take hard decisions on the allocation of scarce resources and to determine priorities within the social services. In reply Bevan denied the time was right for the betrayal of so important a principle as a free health service. The immediate need to control social expenditure, he claimed, arose from the need to finance the rearmament programme for the Korean War and he was confident that from the overall cost of that programme (£1250 million) savings could be made of some £13 million, the estimated revenue to be raised from charges in their first year. Charges were therefore financially unnecessary, whilst the political damage to the Labour government would be immense. To abandon the principle of a free health service would be 'a shock to their supporters in the country and a grave disappointment to socialist opinion throughout the world'.[24] The Conservative Party would also take the Labour government's action as a precedent to justify the further erosion of the NHS by the introduction of prescription charges.

There was considerable justice in both Bevan's and Gaitskell's case. Bevan was correct, in the short term, to predict that the rearmament budget would not be fully spent and that the Conservatives would introduce further charges. Gaitskell was equally correct, for the longer term, to insist that the resources available to the social services in general and the NHS in particular were limited and that priorities had to be determined. The tragedy was that reconcliation could not be reached and that Gaitskell's victory led to no constructive attempt by the Treasury to determine the criteria on which resources should be allocated to and within the NHS. All his victory ultimately signified was the end of the special treatment that the NHS had enjoyed since 1948.

Both the intensity and the resolution of the dispute within the Labour cabinet over charges illustrate how welfare policy is influenced and ultimately determined by wider political forces (see introduction to Chapter 4). The dispute was exacerbated by the wider battle Bevan was fighting over the speed at which the government should move towards 'socialism' (see Section 4.3) and his personal anger at being overlooked for higher office (and especially the chancellorship of the exchequer, which went in October 1950 to Gaitskell, some nine years his junior with 16 years' less experience in the House of Commons). Its resolution was eventually determined not so much by principle as by circumstance and personality. Attlee was ill during the budget discussions and in the absence of his skilled chairmanship the long-standing exasperation of Bevan's colleagues began to boil over, especially when he indulged both publicly and privately in displays of personal pique against Gaitskell.[25] He became virtually isolated and was able to secure only the resignation of one Cabinet colleague and three votes in the House of Commons for what he portrayed as an attack not only on the NHS but on the welfare state as a whole. In contrast Gaitskell remained relatively calm and conciliatory and, by an increase in retirement pensions, demonstrated that there was to be no fundamental attack on welfare expenditure.[26]

Complications at birth

The establishment of the NHS was, for so idealistic an institution, remarkably unaltruistic.[27] Its planning was taken by the medical profession as the opportunity to advance its own self-interest, whilst its early development was the occasion for bitter infighting within the Labour Cabinet. Its first years were dominated by the charismatic personality of Bevan, and to him must go the credit for both the actual establishment of the service and the winning for it of the lion's share of available resources. In no other Western country were the whole population and the full range of medical need (Beveridge's principles of universalism and comprehensiveness) so quickly realized by a *free* service. Even in the 'advanced' social democratic welfare state of Sweden, where continuing control by local government offered a degree of direct democratic accountability, charges were – and remain – payable not just for medicine but also for hospital stays and visits to GPs; and until 1970 they were sufficiently high to deter the poor from seeking treatment. Bevan's legacy, however was not wholly benevolent. His eventual choice of administrative structure impeded the development of a more cost-effective and equitably distributed service: its tripartite division, the devolution of power to the medical profession and, above all, the failure to develop specialist managerial skills at the centre discouraged rather than encouraged the greater coordination and efficiency that was the principal justification for nationalization. The policy of 'universalizing the best' encouraged high hopes which could only lead to demoralization when, inevitably, they were not met. Finally, the initial overspending of the budget permanently labelled the NHS – whatever the contradictory finding of the Guillebaud Report in 1956 – with a reputation for extravagance. Bevan's ultimate legacy was, therefore, an administratively flawed service which, despite its close public identification with the welfare state, was to be denied direct representation in Cabinet for the next 11 years.

7.2 CONSOLIDATION AND RECONSTRUCTION, 1951–74

After the traumas of its establishment, the NHS experienced a decade of consolidation before its structure, if not its ideal, came under increasing attack. The period of consolidation was epitomized by the content of, and the reaction to, the report of the Guillebaud Committee which had been appointed in 1953 to examine 'the present and prospective cost of the NHS'. To the exasperation of those who had commissioned it, it concluded that there was – and had been – no 'widespread extravagance' in the NHS and that accordingly there was no need for any major reorganization. 'No fundamental changes recommended', proclaimed the Ministry of Health press release, 'Service needs time to settle down'.[28] By 1962 that time had evidently passed. The Conservative government drafted an ambitious ten-year plan to modernize the hospital service; and the medical profession itself, in the Porritt Report, recommended the full integration of the three separate services within the NHS. The former was a major attempt from the centre to determine priorities and to allocate resources within the service, whilst the latter was the first stage in a lengthy campaign which was to culminate (amidst escalating pressure from both within and outside the NHS) in its wholesale reorganization.

The 1956 Guillebaud report

The Guillebaud Report has been accorded a strangely mixed reception. To some it has appeared an 'impressive document', to others a 'bluebook full of whitewash'.[29] These different judgements arise from the competing criteria used. The first is based on the Report's pioneering achievement in relating health expenditure to inflation and economic growth, so that its real and relative cost could be properly established – an achievement that depended on the work of two rather incongruous research officers for an intended Conservative cost-cutting exercise, Abel-Smith and Titmuss. As a result of their research, the Report could authoritatively dispel the myth that the real cost of healthcare had escalated since 1948 and would escalate further owing to the 'ageing' of the population. Rather, it concluded, NHS expenditure per head had been virtually static between 1948 and 1954, and in relative terms had actually fallen from 3.75 per cent to 3.25 per cent of GNP; capital expenditure on hospitals, far from being extravagant, had fallen dangerously to only 33 per cent of prewar levels; and the additional health costs incurred by an ageing population could easily be accommodated by the expected rise in economic growth. Consequently, the Report dismissed demands for radical reorganization. There was, it admitted, some administrative inefficiency, arising in particular from the tripartite division of the NHS, but such inefficiency had been even greater before 1948 and was inherent in any large organization. What was required was not another administrative upheaval, but time for attitudes to change. More, rather than less, expenditure was needed.

Such conclusions naturally appalled the Treasury (which had been anticipating major savings) and in retrospect they have been criticized as overcomplacent. After the imposition of a ceiling on NHS expenditure and the introduction of charges, it is argued, financial control might at last have become 'sufficient'. Was it, however, 'efficient'? Did it, in other words, ensure full value for the very large sums of money devoted to healthcare? In this respect the Report has been attacked on three main grounds. First, on the critical issue of how demand should be regulated in a 'free' service, the Report dismissed Bevan's implicit assumption that there was an objective standard of 'adequacy', but it offered little guidance on how governments should determine the percentage of GNP to be allocated to healthcare. Second, although the Report encouraged the building of homes for the elderly (as an alternative to hospital care) and conservation in dentistry (including fluoridization), it largely accepted the medical profession's bias towards hospitals and curative medicine. Indeed it maintained that 'those who have criticised the Health Service for spending far too much on disease and far too little on prevention have tended to overstate their case'.[30] Finally, it rejected most of the expedients for raising additional income (which were to remain remarkably constant between the 1940s and the 1980s): the raising of existing charges; the introduction of a hospital boarding charge; the extension of pay beds; and the exclusion from the NHS of the 'non-central' ophthalmic and dental services. In fact it recommended the abolition of the Labour government charges on ophthalmic and dental care on the grounds that they were seriously discouraging treatment – although it conversely argued that the prescription charge, introduced by the Conservatives, had no such deterrent effect. Given such negative advice it is hardly surprising that the committee's critics have concluded that it was mesmerized by the *status quo*.

Preventive medicine

Any reforms which Conservative governments might have introduced in the 1950s were first delayed by the deliberations of the Guillebaud Committee and then discouraged by its recommendations. Nevertheless, serious consideration was given to the redeployment of resources from curative to preventive medicine; but it foundered not just on the vested interests of hospital consultants but also, more surprisingly, on those of Treasury officials. They recognized that preventive medicine represented the best value for money within healthcare, but their principal concern was not the cost-effectiveness but the control of public expenditure. This required that new expenditure must be balanced by cuts elsewhere in the health budget (which, owing to Bevan's reforms, consultants had the power to resist) and that increased grants should not be made to local authorities (which the Treasury could not directly control).

A return to social insurance?

A second potential reform, which was initially a centrepiece of the Conservatives' drive for an 'opportunity' as opposed to a 'welfare' state, was a return to the principle that the NHS should be fully funded through contributory insurance. The proposal was strongly supported by Macmillan as prime minister. Beveridge had anticipated that insurance contributions would provide one-third of the costs of the NHS and it was a popular misconception that they covered the full cost. By 1956, however, they in fact contributed only 6.4 per cent; and it was felt that a move to total funding by insurance would not only enable income tax to be reduced (thereby increasing work incentive) but also instil into both doctors and patients a new sense of responsibility. If, as in social security, a direct link could be established between contributions and benefit, doctors would be more restrained in their prescriptions and patients in their demands. Thus an effective antidote would have been established to the policy of 'universalizing the best'.[31]

There were, however, major practical drawbacks to such a policy. As Beveridge himself had recognized, the cost of a comprehensive health service was so great that it could not be financed by a flat-rate insurance scheme based on what the poorest contributor could afford. Moreover, in the late 1950s insurance contributions were already being raised to offset the cost of old age pensions (which were seen as an ever greater threat to government solvency) and so there was a very real problem of non-compliance. Finally, if some individuals failed to pay their premiums, could they really be denied medical care? The proposal was therefore reluctantly dropped although (as Table 7.3 illustrates) the relative contribution of the Insurance Fund to the NHS in the 1960s did significantly increase.

The 1962 Hospital Plan

The 1960s, in the wake of the Plowden Report, were characterized by a greater confidence in economic planning (see Section 5.2); and this led within healthcare to the drafting and extensive promotion of an overtly ambitious plan to modernize the hospital system. As has been seen, the NHS inherited (largely from the Poor Law and the increasingly bankrupt voluntary sector) an ill-assorted, ill-equipped and ill-distributed collection of hospitals, and capital

Table 7.3   NHS sources of finance, 1950/1–1974/5 (%)

Financial year	Taxation	Insurance	Charges
1950–1	87.6	9.4	0.7
1952–3	87.6	8.0	4.0
1954–5	86.9	7.9	5.0
1956–7	88.7	6.4	4.7
1958–9	80.3	14.4	5.0
1960–1	81.9	13.3	4.5
1962–3	77.1	17.2	5.5
1964–5	79.6	15.0	5.1
1966–7	84.8	12.4	2.4
1968–9	84.8	11.8	3.1
1970–1	85.8	10.8	3.2
1972–3	87.0	9.0	3.6
1974–5	91.3	5.7	2.6

Note: Figures exclude local authority health expenditure.
Source: A. Leathard, *Health Care Provision* (1990) p. 38.

expenditure upon them during the 1950s had been well below the minimum recommended by the Guillebaud Committee. The hospital service therefore presented the ideal challenge for both the planned expansion of welfare expenditure (as advocated by Plowden) and a Ministry of Health revitalized by the simultaneous appointment in 1960 of a new minister (Powell), a new permanent secretary (Sir Bruce Fraser) and a new chief medical officer (Sir George Godber).[32] The last, as a doctor committed to the more equal distribution of healthcare, brought to the Ministry the expert drive that had characterized Whitehall's wartime success. The planning credentials of Powell (who had resigned in 1958 with Thorneycroft over excessive welfare expenditure) and Fraser (the Treasury official formerly responsible for containing health expenditure) were, however, less apparent.

Both nevertheless played a constructive part in the development of the Hospital Plan. The Plan's overriding object was to guarantee access for both the medical profession and the public to the most modern and comprehensive facilities. Accordingly 1250 hospitals were to be closed and, at the cost of £500 million, 360 extended and 90 new ones built to provide a national network of 600- to 800-bed district general hospitals, each serving a catchment area of between 100,000 and 150,000 people. It was the role of Powell to persuade each RHB to draft an appropriate plan for its area and to determine the principles on which it should be integrated into a national plan. Fraser's role was to persuade the Treasury that, through a more concentrated and capital-intensive service, better medical care could be provided at a relatively low cost.

One critical deal that they did strike was a change in the balance between current and capital expenditure, which resulted in the relatively unpopular decision of the Conservatives in 1961 to raise health charges considerably and of Labour in 1968 to reintroduce prescription charges only four years after abolishing them.

Despite a rise in capital expenditure on hospitals from 3.1 per cent to 7.8 per cent of the health budget (see Table 7.1), however, neither the promised savings nor indeed the full complement of district general hospitals had been achieved by the time of the Plan's abandonment in 1973. Was the Plan there-fore, as the New Right would assume, a clear example of 'government fail-ure'? This has certainly been the conventional conclusion. 'A command-and-control bureaucracy', it has been agreed, 'moved with sloth-like speed to produce a set of half-built, cumbersome and inflexible hospitals which the nation could not afford'.[33] Such a conclusion is somewhat exager-rated. The Plan did provide a long-term political commitment which insu-lated the much-needed modernization of the hospital system from the more severe public expenditure cut backs in 1960s. New hospitals were built and a modest redistribution of resources achieved. Unquestionably, however, expectations and faith in centralized planning were disappointed.

The reasons for disappointment were many. As Plowden's critics had predicted, the 'rationality' of long-term building programmes was disrupted – albeit not halted before 1973 – by short-term expenditure cuts (necessitated by successive economic crises) and by rising inflation. As Plowden himself had feared, there was also an absence of the requisite sense of political and public responsibility. Despite Powell's reputation for integrity, the Plan was knowingly based on highly questionable assumptions. The aggregate sum of £500m, for example, was derived not from any objective calculation of need but from an estimate of the resources likely to be available; and the promise that capital investment would reduce current expenditure was dismissed by the Treasury (quite correctly in the event) as 'guff'. Indeed the whole exercise might be dimissed as a cynical charade as the extra annual revenue raised by charges (£66m) exceeded the projected 'increase' in capital expenditure (£50m).[34] For its part, the medical profession provided little constructive guidance to the planners on how to meet their clinical needs. For its own convenience, but regardless of the potential cost for patients (in travel time) and the tax-payer, ever larger hospitals were typically demanded.

The inherent limitations of centralized, technocratic planning were also exposed. Inevitably there were public protests at the closure of local hospitals, thereby contradicting Bevan's belief that it was better to be 'kept alive in the efficient if cold altruism of a large hospital than expire in a gush of warm sympathy in a small one'. As one outraged protester insisted:

> The ideological centralization proposed in the Hospital Plan is about as realistic as would be a plan to scrap all the ships in the fleet except the aircraft carriers, and about as moral as would be a plan to close all the parish churches on the grounds that the work done in them could be more efficiently organized in cathedrals. [35]

However planning also failed because, as Hayek had predicted (see Section 2.2.3), it was dependent on imperfect knowledge. The Plan was an aggregation of proposals put forward by RHBs in unseemly haste and *inter alia* without any clear understanding of future population distribution or agreement on planning norms. Amongst the latter was the ratio of beds to population, although its utility was not uncontroversial. It was, agreed some doctors, a 'useful tool . . . rather like giving a blind man a stick – it may help him even though it won't improve his sight'. In any case, it was arbitarily reduced from the ideal of seven acute beds per 1000 patients (as defined in 1948) to 3.3.[36] As a result of such improvisation, the Ministry's deputy secretary could but conclude that the Plan 'instead of being founded on calculation, reason, logic and mathematical projection . . . rest[ed] on no ascertained facts whatever'. Moreover, little serious forethought was given to the capacity of the construction industry or to the availability of appropriate sites, let alone to the standardization of hospital design. Hence hospital construction did not repeat the success of the 1950s school-building programme. Rather it resulted in the bankruptcy of many contractors and both a slowness of completion and a poor quality of finish that had few international parallels. The Hospital Plan, in short, did little to advance faith in centralized planning

> The success of the Hospital Plan was also dependent on the implementation of a complementary programme, outlined in the 1963 and 1966 white papers *Health and Welfare: the development of community care*, which was designed to reduce pressure on district general hospitals by providing alternative accommodation for the elderly, the mentally handicapped and the convalescent. By 1972 it was intended that £200 million would have been spent on the building of 1000 new residential homes and 1000 new training centres for the mentally and physically handicapped, and that there would have been an increase of 45 per cent in local authority staff (such as health visitors) to provide care for people in their own homes. As with the Hospital Plan, however, achievement fell far short of these objectives, and consequently many patients had to remain in the district general hospitals, where their treatment was not only more expensive but also less effective.

The 1974 reorganization

The conclusion drawn by government from the experiences of the 1960s was not that centralized planning was defective but rather that, in the light of the failed community care programme, greater unification and centralization were needed. Community care was the responsibility of local government which, given its independent financial and electoral base, could not be easily brought into line. Accordingly one of the principal objectives of the major reorganization of the NHS which was finally implemented in 1974 was the integration of the remaining local government health services into the NHS.

This reorganization has been deemed an even more unqualified failure. Indeed it can hardly be judged otherwise. It had to be severely modified as early as 1982 and so survived unscathed for an even shorter period than Bevan's own reforms, which it was designed to replace.

The underlying pressure for reform came from two main sources – the medical profession and the Ministry of Health. The former was dissatisfied with a tripartite division of healthcare that not only filled highly capitalized hospitals with inappropriate, long-stay patients but also discouraged the joint development of preventive and aftercare services which GPs (on the retirement of their interwar cadre) and local authorities were now increasingly ready to provide. The Ministry of Health desired, above all, clearer lines of management communication. Accordingly, in the initial restructuring plan, it was proposed that under the Ministry there should be some 40–45 area health authorities (AHAs) each responsible for the *full* range of healthcare within a given locality. They should also be coterminous with the major local authorities, which the Royal Commission on Local Government was expected to recommend (see Section 4.4), because it was recognized that closer coordination with social workers was necessary if many of the underlying problems giving rise to ill-health and disrupting convalescence were to be resolved. It was even hoped that by these means healthcare could be returned to the control of local government and thus direct democratic accountability.[37]

By 1974, however, this simple structure had been changed beyond recognition. The AHAs had been adjudged too small for planning purposes and too large for the detailed implementation of policy. The Royal Commission on Local Government had also recommended smaller local government units than anticipated. Consequently, the final plan for England and Wales proposed 90 AHAs which were to be coterminous with the new local government units responsible for social work. Above them, responsible for planning, were to be 14 regional health authorities (RHAs, coterminous with the old RHBs), and beneath them, responsible for the actual implementation of policy, a further 200 district management teams, each shadowed by a community health council to give expression to public opinion. Medical care was no longer to be unified because the executive committees for GPs, dentists and opticians (renamed family practitioner committees) were excluded from the remit of the AHAs, and managerial lines of communication were no longer to be clear because membership of the various authorities was based not purely on managerial but also on representative criteria. Members of the AHAs for example were to be drawn in equal proportion from the nominees of local government, the medical profession and the state. The overriding objective of this restructuring was identified as the 'maximum delegation downwards, matched by accountability upwards', but in fact what was created was a Byzantine structure in which there were too many tiers of administration and in which senior executive officials were responsible to authorities which might include among their members one of their subordinates.[38] 'An attempt to please everyone', as Klein has concluded, 'satisfied no one.' It was a disaster.

7.3 THE DELIVERY OF HEALTHCARE

Neither the pragmatism of the 1950s nor the centralized planning of the 1960s could rapidly make good the defects in either individual services or the overall structure of the NHS, inherited respectively from the interwar years and the 1940s.

- How did this failure adversely affect those working within the service?
- How did it affect those who received treatment?

The producers of healthcare

In a profession notorious for understaffing and low pay, all those within the service unquestionably benefited from state control. Between 1948 and 1973 staff costs rose from 60 to 70 per cent of an expanding budget, and the number of staff rose to almost one million. The improvement in morale that should have resulted from these advances was, however, dissipated by the unevenness of pay awards, the disappointment of expectations (built in part upon the unrealistic hopes of the 1940s) and bad management. The formidable number of enquiries into the pay, training and conditions of work of not only consultants, GPs, dentists, doctors and nurses but also administrators and ancillary staff reflected both the size and the historical complexity of the problems facing each branch of the profession – and the continuing inability of the NHS managers to resolve them.[39] As a result militancy grew. In the mid-1960s GPs threatened to withdraw from the service (only to be appeased by the granting of a 'GPs' charter'); in 1966 junior hospital doctors formed their own association; following a pay freeze in 1962 nurses grew increasingly united and defied tradition to mount an aggressive campaign in 1969 to improve their conditions; and in 1973 ancillary workers (whom trade unions had only started to organize seriously in the late 1960s) held their first national strike. The junior hospital doctors and then the consultants threatened similar action two years later. There was thus little of the altruism which Titmuss had presumed would be fostered by the welfare state in general and the NHS in particular.

A good illustration of the mixed impact of the NHS upon its workforce is the experience of GPs, whom Bevan rather belatedly recognized as 'the most important' people within the service.[40] British GPs retained their unique status after 1948, neither developing particular specialisms nor undertaking more hospital work as did their European and American counterparts respectively. Exclusion from specialist work was in part a result of the social prejudice of hospital consultants and the increasing sophistication of surgery; but it also reflected the fact that after 1911 the capitation fee paid by the state enabled doctors in Britain, in contrast to those abroad, to earn a living from general practice. However, the GPs' insistence in 1948 on the continuation of capitation fees – to the exclusion of salaries – had some major disadvantages: a flat fee for each patient on their list provided no reward for the good care of patients, the responsible prescription of drugs or the purchase of modern equipment.

Accordingly GPs found themselves in an increasingly disadvantageous position. Denied their former right to sell the goodwill of their practices upon retirement, and with little private practice, they enjoyed few market incentives. On the other hand, without a clear salary structure they were denied the incentives of promotion and merit awards which hospital doctors enjoyed after 1948. Cut off from the glamorous world of hospitals (upon which the media concentrated) and with inflation gradually eroding the value of the generous Danckwerts award of 1950 (which, at the cost of £40 million, far exceeded the value of any economy achieved by the Conservative government), GPs felt increasingly isolated and demoralized in the 1950s.

This demoralization was countered by the 1960 Pilkington pay award, the institution of an annual pay review and, above all, by the 1965 GPs' charter which, through the provision of cheap loans and a basic salary to underpin capitation fees, encouraged the modernization of surgeries and offered some reward for initiative. As GPs gradually abandoned their initial hostility towards health centres, there also opened up for them the possibility of a constructive new role, not as junior hospital consultants (which they had been in danger of becoming in the 1930s) but as senior social workers (at the head of a team of district nurses, health visitors and midwives) promoting 'community' or 'positive' medicine.[41] Thus from a base in 1948, when they had at least secured their historical objectives of minimum financial security and clinical freedom, they had the chance to rebridge the gulf between curative and preventive medicine and to establish, as the unique hallmark of the British NHS, the provision of healthcare by doctors alive not only to their patients' medical but also to their social needs. That GPs were unable fully to rise to this challenge was another of the missed opportunities of the 1960s.

> The nursing profession provides a further example of a lost opportunity both for the NHS and for the creation of a satisfying career for women. Growing in number to some 300,000 by the early 1970s, nursing offered both the means of ensuring the cost-effective delivery of services within hospitals and a challenging career for women (and from the 1960s to an increasing number of men).[42] Advances in medical science required a specialist elite who could administer an increasingly complex organization and mix of treatments. They required also a body of trained carers who, on the consultants' behalf, could monitor patients' progress. The consequent opportunity to restructure the profession had been identified during the war. It was not taken. In part this was the fault of male consultants, jealous of their power, and of short-sighted government economies. The major blame must rest, however, with the nurses' national and local leaders who – in contrast to evolving practice abroad – continued to favour 'character' and discipline over training and flexible work patterns. Serious recruitment problems, which increased immigration did not solve, and high wastage
>
> →

rates ensued. Undeniably there were some advances. Following the 1949 Nurses Act, for instance, the pay, hours and conditions of work were stan- dardized and improved. The 1966 Salmon and the 1972 Briggs Reports also pointed the way forward to greater administrative responsibility and better education for nurses. Such advances were cloaked, however, by frustration and demoralization which boiled over into a first display of militancy in 1969.

The consumers of healthcare

Like the conditions of those working within the service, the general standard of health also improved between the 1940s and the 1970s.[43] In England and Wales the death rate, for example, declined by 16 per cent (if the changing age structure of the population is taken into account); life expectancy at birth increased from 66.4 to 69.6 years for men and 71.5 to 76 years for women; and infant mortality between 1940 and 1975 fell from 56 to 16 per 1000 live births. Illness (morbidity), as measured by absence from work, increased rather than decreased (as Beveridge had assumed), although this might simply have reflected changing attitudes to health and to work once full employment had been achieved. Most of the major killer diseases also declined, although they were then replaced by others, such as lung cancer and heart disease, which arose either from an unhealthy life-style or old age.[44]

Amidst the general improvement, however, there were two significant grounds for concern. First, by international standards Britain's progress was slow. For example infant mortality (although decreasing) was relatively high and becoming even higher in relation to countries such as the Nertherlands, which did not have a national health service. Second, despite the more equi- table geographical distribution of consultants and GPs at least until the 1960s, there was little advance towards the greater equality of health standards between regions or between social classes. This had been one of the principal objectives of the NHS. It has been estimated, for example, that in 1970 the chances of a child of an unskilled worker (Registrar General's Class 5) dying within one month and one year of birth were, respectively, twice and over three times as high as a child of a professional worker (Registrar General's Class 1). Moreover, people in Class 5 were in general two and a half times more likely than people in Class 1 to die before retirement age – reflecting not a decline but a growing disparity in mortality rates between the classes.

Not all the blame for these disappointing trends should be placed on the NHS. The poor international comparisons can be explained in part by Britain's relatively low economic growth rate whilst increasing inequality also reflected conservative attitudes towards diet and exercise. Even in relation to diet and exercise, however, the NHS must shoulder some blame because of its failure to promote a more effective health education policy. Indeed, histori- cally the most effective health education programmes had been provided by local authorities (especially through their mother and baby clinics); and this was, of course, the very area of health which became demoralized and suffered most from the postwar diversion of resources into hospitals.

Arguably, however, the most disadvantaged group of NHS patients was the mentally ill. It was the intention of successive governments to capitalize on new drugs (such as phenothiazine) to control mental illness and consequently to release patients from the large Victorian asylums, where at best care rather than a cure was provided. This was the explicit purpose behind the 1959 Mental Health Act and one of Powell's principal objectives in the 1962 Hospital Plan.[45] However, owing to the slow provision of residential and training centres under the community care programme, the release of patients was delayed. Then, after the 1967 Ely Hospital (Cardiff) scandal over the maltreatment of patients, a series of abuses was exposed in other mental hospitals. The mentally ill represented exactly the type of (largely) inarticulate patient for whom the NHS should have been able to cater far better than the market, and it is to the personal credit of successive ministers (most notably Powell, Crossman and Joseph) that a problem long hidden from public view and carrying no obvious electoral advantage should have been brought into the open. Their best efforts were, however, frustrated by a general lack of interest within the medical profession, obstruction from their civil servants and the conservatism of public opinion. The medical profession was attracted towards more glamorous responsibilities whilst, to stimulate greater official and public concern, governments had to subsidize pressure groups such as MIND to expose the shortcomings of their own hospitals. This strategy well represents the irrationality into which professional vested interests, Bevan's paternalistic administrative structure and poorly informed public opinion had plunged the NHS by 1974.

Women, having been largely excluded from national health insurance in the 1930s, were among the major beneficiaries of the NHS. However, as argued in Section 2.3.3, there were surreptitious ways in which, both as workers within the service and as patients, they were disadvantaged. The decline in the number of maternity clinics run by local authorities was one example of an actual decline in service. More significantly, between the mid-1940s and the 1970s childbirth within hospital rose from approximately 50 to 96 per cent of all births. This had not been the intention of government. Rather it was the consequence of the determination of hospital consultants to wrest responsibility from GPs whom (with some justice) they regarded as ill-trained; and initially mothers themselves appeared to favour hospital deliveries. However, when housing conditions improved and mothers' attitudes changed, a policy designed to help women physically became one which could damage them psychologically; and its retention smacked of an insensitive paternalism which also discouraged open parental access to children in hospitals and husbands' attendance at births. The lack of resources assigned to family planning and abortion, after state provision of both was legalized in 1968, also reflected the low priority accorded to health services required exclusively by women.

7.4 CONCLUSION

'A free health service', Bevan proclaimed after his resignation, 'is a triumphant example of the superiority of collective action and public initiative applied to a segment of society where commercial principles are seen at their worst.'[46] In interwar Britain commercial principles had indeed intruded into healthcare and the results had left much to be desired. Many present-day economists would also agree that, in theory at least, state provision of healthcare is more efficient than either private or social insurance (see Section 3.2.1). The establishment of the NHS in 1948, therefore, certainly provided an opportunity to demonstrate the superiority of collective action and public initiative.

This opportunity was not fully seized. The NHS did admittedly establish in Britain, far sooner than in any other country, a universal, comprehensive and relatively free system of healthcare. It also succeeded in retaining the affection of the public. It failed, however, to resolve two fundamental administrative and political challenges which were critical to its future success. In the absence of a suitable system of local government, hospitals had to be nationalized; and nationalization required the development of both an organizational structure to integrate hospitals with the other health services and new administrative skills within Whitehall. In the inevitable absence of sufficient resources to satisfy all medical demands, clear criteria had also to be developed to determine priorities and to ensure the efficient allocation of scarce resources. The NHS, as originally designed by Bevan, was unable to rise to these challenges. As the medical profession had itself come to recognize in 1962, the tripartite system discouraged rather than encouraged cooperation and only in the 1960s did the Ministry of Health start seriously to develop the skills by which the relative merits of centralized planning (as opposed to those of the market and local initiative) could be truly tested. The policy of 'universalizing the best' was also retained in order to maintain consensus, long after it had been exposed as essentially meaningless. Sufficient resources only existed to provide either the best in a given area (be that geographical or medical) or to 'universalize the adequate'.

Given its benighted legacy (in terms of a backlog of ill-health, entrenched professional prejudice and dilapidated facilities) it is perhaps unsurprising that the NHS was not immediately successful. However, its difficulties were increased rather than decreased by certain early developments. For example the altruism latent in certain sections of the medical profession, which might have provided the bridgehead for a more enlightened service, was dissipated by the bitter negotiations between the Labour government and the medical profession. The genuine political will that existed in the 1950s to improve preventive medicine and the care of the mentally ill was frustrated by the institutional power earlier conceded to hospital consultants. 'A vested interest in denigration' had also developed amongst those working within the service (despite their unquestionably improved conditions) as a result of the exaggerated hopes excited in the 1940s. In the absence of any market criteria, the disappointment of these hopes was blamed not on a genuine lack of resources but on the perfidy of politicians and the incompetence of senior administrators.[47] By the time a concerted effort was made to revitalize the service in the 1960s, not only were the techniques of centralized planning still seriously underdeveloped but the economic and the cultural climates had also become far less favourable (see Sections 4.4 and 4.5). Other countries, whose more selective services often offered higher standards of treatment, appeared better able to adapt and erode the NHS's comparative advantage. Medicare and Medicaid were introduced in the USA, for example, in 1965; the range of people and services covered by social insurance in Germany was significantly extended; and, as has been seen, charges in Sweden were greatly reduced in 1970.

Many theoretical reasons have been advanced for the relative failure of the NHS (see Sections 2.2 and 2.3). From a pluralist perspective, however, what is outstanding is the close identification of the NHS with the welfare state as a whole. To contemporaries the two institutions often appeared synonymous. To the historian the inability of the NHS to develop the requisite administrative structures, to forge a firmer professional commitment and to nurture informed public support equally mirrors the larger failure of the welfare state effectively to respond to the new positive responsibilities placed upon government after the Second World War. As a consequence, confidence in both the NHS and the welfare state was not reinforced by a series of proven successes but undermined by a series of perceived failures.

7.5 FURTHER READING

The NHS is well served by introductory texts. Among the best are R. Klein, *The New Politics of the NHS* (1995); and B. Watkin, *The National Health Service: the first phase, 1948–74 and after* (1978). Both contain good bibliographies, as does the broad survey by V. Berridge, *Health and Society since 1939* (Cambridge, 1999). They can be supplemented by the well-documented official history, C. Webster, *The Health Services since the War* (2 vols, 1988–96). D. M. Fox provides useful comparisons in *Health Policies, Health Politics: the British and American experience, 1911–1965* (Princeton, NJ, 1986).

The origins of the NHS have attracted much attention. In addition to the texts cited above, H. Eckstein, *The English Health Service* (Cambridge, MA, 1958) presents an American perspective, whilst insider accounts are J. E. Pater, *The Making of the National Health Service* (1981) and more briefly, but with equal illumination, P. Benner, 'The early years of the National Health Service', in T. Gorst, L. Johnman and W. Scott Lucas (eds), *Postwar Britain* (1989). The various interpretations are dissected in C. Webster, 'Conflict and consensus: explaining the British Health Service', *Twentieth Century British History*, 1 (1990) 115–51. The political battle over the early financing of the NHS is recorded in M. Foot, *Aneurin Bevan*, vol. 2 (1973) and, rather more reliably, in P. M. Williams, *Hugh Gaitskell* (1979).

On particular aspects of healthcare, general practice is particularly well covered by A. Digby, *The Evolution of General Practice, 1850–1948* (Oxford, 1999) and I. Loudon, J. Horder and C. Webster (eds), *General Practice under the National Health Service* (Oxford, 1998). So too are hospitals by J. Mohan, *Planning, Markets and Hospitals* (2002). Rather more impressionistic is P. Hall, 'The development of health centres', in P. Hall, H. Land, R. Parker and A. Webb, *Change, Choice and Conflict in Social Policy* (Aldershot,1986). Also impressionistic but invaluable is the recreation of the experiences of the consumers and producers of less glamorous health services such as pharmacy, midwifery and district nursing in J. Bornat, R. Perks, P. Thompson and J. Walmsley (eds), *Oral History, Health and Welfare* (2000). C. Ham, *Health Policy in Britain* (Basingstoke, 1999) identifies the main theoretical approaches to the history of the NHS as does, in a challenging comparative perspective, M. Moran, *Governing the Healthcare State* (Manchester, 1999).

Education

CONTENTS

1943 *Education Reconstruction* white paper (Cmd 6458) – wartime blueprint

1944 Education Act – only major wartime legislation on welfare

1946 Barlow report, *Scientific Manpower* (Cmd 6824) – need to double science graduates

1947 School leaving age raised to 15

1953 Grants to university students made mandatory

1954 *Early Leaving* report – first questioning of 11-plus exam

1956 *Technical Education* white paper (Cmd 9703) – five-year expansion plan

1958 *Secondary Education for All* white paper (Cmnd 604) – another five-year plan

1959 Crowther report, *15 to 18*, on the missing link

1963 Newsom report, *Half Our Future*, on average and below average 13–16-year-olds. Robbins report, *Higher Education* (Cmnd 2154) – plan to expand universities greatly

1965 Circular 10/65 – drive to introduce comprehensives. Industrial Training Act – drive to improve productivity

1967 Plowden report, *Children and their Primary Schools* – recommends positive discrimination

1968 Widespread student protest, following LSE sit-in in 1967

1969 First Black Paper heralding backlash. First polytechnics opened and Open University founded

1970 Circular 10/70 – Conservatives revoke 10/65

→

1972	*Education: a framework for expansion* white paper (Cmnd 5174) – Mrs Thatcher's expensive plans. School leaving age finally raised to 16		later being made mandatory by 1976 Education Act
1973	Retrenchment starts. Employment Training Act transfers vocational training from schools to industry (the Manpower Services Commission)	1975	Abolition of direct grant schools. Progressive methods discredited by events at William Tyndale school and Polytechnic of North London. Bullock report, *A Language for Life*, identifies some declining standards
1974	Circular 4/74 – Labour revokes 10/70, with comprehensives	1976	James Callaghan's Ruskin College speech – call for a core curriculum and less anti-industry bias

Education initially attracted as much popular enthusiasm as the NHS and, until the 1970s at least, it was more successful in attracting public finance. Its exceptional degree of political support was demonstrated by the fact that the 1944 Education Bill was the only major piece of reconstruction legislation to be enacted during the war and, in its wake, public opinion was recorded as providing 'overwhelming support for extra expenditure on education'.[1] The war thus reversed, if only temporarily, the widespread popular indifference – and even hostility – to education which had followed the introduction of compulsory schooling in 1880. Because of full employment, children's earnings were no longer so vital to family income. Consequently, many parents were able for the first time to regard education not as a short-term financial loss but as an opportunity for their children to secure a good job and hence long-term financial security.

Partly because of this increased popularity, expenditure on the formal education system grew faster in the 1950s and 1960s than on any other social service.[2] Between 1951 and 1975 it rose from 6.8 per cent to 12.5 per cent of public expenditure and from 19.5 per cent to 23.1 per cent of social expenditure. Education thereby permanently supplanted the NHS as the second most expensive social service after social security (see Appendix, Tables A.3, A.4, A.5). There were two other explanations for the increased size and the changing structure of the education budget (see Table 8.1). The first was demographic. The baby boom of the mid-1940s required the expansion of primary education in the early 1950s, secondary education in the late 1950s and higher education in the early 1960s. This cycle was repeated after the unexpected baby boom of the late 1950s (see Section 4.2). The other was increased educational attainment. In the 1960s especially, Britain was fully part of an 'educational explosion, probably . . . unique in the western world'.[3]

Despite this explosion, the education service soon became the subject of informed criticism, mounting disillusion and political disagreement. As early as 1956 the very system of secondary education, through which the 1944 Act had been expected to secure greater 'equality of opportunity', was attacked by

Table 8.1 Education: selected current and capital expenditure, 1951–77

	1951–2		1961–2		1966–7		1971–2		1976–7	
	£m	%	£m	%	£m	%	£m	%	£m	%
*Current expenditure:**										
1. Schools of which:	220	53.9	531	50.1	883	48.3	1401	44.4	4,148	54.3
2. Nursery	–	–	2	0.1	–	–	8	0.3	153	2.0
3. Primary	122	29.9	246	23.2	366	20.0	639	20.3	1,542	20.2
4. Secondary	91	22.3	269	25.4	413	22.6	699	22.2	2,012	26.4
5. Further and adult education	23	5.6	87	8.2	186	10.2	351	11.1	940	12.3
6. Teacher training	8	2.0	25	2.4	69	3.8	129	4.1		
7. Universities	31	7.6	87	8.2	187	10.2	336	10.7	627	8.2
8. Total current expenditure	338	82.8	877	82.7	1,521	83.3	2,661	84.4	6,960	91.2
Capital expenditure:										
9. Schools	52	12.7	114	10.7	160	8.8	327	10.4	483	6.3
10. Further and adult education	9	2.2	31	2.9	37	2.0	64	2.0	88	1.2
11. Teacher training	1	0.2	12	1.1	11	0.6	12	0.4		
12. Universities	6	1.5	26	2.5	80	4.4	81	2.6	102	1.3
13. Total capital expenditure	70	17.2	183	17.3	306	16.7	493	15.6	673	8.8
14. Total public expenditure	408	100.0	1,060	100.0	1,827	100.0	3,154	100.0	7,633	100.0

* Excludes grants to students.
Note: For 1951–2 and 1966–7, lines 1–7 and 9–12 exclude Northern Ireland.
Source: *Social Trends* (1970, 1979).

Crosland as 'divisive, unjust and wasteful'. In the same year the paucity of technical education was also identified by the Prime Minister as a major reason for Britain's declining international competitiveness. 'The prizes,' Eden warned, 'will not go to the countries with the largest population. Those with the best systems of education will win. . . . Our scientists are doing brilliant work. But if we are to make full use of what we are learning, we shall need many more scientists, engineers and technicians.'[4]

The launching by the Soviet Union of the first space satellite (Sputnik) in 1957 came as a profound shock and was taken as confirmation that, because of the backwardness of its education system, Britain was in no position to 'win'. There was a brief return to wartime optimism and political consensus in the early 1960s, but disillusion and party disagreement returned. This was principally because of the perceived incompatibility of the three continuing objectives of policy:

- equality of opportunity
- improved technical education
- the maintenance of educational standards.

There was in theory no reason why these objectives should have been – or should have been seen to be – incompatible. Education had long been recognized as a public good (see Section 3.2.1). Hence any increase in equality of opportunity, by enabling more children to reach their full potential, was acknowledged to be in the national interest. Technical education had in the past been popularly regarded as a subtle device to divert children from humbler backgrounds away from prestigious and well-paid administrative jobs. Given the shortage of skilled manpower and, consequently, the high wages it could command, this suspicion was no longer valid. Finally, any lowering of standards to obtain a spurious equality would have denied children a genuine opportunity to develop their talents fully. It would also have undermined Britain's industrial competitiveness, the creation of wealth and thus the buoyancy of government revenue upon which all welfare services ultimately depended.

Such interdependence was recognized by the advocates of educational reform within both the major political parties. Crosland, for example, steadily maintained that greater equality of opportunity was the key to increased educational attainment and faster rates of economic growth. Eccles, Eden's minister of education, likewise identified educational expenditure as the 'wisest investment'. It would not just satisfy industry's technical needs and enable everyone to respond to market opportunities, it would also instil that sense of personal responsibility for which the 1944 *Employment Policy* white paper had called. 'Problems such as forestalling inflation, preventing and settling strikes and abandoning restrictive practices', he insisted, 'will, in the end, only be solved by better education.'[5]

Beneath such apparent consensus, however, there lay a deep political divide. Crosland (as a democratic socialist) ultimately sought to employ educational reform as a means of creating a 'classless society'. In contrast

Eccles (as a reluctant collectivist) sought to maintain as much as possible of the *status quo*. Accordingly he advised his colleagues that any 'political party, aiming to poll more than half the votes at future general elections, must be clearly identified with one sector of the sprouting Welfare State, and ... education is a service marked out as peculiarly Conservative in purpose'. Such conflicting objectives raise fundamental questions about the ultimate purpose for which the two parties were seeking greater equality of opportunity and improved technical education and, above all, about the contemporary criteria by which 'educational standards' were judged. Any assessment of the achievements of the postwar education system must, therefore, be prefaced by an examination of the precise political nature of the Act which provided its statutory basis.

This chapter will be based almost exclusively on England and Wales. Northern Ireland and in particular Scotland enjoyed very different, and in many ways superior, systems of education (as described in Section 4.4). Only their major divergences from innovations in English and Welsh policy and practice will be noted.

8.1 THE 1944 EDUCATION ACT AND ITS CRITICS

The 1944 Education Act, as has been seen, enjoyed exceptional popular and political support during the war. It was also to provide the statutory basis for the education system over the following 40 years. It is little wonder, therefore, that it was once described as the 'greatest measure of educational advance since 1870, and probably the greatest ever known'. However, as defects came to be perceived in postwar education provision, criticism mounted. One educational historian has even gone so far as to attack the Act as a 'clever exercise in manipulative politics by a past master of the art (of the possible) with the aid of a state bureaucracy devoted to highly conservative objectives'.[6] Which of these assessments is the more accurate? To answer this question three basic issues have to be resolved:

- What precisely did the Act propose?
- What did it deliberately, or accidentally, omit?
- Were the perceived deficiencies in postwar education directly attributable to the Act itself or rather to those who implemented it?

Prewar confusion

The interwar system of state education in England and Wales, which the Act sought to reform, was as confused and confusing as the interwar health services. There were two particular sources of confusion.

The *first* was the uneasy distinction between 'elementary' and secondary or 'higher' education. The latter did not (as today) cover all children over the age of 11, but only those who attended grammar schools – be they the old,

privately endowed foundations or the schools established by local government after 1902. Fees were chargeable at these schools (although by 1938, 48
per cent of places were free) and they were attended by only 20 per cent of
children between 12 and the minimum leaving age of 14. All other children
remained within the free 'elementary' education system – and often within
the same 'all-age' school which they had attended since the age of 5.

The *second* major source of confusion, within both elementary and
secondary education, was the 'dual' nature of the schools. Until local government was itself permitted to provide elementary and 'higher' education (in
1870 and 1902 respectively) voluntary organizations, and in particular the
churches, had been responsible for its provision – with the government's role
limited to the payment of subsidies. Throughout the interwar period the
voluntary sector (despite increasing financial difficulties) survived.
Consequently in many schools the appointment of staff, the overall organization of the school and all new buildings were the responsibility of independent boards of governors and not the local education authorities (LEAs). In
1938, for example, one-half of schools in the elementary sector, catering for
just under one-third of children, were voluntary.[7]

> Prewar confusion and rivalry was institutionalized, and exemplified, by
> responsibility for 'elementary' and 'higher' education being assigned to
> different tiers of local government. Secondary education was solely the
> responsibility of county councils and county boroughs. Within the counties
> 'elementary' education was often the direct responsibility of the much
> smaller and potentially less efficient non-county boroughs and urban
> districts.

The Act's objectives

The principal purpose of the Act was to end this confusion. Accordingly there
were four major *administrative* changes:

- Responsibility for the implementation of policy was placed solely on
  county councils and county boroughs, thereby more than halving the
  number of LEAs from 315 to 146.
- Voluntary schools were not nationalized (as was to be the case with voluntary hospitals) but their independence was reduced and their financial
  problems alleviated by two new types of subsidy for 'aided and 'controlled'
  schools.
- In order to ensure standardization of educational provision, the Board of
  Education was elevated into a ministry with the authority not just to
  'superintend' but to 'control and direct' LEAs.[8]
- All teachers were to be paid uniformly according to the nationally negotiated Burnham pay scales.

'Aided' schools were those whose governors were prepared to pay half the cost of alterations, improvements and external repairs (with the LEA meeting all other costs).[9] In return the governors would be permitted to retain control over the appointment and dismissal of teachers and the nature of religious instruction. 'Controlled' schools were those for which LEAs assumed full financial responsibility, with the rights of the governors limited to consultation over the appointment of the headmaster and teachers responsible for religious instruction. Only 500 Church of England schools were expected to opt for 'aided' status but eventually 3000 did.

These administrative reforms were a necessary precondition for major advances in both the *nature* and *quality* of state education:

- It was for the first time made entirely free.[10]
- The school leaving age was raised to 15, with the proviso that it should be raised to 16 as soon as was 'practical'.
- A clear break was also introduced at the age of 11 between 'primary' and 'secondary' education, so that all children had the same potential 'ladder' to university.
- For those who left school at the minimum age there was to be compulsory attendance at county colleges.
- Local authorities were required to provide further education courses in technical, commercial and art education.

As practical measures to increase equality of opportunity, there were to be increased provision of nursery education; free school meals, milk and medical inspection (to ensure that all children were physically able to benefit from their education); and a major upgrading of facilities in primary schools.

The Act therefore represented – as was clearly recognized at the time – a major step towards the creation of an efficient, cost-effective and just education system. With regard to *efficiency,* the concentration of responsibility on county councils and county boroughs created within each locality a single authority for primary, secondary and further education with a sufficiently large population and financial base to ensure a fully comprehensive service.[11] Should any authority prove recalcitrant, then the ministry had the ultimate power to 'control and direct' it. With regard to *cost-effectiveness,* the new deal for voluntary schools retained within the state system a much-needed source of non-government finance, whilst removing the major impediment to the upgrading of primary schools and the provision of specialist secondary education. For example, the poor facilities for children aged between 7 and 11 in voluntary schools had been highlighted by *Educational Reconstruction,* the white paper which preceded the 1944 Act. Lack of finance had also led to the inequitable position that only 16 per cent of their pupils received specialist 'post-primary' education, whereas the comparable figure in the state sector was 62 per cent.[12]

Finally, *equality of opportunity* was advanced even more explicitly through the abolition of fees and the raising of the school leaving age. The former made the criterion for educational advance children's ability, rather than their parents' financial or social status. The latter, by ensuring four years of specialist secondary education, significantly reduced the disparity between the amount and quality of education received by children from different classes. Increased support for voluntary schools also reduced another source of inequity which wartime evacuation had exposed: the considerable difference in the quality of education provided in the countryside (where church schools predominated) and the towns.

The Act criticized

Despite such achievements, the 'progressive' nature of the Act has been seriously questioned. There have been three main criticisms:

* it attempted little that was new
* it halted an existing momentum towards the expansion of technical education
* it was innately conservative.

Unoriginality. In relation to secondary education, the charge here is that the raising of the school leaving age to 15 (with a clear distinction between primary and secondary education at the age of 11) had already been recommended by the Hadow Report of 1926. In the implementation of this report, so it is argued, not only was the school leaving age scheduled to be raised in September 1939, but local government had grudgingly started to replace 'all-age' schools with specialist junior technical and central 'modern' schools. Moreover, through the increasing provision of free places in grammar schools, the whole of 'post-primary' education had in certain areas effectively become free.

The weakness of such an argument, however, is that interwar progress was gradual and geographically uneven – not least because it was constrained by the financial weakness of the voluntary sector and by the latent antagonism both between voluntary and state schools and between the two responsible levels of local government. A major achievement of the Act was that it removed these historic impediments to progress and thereby enabled interwar ideals to become postwar reality.

Technical education. A long-overdue expansion of technical education had been vigorously advocated in 1938 by the Spens Report. The *Educational Reconstruction* white paper fully acknowledged the justice of Spens's case, admitting that:

> Too many of the nation's abler children are attracted into a type of education which prepares primarily for the University and for the administrative and clerical

professions; too few find their way into schools from which the design and crafts-manship sides of industry are recruited. If education is to serve the interests both of the child and of the nation, some means must be found of correcting this bias.[13]

By encouraging the development of technical schools, making continuing education compulsory and placing a requirement on local government to provide further technical education, the Act also appeared well designed to redress the balance.

Nevertheless. there is some validity in the charge that – as in other propos-als for industrial reconstruction – 'the wartime coalition and its civil servants came, they saw, and they shirked' this particular challenge.[14] In contrast to the zeal with which he tackled the problem of church schools, for example, Butler (the Conservative minister principally responsible for the Act) quickly passed the question of technical education to his officials. The one initiative he took was to appoint the Norwood Committee on the secondary school curriculum and when, as expected, its report provided a strong defence of the traditional qualities of public and grammar school education, he expressed his satisfac-tion. 'This well written report', he noted, 'will serve our book very well – particularly the layout of the secondary world. Spens will be furious.'[15] The political drive to galvanize Whitehall into a radical reappraisal of technical education was therefore clearly lacking.

In practical terms, however, what more could the Act have done to instil into the education system, and into society at large, a new industrial culture? Within the Labour Party Bevin had proposed that all school-leavers should be sent at 14 to boarding schools and then, at 16, into industry for four years of compulsory training. Within the Conservative Party a powerful advisory committee had simultaneously recommended *inter alia* compulsory technical and vocational training for all 14–18-year-olds and the replacement of classics by a national curriculum of science and technology. With some justice such proposals were dismissed at the time – and have been dismissed since – as 'semi-fascist'.[16] They were clearly impractical.

Whilst the traditionalism of Butler and his civil servants should be acknowl-edged, it is unclear what more they could have done in relation to techni-cal education. Correlli Barnett, one of the Act's foremost critics, may be justified in arguing that:

> The vaunted 1944 Education Act offered not so much an executive oper-ational framework as an open gate to an empty construction site on which local authorities might or might not (depending on their zeal and the effectiveness of the Ministry's nagging) build the technical and further education system that Britain so desperately needed.[17]

However, at least the gate had been fully opened. The critical question is, therefore, not why the Act's proposals were so insubstantial but why, given the nagging of Conservative governments throughout the 1950s, the opportunities they offered were never fully seized.

Innate conservatism. The war, so it is argued, provided an unparalleled opportunity for four radical reforms:

- the abolition of public schools
- the secularisation of state education
- the raising of the school leaving age to 16
- the unification of secondary education within multilateral or comprehensive schools.

None of these reforms was achieved. Public schools, which had been in serious financial and political trouble in 1940, survived to gain in strength after the war. The place of religion was consolidated, as part of the deal with voluntary schools, with the obligation on all schools to hold daily corporate acts of worship. Such an obligation was exceptional in advanced welfare states. The raising of the school leaving age to 16 was deferred until 1972. Finally, the Act's endorsement of diversity within secondary education ensured the survival of the grammar school and thus, within the state sector, a sense of educational privilege and hierarchy – in place of the 'popular culture' and democratic values which, it was believed, multilateral or comprehensive schools would disseminate.

There is again some justice in these criticisms. Senior civil servants initiated reconstruction planning with the explicit intention of forestalling more radical change and later many assumed 'the mantle of spokesmen within the government' for the independent and grammar schools.[18] One of the main reasons, for example, why 11 was chosen as the age at which to divide primary and secondary schooling – despite the doubts of educational psychologists and Butler himself – was the defence of the traditional structure and curriculum of grammar schools. Butler (a governor of Felstead, with two sons at Eton) also advised the representatives of public schools on how to deflect public hostility and later admitted that he had appointed the Fleming Committee – which reported on the future of public schools in June 1944, just after the third reading of the Act – to minimize public discussion. Indeed it was his commissioning of this, and of the Norwood Committee, which has led directly to the charge that the Act was a 'clever exercise in manipulative politics'.

A 'multilateral' school embraced the principle which later became identified with comprehensives. Children of every ability, or aptitude, should be taught within the school albeit within streamed classes. Comprehensives also incorporated streaming although many of their proponents argued that, in their purest form, they should have only mixed-ability classes. During the war, the multilateral school was quickly recognized within the wartime Board of Education as 'the only full solution to the problem of a truly democratic education'. Grammar schools, it was acknowledged, had not fully thrown off their nineteenth-century legacy as schools for middle-class children. Moreover, they were imbued with the Platonic ideal of 'education for leadership': they, together with the public schools, should train the country's chosen elite, whilst it was the duty of all other schools to provide the willing followers.[19]

Progressive or conservative?

What such a barrage of criticism overlooks is that manipulation was needed not just to thwart radical reform but to achieve any reform at all. It was not preordained that the only piece of reconstruction legislation to be passed during the war should be the Education Bill. That it was enacted was a triumph for, and a tribute to, Butler's political skills. His predecessor at the Board of Education had after all been dismissed for being too radical and his own initial proposals had been rejected by Churchill because they raised party controversy 'in the most acute and dangerous form'.[20] Without the prime minister's backing (usually a prerequisite for any major reform), Butler had also to reconcile the conflicting interests of Conservative and Labour back-benchers. The potential hostility of the former was demonstrated by their successful defence of direct grant schools (which Butler wished to abolish), whilst the radicalism of the latter was reflected by their imposition on Churchill, during the passage of the Act, of his only wartime parliamentary defeat (over equal pay).[21] In such circumstances the achievement of so substantial an Act cannot be dismissed simply as a triumph for conservatism. It was a genuine triumph for reform.

Although its radicalism may have at times been exaggerated, therefore, the Act did represent a major advance in education policy. It swept aside the historic impediments to change and, by guaranteeing to all children four years of specialist secondary education, it ensured a significant increase in educational opportunity. Certain controversial issues, such as public schools, were deliberately evaded. Others, such as technical education, were not incisively handled. Moreover, in relation to multilateral education (which was favoured by an articulate but unrepresentative minority), the Norwood Report was deliberately commissioned and published to signal the government's hope that, whatever its possible educational and social disadvantages, the postwar education system would be a tripartite one.

However, even if Butler and his officials thereby revealed an innate conservatism, it is of equal significance that – as with technical education – they left all options open. They were never as dogmatic as were, for example, Beveridge and Bevan in their respective spheres. Indeed the perfect riposte to those who criticize the conservatism of the Act is the later complaint from the New Right that, 'as a giant umbrella under which all sorts of experiments could flourish', the Act 'hardly suggested a coherent Conservative policy for education'.[22] The essence of the Act, therefore, was its pragmatism. In consequence, its ultimate impact on policy was determined not by its authors but by those who implemented it.

8.2 EDUCATION AND EQUALITY

The overriding objective in the implementation of postwar education was greater equality, but its attainment was complicated by a perceived conflict

with the maintenance of educational standards and, above all, by a fundamental redefinition of equality. In 1944 equality had essentially meant 'equality of opportunity' (the assurance that no accident of parental circumstance,
place of residence or sex would prevent children from developing their talent
to the full) and 'parity of esteem' (the equitable distribution of resources
between children of different aptitudes). To these definitions had been added
by 1975 'equality of outcome' (the reduction of differences in educational
achievement between children of different social groups, so that the educational system did not simply reflect and reinforce existing class differences).
The means of attainment also changed, most dramatically within secondary
education where the tripartite system was progressively supplanted by
comprehensive schools.

- What were the major phases in the implementation of educational policy?
- Why did the tripartite system collapse so quickly?

Three policy phases

1945–54.   The simple priorities during the immediate postwar years were to
maintain prewar standards and to lay the foundations for the achievement of
'equality of opportunity'. To maintain standards one-third of school buildings
had, as a result of war damage, to be either rebuilt or repaired; and, as a result
of the baby boom, extra resources had to be assigned to primary education to
meet the needs by 1954 of almost one million extra children (see Table 8.2).[23]
To achieve greater equality the school leaving age was raised to 15 in 1947,
grammar school fees were removed, grants to university students made
mandatory in 1953 (albeit under varying local conditions) and the provision
of school milk and meals was expanded.[24] These reforms were extremely
expensive in terms of manpower and money and, in the given economic
circumstances, major achievements.

In 1951, however, the incoming Conservative government – despite
Butler's authorship of the 1944 Act – apparently felt no such commitment to
educational provision. To reduce public expenditure the Chancellor of the
Exchequer advised his colleagues that they should 'plan changes in policy as
well as constant pruning'; and amongst the economies considered, but ultimately rejected, by Cabinet were the raising of the school entry age from 5 to
6 (as on the continent), the reversion of the school leaving age to 14, and the
charging of fees not only in secondary but also in primary schools.[25]
Remarkably the chancellor was none other than Butler himself.

Within the Labour Cabinet the raising of the school leaving age provoked
considerable heart-searching. This was because, at a time of acute
manpower shortage and restrictions on public expenditure, it both
deprived the labour market of 400,000 school leavers and required the

➔

Table 8.2 Maintained nursery and primary schools in England and Wales, 1946–75

	Nursery schools				Primary schools			
	Number	Pupils (000)	Teachers	Pupil/ teacher ratio	Number	Full-time pupils (m)	Teachers	Pupil/ teacher ratio
1946	75	6	229	–	23,991	3.7	116,820	32.0
1950	416	21	905	–	23,133	4.0	130,046	30.4
1955	464	23	1,168	–	23,664	4.6	148,739	30.9
1960	454	24	1,082	–	23,488	4.2	144,693	29.0
1965	461	28	1,085	22.0	22,882	4.3	151,084	28.3
1970	482	34	1,307	19.4	23,075	4.9	180,008	27.4
1975	612	48	1,481	21.4	23,280	5.1	213,055	24.2

Note: The statistics for nursery schools exclude direct grant schools. Figures for pupils include part-time pupils in nursery schools but exclude them for primary schools. Figures for teachers are full-time equivalents.

Source: Department of Education and Science, *Statistics of Education* (1978) vol. 1, Historical Tables.

emergency training of an extra 35,000 teachers, together with the diversion of scarce building labour and materials to the extension of schools (in the famous HORSA operation). As the Minister of Education admitted at the time, it was an 'act of faith rather than an act of wisdom'.[26] However, by honouring the 1944 commitment, the Attlee government revealed its ultimate determination not to sacrifice long-term social need to short-term economic demands – as had happened after the First World War.

1954–63. By late 1954 the economic situation had eased, building labour and materials had become more plentiful (with the peaking of Macmillan's housing drive) and a new minister, Eccles, was appointed who was committed to 'bringing the Butler Act to life'.[27] This was to be the priority for the next decade. Under the stimulus of the 1958 white paper *Secondary Education for All: a new drive* (which committed the government to planned capital expenditure of £300 million over five years), a major attempt was made to modernize secondary education. There was a belated reduction of all-age schools between 1954 and 1963 from 3528 to 411 (catering for 93,000 as opposed to 636,000 pupils) and the building of over 2000 new schools, mainly secondary moderns. Primary education obviously benefited from such rationalization, as it did also from the ebbing of the birth rate, but by the late 1950s the effect of the postwar baby boom was starting to be felt in higher education. The decade from 1954 to 1963 was therefore one of unprecedented educational expansion. It also marked 'the high point for popular belief in the state system of education'.[28]

It was, however, also the time at which serious misgivings began to be widely expressed about not only the lack of technical education (which will be examined in Section 8.4) but also the structure of secondary education. These doubts were fuelled by the conclusions of a succession of official enquiries, which resulted in three particularly significant reports:

- the 1954 report, *Early Leaving;*
- the 1959 Crowther Report on the education of young people between 15 and 18; and
- the 1963 Newsom Report, *Half Our Future,* on the education of children of average or below average ability between the ages of 13 and 16.

These reports did not directly attack tripartism. They did demonstrate, however, that the accident of parental circumstance still greatly influenced children's chances of entering grammar school and their subsequent academic performance; and that (given the failure to implement two of the 1944 Act's proposals, county colleges and the raising of the school leaving age to 16) many children were still not realizing their full potential.

These academic findings had two major political consequences. First, they confirmed the practical misgivings and complaints about the 11-plus examination (by which children were allocated to different types of secondary school) expressed by LEAs and many parents – not least those whose children had 'failed' the examination. Because of these objections well over half of LEAs were actually planning to introduce comprehensive schools by 1963.[29] The findings also helped to validate a switch in Labour Party policy after 1953 from the nominal support of multilateral schools to a commitment to comprehensive education in which (for both educational and social reasons) academic 'streaming' would be kept to a minimum.

> The expansion of higher education started with the upgrading of certain university colleges such as Exeter, Hull, Leicester and Southampton. Seven new universities (Sussex, East Anglia, York, Essex, Lancaster, Kent and Warwick) were then sanctioned. All this occurred before the commissioning in 1961 of the Robbins Committee on Higher Education.[30] Robbins recommended an increase in student numbers from 8 per cent to 17 per cent of the relevant age group; and so enthusiastic was its reception that within 24 hours the government had accepted its interim recommendation that numbers should be virtually doubled within ten years.

1964–76. This final phase saw a sustained attempt, at all levels of education, to engineer greater educational and social equality.

Most notoriously, Crosland (as secretary of state for education) requested all LEAs in 1965 to submit 'plans for reorganising secondary education in their areas on a comprehensive basis' in order to realize the Labour government's 'declared objective to end selection at 11-plus and to eliminate separatism'. In the same year a Public Schools Commission was established to re-examine the proposals of the wartime Fleming Committee on private schools with particular emphasis on the need to reduce 'the divisive influence they now exert'.[31] Within the primary and nursery sector there was a further official enquiry which resulted in the 1967 Plowden Report on *Children and their Primary Schools*. It was generally complimentary, but expressed serious concern about the continuing disadvantages suffered by children from 'deprived' backgrounds. Heavily influenced by the contemporary War on Want programme in the USA, it recommended the establishment of educational priority areas in which positive discrimination could be exercised in favour of such children by means of extra money and staff. This policy was duly implemented by the Labour government. Finally, within higher education the Robbins targets were not only met but exceeded, with the number of students expanding between 1962–3 and 1970–1 not by 59 per cent but by 104 per cent.[32]

> In higher education, Labour did not introduced the proposed 'unitary' system, by which the majority of students would have been taught in some 60 self-governing universities. Instead it established a 'binary' system with
>
> ➜

the creation between 1969 and 1973 of 30 polytechnics under local government control. As Robbins himself remarked, it appeared to be a 'supreme
paradox' that a government 'pledged to abolish artificial hierarchy and
invidious distinctions in the schools' should create them in higher education. The divide was nevertheless defended by Crosland on egalitarian
grounds. The polytechnics, he argued, would ensure a less elitist and a
more socially responsible and responsive form of further education. Only
one new university was indeed to be sanctioned after 1965, and it was a far
from traditional one – the Open University, founded in 1969 and enrolling
its first students in 1971.

Labour's deliberately egalitarian measures were – somewhat surprisingly –
sustained after 1970 by the incoming Heath administration. Admittedly the
attack on private education was halted and LEAs were no longer requested –
or, as had been the intention of Labour's draft 1970 Education Bill, compelled
– to introduce comprehensive education.[33] Rather, ministers encouraged and
then used parental opposition to reject LEA proposals for the closure of individual grammar schools, thereby undermining the social and educational
logic of many reorganization plans. Nevertheless over 3000 comprehensives
were established and in 1972 the school leaving age was finally raised to 16,
as had initially been proposed by the 1944 Act.

Simultaneously the government announced its intention, in the white
paper *Education: A Framework for Expansion* (Cmnd 5174), to maintain the
momentum of the 1960s by increasing education expenditure by 50 per cent
over the next ten years. The main beneficiaries, in accordance with the recommendations of the Plowden Committee, were to be nursery and primary
education. However, within higher education – where the Open University
had been saved, almost literally, over the dead body of the Chancellor of the
Exchequer – the number of full-time students was also to rise from 15 per cent
to 22 per cent of the relevant age group. Each of these measures was justified
in egalitarian terms. The Secretary of State for Education, for example,
defended the Open University because it provided 'educational opportunity
for those prepared to work for it' and increased expenditure on nursery
education on the ground that it could 'help redress the balance of those born
unlucky'.[34] No less remarkably than in the early 1950s, when Butler (as chancellor of the exchequer) seemed intent on destroying his own Act, the secretary of state for education between 1970 and 1974 was none other than
Margaret Thatcher.

Between 1970 and 1974, 3612 proposals for the reorganization of
secondary schools on comprehensive principles were submitted to government. Only 326 were ultimately rejected. As a result, the proportion of

→

secondary school children within comprehensive schools rose from 32 per cent to 62 per cent (see Table 8.3). Thus, just as the peak of council house building was reached between 1951 and 1955, so more grammar schools were closed between 1970 and 1974 than in any comparable period. The double irony is that both these 'social democratic' achievements were not only achieved under Conservative governments but that the responsible ministers were respectively Macmillan and Mrs Thatcher, who represented very different strands of Conservatism.

Table 8.3 Maintained secondary schools in England and Wales, 1946–75

	1946	1950	1955	1960	1965	1970	1975
Secondary modern							
Schools	2,843	3,227	3,550	3,837	3,727	2,691	1,216
Pupils (000)	719	1,095	1,234	1,638	1,555	1,227	697
Teachers	–	47,759	56,770	74,281	78,567	65,259	38,702
Pupil/teacher ratio	–	22.9	21.7	22.1	19.8	18.8	18.0
Grammar							
Schools	1,199	1,192	1,180	1,268	1,285	1,038	566
Pupils (000)	488	503	528	672	719	605	344
Teachers	–	27,155	29,195	36,365	41,879	36,940	21,367
Pupil/teacher ratio	–	18.5	18.1	18.5	17.2	16.4	16.1
Technical							
Schools	324	301	302	251	172	82	29
Pupils (000)	60	72	87	102	85	44	18
Teachers	–	4,362	5,083	5,517	4,965	2,719	1,102
Pupil/teacher ratio	–	16.6	17.6	18.5	17.0	16.1	16.4
Comprehensive							
Schools	–	10	16	130	262	1,145	2,596
Pupils (000)	–	8	16	129	240	937	2,460
Teachers	–	386	807	6,709	13,403	53,732	145,506
Pupil/teacher ratio	–	20.7	19.7	19.2	17.9	17.4	16.9
Total							
Schools	4,366	4,765	5,144	5,801	5,863	5,385	5,035
Pupils (000)	1,269	1,696	1,915	2,723	2,819	3,046	3,827
Teachers	58,455	80,545	94,390	131,591	150,736	171,343	222,591
Pupil/teacher ratio	21.7	21.1	20.3	20.7	18.7	17.8	17.2

Note: The 'total' figures include a small number of hybrid schools and, after 1968, middle schools 'deemed secondary'.

Source: Department of Education and Science, *Statistics of Education* (1978) vol. 1, Historical Tables.

   The seeds of the 'Thatcherite revolution', however, had been sown. During the surreptitious expansion of comprehensive schooling in the late 1950s there had developed a local populist movement (which increasingly found expression at Conservative Party conferences) to defend grammar schools.[35] As a result of student unrest in the late 1960s a series of 'Black Papers' was published attacking 'progressive changes' initially in universities, but then in primary and secondary schools. Finally, after the Conservative government's encouragement of parental opposition to comprehensive reorganization and its electoral defeat in 1974, there was a media attack on declining educational standards which culminated in the exposure of two 'scandals' in London: at the William Tyndale primary school and the Polytechnic of North London, where progressive teaching methods and student participation respectively were seen to have resulted in anarchy.

   This attack finally drove the Labour Prime Minister, Callaghan, to launch a 'great debate' on education in a speech at Ruskin College, Oxford, in October 1976 which called for a more disciplined structure of learning at all levels of education, within which the educational benefits of modern teaching methods could be more effectively realized. Just as the 1973 oil crisis (by halting the planned increase in expenditure) had foreshadowed a new era of educational 'cuts', so this speech (with its references to a 'core curriculum' and the need for greater vocational training) was a portent of the future.

Controversy: falling standards?

Beneath the ideological rhetoric of the educational backlash, there were two issues of substance. The first concerned standards. Superficially there would appear few grounds for doubting the dramatic improvement in educational standards after 1944. For example:

- Between 1948 and 1964, the average reading age for 11-year-olds improved by 17 months and for 15-year-olds by 20 to 30 months.[36]
- The number of children voluntarily staying on at school for a fifth year rose to 60 per cent by 1972 – incidentally making the raising of the school leaving age a far less traumatic event than in 1947.
- The number of children gaining academic qualifications also soared. This was particularly true for the years between 1970 and 1976, when those leaving school with no graded results fell from 44 per cent to 19 per cent.

Complaints about falling standards would therefore appear to reflect sheer prejudice against the greater equalization of educational opportunity and the slow erosion of traditional values for which wartime reformers had called.

   Such prejudice did exist, and was expressed most vividly by novelists such as Kingsley Amis, who repeated in the first Black Paper of March 1969 his earlier charge that 'more means worse', and Evelyn Waugh, who had ironically written in relation to Amis and his peers in the 1950s:

Have you heard of the Butler Education Act? In it he provided for the free distribution of university degrees for the deserving poor. I could make your flesh creep by telling you of the new wave of Philistinism with which we are threatened by these sour young people who are coming off the assembly line in their hundreds every year and finding employment as critics, even as poets and novelists.[37]

A similar prejudice was also expressed more sinisterly by educational psychologists such as Burt and Eysenck, who continued to insist in the Black Papers that there was a 'fixed pool of ability' and that consequently any attempt significantly to increase educational opportunity would merely lower standards.

Nevertheless, there was a modicum of evidence to support the critics' case. For example, a marginal drop in reading standards after 1960 amongst 7-year-olds was identified by the 1975 Bullock Report (which had been commissioned by the Conservatives in 1972). It is also questionable whether, either in absolute terms or in relation to Britain's industrial competitors, educational standards were rising as fast as increases in expenditure and decreases in staff/pupil ratios warranted (see Tables 8.2 and 8.3).

Controversy: defining equality

The second issue of substance arose from the conflicting definitions of equality. To the traditional supporters of the 1944 Act, 'the essential point', as expressed by Sir Edward Boyle (the most undogmatic of Conservative education ministers, whose political career was broken in the 1960s by the populist backlash), was that 'all children should have an equal opportunity of acquiring intelligence and of developing their talents and abilities to the full'.[38] Such an objective required the equal allocation of resources to children of different educational aptitudes. It could also justify a measure of positive discrimination in favour of children from deprived backgrounds.

What such a definition of equality specifically did not condone, however, was the standardization of educational methods and, above all, of results for children of different aptitudes and abilities. Just such a standardization, however, was perceived to be inherent in certain 'progressive' postwar educational developments and especially in unstreamed comprehensives, where particular emphasis was placed on the social integration of gifted children and the stimulus that their presence in the same class could provide for the less able.[39]

Any such attempt to engineer 'equality of outcome', so the critics argued, was pernicious and self-defeating. Rather than advancing justice and increasing educational standards, it denied gifted children both freedom of expression and the opportunity to develop their talent fully. In short, the unequal treatment of equally talented children on purely social and financial grounds (which had been prevalent before the war) would be replaced by the equal treatment of unequally talented children on purely ideological grounds.[40] It would also – at a time of increasing international competitiveness and

decreasing social cohesion – deprive the country of the economic and political leadership of a well-trained elite.

> The creation of an educational elite, so it was argued, was not in itself
> unjust. In accordance with Rawls's theory of social justice, the 'inequality of
> educational outcome' it represented was morally defensible so long as it
> benefited the least advantaged in society (see Section 3.2). The private and
> tripartite state system was held to do just this. It was, for instance, the
> particular mission of public and grammar schools to instil into their 'privi-
> leged' pupils a sense of civic responsibility. Once grammar school fees had
> been abolished, it was also assumed that entry into the educational elite
> was genuinely open.

Inequality between social classes was the dominant issue in the political battle
over educational equality. There were, however, other forms of inequality. As
will be noted in the following section, there were major geographical disparities in the quality and type of secondary schools. Even more seriously there
was widespread gender inequality. For example:

- The 11-plus examination was weighted heavily against girls on the ground
  that they matured earlier.
- Within secondary schools girls were directed by both the formal and a
  'hidden' curriculum into different subjects from boys. Both prepared them
  not for paid work outside but for unpaid work inside the home.
- The percentage of female students fell the more advanced education
  became. As late as 1964, for instance, only a quarter of university undergraduates were women and, at Oxford and Cambridge, the percentage was
  as low as 10 per cent and 13 per cent respectively.

A combination of all these class, regional and gender factors meant that, at the
most extreme, a middle-class boy in Cardiganshire in the early 1960s was 160
times more likely to enter full-time higher education than a working-class girl
from West Ham.[41] It was the realization that inequality on this scale continued to exist some 20 years after the 1944 Act which led to the major discontinuity in postwar education policy – the replacement of the tripartite structure
of grammar, technical and secondary schools with comprehensive education.

8.3 THE COLLAPSE OF TRIPARTISM

Because of Butler's pragmatism, tripartism had not been the explicit objective
of the 1944 Act. It was, however, the clear recommendation of the 1943
Norwood Report. It was also the clear objective of the civil servants responsible for the Act's immediate implementation – if only because of the pressing
economic need physically to base the expansion of secondary education on

existing 'post-primary' and secondary school buildings.[42] Moreover, to the public the specialised training of children in accordance with the three broad types of educational aptitude identified by Norwood – stemming from a child's interest in the 'abstract', the 'mechanical' or the 'practical' – appeared both rational and in line with European experience. Once established, therefore, tripartism attracted little criticism and the plans to consolidate it further in 1958 were largely uncontroversial.[43] Yet within 15 years it had been virtually abandoned and two-thirds of secondary school children were attending comprehensive schools.

   Why was there so dramatic a change? The principal reasons were practical, not ideological, and centred on two issues:

- The continuing failure of technical and secondary modern schools to achieve the promised 'parity of esteem' with grammar schools.
- The fallibility of the 11-plus examination by which children were allocated to a particular type of secondary school.

Parity of esteem

As the only true prewar 'secondary' school, grammar schools had inherited better facilities and higher public esteem than had their rivals and, until 1958 at least, these advantages were officially accentuated rather than reduced. Central government gave higher maintenance grants to grammar schools, for instance, whilst local government found ways of paying grammar school teachers higher wages for special qualifications and 'responsibilities'. Such continuing disparity confounded one of the main objectives of the 1944 Act – that children of different aptitudes should have an equal opportunity to develop their talents fully. Consequently, serious doubts were cast on whether it could ever be attained within a tripartite system.

The 11-plus exam: apparent failings

Of even greater concern was the perceived fallibility of the 11-plus examination. The results of this examination were not necessarily conclusive in the allocation of children to a specific type of school. Their results could be modified by teachers' reports and interviews. Moreover, the examination itself was not uniform throughout the whole country, although it did have a common core of written tests in English, mathematics and 'intelligence'. What did become uniform, however, was the increasing conviction of LEAs and parents (supported, as has been seen, by academic research) that the examination was neither fair nor objective.

   There were, as Michael Sanderson has noted, three particular criticisms of the 11-plus: 'there was too much misallocation of talent, too many extraneous factors impeding the flow of ability and too close a relationship of selection and success with social class background'.[44]

Misallocation. By 1958, for example, it was well established that some 10 per cent of children were misallocated at the age of 11. The clearest proof of this lay in the number and distribution of candidates for the examination specifically introduced in 1951 to maintain academic standards, the GCE 'O' level. By the end of the decade many grammar school children were failing to stay at school until 16 to take this examination, while some 22,000 secondary modern pupils – classified by the 11-plus as non-academic – were sitting it with considerable success.[45] Initial errors of allocation were compounded by the failure to transfer more than 2–3 per cent of children per annum between schools after the age of 11.

Extraneous factors. Foremost amongst the 'extraneous factors' were regional inequality, the date of a child's birthday and home circumstances. The number of grammar school places varied greatly between regions, thereby precluding genuine equality of opportunity. In 1959, for example, there were grammar school places for 35 per cent of children sitting the 11-plus in the south-west of England, whereas the comparable figure for the north-east was 22.4 per cent and in other areas (such as Nottingham) the figure could fall as low as 10 per cent. Given the 11-plus examination was held in February, the age of children could range from 10.6 to 11.5 years, depending on the exact relationship of birthdays to the start of the school year in August. This was clearly of advantage to the older children. Moreover, a close correlation was identified between pass rates and children from small families with supportive parents, who had the opportunity to study in relative peace and comfort.[46] This correlation particularly benefited middle-class children.

Social class. The advantage of middle-class children was increased by two further factors. The first was an unconscious bias in the examination towards concepts and language with which they would be more familiar. The second was the realization by teachers that (contrary to educational psychologists' initial beliefs) coaching could enhance examination performance. The latter was perhaps the more pernicious because it led to widespread streaming in primary and even nursery schools (where 'squirrels', who were neat and accumulated information, were separated from 'rabbits', who were messy and incontinent in relation to learning). Teachers tended to place disciplined, articulate middle-class children in the higher streams after which the expectations implicit in such streaming tended to become self-fulfilling. In short, schooling started from an early stage to reinforce class divisions.

By the early 1960s, therefore, the process – and thereby the principle – of selection had come under sustained attack. The geographical disparity of grammar school places exposed the underlying national purpose of the 11-plus examination. It was the allocation of children within a given mix of schools (which had been largely determined by historical accident) not their selection for a particular kind of education according to proven aptitude.

The correlation between social class and success in the 11-plus also demonstrated that genuine equality of opportunity could not be guaranteed by abolition of grammar school fees alone.

The concept of comprehensive (or at least multilateral) schools won support on traditional educational grounds in the 1950s – regardless of any social, or broader educational, advantages the greater mixing of children of different classes and ability ranges might bring. Comprehensives were built in new housing estates and in rural areas, where there were insufficient children to justify three separate schools. By providing educational facilities on one site for children of all aptitudes and abilities, they could also now be seen to offer a practical solution to the problems associated with 'parity of esteem' and misallocation. In addition, by removing the need to examine children prior to entry into secondary school, they enabled decisions about the nature of the child's education to be delayed until 13. This was the age which many experienced teachers and educational psychologists considered to be more appropriate.[47]

The 11-plus: an unwanted examination

That the 11-plus examination, and thereby tripartism, was so quickly discredited can be explained by two main factors The first was that its importance was largely fortuitous and not at all what the authors of the 1944 Act had wanted. As the 1943 white paper *Educational Reconstruction* insisted, for example:

> There is nothing to be said in favour of a system which subjects children at the age of 11 to the strain of a competitive examination on which, not only their future schooling, but their future careers may depend. Apart from the effect on the children, there is the effect on the curriculum in the schools themselves.[48]

Norwood himself, despite – or perhaps because of – being chairman of the Secondary Schools Examination Council agreed. Like the National Union of Teachers, he favoured selection based solely on teachers' reports. Educational psychologists (who dominated educational thinking in the 1940s) were also scornful of an examination which used an *intelligence* test to identify a child's *aptitude*. The irrationality of the process was duly exposed by the selection of children for technical schools on the basis not of a test of mechanical aptitude but of an IQ which just failed to secure entry into grammar school.[49]

However, some practical means of allocating children between existing schools was required and the 11-plus, with its emphasis on intelligence testing, appeared to administrators in central and local government to provide the best solution. Ironically, the basis of this presumption was the increased use of intelligence tests in the 1930s by progressive LEAs, which wished to counteract social bias in the award of grammar school scholarships.

The 11-plus examination gained its pre-eminence because it was thought, ironically, that it would advance equality of opportunity. In particular its intelligence test, as a perceived measure of a child's 'innate, unalterable and asocial ability', was believed to neutralize the impact on examination results of poor teaching and disadvantaged home backgrounds. It could also counter the bias towards middle-class children inherent in teachers' reports (a bias confirmed by postwar research).[50] In addition, because the tests could be conducted on a standardized national basis, they were less idiosyncratic and less expensive than any practical alternative.

The 11-plus: an unwarranted examination

Faith the validity of results of the 11-plus examination – insofar as they were based on intelligence testing – was, however, ill founded. This was not just because such tests were used incorrectly to diagnose educational aptitude, but because the very assumption that intelligence was 'innate, unalterable and asocial' was scientifically unsound. Postwar research by educational psychologists and sociologists (who came to rival the former's influence on policy-making) increasingly suggested that, whereas the limits of an individual's intelligence might be biologically determined, varying social or 'environmental' factors would determine how quickly a child's potential had been realized by any given time.

This new orthodoxy was summarized by Jean Floud in her submission to the Robbins Report. She wrote that an individual's IQ was the 'result of a cumulative process of development which is not unilinear throughout childhood, which proceeds at an irregular pace, does not stop at any particular age, and is susceptible to a startling degree to environmental influences'.[51] If this were true, it was hardly surprising that the 11-plus tended to favour middle-class children (or at least children with supportive parents) and that it failed to identify 'late-developers' who were accordingly branded as 'failures'. In consequence the 11-plus was being condemned by the early 1960s as not only scientifically inappropriate but also scientifically invalid.

This condemnation was based largely on practical and theoretical considerations, but there was also an ideological dimension – as became apparent with the contribution of Burt and Eysenck to the Black Papers. The concept of general intelligence, and the confidence that it could be measured, had first developed within the eugenicist movement at the end of the nineteenth century and had been concerned initially with the measurement of racial differences and mental subnormality. After the First World War it had been applied to vocational training and eventually to education, where it had had a considerable influence on the Hadow and Spens Reports. If innate intelligence could be accurately measured, it was rational to test children so that they could be provided with the most appropriate education and guided into the most suitable occupations.

The trouble was that the assumptions underlying this 'scientific' process were highly circular. Members of each vocational category, and hence social class, were assumed to have a similar IQ. Most non-manual workers, for example, would have an IQ over 115 and most manual workers an IQ under 115. A score of 115, however, was the minimum one required to ensure a place at grammar school. Consequently, if intelligence were genetically determined, it was inevitable that most grammar school places would be awarded to children of non-manual workers – who would then qualify for middle-class occupations. Only the exceptional working-class child would be recruited into grammar school and hence into the educational elite. Even more perniciously, this reasoning could justify higher expenditure on middle-class children because they had the innate intelligence which could – and in the interest both of the individual and the nation should – be developed the furthest. It was on such grounds that IQ testing, and thereby tripartism, was condemned for being highly conservative. Instead of providing genuine equality of opportunity they both reflected and reinforced social inequality. [52]

Tripartism deposed

Tripartism was the principal victim of the postwar commitment to equality. Initially this commitment appeared to pose little threat either to existing educational practice or to the existing social order. The assumption was that through a scientific examination all children would be allocated to the secondary school most suited to their educational aptitude. Consequently, no talent would be wasted. Because intelligence was believed to be genetically determined there would not automatically be an even social mix in every type of school or at each level of education. The opportunity would be available, however, for exceptional children from the lower classes to rise up through the educational system to join, and thereby reinforce, the economic and political elite.

By the 1960s, however, such conservative assumptions had been undermined by both practical experience and sociological research. The agreed objective of 'equality of opportunity' had also been challenged by the contested concept of 'equality of outcome' and there was a growing political move to engineer a more equal society through the educational, as well as the social security, system. This combination of practical, theoretical and political challenges made irresistible the momentum towards the replacement of tripartism by comprehensive, or at least multilateral, schools.

8.4 THE MAINTENANCE OF EDUCATIONAL STANDARDS

Some indication of the overall advance in postwar standards has already been given in Section 8.2. The record was impressive, although by 1975 there was some evidence of a slowing down (or even decline) in the attainment of young children, especially from poorer homes. There were also some grounds for questioning the cost-effectiveness of educational investment. What, however, was the specific record of achievement at each level of education in both the public and private sector?

Nursery education

Nursery education represented a 'black hole' in postwar policy. It could have developed in one of three forms:

- day nurseries, open throughout the hours parents were at work
- specialist nursery schools, open during conventional school hours
- nursery classes attached to primary schools.

Before the war the first – as in many other countries – had been discredited as a receptacle for 'problem children'. Nursery classes were opposed by the educational establishment. It was therefore to nursery schools that the Churchill coalition turned, both to release women for war work and to counteract, after the war, the social deprivation of inner-city children that had been highlighted during evacuation.[53] After the war, however, nursery schools fell victim not only to economic retrenchment but also to an underlying political and medical prejudice that young children were best cared for by their mothers. Consequently, their numbers contracted rather than expanded.

This experience was repeated in the 1960s. Then nursery schools came to be recognized as an 'outstandingly economic and efficient way' to counteract deprivation and, in 1972, the Conservative government committed itself to the fulfilment of the Plowden recommendation that nursery school places should be made available for 50 per cent of 3-year-olds and 90 per cent of 4-year-olds.[54] Economic retrenchment after the 1973 oil crisis, however, thwarted their expansion.

> Nursery education was never fully developed under the classic welfare state. Admittedly the number of children catered for in England and Wales doubled between 1960 and 1975 (see Table 8.2). The most sustained expansion in pre-school care, however, occurred within the private sector under the aegis of such self-help initiatives as the Pre-School Playgroups Association. Expansion was therefore greatest where social deprivation was least.

Primary education

Primary education enjoyed both a mixed reputation and mixed fortunes after 1944. England and Wales were widely recognized as pioneers in child-centred learning, based on individual activity and experience rather than the desk-bound accumulation of facts. 'Progressive' educational theory had become predominant in the 1930s and its practice had been unexpectedly accelerated

during the war as a result of the lack of conventional facilities in many evac-
uated schools. Consequently the Plowden Committee could report in 1967
that, in sharp contrast to prewar elementary schools, only 5 per cent of
primary schools were 'markedly out of touch with current practice and
knowledge'.[55]

However, the actual extent to which child-centred teaching was practised
and the quality of education thereby provided varied greatly. To be fully
effective, it required adaptable premises, classes of under 30 pupils, well-
trained teachers and freedom from a set curriculum. In very few areas were
all these conditions fulfilled. Despite a steady programme of school building
(peaking in 1952 and 1968 with 439 and 736 completions respectively) many
premises remained outdated. As late as 1976, for instance, 20 per cent of
pupils were being taught in schools built before 1900. Despite falling
staff/pupil ratios, a high turnover of teachers conspired to keep the size of
most classes above 30. Above all, as a consequence of the 11-plus most pupils
were streamed.

The objective of the Plowden Committee, which made primary education
a political priority for the first time since the war, was to resolve these difficulties by minimizing inequality and extending good practice. The expansion
of primary education in educational priority areas, however, largely failed
because of lack of support from:

- parents, whose indifference lay at the root of their children's disadvantage
- teachers, who generally opposed the appointment of parent–teacher associations and of untrained aides
- government, which restricted public expenditure after the 1967 devaluation
  crisis.

Retrenchment after 1973 similarly aborted the Conservative commitment to
replace all Victorian buildings. On the other hand 'progressive' teaching
methods were able to advance rapidly as the 11-plus examination was withdrawn.

The impact on primary education of the ending of the 11-plus examination
was dramatic. Whereas only 4 per cent of schools had been unstreamed in
1964, by 1978 only 4 per cent of 8-year-olds were being streamed.[56] Such a
dramatic change inevitably made primary education a principal target for
the Black Papers. 'Progressive' methods, it was more widely argued, might
promise much in principle. In practice, however, standards were perceived
to be falling behind those not only of Europe but also of Northern Ireland
and Scotland, where they were less pervasive.

Secondary education

Within the secondary sector, there were six types of school:

- public (independent) schools
- direct grant schools
- grammar schools
- technical schools
- secondary moderns
- comprehensives.

There were some 150 direct grants schools, such as Manchester Grammar School, which received direct subsidies from central government but were outside local government control and were permitted to enrol fee-paying students. They, like independent schools, had been highly criticized during the war for their elitism and had even appeared anomalous to Butler (see Section 8.1, note 10). They were abolished in 1975, following the report of the Public Schools Commission, established by a previous Labour government a decade earlier. The other vulnerable school was the third prong of the tripartite system – the secondary technical school. They had been designed to train a new technocratic elite but at their peak they catered for only 2 per cent of students and after 1958 their establishment was officially discouraged. The vast bulk of secondary school children were, therefore, taught in one of the other four other types of school (see Table 8.3 for the actual distribution between state maintained schools).

(i) Public schools

The postwar future of public schools was far from secure. Before 1939 they had been in considerable financial trouble, with falling rolls obliging headmasters to spend 'half their time in commercial travelling ... touting on preparatory school doorsteps'.[57] In 1940 they then became the target for much political venom because the qualities of leadership, which they were supposed to instil in their pupils, had been found wanting by the failure of appeasement and the retreat to Dunkirk. 'They had been trained to lead', railed their foremost critic (himself inevitably an ex-public schoolboy), 'and they had led us up the garden.' Further vehement attacks were launched in the 1950s and 1960s. Crosland (another ex-public schoolboy) identified them as the 'strongest remaining bastion of class privilege'. Then in the early 1960s, when the institutional impediments to growth came under scrutiny, Eccles (yet another, and more seriously a Conservative minister) was moved to reflect that 'a small minority of children coming from more or less the same kind of homes and receiving an exceptional kind of education is bad for our society'.[58] The corollary was the appointment of the Public Schools Commission in 1965.

Public, unlike direct grant, schools survived the Commission's report although they lost some of their tax privileges.[59] This was due to three factors:

- covert official support
- the schools' adaptability
- public demand.

Official support did not include the widespread payment of state bursaries as proposed by the wartime Fleming Committee and by the Public Schools Commission. These were rejected – by the schools themselves as a threat to their independence, by local authorities because of the expense, and by work-ing-class parents on account of the social pressures to which their children would be subjected. Rather, abolition was dismissed because it would have infringed individual freedom and because the official conviction was that the schools were centres of educational excellence and experiment which provided a rounded education particularly for their boarding pupils. Public schools also proved to be *adaptable* to changing need, not least because of a £2 million subsidy from industry (channelled to them through the civil service) to improve their science facilities. Indeed by the 1960s more school leavers were joining industry and business than the professions.[60] Finally there was *public demand*. Increasing affluence enabled those middle-class parents who so desired to buy the social privilege for which public schools were condemned. The most powerful parental motivation, however, was the desire to secure the 'best possible' education for their children, and this motivation increased as standards in state schools were perceived to fall. Between 1947 and 1976 the percentage of children attending private schools almost halved from 10.2 per cent to 5.7 per cent, but as the number of comprehensive schools expanded so too did the demand for private education.[61]

> One significant reason for the continuing popularity of public schools was their success with students who had 'failed' the 11-plus examination. In the 1950s, 70 per cent of those 'failures' attained five or more 'O' levels, and 25 per cent two or more 'A' levels.

(ii) Grammar schools

As the traditional guarantor of both academic excellence and working-class upward mobility, grammar schools continued in the 1950s to retain the fierce loyalty of teachers, parents and many Labour councillors. With the onset of comprehensive education after 1965, however, their number also began to fall, although (as has been seen) they provided in many areas the focus for popu-lar resistance.

Essentially their decline reflected their inability to match the adaptability of public schools. The 11-plus examination was designed to supply them with children from all classes 'interested in learning for its own sake'. GCE 'O' and 'A' levels had also been introduced in 1951 specifically to ensure the mainte-nance of high academic standards until the age of 18, when (it was assumed) the majority of their pupils would progress either to university or into the professions. As research soon demonstrated, however, the 11-plus examina-tion was flawed and, of those working-class children who did gain admit-tance a disproportionately high percentage either left at 15 or performed poorly in the sixth form.

Various expedients were tried. Fines were even proposed for parents whose children left early. Scientific subjects were also expanded as much to maintain the interest of the academic 'misfit' as to assume the training of a technocratic elite from the unloved technical schools.[62] Many working-class children and parents, however, continued to be alienated by the traditions, discipline and social values permeating grammar schools. In short, despite many individual successes, grammar schools as a whole failed to bridge the two critical gaps between the arts and the sciences and between middle-class and working-class culture.

> High wastage rates in grammar schools were first identified in the 1954 report, *Early Leaving*. So great did it remain that as late as 1967 three-quarters of all sixth-formers were in public schools.[63]

(iii) Secondary moderns

Secondary modern schools, which catered for three-quarters of pupils in the 1950s, represented one of the saddest failures of postwar policy. The intention behind them had been liberal. Teachers, in conjunction with parents and local industrialists, were to design courses free from a centrally imposed curriculum which would best suit their particular pupils. Secondary moderns, in other words, were to enjoy the essential qualities which, in the German tripartite system after the war, were to make the vocationally oriented Hauptschule so great a success.

In Britain, however, the experiment failed.[64] This was in part because secondary moderns were identified with prewar elementary schools and were denied adequate resources. As late as 1960, for instance, only 10 per cent of schools were purpose-built and one-fifth of teachers graduates. The commitment made in 1958 to honour the wartime pledge of 'parity of esteem' came a decade too late.

More pertinently, secondary moderns came to be judged by wholly inappropriate criteria. Very reluctantly central government had been persuaded in 1953 that, rather than being transferred to grammar schools, 'academic' pupils should be permitted to sit GCE 'O' levels within secondary moderns. Thereafter – to the detriment of the majority of pupils – the interest of teachers, the ambition of parents and the reputation of the school became focused on these results (which could on the whole only be inferior to those of grammar schools).

Equally reluctantly central government consented in 1965 to the introduction of a new national examination for the majority of secondary modern pupils, the CSE. As had been warned, such an examination

on a national basis would induce uniformity of syllabuses, curriculum and methods at stages and ages where uniformity would be most undesirable. Schools would feel unable to resist pressure to enter pupils for it . . . it would prejudice the more widespread development of the varied and lively courses already to be found in the best modern schools. There is also a risk that it would be regarded as an index to the efficiency of schools, a conception which would be unrealistic and even oppressive in view of the wide differences in circumstances and in the range of ability of their pupils.[65]

A large amount of local variety and teacher assessment was built into the examination, but this merely became one of the reasons why it came to be regarded as inferior to the GCE.

Secondary modern schools, in short, fell victim to a lack of imagination and conviction on the part of educationalists and parents. Neither group was willing to accept that equality could best be achieved through the development and rigorous testing of different, but equally valuable, aptitudes and skills.

(iv) Comprehensives

Comprehensive schools, as has been seen, rapidly replaced grammar and secondary modern schools after 1965 (see also Table 8.3). For all the speed of their advance, however, their positive educational purpose was never clear. Comprehensive education had long been advocated within the Labour Party on educational, social and economic grounds. Through the education of children of all abilities and classes within one school, it was believed, genuine equality of opportunity could be provided and class barriers eroded with the result that individual fulfilment, social cohesion and economic efficiency could be maximized. However, given the nature of existing school buildings and of vested interests both inside and outside the teaching profession (which it was the ultimate purpose of comprehensivization to change), the implementation of policy posed many practical problems.

The postwar Labour governments, for example, despite the opportunities offered by the 1944 Act, actually rejected plans for comprehensivization drafted by exceptional LEAs such as Middlesex. Their basic reasons were that at a time of economic stringency other educational policies should take precedence and that it would be imprudent to replace wholesale a proven avenue of working-class upward mobility (the grammar school) with an untried experiment.

One practical issue which discouraged early acceptance of comprehensive schooling was the question of size. To ensure an adequate sixth form, it was calculated, a comprehensive school would need to have at least 750 pupils – whereas the average size of grammar and secondary modern schools as late as 1964 was only 560 and 420 respectively.[66] In so large a school, would there be adequate pastoral care for the disadvantaged? Moreover, would headteachers be able to 'control and inspire' the educational development of all pupils, and especially the academic minority? It was because of such concerns that the largest teaching union, the National Union of Teachers, did not vote in favour of comprehensive education until 1965.

Similar problems attended the implementation of Crosland's Circular 10/65 which, because it provided neither a positive educational lead nor any new injection of finance, has been condemned as a 'toothless tiger'.[67] The momentum for reform, as has been seen, gathered pace for largely negative reasons – such as the prevention of misallocation and the removal from children (and their parents) of the stigma of having 'failed' the 11-plus. Until 1975 no government was willing to intervene directly in 'professional' matters such as the nature of the curriculum or the age of selection for specialist training. Moreover, even the most progressive LEAs became increasingly concerned at the damage to teachers' morale caused by over-speedy and under-funded reform which might result in split-site schools with a small sixth form, presided over by an unenthusiastic head-teacher.[68]

Consequently, the positive social and educational purpose behind the ideal of comprehensivization tended to be obscured. Given the continued existence of grammar (let alone public) schools, under half of comprehensives in the early 1970s could claim to be teaching children of all abilities within their locality. In addition, given the continuing demand on educational grounds for streaming from parents, teachers and even ministers (such as Crosland himself), under a quarter provided mixed ability teaching even in their first year. Comprehensivization may thus have provided the structure in which certain failings of the tripartite system could be remedied. However, it remains an open question whether all the emotional, financial and political capital expended might not have been put to a better educational purpose.[69]

Comprehensive education had the potential to increase as well as reduce social inequality. For example, the introduction of the CSE examination (which was designed to cater for the middle band of pupils, whilst the top 20 per cent sat GCE and the bottom 40 per cent nothing) encouraged streaming. Such streaming was by teacher assessment which, as has been seen, could be class biased. Moreover, the creation of 'neighbourhood' schools threatened to end a traditional avenue of upward social mobility. As was argued by a former Conservative minister in 1965: 'universal comprehensive schooling might even intensify the class barriers which are so often co-terminus with geographical barriers . . . .. The brilliant child from a tough area, who will now often find his way to a good grammar school a short distance away, could find himself [sic] handicapped by confinement to his home area from which the comprehensive's pupils are recruited'. Class exclusiveness could, and was, intensified by the movement of middle-class parents to the catchment area of schools with good results.[70]

The teaching profession

A predominant influence on educational progress was the quality of teaching. The period between 1944 and 1975 has been identified as the 'golden age of teacher control'.[71] The 1944 Act had laid down no specific requirements for the curriculum outside religion. When a measure of greater central control was mooted in the early 1960s, it was rebuffed by the creation of a Schools Council for the Curriculum and Examinations which further consolidated teachers' authority. Then, in the development of comprehensive education, Crosland duly confirmed that government influence over the content of education would be limited to inspection and sponsored research. Consequently the 'key to the secret garden of the curriculum' was not actively sought until Callaghan's Ruskin College speech in 1976.[72]

Given such autonomy it was essential for sustained educational progress that teachers should be well trained, well paid and well regarded. None of these criteria were fully met. The most serious failure was training. During the war (and again in the Robbins Report) an attempt was made to enhance the quality of training by associating it more closely with universities. Preoccupied by other issues, however, they were largely unenthusiastic. Instead, in the 1950s training was overshadowed by the interwar legacy of small, isolated and single-sex voluntary institutions. Then when it was expanded under greater central control in the 1960s, it was subject to a 'deliberate policy of overcrowding' and absurd fluctuations which led to a trebling of student numbers between 1960 and 1969 and a subsequent halving between 1975 and 1978. Indeed, in the late 1960s the Department of Education and Science had no reliable statistics on the number of trainees, let alone on the quality of their training.[73] In consequence, the quality of teaching could act as a constraint on educational progress particularly in the state sector.

Higher education

Until the first polytechnics were opened in 1969 higher education was dominated by universities and, as has been seen, they expanded dramatically after the war with:

- the opening of Keele in 1951
- the upgrading of five university colleges and the commissioning of seven new universities, even before the publication of the Robbins Report
- the raising to university status in 1965 of the nine colleges of advanced technology (CATs).[74]

Aided by the mandatory provision of grants, which established the 'tradition' of English students studying away from home, the number of students tripled between 1951 and 1975 (see Table 8.4). Such an expansion was not openly sought by the universities, but was forced upon them by international trends, the needs of industry and, above all, by popular demand.

This imbalance between supply and demand reflected universities' innate conservatism. Ministers and civil servants in the Department of Education and Science (to which universities became responsible in 1962) had a particular vested interest in exaggerating this conservatism. Indeed they used it to justify the concentration of post-Robbins expansion in the more 'socially responsive and responsible' polytechnics. They resented the fact that universities, whilst becoming increasingly dependent on government finance after 1945, had succeeded through the University Grants Committee (UGC) in maintaining their autonomy.[75] Nevertheless there was some justice in the charge. Despite the international reputation of certain research centres, undergraduate curricula and teaching methods were frequently outdated, the number of female undergraduates (as has been seen) was indefensibly low and the development, at government's request, of teacher training and applied (as opposed to pure) science was less than enthusiastic.

Consequently, when expansion was forced upon them, universities did not handle it particularly well – although the UGC, pressurized by the government's insistence on precipitate change and by uneven funding, did remain a more effective planning agency than any devised by the Department of Education and Science.[76] The result was the student unrest of the late 1960s and the drop in public esteem which led to the backlash of the mid-1970s.[77]

The need for university expansion was demonstrated by the fact that, by 1961, 6.9 per cent of 18-year-olds were qualified for university entrance. In comparison with the USA where the comparable figure was 18 per cent, however, there were places for only 4 per cent. The number of 11-plus failures alone, who were qualified, was sufficient to fill Leicester University (though, contrary to some rumours, this never actually happened).

Table 8.4 Students in further and higher education, 1951–75 (thousands)

	1951	1955	1960	1965	1970	1975
Further education						
Full-time/sandwich	46	58	117	186	271	387
Part-time, day	298	391	488	680	749	743
Evening	550	634	713	796	736	802
Teacher training	25	25	34	73	111	99
Universities						
Students		82	85	108	169	228	261

Note: Figures for further education are for England and Wales only; for universities, the whole of the UK.

Sources: Department of Education and Science, *Statistics of Education* (1977) vol. 3; B. Simon, *Education and the Social Order, 1940–1990* (1991).

Further education

Further education embraced a bewildering array of institutions, run largely by local government, which catered for an equally bewildering array of students studying for:

- pleasure
- individual self-improvement
- within structured day-release or 'sandwich' courses.

Institutional restructuring and upgrading were a constant feature of this sector. For example, there was the merger in 1956 of technical colleges into CATs (which duly became universities in 1965) and the amalgamation of a further 94 colleges into 30 polytechnics between 1969 and 1973.

Absent from all this restructuring, however, was any sustained attempt to reduce what the 1959 Crowther Report had termed the 'no man's land' between formal education and employment – to create, in other words, the county colleges envisaged in the 1944 Act (and duly developed in postwar Germany) to which school leavers, whilst being trained by employers in particular skills, might be systematically released to acquire a more rounded understanding of theoretical, business and social issues. The money spent on raising the compulsory age of formal schooling could well have been better spent on developing this area of further education.[78] Moreover, stronger central support should have been given to polytechnics – and to a lesser extent CATs – to prevent them, under popular demand, from repeating the mistake of the CSE examination in relation to GCE: the increasing imitation of academic university courses.

Final assessment

Whilst there was an unquestionable improvement on prewar standards at each level of education, the record was by no means unblemished. The most successful initiatives were in the private sector, be it in pre-school playgroups or public schools. Within the public sector the full benefit of equally valuable initiatives such as secondary modern, technical and comprehensive schools was denied by a lack of sustained support and resources. Elite institutions, such as grammar schools and universities, were also insufficiently flexible to adapt adequately to changing economic and social needs.

8.5 TECHNICAL EDUCATION

Within the varied record of educational achievement, the most notable failure was that of technical education which in its broadest sense can be defined as:

- vocational training within schools for non-academic children
- a balanced programme of industrial training

- day-release courses for school leavers and an emphasis on applied, as opposed to pure, science in higher education.

What was the cause of this failure?

Wartime momentum

Before the war the need to reshape secondary education to meet the needs of a more technocratic society had been recognized by the 1938 Spens Committee, and its concern was shared by the 1943 white paper *Educational Reconstruction* (see Section 8.2). The war itself also highlighted the need both to forge closer links between industry and universities and to expand the supply of skilled managers and technicians. Consequently two major reconstruction plans were drafted. The 1945 Percy Committee on Higher Technological Education anticipated the binary principle of the 1960s by proposing a national network of technical colleges, to run parallel to universities, which would offer diplomas and degrees validated by a National Council of Technology. Somewhat contradictorily the 1946 Barlow Report on Scientific Manpower (Cmd 6824) recommended a rapid doubling of scientific graduates within the existing university structure – albeit one strengthened by the establishment of a new technological university and three institutes of technology with the authority to supervise postgraduate research.

Peacetime reforms

By the mid-1950s the 'critical mass' for technical education – by which, it was hoped, Britain's culture and thereby its international competitiveness would be transformed – had failed to materialize and the Conservative government (as has been seen) was expressing increasing concern. Few technical schools had been built by LEAs and the experiment was abandoned. Instead, the teaching of science was strengthened in all other schools in both the public and private sector.

In higher education exactly the opposite happened. Initially an attempt had been made to expand the existing system. Imperial College (London), for example, was given increased resources and status, although no new technological university or institute was founded (to the anger of Churchill's scientific adviser Lord Cherwell who resigned from the Cabinet in 1953). Advanced work was discouraged in local authority colleges, despite pressure from demobilized ex-servicemen, for fear this would lead to 'cut-throat competition' with universities.[79] In 1956, however, the Conservatives announced an ambitious five-year programme to create, in line with the Percy Report, a hierarchy of technical colleges outside the university system.

The structure of technical education proposed in 1956 had three tiers. Local and area colleges provided teaching up to the level of Ordinary National Certificate. Some 25 to 30 regional colleges concentrated on preparing full-time students for the Higher National Diploma. Finally, at the apex, ten CATs preparing students for a new National Diploma of Technology overseen by a National Council of Technical Awards (the Hives Committee).[80]

In the 1960s there was a temporary reversion to the Barlow principle with the transformation of CATs into technological universities by the 1964–70 Labour government. This government, in its desire to generate the 'white heat' of a scientific revolution, also despaired of voluntaryism within industry. It duly passed the 1965 Industrial Training Act which established within each industry an Industrial Training Board with the power, for the first time, to impose a levy on all employers from which companies with a structured training programme could be subsidized.[81] The Act had in fact been drafted under the Conservatives and, on their return to power, they tightened its provisions. Their 1973 Employment Training Act gave significant new powers to the semi-independent Manpower Services Commission, and thus initiated a shift in responsibility for training from the educational establishment to industry, which was to be dramatically accelerated after 1976.

Policy failure

These structural changes had some beneficial effects. The number of arts and science undergraduates, for example, rose roughly in parity and so, with the explosion of the total student population, the absolute number of scientists and technologists significantly increased. In relation to Britain's competitors, however, neither the rate nor the rigour of the advance was adequate within schools, industry or further education.

In the school sector, as has been seen, academic examinations were introduced – contrary to the intention of wartime planners – first into secondary modern schools and then for the less able pupils in comprehensive schools. As a consequence the vocational needs of non-academic pupils were neither clearly defined nor satisfied. An expensive initiative by the Schools Council in 1967 to revolutionize the teaching of technology was also submerged beneath the organizational problems posed by comprehensivization.

Within industry, even after the establishment of Industrial Training Boards, the nature of training on the shop floor remained highly conservative and unleavened by the broader perspectives that the 1944 Act had intended to, and German practice did, introduce through day-release courses. Moreover, largely as a result of industrial restructuring, the number of apprenticeships actually collapsed from 240,000 in 1965 to 140,000 in 1974.[82]

Even at the higher level, the swing towards science, for which the planners in the 1940s and 1960s had hoped, failed to materialize. The Robbins Report had recommended that two-thirds of the increase in university students should be in science and technology. By 1967, however, the UGC had had to admit that expansion could only be sustained by admitting more arts and social science students. Two further committees, Dainton (Cmnd 3541) and Swann (Cmnd 3760), were appointed and reported in 1968 on why the demand for degrees and employment in science, engineering and technology was so deficient.

Policy failure resulted in Britain having a relatively unqualified workforce and low productivity. Whereas in the mid-1970s the number of university graduates within British and German industry was broadly similar, two-thirds of German workers had 'intermediate' qualifications, compared with only one-third of British workers. These proportions were reversed for those with no qualifications. 'The Germans', as Sanderson had noted, were 'much better at educating the lowest half of the ability range and they have successfully developed from within that half much of the technically skilled labour force on which their industrial strength rests'.[83]

Reasons for failure

There were five major reasons for policy failure:

- the bias and competence of policy-makers
- the hesistancy of local government
- the conservatism of the teaching profession
- lack of public demand
- the negativism of industry.

The composition of the Robbins Committee, which included only one scientist, was symbolic of a latent bias amongst *policy-makers* which consistently impeded the development of technical education. Although the need to redress the balance of the British educational system was well recognized, the principal danger (reinforced by the experience of Nazism) was still identified as 'unbridled scientism' rather than the absence amongst political and industrial leaders of scientific understanding and business skills. Hence the first postwar university was not the technological university planned by Barlow but a centre of liberal studies, Keele. Moreover, when the new universities were commissioned before the Robbins Report, their sites were in historic rather than industrial centres. Proposals for a University of Scunthorpe excited little enthusiasm.

In addition to this residual bias, policy-makers also simply lacked the competence to plan and direct the necessary transformation. Butler, as has been seen, quickly passed the issue to his officials and it is to their lack of expertise and drive that the failure successfully to develop technical and secondary modern schools has conventionally been attributed. To dispense, for example, with a fixed national curriculum and to proclaim of secondary moderns (as did the 1943 white paper *Educational Reconstruction*) that 'their future' was 'their own to make' may have displayed commendable liberalism. Less charitably however, it could be argued that it also revealed a culpable lack of positive purpose. In the place of a centralized curriculum, what these schools needed for their success was a central source of expert advice, committed support and, above all, an unequivocal guarantee of equal resources.[84]

Policy-makers alone, however, were not responsible for the failure of technical education. *Local government* remained extremely reluctant either to build technical schools or to relax its historic control over technical colleges and so the colleges could not readily aspire to national (let alone international) standards of excellence.

The *teaching profession* as a whole also proved extremely conservative. This was not only in universities, where few sought to build links with local industry (other than Warwick) or to bridge the disciplinary gap between arts and science (other than new technological universities, such as Aston and Salford, which introduced compulsory social studies units). It was true also in further education, where the profession remained wedded to a mass of arcane qualifications, and in schools, where any variation in professional practice to achieve a greater exchange of ideas and personnel between education and industry was resisted.

On the *demand side* parents in the 1950s showed as little enthusiasm for technical and secondary modern schools as did students in the 1960s for the post-Robbins expansion in science and technology. Social, rather than applied, science was so much the preferred area of study that by 1974 one-third of students in the new 'technological' universities were not studying technology. Even the increase in the training of 16–18 year olds under the MSC after 1973 was hardly a positive move. For most it was an 'emergency alternative' to the reality of rising unemployment.[85]

Most damaging of all, however, was the negativism of *industry*. Even during the war employers had displayed a preference for poaching skilled workers from other firms rather than for developing their own training programmes. When a modicum of compulsion was imposed on them in the 1960s, their response lacked the positive endorsement of national standards and the virtues of day-release courses which characterized their German counterparts. Moreover, by accepting the academic GCE and CSE as the recognized certificate for school leavers, they – as much as universities – discouraged the development within schools of vocational skills.

In the 1956 white paper, *Technical Education,* the Conservative government had stressed that the support of parents and industry was vital for the success of their policy.[86] Short of the 'semi-fascist' methods which had been rejected during the war, it remained far from clear how in the face of such indifference and overt hostility this support could be generated.

8.6 CONCLUSION

Education has historically been regarded as one of the most important areas of state intervention. Classical economists, even in the nineteenth century, excluded it from their general demand for *laissez-faire*, and communist regimes have traditionally accorded it high priority. The Second World War in Britain proved no exception. Education was regarded as being of central importance to the achievement of the dual reconstruction aims of building a more meritocratic and technocratic society. Accordingly, after 1945 it rapidly became the second most expensive welfare service. As a result, and in common with the experience abroad, formal educational achievements by 1975 had exceeded all possible prewar expectations – and such an achievement did not reflect, as some insinuated, any general decline in standards.

The consensus which supported this educational expansion was, for so political an issue, remarkable. It did, however, conceal areas of considerable disagreement.

- Pedagogically, was an individual's independence best secured by a training in 'liberal' values or in marketable skills?
- Politically, was the ultimate objective of education to reinforce traditional social values and structures or to engineer social change?

Such questions, which went to the heart of the conflict over whether the fundamental purpose of the welfare state should be to improve the functional efficiency or the equality of society, had been left unresolved by the 1944 Education Act. Innately conservative, it had nevertheless prescribed no rigid structure for schools nor – uniquely in Western Europe – a centralized curriculum. It had merely removed the historical impediments to reform.

The opportunity thus offered was not seized as effectively as it was in other countries. Policy-makers clearly identified the key issues and the full range of relevant policy options. New initiatives, however, were abandoned before they had had the opportunity to achieve their objectives (such as technical and secondary modern schools). Alternatively, they were compromised by over-hasty implementation and underfunding (such as the expansion of comprehensive and higher education). Other policies such as tripartism and intelligence testing (as one amongst many tools for determining children's schooling) were also abandoned for no good educational reason. Tripartism after all remains the organizational principle behind the highly effective German education system and intelligence testing (under the guise of 'verbal reasoning') is still employed within British schools to measure children's progress.

Each policy initiative, however, fell victim to an ill-conceived attempt to resolve by structural means the fundamental educational and social dilemma of how to meet children's individual needs without reinforcing social divisions. Such an attempt evaded rather than resolved the issue. By reinforcing the bias against vocational training, it also discouraged the development of an 'industrial' culture upon which international competitiveness and ultimately individual welfare depended.

Policy-makers within central government were not solely responsible for these failures, although they did fail to ensure one of the preconditions of success: the proper payment and training of teachers. Their chosen policy was not to employ their residual power to 'control and direct' but to allow the implementation of policy to be determined, under the aegis of LEAs and the UGC, by public demand, the vested interest of the teaching profession and the apathy of industry. When such decentralization failed, especially in relation to technical education, the demand for greater centralization became inexorable.

8.7 FURTHER READING

The history of education has spawned a large and varied literature. It is best summarized, albeit with a clear political bias, in two books by Roy Lowe, *Education in the Postwar Years* (1988), and *Schooling and Social Change, 1964–1990* (1997); and in B. Simon, *Education and the Social Order, 1940–1990* (1991). Additional information, particularly on unglamorous but essential issues, such as curricula and examinations, is provided in P. Gosden, *The Education System since 1944* (1983). The journal *History of Education* contains the latest research.

The war period is definitively covered by P. Gosden, *Education in the Second World War* (1976), and the same author, together with P. R. Sharp, has provided a good case-study of policy implementation in *The Development of an Education Service: the West Riding, 1889–1974* (1978). The issue of equality is covered incisively in M. Sanderson, *Educational Opportunity and Social Change in England* (1987) and further education authoritatively in W. A. C. Stewart, *Higher Education in Postwar Britain* (1989).

The latter covers technical education, a subject long neglected by historians as well as educationalists until the changed priorities of the 1980s. C. Barnett in *The Audit of War* (1986) led the offensive to which a riposte, together with a bibliographical guide to the debate, has been provided by D. Edgerton, *Science, Technology and Britain's Industrial 'Decline', 1870–1970* (Cambridge, 1996). Good historical analysis is provided by G. McCulloch, *The Secondary Technical School* (Lewes, 1989) and M. Sanderson, *The Missing Stratum: technical school education in England, 1900–1990s* (1994), whilst industrial training is covered by D. H. Aldcroft, *Education, Training and Economic Performance, 1894 to 1990* (Manchester, 1992), and, in an international context, by D. King, *Actively Seeking Work?* (Chicago, 1995).

There is also a rich supply of contemporary literature. An insight into the earlier period is provided by O. Banks, *Parity and Prestige in English Secondary Education* (1955), while the optimism of the 1960s is well captured in J. Vaizey, *Education for Tomorrow* (1962) and R. Pedley, *The Comprehensive School* (1962). The ambitions and frustrations of two reforming ministers of education, Sir

Edward Boyle and Anthony Crosland, are recorded in M. Kogan (ed.), *The Politics of Education* (1971). Finally, two excellent collections of primary sources, for official reports and educational research respectively, are J. S. Maclure, *Educational Documents* (5th edn, 1986); and H. Silver, *Equal Opportunity in Education* (1973).

CONTENTS

1942	Scott report, *Land Utilisation in Rural Areas* (Cmd 6378) – supports stricter planning. Uthwatt report, *Compensation and Betterment* (Cmd 6291) – recommends nationalization of development rights
1944	*Control of Land Use* white paper (Cmd 6537) – compromises on earlier reports. Dudley report on housing standards
1945	*Housing* white paper (Cmd 6609) – sets Labour's objectives
1946	New Towns Act. Civil disobedience – outbursts of squatting in London and disused army camps
1947	Town and Country Planning Act – establishment of Land Commission and 100 per cent betterment tax
1948	National Parks Act
1951	Conservative election commitment to build 300,000 houses annually
1952	Town and Country Planning Act – abolition of Land Commission, creation of dual market in land
1956	Suspension of general housing subsidy. Subsidies tailored to encourage high-rise building
1957	Rent Act – starts deregulation
1959	Town and Country Planning Act – councils have to purchase land at market value. Subsequent explosion in land prices. Mandatory improvement grants – to encourage renovation (effective only after 1968) →

1961 Parker-Morris report, *Homes for Today and Tomorrow* – recommends new minimum standards	*Home* tv drama). Land Commission Act – re-establishes Land Commission and betterment tax (abolished again in 1971)
1963 Rachman scandal. Owner occupiers no longer taxed on imputed rent.	1968 *Old Houses into New Homes* white paper (Cmnd 3602) – prioritizes renovation. Ronan Point collapses – abrupt end to high-rise building
1964 Housing Corporation established to encourage housing associations	
1965 Milner Holland report, *Housing in Greater London* (Cmnd 2605) – finds no widespread abuse of 1957 Rent Act. Rent Act – introduces fair rents. *Housing Programme, 1965–1970* (Cmnd 2838) – Labour accepts owner-occupancy as 'normal'	1972 Housing Finance Act – subsidizes people not buildings. Leads to suspension of Clay Cross councillors in 1973
	1974 Labour freezes council house rents. Housing Action Areas – to refocus help on needy
1966 Shelter founded as pressure group for the homeless (later boosted by 1967 *Cathy Come*	1975 Community Land Act – renews local authorities' right to buy land below full market value

In contrast to education, housing policy enjoyed little wartime consensus and remained throughout the postwar years at the heart of party conflict. During the war, admittedly, a white paper had been published on the related issue of land use; and after the mid-1950s the Labour Party endorsed the Conservatives' earlier call for a 'property-owning democracy'. However, the wartime coalition was unable eventually to agree upon the white paper's proposals and the ownership of land, as Michael Foot has remarked, became 'the rock' upon which it was broken.[1] Thereafter it was to remain a key election issue. So too were the management and finance, if not the principles, of the housing programme. In the 1951 and 1964 elections, for example, the Conservative and Labour Parties respectively used the promise to build 300,000 houses a year and the Rachman scandal over the terrorizing of private tenants to discredit the 'socialist' and 'free-market' approaches to housing and thereby their opponents' overall attitude towards the welfare state.

The interest of the electorate itself was initially intense, with 41 per cent of those polled in 1946 identifying it as their principal concern (whilst only 15 per cent chose full employment).[2] Despite a steady improvement in housing standards, however, disillusion soon became endemic. A survey of public attitudes towards the welfare state in 1956 revealed that it was 'the only service about which there were widespread complaints'; and dissatisfaction mounted with the rapid increase in high-rise estates (which were the mirror image of people's stated preferences) and the reports of corruption which affected this area of the welfare state alone. Such reports were particularly justified in Northern Ireland and Scotland where, as has been described in Section 4.4, the implementation of policy was distinct from that in England and Wales. The distribution of subsidies also provoked dissatisfaction. In middle-class demonology, scroungers on the dole queue were quickly replaced by tenants in subsidized council housing with 'private cars outside and television aerials which festooned the roofs'. On the left, a similar hatred was reserved for private landlords and property developers.

Such widespread antagonism and resentment were a reflection of the extent and complexity of government intervention in the housing market. Within the constraints set by private landlords, financial institutions, the construction industry and local authorities, central government was expected to implement a wide range of controls (covering, for example, land use, housing standards and rent) and to provide extensive subsidies for both the public and private sectors.

State intervention on this scale was not unique to Britain. Subsidization of housing, for example, was – and is – common to all Western countries, in part because the costs of construction are high in relation to average wages and in part because housing is recognized to be a public good (see Section 3.2.1). As the One Nation group of Conservative backbenchers acknowledged in 1950, for instance, good housing can both assist labour mobility (and hence economic growth) and also reduce expenditure on other social services (by improving health and enhancing the quality of life – thereby reducing the number of broken marriages and, arguably, crime).[3]

Where Britain was unique, however, was that subsidies were not spread evenly – as elsewhere – through a wide network of agencies, and government itself owned much of the housing stock (the comparable figures for Britain and France in the early 1970s, for example, being 31 and 0.5 per cent). Consequently the opportunity for political antagonism in Britain was far greater. Moreover, in Britain there was until 1973 the anomaly that only two of the three major types of housing tenure – council housing and owner-occupancy – were subsidized. The third – private rented accommodation – was not, although ironically it was the one to which the poorest traditionally had the most recourse.

The extent and complexity of government intervention makes the accurate assessment of housing costs over time extremely difficult. As demonstrated in Table 9.1, current expenditure consists largely of loan repayments to private financial institutions and is offset by both subsidies (from tax-payers and rate-payers) and by rent paid by tenants. More particularly, tax relief on mortgage interest payments – as a prime example of 'tax expenditure' – is not recorded in conventional government accounts (see Appendix A.4) and its full cost was only made public in the 1970s as a result of public pressure following the dramatic increase in house prices, and thus in the government's liability. Aggregate figures do, however, clearly demonstrate two underlying trends. *First*, as conventionally defined, housing expenditure declined between 1951 and 1971 from approximately 20 per cent to 10 per cent of social expenditure, before rising again to 16 per cent in 1976. *Second*, it was extremely volatile as a result of its sensitivity to both political fashion and the needs of the managed economy. In the 1950s, and again after 1974, its growth was less than

Table 9.1   Housing: selected current and capital expenditure, 1951–76 (£m)

	1951–2	1956–7	1961–2	1966–7	1971–2	1975–6
Current expenditure						
Local Authority housing (net)	15	30	45	75	72	189
Repairs, maintenance, etc.	47	65	97	114	284	764
Loan charges	81	167	258	420	701	1,524
Less: rent received	–84	–154	–232	–396	–681	–1,236
Government subsidies	–38	–67	–78	–101	–232	–863
Total current expenditure	78	108	137	187	348	1,534
Tax relief on mortgages	–	–	–	–	328	770
Capital expenditure						
Local Authority	298	293	279	679	673	2,041
Public Corporation	21	32	25	54	73	298
Total capital expenditure	340	382	431	825	917	2,966
Total public expenditure on housing	417	490	568	1,012	1,265	4,500

Sources: Social Trends (1970, 1977); Annual Abstract of Statistics (1964).

any other welfare service, whereas in the early 1970s it expanded at almost double the average rate (see Appendix, Tables A.4 and A.5).

In comparison with other welfare services, therefore, postwar housing policy was not only more politically contentious and publicly disliked but also more administratively complex and economically volatile. Its four principal object-ives nevertheless remained relatively consistent: the provision of

- a sufficient number of houses
- in a well-planned environment
- of an adequate quality
- at a fair price.

It is against these criteria that its record will be assessed.

9.1 PLANNING

The one area in which the war did achieve a continuing measure of consensus was, ironically, the most contentious: land ownership. Before the war, only 3 per cent of land had been effectively subject to planning permission. After the war, no land could be developed without prior consent from local or central government. This was a revolutionary restriction on the traditional rights of private property and, together with the Beveridge Report and the Keynesian input into the 1944 *Employment Policy* white paper, may be seen as a classic example of the confidence of 'disinterested' experts that they could use the dislocation of war to realize reforms long championed by informed opinion.

- How was this modicum of consensus achieved?
- Why was consensus not more extensive?
- How effectively was planning policy implemented?

Wartime truce

The acceptance of planning permission was a consequence of both long-term trends and short-term need. Since the turn of the century there had been growing concern about uncontrolled urban development. Pressure groups had been formed, such as the Town and Country Planning Association and the Campaign for the Preservation of Rural England, to encourage better urban planning and to discourage urban sprawl. They had met with partial success. Locally, for instance, the London County Council had adopted in the 1930s the principle of green belts and satellite towns. Nationally, the 1940 Barlow Report had advocated the creation of a 'central authority' to oversee the dispersal of industry and people from congested areas.[4] The war reinforced such trends. Detailed legislative change was considered by two reconstruction committees, the Scott Committee on Land Utilization and the Uthwatt Committee on Compensation and Betterment.[5] Even more importantly, extensive bomb damage created an urgent need for redevelopment. In a last flowering of Victorian optimism and utopianism, planners such as Patrick Abercrombie (who was responsible for the 1945 Greater London Plan) exuded the confidence that they could mastermind such redevelopment.

The minimum power they needed, it was agreed, was the power to forestall the worst excesses of unrestricted 'market' forces. More extensive powers to permit an active government role in urban redevelopment, however, aroused great controversy. This was because they went to the heart of the ideological differences between the Conservative and Labour Parties over whether power should lie ultimately in the market or with the state. Three particular issues were to dog policy-makers.

- Should betterment (the large increase in the value of land once it had been granted planning permission) be enjoyed by the private landowner or by the community?
- How could a steady supply of land for development be ensured, especially if the owner were to be denied betterment?
- How successfully could central and local government adjust to, and discharge, their new positive responsibilities? Both would acquire more power as the rights of private property declined and need to acquire new skills (such as the valuation of land in the absence of clear market criteria).[6]

In order to maintain political unity, the Coalition's 1944 white paper *Control of Land Use* sought to resolve these problems by steering a middle course between the traditional Labour and Conservative preferences for the nationalization of, and a free-market in, land. It rejected the outright nationalization of land or of development rights (as recommended by Uthwatt); but, whilst thus defending private ownership, it agreed that no land should be developed without planning permission. Owners should be compensated for the loss of any anticipated profit from the unrestricted development of their land. Should they thereafter be granted planning permission, however, they should be subject to a betterment tax equivalent to 80 per cent of the increased value of their land. Finally, the white paper proposed a land commission to oversee both the levying of this tax and the payment of compensation.

The authors of the white paper were fully alive to the political sensitivity of their proposals. As the introduction stated: 'proposals for controlling the use of land are bound to raise again issues which for many years have been the subject of keen political controversy. . . . No proposals on this subject – on which widely divergent views are held with conviction – can be wholly satisfactory to all shades of opinion.' At the same time, however, they were aware that agreement was urgently needed were a repetition of interwar failures to be avoided. The proposed compromise, they felt, successfully reconciled the 'rights of land tenure . . . with the best use of land in the national interest'.[7] Landowners were to be denied windfall profits from decisions by local government to zone certain areas, but not others, for development. The supply of land would be maintained because nationalization (with its attendant political and financial problems) was to be avoided and owners were to retain 20 per cent of the enhanced value of their land. Finally, the land commission would not develop into a bureaucratic monster, as it would not itself own or develop land (again as Uthwatt had proposed) or acquire a large independent income (as revenue from betterment tax would be matched by outgoings on compensation).

Resumption of party hostilities

After the war, however, neither Labour nor Conservative governments endorsed this compromise and, to the detriment of their respective housing programmes, followed sharply divergent policies. Labour government policy was dominated by two main principles. *First*, the community rather than the private landowner should enjoy the major benefits of betterment. Consequently, in its major legislation – the 1947 Town and Country Planning Act, the 1967 Land Commission Act and finally the 1975 Community Land Act – a betterment tax was introduced at the respective rates of 100 per cent, 40 per cent and 60 per cent. *Second*, government should have the ultimate right to buy and develop land, so that a ready supply could be guaranteed for house-building. Hence in 1947 and 1967 a Land Commission was established, and in 1975 local authorities were empowered to buy land below its full 'developmental' value.[8] This land could then either be used for public building, thereby reducing *inter alia* the cost of council housing, or it could be sold to private developers at its full market price, thereby generating a profit from which 'unprofitable' but socially desirable developments, such as recreational facilities, could be financed.

The need for Labour governments to introduce three separate acts reflected the antipathy of intervening Conservative governments towards any interference in land development beyond planning permission. They maintained that, once the worst war damage and the absolute shortage of housing had been made good, the supply and price of land could best be determined by the free market. Thus, on their return to office, the two Land Commissions were abolished (in 1953 and 1971 respectively) and after 1959 local government was required to purchase land for development at its full market price, with all betterment accruing to the landowner. In the 1970s the justification for such a policy was that any private profit would be subject to capital gains, or to the later development gains, tax.

The failure of 'socialist' policy

The policies of both parties were a failure.[9] Labour's imposition of a 100 per cent betterment tax in the 1940s removed all incentive from landowners to sell and consequently there was a 'development strike'. Moreover, the Land Commission was unable to guarantee the supply of land since the money at its disposal (£100,000 in the first year) was derisory and its powers of compulsory purchase were ill-defined. In the 1960s the new Land Commission traded constantly at a loss and, by the time of its abolition, had sold only 913 acres of land. Similarly, under the Community Land Act only 6000 acres were purchased by local authorities and by 1979 they had accumulated debts of £33 million. Labour's practical achievements were therefore minimal.

It might be argued, especially of the 1967 and 1975 Acts, that this failure was due not to any inherent defect but to the ideological bias of incoming Conservative governments which repealed them just as they were about to bear fruit. Such an argument would, however, be fallacious because within each Labour government there were major obstacles to, and serious reservations about, the full implementation of policy. *Economically*, each piece of legislation coincided with a sterling crisis which strictly limited the money available for land purchase. *Politically*, grave concern was expressed about any policy which – whatever its long-term gains – might in the short term delay the release of land and thus disrupt the housing programme. It was also significant that in the 1940s and 1960s the ministers responsible for so radical a new policy (Silkin and Willey) were denied seats in the Cabinet and that in 1976 the Office of Planning and Local Government was abolished as soon as the requisite legislation had been passed. *Administratively*, the instinct and advice of officials (even in the Land Commissions) were to defend the private market; and the Treasury was vehemently opposed to the creation of any new body which had the right to raise, and to dispense the proceeds of, taxation.[10] *Constitutionally*, there were also serious reservations about an unelected body such as the Land Commission usurping the power of local government to buy and to plan the development of land. Consequently Labour policy ultimately failed because, whilst paying lip-service to manifesto commitments, ministers and their officials remained resolutely opposed to their practical implementation.

The failure of market solutions

The policies of successive Conservative governments were even more disastrous. The need was acknowledged for planning permission and even for compulsory purchase in exceptional circumstances. Their major objective was, however, to ensure that landowners received the full market price of their land; and this led first to the anomalous 'dual' market between 1954 and 1959 (when the full price of land could be charged to private developers but not to local authorities) and then to an unprecedented explosion in land and ultimately in house prices in the early 1960s and the 1970s (when local authorities were obliged to pay the full cost).

The Conservatives' faith in the market was confounded by the excessive demand in the 1960s for industrial and residential land and in the 1970s for commercial land. In a rising market landowners and land speculators delayed the sale of land in order to reap higher profits and thereby increased still further both the shortage and the price. In the 1970s such speculation reached exceptional heights because, in its attempt to stimulate industrial growth, the Heath government deliberately made money for investment more readily available. Investors rapidly discovered, however, that easier – and less heavily taxed – profits could be made from property. Consequently, not only individual speculators but also all major institutional investors became heavily involved in the property market. Ministers quickly recognized their mistakes. Thus in the 1960s the reintroduction of a betterment tax was seriously debated within Cabinet, and in the 1970s a freeze on office rents was imposed (until it threatened the whole credit structure of the City of London) and then a new tax on development gains. Such remedies were, however, either too little or too late. Whilst betterment accrued solely to the landowner or speculator, the cost of land escalated so sharply that whereas in the 1950s it had accounted for only 3 per cent of the capital cost of a house, by 1975 it accounted for 19 per cent.[11]

New towns

Despite the failure of both Labour and Conservative governments to regulate land use, there were two relatively minor but successful planning initiatives. The first was the New Towns Act of 1946. The concept of new towns as well-planned, self-contained and communally owned settlements had been privately pioneered before the war at Letchworth and Welwyn Garden City and it was identified by postwar governments as a means of both relieving congestion in major conurbations and stimulating economic growth in relatively depressed areas. As with other interwar ideals, its implementation was initially over-paternalistic (with the appointed – rather than elected – new town corporations, for example, encouraging art galleries and museums but actively discouraging cinemas). It was also neglected in the 1950s. Between 1946 and 1970, however, 31 new towns were designated and they have been described as 'the single, most ambitious planning experiment in postwar Britain'. Nevertheless their significance should not be exaggerated. They accounted for only 3.5 per cent of the houses built during this period.[12]

Fourteen new towns were designated between 1946 and 1951. The majority were near London (such as Stevenage, Crawley and Hatfield) but others were built near Newcastle (Newton Aycliffe and Peterlee), near Glasgow (East Kilbride) and in South Wales (Cwmbran). In the 1950s, only Cumbernauld, near Glasgow, was commissioned; but in the 1960s a further 16 were approved either on green-field sites (most notoriously, Milton Keynes) or at the centre of depressed or relatively slow-growing regions (such as Warrington, Peterborough, Northampton and Londonderry).

National parks

The second initiative was the National Parks Act of 1949 which led to the realisation of another interwar ideal: the creation of national parks and the designation of 'areas of outstanding natural beauty'. This initiative was the consequence of increased popular leisure and, to a lesser extent, of the latent hostility to propertied privilege which had been demonstrated by the 'mass trespass' in the Peak District in 1932. It also represented an early concern for conservation which, in an urban setting, was to be reflected in the foundation of the Civic Trust in 1957 and the creation of conservation areas a decade later.

The national parks legislation was restricted to England and Wales. The first parks to be established in the 1940s and 1950s were the Brecon Beacons, the Pembrokeshire Coast and Snowdonia in Wales; Dartmoor and Exmoor in the west of England; Northumberland, the North Yorkshire Moors and the Yorkshire Dales in the north-east; the Lake District in the north-west; and the Peak District in the midlands. Amongst the initial areas of oustanding natural beauty were the Gower Peninsula in Wales and the Quantock Hills in the west of England. The Antrim Mountains in Northern Ireland were proposed, unsuccessfully, as a national park in the 1960s. None were designated in Scotland until after devolution.

Implementing policy: local government on trial

Constant legislative change consumed much political and administrative energy in Westminster and Whitehall. Actual responsibilty for the implementation of policy, however, fell largely to local government. How successfully did local government rise to this challenge?

Judged by one principal aim of interwar reformers, it was remarkably successful. Urban sprawl was contained, with the annual conversion of land from agricultural use being reduced from 25,000 to 16,000 hectares, or to 0.1 per cent of Britain's land surface.[13] Two serious weaknesses, however, soon became apparent. First, neither the faith of interwar planners nor the 'scientific' techniques of their postwar successors proved sufficient, in the drafting of local development plans, to anticipate changing economic and social needs. Planning disasters consequently ensued. In the short term 'planning blight' descended on many areas awaiting redevelopment, whilst in the long term serious damage was inflicted by the destruction of historic city centres. This weakness was compounded by planners' innate paternalism and secretiveness, which became so notorious that after 1968 they were legally obliged to demonstrate that public opinion had been taken into account during the drafting of plans. The second major weakness (which was in part outside councils' control) was the negativism of public planning. Constrained after 1959 by the high cost of land and denied the proceeds of betterment, local government lacked both the opportunity to develop ambitious public projects and the power to enter into a more constructive partnership with private developers. Given the weakness of local government (as described in Section 4.4) and the succession of postwar planning disasters, such restrictions might be regarded as fortunate; but private development was itself, both before and after the war, far from perfect. A better-planned environment could well have been achieved had a better balance been maintained between public opinion as expressed imperfectly through the ballot box and through the market.

The 1947 Town and Country Planning Act (like the earlier Education Act) concentrated responsibility in England and Wales on county councils and county boroughs and thereby reduced the number of planning authorities from 1441 to 145. This remained the situation until 1975, although in the 1960s county councils were given responsibility solely for the strategic 'structure plan' whilst their constituent districts were charged with its detailed development. In Northern Ireland, planning remained the responsibility of 37 small authorities until centralized under the Department of Environment in Belfast in 1972. In Scotland, the county councils, large burghs and two small burghs answered to the Scottish Office.

9.2   HOUSING CONSTRUCTION

The construction of housing generated far less political controversy than planning, although it equally defied the logic of wartime planners.[14] During the war it had been assumed that, once bomb damage had been repaired, the stabilization of – or even decline in – the number of households would restrict public building largely to the replacement of slums. Then, given the known size of slum areas, this task could be completed. In reality, however, the number of households increased rapidly as a result of changing demographic trends and greater affluence (see Section 4.2). Greater affluence also raised public expectations about the size and quality of housing. As a consequence not only did the demand for new housing rise, but so too did the standards by which property was adjudged fit for human habitation. This happened, moreover, at the very time that more of the old housing stock was falling into serious disrepair as a result of the low quality of much speculative building in the late Victorian and Edwardian periods. Slum clearance, it was gradually realized, was not a finite but a continuing problem.

Government policy to meet these evolving challenges fell into three broad phases. Each covered both Labour and Conservative governments and so reflected a measure of underlying, bipartisan agreement. Within each phase, however, a change of government could – and did – result in a change of tactics and emphasis. Their combined impact was nevertheless a revolution in the nature of both housing and housing tenure.

1945–56: attacking the housing shortage

The consistent objective of the first phase of policy, despite its punctuation by a severe – and effective – attack on the record of the Attlee government by the Conservatives in the 1951 election, was the eradication of the housing shortage inherited from the war. The Labour government and in particular Bevan (who was the minister responsible for housing between 1945 and January 1951) did not wholly deserve the criticism to which they were subjected. Almost half a million houses had been destroyed or rendered uninhabitable during the war and a further 3 million had been damaged. In addition few new houses had been built and few slums cleared (other than by courtesy of the Luftwaffe). There was, therefore, a severe housing shortage. Moreover, in a straitened economy any housing drive had to compete for scarce resources with the building requirements of industry and the other social services. The 1947 convertibility crisis, for example, greatly reduced the import of timber (for which dollars had to be paid) and the public expenditure cuts associated with devaluation in 1949 hit capital expenditure particularly hard.[15]

In addition, there was an irreconcilable conflict of interest within the housing programme itself. To whom should priority be given? The rival claimants were:

- Industrial workers, so that labour mobility and thereby economic growth could be increased.
- Returning soldiers, as Churchill wished, in order to avoid the obloquy that was heaped upon Lloyd George after the First World War for his failure to provide 'homes fit for heroes'.[16]
- The most needy, in accordance with traditional Labour Party policy.

Bevan eventually decided upon the last option and consequently the vast majority of building licences (ranging from 90 per cent in 1946 to 80 per cent in 1950) were reserved for the construction of high-quality council houses. The result was that the annual number of council houses completed reached a historical high. At their prewar peak in 1938, 122,000 had been built. In 1948 the total was 217,000 and, despite public expenditure cuts, the figure never fell below 175,000 (see Table 9.2).

Table 9.2 Houses constructed and demolished in the UK, 1938–76 (thousands)

	Houses built			Houses demolished
	Local Authority	Private	Total	(GB only)
1938	122	237	359	–
1948	217	34	251	–
1951	176	25	202	–
1956	181	126	308	39
1961	122	181	303	67
1966	187	209	396	79
1971	168	196	364	87
1976	170	155	325	51

Note: Figures are rounded to the nearest thousand.
Sources: D. and G. Butler, *British Political Facts, 1900–1985* (1986) pp. 332–3; S. Merrett, *State Housing in Britain* (1979) p. 120.

Bevan justified his decision not just by individual need but on the ground that local government, rather than private builders, could be trusted to honour planning agreements. On the quality of housing, he also argued with prescience that while the Labour government 'would be judged for a year or two by the number of houses we build, we shall be judged in ten years' time by the type of houses we build'.[17] However, as with the NHS, Bevan's housing record has been criticized as inherently conservative despite its veneer of radical rhetoric. Above all, its almost total reliance on local authorities led to the neglect of other equally positive ways to ensure the right to, and equitable distribution of, affordable housing.

There were, however, two major flaws in Bevan's policy, which fostered public disillusion and gave substance to the Conservatives' later attack. First, the rehousing programme started slowly; and out of frustration there was an unprecedented outburst of squatting both in the West End of London in 1946 and more permanently in disused army camps.[18] Whatever Labour's later achievements, it was to these acts of defiance that popular memory constantly returned. Second, private building was restricted by 1951 to a mere tenth of its annual output in the 1930s. Consequently, the *total* number of houses built was only just over half the prewar average.

This shortfall, so the Conservatives argued, was essentially the result not of economic constraints but of mismanagement. Labour, so the jibe went, had only 'half a Nye' on housing. Distracted by battles over the NHS, Bevan failed to coordinate policy in Whitehall (where responsibility was divided between five ministries), to provide clear targets (a strange oversight for someone supposedly committed to planning) and, as in the NHS, to utilize private sources of initiative (such as non-profit-making housing associations). It was, so Conservatives were later to claim, because of their greater pragmatic willingness to harness any agency that could contribute to their housing drive that they were able to exceed Labour's achievements and thereby all but end the housing shortage.

When the Conservatives returned to power in 1951, one of their principal welfare commitments was to build 300,000 houses a year and this target they duly achieved.[19] Despite recurring balance of payments crises, Harold Macmillan (as housing minister) was able to win a disproportionate share of scarce resources by capitalizing upon the Prime Minister's support and the fear that any shortfall in production targets might lead to a questioning of the party's commitment to the welfare state, and thereby jeopardize its future electoral success.

The key to Macmillan's success was the flexibility of his approach. Rather than restraining the construction of council housing, he encouraged it so that – just as the largest number of comprehensive schools was opened while Margaret Thatcher was education secretary – the greatest number of council houses ever to be built within a four-year period was achieved under the Conservatives between 1952 and 1956. Simultaneously private initiative was encouraged by the lifting of restrictions on land use and the abolition of building licences by 1954. As a result the 300,000 target was achieved as early as 1953 and the annual completion figure was never again to fall below this level until 1978, with the brief exception of 1958 and 1959.

The only major blemish in Macmillan's record was a drop in the quality and size of housing. In the public sector, for instance, terraces replaced semi-detached housing and average house size fell from just over 1000 to 900 square feet. Even here, however, it should be remembered that the average size of council houses in the 1930s had only been 750 square feet and that the cuts had initially been planned by Bevan's successor as housing minister, Hugh Dalton.[20]

The disproportionate share of resources accorded to housing angered other social service ministers and particularly the chancellor of the exchequer (Butler) who was Macmillan's leading rival for the future leadership of the Party. This was an uncanny repetition of Bevan's battles over NHS funding. Macmillan's permanent secretary and the head of the civil service were also antagonized by the unconventional means he employed to achieve results. In an all too rare insight into the administrative changes demanded by the government's new positive welfare role, they were dismissed by the assertion that his was 'a war job. It must be tackled in the spirit of 1940.'[21] The nature Macmillan's response to these political and administrative challenges helps to explain why he rose to the leadership of his Party, but Bevan did not.

1956–68: creating a 'mixed economy' of housing

By 1956 the housing shortage in England and Wales was considered to have been all but resolved. As priority in welfare expenditure was therefore transferred to education, housing policy reverted to the principles of the 1930s: the maintenance of a 'mixed economy' housing market in which the private sector satisfied any 'natural' increase in demand whilst the public sector concentrated on slum clearance.

To achieve the desired balance the role of the public sector was reduced in two ways. First, subsidies for construction were reduced after 1954 and restricted in 1956 solely to meeting the 'special needs' of the elderly, slum clearance and new towns. Second, local government was fully exposed to market forces by the ending of both cheap loans in 1955 and, as has been seen, preferential land prices in 1959. In contrast demand in the private sector was boosted with a series of tax concessions (which will be discussed in the next section) and, after 1959, increased pressure upon local government to sell council houses, to provide mortgages and to distribute mandatory grants for house improvements.

The major increase in construction was, however, expected in private rented accommodation which, as illustrated in Table 9.4, had declined between 1945 and 1956 from 54 per cent to 36 per cent of the housing market. The principal reason for the decline was believed to be the continuation of wartime rent controls which, in a period of increasing inflation, had restricted the level of rent chargeable to that applicable in 1939 and, in many cases, 1915. A Rent Act was duly passed in 1957 which immediately decontrolled half a million houses and permitted controls on many more to be lifted on a change of tenancy. Rents on all remaining controlled property were also permitted, within certain limits, to be increased to enable landlords to make both essential repairs and a reasonable profit.

The private rented market, however, did not revive and under Labour taunts the Conservatives grew increasingly concerned about an increasing housing shortage, especially in the rented sector. To accelerate construction they partially reversed earlier policy by permitting local government in 1962 to build again for 'general purposes' and by encouraging more ambitious programmes of redevelopment, in particular through the use of prefabricated building units. The Housing Corporation was also established in 1964 to channel funds to non-profit-making housing associations which provided rented accommodation.[22]

This construction strategy was not overturned but rather reinforced when the Wilson government took office in 1964. Its vitriol was reserved for the Conservatives' Rent Act which had led, so it believed, to the exploitation of private tenants. However, it no longer sought – as it had before the war – to take the private rented sector into public ownership. Nor did it seek, as it had in the 1940s, to concentrate construction in the public sector. On the contrary, its first major policy statement *The Housing Programme, 1965–1970* explicitly confirmed the concept of a 'mixed economy' housing market. The only major change made by Labour was, therfeore, quantitative. The annual output of houses was to be raised to 500,000, a target which it came closest to meeting in 1968 when 426,000 houses were built.

The Labour Party's ideological opposition to owner occupation was formally dropped in 1965. 'The expansion of the public programme now proposed', its *Housing Programme* white paper admitted, 'is to meet exceptional needs. The expansion of buildings for owner occupancy on the other hand is normal; it reflects a long-term social advance which should gradually pervade every region.'[23] This change of policy was reflected at the building peak in 1968 by the fact that construction was shared almost equally by the public and the private sectors.

1968–75: renovation

The twin priorities of the third phase were renovation and (within the public sector at least) a concentration of resources on the most needy. This change of policy was announced in the Labour government's white paper, significantly entitled *Old Houses into New Homes*, which stated boldly that 'within a total public investment in housing at about the level it has now reached the greatest share should go to the improvement of old homes'.[24] Such a pronouncement revealed three things:

- In the aftermath of the devaluation crisis, the new policy was designed to save money. Constant expenditure in cash terms during a period of inflation meant a fall in the real level of housing investment.
- In direct contradiction to earlier Labour policy, construction targets – especially in the public sector – were to be cut. This was effected especially after 1972 when the Conservatives again withdrew 'general purpose' subsidies.
- Large-scale slum clearance ,which had been so strongly encouraged in the

1960s, was to be abandoned – although ironically, because of existing contracts, the number of houses demolished did not peak until 1971 (see Table 9.2).

There were many good reasons for this new emphasis on renovation rather than redevelopment. The largest area of poor-quality housing had already been cleared by 1968 and so, logically, a new strategy was required. Public concern was at last being expressed about the demolition of historic and structurally sound, if poorly maintained, buildings; and the conservation of the environment (as well as of grammar schools) had helped the Conservatives to sweeping victories at the local elections of 1967. There were also growing doubts about the social costs of large-scale redevelopment, especially the construction of the new 'high-rise' estates. The new technique of cost–benefit analysis could provide some measure of these costs (see Section 3.2.2) and, when combined with the additional cost of rebuilding over renovation, they made redevelopment appear far from cost-effective.[25] Finally, there were even serious doubts about the very safety of high-rise flats after the partial collapse of the Ronan Point tower block in East London in 1968. Political expediency, environmental concern, economic logic and even public safety, therefore, all combined to encourage a change of policy.

The major new policy instruments were improvement grants and the creation of 'general improvement areas'. Investment grants had been introduced by Bevan as early as 1949 and had been made mandatory in 1959. General improvement areas, introduced in 1969, were discrete localities of between 200 and 300 houses in which private renovation could be matched by small public improvements to the environment (such as tree planting). Once such areas had been created the number of grants awarded to private owners trebled, peaking at 260,000 in 1973. Within the 964 areas sanctioned by 1975, one-quarter of the 280,000 houses had received grants.[26]

There was one major drawback to a policy so heavily dependent on private initiative for the disbursement of public funds. Those people, and indeed those properties, most in need of aid tended to benefit least. Remedial action was duly taken under the Conservatives. In 1973 stricter conditions were imposed on grants, with the result that their number quickly fell back to pre-1968 levels. In addition, and in accordance with its greater emphasis on selectivity in social security (see Section 6.3), the Conservatives drafted legislation to create 'housing action areas' in which resources would be directed to the most needy areas. The parliamentary passage of the requisite legislation was interrupted by the 1974 election, but it was completed by the incoming Labour government, thereby maintaining the essentially bipartisan approach to postwar construction policy. This initiative was crucial to the regeneration of housing policy in Scotland.[27]

Ending the crude housing shortage

These three phases in bipartisan policy transformed the nature of housing in Britain. First, the *absolute* shortage of housing was eradicated in England and Wales by the 1960s (as demonstrated in Table 9.3), in Scotland by 1970 and in Northern Ireland by 1979. This did not mean that there was no *actual* shortage. Some houses were second homes. Some lay empty. Others were simply in the 'wrong' place. More separate households might also have been formed, had additional accommodation been available. The recorded number of homeless people, at 1 per cent of the population, was nevertheless extremely low – although, as was discovered in 1977 when care for the homeless was for the first time made a statutory responsibility of local government, such statistics are also sensitive to changing public perception and definition.[28]

Table 9.3 Households and dwellings in England and Wales, 1951–76 (thousands)

	1951	1961	1971	1976
Total dwellings	12,530	14,646	17,024	18,100
Total households	13,259	14,724	16,779	17,600
Surplus(+) or deficiency (–)	–729	–78	+245	+500

Source: P. Malpass and A. Murie, *Housing Policy and Practice* (1987) p. 75.

Revolutionizing ownership

The second major change, as demonstrated by Table 9.4, was in housing tenure. Despite the efforts of successive Conservative governments, the private rented market collapsed and was replaced first by council housing (as a result of construction in the public sector outstripping that in the private sector until 1959) and then by owner-occupancy. One reason for this collapse was the continuation of wartime controls and the fear that they might be intensified by Labour governments. A more important reason, however, was that – unlike in Europe – private rented accommodation enjoyed few of the subsidies or tax concessions accorded to other tenures. In contrast owner-occupancy received increasingly generous subsidies and by 1970 accounted in Britain as a whole for over half of the housing stock. This was a level far in excess of contemporary European experience where, as late as 1978, the comparable figures for France and Germany respectively were only 47 per cent and 37 per cent.

Improving quality

The third major achievement under the classic welfare state was the improved

Table 9.4   Housing tenure in Britain, 1945–76 (%)

	Owner-occupied	Public rented	Private rented	Other
1945	26	12	54	8
1951	30	18	45	8
1956	34	23	36	7
1961	42	27	26	6
1966	47	29	19	5
1971	51	31	19	
1976	53	32	15	

Note: 'House' is defined as a building or part of a building which provides struc-
turally separate living quarters.
Source: Royal Commission on the Distribution of Income and Wealth, *Seventh
Report* (Cmnd 7595, 1979) p. 133.

quality of housing. The extent of such improvement is perhaps surprising in the light of the deliberate reduction in standards during the Macmillan housing drive and its subsequent condemnation by the official Parker Morris report, *Homes for Today and Tomorrow*, in 1961. 'Homes are being built at the present time', it complained, 'which not only are too small to provide adequately for family life but also are too small to hold the possessions in which so much of the new affluence is expressed.'[29] It advanced new minimum standards of space and heating which, it stressed, should not be regarded as maximums. This, however, is inevitably what happened when they were eventually given statutory force by the Labour government in 1968. Nevertheless, in both absolute and relative terms, the quality of housing rose sharply. Reliable statistics on the number of houses unfit for human habitation were – perhaps significantly – not collected until 1967, but thereafter the number so recorded fell sharply from 1.8 million to 0.9 million in 1975 or from 12 per cent to 5 per cent of the total housing stock.

The authors of the Parker Morris report would no doubt have been unimpressed by these figures. Just as the contemporary poverty lobby had argued for a relative standard of poverty, so they had maintained that the quality of housing should be judged not by low prewar standards but by rising expectations. 'There was a time', they asserted, 'when for a great majority of the population, the major significance of the structure in which they made their home was to provide shelter and a roof over their heads. This is no longer so. An increasing proportion of people are coming to expect their home to do more than fulfil the basic requirements.' A revised list of five 'basic amenities' was drafted in 1970 to include a fixed bath or shower, a lavatory with an inside entrance, a wash-hand basin, hot and cold water at three points and a kitchen sink. By this new list, the number of substandard housing units had declined by 1975 from 3.9 million to 1.6 million. Considerable problems still remained, therefore, but the pace of rehabilitation had been fast. As Donnison and Ungerson have concluded: 'the biggest slum clearance and grant-aided improvement programmes to be attempted anywhere in the world [had] gone far to eliminate the worst conditions'.[30]

High-rise building

There was, however, one way in which slum clearance rather than enhancing housing standards actually threatened to reduce them: the building, by experimental prefabricated methods, of large impersonal estates of high-rise buildings, lacking many of the amenities common in similar developments on the continent. The irony was that no-one actively sought these estates. The One Nation group of Conservatives in 1950, for instance, had condemned 'the building of such family nightmares as blocks of flats without balconies or gardens'. Their instincts were confirmed by a Greater London Council survey in 1967 which revealed that 75 per cent of council house applicants wanted a house with a garden, whereas only 9 per cent of the GLC's housing stock fell into this category.[31] Their construction was, therefore, largely fortuitous and the consequence of the convergence of a wide variety of independent factors:

- architectural fashion and perceptions of 'modernity'
- conservationists' determination to halt urban sprawl
- the desire of inner-city Labour councils and Conservative councils respectively to keep or rebuff traditional Labour voters
- the high cost of land, especially after 1959
- the insistence by central government, especially in the early 1960s on quick results.

In the light of such a potent combination of factors, the large construction companies identified their own interests as being to persuade local authorities to undertake large-scale redevelopment and to sanction new construction techniques which were beyond the capacity of local contractors. In addition, through high-pressure salesmanship and (in certain cases) corruption, they persuaded the larger authorities to set a trend which the smaller ones felt bound to follow. They were even assisted by the structure of government subsidies. Official policy was to encourage the construction of 'mixed' estates and, in order to persuade conservative councils to build a certain minimum of high-rise flats, subsidies progressively favoured taller buildings. Hence 15- and 6-storey blocks of flats attracted subsidies which were, respectively, three times and twice as generous as those provided for houses. These subsidies proved to be so attractive that, in conjunction with the construction companies' powers of persuasion, they not only eroded councils' conservatism but also led to a wholly unexpected concentration on high-rise building.

The replacement of slums by high-rise prefabricated flats was largely confined to a relatively brief but intense period of construction in the 1960s. As soon as the unintended consequences of the subsidy structure were fully appreciated, remedial action was taken in the 1967 Housing Subsidies Act.

Consequently, the decline of high-rise buildings had started even before the partial collapse of Ronan Point in 1968.[32]

> The period of high-rise construction, brief though it was, graphically illustrated two broader features of construction policy. First, it was a prime example of incrementalism. Subsidies and grants designed to achieve a given end frequently resulted in the achievement of another. Second, a vigorous housing policy did not automatically – as the Conservatives had hoped – resolve social problems. It could, and often did, actually intensify them.

9.3 HOUSING COSTS

As may be inferred from the preceding sections, government is able to influence the cost of housing by three means:

- subsidizing construction
- subsidizing owner-occupation
- rent controls.

Between 1945 and 1975 the first two methods proved to be relatively uncontroversial but the latter excited much political controversy.

Subsidizing construction

The direct way in which government has traditionally influenced construction costs is through the payment of subsidies. Subsidies may be used for a wide variety of purposes: to vary the range of building (as with the switch from 'general' to 'special' purposes in 1956), the types of building (as with the progressive storey-height subsidy in 1956) or the type of investor (as with the granting of subsidies to housing associations after 1962).[33] Their principal purpose after 1945, however, was to regulate the pace of construction. Thus, at the start of Macmillan's housing drive in 1952, the subsidy on new houses was virtually doubled to £26.70 per annum. Then, when the housing shortage appeared to have been resolved, it was halved in 1955. Construction was encouraged in this way because subsidies were payable annually over 60 years and so the future cost to local government was greatly reduced.

Such long-term subsidies, however, have one serious flaw. In periods of inflation, such as the 1960s, their real value falls and so local authorities are faced with the need dramatically to increase either council-house rents or the rates. To forestall just such an eventuality, the Conservative government in their 1972 Housing Finance Act cancelled all existing subsidies and replaced them with a new grant which was to be adjusted annually to meet the difference between a council's 'reckonable' (that is, approved) housing expenditure

Table 9.5   Cost of building subsidies in the UK, 1952–77 (£m)

	Central government subsidies to		Local authority subsidies	Total
	Local authorities	*Housing associations*		
1949–50	34	2	14	50
1964–5	89	9	53	150
1973–4	299	44	89	432
1976–7	987	171	185	1,343

Source: A. H. Halsey (ed.), *British Social Trends since 1900*, 2nd edn (1988), table 10.27.

and rent income. The original purpose behind this reform was to reduce the subsidies from central government but, as can be seen from Table 9.5, it was singularly unsuccessful in this respect. As land prices and interest rates soared, so too did 'reckonable' expenditure, and both council tenants and rate-payers received unprecedented assistance from the general tax-payer. This unintended consequence of the 1972 legislation was a prime example of incrementalism, with the planned objectives of direct subsidization being distorted by the unplanned and indirect effects of planning and monetary policy.

Subsidizing owner-occupation

The cost of housing for owner-occupiers was reduced, particularly in the 1960s, by both Conservative and Labour governments. The first major conces-sion to owner-occupiers – tax relief on mortgage interest payments – had been made in 1921, but until the 1950s its impact had been slight. Because of rela-tively high tax thresholds and low house prices, both the number of benefi-ciaries and the value of the tax allowance had been low. Tax was also levied on the 'imputed' rent (the income which home-owners would theoretically gain from their property should they rent it out) and, in any case, interest payments on all loans were treated similarly. All this changed in the 1960s. With tax thresholds dropping and house prices rising, the number of benefi-ciaries and the value of their hidden subsidy began to escalate.[34] A series of tax reforms also saw the withdrawal of tax liability for 'imputed' rent in 1963; the exemption from capital gains tax in 1965 of profits from the sale of a person's 'principal' home; and the withdrawal in 1968 of tax relief on interest for all loans other than mortgages. In addition improvement grants were provided so that home-owners could increase the value of their properties at the tax-payer's expense; and, finally, building societies were provided with subsidies in 1959 and 1974 respectively to encourage loan-advances on pre-1919 property and to insulate mortgages from rises in interest rates.

All these concessions were extremely expensive. In 1975–6, as can be seen from Table 9.1, the annual cost of tax relief on mortgages was estimated to be £770 million. Simultaneously the estimated cost of exemption of house sales from capital gains tax was £500 million and the estimated amount of tax-free 'imputed' rent was well over £2000 million. The Treasury not surprisingly objected to so great a loss of revenue. It had also initially opposed increased owner-occupancy on the grounds that it could *inter alia* distort investment, encourage personal indebtedness and increase wage claims. Why then were such costly concessions made?

The reason was largely political. After the war, with the perceived advance of socialism, Conservative politicians became convinced that the creation of a 'property-owning democracy' was essential to foster individual initiative and thus economic efficiency and political stability. In the 1950s, when they developed the concept of the 'opportunity state', tax concessions on mortgage interest (as on occupational pensions) were also justified as a means to achieve their ends – even if they did distort both the housing market and industrial investment.[35] Likewise, in the 1950s the Labour Party (partly as a result of the ambitions of 'affluent workers' as recorded by opinion polls) came to accept home-ownership as a natural instinct. It was also fully aware that, given the many articulate interests involved, it would be politically inexpedient to withdraw any concessions despite their unexpected high cost.

> In view of the predominance of rented accommodation even for middle-class households in the nineteenth century, some doubt has been cast over whether home-ownership is indeed a response to 'natural' instinct. Might it not be the 'creation' of preferential treatment?[36] Such treatment was certainly provided under the classic welfare state as the financial incentives provided by successive governments reduced the cost of home-ownership well below its 'market' cost. These incentives were also highly regressive and expanded fastest in the 1960s at the very time when other policies were being constricted because of a perceived lack of resources. Owner-occupiers thus quickly became some of the most privileged recipients of state welfare.

Re-establishing market rents

Such favourable treatment was certainly not accorded to tenants in either the private or the public rented sector. Under Conservative governments, the pre-eminent objective of policy was to ensure that both sets of tenants paid a full market rent. This would encourage those council tenants who could afford it to opt for home-ownership. Their places could then be taken by poor families 'shaken out' of the private market. Such a rationalization of the private sector might cause short-term hardship. In the long term, however, it was deemed necessary for three reasons:

• to achieve greater equality between tenants, with the ending of fortuitous differences between the various controlled tenures
• to ensure the most economical use of housing
• to provide landlords with sufficient profits to halt the accelerating degeneration of their property.

The 1957 Rent Act and the 1972 Housing Finance Act were the principal means by which the Conservatives planned to attain their objectives. The former, as has been seen, decontrolled 500,000 houses and prepared the way for either decontrol or rent increases in all the others. The latter sought to target subsidies more effectively by obliging local authorities, for the first time, to charge all their tenants a full market rent and then to distribute rent rebates to those in genuine need.

> By 1956, it was estimated that for the 1.9 million and 3.3 million properties which fell respectively under the 1915 and 1939 Rent Control Acts, rents were on average 150 per cent and 80 per cent below their 'true' level. Such a loss of income, it was believed, had to be staunched were conditions in the private rented sector ever to improve.[37]

Both pieces of legislation infuriated the Labour Party. It had traditionally equated private landlords with exploitation, and the 1957 Rent Act appeared fully to confirm its suspicions. Several unscrupulous landlords, most notoriously Perec Rachman in London, either bribed or terrorized sitting tenants to leave their homes, which could then be decontrolled and either sold or re-let at a considerable profit. Such exploitation, as an official report later confirmed, was actually rare; but nevertheless, because Rachman had links with certain spy and sex scandals which went to the heart of the Conservative Party, Labour politicians were able effectively to capitalize upon it in the 1964 election.[38] In victory they intensified restrictions on private landlords in three ways. They extended the authority of rent tribunals, which had been set up in 1946 to monitor rents, from unfurnished to furnished property; they granted tenants security of tenure; and they appointed rent officers who might review contracts every three years to ensure that tenants were only being charged a 'fair' rent.[39]

The Labour Party's reaction to the 1972 Housing Finance Act was more tortuous, if no less passionate. On the one hand the Party was concerned that council tenants should be as well subsidized as owner-occupiers. It was also suspicious of any further infringement by central on local government. On the other hand leading ministers had largely come to agree with the

Conservatives that local authorities should be obliged to concentrate subsidies on the most needy. 'Help for those who most need it', declared *The Housing Programme, 1965–1970*, 'can only be given out if the subsidies are in large part used to provide rebates for tenants whose means are poor.'[40]

Labour's dilemma, moreover, was intensified by the fact that rent rebates – which had been urged on local government since 1930 – were unpopular with both local authorities and their more prosperous tenants. The former preferred subsidies to the needy to be disbursed by centrally funded agencies such as the Supplementary Benefits Commission, whilst the latter resented any redirection of resources to their 'less prudent' neighbours. In the end, when the party was returned to office in 1974, the increase of council rents to market levels – without which the funds could not be found to finance rebates – was halted. Over the next five years rents, which had risen strongly under the Conservatives (albeit never to a level above 10 per cent of average family income), fell in real terms by 25 per cent.

Attempts to introduce rebates had traditionally been met by violent protests, be it in Leeds and Birmingham in the late 1930s or in St Pancras in the 1960s. The early 1970s proved no exception. The Labour councillors at Clay Cross in Derbyshire refused to implement their mandatory responsibilities under the 1972 Act and were duly suspended.[41] After much heart-searching the Labour Party supported their stand.

A dog's breakfast

The influence of central government over the ultimate cost of housing for both owner-occupiers and council tenants was extensive and extremely complex. Indeed, with characteristic suavity, Anthony Crosland described it as a 'dog's breakfast'.[42] What was incontrovertible was that there was no longer any 'free market' in housing and that any attempt, or pretence, to revive one was either misguided or pernicious. Britain was not unique in having such extensive subsidies. What was unique to Britain was that one group of tenants – those in private rented accommodation – were largely assisted by paternalistic controls, whilst in all other tenures the range of subsidies was unduly complex.

9.4 CONCLUSION

Housing has been described as the 'extreme instance of irrationality among all the social services'.[43] It has also aroused extreme political passions and caused deep public disillusion. This is perhaps not surprising. On the one hand central government has had to share power with an exceptionally wide range of independent or semi-independent agencies. As a result opportunities, especially in the long term, were rife for the initial intentions behind legislation to become distorted during its implementation. This was the case with the unsuccessful attempts in the 1950s to revive the private rented sector, in the 1960s to build 'mixed' council estates and in the 1970s to rationalize subsidies. On the other hand policy has had to address an equally wide range of issues which, like the rights of private property and the need for shelter, went to the heart of political power and individual security. Planning and rent control policy were clearly affected by these pressures.

Despite these complexities and latent conflicts, a 'mixed economy' housing market did successfully evolve between 1945 and 1975. The worst excesses of unplanned development between the wars were avoided. The absolute housing shortage was resolved. General standards of housing also improved remarkably, albeit from a very low base. For all its weaknesses, in other words, housing policy well reflected the pragmatic strength of the classic welfare state.

For the more idealistic supporters of collectivism, however, there were two ominous developments. The striking growth of owner-occupancy signified a retreat from the communal values which policy-makers had initially tried to foster. In the 1970s there was also in housing legislation – as within the original NHS and the shift in education policy towards a core curriculum – a distinct move by central government to erode local democracy. Both those developments were to gather even greater momentum after 1975.

9.5 FURTHER READING

Two good general introductory books are J. R. Short, *Housing in Britain: the postwar experience* (1982); and D. Donnison and C. Ungerson, *Housing Policy* (Harmondsworth, 1982). The latter is strong on international comparisons, as is M. Daunton, *A Property-Owning Democracy?* (1987) which also places postwar developments in historical perspective. Another excellent introduction, within an explicit Marxist framework, is S. Merrett, *State Housing in Britain* (1979), whilst P. Malpass and A. Murie, *Housing Policy and Practice* (1994) has a useful historical introduction and an even more useful bibliography. The Scottish experience is well summarized by A. Gibb, 'Policy and politics in Scottish housing since 1945', in R. Rodger (ed.), *Scottish Housing in the Twentieth Century* (Leicester, 1989).

The definitive political history of planning is A. Cox, *Adversary Politics and Land: the conflict over land and property in postwar Britain* (Cambridge, 1984). This may be supplemented by G. Cherry, *The Politics of Town Planning* (1982) and M. Aldridge, *The British New Towns: a programme without a policy* (1979). Three other classic works are: P. Dunleavy, *The Politics of Mass Housing in Britain, 1945–75* (Oxford, 1981); M. Boddy, *The Building Societies* (1980); and on Rachman and rents in the 1960s, K. G. Banting, *Poverty, Politics and Policy* (1979).

The complexities of policy can be enlivened by the exploits of three particularly charismatic housing ministers recorded, respectively, in M. Foot, *Aneurin Bevan*, vol. 2 (1973); H. Macmillan, *Tides of Fortune, 1945–1955* (1966); and R. H. S. Crossman, *Diaries of a Cabinet Minister*, vol. 1 (1975).

The Personal Social Services

1945	Death of Dennis O'Neill – highlights plight of foster children	1959	Mental Health Act – encourages release of patients into community
1946	Curtis report, *Care of Children* (Cmd 6922). Charity Organization Society renamed Family Welfare Association	1960	Ingleby report, *Children and Young Persons* (Cmnd 1191)
1947	Marriage Guidance Council established	1963	Children and Young Persons Act – implements Ingleby, permits preventive action. 'Generic' social work training standardized to unify profession
1948	Children Act – implements Curtis, all local authorities to have specialist children's committees. National Assistance Act – limited responsibilities for local authorities. Beveridge, *Voluntary Action*		
		1965	New wave of voluntary action – Child Poverty Action Group (CPAG) and Disabled Income Group (DIG) founded
		1966	Shelter and National Association for the Care and Resettlement of Prisoners (NACRO) founded
1953	Samaritans founded		
1957	Boucher report – encourages removal of frail elderly from NHS to local authorities	1968	Seebohm report, *Local Authority and Allied Services* (Cmnd 3703). ➜

Social Work (Scotland) Act – implements 1964 Kilbrandon report, pioneers 'child hearings'

1970 Local Authority Social Services Act – implements Seebohm, unifies social services departments in all local authorities. Chronically Sick and Disabled Persons Act – introduces mobility and attendance allowances

1971 *Better Services for the Mentally Handicapped* – wishful thinking

1972 Home Office, Voluntary Services Unit established – official support for voluntary work

1973 Death of Maria Colwell – discredits Seebohm reforms

1974 *Better Services for the Mentally Ill* – more wishful thinking

1978 Wolfenden report, *The Future of Voluntary Organisations* – new rationale

The personal social services are one of the most ill-defined, neglected and yet vital parts of the welfare state. The term covers essentially the residual services provided by, or through, local government for groups such as the elderly, the physically and mentally handicapped, children and 'problem' families.

Since the war – and in sharp contrast to earlier Poor Law practice – the ordinary needs of individuals within such groups have been catered for, as for everyone else, by the main welfare services. Moreover, many of these main services (and most notably general practice within the NHS) provide a sympathetic 'personal' service. What is distinctive about the personal social services is that they provide for *extraordinary* individual need. They have also been concerned, particularly since the 1960s, not with one specialized area of care but with their clients' *overall* welfare. Their essential purpose is to ensure that those in need of care can enjoy as normal a life as possible and that those deemed to require 'control' can adapt to, or at least come to terms with, society at large.[1]

Between 1945 and 1975 the personal social services were relatively neglected. They lacked three key qualities:

- professional identity
- political weight
- public recognition.

In relation to *identity*, those working within the sector were initially recruited from a diverse range of sources (including private charities, voluntary hospitals, local public assistance committees and the Assistance Board). They represented an equally diverse range of specialisms, each seemingly in constant dispute with the others. In addition, social work as an academic discipline – unlike medicine or teaching – lacked an agreed body of theoretical knowledge and thus clear criteria by which to guide policy or to measure success. In relation to *political weight*, the sector lacked a strong professional lobby and its clientele, by definition, could exert little political influence. As a responsibility of local government, it was also divided and decentralized. Finally, with regard to *public recognition*, the presumption remained widespread that the problems for which the sector was responsible should not be the concern of government. Should they not be resolved by families or charity?

As a result of these handicaps, the personal social services were poorly funded. As late as 1966, for example, they were apportioned only 1.7 per cent of public expenditure. The situation started to improve with the growth of professionalism in the early 1960s and, above all, with the publication of the Seebohm Report on Local Authority and Allied Personal Social Services in 1968.[2] Thereafter greater coordination was achieved both in administration and training and the personal social services became the fastest growing area of welfare (see Appendix, Tables A.3, A.5). Even so, by 1976 they still consumed only 3.9 per cent of social expenditure and tended to attract adverse publicity.

That the personal social services enjoyed so little public esteem was the more unfortunate because their role was in many ways central to the evolution of the welfare state. They cared directly for many of the most vulnerable members of society (by whose treatment the humanity of any country's social services should ultimately be judged). They also raised fundamental questions about the proper role of the state and the individual and, in particular, about the respective 'rights' and 'duties' of the citizen. In the past those in need had conventionally been blamed for their misfortunes. They had been discouraged from seeking help from the state and punished if they did so. After the war such attitudes were – in theory at least – totally reversed. All claimants were to be regarded as full citizens, encouraged to identify both their problems and their needs, and helped by the state as much as possible.

Even had such principles been immediately accepted, however, two main questions would have remained:

- What was the proper relationship between the state and those families and voluntary organizations which had traditionally provided and continued to provide so much care for those in need?
- To what extent should behaviour deemed 'aberrant' be controlled (as was clearly necessary, for example, in relation to convicted offenders on probation or parents found guilty of child neglect)?

With regard to the *role of the state*, it was clearly desirable to maximize 'community action' both to save the tax-payer money and to maintain an active and caring society. However, one of the principal objectives of the welfare state was to ensure uniformity of care throughout the country. Dependence on non-state agencies, whilst satisfying the needs of certain groups in certain areas, might lead to the neglect of others elsewhere. If state provision were then to be targeted only on those areas of neglect, might it not lead to charges of inequity and even to the erosion of voluntary provision in the original areas? With regard to the *role of social workers*, to what extent (as employees of the tax-payer) should they require their clients to conform to conventional norms? Conversely, to what extent (in serving the interests of their clients) should they campaign for legislative change or even challenge – and encourage their clients to challenge – society's norms?

The purpose of this chapter is to look first at the evolution of the statutory social services in the light of such dilemmas and then at the development of voluntary provision. Voluntary action was the subject of the third – and least satisfactory – Beveridge Report in 1948.[3] For a time it was widely assumed that, in the guise at least of organized charity, it would be negligible. However, as will be seen, the size of the problems facing the statutory services were such that voluntary provision, on both a formal and an informal basis, was soon recognized to be a vital supplement and complement to state welfare.

10.1 THE STATUTORY SERVICES

The period from 1945 to 1976 was, far more than for any other service, one of experiment for the personal social services with a watershed being provided in 1968 by the publication of the Seebohm Report and the enactment of the Social Work (Scotland) Bill.

- What was the nature of the service before 1968?
- Why was the Report commissioned and the Act passed?
- What did the one recommend and the other require?
- How fully were they implemented?
- Most importantly, what effect did they have on the care of those in need?

Relative stagnation, 1945–60

In the main the 1940s and 1950s were a far from heroic period. The formulation and implementation of policy were impaired by three major groups of factors: administrative and professional divisions; the persistence of prewar attitudes and institutions; and both economic and legislative constraints.

Administrative division. Within Whitehall responsibility for policy in England and Wales was divided between the Home Office (which oversaw the probation and the children's service), the Ministry of Health (which was concerned with the care of the elderly and the handicapped) and several other ministries such as Education. These divisions were replicated at a local level. After 1948 each English and Welsh local authority had to have a separate children's committee. Responsibility for other welfare functions, however, was divided between health and welfare committees (which might be separate or combined) and the housing and education committees.

Professional divisions. The various political committees of local government were served by separate administrative departments, which in turn were staffed by different groups of professional workers. Each had their own distinct traditions, assumptions and training. Such disunity inevitably impaired the coordination of policy. It also led to a multiplicity of visits to those in need by a succession of officials, each concerned with only one specialist aspect of care. This was not only extremely confusing and irritating for their clients, but also highly inefficient.[4] The situation in Northern Ireland and Scotland was little better than in England and Wales, although separate children's departments were not required there. Moreover, after 1954 'unified' social work departments were established in Northern Ireland which encouraged professional collaboration.

The prewar legacy. Implementation of policy was further impaired by the widespread survival of prewar attitudes, not least in Scotland. The belief persisted that individual care for the needy should, and could, be provided only by families and charities.[5] In addition, training was disparaged by those who still considered success to depend solely upon a good rapport with people and an ability to 'take a firm line and to stand no nonsense'. Moralistic judgements and an overriding concern for social discipline also persisted – with, for example, some senior officials in the mid-1950s defining their principal role as being to 'ensure that people do as they are told and to make them realize they will be punished if they don't'.[6] Such attitudes inhibited the allocation of scarce resources to the personal social services. When held at a political level, they left councillors unconvinced of the value of statutory provision. When held at an administrative level, they prevented any incontrovertible success, which might have allayed political suspicions. As a result case-loads mounted and the opportunity for 'success' receded.

Scarce resources. A further impediment, which was not self-inflicted, was a lack of building material and labour (which, as has been seen, were monopolized by the housing and school-building programmes). A rare area of increasing professional and political agreement was that prevention was better than cure and that 'community' was preferable to institutional care. However, the resources simply did not exist to provide the necessary facilities.

> The inability of the personal social services to win their fair share of scarce resources stifled what few progressive possibilities there were. One of the principal objectives behind the 1948 Children Act, for instance, had been to ensure that all children taken into care should be individually assessed in 'reception centres' before being transferred either to foster care or to a small, substitute 'family home'. However, by the early 1960s over one-third of local authorities had still been unable to build any reception centres and, given a similar shortage of family homes and only half the required number of foster parents, many children were still confined to large residential institutions. The situation was similar with the elderly. Even where there was the political will, sufficient nursing homes and sheltered accommodation could not be built, with the result that as late as 1960 over half of elderly people in local authority care were still living in former Poor Law buildings.[7]

Legislative restriction. A final constraint was legislative. The two major acts which defined local government's responsibilities in England and Wales, for example, were the Children Act and the National Assistance Act of 1948. The Children Act was in many ways progressive. By insisting on separate children's departments it ensured coordination of policy. It also revolutionized attitudes towards childcare. As late as the 1930s the major objective of policy had been defined as 'to set to work and put out as apprentices all children whose parents are not . . . able to keep and maintain' them. It insisted instead on the furtherance of each child's best interests and the proper development of their 'character and abilities'.[8] The Act failed, however, to make any provision for the *prevention* of neglect or abuse. Parental rights were scrupulously respected and material help, such as cash payments or rehousing, was expressly forbidden. No move to lift these constraints was made until after the report of the Ingleby Committee in 1960 (Cmnd 1191) and the subsequent Children and Young Persons Act of 1963.

The National Assistance Act (which dealt with most other people in need) was equally restrictive. It left local authorities with 'limited power and limited guidance to develop their services as they felt inclined or able'. Given the long-standing weakness of local government which was noted in Chapter 4, most local authorities felt 'inclined or able' to do very little.[9] Even where they were so motivated, however, they were prevented from providing the elderly with anything more than residential accommodation or home help. Other forms of domiciliary care, such as meals on wheels and chiropody, were explicitly reserved for voluntary care.

Forces for change, 1960–68

By the late 1950s attitudes started to change. The Ingleby Report, by recommending preventive work, represented a significant advance in official thinking. So too did the 1957 Boucher Report and, above all, the 1959 Mental Health Act. The former sought, by placing responsibility firmly on local authorities, to resolve the rather demeaning dispute between the NHS and local government over who should care for the 'frail' elderly – those who were not confined to bed but who nevertheless required considerable periods of care in bed. The latter made mandatory, rather than permissive, local authorities' responsibilities for the mentally and, by extension, for the physically disabled. One motive behind each of these 'advances' was unquestionably economy. With the rise in juvenile delinquency and in the number of elderly people (see Section 4.2), preventive childcare and local government services for the elderly and handicapped were seen to be more cost-effective than policing and care within the NHS.

Economy, however, was not the only motive. More positively, changes in professional and public attitudes played their part. In 1954 the London School of Economics had launched a 'generic' training course for social workers with the potential to unify the profession by providing a common core of knowledge on which to build later specialization. Following an exhaustive enquiry chaired by Eileen Younghusband, such courses became standard in 1963. Simultaneously the profession as a whole drew closer together within the Standing Conference of Organizations of Social Workers. There was a similar liberalizing of public attitudes where, as Younghusband herself claimed, 'curiosity broke free from static and moralistic assumptions'.[10] Greater affluence and the satisfaction of the initial objectives in each of the other welfare services permitted some relaxation of traditional anxieties and thus the expenditure of greater sympathy and resources on those in need.

These changes in attitude, moreover, were underpinned by scientific advance. The development of new drugs, for example, enabled the mentally ill to be released from Victorian asylums and treated more safely within the community. Better care for Down's syndrome children and victims of cerebral palsy was also made possible by the realization that they were, respectively, educable and not mentally handicapped.

As a consequence of the changed climate of opinion, real expenditure on the personal social services (which had remained largely static in the 1950s) started to grow and actually doubled between 1960 and 1968.

The commissioning of Kilbrandon and Seebohm

The most notable initiatives in the early 1960s were taken in the probation and children's services; and it was pressure from within these services which led directly to the establishment of the Seebohm Committee in 1965 and the passage of the Social Work (Scotland) Act in 1968.

To minimize juvenile delinquency, the growing conviction was that each local authority should have a 'family service' which could identify aberrant behaviour at an early stage and treat it within the family. This was certainly the conviction of the 1964 Kilbrandon Report (Scotland's equivalent of Ingleby) which went so far as to recommend – in line with practice in Sweden and the USA – that notions of 'guilt' and 'punishment' should be replaced by 'failure of upbringing' and 'education'. The family was to be regarded as the prime source and basis for all remedial action. Herein lay the origins of Scotland's radical system of 'child hearings', established by the 1968 Act, whereby specially appointed juvenile panels heard all relevant cases and had their decisions implemented not by the courts but by local authorities.

Not all recommendations of the Kilbrandon report were implemented. It had advocated a separate children's service. Instead the innovative 1968 Social Work (Scotland) Act, in advance of England and Wales but following the precedent of Northern Ireland, established 'unified' social service departments which catered for the elderly and the handicapped as well as for children.[11]

A parallel 'slippage' occurred in England and Wales where the original terms of reference for the Seebohm Committee had been not just 'to review the organization and responsibilities of the local authority personal social services in England and Wales' but also 'to consider what changes are desirable to secure an effective family service'.[12] Its members, however, were well aware that many leading academics – including Titmuss – opposed such a development on the ground that it would create further artificial divisions within social work. Consequently they evaded their terms of reference. As their report later admitted: 'We decided very early in our discussions that it would be impossible to restrict our work solely to the needs of two or even three generation families. We could only make sense of our task by considering also childless couples and individuals without any close relatives: in other words, everybody.'[13]

The Seebohm Report

The Seebohm Committee's eventual recommendations were relatively straightforward and contained three main sets of proposals in relation to the organization, duty and academic underpinning of social work.

Organizationally, it argued, each local authority should not have a family service. Instead, as in Scotland and Northern Ireland, there should be an enlarged social service department which could unite the various social work professions, coordinate field work (so that both the 'total requirements' of clients could be identified and the service made more 'accessible and comprehensible') and pack sufficient political weight to attract adequate resources.[14] The *duty* of this new department should be to ensure that it did not become 'a self-contained unit but . . . part of a network of services within the community' coordinating, in particular, the work of volunteers. *Finally*, 'generic' training and further sustained research was to be encouraged. The former was required to further professional cooperation and eventually to ensure that 'as a general rule, and as far as possible, a family or individual in need of special care should be served by a single social worker'. The latter was urgently needed to guide policy at both central and local level. 'Social planning', the Report insisted, 'is an illusion without adequate facts; and the adequacy of services mere speculation without evaluation.'

Seebohm's failings

Because of their relative simplicity and the pioneering work already completed in Scotland, the Seebohm proposals were speedily translated into law by the 1970 Local Authority Social Services Act. In the short term, therefore, the Report was highly successful and the personal social services were able to avoid the tortuous negotiations which stifled the Labour government's simultaneous attempts to reform pensions, local government and the NHS. In the longer term, however, its success was far less clear-cut. The most substantial criticisms of the Report concerned its:

- intellectual shortcomings
- unresolved practical contradictions
- defective methodology.

Intellectual shortcomings.   The report evaded crucial decisions, so it has been argued, by providing no explicit justification of social work, identifying no criteria by which priorities could be determined and giving no clear indication of where power should ultimately lie. It was for example self-deprecatory, typically admitting at one stage:

> although we often do not know how to prevent social distress or where our efforts can best be concentrated it is right to strive towards prevention . . . . We must act on the best information and regard what is done as an experiment, in the broadest sense, from which to learn.[15]

Such modesty initially antagonized the Labour Cabinet, which had been looking for a strong lead. It also listed a large number of desirable objectives and clients' rights but neither estimated their cost nor considered the means, and the consequences, of raising potentially large sums of money to finance them. Consequently, as one critic has noted, 'expectations raced ahead of available resources and the Babel of universalist aspirations overwhelmed the language of priorities'.[16]

The intellectual shortcomings of the Seebohm Report was reflected in its evasion of the key issue of where power ultimately lay. This was apparent in its brief for the social service departments in their key role of 'community development' – to plan from the centre and simultaneously 'to ensure genuine consumer participation'. Such a formula was dangerously reminiscent of the unresolved dilemmas in the 1940s concerning the implementation of 'democratic' economic planning (see Section 5.3). Given that the wishes of the planners and consumers must at times conflict, how were they to be reconciled?[17]

Unresolved contradictions.   Many detailed reservations were voiced by social workers. Administrative duplication was not eradicated, they argued at the time because their responsibilities continued (perhaps inevitably) to overlap with other services – especially housing. The required balance between genuine social work (the identification through casework of individuals' needs) and welfare work (the provision of practical help through the coordination of relevant services) was also left unclear. So too was the balance between generalist and specialist skills.[18] Moreover, by recommending that the Secretary of State for Health and Social Security should sanction the appointment of the heads of all the 'unified' departments, greater centralization appeared to be favoured over local initiative, which was concurrently being promoted by the Royal Commission on Local Government.

Methodology. Most damning of all, however, was the means by which the Committee reached its conclusions. Like Beveridge in the 1940s, it determined the basis of its report (the creation of a unified social service department in each local authority) before it took any evidence. When evidence, however powerful, contradicted this assumption (as it did, for instance, over specialization) it was rejected. Moreover, no independent research or survey of clients' opinions was commissioned. Whatever the premium on the production of an early report, such behaviour was – to say the least – peculiar for a committee which placed such weight on the dispassionate analysis of scientific research and active popular participation. In short, and very surprisingly given its membership and remit, it was a prime example of the professional elitism and conceit which so tarnished the reputation of the classic welfare state.

Disillusion

Such shortcomings within the Report would have confounded the implementation of policy, but the initial work of the new 'unified' departments was further complicated by two administrative upheavals (in 1971 and again in 1974, following the reorganization of local government). These upheavals admittedly resulted in a greatly increased number of social workers. They were nevertheless damaging because, in the scramble for position and increased salaries, professional self-interest was seen to swamp clients' needs.

The public reputation of the departments was tarnished in two other ways. First, as a deliberate act of policy, resources were diverted to previously neglected areas from well-respected and proven services, such as childcare. In consequence an increasing number of specialists resigned – some actually transferring to the voluntary sector where they felt there was greater scope for personal initiative. Second, amongst those who remained, an articulate minority (most notably in the Community Development Programme) were committed to the need 'to change society' and so brought social work into still greater political disrepute. Rather than heralding a new dawn, therefore, the implementation of the Seebohm Report appeared to confirm the worst fears of its critics – the social service departments were 'an expensive waste of time, which left much human misery unalleviated'. Disillusion in Scotland was equally swift.[19]

Client care

Was such disillusion justified by any deterioration after 1968 in the standard of care for those in need? The most important groups of clients were:

- children
- the elderly
- the disabled.

The most emotive of these clients for the social service department were *children* of whom, by 1974, 91,300 were in care and a further quarter of a million under supervision.[20] Just as the classic welfare state had opened with a tragedy (the death in 1945 of Dennis O'Neill at the hands of his foster parents) so it drew to a close with another (the murder in 1973 of Maria Colwell by her stepfather). There was, however, a significant difference. The first tragedy had preceded – and even accelerated – the pioneering Children Act and the establishment of expert children's departments. The latter succeeded the establishment of, and thereby discredited, the new unified social service departments in which children in any case no longer had formal preference. The quality of childcare was therefore seen at the time to decline. This remains the verdict, particularly given the continuing revelation of abuse in children's homes, although the Scottish legislation on children's hearings and its pale English imitation (the 1969 Children and Young Persons Act) did to an extent maintain the momentum of postwar reform.[21]

In contrast the standard of care for the largest group of clients – *the elderly* – is generally agreed to have improved. Their needs had been traditionally neglected by government, other than through the payment of pensions. They had also tended to be neglected by social workers, in part because – with the near-certainty of constant deterioration and the absolute certainty of only one 'cure' – the work was regarded as thankless. After 1971, however, greater attention was turned to the 2.5 million people aged over 75 and a wider range of domiciliary care became mandatory for local authorities. Social work admittedly remained crisis-orientated and geared to the provision of physical help rather than to the combating of mental deterioration. Nevertheless the standard of care throughout the country as a whole undoubtedly rose.

Services for the elderly had so improved by 1975 that for every 1000 people over 75, there were 17 home helps and 15,520 meals distributed annually.[22] Moreover, in one of the few surveys of the elderly living outside residential care, those polled expressed considerable satisfaction with both their accommodation and the services provided.[23]

One group of the elderly who did not benefit from this general improvement was the frail elderly or, in the more pejorative terminology of the late 1960s, 'bed blockers'. They needed either constant nursing but not medical care, or needed both but not constantly. They were, therefore, the indisputable responsibility of neither the NHS (required after 1948 to care for those needing constant medical and nursing attention) nor local authorities (required to provide 'care and attention'). Both proceeded to pass the buck. Doctors wanted to concentrate on acute care, local authorities on the less frail through the upgrading and expansion of residential homes inherited from the Poor Law. The Ministry of Health covertly, and with the use of questionable evidence and logic, sought to shift the frail from hospitals into the community. A low ceiling on geriatric hospitals beds was justified, for example, on the grounds that speedier rehabilitation through improved geriatric medicine would accelerate through-put. Geriatrics, however, was actively scorned and under-resourced in most hospitals.

→

Ministry policy was covert because openness would have caused a furore – not least because they were seeking to transfer the frail from hospital care (which was free) to institutional or domiciliary local authority care (which was not). This was a dilemma that, having been fortuitously resolved in the 1980s, was to return with a vengeance in the 1990s. In the meantime, the frail suffered not just from uncertainty but deliberate misclassification. In the late 1950s, for example, it was officially admitted that quite unjustifiably they made up 14 per cent of patients in mental hospitals.[24]

The final significant group of clients was the *disabled*. They, like the elderly, had previously been neglected by government and the Seebohm Report had commented in particular on the 'urgent need' for greater care of the *physically disabled*.[25] A start was made with the 1970 Chronically Sick and Disabled Persons Act, which required all local authorities to register the disabled and to publicize the services available to them. A full range of cash benefits for them and their carers, as noted in Section 6.4, was also introduced but they were chronically under-resourced. The *mentally disabled* fared little better. This was particularly dispiriting because, as was seen in Section 7.3, community care for the mentally ill had – with the support of powerful ministers such as Enoch Powell – been one of government's supposed priorities.

The disabled were less well treated than the elderly because the legislation, which was designed to meet their needs, was inadequately resourced. For example, neither the 1970 Act itself nor the new benefits were properly funded (see Section 3.1.3). This led to intense anger. Money was so tight that in certain localities sample surveys were substituted for registers and so there are not even accurate national figures for the number of disabled at this time. Likewise the targets in the 1971 programme, *Better Services for the Mentally Handicapped,* had not been realized by 1975. Consequently the parallel document, *Better Services for the Mentally Ill*, concluded in 1975 that 'by and large the non-hospital resources are still minimal'.[26]

Qualified advance

After the relative stagnation of the 1950s, legislative change in both England and Scotland failed fully to capitalize upon the more liberal attitudes of the 1960s. In particular the Seebohm Report was unable to effect an immediate revolution in the personal social services similar to that achieved in social insurance by the Beveridge Report.

This was perhaps inevitable because – despite its traditions stretching back to the nineteenth century – social work lacked the basic infrastructure, the tried methods and, above all, the universal appeal of social security. An organizational framework was created within which the profession could unite. As in so many areas of welfare policy, however, organization alone could not resolve conflict over fundamental values and the allocation of scarce resources. The basic research, by which the better identification and treatment of given problems could be translated permanently into effective prevention and cure, also remained undone. Amongst both professionals and the public disappointed expectations bred further disillusion. This in turn obscured the real, if rather mundane, achievement of the early 1970s: a general levelling up of standards in previously neglected areas of care.

10.2 VOLUNTARY PROVISION

The statutory services supported, and were in turn supported by, a range of non-statutory or 'independent' services which was so diverse as to defy adequate description, let alone accurate quantification.[27] There were three broad categories:

- commercial services run for profit
- 'informal' care provided by family or friends
- voluntary care, provided either by unpaid workers within the statutory services or by formal non-profit-distributing organisations.

Commercial (with-profit) services

Commercial services had been widespread before 1945. They were especially prevalent in the fields of medical care and burial insurance where, as has been seen, they were attacked by Bevan and Beveridge on account of their exploitative nature and administrative inefficiency.[28] One of the initial objectives of the NHS and national insurance (with its statutory death grants) had been their elimination. However, as demonstrated by the retention of pay-beds in NHS hospitals and the growth of occupational pensions, they continued after 1948 and were even subsidized through tax concessions (see Section 6.3). The one consolation was that they were now concentrated on the welfare of the better-off and before 1975 there were no serious attempts to target those in real need. Until 1975, therefore, non-statutory care was not of a commercial but essentially of an informal or voluntary nature.

Informal care

Informal care was the traditional source of 'care and tending' and after 1945 it continued to dwarf all other forms of provision. In the 1950s, for example, a PEP poll recorded that 'in times of trouble' one-half of mothers received help from relatives and a further one-third from friends.[29] The majority of these carers were women and, as feminists have argued, their responsibilities represented a huge potential loss to their own welfare both in time and employment opportunities forgone.

The continuation of informal care on such a scale after the war confounded contemporary predictions. It was assumed that it would wither away as a result either of increased state welfare or of a range of social trends (such as the break-up of families, the increasing number of working women and the destruction of tightly knit communities by housing redevelopment).[30] That it survived, and even expanded, was the result of several factors. There was greater need, for example, with the increasing number and longevity of the elderly. There was a lack of statutory care services in relation to more advanced 'social democratic' welfare states.[31] It was also rather conversely the consequence of improved statutory services, such as the personal social services and the social security system. This was because they enabled those in need – both physically and financially – to remain longer in their own or their relatives' homes. In Britain, in other words, the proper role of the personal social services was seen to be the support, and not the supplanting, of informal care.

The continuing importance of informal care was fully revealed in the late 1980s, when reliable estimates of the value of care first became available. Total annual expenditure by government on the personal social services was approximately £4,300 million. Charities spent some £400 million. The value of services provided by informal care dwarfed both at an estimated £24,000 million.[32] Moreover 6 million people, or 14 per cent of the adult population, were deemed to be 'carers'.

Voluntary (non-profit-distributing) care

The continuation of voluntary care on a formal rather than an informal basis was initially more controversial, for both political and functional reasons. *Politically* the belief of many was that social security, in its broadest sense, was an inalienable right which could be guaranteed only by a universal, democratically controlled service. 'How', enquired Bevan, 'can the state enter into a contract with a citizen to render a service through an autonomous body?'[33] Many Labour supporters and sympathizers were also hostile to working with organized volunteers because of their past record of social exclusivity and condescension towards manual workers. *Functionally*, as was well illustrated by voluntary hospitals in the 1930s, private charity lacked the sufficient, regular income either to deploy an adequate number of trained staff or to provide the comprehensive care (in terms of both need and geographical coverage) which the electorate increasingly expected. The experience of evacuation had made the provision of standardized national services a postwar prerogative. This clearly could not be achieved by a patchwork of competing, and often excessively competitive, agencies.

In the 1960s, however, attitudes towards formal voluntary care began to change and a consensus to form, albeit somewhat uneasily, on both its political

virtues and practical value. Politically, the fundamental assumption of both
'reluctant collectivists' and the New Right had always been that voluntary
care was an essential characteristic of a free and dynamic society. Statutory
services, they argued, embodied a *passive* concept of citizenship. The better-
off discharged their 'duty' by the simple payment of taxes whilst those in
need were entitled to, but did not always receive, 'rights'. Voluntary care, in
contrast, represented an *active* concept of citizenship whereby the better-off
directly helped those in need with the positive purpose of restoring them to
self-sufficiency and thus 'full citizenship'. The one was symptomatic of an
impersonal and demoralized society, the other of a vigorous and highly ethical one.

These views started to be expressed again with increasing confidence not
just amongst Conservatives but also within Labour Party. Admittedly, they
had never been wholly anathema to those on the right of the Party. In the
1940s, for example, one minister in the debate on Beveridge's *Voluntary
Action* had fully accepted that 'the voluntary spirit is the life blood of democracy'.[34] What was new in the 1960s was that, because of the evolving nature
of voluntary care, somewhat similar views came to be advanced by those on
the left of the Party. The increasing number of self-help and pressure groups
were seen to be an embodiment of participatory democracy – or even a
means of effective protest against the 'capitalist state'.[35] The net result was
that, from competing ideological positions, a political consensus started to
develop in favour of formal voluntary care.

A similar uneasy consensus formed over its practical advantages. These
were later summarized by the independent Wolfenden Report as the ability
to 'complement, supplement, extend and influence' informal and statutory
care.[36] Since the war voluntary organizations had consistently comple-
mented the other services in areas where there was either little political
sympathy or opportunity for self-help (such as the care of vagrants and drug
addicts) or where government action was considered to be inappropriate.
They had also supplemented informal and statutory care by making available additional money, manpower and facilities.

What really excited reformers in the 1960s, however, was the way in
which voluntary care could 'extend and influence' state welfare. Self-help
groups, for example, by increasing public participation – and above all
increased participation by the 'consumers' of welfare and their carers – identified 'real' needs, to which the state had then to respond. Voluntary agencies
were also able to pioneer new techniques and methods of care. This was
because, unlike their official counterparts, they had not always to ensure
equity or to consider possible political objections. Finally, all those involved
in the delivery of care formed a body of informed opinion which could both
champion services (which might otherwise be overlooked politically) and
directly improve their quality. As the Wolfenden Committee noted, for
example, within each service 'the very presence of outsiders can prevent
possible abuses of power and stimulate higher standards of provision'.[37] The
Seebohm Report concurred. 'A certain level of mutual criticism between local

authority and voluntary organisations may be essential', it admitted, 'if the needs of consumers are to be met more effectively and they are to be protected from the misuse of bureaucratic and professional power in either kind of organisation.'

Examples of voluntary care providing a service deemed inappropriate for state intervention are the provision of impartial information on individual rights by Citizens' Advice Bureaux (founded in 1938) and of personal counselling by both the Marriage Guidance Council (founded in 1947) and the Samaritans (founded in 1953). The vital support the voluntary sector gave statutory services is illustrated by its direct responsibility as late as 1967 for 15,000 of the 80,000 children, and 11,000 of the 95,000 elderly, in residential care.[38]

During this evolving consensus, the three principal forms of voluntary care had a very different reception. These three forms were:

- unpaid volunteers within statutory services
- self-help groups
- formal charities.

(i)   Unpaid volunteers

The least contentious type of formal care was the work of unpaid volunteers within the statutory services, such as that undertaken by the 'friends' of hospitals. The major advantage of this type of voluntary work was that it was not seen to challenge the legitimacy of the state services. Rather it strengthened them by relieving professional staff of routine tasks, which they either lacked the time to perform or could perform only at the expense of more specialist work.

The major disadvantage was that volunteers – in the old philanthropic tradition – could at times be unduly moralistic or inefficient (or even both). Some attempt was made to remedy these weaknesses after 1969, once the independent Aves Report had suggested ways in which the recruitment, training and deployment of volunteers could be made more professional. Indeed the Seebohm Report recommended that the new social service departments should become the 'focal point' for their recruitment By 1975, some 140 volunteer bureaux had been duly established.[39]

Volunteers tended to be middle-aged. As part of the 1960s revolution, younger people were increasingly recruited by agencies such as Community Service Volunteers (founded in 1962) and Task Force (founded in 1964).

(ii)   Self-help groups

The next least contentious form of voluntary care was self-help groups. Mutual aid had been the form of voluntary action favoured by Beveridge, but in the field of insurance the old nineteenth-century friendly society was already in terminal decline by the 1940s and any expansion of voluntary insurance thereafter was strictly on commercial lines. In the 1960s, however, there emerged a different kind of self-help group, which provided practical care and support for its members. They ranged from highly localized and transient groups to the local branches of national organizations, serviced by highly professional coordinating committees.

The advantage of such self-help groups was that they displayed personal initiative which could act as a therapy for their members. They could also provide cheap and adaptable services to supplement those funded by the state. Their disadvantages were the traditional ones. Both the standard of their service and their geographical coverage could be extremely uneven. They were also a potent source of political controversy. To some they represented a welcome rejection of dependency upon government. To others they provided an equally welcome vehicle for protest through which greater resources could be extracted *from* government.

Foremost amongst the national self-help organizations were Age Concern, which had 11,000 local groups by 1975, and the Pre-School Playgroups Association. The latter by 1975 had 9400 groups catering for 360,000 children and actively involved three-quarters of their parents under the guidance of leaders, nine-tenths of whom were trained.[40] Nevertheless, as argued in Section 8.4, it still demonstrated the inherent weakness of voluntary care. It was strongest in middle-class areas where the need for extra child support was least.

(iii)   Charities

The most contentious form of voluntary care was that provided by long-established charities (such as Dr Barnardo's and the National Society for the Prevention of Cruelty to Children) or by organizations directly funded by government (such as the Women's Voluntary Service (WVS), founded in 1938 to meet civil defence needs and retained after 1945 as part of the contingency planning for future wars).[41] These major charities had long realized that they lacked the resources to compete with, or to dominate, state welfare as they had done in the nineteenth century. Indeed since the First World War they had largely welcomed the lifting from them of the impossible task of relieving primary poverty and the opportunity to work constructively with government. This change of attitude was epitomized by the Charity Organisation Society (COS). Before 1914 it had been the leading proponent of minimum government. By the Second World War, however, its secretary was arguing that 'social workers can double their usefulness by working for an official body with public funds behind it'.

After metamorphosis of the COS into the Family Welfare Association in 1946, the object of its pioneering casework also changed. It was no longer to distinguish between those who were 'deserving' or 'undeserving' of charitable assistance but to help 'problem families' adjust to the world around them.[42] Despite such changes, however, the continuing presence of charities was still widely resented. They were seen by many as either a potential obstacle to the provision of universal and comprehensive services by the state or as a vehicle for the imposition of class, as opposed to democratic, values.

There was some justification for these fears in the 1950s because within organized charities, as within local authorities, old assumptions and habits died hard. Their services were, nevertheless, needed to make good the gaps left by the financial and legislative restrictions upon the statutory services. Hence the specialist needs of certain minority groups (most notably the blind and the deaf) continued to be largely catered for by private charities. In the rapidly expanding area of care for the elderly, the vast majority of new initiatives (such as meals on wheels and day centres) were also pioneered by voluntary organizations.[43]

> To fill gaps left by the state, the NSPCC undertook most of the preventive work in relation to the neglect and abuse of children. In addition, the WVS – in conjunction, and often in open rivalry, with other organizations such as the National Old People's Welfare Council (later Age Concern) and the Red Cross – provided domiciliary care for the elderly.

Renaissance: 1965–75

The 1950s were not wholly bereft of new initiatives. As the Wolfenden Committee admitted, however, it was essentially a period of 'marking time'. In the 1960s, by contrast, voluntary organizations played their full part in the explosion of 'creativity, ingenuity and energy'.[44] The traditional agencies were joined by new pressure groups, such as the CPAG and the DIG (both founded in 1965) and Shelter (founded in 1966). New service-providing organizations were also established, most notably the National Association for the Care and Resettlement of Offenders (NACRO) which was founded in 1966.[45]

Equally significantly the assumptions and practices of the traditional agencies themselves were transformed. In 1969, for example, Dr Barnardo's changed its emphasis from residential homes to care within the family. It also increasingly concentrated upon the needs of problem children and the most deprived areas. Similarly the NSPCC, whose inspectorate had previously been predominantly male and recruited from the police force, was employing by the early 1970s an equal number of men and women as inspectors. In addition they were no longer expected to wear uniform.

Such a transformation in attitudes made the provision of care by voluntary agencies more acceptable. What, however, really accelerated their acceptance was a growing awareness of shortfalls within, and the shortcomings of, state provision. As with private charity in the nineteenth century, so with state welfare in the twentieth, it was finally recognized by experts and politicians alike that there were insufficient resources to meet all needs. Moreover, statutory care could be both insensitive and inflexible. Hence the Seebohm Committee's enthusiasm for a 'mixed economy' of welfare. Constructive rivalry between voluntary and statutory care could offset the weaknesses inherent in both. Hence also the more open acceptance by both political parties of voluntary care. It provided both a means of counteracting the relentless rise in public expenditure and an antidote to the vested interests of professional social workers.

By the mid-1970s, therefore, formal voluntary care was almost wholly rehabilitated. A Voluntary Services Unit was established in the Home Office by the Conservative government in 1972 to coordinate policy and an increasing number of local authorities started willingly to employ voluntary bodies on an agency basis to discharge their statutory responsibilities. The major national charities had also expanded so fast that by 1976 they were employing a permanent staff which was equivalent in size to one-fifth of that working for the social service departments. It was equally well trained.

Potential dangers, of course, attended this increasingly close identification of statutory and voluntary care.

- With income from private donations (despite tax concessions) falling by 1976 to under half of their revenue and with fee-income rising to 37 per cent, could the major charities maintain their independence and their ability to experiment?[46]
- With increasing centralization and bureaucratization, could they maintain the local spontaneity and enthusiasm which were amongst their key assets?
- Might not local government lose the first-hand experience it needed to monitor effectively the discharge of statutory duties by outside agencies on their behalf?

That such questions were being asked, however, represented a remarkable transformation in the position of voluntary organizations. In the 1950s their very future had appeared to be in jeopardy.

10.3   CONCLUSION

During the 1960s and 1970s, as Younghusband has remarked, the statutory personal social services 'leapt from the margins to the centre' of welfare policy. In consequence, a more comprehensive and professionalised service was provided for all those in need.[47] However, the Seebohm Report, which was central to this transformation, was not without fault. It might be taken as a leading example of the besetting sin of the classic welfare state – professional self-interest. It also failed to dispel long-standing misgivings about the ability of social workers to discharge all the responsibilities which they sought to reserve for themselves. Indeed, many still remained to be convinced in the 1970s that social work was entitled to call itself a profession.

The implementation of the report was also contentious. Its major recommendation, the creation of unified social services departments, was accepted. However, hard decisions over priorities continued to be evaded and the effectiveness of individual policies was neither systematically monitored nor evaluated. For instance, it was not until 1976 that the first public statement of 'rational and systematic priorities throughout the health and personal social services' was published; and even then it was exposed by the concurrent economic crisis as unrealistically optimistic.[48] By 1975, therefore, the role and future of the social service departments were still far from secure.

The statutory social services were dwarfed by the care provided for those in need by family and friends. They in turn, however, did come to dwarf their historical adversary: organized voluntary care. The latter, after a period of stagnation, was nevertheless revitalized in the 1960s. Its expansion was encouraged with a new enthusiasm by successive governments, which saw it to be both cost-effective and an antidote to bureaucratic self-interest. Beneath an apparent political consensus, however, there was a deep ideological divide. This went to the heart of the unresolved dilemma concerning the proper role of government and the individual within the welfare state. Was increased voluntary provision to be welcomed as an expression of greater individual initiative which would reduce state intervention? Or was it to be seen as a vehicle for collective action which would ultimately expand, or even transform, the role of the state?

Before 1975 this fundamental conflict was not openly addressed and voluntary care mainly expanded only at times when, and in places where, the statutory services themselves were strong. The critical battle, over what the state should not as well as could not do, was not to be fully joined until the 1980s.

10.4   FURTHER READING

The history of the personal social services is covered more fully than in most texts by D. Gladstone (ed.), *British Social Welfare* (1995), and exhaustively in the encyclopaedic E. Younghusband's *Social Work in Britain, 1950–1975*, 2 vols (1978). A similar service is provided for Scotland by J. Murphy, *British Social Services: the Scottish dimension* (Edinburgh, 1992). The chapter by H. Glennerster et al., in J. Hills (ed.), *The State of Welfare: the welfare state in Britain since 1974* (Oxford, 1990) provides an authoritative summary of the state of the personal social services in 1975, whilst H. Glennerster, *Paying for Welfare* (Hemel Hempstead, 1997) is illuminating on both its funding and that of the voluntary sector.

A full analysis of the Seebohm Report is provided in P. Hall, *Reforming the Welfare: the politics of change in the personal social services* (1976), whilst other primary material can be found in B. Watkin, *Documents on Health and Social Services: 1834 to the present day* (1975). Services for children are well covered by the draftsman of the Seebohm Report, R. A. Parker, in 'The gestation of reform: the Children Act 1948', included in P. Bean and S. MacPherson (eds), *Approaches to Welfare* (1983); and in J. Packman, *The Child's Generation: childcare policy from Curtis to Houghton* (1975). A full bibliography is provided in H. Hendrick, *Children, Childhood and English Society, 1880–1990* (Cambridge, 1997). Services for the elderly are equally well covered up to 1971 by R. Means and R. Smith, *From Poor Law to Community Care* (Bristol, 1998), and thereafter by the same authors with Hazel Moberly in *From Community Care to Market Care?* (Bristol, 2002). P. Bridgen and J. Lewis, *Elderly people and the Boundary between Health and Social Care 1946–91: whose responsibility?* (1999) provides a model of how to place a particular present-day issue into historical perspective. P. Thane, *Old Age in English History* (Oxford, 2000) provides a similar service for the totality of the elderly's experience. A contemporary classic is P. Townsend, *The Family Life of Old People* (1957).

The history of voluntary provision has a counterpart to Younghusband in G. Finlayson, *Citizen, State and Social Welfare in Britain, 1830–1990* (Oxford, 1994). Some may find his 'A moving frontier: voluntarism and the state in British social welfare', *Twentieth Century British History*, I (1990) 183–206, a valuable introduction. The history of the Family Welfare Association by J. Lewis, *The Voluntary Sector, the State and Social Work in Britain* (Cheltenham, 1995) is an incisive commentary upon the evolving relationship between all three. P. Starkey, *Families and Social Workers: the work of Family Service Units, 1940–1985* (Liverpool, 2000) is another illuminating case study of a particular charitable organization. Other books which put the role of voluntary provision in historical perspective are M. Brenton, *The Voluntary Sector in British Social Services* (1985); A. Ware (ed.), *Charities and Government* (1989); and F. Prochaska, *The Voluntary Impulse: philanthropy in modern Britain* (1989).

The Achievement

CONTENTS

The classic welfare state evolved in the 1940s for a variety of reasons. As has been seen, the least contentious of its initial objectives were functional: to make good 'the failure of the market to control avoidable ills' (which had become all too apparent between the wars) and to standardize the quality of public services, (which evacuation had exposed as unacceptably uneven).[1] Even so pragmatic an expansion in the role of government, however, had revolutionary consequences. All citizens were effectively guaranteed, for the first time in British history, equal welfare rights. It was on the basis of such a guarantee – reflecting, so it was believed, a heightened sense of community during the war – that many then came to argue, more contentiously, that the essential objective of the welfare state was the creation of a more equal and altruistic society. Consequently, the record of the classic welfare state has come conventionally to be judged by the twin criteria of *efficiency* and *equality*.

By such criteria, no definitive conclusion can be reached about its relative success or failure. This is because:

- They potentially conflict. Universal welfare policies designed to achieve *equality* have, for example, been widely condemned as an *inefficient* way of targeting help on those in need.
- There is no agreed definition of the terms 'efficiency' and 'equality'.
- There are problems of measurement.
- There are counterfactual problems.

Between 1945 and 1975, there were – as there still are – conflicting *definitions* of equality. The concept of equality went to the heart of party conflict. For instance as Gaitskell (the leader of the Labour Party) wrote in 1956: 'If you don't feel strongly about equality, then I think it is very hard to be a genuine Socialist, and if we were to abandon this, then I think there would be very little left to distinguish us from the Tories.' What, however, did he mean by equality? His definition was a levelling not just of income and wealth but also of social status and power. This was anathema to the contemporary Conservative Party. 'We are frankly opposed', admitted the One Nation group of back-benchers, 'to policies which make everybody more or more nearly equal.'[2] The Conservatives, nevertheless, were not wholly inegalitarian. They (like New Labour) openly championed another type of equality – equality of opportunity.

Likewise, efficiency can be defined in a variety of different ways It can alternatively mean:

- the optimum allocation of aggregate resources
- the cost-effective delivery of specific policies
- the successful encouragement of 'desirable' personal attitudes, be it greater altruism or self-sufficiency.

The *measurement* of equality and efficiency is equally contentious. For example, conventional microeconomic analysis can provide some measure of the efficiency of both individual policies and aggregate welfare expenditure (see Section 3.2). Within individual policies, however, certain 'inputs' and 'outputs', such as the cost of unpaid carers or the benefit of humane care for the dying, have no market price. They have to be valued subjectively. Similarly any measure of the efficiency of aggregate expenditure has ultimately to depend on the perceived political purpose underlying state welfare.

Problems of measurement are well illustrated by the NHS. To maximize the *economic* return on investment in the NHS, for example, care would have to concentrate on 'relievable need' amongst the existing and future workforce – to the exclusion of the elderly, the disabled and the dying. Could any government openly espouse such a policy? If not, what alternative measures of efficiency are available? In the absence of an agreed alternative, the NHS is inevitably judged on market criteria. This is ironic because the very justification for its existence (like that of the welfare state as a whole) is the proven inability of the market, in given areas of welfare, to allocate scarce resources efficiently.

The final obstacle to a definitive assessment of the achievement of the classic welfare state is the counterfactual question: what would have happened had it not existed? Given the buoyancy of world markets and the breakthroughs in medical science, for example, would not 'full' employment and improved standards of health have been achieved anyway? Can their attainment be legitimately accredited to the welfare state? Conversely, as the white papers *Employment Policy* and *Technical Education* warned in 1944 and 1956, a prerequisite for 'full employment' and educational reform was the positive support of employers, trade unions and the general public. Given the innate conservatism of postwar Britain, could any form of government have achieved more?

The answers to such conceptual, technical and historical questions ultimately depend on personal judgement. The purpose of this chapter is to provide the material upon which such judgements can be based.

11.1 EQUALITY

Equality is a highly controversial concept. It can mean:

- Equality of treatment by the state, as implicit in the Beveridge Report.
- Equality of opportunity, as promoted by the 1944 Education Act and later by the Conservative Party.
- Equality of outcome, as increasingly desired in the 1960s by those seeking to reform the social security and education systems.

Similarly it may refer to equality of:

- social status
- power
- income and wealth.

It is by the third definition in both of these categories that equality can be most easily quantified. Consequently, it is by the recorded figures for the distribution of income and wealth that the welfare state has most frequently been judged. This has consequently taken precedence over the issue of gender equality where, as argued in Section 2.2.3, welfare provision has both reduced and reinforced inequality in the private sphere. It has also taken precedence over regional equality where, as demonstrated in Table 4.5, resources were redistributed from the centre to the periphery.[3]

- To what extent, therefore, has welfare policy affected the distribution of income and wealth?
- How valid is such a test for the overall achievement of the classic welfare state?

Equality of income

The most authoritative estimates of the distribution of personal income is summarized in Table 11.1. They confirm the persistence of inequality throughout the period. Between 1949 and 1975–6, for example, the percentage of post-tax income enjoyed by the bottom 50 per cent of income earners only

Table 11.1   Distribution of personal income in Britain, 1949–75/6

Per cent	1949	1954	1964	1970/1	1975/6
Before tax					
Top 1	11.2	9.3	8.2	6.6	5.6
Top 10	33.2	30.1	29.1	27.5	25.8
Next 40	43.1	46.9	48.2	49.0	49.9
Bottom 50	23.7	22.0	22.7	23.5	24.3
Gini coefficient	41.1	40.3	39.9	38.5	36.6
After tax					
Top 1	6.4	5.3	5.3	4.5	3.6
Top 10	27.1	25.3	25.9	23.9	22.3
Next 40	46.4	48.4	48.9	49.9	50.3
Bottom 50	26.5	26.3	25.2	26.1	27.4
Gini coefficient	35.5	35.8	36.6	33.9	31.5

Source: Cmnd 7595, Royal Commission on the Distribution of Income and Wealth, Report no. 7 (1979), table A.4.

rose marginally from 26.5 per cent to 27.4 per cent. By contrast, in 1976 the top 1 per cent enjoyed 5.5 times the mean for personal income and wealth.[4] Why was the pace of recorded change so slow with the Gini coefficient (a measure which, as explained later, denotes greater equality as it declines towards zero) actually increasing for post-tax income before 1964? The conventional explanation is the *decreasing progressiveness* of both *taxation* and the *benefit system*.

Redistributing income: taxation

Soon after the war the Inland Revenue acknowledged, as must all welfare analysts, that the way in which government *raises* money is as important to individual welfare as the way in which it spends it. As it advised the 1951–5 Royal Commission on the Taxation of Profits and Income:

> Tax is no longer simply a matter of raising the revenue required with the minimum disturbance to private and public interests. The social and economic effects of tax are so great and the possibility of the deliberate use of taxation to achieve social and economic ends so important that it is no longer possible to deal with tax purely, or in some instances even primarily, in a fiscal sense.[5]

However, it thereafter lacked both the resources and the will to monitor the redistributive effect of tax changes. Consequently there are no authoritative contemporary estimates. Undoubtedly, however, taxation was decreasingly progressive. This was for three rather complex reasons:

- modifications to the overall tax structure
- the changing incidence of individual taxes
- the expansion of 'fiscal' and 'occupational' welfare.

(i) The changing tax structure

The major structural change was a switch from the taxation of companies and personal wealth to the taxation of those on average, or below average, incomes. Between 1955 and 1964, for example, and again between 1965 and 1974 the percentage of total tax revenue raised from companies was halved.[6] Simultaneously, the effectiveness of death duties, which had initially been so swingeing that the heirs of a £2 million estate could expect to receive only £400,000, was eroded by legal avoidance. To make good the resulting short-fall government revenue became ever more heavily dependent on the proceeds of income tax (despite the Conservative Party's concern for the maintenance of incentive), employees' national insurance contributions (as the Treasury's own contribution plummeted) and indirect taxes (such as excise duty on beer and tobacco, and other sales taxes). The latter were particularly regressive and by the 1970s were responsible for the immediate return to the Treasury of approximately one-fifth of a subsistence pension.

(ii) The incidence of taxation

The nature of individual taxes on expenditure and income also changed and thus the way in which they affected ordinary people (their incidence). For example purchase tax, when it was introduced in 1940, was levied at different rates. Luxury goods were taxed the heaviest. However, as Britain grew more affluent, it was not adapted to changing consumption patterns and so it differentiated less between the rich and the poor. Finally, following Britain's entry into the EEC in 1974 it was replaced by VAT – a flat-rate tax which did not distinguish at all between luxury and ordinary goods.[7]

Simultaneously, income tax became less progressive. This was due to changes both to the rate at which it was levied and the level of income at which it became payable (the tax threshold). Between 1945 and 1975, for instance, the standard rate of income tax fell from 50 per cent to 35 per cent. This was of greatest advantage to those on high and middle incomes. Meanwhile the 'reduced' rates of tax, at which the lower paid entered the tax system, were successively withdrawn after 1962 so that by 1970 those with sufficient income just to cross the tax threshold had to pay the full standard rate.[8] This anomaly was accentuated by inflation which, by increasing money incomes and decreasing the value of personal tax allowances, drew an increasing number of people into the tax system (fiscal drag). As a result, between 1945 and 1975 the number of income tax-payers increased from 17.5 million to 20.5 million.

The net result of these changes to the incidence of individual taxes was that a far greater weight of taxation fell on the lower paid. In addition the lowering of the tax threshold created two socially indefensible anomalies. First, people living below the poverty line became liable not just to indirect taxation but also to income tax. Second, the low-paid were subject to the highest marginal rates of taxation (the percentage of income lost when increased earnings either take the low-paid across the tax threshold or make an existing tax-payer liable to a higher rate of tax). These anomalies lay at the root of the unemployment and poverty traps in the 1970s and led to the unavailing calls for a merger of the tax and benefits systems (see Section 6.3).

The increased incidence of taxation is well illustrated by the fact that in 1949 the earnings of a married man with two children had to reach 103 per cent of average earnings before he became liable to pay any income tax. Because of the reduced rate of taxation (see note 8 for details) they had to reach 187 per cent before he had to pay it at the standard rate. In 1975 married men with two children became liable to tax at the full standard rate when their earnings reached only 44.6 per cent of the national average.

The resulting injustice is evident from the treatment of the poor. In 1976 the poverty line for a married man with two children was £43.50 when in work (the family income supplement level) or £35.05 when out of work (the supplementary benefit level). However, he crossed the tax threshold when his earned income reached £31.40. Money received from family income supplement had, in other words, to be passed back immediately to the Inland Revenue. This is a prime example of why, in any calculation of the redistibution of income by government, attention has to be paid to the *financing* as well as the targeting of benefits.[9]

(iii)   Fiscal and occupational welfare

The final reason for the decreasing progressiveness of taxation was the expansion of tax allowances. They had been overlooked by Beveridge as a source of welfare, but their importance was highlighted in 1955 by Titmuss in his famous lecture on the 'social division of welfare'.[10] He distinguished between three kinds of welfare:

- state welfare
- fiscal welfare
- occupational welfare

State welfare involved the overt and audited transfer of resources to individuals either in kind (such as healthcare) or in cash (such as supplementary benefit). Fiscal and occupational welfare, by contrast, involved the covert and unrecorded transfer of resources to individuals and companies through the exemption from taxation of that proportion of income spent in an approved manner. The most notorious form of fiscal welfare was tax relief on mortgage interest payments which, as was shown in Section 9.3, was costing government an estimated £770 million by 1975. Examples of occupational welfare were the exemption of company contributions to occupational pensions (enjoyed by 11.4 million employees by the mid-1970s) and subsidies on company cars and meals (enjoyed by an estimated two-thirds of senior management).[11]

Fiscal and occupational welfare clearly favoured the better-off. In addition they were socially divisive. On the one hand those on high incomes could take maximum advantage of the allowances. This had the added advantage of enabling them to minimize the proportion of their income liable to higher rates of tax. The tax-base was thereby reduced and, to maintain its revenue, government had to raise additional money from those on below-average wages.[12] On the other hand salaried workers were favoured over wage earners. Differences in social status were consolidated, for example, by subsidized cars and entertainment. Those able to afford a mortgage were also assisted in the purchase of a capital-appreciating asset which would have significant consequences for the later distribution of wealth. The irony was that as state-financed benefits for the well-off were increasingly sought (and financed), state-financed benefits to those in genuine need were increasingly stigmatized (and restricted).

One of the most serious objections to fiscal welfare at the time was that it undermined the cross-class interest in state welfare that universalism was designed to foster. This can be seen with one of the first tax allowances granted, child allowance. Initiated in 1909 to minimize divergences between the disposable income of parents and childless couples (horizontal or contingency equity), tax-payers continued to enjoy it until 1976 in addition to family allowances (introduced in 1946 and paid in cash over the counter at Post Offices). Those sufficiently rich to pay tax, therefore, recieved considerably more child support than the poor. This was one of the reasons why there was only a muted protest against the falling real value of family allowances throughout the period.

Redistributing income: state benefits

If, as was generally recognized by the 1970s, taxation had become increasingly regressive, the assumption persisted that the welfare state as a whole was still progressive because resources were being transferred from the rich to the poor by the social services. This was the conviction of certain Conservative ministers in 1955 when, following Titmuss's lecture, they asserted: 'substantial social service benefits were being enjoyed by a large number of people who, because of full employment, were not now in real need of them. The burden of providing these benefits fell most heavily on the middle classes.'[13]

Twenty years later it remained the conviction of one of the members of the Royal Commission on the Distribution of Income and Wealth, Sir Henry Phelps Brown, who reflected that:

Taxes as a whole fall on households almost proportionately throughout the top 70 per cent; only the bottom 30 per cent are in some measure spared, but even the poorest tenth contribute a fifth of their receipts. . . . Evidently, if the business of redistribution is to be done effectively, it is the provision of benefits that must do it.

This responsibility, he felt confident, was being discharged by welfare policy. In 1977, for example, he estimated that 'with remarkable consistency' the top 60 per cent of income earners received benefits from government worth £1000 per household. In comparison, the bottom 40 per cent received benefits worth up to twice that amount. As a result, 'the top 60 per cent gave up nearly 17 per cent of their original income to be transferred to their poorer neighbours'. This was 'markedly progressive'.

Such cofidence has not gone unchallenged. *Cash benefits*, it is agreed, do benefit the lower-paid disproportionately – although, with the introduction of universalism in 1948, the better-off did enjoy some remarkable windfalls. For example, a man aged 55 in 1948, whose income had previously been sufficiently high to exempt him from compulsory insurance, became entitled in 1958 to a pension worth ten times the actuarial value of his contributions (see Section 6.3).

The redistributive effects of *benefits in kind* are, however, more contentious. Many argued, then as now, that they disproportionately favour the better-off. In healthcare, for example, the middle class in general is believed to have easier access to better facilities (owing in part to the historical location of hospitals and the preference of GPs for middle-class areas). They are also believed to enjoy longer periods of consultation with doctors, owing to greater articulacy and perhaps social affinity, and, in addition, more advanced and expensive treatment. Similarly in education a disproportionate number of middle-class children stay on after the end of compulsory schooling to enjoy high-cost further education. In 1958 Abel-Smith calculated that the cost of three years' university education was equivalent to that of ten years' primary and secondary schooling. This he used as one of his justifications for the charge that 'the major beneficiaries of postwar changes in the social services have been the middle classes'.[14]

Twenty-five years later this verdict was endorsed by Le Grand. He calculated that, in the late 1970s, the top 20 per cent of income earners were receiving educational and health services worth respectively three times and two-fifths as much as those received by the bottom 20 per cent. 'Almost all public expenditure on the social services in Britain', he concluded, 'benefits the better-off to a greater extent than the poor'.[15] Under the classic welfare state, determined attempts had been made to equalize provision, such as Education Priority Areas, Housing Action Areas and the the work of the Resources Allocation Working Group in healthcare after 1976. Quantifiable results, if any, had clearly been limited.

Redistributing income: tentative conclusions

Disagreement over the rebistributive impact of the tax-benefit system as a whole, it had been hoped in the 1960s, could be resolved scientifically. To determine if and how redistribution occurred, household income was divided into five categories:

- original income (derived from employment and investment)
- gross income (original income plus cash benefits)
- disposable income (gross income minus direct taxes)
- post-tax income (disposable income minus indirect taxes)
- final income (post-tax income plus benefits in kind).

The initial findings from such calculations confirmed that a redistribution of income did occur over an individual's lifetime (enforced thrift). There was also some redistribution within economic classes from, say, the healthy to the sick (contingency redistribution). Less conclusive was the evidence about the extent of vertical redistribution from rich to poor (class redistribution).[16]

Some degree of vertical redistribution, however, has been confirmed by more recent analysis. It has been calculated, for example, that in 1975 the Gini coefficient fell from 45 to 31 between original and final income. Nevertheless, retrospective analysis does not provide a wholly 'progressive' picture. It has underlined the retrogressive nature of indirect taxation (with post-tax income being less equal than disposable income). It has also provided little evidence of increasing equality over time. Wartime changes were simply maintained in the 1950s. Thereafter there was only a slight decrease in inequality. For all the bureaucratic 'churning' of money, as it was raised through taxation and then dispensed in benefit, the results – in terms of equality – were extremely limited.

Even such tentative conclusions, however, must necessarily be treated with caution because of the way in which data is collected and processed, and the findings presented. Most of evidence derives from the Family Expenditure Survey. Its basic limitations have already been identified in Section 6.2. In addition, it is unable to provide information on the redistributive effects of many taxes (such as employers' national insurance contributions) and of much public expenditure (especially that on public goods). Its assumptions about the take-up of many benefits in kind are also hypothetical.

Calculations of personal income are dogged by similar technical problems, as was admitted by the authoritative 1975–9 Royal Commission on the Distribution of Income and Wealth. They exclude, for example, non-monetary income (such as perks). They are based on individuals rather than households (and therefore record a large number of 'non-earning' housewives). Being on an annual basis, they also overlook the irregularity of many people's income (such as the royalties for impoverished authors of books on the welfare state which have taken too long to write).[17] All such conventions again tend to exaggerate the degree of inequality. Moreover, because other countries work to different assumptions on each of these issues, they make accurate international comparisons extremely difficult.

Finally, there are additional technical problems when either national or international data are expressed. One of the most effective forms of presentation is the Lorenz curve, which plots the proportion of personal income held by any given percentage of the population (see Figure 11.1). Total parity is represented by the diagonal line and the Gini coefficient is the measure of the area between the curve and the diagonal. As income equality increases, so the curve will shift to the left towards the diagonal and the Gini coefficient will move nearer to zero. One of the weaknesses of this measure, however, is revealed by the graph. In 1964 the distribution of income as measured by the Gini coefficient was more equal in Britain than in West Germany. This result, however, was only achieved because of a more equal spread of income amongst the top 50 per cent and despite the income of the bottom 50 per cent being further from the average than in Germany. In other words the Gini coefficient (as used in Table 11.1) is an aggregate measure and may obscure the actual experience of different income groups.

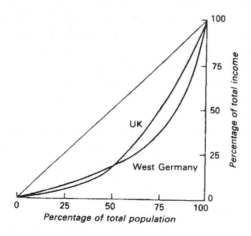

Figure 11.1   Lorenz curve for the UK and West Germany, 1964.
Source: A. B. Atkinson (ed.), *Wealth, Income and Inequality* (1980) p. 41.

Equality of wealth

Estimates of wealth are bedevilled by similar technical problems. This is because, in the absence of an annual wealth tax, they are conventionally calculated by the so-called 'estate multiplier method'.[18] In any one given year the number of people dying and leaving an estate liable to taxation is taken to be a representative sample of all wealth holders in the country. An aggregate figure is then determined through the application to each group of a special multiplier which is sensitive to differences of gender, age, wealth and locality. The potential weaknesses of such a convention are many. Half the number of people dying in any one year, for instance, do not have any taxable wealth. They do nevertheless own some wealth (estimated by the Royal Commission at some £700m in 1972). How is this wealth to be incorporated?

More seriously the calculations ignore altogether certain types of wealth, such as the right to social security. This should be regarded as a form of wealth because, before the welfare state, such security was enjoyed only by the wealthy. Had pension rights alone been included in the conventional calculations for 1972, so the Royal Commission estimated, the share of the bottom 80 per cent of wealth holders would have jumped from 19.2 per cent to 40.7 per cent. Finally, the figures are based on individuals and are not age-specific, and therefore ignore the wealth which many enjoy but do not actually own (such as the spouse or dependants of a rich individual) and the wealth which a young person may eventually acquire. Each of these weaknesses, it should be noted, again greatly exaggerates the degree of inequality that is recorded.

With these reservations in mind, it would would appear that throughout the welfare state personal wealth was far more unequally distributed than income (see Table 11.2). So far as can be judged, the proportion of wealth held by the bottom 80 per cent of wealth holders remained static until 1970, after which it increased to a mere 23 per cent. In 1976, whereas the top 1 per cent enjoyed 5.5 times the mean for personal income, the top 1 per cent owned 25 times the mean for personal wealth.[19]

Alternative measures of equality

Technical problems reduce the confidence with which recorded figures of income and wealth can be used to judge the classic welfare state. So also should their conceptual limitations. Above all, are income and wealth an appropriate proxy for welfare? There are, after all, many instances in which a reduction in income can represent an increase, not a decrease, in individual

Table 11.2 Distribution of personal wealth in England and Wales, 1950–76

Per cent	1950	1954	1964	1970	1976
Top 1	47.2	45.3	34.5	29.7	25.0
Top 5	74.3	71.8	58.6	53.6	46.0
Top 10	–	–	71.4	68.7	60.0
Top 20	–	–	84.3	84.5	77.0
Bottom 80	–	–	15.7	15.5	23.0

Source: Cmnd 7595, Royal Commission on the Distribution of Income and Wealth, Report no. 7 (1979), table 4.5.

welfare. For example, a woman may give up work to have, and look after, a child. Students may consciously forgo higher earnings in order to gain qualifications which may maximize their future earnings – or even their personal fulfilment. In a distinctly different case (of course) an individual's preference might be for leisure over work. How accurately, therefore, can figures for the mere distribution of income and wealth reflect the distribution of individual welfare?

Moreover, recorded figures for income and wealth can reveal little about the equally important (albeit less easily quantifiable) issue of the distribution of power and social status. It is here that the achievements of the classic welfare state, particularly in relation to previously disadvantaged groups, are perhaps in most danger of being underestimated.

The very acceptance by the wartime Coalition of the bulk of the Beveridge Report represented, after all, a marked shift in effective *power* from Conservative ministers and Treasury officials. The subsequent attainment of full employment has also been described as a 'transfer of power . . . on a momentous scale' not just on the shop-floor (where scarcity of labour gave trade unions greater bargaining power) but also in political decision-making (as corporatist negotiations began to proliferate).[20] Moreover, it has been argued that industrial management underwent a 'psychological revolution' as a result of the increased power of both the state and the consumer. In consequence, it became increasingly sensitive to public, as opposed to short-term private, welfare.

With regard to *social status*, the Beveridge Report – by guaranteeing social security to all – effectively recognized, in T. H. Marshall's words, everyone's 'equal social worth'.[21] The establishment of universal services such as the NHS reinforced this breakthrough, as did other less publicized reforms such as legal aid (which after 1949 gave to those previously unable to pay lawyers' fees a real – as opposed to a merely theoretical – equality before the law). Finally, full employment and consequent affluence reduced the visible differences between the members of each social class and, as has been seen in Section 4.5, led in that respect to the creation of a largely classless culture.

So optimistic a summary might with some justice be challenged. Given the gradual reimposition of Treasury control after 1947, was there really a permanent redistribution of administrative power? In corporatist bodies was there any constructive sharing of power or did the three sides merely talk past, rather than to, each other? Did management's attitude really change? Did the concept of 'equal social worth' stretch to a redistribution of responsibility within the private sphere of the home? More damagingly, as earlier chapters have shown, welfare policy itself could even accentuate inequalities. Fiscal and occupational welfare could underpin and even exaggerate status differences. Likewise, contributory insurance and work practices within welfare services could reinforce women's dependence on men and the sexual division of labour.

One example of the inequality generated by the classic welfare state was the increasing power of pension funds. As a result of fiscal concessions and the contracting-out clauses in successive insurance acts, these funds accumulated massive reserves which gave the old financial elite an even stronger control over investment and thus the future structure of the economy. This was far removed from the purpose behind Beveridge's initial intention and desire to encourage 'socially desirable forms of thrift' and diffuse power through small, democratically controlled friendly societies.[22]

Nevertheless it is undeniable that the classic welfare state achieved a significant redistribution of both social status and power. Freedom from fear of absolute poverty and universal access to services such as the NHS and secondary education dramatically improved the quality of the lives of many. So too did the comparative job security and, above all, the sustained rise in average living standards that emanated from full employment. Tables for the distribution of income say nothing about *actual* living standards; nor do they reveal how apparently insignificant sums amongst the lowest paid can have – in terms of genuine social and political independence – a significance far beyond their monetary value.[23] As for the distribution of power, the record of the classic welfare state has only to be set beside that of the 1930s and the years after 1975 for its relative achievement to be apparent. All these advances, moreover, enabled long-standing and deep-seated sources of inequality, particularly those affecting women and ethnic minorities, to be fully faced for the first time. The identification of problems should not be confused with their intensification.

Equality as an ideal

The conclusion to be drawn from these complex technical, conceptual and political issues is relatively straightforward. Any estimate of the welfare state's achievement in relation to equality must clearly include a full analysis of the tax system and the recorded distribution of income and wealth. This is particularly important to correct eroneous contemporary assumptions about the 'progressive' nature of the classic welfare state. Equally, however, it is wrong to judge its record too precipitately on such evdence alone. Other evidence of a qualitative as well as a quantitative nature is equally relevant.

One final caveat remains. It should be remembered that greater 'equality of outcome' was not an initial objective of the welfare state. Nor was it ever an objective of the Conservative Party, which held effective power for much of the period. Nor indeed, did it have any 'great popular appeal' even amongst the supporters of the Labour Party – as Gaitskell himself had to admit.[24] Skilled workers, with their vested interest in wage differentials, were amongst its leading opponents. Unskilled workers also stubbornly remained interested more 'in the inequality of horses than the equality of men'. On what grounds, therefore, should equality of outcome – as suggested by academic concentration on the distribution of income and wealth – be the predominant criterion on which the record of the classic welfare state is judged?

Divisions within the Labour Party over equality as a practical ideal led to a bitter row in the 1960s between Crossman, as secretary of state for health and social security, and those responsible for the 'rediscovery' of poverty. 'In wartime', he argued, 'it is just possible to persuade democratic communities to accept the fair shares of a national siege economy and even to welcome the drastic restrictions and heavy sacrifices involved. But this readiness to share is only ' "for the duration".'[25]

11.2   EFFICIENCY

The efficiency of the classic welfare state both in aggregate and in relation to the delivery of individual services is similarly the subject of ideological and technical dispute.

Ideological differences are at their most acute over the aggregate efficiency of the classic welfare state. As demonstrated in Section 2.2, the basic belief of democratic socialists is that the state is better able to promote welfare than the market. This is because the latter inherently undersupplies public goods, is unable sufficiently to measure externalities and, in the real world, is handicapped by both imperfect knowledge and imperfect competition. In contrast the fundamental assumption of the New Right is that state provision – as opposed to state financing – of welfare services is inherently inefficient. Centralized bureaucracies cannot be as efficient as the market in the collection of information, the synchronizing of demand with supply, or in their response to changing consumer demand. Despite the assumptions of Beveridge and Keynes, bureaucrats are not disinterested. Nor, despite the theories of Weber, are they rational and expert. Risk-taking and the will to work are also discouraged by high taxation and the creation of a dependency culture.

Following the mass unemployment and poverty of the 1930s, the former set of beliefs was widespread and underpinned the rapid expansion of state welfare in the 1940s. By the 1960s and 1970s, however, the latter attracted increasing support. Was the misallocation of resources by the classic welfare state really so bad as to justify this dramatic reversal of political and public opinion?

Technically, a standard framework for the measurement of the efficiency of individual services has been developed whereby the input into a given service can be measured against intermediate outputs and final outputs or 'outcomes'. Such a framework cannot, however, resolve the problem of pricing which has already been identified (see Section 3.2.2). It also raises problems of its own, as can be demonstrated in relation to the NHS.

In the NHS an example of an 'intermediate output' is the number of beds provided by hospitals. An example of final outcome is morbidity (or recorded illness). Does a decrease in the relative number of hospital beds (as happened after 1945) represent a decline in output and thus in health-care? Alternatively, does it signify a faster and more efficient 'throughput' of hospital patients as a result of better management? Similarly does increased morbidity, as measured by absence from work through sickness (which again occurred after 1945), signify a real fall in health standards or merely a change in the 'perceived level of acceptable wellbeing'?[26] More fundamentally, are final outcomes a fair test of efficiency? Do they not for example depend less on government policy than on decisions by individuals – in relation, for instance, to personal fitness and diet?

The efficiency of the welfare state in aggregate

The historical consensus is that neither 'aggregate nor comparative data on growth rates of social expenditure and GDP provide clear support for the argument that expansion of the welfare state in Britain . . . has sapped incentives or retarded economic growth'.[27] In the 1960s and 1970s, after all, the countries with the fastest growing welfare expenditure and the highest percentage of GDP committed to welfare were respectively Japan and Germany. They also had the fastest rates of economic growth. In other words, as Beveridge had argued, welfare expenditure – properly targeted – is not incompatible with economic growth. It can even be a precondition for it.

No reliable data exist to suggest that British welfare policy was poorly targeted in either the way it was financed or delivered. Housing may have been oversupplied because of public provision and, above all, fiscal incentives to owner-occupiers. Relatively high marginal rates of tax may have, at the margin, discouraged risk-taking, although repeated enquiries provided no incontrovertible proof. What is clear, however, is that the will to work – despite repeated assertions to the contrary – was not generally sapped by high benefits. The ratio in Britain between benefit and the average industrial wage (the replacement rate) was amongst the lowest in advanced welfare states. Moreover, as Esping-Andersen's typology suggests, the British welfare state was one of the least generous by 1975. Any economic analysis which contests this is based more on polemic than empirical evidence. Indeed, if the classic welfare state is to be criticized for having any adverse effect on economic growth in an aggregate sense it may well have been because it was too small rather than too large.

Comparative figures quickly disprove the assertion that Britain's welfare system was over-generous and undermined the will to work. In 1975, for example, unemployment benefit for a single person and for a married man

→

with two children was well below the official poverty line at respectively 19 per cent and 41 per cent of the average wage. Supplementary benefit was equivalent to 38 per cent and 60 per cent. In the USA the comparative figure for both types of claimant was 50 per cent, in Japan and Germany 60 per cent and in France up to 90 per cent.[28]

The efficiency of individual services

In relation to individual services there were, as earlier chapters have shown, abundant examples of inefficiency. Technical deficiencies, for example, frequently caused demand management to be destabilizing. The initial administrative and power structure of the NHS discouraged the cost-effective allocation of resources and later attempts at reorganization, most notably in 1974, were little short of disastrous. Education expansion in the 1960s failed to remedy Britain's traditional weakness in technical education and was so precipitate as to provoke a serious backlash. In the slum-clearance programme, the encouragement of prefabricated high-rise buildings solved short-term problems only at incalculable long-term cost. In the personal social services, the Maria Colwell tragedy became a focus for justified fears about the efficiency of the reforms following the Seebohm Report. Finally, and perhaps most seriously of all, there developed – as a result of the increasingly regressive tax system and the expansion of means-tested benefits – so complex a system of social security that by the mid-1970s officials were deliberately discouraging take-up in order to make their workloads tolerable.

In a symbolic expression of growing public disillusion with the welfare state as a whole, the Department of Health and Social Security became popularly known in the 1970s as the Department of Stealth and Total Obscurity.

Efficiency gains

Does such a catalogue of inefficiency in individual services reflect the true record of the classic welfare state? There were, after all, equally numerous examples of the efficient exercise of state power, such as the Macmillan housing drive and the Ministry of Education's school-building programme in the early 1950s. When the public sector was opened up to scrutiny from private business in the early 1980s (the Rayner exercise), the annual 'efficiency' savings achieved were equivalent to less than one-quarter of 1 per cent of total public expenditure.[29]

There was also, by any historic standard, a dramatic and sustained improvement in policy output, be it measured in terms of:

- the rate of economic growth
- the absolute living standards of the poor
- the standard of health
- the attainment of educational qualifications
- the quality of housing
- the care of traditionally neglected groups, such as the disabled.

These achievements were collectively far superior to those of the 1930s when, for instance, the reality of poverty and mass unemployment was accentuated by the absence of a comprehensive health and social security system. They were superior also to the decade after 1975 with the return to mass unemployment and escalating inequality.

These achievements, moreover, were dependent on the peculiar nature of the classic welfare state. Economists, as has been seen, have identified specific areas of policy in which state welfare is inherently more efficient than the market. Foremost is healthcare where the cost – and the percentage of GDP consumed – was low by international standards. This was something of which to be proud rather than ashamed. It represented a highly efficient use of resources with administration typically consuming only 5 per cent of the total expenditure in contrast to 8–9 per cent in the insurance-based system of France and Germany and 15–20 per cent in the market-led system of the USA. It also represented a tighter control over the expenditure of health professionals than achieved by the market or by social insurance funds elsewhere. Such advantages, however, were not confined to the NHS. 'With a public service presence in education and housing high by international standards', as another commentator has concluded, 'the postwar British welfare state was able from the start to pursue its objectives and force political control.'[30]

Economists have decribed the relative theoretical efficiency of the NHS in the following way: 'on the demand side, decisions are made by doctors, thus alleviating the effects of consumer ignorance; the problems of private insurance are resolved by abandoning the insurance principle even as a fiction; and treatment is largely free at the point of use, which reduces the externality problem and goes a long way towards eliminating the influence of income distribution on consumption. On the supply side, doctors are not as a rule paid a fee for service, thus removing the financial incentive to oversupply.'[31]

Such relative achievements in aggregate and in relation to individual services, it could be argued, were largely the consequence of a fortuitous combination of uniquely favourable factors such as buoyant world markets and advances in medical science. In many ways, however, circumstances were far from propitious for the development of state welfare. Between 1945 and 1975, for example, neither political party provided a sufficiently bold or principled lead. The civil service was tardy in developing the requisite administrative structures and management techniques. Moreover professionals within the social services, especially after the mid-1960s, failed sufficiently to curb their self-interest.

Such real-world failings, of course, cannot be used to excuse any weakness in the classic welfare state. It was, after all, the essential logic behind the increase in state welfare that resources could be allocated more efficiently by the joint decisions of politicians, civil servants and professionals rather than by the decisions of individual consumers and producers freely expressed through the market. Nevertheless it is equally important to remember how far policy-makers were influenced by Britain's liberal past. It was also constantly constrained by a conservative public opinion which – as affluence increased – grew ever more interested in short-term rights as opposed to long-term duties. Indeed if there was one area in which the classic welfare state did incontrovertibly perform inefficiently – especially in relation to the period after 1975 – it was in the way in which its energy (and tax-payers' money) was used to nurture a supportive welfare, as opposed to an entrepreneurial, culture.

11.3 CONCLUSION

By definition, any conclusion about the achievement of the classic welfare state must be a personal one. A balanced review of the evidence, however, can explode certain myths. Just as for prewar, so for postwar Britain the empirical evidence simply does not exist, for example, to support the frequent assertion that state welfare, by misallocating resources and sapping the will to work, undermined economic efficiency.[32] It can also prevent the isolation of a single aspect of welfare policy and its subsequent unfavourable comparison to foreign practice without due reference to the overall structure of welfare policy and Britain's distinct cultural heritage. Most important of all, however, it can ensure that judgements are made not against some abstract ideal but against a balanced assessment of what, at any given time in the past, was realistically possible.

In the 1960s, as Enoch Powell recognized, professionals within the welfare services compared their situation to an unattainable ideal. As a result, despite historically high standards of salaries and resources, there developed a vested interest in the denigration of the classic welfare state.[33] There is no reason why historians should fall into the same trap.

11.4 FURTHER READING

The tension between equality and efficiency as goals of welfare policy has attracted ever-increasing attention. Good theoretical introductions are provided by J. Le Grand, C. Propper and R. Robinson, *The Economics of Social Problems* (Basingstoke, 1992); N. Barr, *The Economics of the Welfare State*

(Oxford, 1993); and the short classic by A. M. Okun, *Equality and Efficiency: the big trade-off* (Washington, DC, 1975). The best theoretically informed historical summaries are R. Middleton, *Government versus the Market* (Cheltenham, 1996) and, more briefly P. Johnson, 'The welfare state', in R. Floud and D. McCloskey (eds), *The Economic History of Britain since 1900*, vol. 3 (Cambridge, 1994) which has been updated as 'The welfare state, income and living standards' in the third edition of that work, now edited by Floud and Johnson himself (Cambridge, 2004). A useful empirical overview is also provided by R. Parry, 'UK', in P. Flora (ed.), *Growth to Limits: the Western European welfare states since World War II* (Berlin, 1986).

The concern for equality was particularly acute in the 1970s and the Royal Commission on the Distribution of Income and Wealth (1974–9) pioneered much valuable theoretical and empirical research. The reports which are of most relevance to the classic welfare state are no. 1 (Cmnd 6171, 1975), no. 5 (Cmnd 6999, 1977) and no. 7 (Cmnd 7595, 1979). One of its members, Sir Henry Phelps Brown, subsequently wrote the wide-ranging *Egalitarianism and the Generation of Inequality* (Oxford, 1988). An extremely valuable collection of readings is A. B. Atkinson (ed.), *Wealth, Income and Equality* (Oxford, 1980), and some of Atkinson's own major essays are published in *Incomes and the Welfare State* (Cambridge, 1995). Three more popular works are A. B. Atkinson, *Unequal Shares: wealth in Britain* (Harmondsworth, 1974); F. Field, M. Meacher and C. Pond, *To Him Who Hath: a study of poverty and taxation* (Harmondsworth, 1977); and W. D. Rubinstein, *Wealth and Inequality in Britain* (1986). A stimulating approach to the measurement of equality, albeit applied to Britain in the late 1970s, is provided in J. Le Grand, *The Strategy of Equality: redistribution and the social services* (1982). Meanwhile the first serious archivally based history of postwar taxation has been provided by M. Daunton in *Just Taxes: the politics of taxation in Britain, 1914–79* (Cambridge, 2002).

A leading theoretical attack on the efficiency of welfare policy is P. Minford, *The Supply Side Revolution in Britain* (1991). More applied critiques have been advanced by the Institute of Economic Affairs, best summarized in: A. Seldon (ed.), *The Emerging Consensus* (1981); R. W. Bacon and W. A. Eltis, *Britain's Economic Problem: too few producers* (1978); OECD, *The Welfare State in Crisis* (Paris, 1981); and, for the early postwar years, C. Barnett, *The Audit of War* (1986). When subject to closer empirical and comparative examination many of their conclusions have appeared, at best, unproven. The evidence for more balanced judgements is provided by the books on individual policies cited in earlier chapters.

Part III

The Welfare State since 1976

chapter 12

The Rise of 'Thatcherism', 1976–1997

CONTENTS

Old Labour

1975 Cash limits on all public expenditure

1976 Unemployment reaches 1.5m. IMF loan. Callaghan speeches abandoning full employment and suggesting core curriculum. Direct grant schools abolished

1978 Wolfenden report, *The Future of Voluntary Organisations*. Supplementary Benefits Review – extension of means testing

1979 **Mrs Thatcher**, following winter of discontent, becomes prime minister (re-elected 1983, 1987; resigns 1990)

1980 Medium term financial strategy (MTFS) formalizes monetary policy. Social Security Act – earnings-related and automatic indexing of benefits to end in 1982. Education Act – assisted places in secondary schools and GCSE introduced. 'Right to buy' council housing. Black report, *Inequalities in Health*

1981 (Toxteth, Brixton riots.) Deflationary budget splits Cabinet. *Growing Older* white paper (Cmnd 8173) redefines community care

1982 (Falklands war.) Radical plans to privatize higher education and NHS rejected. Eight months of industrial disruption within NHS

1983 Unemployment exceeds 3m (until 1987). Griffiths report – starts managerial revolution in NHS

1985 (Further inner city riots; defeat of miners' strike; GLC abolished.) MTFS abandoned

1986 Social Security Act implements

➜

earlier Fowler review (Cmnd 9517–9, 9691) – introduces income support, social fund, housing benefit and family credits. Audit Commission report, *Making a Reality of Community Care* – record of past failings. City technology schools introduced. Prolonged teachers' strike

1987 Cleveland scandal discredits social workers

1988 (Next Steps – civil service split into executive agencies.) Education Act – introduces core curriculum and opting out of local authority control. Housing Act – tenant's choice. Griffiths report, *Community Care: agenda for action* foreshadows internal market. Top rate of income tax halved to 40 per cent

1989 *Working for Patients* (Cm 555) foreshadows internal markets in NHS. Children Act – prioritizes parents over state. Free eye and dental checks cancelled

1990 (Poll tax riots.) Recession starts and lasts to 1994. NHS and Community Care Act – introduces internal markets to both

services. Student loans. **Major** prime minister (November, re-elected 1992). Disability living and working allowances introduced

1991 Citizen's Charter. *Competing for Quality* (Cm 1730) – all public services to be 'market-tested'. Child Support Agency set up

1992 Black Wednesday (16 Sept) – EMS abandoned. NEDC abolished. Education Act – publication of league tables. Further and Higher Education Act – polytechnics can become universities. *Health of the Nation* white paper (Cm 1986) – health targets

1993 (Council tax replaces poll tax.) Portillo and Lilley 'fundamental review' of social security. Attack on single parents. Incapacity benefit – tightens rules. Wages councils abolished. Teachers boycott attainment tests

1995 Hackney Downs – first taskforce takes over 'failing' secondary school

1996 Jobseekers' Allowance and nursery vouchers introduced

The purpose of this chapter is to provide an overview of the fundamental changes to the welfare state that occurred between 1976 and 1997. It covers, in other words, the time from which a 'sea-change' in favour of the Conservatives was first identified to the election at which, having enjoyed four previous successes, they suffered a cataclysmic defeat with their representation in Parliament being reduced to its smallest size in over a century. The changes to the welfare state have conventionally been accredited to, or blamed on, the rise of 'Thatcherism'. The precise meaning of this term, however, is contested. All Western welfare states at this time, after all, were under common economic, political and philosophical attack. Was there a unique British response during Mrs Thatcher's period as prime minister (1979–90)? This is hard to establish because, as will be shown, there were major contradictions within the reforming rhetoric of her governments as well as between the rhetoric and actual policy decisions.

The possibility is therefore raised that the welfare state underwent a necessary functional change at this time, the nature of which was only incidentally influenced by the ideology of the ruling party. It may even have been obscured by contemporary political claims and counterclaims. This possibility can be left open by avoiding an exclusive concentration on Mrs Thatcher's term in office. Consequently analysis starts in 1976, when 'Old' Labour was in power. It concludes in 1997 when Mrs Thatcher's successor was completing his seventh year as prime minister. This, as John Major himself might have said, was a not insignificant period. His premiership, after all, lasted longer than the postwar Labour governments which laid the foundation of the classic welfare state.

This chapter will re-examine the nature of the mid-1970's 'crisis', identified in the introduction of this book. It will then summarize the broad political and economic context in which welfare policy evolved before contrasting the perceived frailty and resilience of the welfare state as a whole. A definition of 'Thatcherism' and a final assessment of its impact will be reserved until after the detailed examination of each core welfare policy in the next chapter.

12.1 THE WELFARE STATE IN CRISIS

Despite its historic achievements, the welfare state in Britain was – as identified in Chapter 1 – widely perceived to be in crisis in the mid-1970s. The immediate causes were economic. Oil prices quadrupled after the Arab–Israeli war of October 1973. This so accelerated the underlying annual rate of inflation that it reached the unprecedented level of 27 per cent in 1975. Simultaneously, the rate of economic growth declined so sharply that there was an actual fall in GDP in 1973 and 1975. As a result, unemployment rose for the first time since the war to over one million and peaked in 1976 at 1.5 million. The government thus found itself in a vicious economic spiral. Slower economic growth reduced tax revenue whilst demand for welfare continued to increase, not least because of rising unemployment. This created a 'fiscal crisis' as expenditure outstripped income. It bridged the gap by borrowing. This, however, merely undermined foreign confidence in sterling. The value of the pound fell below $2 for the first time ever, and then plunged rapidly to $1.55. This, in turn, increased the cost of imports which further increased inflation.

The response of the Heath (1970–4), Wilson (1974–6) and Callaghan (1976–9) governments to this crisis inevitably affected welfare policy adversely. Each implemented a series of cuts to public expenditure, or at least to planned increases in public expenditure. Such cuts were made more effective after November 1975 by the introduction of 'cash' limits. Since the early 1960s all planning of expenditure had been in 'volume' terms. This meant that, whatever its rising cost, the agreed output (or volume) of policy was assured. Now, if inflation or wage settlements raised the cost of a programme above its predetermined 'cash' budget, either staff or the service itself had to be cut.[1] Finally, reflationary demand management (Keynes' solution to rising unemployment) was abandoned in 1976. The commitment to 'full' employment, as emphasized in Chapter I, was key to the solvency of the postwar social security system. It minimized claims whilst maximizing contributions. Just as cash limits in a period of inflation presaged major cuts in expenditure programmes, therefore, so the abandonment of the commitment to full employment threatened a major contraction in benefits. The 'party', as Anthony Crosland warned local government in 1975, was truly over.[2]

Confidence in the welfare state may have been shaken by these short-term economic shocks. The sense of crisis in the mid 1970s, however, was more deeply rooted and led to a fundamental review of its:

- record
- nature
- legitimacy.

The record

As described in Part II, criticism had mounted of the whole interventionist record of postwar government since the early 1960s, when Britain's relatively low rate of economic growth had been belatedly recognized. The subsequent management of the economy together with the varied record of welfare reform had done little to assuage it. Consequently the standard and cost effectiveness of service in each area of policy came under critical scrutiny. Were they compounding the very problems they were supposed to resolve? One senior Labour minister even went so far as to dismiss the whole of the previous 25 years as a total failure.[3]

The nature of the welfare state

Given this apparently poor record, the conviction was increasingly voiced that the welfare state was not only failing to resolve but also, by its very nature, could not resolve Britain's problems.

In economic policy, for example, the management of the economy had become increasingly corporatist since the establishment of the NEDC in 1962. However, neither side of industry, let alone government, appeared to have the technical capacity to resolve the structural problems of the economy. Nor did they appear to have the will to instil into their members the 'responsible' attitudes for which the 1944 *Employment Policy* white paper had called. The failure of successive prices and incomes policies, and the imposition of a three-day working week during the winter of 1973/4, were taken as proof of the ultimate sterility of all corporatist deals.

Likewise the civil service, rather than being regarded as a source of disinterested expertise (as assumed by Beveridge and Keynes) or a guarantor of efficiency (as assumed by Weber), came to be identified as an impediment to change. Its size (broadly defined) had exploded between 1966 and 1976 from

2.1 million to 3.3 million, or from 8.3 per cent to 13.2 per cent of the work-force.[4] This led to the charge that, through both its numbers and cost, it was 'crowding-out' and thereby stifling wealth creation. It became a common scapegoat for economic decline. In welfare policy, moreover, officials appeared – for the first time since the early nineteenth century – to be more interested in their own welfare than that of the public they were supposedly serving. The implementation of the Seebohm Report and the reorganization of the NHS in 1974, for example, became notorious for the unseemly scramble for positions and pay which they inspired. In addition officials, insulated from growing personal uncertainty in the private sector by such 'privileges' as job security and inflation-proof pensions, appeared unsympathetic and – largely for their own convenience – unresponsive to any consumer demand for change within monopolistic services.

Demographic change and affluence required such change. By the mid 1970s, for example, the postwar 'baby boom' had joined the workforce and formed the most dynamic part of the electorate. They were less reliant than earlier generations on state welfare to maintain their living standards. Rather they started to resent it as increased taxation, at a time of stable (or even falling) real wages, contributed to a disappointment of expectation especially amongst young married owner-occupiers. This resentment was exacerbated by the lack of choice to which affluence accustomed them in the private sector. Resentment of redistribution and rigidity contributed greatly to the 'sea-change' of opinion which bore Mrs Thatcher to power.

Legitimacy

Such practical concerns led to a questioning of the very legitimacy of the welfare state at both a popular and intellectual level. The *popular* challenge came first from some of its apparent beneficiaries. For example students, as in the rest of the Western world, responded to increased educational opportuni-ties in the late 1960s by challenging not only the educational system but also government itself. Workers in the nationalized industries became politicized, with the miners in particular helping to bring down the Heath government in 1974. Other public sector employees also increasingly resorted to strike 'action', culminating in the 1978/9 'winter of discontent' which in turn brought down the Labour government.

The failure of government to deal decisively with these particular instances of militancy generated disaffection amongst the general public because it appeared to confirm that Britain was 'ungovernable'. Its loss of authority was linked with wider social concerns such as escalating crime and renewed terrorism in Northern Ireland. Even the future of key institutions such as the family (given the rising incidence of divorce and illegitimacy) and the nation (following Britain's entry into the EEC and the 1979 referenda on devolution for Scotland and Wales) seemed under immediate threat. In brief, Britain as a welfare state was beginning to be seen by many to be not just politically but morally bankrupt.

Such widespread disaffection reopened fundamental *ideological* questions about the proper role of the state in society which had been stifled by prevailing orthodoxies since the war. In the 1960s, admittedly, 'universalists' within the Labour Party had questioned prevailing beliefs about the nature of the welfare state and sought to redefine the goal of 'equality'. In the 1970s, however, the challenge was far more fundamental. An increasing number of people, in the jargon of the time, began to 'think the unthinkable'.

On the left, the Marxist critique of the welfare state as a vehicle for capital accumulation and the legitimization of capitalist society was vigorously refined (see Section 2.3.2). It underpinned much of the contemporary shop-floor militancy and especially the demand for workers' control, which was later espoused within the Labour Party by Tony Benn. Of even greater significance was the growing assertiveness of the New Right, especially after the establishment of the Centre for Policy Studies by Keith Joseph in June 1974 and the succession of Margaret Thatcher to the leadership of the Conservative Party in the following February. Its specific targets were Keynesian demand management, the 'collusive conspiracy' of corporatism and bureaucracy. Its proffered remedies were a greater control of money supply (monetarism), the 'discipline' of the market and the 'rolling back of the frontiers of the state'.

The New Right in both its liberal and its conservative guise was, as has been seen, inherently hostile to state welfare (see Section 2.2.3, especially note 37). It was seen both to reduce individual freedom and, by empowering previously disadvantaged groups, to challenge traditional authority. Its populist message was that governments in their economic policy should act like housewives and balance their budgets. Likewise, in social policy they should behave like responsible parents and strive for the ultimate independence of those temporarily dependent upon them. If those in need were encouraged to look passively to the state for help, they would be denied the invigorating experience of self-help and of family or community care. Moreover, in the country at large, enterprise would be discouraged by higher taxation. As Keith Joseph concluded during his conversion to 'true' Conservatism:

> The only lasting help we can give to the poor is helping them to help themselves; to do the opposite, to create more dependence, is to destroy them morally, whilst throwing an unfair burden on society.[5]

In short, the New Right was committed – just like the Poor Law reformers of the 1830s – to a 'remoralizing' of society. Herein lay the basis of the calls for a return to 'Victorian values'.

Conservative concerns with 'remoralizing' the poor allied the Party with the re-thinking of welfare policy in the USA which was to mature in the 1980s with Charles Murray's *Losing Ground* (1984), Lawrence Mead's *Beyond Entitlement* (1985) and David Ellwood's *Poor Support* (1988). They in turn

➜

laid the basis for the 'welfare to work' schemes, which were to provide a measure of consensus in both Britain and the USA in the 1990s. The Conservatives tentatively moved towards requiring those on benefit to work or train – an objective, it should be remembered, of Beveridge – through a variety of initiatives from Restart (1986) to Workstart (1994). New Labour systematized these initiatives in its 1997 New Deal.

American analysis was contested as well as unevenly researched. Murray, for example, believed that claimants acted rationally and current benefits provided the able-bodied with 'perverse incentives' not to work. They should be very closely monitored or cancelled. Mead's view, on the other hand, was that claimants were 'dutiful but defeated'. To break the 'poverty culture' welfare should both 'help and hassle' them back to work, self-respect and independence. Ellwood developed a sophisticated mix of incentives (such as tax credits) as well as goads (time-limited benefits) to ensure this happened.

This debate over ends and means provided the bounds for a new consensus in the 1990s within the USA and Britain. Under the Conservatives, the pillorying of lone mothers in 1993 was directly inspired by Murray. The prime example of 'perverse incentives', however, was a clarification of regulations in the early 1980s that the social security system was liable to pay the full cost of nursing home care for those with limited assets. The old duly transferred their assets and relieved relatives of traditional responsibilities. The social security bill for residential care rocketed from £10 million in 1979 to £2072 million in 1991. It was, of course, the 'welfare dependency' of the middle class which this 'perverse incentive' mainly reinforced.[6]

The welfare state in the mid-1970s, therefore, came under sustained political, popular and philosophical attack. This raised the following fundamental questions:

- Were its perceived weaknesses merely superficial? Could they have been remedied, as they appeared to be remedied at the time in continental Europe, by better management?
- Was improved management insufficient? Was a more fundamental modernization needed to adapt the welfare state to changed political and economic circumstances? Did such restructuring or 'recalibration' require, in addition to new methods of policy delivery and new policy targets, a new accommodation with market capitalism?
- Alternatively, had the restructuring of the economy and globalization so destroyed the necessary preconditions for state intervention that the 'classic' welfare state had to be dismantled? Was the only viable alternative a 'forced march' back to the policies of the 1930s – from which the welfare state had been deliberately designed as an escape?[7]

It is in the light of such questions that the development of welfare policy as a whole should be examined.

12.2 THE POLITICAL AND ECONOMIC CONTEXT

After 1976 welfare policy was subject first to an 'economic hurricane' and then to an 'ideological blizzard'.[8] As has been seen, the newly elected Labour government in 1974 inherited a severe economic crisis. Its response was a series of economic cuts culminating, after negotiations with the IMF, in the reduction of planned public expenditure by £2 billion in 1976. This action temporarily restored the economy but not its own political fortunes. It was heavily defeated in the election of May 1979 (see Table 12.1).

The incoming Conservative government inherited and then, through its monetarist policies, intensified a new economic crisis. By 1982, however, a revival was under way and between 1984 and 1989 Britain enjoyed a faster rate of growth than any other European country (see Table 12.2). This was a remarkable reversal of fortune which not only transformed the reputation of the country abroad but also established that of Mrs Thatcher as prime minister. Recession struck again between 1990 and 1994. It drove Mrs Thatcher from office, discredited her successor John Major and intensified the debate within the Party over whether the welfare state should be restructured or dismantled.

The last days of 'Old Labour', 1976–95

The initial priority of the Labour government in 1974 had not been to resolve the immediate economic crisis but *inter alia* to give substance to its 'social contract' with the unions and thereby increase public expenditure. It was consequently a time when, in the words of one despairing Treasury minister, the government seemed to spend money 'we did not have'.[9] Only in June 1975 were the economic problems finally addressed with the introduction of a

---

Table 12.1   Election results, 1979–97

| | Labour | | Conservative | | Others | Elected prime minister |
	Seats	%vote	Seats	%vote	Seats	
1979 May	269	36.9	339	43.9	27	Thatcher
1983 June	209	27.6	397	42.4	44	Thatcher
1987 June	229	31.7	376	43.4	45	Thatcher
1992 April	271	35.2	336	42.3	44	Major
1997 May	419	44.4	165	31.4	75	Blair

Note: The number of seats increased by 15 in 1983 and by one in 1992.
Source: D. and G. Butler, *British Political Facts, 1900–1994* (1994) pp. 218–19.

Table 12.2   Comparative annual growth rates, 1979–97

	UK	G7	US	Japan	Germany	France
1979–83	0.9	1.8	1.3	3.4	1.2	1.8
1984–88	4.0	3.8	4.0	4.3	2.5	2.5
1989–93	0.4	1.9	1.7	3.0	3.1	1.5
1994–97	3.0	2.3	2.5	1.7	2.0	2.2
1979–97	2.1	2.4	2.4	3.2	2.2	2.0

Note: G7 was the formal group of the seven leading industrial nations.
Source: S. Wilks, 'Conservative governments and the economy', *Political Studies*, 45 (1997) 690.

voluntary prices and incomes policy and the imposition of both cuts in and cash limits on public expenditure.

After Harold Wilson's surprise resignation in March 1976 the same policies were maintained by the new prime minister, James Callaghan. He soon came under attack from foreign bankers but they were quickly assuaged by the terms of the IMF loan and the revival of the economy. Balance of payments problems were relieved by the coming on stream of North Sea oil. Unemployment began to decline. By early 1978 inflation had also fallen below 10 per cent, whilst the value of the pound had risen above $2. Callaghan began to exude confidence and to taunt the Conservatives – who had been out of power for 12 of the previous 14 years – that Labour were the 'natural party of government'. The welfare state, it seemed, might not be exposed after all to the 'ideological blizzard' of the New Right.

Such confidence was, however, misplaced. The government had lost its over-all majority as a result of by-election defeats and defections. It had had to make a pact with the Liberal Party in order to survive.[10] More seriously, party activists were increasingly aggrieved. In general, they demanded the 'funda-mental and irreversible' shift in wealth which had been promised by the 1973 *Labour's Programme for Britain* and was implicit in the social contract. In partic-ular they were angered that, as a result of successive expenditure cuts, wage restraint under the social contract was not being matched by compensatory increases in the 'social' wage. Eventually, in October 1978, a Labour conference rejected a further extension of the government's prices and incomes policy and, despite their affiliation to the Labour Party, the public sector unions launched their 'winter of discontent'. This demonstration of militancy destroyed not only the incomes policy but also the government's chances of re-election.

A power struggle within the Labour Party had been fermenting since vari-ous changes to its constitution in the early 1970s and it continued to divide the Party in the early 1980s. Many moderate members left to form the Social Democratic Party in 1981 and, after Callaghan's resignation, Michael Foot's leadership became hopelessly compromised. This had serious consequences for welfare policy because there was no effective opposition to the Conservative Party's doctrinaire monetarism when it was at its most vulnerable in the early 1980s. Indeed, as has been remarked of the 1983 general election: 'amongst the forces ranged against the most unpopular leader of modern times' was 'a party that was unelectable' and 'a grouping that was destined merely to be a vote splitter. No radical visionary ... could have asked for more.'[11] Not until the constitutional changes were reversed between 1991 and 1995 (with the expulsion of Militant Tendency, a weakening of the link with the trade unions, and the revision of Clause 4 committing the Labour Party to wholesale nationalization) were the Conservatives again to be faced with a serious electoral challenge.

Mrs Thatcher in power, 1979–90

The effective absence of an alternative party of government helps to explain a major paradox of the 12 years of Conservatism under Mrs Thatcher. The Prime Minister certainly had a fundamentalist, radical vision. She was also driven forward by immense energy and an 'inner conviction' based on her certainty about what was 'right' and 'wrong'.[12] This meant that, even during the initial crisis into which her monetarist policies plunged the economy, she was not tempted – as had been her Conservative predecessor – to perform a 'U turn'. To Edward Heath the 'free market' policies which he had adopted between 1970 and 1972 were a means to an end – greater international competitiveness as a necessary precondition for long-term full employment. If they failed to achieve this objective, they were expendable. To Margaret Thatcher, however, monetarism with its eternal truths (such as the iniquity of spending more than one earned) was an end in itself. Nevertheless, for a populist leader, she remained remarkably unpopular both amongst the general public and, despite many ministerial reshuffles, within her own Cabinet. This placed a major constraint on what she could achieve. It was not until her third election victory in 1987 that such opposition was effectively quashed. Even then, after three years, she was to be forced by party pressure to resign.

The 12 years of Conservative government under Margaret Thatcher were divided into three administrations: 1979–83, 1983–7 and 1987–90.

1979–83.   During Mrs Thatcher's first administration, the boldest decision in domestic policy was the introduction of the medium-term financial strategy (MTFS) in the 1980 budget and its retention during the subsequent economic collapse. This, in theory at least, laid down clear targets for monetary growth and thus for public expenditure which, as an early white paper had notoriously proclaimed, was perceived to be 'at the heart of Britain's economic difficulties'.[13] Between 1979 and 1981 industrial output and GDP fell respectively by 16 per cent and 5 per cent, whilst inflation peaked at 22 per cent and unemployment rose inexorably towards 3 million. Despite such disasters, however, the Prime Minister warned the 1980 Conservative Party conference in o.. her few memorable, if manufactured, phrases that 'the lady's not for turning'.

The economic damage was duly exacerbated by a deflationary budget in 1981. A Cabinet rebellion did then forestall a further proposed round of cuts and a more moderate budget was secured for 1982. Moreover, due in part to a near cabinet riot and a judicious leak to *The Economist*, a report from the Central Policy Review Staff recommending a radical restructuring of welfare policy was speedily withdrawn.[14] This had floated the idea, amongst others, of ending the public funding of higher education and the replacing the NHS by private health insurance. Margaret Thatcher's prestige, however, was little impaired because in the meantime the Falklands War had been fought and won.

1983–1987. Margaret Thatcher's second term of office, despite a parliamentary majority of over 140, was surprisingly restrained. In the mid-term there was even talk of consolidation – a concept which had affronted her 'fellow' radical, Aneurin Bevan, in the late 1940s – and the notion gained credence that 'the Thatcher style was to talk radical and to act conservative'.[15] The government even appeared accident-prone, with Michael Heseltine's resignation in January 1986 over the Westland affair portraying the Prime Minister in the unaccustomed light of being unpatriotic, incompetent and dishonest.

There were, however, notable successes. The miners were decisively beaten in March 1985 after a year-long strike, and high-spending metropolitan counties, in particular the Greater London Council (GLC), were abolished. Such 'victories' reassured those who, following the perceived breakdown in law and order during the 1970s, were desperate to see the restoration of traditional authority. More positively, there were continuing cuts in income tax (so that, by 1988, the top rate had been reduced from 83 per cent to 40 per cent and the standard rate from 33 per cent to 25 per cent); an escalation in the sale of council houses; and the successful launch of a shareholder democracy with the privatization of British Telecom and British Gas.[16] Each initiative deliberately created a distinct client group that was likely in the near future to vote Conservative.

However, the key to another sweeping election victory in 1987 (albeit with a reduced majority) was the sustained recovery of the economy. This did not represent a triumph of the MTFS, officially abandoned as impractical by its architect (Nigel Lawson) in the 1985 budget. Nor did it signify a decrease in unemployment which, despite a doctoring of the figures, remained relentlessly over 3 million.[17] Rather it reflected the successful containment of inflation below 5 per cent and the achievement of a high and sustained rate of growth which increased real earnings by 14 per cent.

1987–1990. A third election victory revived Margaret Thatcher's radicalism and led her to 'vow vengeance' on those who had earlier obliged her to abandon strict monetarism and forgo such favoured reforms as the privatisation of water and the cancellation of state earnings-related pensions.[18] The result was a managerial revolution which, as will be seen, saw the introduction into all major areas of policy of 'internal markets' and a 'purchaser–provider' divide. Government was to continue to finance, but no longer to directly deliver welfare services itself. In the NHS, for example, hospitals were no longer to receive their funding from government. Funding would go instead to District Health Authorities or (increasingly) to GPs who, acting on behalf of their patients, would *purchase* care from whichever hospital they judged would *provide* the optimum service. That hospital could be within or outside their health region and in either the public or private sector. The system, in other words, was designed to make actual service providers compete as if in an open market. This, it was hoped, would realize the perceived benefits of markets: greater cost-effectiveness and responsiveness to consumers. Such a reform was only managerial. It did not automatically reduce state funding (although greater cost-effectiveness might have that consequence). Nor did it 'roll back the state' (although it was immediately attacked as laying the foundations for privatization). It was, however, the major legacy to the welfare state of Mrs Thatcher's 12 years in power.

Of greater short-term significance was the introduction of a new system of local government finance – the community charge or 'poll tax'. This was a brave initiative and one to which Mrs Thatcher had been publicly committed since 1974. The current system of rates, based on property values, offended the conventions of public finance in two ways. It was levied only on the householder. The majority of the local electorate could, therefore, vote for increases in expenditure without directly suffering any adverse changes in taxation. Secondly, the revenue flow was so restricted that central government had to fund the majority of local expenditure. Local authorities could, therefore, increase expenditure without suffering any direct electoral consequences. The requirement was a simple system which would foster the fiscal responsibility of both local electorates and the local authorities. A perceived partisan bonus of such a system, moreover, was the curb it would place on high-spending Labour councils.

It was, however, discontent amongst Conservative voters in Scotland at a revaluation of their property, and thus a prospective rise in rates, that finally ensured the nettle was seized. A plan to levy a flat-rate charge on all local electors was duly framed and, unusually for such legislation at this time, passed through a full administrative and political scrutiny. However, the failure to identify the plan's basic flaws (particularly in relation to equity) demonstrated how the traditional integrity and robustness of the policy-making process had been compromised over the previous decade.[19] A campaign of non-registration in Scotland forewarned the government of difficulties. When applied to England and Wales it provoked a violent riot in London. Thus, combined with renewed anger at her 'presidential' style, her negativism towards the EEC and, above all, a deterioration of the economy, it was the fiasco of the poll tax which provided the pretext for Mrs Thatcher's enforced resignation in November 1990.

In retrospect Mrs Thatcher wrote that, at the 1987 election, 'we had to dispel any idea that we were stale ... We therefore had to advance a number of clear, specific, new and well-worked out reforms.'[20] Economic policy, trade union reform and privatization had taken precedence. Now, as her recollection suggests, welfare policy had priority *faut de mieux.*

The quote also reflects the perceived political need for an almost Maoist sense of continual revolution which, after its initial beneficial shock to complacency, disrupted and ultimately demoralized those responsible for delivering services. More damningly, it exaggerates the coherence with which reform was planned. The 1990 NHS and Community Care Act, for example, introduced the internal market to those two services. The concept had, however, been developed in relation to the NHS by the American economist, Alain Enthoven, as early as 1985. It was ultimately adopted largely as a measure of desperation as the impracticality of alternative reforms was exposed. In addition, as will be seen, it was opposed by Mrs Thatcher to the last. Similarly the concept had been applied to community care by Mrs Thatcher's personal adviser, Sir Roy Griffiths, in early 1988. To the author's fury, it was disregarded for 18 months. This was not least because logic required that the empowered purchasers should be the local authorities, which the prime minister so despised.

John Major, 1990–97

Mrs Thatcher's successor was, to his and everyone else's surprise, John Major. Equally to everyone's surprise, he led the Conservative Party to a narrow election victory in 1992.

At first, in part perhaps because of his own disadvantaged background, he appeared sympathetic to welfare policy. The welfare state, he claimed, was an 'integral part of the British instinct' and the creation of a 'classless society' one of his ideals. Amongst his first acts was the unfreezing of child benefit and the release of money to haemophiliacs who had contracted HIV through blood transfusions. Unlike Mrs Thatcher he was also proud to admit that he was an NHS patient. Accordingly the service could feel genuinely safe in his hands, as was confirmed by the emphatic pledge to his Party conference in 1991: 'no privatisation of healthcare, neither piecemeal, nor in part, nor in whole, not today, not tomorrow, not after the next election, not ever while I am prime minister'.[21] Even his talismanic reform, the Citizen's Charter, could be depicted as a rejection of his predecessor's underlying philosophy. It was designed to maintain an even balance between the 'consumers' and 'producers' by making explicit the standards of service all consumers of welfare had the right to expect. The balance, significantly, was to be maintained not by open competition but by the agreement and monitoring of performance targets.

The prime minister's authority, however, was eroded by the economic recession he had inherited. By 1992, there was an economic and fiscal crisis on the scale of the mid-1970s. Unemployment soared to over 2.5 million and the budget deficit reached £46 billion. The one difference was that the principal victims were not those who might be blamed for relative decline but those who had participated in the economic boom of the 1980s. This was made explicit by the experience of owner-occupiers, whom housing policy in the 1980s had deliberately moulded into core Conservative voters. By 1992, 351,000 fell over six months in arrears with their mortgage repayments and the annual rate of repossession peaked at 75,540. A further 1.7 million saw the value of their houses fall below that of their mortgage ('negative equity').

Such experiences, combined with an influx of new 'Thatcherite' MPs as a result of the 1992 election, created a deep animosity within both the party and government to welfare expenditure. This was exacerbated when, in direct defiance of election pledges, taxes had immediately to be raised to meet its cost. A 'fundamental review' of policy was duly launched by Michael Portillo and Peter Lilley in 1993, which opened the distinct prospect that radical change to the welfare state might extend beyond the merely managerial to an actual reduction in both the state's financial and statutory commitments.

Robust support for the welfare state still remained in Cabinet, not least in the powerful form of Kenneth Clarke who was chancellor of the exchequer from May 1993. However, it became as divided on welfare as it was on Europe and, as with Europe, the Prime Minister proved unable to 'bridge the unbridgeable'. Hence, influenced by Charles Murray's polemic, the attack at the 1993 Party conference on vulnerable groups, such as single parents, on account of their welfare dependency. Incapacity benefit and the Jobseekers' Allowance (incorporating the goads but not the incentives of workfare programmes in the USA) were introduced to tighten the conditions on which benefits could be claimed. The prospect of privatization was simultaneously advanced by the requirement that 85 per cent of the residential care 'purchased' by local authorities after 1993 should be in the private sector and the later agreement that vouchers for nursery education, introduced in 1996, could pay for existing private provision. Despite the Prime Minister's ideal of a classless society, he also failed significantly to reverse a dramatic rise in inequality unparalleled in the Western world.[22] Even his own rhetoric started to denigrate welfare policy. In the foreword to the 1997 election manifesto, for example, he criticized 'the dead hand of the state' and extolled 'the self respect and independence that comes with being self-sufficient from the state'. Then the twin evils of state welfare and Europe were linked in an attack upon Labour. 'A stark choice', it was claimed, lay 'between the British way – of trusting the people and unleashing enterprise – and the failing social model, practised on the continent, which the Labour Party wants to impose on us here under the guise of "stake-holding".'[23]

The 1997 election resulted in a landslide defeat. Antipathy towards the Conservatives was so great that they failed to win a single seat in either Wales or Scotland. This was only in part because of the attack on the welfare state which, as the Prime Minister had initally acknowledged, was an 'integral' part of national culture – most especially in Wales and Scotland. More important was the government's loss of trust. This occured not just because taxes were raised contrary to election pledges but because on 'Black Wednesday', 16 September 1992, market pressure forced the abandonment of its central economic strategy (membership of the European Union's exchange rate mechanism). This not only represented a *volte face* but also incurred a huge financial loss. Yet unforgivably there were no ministerial resignations. Thereafter the media hounded a government that was deeply split over membership of the European Union, besmirched with 'sleaze' and beset by a relentless series of crises from fat cats to mad cows.[24] Plans to dismantle the welfare state accordingly took place in rather an unreal atmosphere.

12.3 THE DISMANTLING OF THE WELFARE STATE?

To what extent did this sequence of political and economic events effectively lead to the dismantling of the classic welfare state? There were three notable casualties:

- corporatism
- the professions
- the Keynesian commitment to full employment

Corporatism

The 1974–9 Labour governments remained committed to corporatism, as was demonstrated by the social contract and their ambition to restructure industry through the National Enterprise Board. Margaret Thatcher, however, was rigidly opposed to trade unions (whose legal immunities were curtailed by a succession of employment acts) and corporatist industrialists (to whom she measurably preferred self-made entrepreneurs in the mould of Lord King, who successfully rationalized British Airways).

After the 1983 election the TUC tried to rebuild bridges with a policy of 'new realism'. This vindicated the 'softly, softly' approach of Margaret Thatcher's first secretary of state for employment and her principal opponent within Cabinet (James Prior). Reconciliation, however, was deliberately sabotaged by the banning of trade unions in a government defence establishment (GCHQ). Consequently, having crossed the threshold of Number 10 Downing Street only three times since 1979, the TUC general secretary (Len Murray) opted for early retirement. Disaffected industrialists likewise launched a despairing attack on government in 1985.[25] The last rites were duly performed in the 1990s with the abolition of NEDC in 1992 and a simultaneous weakening of the Labour Party's links with the trade unions.

The professions

It was not only the industrial participants in corporatism who felt the full force of Conservative disdain, but also those institutions which broadly supported it. The civil service was a principal victim. Its cause was not noticeably advanced when, at a party in 1980 designed to achieve greater mutual understanding, Mrs Thatcher issued a clarion call for a coordinated attack on 'the system'. 'But', replied the head of the civil service rather lamely, 'we are the system.'[26]

By the mid-1990s, however, the civil service itself could hardly be described as a system any more, having summarily lost the national unity that had been painfully constructed since the turn of the century. In 1988 the *Next Steps* report recommended the separation of a small core of policy advisors from the delivery of policy, which was to be entrusted to semi-autonomous executive agencies. By the late 1990s over 80 per cent of officials worked in such agencies, which were able to determine independently the grading, pay and conditions of work of their employees. Then in 1991, under Major, the *Competing for Quality* white paper (Cm 1730) required all state responsibilities to be 'market-tested'. The result was that many were 'contracted-out' of the civil service or fully privatized. Security of tenure and transferability of jobs within the service became things of the past.

The higher civil service avoided the worst of the treatment it meted out to its subordinates. Its pay remained 'comparable' with outside work (a statutory requirement which was abandoned for the rest of the service in 1981 at the cost of a lengthy strike). In 1994 agreement was also reached that most of its posts would be filled by internal promotion. However, some were publicly advertised and, following the increased delegation of authority, a significant number were lost. The Treasury, for example, contracting by almost a third. Its role as the principal channel of balanced and disinterested advice to ministers was also usurped by a series of special advisers, recruited from industry or innumerable 'think tanks' – to whom, to the ultimate disadvantage of decision-making, balance and disinterest came rather less naturally. Indeed one of the most demoralizing features of the years after 1979 was the scarcely veiled contempt in which many of the traditional values of the civil service, and in particular its public service ethos, was increasingly held.

A wide range of professionals, other than accountants, were treated with equal disdain. Any claim they had to expertise or altruism, as Wilding has remarked, was thrust aside. Rather, they were dismissed as 'another "producer interest" to be treated with the same hostility as any other branches of organised labour'.[27] Thus doctors and teachers alike were excluded from the major reviews of health and education policy in the late 1980s.

The Church of England was another victim, especially after the publication in 1985 of *Faith in the City*, which questioned the government's emphasis on individual rather than collective responsibility. So too was academia, which was denied its accustomed privileged access via royal commissions to policy-

3   Dismantling the welfare state, 1987
A third election victory finally let the Conservatives loose on the welfare state. Here, led by Mrs Thatcher, they display all the finesse of their other *bête noir*, football hooligans.
Source: © Kal (Kevin Kallaugher), *Sunday Telegraph*, 4 October 1987.

making and experienced a major reduction in its conditions of employment (such as the loss of tenure in 1987) without any compensation. It replied with sustained attacks on government policy, such as the letter signed by 364 economists in opposition to the 1981 budget. There were also token gestures of defiance, such as the denial to Margaret Thatcher of an honorary Oxford degree in 1985. All were paying a very high price for the lack of openness and elitism, and the stifling of genuine debate, which had been a principal failing of the classic welfare state.

> The education and medical professions were a prime, and deliberate focus for public displays of government contempt. In introducing his 1988 Education Act, for instance, Kenneth Baker attacked 'the smug complacency of too many educationalists'. A successor (John Patten), rather more bluntly, using his full ministerial authority publicly to dismiss a chief educational officer as a 'nutter'. This was a term that might have been used by, or even of, the abrasive head of the new independent schools inspectorate,
>
> →

Ofsted (Chris Woodhead), who was happy to condemn 5 per cent of teachers as 'hopelessly incompetent' and one-eighth of head teachers as 'not up
to the job'. In response Lord Annan, an archetypal academic member of
'the great and the good' in earlier days, accused the government in the
reform of higher education as treating 'universities like so many piles of
dung'.

Likewise during the reform of the NHS, Kenneth Clarke confronted the
BMA even more vigorously than Bevan. He dismissed it retrospectively as
one of the nastiest trade unions he had ever dealt with. At the time he
caused even greater offence by requesting GPs to 'stop feeling for their
wallets' every time reform was mentioned. The BMA retaliated with a
nationwide poster campaign enquiring 'What do you call a man who
ignores medical advice?'. The answer, naturally, was 'Mr Clarke'.[28]

The commitment to full employment

Another major casualty was the postwar commitment to 'full' employment,
which Beveridge had seen as essential for both the maximization of individual welfare and the solvency of social insurance. As Callaghan's speech to the
1976 Labour Party conference illustrated, the monetarist contention was
accepted that there was a 'natural' rate of unemployment. Counter-cyclical
Keynesian demand management could only reduce it in the long term by
injecting ever larger doses of inflation into the economy.[29] The role of government consequently reverted to what it had been before the war: the discharge
of an indirect responsibility for employment, through the provision of the
conditions in which the market should work with optimum efficiency. This
entailed cuts in both direct taxation and public expenditure and the removal
of impediments to competition imposed in particular by trade unions.

As the abandonment of the MTFS in 1985 showed, doctrinaire monetarism
proved in the real world to be as impractical as Keynesian demand management (see Section 5.2). The use of fiscal policy to manipulate demand also
remained irresistible, especially before elections. After 1979, however, the
government showed no undue urgency to reduce the level of unemployment
to 5 per cent, which had been Keynes's own definition of 'full' employment.
The public appeared uninterested and electoral success was no longer
adjudged to depend on the eradication of unemployment. Even the Labour
Party dropped the commitment in 1990.[30]

12. 4 THE RESILIENCE OF THE WELFARE STATE

Throughout this carnage the social services, nevertheless, remained surprisingly unscathed. Successive cuts in central and local budgets did reduce
projected increases in expenditure. As has been seen, there was also a
managerial revolution within each service. However, despite the explicit

commitment of Conservative governments after 1979 to 'roll back' the state, to end the 'dependency culture' and to reduce taxation, public expenditure steadily rose in real terms with the sole exception of 1985/6 and 1988/9 (see Table 12.3).

Likewise expenditure on social policy only suffered two real cuts (in 1977/8 and 1988/9) and, as a percentage of GDP, only fell temporarily in the second half of the 1980s (see Table 12.4). To finance this expenditure, the percentage of GDP taken in both direct and indirect taxation (the 'tax take') rose from 33.5 per cent in 1978 to 36.7 per cent ten years later before falling back to 35 per cent in 1994.[31]

There were three principal reasons for this resilience:

- technical factors
- political support for the welfare state
- popular support for the welfare state

Table 12.3   Public expenditure, 1974/5–1995/6

Fiscal year	£bn	Percentage of GDP
1974–5	220.9	46.75
1975–6	221.5	47.25
1976–7	215.7	44.75
1977–8	205.3	41.5
1978–9	215.7	42.25
1979–80	223.1	42.5
1980–1	227.1	44.75
1981–2	229.9	45.5
1982–3	235.9	45.5
1983–4	240.8	44.75
1984–5	248.3	45.25
1985–6	246.6	43.25
1986–7	252.3	42.25
1987–8	253.7	40.5
1988–9	248.5	38.0
1989–90	254.6	38.25
1990–1	258.6	39.0
1991–2	266.9	41.0
1992–3	282.9	43.5
1993–4	289.1	43.25
1994–5	295.6	42.5
1995–6	299.8	42.25

Note: £ at 1995–6 prices.
Source: HM Treasury, *Public Expenditure* (Cm 3601, 1997) table 3.1.

Table 12.4   Social expenditure, 1975/6–1995/6

	Year on year change (%)	Percentage of GDP
1975–6	2.5	25.4
1976–7	3.7	25.5
1977–8	–4.7	23.7
1978–9	1.5	23.2
1979–80	1.1	22.9
1980–1	1.0	24.0
1981–2	1.1	24.3
1982–3	1.9	24.2
1983–4	4.9	24.5
1984–5	1.2	24.3
1985–6	1.4	23.7
1986–7	4.4	24.0
1987–8	<u>1.0</u>	<u>23.2</u>
1988–9	(–2.0)	21.5
1989–90	2.5	21.7
1990–1	2.2	22.2
1991–2	8.9	24.6
1992–3	6.2	26.1
1993–4	3.5	26.3
1994–5	2.4	26.0
1995–6	1.7	25.8

Note: 1975/6–1987/8, £ at 1987/8 prices; 1988/9–1995/6, £ at 1995/6 prices.

Sources: J. Hills (ed.), *The State of Welfare* (Oxford, 1990) p. 339; HM Treasury, *Public Expenditure* (Cm 3601, 1997) tables 3.3, 3.4.

Technical factors

There were many technical factors which sustained the level of social expenditure. As Beveridge had warned, the abandonment of 'full' employment sharply raised the cost of unemployment insurance and other related benefits. By increasing unemployment in the early 1980s, therefore, monetarism ironically also increased social expenditure. So too did the recession between 1990 and 1994. Demographically, the number of elderly people requiring pensions and expensive healthcare increased (although admittedly the number of schoolchildren did fall in the 1980s by 10 per cent). With the increasing breakdown of marriage, informal care also required increased subsidies. So too did the fifth of all families with children which were headed by a single parent by the 1990s. Finally, in a period of rapid inflation, the relative price of labour-intensive services rose disproportionately.

In short, with a volatile economy, an ageing population and changes to traditional family structures, social expenditure had to increase simply to maintain a given level of service. Moreover, public expenditure as a whole did not decline automatically in line with the withdrawal of the state provided services. This was because private provision typically required substantial subsidies, as the rising cost of tax subsidies to owner-occupiers (to which Mrs Thatcher was committed) demonstrated.

Political support

The principal safeguard of social expenditure was not technical but, despite the rhetoric and perceptions of electoral opinion, the continuing political and popular support it enjoyed. Politically, as has been seen, the Cabinet in 1982 swiftly defeated the dismantling of the welfare state proposed by the Central Policy Review Staff. Then, when a measure of radical reform was achieved after 1987, it was restricted essentially to management.

Political rejection of radical action was due in part to Mrs Thatcher's lack of overall strategy. As has been argued:

> She was not by habit a strategist. Although she had pictures in her mind of the kind of place she would like Britain to become . . . the common experience of those who worked closely with her was that she did not instinctively relate present problems to some grand conceptual plan. Because of her . . . emphatic way of speaking, she was usually depicted otherwise. . . . But this was propaganda, put about not so much by her staff as by an adoring press.[32]

This shortcoming was compounded by her methods which, to say the least, did little to encourage the informed and detailed planning required to ensure that – in the face of inevitable opposition from vested interests – radical change was both practical and able to sustain support.

The last fully researched attempt to reform welfare policy in the 1980s was the 1985 Fowler review of social security. It was not the new Beveridge Report, as widely proclaimed at the time, but it did at least share its respect of detailed research and consultation. Thereafter, such thorough planning was actively discouraged– not least perhaps because the Fowler review, in exposing the impracticality of some of the Prime Minister's favoured hunches (such as the ending of SERPS) confirmed her suspicion of the inherent negativism of official advice. Thus the 1988 Education Bill, which introduced the internal market into schools, was submitted to Parliament after the briefest of consultation periods with 137 clauses. It emerged, largely as a result of the government's own amendments, with 238. Its guiding principle, in the words of one affronted commentator, appeared to be 'action before words, decision before debate'. Kenneth Clarke also did little to disarm opposition to the 1990 NHS and Community Care Bill by cheerfully admitting that 'he was making it up as he went along'.[33] The poll tax fiasco was the inevitable consequence of such methods.

The major radical reform of the the 1980s, the introduction of 'internal markets' to all major welfare services, appears in retrospect to have been the result of a coherent strategy. In reality, this was anything but the case (see above, p. 327). A vivid first-hand account of how the principle came to be incorporated into the 1990 NHS Act has been provided by Kenneth Clarke. A review of the NHS had been announced, to the total surprise of the Cabinet and Whitehall, on a television programme in January 1988. It was then carried out by a committee of five ministers, backed by special advisers, which was not – and therefore did not follow the practices of – a formal Cabinet committee. The result was that Mrs Thatcher was 'at her worst . . . We would have two- or three- hour meetings and she would end up screaming like a fishwife. and complaining about the bloody consultants and the hospitals, and her doctor friends had told her this, or told her that, or we would end up with unbelievably rambling conversations in which we failed to get to grips with anything'.[34]

In the main, however, the dismantling of the welfare state was resisted for a more positive reason. A significant number of Cabinet ministers remained convinced the existing social services were relatively efficient, necessary and ideologically justified. The privatization of SERPS, for example, was opposed by the Treasury on the grounds that it would cost an additional £1b (mostly in revenue foregone as a result of the tax allowances deemed necessary to encourage people to become 'independent' of the state). The Treasury also persistently defended the NHS on the grounds that it was more cost-effective than one based on insurance.[35] Education vouchers were equally opposed because were they to subsidize private education (as was indeed to be the case with nursery vouchers in 1996) they too would increase rather than reduce public expenditure.

Collective provision, it was therefore argued, was more cost-effective. It was also adjudged functionally necessary. The privatization of SERPS, for example, was defeated not just on cost but because of opposition from insurance companies and employers. They took fright at the prospect of taking on, respectively, more high-risk cases and administrative responsibilities. Placing the NHS on an insurance basis similarly posed practical difficulties because, unlike in continental Europe, large social insurance funds had been disbanded in 1948. The private insurance industry was again not over eager to respond to the new challenge, as demonstrated by the few policies issued to the elderly after 1988 (after Mrs Thatcher had compelled a reluctant Treasury to provide tax allowances for their private health cover). Indeed, throughout the whole field of welfare policy the private market appeared persistently reluctant to replace state provision. As will be seen, industry failed to provide the anticipated funds for city technology colleges in 1986, the banks declined to administer student loans in 1988 and private landlords were not enamoured with the prospect of taking responsibility for 'sink estates' as permitted after 1988. In short, once the dismantling of the welfare state was broached, there appeared simply to be no alternative.

There were also serious reservations about why there should be an alternative. Welfare policy continued to be seen, as Beveridge had viewed it, not as a threat to the market but as a precondition for its efficient working. As Mrs Thatcher's own adviser on social policy later argued, state welfare should be viewed 'not as an interference with the free market but as helping to preserve it'. It was also 'an expression of solidarity with our fellow citizens'. These 'market and community arguments', he concluded, 'together explain the remarkable consensus in most advanced Western nations that some sort of welfare state is both necessary and desirable'.[36] The Conservative challenge, therefore, should not be to dismantle but to restructure it.

Popular support

Political support for the welfare state was also expedient. This was because evidence from a wide variety of opinion polls confirmed continuing support for higher expenditure on welfare policy, even at the cost of higher taxation.[37] Despite the Thatcherite rhetoric, less than 10 per cent of these polled after 1979 favoured a reduction in spending and taxation. Until 1983 the majority favoured the *status quo*. Thereafter a majority, peaking in 1991 at 65 per cent of those polled, favoured higher spending *and* taxation. This was the view, therefore, not just of those who benefited directly from the welfare state, such as the poor and public employees responsible for its implementation (as argued by the New Right) but also by the better-off and many Conservative voters.

A number of explanations have been advanced for this phenomenon. Taylor-Gooby in particular has argued that it was driven by self-interest. Support was greatest for universal services, such as pensions and the NHS, which everyone enjoys. They are recognized to be more cost-effective than the alternatives provided by the market. On the other hand, benefits targeted at 'undeserving minorities' such as the unemployed or single mothers command less support. Others, however, have noted a measure of altruism which would have delighted Titmuss (see Section 2.2.2). Many of those expressing support for higher taxation were reported as believing that the country as a whole rather than they themselves would be the beneficiary. Were this true, it would have refuted the thesis advanced by J. K.Galbraith in *The Culture of Contentment*, which became brifly fashionable after the 1992 election. The two-thirds of the population which was comfortably off, he argued, would resist any attempt at their expense to help the poor.[38]

The evidence of opinion polls must always be subject to qualification. Respondents notoriously tell pollsters what they think they want to hear. How they vote and how they publicly express their views may differ considerably. The sample may be small and unrepresentative. Moreover those appearing to act altruistically may well be ultimately motivated by self-interest. Higher expenditure on education and unemployment benefit for example could well be viewed, in Joseph Chamberlain's words, as the 'ransom' the better-off have to pay for a productive and cohesive society. Changing opinions can also simply reflect a changing *status quo*. For instance, growing support for higher expenditure and taxes in the late 1980s could simply reflect the fact that direct taxes were falling sharply and services also appeared to be doing so.

There is, however, little in the poll evidence to suggest success for the cultural revolution for which Mrs Thatcher was striving. If she did achieve any success it was in reforming the views of the Labour Party. Its 1997 manifesto laid heavy emphasis on New Labour being 'wise spenders not big spenders'. Ministers were to be required 'to save before they spend'. Conservative spending targets were not to be exceeded for two years. There was also to be no increase in rates of income tax before the next election.[39] Such 'prudence' might have been a reasoned response to the need to adapt social democratic policy to the changed realities to which the welfare state had been exposed since the 1970s. It was not, however, justified by the polls which, on balance, reflected attitudes to welfare more precisely than election results because the latter, after all, were influenced by many considerations other than welfare. What the opinion polls clearly showed is that there had been no 'Thatcherite' revolution at a popular level. The market's inability to replace any of the state's major welfare responsibilities demonstrated that the values of the welfare state were institutionally embedded in Britian. They were also culturally embedded.

12.5 CONCLUSION

Despite the abandonment of corporatism, the abuse of professional 'producers'of welfare and the suspension of the commitment to 'full' employment, the social services remained surprisingly unscathed after 1976. Under the continuing influence of egalitarian thinking, they were initially earmarked for expansion by the Labour government but such plans were hit hard by the world economic crisis. There was a gradual relaxation in the later 1970s. Any hope of significant expansion, however, was hit hard again by the blunt weapon of monetarist policy. Even in the absence of any welfare strategy, constant economies were required in order to meet monetary targets; and given rising demands for welfare (caused not least by the impact of monetarism on employment) this created an impression of a major contraction of services, although aggregate figures prove otherwise.

1987 was the year when, for welfare policy 'the dog finally barked'.[40] Radical reform, however, was restricted largely to the management. The main ideological assault did not commence until a second 'fiscal crisis' in the early 1990s. Even then it was robustly contested within Cabinet. Such political support, combined with the weakness of the market and the strength of public opinion, meant that attention essentially remained focused on restructuring rather than dismantling. This is the broad framework in which the evolution of individual policies needs to be studied.

12.6 FURTHER READING

There are few balanced histories of the 1974–9 Labour governments. D. Coates, *Labour in Power? A study of the Labour government, 1974–79* (1980) is a contemporary assessement which can be matched with A. Seldon and K. Hickson, *New Labour, Old Labour: the Wilson and Callaghan governments, 1974–79* (2004). There are, however several good insider accounts, the most valuable of which are: J. Barnett, *Inside the Treasury* (1982); B. Donoughue, *Prime Minister: the conduct of policy under Harold Wilson and James Callaghan* (1987), later updated in *Heat of the Kitchen* (2003); and D. Healey, *The Time of My Life* (1989). K. Morgan, *James Callaghan: a life* (1997) is the authorized biography.

Both Mrs Thatcher and John Major have written autobiographies: *The Downing Street Years* (1993), and *John Major: the autobiography* (1999). Pre-eminent amongst the biographies of Margaret Thatcher are H. Young, *One of Us* (1993), and J. Campbell, *Margaret Thatcher* (2 vols, 2000 and 2003), which provides invaluable correctives to ministerial self-delusions. They may be supplemented by two exceptionally full insider accounts, N. Lawson, *The View from No. 11* (1992) and G. Howe, *Conflict of Loyalty* (1994). Context is provided by D. Kavanagh, *Thatcherism and British Politics: the end of consensus?* (Oxford, 1990); A. Gamble, *The Free Economy and the Strong State: the politics of Thatcherism* (1994); and D. Kavanagh and A. Seldon (eds), *The Thatcher Effect* (1989). The same editors have produced *The Major Effect* (1994), whilst Selson has authored by himself the sympathetic *John Major: a political life* (1997). Finally, a basic framework in which to place the conflicting evidence is provided by D. Childs, *Britain since 1945: a political history* (1997).

Two accessible introductions to economic policy at this time are A. Cairncross, *The British Economy since 1945: economic policy and performance, 1945–1990* (Oxford, 1992) and R. Middleton, *The British Economy since 1945* (Basingstoke, 2000). A far fuller analyis is provided in R. Floud and P. Johnson (eds), *The Cambridge Economic History of Modern Britain* (Cambridge, vol. 3, 2004) whilst, no doubt to the relief of many, an excellent brief survey is S. Wilks, 'Conservative governments and the economy, 1979–97', *Political Studies*, 45 (1997) 691–703. All have good bibliographies. The key turning point is well analysed in K. Burk and A. Cairncross, *Goodbye, Great Britain: the 1976 IMF crisis* (1991), whilst the contemporary mood exudes from W. Keegan, *Mrs Thatcher's Experiment* (1984), and *Mr Lawson's Gamble* (1989).

chapter 13

The Impact of 'Thatcherism' 1976–1997

CONTENTS

The detailed examination of welfare policy after 1976 follows a broadly similar pattern to that used for the classic welfare state. There are two changes. First, because economic policy reassumed its interwar antipathy to social expenditure, attention has been restricted to its impact. That was covered in the previous chapter. Second the personal social services are the second service to be examined after social security, rather than the last. This is not because they were the fastest expanding area of policy in the mid-1970s. Rather it is because they became more closely linked with social security as a service for the poor. They were thus identified together within the narrower definition of the welfare state which, under American influence, was becoming more fashionable (see Section 2.1, especially note 2).

Such semantic changes were of increasing importance to welfare policy after 1987, or more particularly after the first (none too successful) appointment of a New Right adherent, John Moore, to the Department of Health and Social Security. They may be viewed positively as a subtle attempt to change outdated assumptions. Alternatively they may been seen as a cynical ploy to disguise the true extent of the 'new austerity'.

13.1 SOCIAL SECURITY

The service which was potentially most vulnerable to radical economies and reform after 1976 was that which had been the central concern of the Beveridge report and so lay at the core of the classic welfare state: social security. As by far the most expensive service, it was the one where cuts had to be made were significant economies to be achieved. As a service for the poor (with the exception of pensions), it was also of little direct appeal to the middle-class electorate. Moreover, as the service demonized by American conservatives as the cause of a dependency culture, it was the prime target for ideological assault. This came in the person of a new secretary of state for health and social security, John Moore, after the 1987 election. He started linguistically to undermine conventional assumptions. 'Social security' was re-termed 'welfare'. The 'benefit culture' also replaced the 'poverty trap' as the principal target for reform.[1]

Despite these potential handicaps, however, the social security budget did not suffer a permanent cut. Real expenditure on it rose from £50.7 billion (at 1995–6 prices) in 1978–9 to £93.1 billion during the economic recovery of 1995–6.[2] What did this signify?

- Despite the rhetoric, did these services become more generous?
- Alternatively, did they expand simply to meet increased need?
- If the latter, how effectively was need met?

These are the broad questions which this section will address.

The record

In the mid-1970s the enhancement of social security was a principal objective of the Labour government as a result of its social contract with the trade unions. Three major acts were passed in 1975. The Social Security Act placed all social insurance benefits on an earnings-related basis. The Social Security Pensions Act guaranteed everyone an inflation-proof flat-rate and earnings-related pension.[3] Finally, the Child Benefit Act gave mothers an inflation-proof weekly payment for all their children, with additional benefits for single parents.

The common purpose behind this legislation was to reduce means-testing and to redistribute resources in favour of the low-paid. The extension of the earnings-related principle, for instance, was designed to guarantee the relative value of benefits over time. This would realize Beveridge's aim, albeit in a manner of which he would have disapproved, that all claimants should have an automatic right to an 'adequate' benefit. The detailed changes to pensions legislation (such as the determination of the size of the earnings-related pension by the best, not the last, 20 years of a worker's earnings) also favoured those who, like manual workers, enjoyed their peak earnings when young.

Women were amongst the principal beneficiaries of this legislation, fashioned by Barbara Castle. For example, in the calculation of pension entitlement, they were credited with contributions for the years spent at home bringing up children. Above all, they benefited from the increased value of child benefit. This was to be financed, however, by a switch of money from the 'wallet' to the 'purse': the withdrawal of child tax allowances, which had been enjoyed largely by fathers, and the payment of the enhanced cash benefit largely to mothers. This was a major challenge to the 'male breadwinner' concept of a welfare state. Callaghan, as the new prime minister, dismissed Castle before the reform was operative. Then, fearful of the trade unions' reaction, he sought to postpone it indefinitely. He was defeated by the unprecedented leaking of Cabinet minutes to the press.[4]

These reforms were expensive and, following the economic crisis of 1976, both Labour and Conservative governments fought to contain their immediate and future cost. Under Labour the principal objective was to husband scarce resources both by administrative economies and by the better 'targeting' of those in greatest need. This, as the 1978 Supplementary Benefit Review made explicit, meant a renewed emphasis on means-tested benefits.[5] Under the Conservatives the initial motivation was economy. After the appointment of Moore and the popularization of Charles Murray's work, however, there was also an explicit ideological dimension. This reached its apogee in the 'fundamental review' of policy mounted by Portillo and Lilley in 1993. Dividing these two phases was the 1986 Fowler review.

Conservative strategy

In office the Conservatives followed three main strategies:

- cutting the real value of benefits
- cutting the number of claimants
- cutting bureaucracy.

(i) Cutting the value of benefits

The principal methods of reducing the value of benefits were the ending of earnings-related supplements, the modification of indexing and simple abolition. In 1982, for example, earnings-related supplements to all short-term benefits (such as unemployment pay) which had been introduced in 1966 were cancelled – although, to maintain government revenue earnings-related *contributions* were retained. This was the first time a 'right', supposedly guaranteed by insurance contributions, had been withdrawn. In relation to indexation, the annual uprating of benefits in line with inflation was regularly frozen, delayed or only partially implemented. In 1981 and 1988, for instance, child benefit was frozen. Between 1981 and 1983 short-term benefits were also increased by 5 per cent less than the rise in prices. The shortfall was only restored once the benefits had been made taxable – which saved £400 million per annum on unemployment insurance alone, a sum equivalent to one-tenth of payments to the unemployed.[6] Finally, death and maternity grants in 1986 were among those benefits withdrawn.

Pensions suffered the most swingeing cut in value. In 1982 their uprating was linked to prices rather than earnings. As a result, their relative value fell from 23 per cent of average male earnings to only 15 per cent in 1995. Their overall cost was simultaneously reduced by one-third, at an estimated saving to government of £43 billion between 1980 and 1992. Moreover, the redistributory nature of the State Earnings Related Pension (SERPS), painfully negotiated in 1975, was eroded by various means, thereby cutting its long-term cost by half.[7]

(ii) Cutting the number of claimants

The Conservatives' second strategy was to restrict the number of claimants for benefit. This was effected continuously by a succession of small cuts. There were, however, two coordinated bursts of regulation in 1986 and 1993 as part of, respectively, the Fowler and the 'fundamental' review. In 1986, for instance, those aged between 16 and 18 lost their right to claim income support (the revamped system of supplementary benefit). Their mothers simultaneously lost the right to child benefit for those not in full-time education. Meanwhile, the right to housing benefit was restricted to those on incomes broadly equivalent to the level of income support – a cut which secured an annual saving of £450 million.[8] In 1993 stricter medical tests were introduced when aid to the disabled was consolidated in Incapacity Benefit. This removed 200,000 claimants. Arrangements were also made to delay the payment of women's pensions until they reached the age of 65 rather than 60. Gender equality was to be achieved by eroding women's rights not enhancing men's.

Unemployment benefit was a prime target for these cuts. Eligibility was constantly tightened after 1978 and after 1986 staff were particularly left in no doubt that they should follow a 'benefit control' rather then 'welfare' model of administration. The 1986 Restart programme introduced compulsory interviews for the long-term unemployed, which cut claimants by 8 per cent. The availability of benefit for those under 25 was simultaneously restricted. Then in 1988 the right to benefit was removed altogether from those aged 16 and 17. Between these two years, it was estimated, stricter criteria for benefit cut the number of registered unemployed by half. In 1993, in the build up to the introduction of the Jobseekers' Allowance, the entitlement to benefit earnt by insurance contributions was halved to six months. This was designed to remove 165,000 claimants at an annual saving of £180m.[9]

(iii) Cutting bureaucracy

The Conservatives' third strategy was to simplify and thereby reduce the cost of administration. One major change, to bring Britain in line with continental Europe, was the requirement on employers to administer sickness and maternity benefit after 1982 and 1986 respectively. The objective was both to reduce the size of the civil service and to combat fraud more effectively. Initially employers had only to administer the schemes for eight weeks and their costs were reimbursed. Their responsibilities, however, were soon increased to 28 weeks and, amid considerable furore, reimbursement was halted in 1994.

Another major change after 1988 was the delegation of responsibility for the delivery of services to executive agencies, so that by 1996 all but 3 per cent of DHSS staff were employed in such agencies. Indeed, the Employment Service (responsible for the delivery of embryonic 'welfare-to-work' measures) absorbed so many of the staff of the Department of Employment that the Department was disbanded in 1995. For 80 years (initially as the Ministry of Labour) it had been the advocate of trade unions and, more recently, of active labour market policies. Its disbandment was symbolic.

The most significant administrative changes, however, were those effected in 1986 following the Fowler review. The means-tested system (renamed Income Support) was greatly simplified by the establishment of two benefit rates, one for the over-25s and the other for the under-25s. Additional premiums were to be paid for families, the disabled and the elderly. A variety of other benefits were consolidated into Family Credit and Housing Benefit. The result was a system 'less sensitive to individual need, but easier to understand and administer' – and computerize.[10] The review also revolutionized the administration of the 'exceptional payments', to which claimants of means-tested benefit were entitled in addition to standard benefit. These payments were ruthlessly concentrated into the Social Fund. All payments were to be at the discretion of officials and claimants had no right of appeal. Moreover, 70 per cent of grants were in the form of loans. Each DHSS office was also cash-limited so that money for those living below the official poverty line could, and often did, run out. By such restrictions, expenditure was cut by two-thirds

> The system of 'exceptional payments' undoubtedly needed some, although perhaps not such draconian, modernization. Owing to an injudicious decision soon after the Conservatives had taken office, the statutory right to such payments had been codified. The resulting 16,000-paragraph rule book became a gold mine for claimant groups. Expenditure rose from £41 million to £222 million by 1984, with two-thirds of claimants receiving such payments 'as of right'. This begged the question of whether they were truly 'exceptional'.

Policy failures

Collectively, these three strategies were far from successful. Administrative efficiency did not uniformly improve, aggregate costs were not reduced and there was no radical redirection of policy. In short, in direct contradiction to Conservative strategy, there was:

- increasing bureaucracy
- increasing costs
- increasing confusion.

(i) Increasing bureaucracy

Policy, as has been seen, was often framed in disregard or even ignorance of the full complexity of the situation. As a result administrative chaos frequently ensued. This contrasted starkly to the relatively smooth expansion of contributory insurance after the Second World War and, even more damningly, to the efficient introduction of social insurance after the assiduous planning of Edwardian civil service. Against increasingly stiff opposition, *The Times* concluded, the introduction of housing benefit in 1986 was 'the biggest administrative fiasco in the history of the welfare state'. Across the country, 'dozens of council housing offices closed their doors early, took their phones off the hook and locked long queues outside as they attempted to sort out backlogs which left claimants without rent and rate payments for weeks and in some cases for months. In places the police had to be called to quell disturbances'.[11] Increasing bureaucracy (in the pejorative sense of the term) led to increasing costs, as expensive concessions had swiftly to be made.

Things did not noticeably improve with the introduction of the *Next Steps* reforms. For example, the introduction of the key reform resulting from the fundamental review of 1993, the Jobseekers' Allowance, was disrupted by a prolonged pay dispute within the Employment Service. Constant 'market testing' of their work (to see whether it might be contracted out or even privatized) left staff as demoralized as their benefit claimants were alleged to be. 'The biggest administrative fiasco' in this respect, however, was the Child Support Agency (CSA) which – again against stiff competition – became 'the most vilified public body in the land'.[12]

The CSA demonstrated how poor policy-making could translate emerging consensus into conflict. Between 1974 and 1989, the number of single parents escalated to 1.15 million, one-fifth of all families with children. Two-thirds claimed income support. Less that a third, however, received any maintenance. It was widely agreed that, on moral and financial grounds, the tax-payer should not effectively subsidize the absent partner (who was usually the father). It was also agreed that the mother should have an adequate income although, as has been seen, under Murray's influence single mothers were starting to be regarded by some as villains rather than victims.

→

Since effective solutions had been already been pioneered in the USA and Australia, the problem should have been easily resolved. It was not. In 1992, the CSA assumed from the courts full powers to assess, collect and enforce maintenance payments. Three mistakes were then made. First, the powers were made retrospective. The CSA consequently overstretched itself reviewing past settlements – an unnecessary burden which achieved little more than greatly offending many law-abiding parents who considered their obligations to have been legally and fairly settled. Second, at the Treasury's insistence, income support payments to the single parent were reduced by the full value of any enhanced maintenance payment. This gave the recipient no incentive whatsoever to incur the unpleasantness (and even danger) of providing the CSA with the details of the absent partner. Finally, in order to ensure that children in the 'second' families of absent partners did not suffer, complicated rules were devised with which the CSA's computers, let alone staff or parents, could not cope.

In short the CSA, which was radically overhauled in 1995, illustrated the relative poverty of policy-making at this time. It also begged the question of whether Conservative policy was designed to improve customer care (as promised by the Citizen's Charter) or simply to reduce costs.[13]

(ii) Increasing costs

Rather than contracting, the aggregate cost of social benefit – as has been seen – also doubled in real terms. On the positive side, this reflected the targeting of more generous benefit on previous disadvantaged groups. Expenditure on the disabled, for example, quadrupled in real terms between 1979 and 1996, particularly after the introduction of Disability Living and Working Allowances in 1990. When child benefit was unfrozen in 1991, additional payments were made to the first child. The real value of most benefits, for those who retained the right to claim them, also rose over time (often as the result of impending elections).[14]

In the main, however, the reasons were more negative. They included not just administrative incompetence but also increasing need as a result of social change (such as the increase in one-parent families) and, above all, economic change (such as higher unemployment and the casualization of the labour force). Moreover, the number of those drawn into the social security system was not matched by the number of those whom, it had been hoped, would be liberated from it. Radical reforms, aired between the 1982 CPRS report and the 1993 fundamental review, included the ending of universal child benefit, the privatization of SERPS and sickness pay, and the ability to 'opt out' of unemployment and maternity benefits. Each was adjudged to be politically impossible. Indeed, one of the successful objects of the Fowler review had been to parry an attack by the Treasury on both the structure and cost of social security, and to keep its budget largely intact.

(iii) Increasing confusion

The fundamental impediment to reform, however, was a contradiction in policy aims. Two have already been mentioned. First, there was the confusion over whether the ultimate object was to improve the quality of service or to reduce their costs. It was not only the CSA that was destabilized by this but also the Employment Service. After 1994, in the build up to the Jobseekers' Allowance, for example, it had to employ 'performance measures' to assess whether claimants were making effective applications for work. Was this genuinely to assist claimants in their search for employment or a reinvention of the interwar 'actively seeking work test' designed to disqualify as many claimants as possible? Perhaps one of the political attractions of 'hiving off' executive agencies was that such dilemmas could also be hived off.

The second contradiction was that encouraging people to 'stand on their own feet' by switching from social to private insurance was not always a cheap option. Large subsidies, as has been seen, had to be paid to encourage the switch. This was because the private market was frequently reluctant to shoulder the full risk. In an attempt to decrease middle-class dependence on the state, it is true, many tax allowances were gradually reduced. Mortgage interest relief, for example, was reduced in 1988 and more particularly in 1993 (although more radical changes had been persistently vetoed by Mrs Thatcher, who wanted to retain this perk 'for our people').[15] However the annual cost of the allowance to induce people to leave SERPS rose so steeply that by the mid-1990s it was equivalent to one-third of the total cost of providing the basic state pension.[16]

Similarly the attempt to target benefit on those in greatest need through means tests contradicted a range of other objectives. Means testing, for example, contradicts the aim of reducing administrative costs because it is labour intensive. As a result, over 40 per cent of the cost of the Social Fund was typically consumed on administration while the equivalent figure for universal child benefit was just over 2 per cent.[17] Means-testing also, as demonstrated in Section 6.3, frequently reduces rather than increases work incentives. This is because it creates 'unemployment' or 'poverty' traps. For instance, the dependence of lone mothers on the state was reinforced in the early 1990s by the fact that they gained little additional income by increasing their working hours from 16 to even 55 per week. The Fowler review had admittedly reduced the intensity of the problem but only at the cost of generalizing it.[18]

The contradictory aims of Conservative policy were exemplified by the persistent Party pressure to cancel child benefit. As a universal benefit, it was not targeted on the poor and was deemed unnecessarily expensive. However, its withdrawal would have decreased work incentive. It had, after all, been introduced in its original form of family allowances by a Conservative government in 1945 to ensure that the income of those in work – like those on benefit – reflected family need. Were it to be withdrawn, there was a danger that, for large families, income from benefit would exceed that from work.

These contradictions lay at the heart of the policy battles within the Conservative government after the second fiscal crisis of the early 1990s. Portillo and Lilley in their 'fundamental review' sought a further residualization of the welfare state. Lilley, for example, continually tightened qualification rules to reduce numbers on benefit as well as, justifiably, to attack fraud (deemed to cost at minimum £3.9 billion after 14 years of Conservative administration, or arguably misadministration).[19] In 1997 he then produced his Basic Pension Plus scheme to privatize the pensions of those then joining the workforce – but not of those who had already paid contributions, as cynically alleged by New Labour.

Portillo simultaneously introduced the Jobseekers' Allowance, with all the goads and few of the incentives then being deployed in parallel 'welfare-to-work' measures abroad. The right to contributory benefit was halved to six months and claimants required to prove they were actively seeking work. The 'rebranding' of an 80-year-old benefit (unemployment benefit) was also designed, in the wake of John Moore's semantic sallies, to place greater emphasis on the responsibilities as opposed to the rights of claimants.

However, Kenneth Clarke as chancellor resisted the ideological thrust of such initiatives. He maintained the Treasury's suspicion of the practicality of, and the supposed economies to be gained from, the privatization of core social policies. He also supported incentives (largely in the form of subsidies to employers) to encourage those on benefit back to work. Here was the germ of a new consensus between the Conservative and Labour Parties, if not within the Conservative government itself.

Conclusion

By the mid-1990s, ideological hostility towards the social security system was finally being translated by Portillo and Lilley from rhetoric into a coherent, if contested, plan of action. This, together with the revival of the economy under Clarke's chancellorship, stabilized its aggregate cost. That cost, however, had almost doubled in real terms since 1979. This can be explained in part by underlying demographic trends, the more generous treatment of previously neglected groups and a rise in the real (if not relative) value of many benefits. It was also due, however, to the adverse consequences of economic policy and more especially to an earlier confusion of aims within, as well as confusion in the delivery of, policy.

The net result was that the numbers of those both on means-tested benefit and in poverty rose disconcertingly. Between 1979 and 1990, for example, the number on supplementary benefit/income support rose by two-thirds. Simultaneously, the numbers living on an income lower than 40 per cent of the national average (a conservative definition of relative poverty) increased fivefold to 7.7 million.[20] This was not a record of which to be unduly proud.

13.2 THE PERSONAL SOCIAL SERVICES

The development of the personal social services followed a broadly similar course to that of social security. In the aftermath of the Seebohm Report, real expenditure doubled between 1970 and 1974 and national targets were for the first time set for each major client group.[21] After the 1976 economic crisis, however, this momentum was lost and the targets were abandoned. Real expenditure fell sharply in 1977–8 and did not regain its former level until 1980–1. It would have fallen again had not local government then rejected planned cuts and maintained existing levels of service out of its own resources. This act of defiance contributed directly to the growing confrontation between central and local government which resulted in 1985 in the rate-capping of 'overspending' councils.

Nevertheless real expenditure more than doubled (at 1995–6 prices) between 1978–9 and 1995–6 from £4.1 billion to £9.4 billion. This was a result of demographic pressure (such as the ageing of the population and the decline of the traditional family structures), recognition of the needs of previously overlooked groups (such as carers) and political hesitancy.

The initial motivation behind the initial cuts was largely economic: the need to keep within cash-limited budgets. As with social security, however, there was an added ideological dimension after 1979. This led to a fundamental questioning of:

- the role of social workers
- the role of local authorities.

As a result of such questioning, the personal social services then became a controversial pioneer of the totemic managerial reform of the 1980s: 'internal markets'.

The role of social workers

Conservative ministers, like many members of the public, doubted the competence and were highly suspicious of the underlying motives of social workers. Was their principal purpose to encourage their 'problem' clients to conform to, or to challenge, conventional norms? The fundamental Conservative instinct was that clearly it should be the former, but that in practice it was the latter. Again, in their treatment of the elderly and handicapped were they seeking ultimately to support or to supplant the family and voluntary care? Conservatives were convinced, as evidenced by Mrs Thatcher's choice of Ferdinand Mount as her principal policy adviser in the mid 1980s, that the proper agency for personal individual care was not the state.[22] Rather it was the family or, failing that, charitable organizations (supported, if necessary, by tax concessions) and the market (with its greater sensitivity, in theory at least, to changing individual needs).

When such fundamentalist instincts came to be translated into practical legislation, however, anomalies began to appear. In the increasingly sensitive area of child abuse for example, was the family to be treated as the solution or the cause of the problem? When parents were wrongly accused, as in the 1987 Cleveland 'scandal', government and the public were quick to condemn social workers. On the other hand, when a tragedy did occur (as in 1985 with the death of Jasmine Beckford at the hands of her parents), both government and the public were equally swift to criticize the failure of social workers to take preventive action.

A major piece of consolidating legislation, the 1989 Children Act, sought to resolve this issue. It followed 'one of the most thorough reviews to be undertaken in any field of social welfare for many years' and has been called 'the most far-reaching piece of children's legislation ever introduced'.[23] Its clear verdict was that the 'prime responsibility' for the care of children should lie with parents rather than with government. Even when in local authority care, for example, children should remain in close contact with their parents and be returned home as soon as possible. In cases of suspected child abuse, however, social workers were still left with the appallingly difficult dilemma of when and how to act.

The Cleveland 'scandal' arose from the sending into care of some 200 children on the judgement of two social workers that they were being sexually abused within their families. With characteristic understatement, the *Daily Mail* likened the social workers to members of the Nazi SS. The resulting judicial enquiry can be seen to have significantly altered official attitudes in favour of parental rights and thus prepared the way for the Children Act. Greater powers for social workers to protect children from abuse by parents or guardians had been drafted after the Beckford enquiry, but were then dropped.[24]

The role of local government

An even greater anomaly arose in the midst of the 1980s in relation to community care. The capping of local government capital expenditure limited the residential accommodation available, above all, to the elderly. Voluntary and private agencies filled the void and requested the payment of their fees by the social security system. This was granted on a discretionary and then a standardized basis between 1979 and 1983. Annual social security expenditure, as has been seen, duly rocketed from £10 million for 11,000 claimants to an eventual figure in 1992 of £2.5 billion for 250,000 claimants.[25] Such expenditure, as the Audit Commission argued in its 1986 report *Making a Reality of Community Care*, was wholly illogical. Government had entered into an open-ended commitment to subsidize whatever form of residential accommodation the elderly chose. Meanwhile, the cheaper and more humane option of caring for the elderly in their own home, supported by domiciliary services such as home helps and meals on wheels, was largely ruled out because of the rate-capping of local authorities.

Community care, an apparently consensual objective in the 1970s and 1980s, underwent a subtle change of meaning after 1979. It came to be defined as care *in* the community rather than care *by* the community.[26] For example, patients were no longer to be released from large national institutions (such as geriatric or mental hospitals) into residential or other accommodation provided by local authorities. Rather they had to be cared or largely paid for by their families either at home or in private residential accommodation. In 1996 an attempt was made to 'privatize' care, particularly for the frail elderly, by offering generous tax concessions on insurance cover for the cost of nursing. Take up was low.

The government turned for advice on how to remedy this dilemma to the managing director of Sainsbury's, Roy Griffiths. His recommendations stunned it. He suggested that the subsidies for residential accommodation should be transferred from the social security budget (which government controlled) back to local authorities (with whom it was embattled). To Griffiths' disgust, Mrs Thatcher sidelined the report for 18 months. Then in July 1989 she burst into Cabinet demanding to know one good reason why it should not be implemented. Cabinet ministers 'all just stared back at her', as Timmins has revealed, 'they thought she had been the one good reason'.[27]

What had slowly become apparent was that, were the report to be implemented, central and not local government would be the winner and that expenditure could be cut. For example, local government would no longer be a major provider of services but an 'enabler'. It would appoint 'care managers' for all those in need and, on the basis of accumulated evidence, draft an overall plan for their care. Central government, for its part, would be committed to no expense until it had approved these plans. Its grant towards their cost would also be 'ring-fenced', so that local authorities could not spend it on another service. It would thus, as with executive agencies, regain control over expenditure whilst distancing itself from any difficulties arising from the implementation of policy. Such difficulties, however, should be minimal. Cost-effectiveness was to be assured by the government's two favoured policy instruments: competition and regulation. Voluntary and private agencies were to compete for the local government care contracts and thus keep the cost down. Meanwhile the actual delivery of care was to be monitored by the Audit Commission and a new Social Services Inspectorate.

These proposals were duly incorporated in the 1990 National Health Service and Community Care Bill, although their implementation was delayed until 1993. The delay was occasioned by both imperfect drafting, complications over the poll tax and the simultaneous reform of the NHS. It did mean, however, that implementation coincided with the fundamental review. As a result the terms of the Act were tightened. In each region, for example, a minimum of 85 per cent of care had to be provided by agencies other than the local authority.

The success of this 'internal market' and the 'purchaser–provider divide' has been hotly contested. In terms of policy delivery, the administrative ('transaction') costs of preparing and negotiating the contracts were high. Those empowered were care managers rather than their clients, who had, in addition, lost the free choice of accommodation which they enjoyed courtesy of the social security system. The amount of effective competition, and thus the mechanism to minimize inefficiency, was also limited. The initial objective of the welfare state to ensure standardized levels of national care also appeared in jeopardy. Finally, as Jane Lewis has clinically pointed out, the reforms were ill-suited to their broader aim of reviving civil society. Voluntary bodies competing for contracts in the 1990s were not the embodiment of independent active citizenship, as in Victorian days. Rather they were the creature of government. The need to tender and minimize costs required formalized procedures. It generated tensions between professional and volunteer staff. It also stifled experiment and innovation. In short, it destroyed the unique qualities and the essential benefits that voluntary organizations traditionally contributed to the quality of both civil society and policy delivery. [28]

Conclusion

It is extremely difficult, for the reasons given in Section 3.2.2, to establish statistical evidence by which to measure the input and output, let alone the final outcome, of the personal social services. There are many omissions (such as the number of abused children), inconsistencies (such as the measurement over time of medical need or incapacity) and imponderables (such as the differential rate of inflation in each service). The amount of total care needed is also unquantifiable.

On the best evidence available, however, it is clear that the radical ideals of both the 1970s and the 1980s were disappointed. After 1976 there were neither the economic resources nor the popular support to realize the comprehensive, professional coverage envisaged by the Seebohm Report. The radical intentions of the Conservatives were in turn also frustrated. The balance between the family and the state remained in practice, if not in theory, unresolved. So too did the overall cost-effectiveness of the 'purchaser–provider' divide.

Undoubtedly many benefited from the doubling of real expenditure after 1979. The commissioning between 1976 and 1997 of some 30 reports into child abuse scandals, however, also suggests widespread policy failure. Much of the abuse was of children in residential care, and the chairman of the enquiry commissioned in 1997 to survey the evidence lamented that his task was 'a crash course in human (largely male) wickedness and in the fallibility of social institutions'. The fallibility was not malevolent but, as the enquiry's poll of children's opinions confirmed, it did offend the principle of privileging the consumers over the producers of welfare. As the report commented:

The common theme to our discussions with young people was their very reasonable desire to be treated as people and individuals – which is what the Children's Act intended . . . The inadvertently oppressive nature of professional systems was exposed by the . . . child who said, very simply, 'I don't like people making decisions about me and they think they know what's best for me just by reading my file.'[29]

13.3 HEALTHCARE

Real expenditure on the NHS, as on social security and the personal social services, virtually doubled between 1978–9 and 1995–6. Its budget, at 1995–6 prices, rose from £23.5 billion to £40.7 billion, which represented an increase from 4.6 per cent to 5.6 per cent of GDP. The period also ended with a white paper, *A Service with Ambitions*, which has been described as 'the warmest endorsement ever of the NHS from the Conservative Party'.[30] There was not, however, a smooth evolution of healthcare policy as such indicators might suggest. On the contrary the NHS, as both a political ideal and a deliver of healthcare, experienced a series of crises between 1976 and 1997 which shook it to the core.

The mid-1970s, as in other welfare policies, were a period of innovation. To remedy the organizational weaknesses of the old tripartite system, as has been seen, its administrative structure was thoroughly overhauled. Determined attempts were then made to withdraw Bevan's enforced concessions to the medical profession (such as pay-beds) and to correct, at last, the geographical inequalities inherited from before the war (through the innovatory work of the Resources Allocation Working Party). The economic crisis halted such innovation and ushered in a decade of intense political and financial vicissitude. Every alternative to the funding of the NHS from general taxation was explored. By December 1987 the service as a whole was also technically bankrupt. There then followed the contested introduction of 'internal markets'. This was held by many to have lowered morale and standards of healthcare, thereby leading to Tony Blair's warning before the 1997 election that there was only 24 hours in which to save the NHS.

- What were the major structural changes introduced by the Conservatives?
- How effective were they?
- Why was the NHS persistently considered to be in crisis?

Structural change: the first phase

The first target for attack was the administrative structure introduced by Keith Joseph in 1974. A Royal Commission on the National Health Service, reporting in 1979, generally endorsed the underlying principles of the service. However, it condemned its excessive bureaucracy.[31] Consequently, in 1982 one administrative tier (the Area Health Authorities) was shed. The planning and implementation of policy became the responsibility of Regional and District Health Authorities alone.

A funding crisis simultaneously arose. This provided Roy Griffiths with his first trouble-shooting role. He was highly critical of the style of consensus management inherited from the Conservatives' 1974 reforms (see Section 7.2). 'If Florence Nightingale were to carry her lamp through the corridors of the NHS today', he wrote, 'she would almost certainly be searching for the people in charge.'[32] His solution was a totally new management structure headed by a Health Services Supervisory Board (chaired by the Secretary of State). Beneath it there was to be a NHS Management Board and general managers were to be placed in charge of all district authorities and hospitals.

Within hospitals, the number of managers was substantially increased and made accountable for their budgets. Consultants were also directly involved in managerial as well as clinical decisions. Finally, clear procedures were established for the evaluation and implementation of policy. The former included comparative costing to spread best practice throughout the service. The latter included competitive tendering. This, in the end, principally affected catering services which duly experienced a 30 per cent drop in costs by 1989.

In a last demonstration of 1970s 'worker' power, nurses and ancillary staff had mounted a prolonged pay dispute. They were finally beaten in December 1982. The implementation of the Griffiths Report in 1983 saw a similar defeat for the BMA. With the support of the House of Commons Social Services Committee, it protested that professional judgement should not be subject to the rulings of lay administrators.[33] Its protests were swept aside, as they were to be again in 1985 when the government restricted the range of drugs that could be prescribed.

Sir Roy Griffiths was the managing director of the supermarket firm, Sainsbury's. He typified the businessmen brought into Whitehall on a part-time basis to inject into the civil service the management efficiency, for which British industry had for so long been renowned. Another was the joint managing director of Marks and Spencers, Sir Derek Rayner, who acted as Mrs Thatcher's efficiency adviser from 1979 to 1983. Amongst his less successful manpower economies was the reduction of checks on claimants for unemployment benefit which led to the explosion in fraud that, as seen earlier, was finally tackled in the 1990s. A third was a director of ICI, Sir Robin Ibbs, who was responsible for the *Next Steps* programme of devolving policy delivery to semi-autonomous executive agencies.

Structural change: the second phase

The one thing the Griffiths Report could not resolve was the funding crisis. By 1987 the NHS was technically bankrupt. To keep within their budgets, hospitals had increasingly to defer payment of bills until the start of the new financial year in April. By May 1987, over £400 million was owing. This accounted for up to a quarter of some hospitals' budgets, excluding pay. To save money, beds increasingly had also to be closed as April approached. Given the impending election, such an expedient was discouraged in 1987 although no financial compensation was offered. Consequently, after the election, beds had to be closed earlier than usual. By December, the month during which demand for hospital care traditionally peaks, some 4000 were closed.

The government's response, as has been described in Section 12.1, was improvised. Mrs Thatcher took the decision to mount yet another fundamental review of the service during a television interview. It took the form of an *ad hoc* rather than a formal Cabinet committee and had virtually no civil service input. The committee's members were also in fundamental disagreement. They had been offered a golden opportunity for radical reform by a growing consensus. It was widely agreed both within and outside the medical profession not only that more funding was urgently needed but that the general tax-payer could also not be expected to provide it. As the presidents of the three senior royal medical colleges pronounced, for example: 'additional *and alternative* funding must be found'.[34] No agreement could be reached amongst ministers, however, on what form that alternative funding should take.

The final solution, published in the 1989 white paper *Working for Patients* (Cm 555), focused on alternative forms of management rather than of finance. It was also reached almost by accident. Building on the work of an American health economist, Alain Enthoven, an 'internal' market was to be created through the manufacturing of a 'purchaser–provider' divide. The *purchasers* were initially to be the District Health Authorities. Then, on holiday, it dawned on the new minister of health (Kenneth Clarke) that GPs could better express patients' wishes. Accordingly, they too could become purchasers, so long as they opted to accept a fixed budget from government as 'fund-holding' GPs. The *providers*, competing for business and therefore constantly seeking to drive down costs, were either publicly funded hospitals (encouraged to turn themselves into independent trusts) or private ones. They could be based within or outside the patients' health area. To oversee this internal market, an NHS Policy Board and a Management Executive was to be created This was designed to make managerial accountability transparent in accordance with the principles of *Next Steps* (see Section 12.3). In addition, to streamline management – albeit at the cost of consumer representation – executive managers were to replace local government representatives on the District Authorities.

These proposals were given the force of law by the 1990 NHS and Community Care Act. They were vigorously opposed by the BMA. More surprisingly, they were also opposed at the last moment by Mrs Thatcher who had asked selected businessman, including Rayner and Ibbs, to examine them. They had pronounced them unworkable. She accordingly contracted cold feet. 'It's *you* I'm holding responsible if *my* reforms don't work' she somewhat disingenuously shouted at Kenneth Clarke, who was determined to proceed and succeed.[35]

The ministerial battle over NHS reform exposed the confusion behind the apparently clear-cut and principled New Right alternatives to state welfare. The Secretary of State for Health and Social Security, John Moore, was a committed right-winger (see note 29). He had demonstrated his toughness by referring consistently to the 'healthcare industry' rather than the NHS and by becoming the first postwar health minister to opt for private care, when he contracted pneumonia in November 1987. He favoured an old idea last aired in the 1982 CPRS review: the financing of healthcare by private or social insurance. Mrs Thatcher was sympathetic and, at minimum, sought tax allowances for private health insurance to encourage greater self-sufficiency. Nigel Lawson, as chancellor, vehemently opposed both suggestions. They would, he argued, increase rather than decrease health expenditure. This was because the government would lose revenue as a result of tax allowances. It would also lose control over doctors' expenditure – as was apparent from the higher incidence and cost of hospital treatment in the USA and Germany, which respectively favoured private and social insurance. Lawson's preferred solution was increased charges. Mrs Thatcher vetoed this as politically impractical.

The effectiveness of reform

The purchaser–provider divide was attacked from its inception on grounds similar to those used in community care:

- It increased administrative costs.
- It empowered District Health Authorities and fund-holding GPs rather than patients.
- It jeopardized equity of care by creating a division between fund-holding and non-fund-holding GPs.
- It also reintroduced commercial principles into healthcare.

Each of these criticisms, however, can be turned on its head.

First, ever since 1948, a strengthening of management had been required to ensure that, in the taking of individual clinical decisions, doctors had some regard for the optimum allocation of scarce national resources (see Section 3.2.2). The Griffiths reforms may have increased the cost of management but the involvement of consultants in managerial decision, and especially the greater use of comparative costing, was important for self-discipline. So too – despite the admitted increase in transaction costs – was the need for GPs to plan, and for hospitals to compete for, contracts.

Second, patients suffered from imperfect knowledge (see Section 3.2.1) and GPs at least were well qualified to act as 'informed purchasers' on their behalf. In consequence fund-holding provided a belated and much-needed mechanism for making hospital consultants more responsive to patients' needs.[36]

Third, given the historical legacy of the NHS, geographical equity had always been an aspiration rather than a reality. It was one which the 1976 Resources Allocation Working Party was only slowly realising. A limited measure of competition at last challenged some inefficient monopolistic practices (see also Section 3.2.1). Hence the highly unpopular but necessary geographical rationalization of hospital provision in London in the mid-1990s, with the defeat of entrenched vested interests in such well-known hospitals as Guy's and Bart's. What the 'new system' had done, as one health minister had presciently foretold, was 'force some decisions out of us cowardly politicians who for twenty years have put them off'.[37]

Finally, the initial raw commercialism of the proposals was modified, particularly after Mrs Thatcher's departure from office. In yet another exercise in semantics, 'buyers' and 'sellers' became rather less confrontational 'purchasers' and 'providers'. Moreover, contract negotiators were increasingly encouraged to consider long-term collaboration rather than short-term competitive advantage.

The effectiveness of the system, however, can ultimately only be judged by its impact on the structure of policy delivery and on health outcomes. Both were positive. In relation to policy delivery, only ten hospitals and no more than 100 of the 28,000 GPs were initially expected to opt for trust and fund-holding status. By 1997, the majority of hospitals and at least half of GPs in England had (although significantly not in Scotland). Managers within hospitals were particularly enthusiastic. So too were those GPs who appreciated not just their increased power in relation to consultants but also the opportunity for developing a 'primary care led' service. This was the long-recognized means of transforming the NHS into a genuine health rather than a mere hospital service. Indeed GP contracts soon became the vehicle for attaining specific targets in preventive healthcare, as laid down in the 1992 *Health of the Nation* white paper (Cm 1986). 'This', responded one World Health Organization official, 'is exactly what we would like all countries to do.'[38]

The quality of individual services and health standards also continued to improve after 1990, as it had done irregularly since 1979. Much public criticism was levelled at individual services and in particular at increased charges and hospital waiting lists. Most notoriously, charges were introduced in 1989 for eye tests and dental check-ups – a move reminiscent of the Labour government's economies in 1951. It was justly condemned as a counter-productive attack on preventive medicine, which the government was simultaneously encouraging GPs to expand. In sharp contrast to public belief, however, the average waiting time for in-patient hospital treatment – after a slight increase in the late 1970s – remained stable in the 1980s at 17 weeks. Waiting times rose again slightly in the 1990s, but mainly as a result of the commitment in the Patients' Charter to eliminate all waits of over a year – which were reduced from 200,000 in 1990 to virtually nil by 1995.[39] In the same period, the number of patients treated, admittedly with some increased injection of funds to make internal markets and voting Conservative more acceptable in the 1992 election, increased by 16 per cent between 1990 and 1994.

As for the overall health outcomes, there was a continuing improvement in

basic health indicators, such as the mean age of death. Even more significantly, there was a reduction in the differences of health standards between
social classes and geographical regions. As Hills has concluded: 'the NHS has
been more successful in eliminating barriers to entry than most other healthcare systems and more successful than critics give it credit for'.[40]

The history of prescription charges illustrates how easy it is to misinterpret
the impact of policy changes. Contrary to explicit commitments in the 1979
election, they were increased by 40 times the rate of inflation between 1980
and 1994.[41] The picture however, was not universally black. Charges were
still typically equivalent to only one-half of the cost of the relevant drugs.
The number of patients exempted also rose from 60 to 80 per cent. So all
were helped and there was a redistribution of resources to those in most
need.

Crisis? What crisis?

Given such achievements, why throughout the period was there such a widespread popular conviction that the NHS was in crisis? There are four main
reasons.

First, as before 1976, there was the continuing temptation to measure
performance against an unattainable ideal – the full potential of medical
advance. To this was added after 1976 the realization that other, often more
prosperous, countries offered a range of treatment unavailable on the NHS.
Such calculations often disregarded complimentary facts such as, in the USA
for example, the overall cost of treatment and the inequity of excluding some
30 per cent of the population from any effective healthcare.

Second, after two years of exceptionally high spending between 1974 and
1976, expectations were slow to adjust to a new era in which health expenditure would grow only slowly in relation to GDP. The gap between increasing
resources and need, in other words, gradually narrowed. Indeed, there is
evidence that in the most attritional years between 1983 and 1987 expenditure
per head, weighted for age, temporarily declined.[42] It was, however, only a
temporary decline.

Third, there was – perversely – the success of the NHS in diverting
resources to under-provided regions. This was inevitably at the expense of
other regions where, especially in the south-east of England, there were articulate vested interests. This was particularly true, as has been seen, when in the
wake of the 1992 Tomlinson report resources were diverted from the centre of
London, where the old prestigious voluntary hospitals had been sited, to the
suburbs.

Finally, as previously argued, the medical profession as a whole was at last
and with some reluctance being made fully aware of the real economic
constraints on healthcare. In other words, their involvement in administration

and devolved budgeting had at last exposed the essential emptiness of Bevan's original promise to 'universalize the best'.

Each of these factors, which fuelled professional and popular dissatisfaction, could and should have been countered by rational argument and action. Both, as has been seen, were noticeable for their absence. Doctors and patients alike were antagonized by the 'permanent almost Maoist revolution' to which, in the absence of a clear strategy, the NHS was subjected.[43] There were also fears that the move to accountable management and increased efficiency would lead to privatization.

Such fears had some grounding in the rhetoric of the 1980s and some action after 1993. On the whole, however, accusations of privatization led to explicit commitments to the contrary. For example, even the radical 1989 white paper, which introduced the concept of internal markets, contained a foreword by Mrs Thatcher which promised that 'the National Health Service will continue to be available to all, regardless of income, and to be financed mainly out of general taxation'.[44] The increased efficiency and responsiveness of the service also made it more acceptable to better off patients, who were forcefully reminded of some of the disadvantages of private insurance during the recession of the early 1990s. In short, there was very little justification for Tony Blair's claim that there were only 24 hours in which to save the NHS. Rather, as with 'welfare-to-work initiatives', there were the germs of a new consensus. This included the internal market, to which New Labour did not long remain opposed, but also moves towards evidence-based medicine, national service frameworks and the use of IT to relieve GPs of some of their burden.

13.4 EDUCATION

For a variety of reasons, the full extent and significance of expenditure on education during this period is hard to determine. After the establishment of the Manpower Services Commission (MSC) by the Labour government in 1974, for example, money for vocational training was channelled away from the formal education system. The Department of Education and Science's budget, therefore, no longer provided an accurate picture of aggregate expenditure. There was also a 10 per cent decline in the number of children of school age during the 1980s as a result of the fall in the birth rate after the mid-1960s. This justified some decrease in expenditure. Nevertheless, on balance it would appear that expenditure on education followed the common pattern. It suffered a slight reduction in the late 1970s and the mid-1980s but then enjoyed stable, and eventually increased, funding. From a nadir of £27 billion in 1985–6 it rose to £36.3 billion a decade later, or from 4.8 per cent to 5.1 per cent of GDP.[45]

Educational standards, as conventionally measured, simultaneously improved. For example, between 1979 and 1990 the number of school leavers with five or more GCSE passes at 'C' grade rose from 24 per cent to 38 per cent. Those with three or more 'A' levels simultaneously rose from 9 per cent to 16 per cent. Meanwhile, by 1993 the number of 18- and 19-year-olds in higher education doubled from 14 per cent to 33 per cent. Given the antici-pated decline in undergraduate numbers for demographic reasons, the expan-sion of higher education was exceptional. Its rate of increase between 1990 and 1993 was actually three times as fast as that in the 1960s following the Robbins report.[46]

However, in relation to the ambitious expansion targets of the early 1970s the initial rate of achievement was disappointing. These targets had ironically been most clearly stated in Mrs Thatcher's 1972 white paper, *Education: a framework for expansion*. Within ten years, for example, the majority of 3- and 4-year-olds were to have nursery places.[47] Yet as late as 1990 the figure was still as low as 44 per cent. The nature of educational development in the early 1980s was equally disappointing for the New Right, as was again endorsed by Margaret Thatcher in her new guise as a radical visionary. As she instructed her Party conference in 1986, there was an urgent need to:

> bring back the three Rs into our schools; bring back relevance into the curriculum; and bring back discipline into our classrooms . . . . Education at all levels . . . has been infiltrated by a permissive philosophy of self-expression.

Hence the priority accorded education in the 1987 manifesto, with a commit-ment no less fervent than that of New Labour a decade later. Hence also the maelstrom of change triggered by Kenneth Baker's 1988 Education Reform Bill (or, as it was called, the great educational reform bill so that the acronym GERBIL could be used).

The consistent objective of policy thereafter was threefold, to make education:

- economically relevant
- more responsive to its 'consumers'
- accountable.

Relevance

The realization of this objective required the correction of Britain's historic weakness in the provision of technical education and a radical change to the content of education in both schools and higher education.

The task of modernizing technical education was entrusted largely to the MSC rather than the education establishment. It sponsored the Technical and Vocational Education Initiative (TVEI) within schools and City Technical Colleges funded directly by central government, as well as a myriad of over-lapping and ever-changing youth training schemes.[48] After 1987, Baker insisted against Mrs Thatcher's wishes that technology should become a compulsory part of the national curriculum. Finally, in 1990 the provision of industrial training was transferred to Training and Enterprise Councils (or Local Enterprise Councils in Scotland) which, in a further erosion of corpo-ratism, were administered by employers to the exclusion of trade unions.

The dividends from this constant flow of initiatives, however, were disappointing. Britain still appeared to lag behind her international competitors. The reasons hardly changed. Advanced school education continued to be dominated by academic 'A' levels. The alternative National Vocational Qualifications (NVQs), together with other forms of industrial training, were on the whole poorly taught. There were thus good practical reasons why, as late as 1990/1, 44 per cent of 16- to 19-year-olds in Britain rejected formal education or training, compared with only 22 per cent in Japan, Germany and France.[49]

A second way to improve the economic relevance of education was, as suggested by Mrs Thatcher's conference speech, the better teaching of basic skills such as literacy and numeracy in schools. This is where the 1988 Act genuinely achieved a radical break with tradition. For the first time in British history, a national curriculum was to be prescribed. Attainment standards and tests were to be set for children at the age of 7, 11, 14 and 16. Moreover the test results were to be published in national 'league tables' of schools so that the standard of education throughout the country would be made explicit.[50]

A major battle was joined, within government and with the teachers, over the extent of the national curriculum and testing. Baker finally succeeded in securing the ten-subject national curriculum and the four attainment tests which he wanted. Teachers, however, resented the loss of autonomy and the explosion in bureaucracy this involved. Consequently, his success was short-lived. Tests for 7- and 11-year-olds were restricted in 1990 to mathematics, English and science. Then, in one of the few effective demonstrations of professional power after 1979, teachers boycotted the tests altogether in 1993. They were ultimately retained as was the ten-subject curriculum, but the intensity of both was reduced. The percentage of the school day consumed by the national curriculum, for instance, fell from 70 per cent to 60 per cent for older children.

The same principles of greater relevance and transparency were extended to higher education. The 1988 Act abolished the University Grants Committee through which university funding had been distributed autonomously, albeit within constraints that increased in line with financial dependence on government. It was replaced by the University Funding Council, which could impose contracts on universities. The underlying assumption of such contracts, as has been written, was that universities should 'feed the needs of industry, whilst also mimicking its managerial behaviour. The role of universities as independent cultural and academic institutions with unique purposes and justifications [was] thus resolutely eroded'.[51] At the same time polytechnics, on which government had looked with favour because of their lower unit costs and perceived sympathy for the needs of industry, were freed from control by local authorities. Then in 1993 they were linked to, and permitted to call themselves, universities under yet another new funding body, the Higher Educational Funding Councils. Further pressure was exerted to teach 'relevant' subjects. Greater inspection, which in turn generated league tables of both teaching and research attainment, was also introduced.

The issue of a national curriculum exposed the tension between the liberal and conservative strands of New Right ideology (see Section 2.2.3, especially note 37). Keith Joseph, as education minister, had dismissed the idea on the liberal New Right grounds that it entailed too great an increase in central government's power. Rhodes Boyson, the former comprehensive school headmaster who contributed to the Black Papers before becoming a Conservative minister, agreed. For him the curriculum was 'the ultimate triumph of the comprehensive socialist philosophy, part of the command economy'. However, in order to maintain standards, the need to bring Britain into line with Europe had been discussed in official circles since the early 1960s and had been advocated by Callaghan in his 1976 Ruskin College speech.

Once agreed in principle, the detail of the proposal still exposed the tension. To what extent should government dictate the nature of the curriculum? Both Mrs Thatcher and Kenneth Baker had strong views. Mrs Thatcher wanted it to cover only the three 'Rs'. She also had characteristically emphatic ideas on syllabus content. When the curriculum was expanded as desired by Baker, for example to cover ten subjects, she expressed her 'clear – and as I naively imagined uncontroversial – idea of what history was'. This concentrated on British history, the Empire and great men.

In the end, it was agreed that the curriculum should absorb most of the school day, thereby restricting teachers' autonomy. The content of the syllabus, however, should be entrusted not to central government but to educationalists in a National Curriculum Council. Such a decision was soon to be regretted and made an excuse for the perceived failure of the curriculum to achieve desired ends. Even John Major who, because of his own school experiences, placed such store by education bemoaned the fact that it had been 'hijacked by the devotees of progressive learning'.[52]

Responsiveness

An additional advantage of innovations such as league tables was that they provided some comparative information on which parents and students alike could make rational choices. They were thus a major step towards changing the balance between the producers and consumers of welfare, as presaged for example in the Citizen's Charter. They thereby strengthened 'parental power', which the Conservatives' 1997 manifesto identified as a 'vital force for higher standards'.[53]

A more ideologically driven stimulus, which would have given parents and students as consumers not just the knowledge but also the financial power to shape provision, was education vouchers. They were constantly considered and rejected until the fundamental review of 1993. Then a pilot scheme was launched to provide school leavers with £1000 credits for training. It was followed in 1995 by a voucher of equal value for nursery education.

This nursery voucher proved to be the perfect justification for the earlier rejection of such initiatives. It offended both the Conservative principles of targeting and equity. It was a universal payment which was simply used by those already purchasing private schooling to reduce their outgoings. Consequently no increase in provision resulted from this expenditure of scarce public resources. At the same time provision for the poor did not increase but actually declined. Private provision remained unattainable because the voucher only covered half its cost. Meanwhile the number of free state places was cut because the cost of vouchers was financed by decreased grants to Local Education Authorities. Nursery education had long been recognized, not least in Mrs Thatcher's 1972 white paper, as the most effective way in which to ensure equality of opportunity. This was not the way to do it.

Vouchers, in any case, were not just impractical but had also been made increasingly irrelevant in mainstream education by the structural changes effected by the 1988 Act. The Act encouraged 'open enrolment' whereby parents had greater freedom to choose their children's school. It also extended the principle of Local Management of Schools (LMS), whereby LEAs reduced their detailed control over the school budget and staff appointments. Such control could even be ended if schools opted out of local government control and became 'grant maintained schools' funded directly by government. The theoretical consequence of such changes was that schools had to compete, and with independent budgets had the incentive to compete, for pupils. Each brought with them a given sum of money, underwitten by government. In short, as Hills has argued, the net result of the 1988 reforms was that 'parents effectively had a "voucher" for the state education of their children, with which they can shop around between local schools'.[54]

By providing a proxy voucher, the 1988 Education Reform Act also created an 'internal' market in education. Unlike in healthcare, and despite expectations to the contrary, it did not take off quickly. Nor, as in the sale of council houses, were increased incentives effective. Grant maintained schools, for example, were given disproportionately high funding and increasing freedom to select pupils. Nevertheless only 200 of a possible 24,000 schools had opted out by the 1992 election and 1100 by 1997.

These figures were admittedly biased by the willingness of only 2 per cent of primary schools to opt out and the general refusal of Scottish schools, like Scottish hospitals, also to do so. Such reticence, however, was in many ways logical. Parental choice was not greatly strengthened because of difficulties of increasing the capacity of popular schools. The financial independence of school governors and head teachers was likewise constrained by controls imposed by central government. The vast bulk of their budgets was also consumed by nationally negotiated staff pay rates, over which they had little control.[55]

Accountability

The explicit purpose of the 1988 Act was to make the education profession at all levels accountable to its consumer. The irony, and perhaps its implicit purpose, was that it became more directly accountable to the central government.

The major victim in this reordering of power was not the educational establishment but democratically elected local government. In 1988, it lost its traditional and much prized responsibility for polytechnics, other higher educational colleges and those schools which chose to become grant maintained. Then in 1991 it lost its remaining responsibility for further education and sixth-form colleges. At a time when increasing emphasis was being placed on the revival of civil society, this was a somewhat strange fate for the body which had been its institutional embodiment since Victorian times. It made all the more urgent Griffiths's contemporary proposals to expand the role of local authorities as 'enablers' in the personal social services.

A corollary of local government's declining power was a rise in that of the Department of Education. Indeed it has even been argued that, in accordance with public choice theory (see Section 3.1.2), the changes were in effect not driven by ministers but by officials who feared for their jobs once the heroic period of school building was complete.[56] The Department gradually gained direct control over all levels of education. Funding, and therefore real power, was controlled through a series of new agencies. In England, for example, the Further Education Funding Council was established in 1991; the Higher Education Funding Councils became responsible for universities and former polytechnics in 1993; and the Funding Agency for Schools took over the financing of grant maintained schools in 1994. In relation to the content of education, it had long had responsibility for school inspection and acquired new powers as a result of the national curriculum (although, in the spirit of *Next Steps*, both were exercised thorough executive agencies). After its merger with the Department of Employment in 1995, it then assumed control of the Training and Enterprise Councils (TECs).

Such a concentration of power was a perverse achievement for a government committed to 'rolling back the state'. It was an equally perverse legacy of a prime minister (Mrs Thatcher) who, after her experience as the minister who had overseen the closure of the greatest number of grammar schools (see Section 8.2), had vowed vengeance on the Department of Education.

An example of the increasing power of central government was its sending in 'hit squads' to take over the management of schools which Ofsted deemed to be 'failing'. The equivalent in the 1990s to the scandal of William Tyndale, which sparked off the educational backlash of the 1970s (see Section 8.2) was provided by Hackney Downs school in North London. Its examination results, like its discipline, were appalling except in Turkish – a subject which it did not actually teach. It was a symbol of growing political and popular consensus over education policy that such action was not opposed by New Labour.

An emerging consensus?

Educational reform throughout the period generated intense bitterness. There were three principal reasons. In higher education, there was the reduction in expenditure in the early 1980s when numbers (unlike in other educational sectors) were rising. Then the precipitous expansion of the early 1990s was underfunded with the result that unit costs fell by 25 per cent in five years (reflected by a deterioration in the staff:student ratio of 30 per cent). After 11 years of Conservative government, there may still have been some slack within the system, but hardly on the scale to justify such 'efficiency savings'. The other two reasons, already identified in Sections 12.3 and 12.4, were the grossly improvised nature of much policy and public displays of contempt towards the educational profession, particularly after universities' protests against cuts in 1981 and the teachers' disputes of 1984–6. Red tape and professional demoralization were not noticably judicious ways in which to enhance the implementation of policy

For all the bitterness, however, there was evidence of a growing consensus behind that educational reform. The need for a core curriculum had long been accepted. LMS had been pioneered by the Labour-controlled Inner London Education Authority and the Labour Party as a whole favoured greater parental involvement. After its rebranding as New Labour, it also expressed support for action against failing schools and teachers as well as the 'setting' (if not the actual streaming) of classes to raise standards. As the *Economist* of 9 December 1995 remarked, the government had every right to complain: 'Please Sir, Blair and Blunkett keep copying my work!' Most important of all, however, was the common perception that on both economic and social criteria education expenditure was highly desirable.

13.5 HOUSING

In contrast to other social services, public expenditure on housing appeared to collapse. In 1976–7 it was 4.2 per cent of GDP. By 1996–7 it had been halved.[57] The collapse, however, was somewhat illusory and reflected changed priorities and accounting practices rather than a major fall in aggregate expenditure.

The recorded fall, for instance, in net *current* expenditure from £5.5 billion (at 1995–6 prices) to zero can be explained by a new system of finance. There was, as John Hills has explained, 'a switch from public funding through subsidies towards a mixture of public and private funding (through rent and housing benefit) of gross public *provision*, which . . . actually *increased* in real terms over the period'.[58] In other words the general housing subsidy from central to local government, which conventional public accounts recorded, ended. Instead local authorities were encouraged and then, after 1988, obliged to charge full market rents. For the 60 per cent of tenants who could not afford the increased cost there was entitlement to housing benefit, funded by government but classified as social security rather than housing expenditure. The income of local authorities, therefore remained buoyant from a combination of private and publicly subsidized rents. At the same time outgoings were reduced, as inflation eroded the real value of past debts and consequently the cost of servicing of that debt. In consequence, real spending on the management and repair of council property was able to increase by over 4 per cent a year throughout the 1980s.

The corresponding fall in net *capital* expenditure from £11.8 billion to £3 billion was real but less dramatic than it seemed. The reduction in net expenditure (the difference between outgoings and income) in fact represented only a 37 per cent reduction in the *volume* of expenditure. There were three main reasons for this. First, the sizeable receipts from the sale of council houses reduced the need to raise money on the open market. Second, the relative price effect for once actually worked in favour of a social service: building costs actually fell. Third, and even more significantly, there was – as heralded in 1968 – a switch from house building to the more cost-effective policy of renovation. Thus council house completions, as will be seen, may have plummeted but the annual number of renovations soared from 75,000 in 1976 to 400,600 in 1995.

The trend in housing expenditure, therefore, did not diverge as much as it might seem from that of other social policies. Policy in the meantime was characterized by two objectives:

- the sale of council houses
- the establishment of a private market, or at least of a purchaser–provider divide within housing provision.

Selling council houses

The sale of council houses has been seen conventionally to epitomize 'Thatcherism'. Sales had been permitted since the 1950s. However, it was not until 1980 that tenants were given the explicit right, and sizeable inducements, to buy. These inducements started at a discount of 30 per cent on a property's market value for tenants who had lived there for three years, with an extra 1 per cent deduction for each additional year of the tenancy. By the end of the 1980s, to maintain the momentum of sales, the discount had risen to a remarkable 70 per cent. As a result, annual sales exceeded 100,000 throughout the 1980s and by 1992 approximately 1.75 million tenants had bought their homes. This permanently transformed the nature of the housing stock. Whereas local government had owned a third of properties in 1976, its share by 1995 was only 19 per cent. In contrast, owner-occupancy had soared from 55 per cent to 67 per cent. This placed Britain in the vanguard of a trend which was soon to affect other major Western countries.

Mrs Thatcher, as has been seen, had initially opposed the policy in 1974. Once converted, however, she fully identified herself with it. She even travelled to Forres in the North of Scotland in 1986 to witness the handover of the one millionth property. It epitomized all she stood for. Council estates, in her opinion, were 'breeding grounds of socialism, dependency, vandalism and crime'.[59] Home ownership, in contrast, encouraged 'all the virtues of good citizenship'. These included personal responsibility, self-sufficiency and, of course, voting Conservative. More fundamentally, as argued by Hayek, it also provided a bulwark against an overpowerful state (see Section 2.2.3). When, in a deliberate parody of Labour's slogan of the early 1970s, Michael Heseltine claimed sales represented an 'irreversible shift of wealth in favour of working people and away from the state' he might, therefore, also have added that they represented an irreversible shift in power.[60] Finally, there was the small matter of the £28 billion raised by the sales. This made it the most profitable of all the privatization programmes, exceeding the value of the combined sale of British Telecom, British Gas and electricity. The sales could therefore be presented as a major reduction in net public expenditure.

As with so many initiatives under Mrs Thatcher, however, the policy also had serious internal contradictions. Its economic benefits were questionable. It may have encouraged economic mobility, but it discouraged wealth creation by diverting resources from industrial investment. It may have encouraged personal responsibility, but it also encouraged reckless borrowing and inflation. This, as has been seen in Section 12.2, resulted in the overvaluation of the housing market in the early 1990s and a rash of repossession and negative equity. It also generated inequality, with an ever-widening gap opening up between the personal wealth of those who owned property and those who did not. This was particularly inequitable since 'self-sufficient' owner-occupiers were acquiring their relative wealth at public expense through tax relief on mortgage interest repayments (see above, note 15). Inequality also increased as those living in 'desirable' estates (where sales predominated) became physically separated from those trapped in 'sink' estates (where sales were few). This, as will be seen, had major repercussions when a radical attempt was made to privatize the management of the most deprived estates.

The converse of council house sales was the collapse of council house building. In 1975, there were 145,600 completions by local authorities and new towns. In 1995 the figure had fallen to a mere 1900. The fall was cushioned by a simultaneous rise in housing association completions from approximately 15,000 to 38,500 and, as has been seen, a substantial increase in renovation.

However, a lack of social housing was a major reason for increasing homelessness. Statistics can be misleading because of changes in the method of calculation, but the number of people who were statutorily homeless in Great Britain, and for whom local authorities were bound to find accommodation, appears to have risen from 70,000 in 1979 to a peak of 180,000 in 1992. It then fell away to 135,000 by 1995. The total number of people in England simultaneously being subsidized in private accommodation rose from under 5000 in 1980 to a peak of 63,000 in 1992.

→

A return to the phenomenon of people sleeping rough in city centres has been taken to epitomize 'Thatcherism' as much as the sale of council houses. Mrs Thatcher was unsympathetic to the 'roofless' and particularly the young. They should, she thought, return to their families. This overlooked the fact that there often were no families or that, if there were, it was abuse within them that was the cause of homelessness.

Creating markets

Following the 1987 election, housing – like education, the NHS and the personal social services – was the subject of radical legislation. The 1988 Housing Act has been called the Conservatives' most coherent housing policy since 1953.[61] In relation to short-term results, however, it was the least successful of the four initiatives.

Allusion has already been made to the *financial* objectives and consequences of the Act. Direct government subsidies to local government were to end and council tenants were required to pay full economic rents. They could no longer be subsidized from local authorities' general revenue. The objective was to ensure that the public rental market was competing with the private one on equal terms. To further revive the latter, rent controls were finally removed and two new forms of lease introduced. These were assured tenancies (which guaranteed tenants security and landlords a full 'market' rent) and shorthold tenancies (which guaranteed tenants a 'fair' rent and landlords repossession of their property).

In terms of the *provision* of social housing, construction of new property was to be the responsibility not of councils but of the approximately 34,000 non-profit-making housing associations, which were deemed to be more responsive and responsible institutions. They were required to raise an increasing percentage of their finance from the private sector. As for existing property, two new schemes were designed to relieve councils of their traditional responsibilities. They mirrored the principle of opting out and 'hit squads' in education. Under 'tenants' choice', private landlords and housing associations were to be encouraged to bid for the right to manage council estates. Tenants were then required to vote on whether they wished to 'opt out' of local government control or not. Into those estates for which no-one sensibly would make a bid, Housing Action Trusts (HATs) could be sent under the watchful eye of the Department of the Environment. They were to assume control, renovate and then pass them on to another landlord, provided that it was not a local authority. In short, local government was to be deprived of its role as the provider of housing. As with community care, it was essentially to become an 'enabler'. It would oversee the building, management and allocation of housing in its own area. It would also purchase accommodation for those who were statutorily homeless.

In the short term, the Act had little effect. By 1997, only 230,000 houses had been transferred from local authority control. Neither private landlords and housing associations nor the tenants themselves could be persuaded by incentives which, as in the sale of council housing, were forever increasing. Only five HATs were established. Even the requirement that housing associations should raise money privately backfired, as the cost of borrowing forced rents so high that only those on housing benefit could afford them. This underlined the fundamental contradictions within policy. The sale of council houses had left behind in the 'sink' estates those tenants who were the least likely to take the risk of opting for an alternative form of management. Meanwhile housing associations, which were designed to encourage independence, started increasingly to cater for those dependent on housing benefit. When change eventually came, therefore, it came from an oblique source: councils who were increasingly frustrated by restrictions on their role and wished to end it.

> Mrs Thatcher's immediate reaction to victory in 1987 was that 'we really have a big job to do in the inner cities'. It was left unclear whether this meant political or socio-economic regeneration. The Conservatives did not thereafter capture the inner-city vote. As exemplified by the regeneration of Docklands in the East London, however, they did physically transform many inner cities. Not least because it was achieved by private corporations rather than by local authorities, such regeneration has also been taken to epitomize 'Thatcherism'. Surprisingly it escapes mention in her memoirs.

Conclusion

The record of housing policy after 1976 was not as bleak as has sometimes been painted. The average quality of housing improved. The actual shortage fell from over 1.5m units in 1971 to under half a million after 1986; and the percentage of the population living in houses without the five basic amenities had fallen from 11 per cent to a mere 1 per cent by 1991. The variety of housing stock also improved. Owner-occupancy accounted for over two-thirds and by its expansion had increased the quality of many people's lives. Rented accommodation was divided between the private (amounting to 7 per cent) and social housing, which itself was divided between local councils (at 19 per cent) and housing associations (at 4 per cent). Greater competition led to its better management. Nevertheless social housing had rapidly become a ghetto for the disadvantaged. Combined with the increase in homelessness, housing policy thus provided a physical expression of the increased inequality which was such a pronounced consequence of economic and social policy under 18 years of Conservative government.

13.6 CONCLUSION

'Thatcherism', to the extent that it is defined by the personal views of Mrs Thatcher on welfare policy, was in essence – as Hugo Young argued –a mosaic of basic instincts, albeit underpinned by New Right thinking (largely from the very different world of welfare in the USA). Those instincts were rooted in a fundamental belief in personal initiative and personal responsibility.

Personal initiative was best encouraged and assured by the free market. This required the rolling back of the state's *economic* power through, for example, privatization, the ending of Keynesian demand management and tax reductions. It also required the emasculation of institutional impediments to the effective working of the market, such as those imposed by trade unions and corporatist employers.

Personal responsibility could only be assured by the ending of a dependency culture and the assurance of effective choice in those services which had to be financed by government (either directly or, preferably, through tax allowances and vouchers). This meant a rolling back of the state's *social* responsibilities, with firm limits placed on both its aggregate expenditure and its direct provision of services. It also meant the emasculation of those who institutionally supported an extended state, most notably the unionized and professionalized 'producers' of welfare.

By this definition, 'Thatcherism' was diametrically opposed to the social democratic consensus which was perceived to underpin the evolution of the classic welfare state (see the quotation from Donnison in Section 2.2.2). It had assumed that within 'Middle England' there was a consensus that greater equality could and should be achieved through a combination of higher taxation and more generous social services. 'Government and its social services' were the 'natural vehicles of progress'. Welfare professionals were their 'trusted' instruments. 'Thatcherism', in short, was fundamentally opposed to the basic values and institutions of the classic welfare state. In office, Mrs Thatcher was committed to dismantling it.

During Mrs Thatcher's premiership, the economic foundations of the classic welfare state were indeed dismantled. In social policy, however, there was no such dismantling. The management of each major service was radically overhauled; but the cost and scope of the government's responsibilities remained largely unimpaired. An effective attack was launched on both only after the 'fundamental review' of 1993. The reward was not, as anticipated, ringing endorsement but rather devastating defeat. In the 1997 general election the Conservatives lost 171 seats and, for the first time in its history, failed to win any in Scotland and Wales. Moreover within two years Peter Lilley, one of the authors of the 'fundamental review' and the Party's then deputy leader, was publicly arguing that the Conservatives would not become electable until they 'openly and emphatically accept that the free market has only a limited role [to play] in improving public services like health, education and welfare'.[62] Why, in social policy, was so little 'Thatcherism' achieved while

Mrs Thatcher was prime minister? Why, after it had been more fully implemented, did it appear to be so emphatically rejected?

Despite her public reputation for decisiveness, more radical action was
stalled during Mrs Thatcher's term in office by a combination of confusion,
caution and contradiction. Reforming legislation, particularly after 1987, was
confused. It was neither planned nor presented in the rational way which
would have fostered greater support (outside and within the relevant service)
and ensured efficient implementation. Typically Mrs Thatcher was also
extremely cautious in translating her instincts, and rhetoric, into action. The
classic example was the reform of the NHS after 1987. She appointed the
right-wing John Moore to 'think the unthinkable', but then repeatedly
accused him of proposing the impractical. He was replaced by Kenneth
Clarke, a known adherent of the principle of a tax-funded service to which she
and Moore were opposed. Finally when, against considerable opposition,
Clarke was driving through the introduction of 'internal markets' – the
managerial innovation on which her government's reputation for radicalism
in social policy was to be based – she sought at the last minute to disown him.

Such caution was in part a reaction to the contradictions in principle which
were exposed once the attempt was made to translate instincts and rhetoric
into action. From the many, four may be singled out. Mrs Thatcher desired to
reinvigorate civil society and yet was deeply hostile to local government, its
traditional embodiment. She desired to roll back the state and yet was eager
to regulate behaviour (through, for example, the national curriculum and
greater inspection) or to influence it (especially through tax allowances, which
effectively increased public expenditure). She desired to end welfare dependency and yet championed targeted means-tested benefit which, by discouraging saving and creating the poverty trap, institutionalized dependency.
Finally, she desired to make public services more responsive and yet cut their
budgets and abused their staff.

Such contradictions reflected in turn a broader dilemma with which
'Thatcherism' was confronted: the extent to which support for state welfare
was embedded in both British institutions and culture. Private enterprise and
tax-payers might vociferously demand a rolling back of the state in principle,
but in practice neither was willing to facilitate or support it. Private enterprise, for instance, was consistently encouraged to offer alternatives to state
provision, be it private health insurance and pensions, the private management of council estates or the sponsoring of City Technology Schools.
Typically it declined to do so – or at least demanded so heavy a subsidy without regulation ('red-tape') that public expenditure, but not necessarily expenditure on the public, would have increased.

The public themselves, as polled at and between elections, expressed broad
continuing support for the welfare state. In part this was because it, and the
NHS particularly, was seen as integral to a concept of fairness and thus of
Britishness. In part, and less altruistically, it was also because it was seen to be
to everyone's individual advantage. The welfare state continued to redistribute resources. Redistribution, however, was not merely vertical – from the

virtuous to the 'idle'. Rather, like savings in a 'piggy' bank, it was horizontal – over a person's lifetime. Three-quarters of an individual's payments made into the system, so it has been calculated, was returned to the same individual when it was needed. Thus it made good a loss of earned income (through, for example unemployment or sickness) or met exceptional need (when a parent or in old age).[63] For everyone, therefore, it provided a fundamental sense of social security. For everyone it also provided, as was additionally recognized, a more efficient and cost-effective service than private enterprise could offer. This was consistently confirmed in relation to the NHS by the Treasury.

If 'Thatcherism' did not and could not dismantle the welfare state, therefore, did it successfully restructure it? By the mid-1970s, as has been seen, the classic welfare state was in crisis. As Donnison has written of the internal tension and the political opportunity that then existed:

> In the late seventies, Labour ministers were aware that, although they could never satisfy their critics in the poverty lobbies, the government's aims were generally far more progressive than the electorate's. Their Conservative successors more brutally recognised that the lobby was electorally naked . . . . 'They are not leaders of a movement', said a Cabinet Minister . . . . 'They're crickets in a field'.[64]

Was the resurrection of the welfare state after this crisis due to its effective modernisation? Was there, as Pierson has suggested occurred worldwide, a successful identification of both new policy priorities and more efficient means to deliver of old ones?

New policy priorities were certainly established. Politically, welfare expenditure was capped and a 'new austerity' introduced in response to the taxpayers' revolt of the mid-1970s. Economically, demand management was dropped and new supply-side measures (such as enhanced training and 'welfare-to-work' measures) initiated to enable the market to respond more effectively to the increased competitiveness of a global economy. Socially, the responsiveness of the 'producers' of welfare was enhanced so that the choice and standards of public services could match more closely those to which consumers were accustomed in the private sector.

Such responsiveness was the result of a managerial revolution within the public sector, epitomized by the introduction of internal markets. The power and dominant assumptions of the professions and unions were broken in a series of confrontations – the long strikes, for example, by civil servants in 1981, within the NHS in 1982 and by teachers in 1986. Competitive pressures then ensured a concentration on consumers' needs and cost-effectiveness. These were both qualities in which the classic welfare state had been culpably lacking. The groundwork was therefore laid for the more efficient delivery of traditional goals. As was said of the internal market within the NHS, for example, 'the new system' forced decisions out of 'cowardly politicians' which had for too long been postponed. It might have been added that the professions and administrators had been equally remiss.

Was the ultimate achievement of 'Thatcherism', therefore, not the dismantling of the welfare state but the somewhat ironic one of saving the welfare state from dismantlement? In the 1970s the *classic* welfare state had fallen into disrepute because of its perceived ineffectuality and inefficiency. The very real danger existed that, were no remedial action taken, support for state welfare – despite its embeddedness in popular culture and institutions – might eventually be fatally compromised. Policy priorities and service delivery, however, were 'recalibrated'; and popular support, albeit for a rather different form of state welfare, duly restored. This had certainly been the underlying object of many Conservative ministers who served under Mrs Thatcher and later opposed the ideological thrust behind the fundamental review. Thus Kenneth Clarke, for all his hostility to local government and welfare professionals, announced with characteristic pugnacity on his appointment as chancellor in 1993:

> Anyone who thinks I came into office in order to dismantle the welfare state has not the slightest idea where I come from nor my record . . .. I am not remotely interested in dismantling the welfare state. I have spent my entire lifetime seeking to modernise it, seeking to give it a chance of survival.[65]

Such sentiments, however, could not be ascribed to the person whose own pugnacity and tenacity initially provoked the restructuring. Indeed Mrs Thatcher, rather than saving the welfare state, might be said to have been saved by it. Sporadic rioting broke out in inner cities in 1981 and 1985 and over the poll tax in 1990. Escalating unemployment and inequality could have sustained more prolonged unrest. Social distress, however, was cushioned by the continuing assurance through welfare benefits of a minimum income for all. Although its redistributory function may have been largely horizontal, the welfare state did still transfer some resources vertically. Through a combination of taxation and benefits (in kind as well as cash) the poorest third, so it has been confirmed, were supported by the better-off. 'With the possible exception of higher education spending on students who live away from home', as Hills has concluded, 'the value of benefits and services going to those with lower incomes is greater than the taxes which they pay to finance them (under any plausible allocation of financing costs).'

The welfare state also cushioned the impact of growing inequality.[66] Inequality was admittedly increased by some government action, such as the cutting of direct taxes and of benefits. It was, however, mainly generated by the market. There was an increasing divergence in individual rates of pay as the result of economic restructuring. There was a parallel divergence in family incomes as a result of the simultaneous increase in high-earning professional women and a decrease in skilled male unemployed. As a Marxist might have predicted, in other words, the welfare state did not just support the freer market but modified its consequences.

During the restructuring of the welfare state after 1976, as has been noted, there was the gradual evolution of an alternative to the postwar social democratic consensus. The Labour Party, particularly as the consequence of four election defeats, gradually accepted the new policy priorities and delivery systems. Consequently, in deference to the 'new austerity' its manifesto in 1997 promised that a Labour government would be 'wise spenders not big spenders'. Economically, the commitment to maintain full employment was suspended and supply-side measures to support the market readily embraced, such as 'welfare-to-work' initiatives. Socially, the internal market was accepted. So too were the means of achieving higher standards and better discipline within schools.

However, despite a casual remark of Peter Mandleson in 2002 that 'we are all Thatcherites now', such a burgeoning consensus could not be called 'Thatcherite'.[67] Mrs Thatcher may have provoked the restructuring of the welfare state; but 'Thatcherism', not least because it was geared essentially to dismantlement, could not dictate the nature of its successful modernization. This was true both when she was in power and, more particularly, after 1993. What then were to be the new principles underlying state welfare, once the classic welfare state had been radically transformed in the light of changed economic and social circumstance? That was the key challenge awaiting New Labour in power.

13.7 FURTHER READING

The best introductions to social policy after 1975 are N. Timmins, *The Five Giants* (2001), with its command of oral and newspaper testimony; and H. Glennerster, *British Social Policy since 1945* (Oxford, 2000), with its command of the latest research findings emanating from the London School of Economics. From the same source comes the authoritative H. Glennerster and J. Hills (eds), *The State of Welfare: the welfare state in Britain since 1974* (Oxford, 1998) although some may find the first edition edited by J. Hills in 1990 a more rewarding, if more complex, quarry of information and ideas; H. Glennerster, *Paying for Welfare: towards 2000* (Hemel Hempstead, 1997), the third edition of a classic; and J. Lewis and H. Glennerster, *Implementing the New Community Care* (Milton Keynes, 1996) which provides a forensic examination of the introduction of 'internal markets' in its chosen policy area. The latter can be supplemented by R. Means, H. Moreby and R. Smith, *From Community Care to Market Care?* (Bristol, 2002), written from a local authority perspective. J. Hills, *The Future of the Welfare State: a guide to the debate* (York, 1997) was an illuminating brief survey provided for the 1997 election. Another brief retrospective is P. Wilding, 'The welfare state and the Conservatives', *Political Studies*, 45 (1997) 716–26.

Analyses of individual policy areas are listed in the bibliographies of the above books and in the notes to the chapter. Two works deserve greater prominence. C. Ham, R. Robinson and M. Benzeval, *Health Check: healthcare reforms in an international context* (1990) provides in brief an exceptional comparative account of the reform of the NHS. D. Price, *Office of Hope: a history of the employment service* (2000) is a unique insider account of the administrative confusion and angst created by the managerial revolution in the civil service and the evolution of the 'welfare-to-work' programme. The *Journal of Social Policy* provides, in its back numbers, quarterly summaries of policy developments and, in current editions, the latest research and reviews of relevant literature.

chapter 14

New Labour and Welfare since 1997

CONTENTS

The rise of New Labour

1985 Kinnock attack on Militant Tendency – starts reform of 'old' Labour Party

1987 Election defeat

1989 (Berlin Wall falls – end of cold war)

1990 Commitment to full employment dropped

1992 (Clinton wins US presidency as 'New Democrat'). Election defeat. Smith replaces Kinnock as leader

1993 Windfall tax on utilities proposed. One man one vote (OMOV) for local selection of MPs

1994 Blair leader on Smith's death. Social Justice Commission advocates 'active' welfare state. Giddens, *Beyond Left and Right*

1995 Clause 4 replaced by commitment to equal opportunity and social justice. Union block vote at conference reduced to 50 per cent

1996 (Personal Responsibility and Work Opportunity Reconciliation Act – introduces New Deal in USA)

1997 Election victory: majority 182

New Labour in power

1997 (Chequers seminar on Third Way). Bank of England in charge of monetary policy. EU Social Charter accepted. Windfall and private pensions tax. Social Exclusion Unit established. 47 MPs oppose cuts in lone parent's benefit ➜

1998	First comprehensive spending review (Cm 4001). New Deal launched. *A New Contract for Welfare* (Cm 3895) – emasculated plan, Harman and Field resign. *Partnership in Pensions* (Cm 4179) – stakeholder pensions. School Standards and Framework Act – educational zones. Literacy hour and university student fees introduced. National childcare strategy and Surestart launched		then minimum income guarantee introduced. Standards in Scotland's Schools Act – no opt out
1999	(Scottish Parliament and Welsh Assembly open. Kosovo war. Florence seminar on Third Way). Budget announces 1 per cent cut in income tax, childcare tax credit. Working families tax credit starts. Minimum wage introduced. NICE and CHI introduced to NHS. Numeracy hour introduced. Pledge to abolish child poverty. Sutherland report, *With Respect to Old Age* (Cm 4192). 67 MPs oppose cuts to disability benefit	2001	(World Trade Centre terror attack). Election: majority 167. New Deal – compulsory interviews. Children's tax credit. Learning and Skills Councils replace TECS. Pledge of 50 per cent in higher education
		2002	(Afghanistan war). Budget – major spending increases, increased national insurance contributions. Third comprehensive spending review. Wanless report, *Securing our Future Health.* Jobcentre Plus – unites benefits and jobsearch. Vocational GCSEs introduced. National Care Standards Commission. Community Care and Health Act (Scotland) – free personal care. Confrontation with unions over PFI
2000	(Fuel protest against stealth taxes). Flu epidemic – Blair promises to raise health spending to European average. NHS Plan and concordat with private sector. Second comprehensive spending review and Budget – major public expenditure rises. Pensions rise by 75p	2003	(Iraq war). Child tax credit, working tax credit and pension credit introduced. Vote on foundation hospitals – parliamentary majority reduced to 35
		2004	Ten foundation hospitals established. Vote on university tuition fees – parliamentary majority reduced to 5. Major cuts in Whitehall proposed to fund more frontline staff

The following two chapters must necessarily be more impressionistic than earlier ones. For them some measure of historical perspective was possible. For the period after 1997 and, more particularly, after the 2001 election no such perspective is available. Consequently, both the criteria and information on which analysis is based must be highly provisional. So too must be any conclusion about the broad issues these chapters are addressing:

- What, in terms of redistribution, has been the broad outcome of New Labour's policy? Has the rapid increase in inequality, evident since the demise of the classic welfare state, been halted or even reversed?

- Is it legitimate to talk of a new welfare consensus? On what principles is this new consensus based?
- Has the constructive restructuring of the welfare state continued in response to changed economic, social and political pressures? To the extent that such pressures are international, is it legitimate once again to talk of Britain as a welfare pioneer rather than a welfare laggard?

This chapter, after a brief discussion of the nature of evidence available, will examine the broad economic and political context in which welfare policy developed. It will ask in particular:

- To what extent did the economy permit New Labour, unlike previous Labour governments, to develop its welfare policy freely?
- Given the speculative nature of the 'Third Way' in 1997 (see Section 2.2.4), what was the political process by which rhetoric was translated into reality?
- What conflicts did this process provoke within the Labour Party?

The next chapter will examine the development of policy in each of the core areas of welfare, before drawing some conclusions.

14.1 PROBLEMS OF EVIDENCE

Historians cavilling at the lack of perspective with which to make judgements might be criticized for protesting too much. After all, no historical judgement is anything more than provisional (see Section 2.4). Furthermore, as will be seen, there have been several well-informed journalistic and academic commentaries on New Labour. The input of social scientists has also been critical to many policy initiatives, not least the work of the Social Exclusion Unit established in 1997 to address the root causes of poverty.

Nevertheless social scientists, let alone journalists, should exercise some modesty in issuing instant judgements. The proven frailties of economists in government, for example, should not be forgotten (see Section 3.2). Nor should the way in which perceptions of a welfare 'crisis' in the mid-1970s were coloured by academic debate having become locked into certain inflexible assumptions, be they based on Keynesianism or a structuralist explanation of poverty (see Chapter 1). A classic example of such academic conservatism was the letter written by 364 Keynesian economists to *The Times* in 1981 forecasting disaster at the very time that the economy was about to revive.

A similar incident occurred within six months of the 1997 election. Fifty-four social scientists wrote to the *Financial Times* accusing New Labour of having 'erased redistribution from the map altogether, despite the massive redistribution from poor to rich achieved by the Conservatives'.[1] The focus of their anger was that on taking office New Labour, unlike all previous Labour governments, had refused to make significant increases in cash benefits.

However, in essence, there was little disagreement between the authors and the government. Redistribution was implicit from the start in many policies and it was explicitly acknowledged as a fundamental objective by the Prime Minister in 2002.[2] There was also agreement that effective redistribution required sustained long-term action. Where disagreement arose was over short-term tactics. Given scarce resources, did the cost of long-term action precluded immediate concessions (see Section 3.2.2)? Given the 'new austerity', was a muted strategy essential to retain electoral and financial confidence without which re-election and the realization of long-term policy goals would not be possible? After all, even in more favourable times, the retention of such confidence had not been a notable feature of Labour's traditional redistributive policies.

The letter's logic was that traditional tactics should be retained. Social justice demanded some immediate redistribution. The principle of redistribution had also to be actively championed to win public hearts and minds. Only time can tell whether the government's new tactics were justified by the ultimate achievement of agreed ends. Similarly only new evidence can reveal whether the letter simply damaged the government or, more positively, stiffened minister's suspect resolve. What is incontrovertible, however, is that the letter underlines the permanent tension within much academic research between objective assessment of policy and partisan policy prescription which, by definition, cannot appreciate all contingent factors and unintended policy consequences.

If effective criteria on which to assess policy are elusive, so too is reliable evidence. Where goals are commendably long term, as with the drive to minimize social exclusion and particularly to eradicate child poverty within a generation, this is inevitable. Reliable evidence, however, is also lacking for the monitoring of such programme's progress and the attainment of more short-term goals.

This is in part because of New Labour's heavily criticized and deserved reputation for 'spin' and 'trickery with figures'.[3] A notorious example of this was Gordon Brown's parliamentary speech introducing the 1998 comprehensive spending review. He added together the projected annual increases over the following three years, with no allowance for inflation, and presented them as though they were a one-off increase: 'an extra £21 billion for health and an extra £19 billion for education'. This implied a 50 per cent increase, whereas the real annual rise was only 5 per cent. A desire to gain full political credit for a major investment in public services was understandable given two years of self-imposed restraint (ironically *honouring* an election pledge). Such misrepresentation, however, discredited government.

More seriously, misinformation – or the potential for misrepresentation – is embedded in the policy-making process. Three examples must suffice. Targets, and penalties for service deliverers not meeting targets, quickly became a key measure by which to judge political success and administrative efficiency. As a sequence of whistleblowers and reports from the National Audit Office revealed, the opportunities and incentives were considerable for the non-reporting or misreporting of inconvenient facts. For example, hospital waiting lists (recording those patients awaiting hospital admission having seen a consultant) could be shortened by delaying patients' access to consultants.

Second, in response to long-term criticism that an annual budget drafted in secrecy was a deeply flawed way in which to design and debate so important an issue as public expenditure, a more open planning process has been developed on precedents set by the Conservatives. There is now a comprehensive spending review in the June/July of alternate years providing an outline plan for the succeeding three years. In the November/December of each year, there is then a pre-budget statement detailing the broad objectives and assumptions underlying the forthcoming budget. The budget, in which firm decision are announced, is then delivered in March/April. A perverse consequence of such openness, however, is that policy initiatives can be – and have been – announced three times. This obscures the precise sequence of policy changes, and their combined impact and interrelationship.

Finally, tax credits have become one of New Labour's most favoured policies for alleviating poverty. They are used to redistribute money by either reducing an individual's tax liability or, if that is too low, by providing that individual with additional income. As will be seen, they have many positive benefits for claimants. However, in the climate of 'new austerity' where electorates are perceived to oppose higher public expenditure and taxation, they have an additional political advantage. Just like tax relief on mortgage interest repayments (which traditionally disguised the public subsidy to home owners), tax credits are essentially a form of 'tax expenditure'. In other words they are revenue which government foregoes rather than, like cash benefits, a payment government makes. Consequently, despite their actual cost by 2003 of £1.6 billion, they can – and have – been formally presented as incurring no public expenditure. Indeed they have even been presented as tax cuts. In 2002 an international agreement regularized the situation. Tax reductions are still not formally counted as expenditure, but income supplements are. Nevertheless, this does not clarify the past and it still remains, in Glennerster's words, extremely 'difficult to track' with confidence 'what these massively important changes really cost'.[4]

14.2 ECONOMIC GROWTH

Between 1997 and 2004 the British economy enjoyed, as Gordon Brown was to boast in his 2004 budget, its longest period of sustained growth since the industrial revolution. The annual rate of growth never fell below 2.1 per cent. This was, of course, an immense boon for the development of welfare policy. Public expenditure was not drained away by high unemployment, as it had been in the early 1980s and 1990s. Government revenue rose. Investment in public services could therefore be increased without any significant increase in taxation. Buoyant labour markets also provided the ideal conditions in which to expand the 'welfare-to-work' programmes, which New Labour made central to its drive to modernize the social security system.

Sustained economic growth was not an international phenomenon. There were, for instance, economic crises in the Far East in 1998 and again in both the USA and Japan in 2002. In continental Europe, growth was also more sluggish and unemployment higher than in Britain. In 1997 and 2000, for example, unemployment in the 'Eurozone' was 10.6 per cent and 9 per cent respectively, whereas the comparable figures in the UK were 7.1 per cent and 5.4 per cent.[5] To what extent could New Labour claim credit for Britain's exceptionalism?

Some credit was clearly due. The wholly unexpected transfer of control over monetary policy to the Bank of England (see Section 2.1) was important for the retention of financial confidence, too frequently denied previous Labour governments. So too was the Chancellor's insistence on 'prudence'. This meant abiding by his golden economic rules. These bore an uncanny resemblance to Treasury orthodoxy in the 1930s and included a commitment to balance the budget over the economic cycle; to borrow only to finance capital expenditure; and to keep the size of the National Debt below 40 per cent of GDP.

Indeed when the sale of third-generation mobile phone licences gave him a bonanza of £22.5 billion, it was used not to boost expenditure but to write off debt. The prudence of such a decision was soon demonstrated. As a result of the Iraq war and slower than expected growth, the Chancellor had in his 2004 budget to increase borrowing from the forecasted £27 billion to £37 billion. This sparked inevitable criticism from the press and the City of London. It could easily be rebuffed, however, because the national debt remained both within its agreed limit and one of the lowest in western Europe

There was, however, a limit to the credit New Labour could claim. The period of sustained growth commenced in 1992 under the Conservatives. Indeed it was a measure of their total disarray, not least over welfare policy, that in 1997 they suffered so catastrophic an electoral defeat in such propitious economic circumstances. Growth was also dependent on the flexibility of the British labour market. The foundations for this had been laid before 1997 at the cost of high unemployment and a restriction of trade union rights, which New Labour only partially restored by signing the social chapter of the Maastricht treaty and the European Working Time Directive.

More seriously, Britain's traditional economic weaknesses appeared yet to be solved. Productivity remained low. The industrial sector continued to contract, with the loss of some 150,000 jobs between 1997 and 2001. The visible trade balance also escalated. This all potentially spells serious trouble in the future.

Full employment was a term, like redistribution, initially eschewed by New Labour. The commitment to attain it had been formally abandoned in 1990. It was partially restored in 1997 in the deliberately evasive phrase of a 'high and stable' level of employment, first used in the 1944 *Employment Policy* white paper. 'Full employment' was then revived as an aspiration by David Blunkett and by Gordon Brown at the 1999 Labour Party conference.[6] Its attainment 'in every region' duly became a commitment in the 2001 manifesto.

Such linguistic niceties reflected changing perceptions of what was practicable. By 1999 the trend was established, and by 2002 the reality achieved, of reducing unemployment to 5 per cent (by the agreed international measure) or to 3 per cent (by the traditional British count of those 'out-of-work and claiming benefit'): 5 per cent had been Keynes' definition of full employment; 3 per cent had been that of Beveridge and the Attlee government. In any case, by both definitions the target of 8.5 per cent, assumed in the 1944 white paper, had transparently been surpassed (see Section 4.1).[7]

14.3   POLITICAL EVOLUTION

In 2002, Tony Blair identified three phases in New Labour's evolution.[8] The first he called 'becoming a modern centre-left party'. This lasted from the shock of election defeat in 1992 to the landslide victory of 1997. The second was 'laying firm foundations'. This covered the first two years in office, during which New Labour was bound by election promises to stay within the Conservatives' spending plans. The third was 'driving through reform'. This phase started in April 1999, once the straitjacket had been removed, and may usefully be subdivided in the autumn of 2002 when there was a subtle change in emphasis from the funding to the delivery of services.

This periodization has been attacked as oversimplistic and for suggesting order where little existed. Such dangers are inherent in any periodization.

14.3.1   Creating a modern centre-left party

The development of welfare policy after 1997 was assisted not just by an unparalleled period of economic growth but also by an unparalleled outbreak of discipline within the Labour Party. This was a direct consequence of defeat in the 1992 election, which the Party had confidently expected to win. The momentum of party reform, commenced under Kinnock's leadership (1984–92), was accelerated.

Modernization took two forms. First, there were further changes to the Party constitution to enable the leadership to develop, and retain support for, moderate policies. Thus, to disable unrepresentative cliques, the principle of 'one man one vote' (applied to the choice of Party leader in 1988) was extended to the local selection of MPs. The union block vote at party conferences was also reduced to 50 per cent.

Second, there was the actual development of a moderate policy. The object was to acknowledge the fundamental social and cultural changes since the 1970s and thereby widen the party's appeal beyond its core voters. 'Society changed and we refused to change with it' Blair pronounced on becoming leader.[9] The first fruits of the rethink were the report of the Social Justice Commission in 1994 and the development of the even more moderate 'Third Way' (see Section 2.2.4). Its symbolic victory was the abandonment in 1995 of Clause 4 of the Party's constitution committing it to the 'common ownership of the means of production, distribution and exchange'. By the mid-1990s the Labour Party had finally started to reach the accommodation with postwar capitalism that other European social democratic parties, particularly in Sweden and Germany, had reached in the 1950s.

Modernization, by this definition, was far from all triumphant. After the election victory of 1997, traditional tensions remained within the Party. For example, MPs and trade unions continued to vote against government policy in Parliament and at Conference, particularly on welfare measures. There was also little evidence that the 'Third Way', despite a series of high-profile international conferences, won either hearts or minds. In Peter Riddell's classic phrase New Labour remained 'something of a guerilla band, less the long march than the long seminar'.[10] Moreover, as with the economy, there were some ominous signs for the future. Labour Party membership collapsed after 1997 and public sector workers, represented by the most powerful unions within the Party, became increasingly demoralized. The winning of elections and the delivery of 'world class' public services becomes the more difficult when those, upon whose work success depends, are so disaffected.

Nevertheless, in the short term the leadership was neither as constrained nor as embarrassed as it had been in the past by conference rebellions, trade union intransigence or by industrial disruption. In addition, any shortcomings in relation to modernization paled into insignificance when compared to the state of the Conservative Party. After 1997 it failed to establish any continuity in either its leadership or policy. Three leaders followed Major in quick succession (Hague to 2001, Duncan Smith to 2003 and then Howard). The dilemma bequeathed by Mrs Thatcher remained unresolved over whether the welfare state should be dismantled or restructured – although, typically, the leaders of the 1993 fundamental review recanted (see Section 13.6). This impotence handed power to New Labour, just as the impotence of Old Labour in the 1980s had left Mrs Thatcher unchallenged.[11] Arguably, the Conservatives were further from being a modern centre-right party than they had been when espousing 'One Nationism' under Macmillan in the 1960s.

The limitations of modernization were illustrated by continuing dissension in Parliament and the collapse of Labour Party membership.

In 2003, 121 Labour MPs voted against the government over the Iraq war. Dissent was most common, however, over welfare policy. There were four major rebellions: 47 MPs voted against cuts in lone parent's benefit in 1997; a further 67 rebelled against cuts in disability benefits in 1999; 62 then voted against foundation hospitals in 2003 (reducing the government's nominal majority of 167 to 35); and finally, 72 voted against university tuition fees in 2004 (reducing the majority to a mere 5). Each of these votes reflected deep divisions within the Party. They were confirmed by the use of the union block vote at Conference to defeat policies such as the creation of foundation hospitals (as in 2003).

In 1997, it was hoped that Labour Party membership would reach one million. However it was then at its peak of 405,000. By 2004 it had declined to 248,000, a figure lower than when Blair had become leader ten years earlier.

14.3.2   Laying firm foundations

To win and retain power, New Labour fully realized that it had to win and retain both financial and popular confidence.

Financial confidence had traditionally been denied, or forfeited by, Labour governments because of their 'tax and spend' policies. Consequently, the pre-election pledges not to increase income tax rates and to stay within Conservative spending plans were vital. They were designed to win such trust. Honouring them, together with other actions such as ceding monetary policy to the Bank of England, was also essential for its retention. Fortuitously, they also laid the foundation for continuing the economic growth, from which future increases in spending could be painlessly financed.

Given the 'new austerity', the same two pledges were deemed to be crucial to the winning of electoral support. Even the moderate proposals for increased expenditure in the 1992 manifesto (funded by equally moderate increases in taxation) were believed to have snatched defeat from the jaws of victory.[12] In consequence the exceptional majority of 182 was won on an unexceptional spending programme. Its extreme modesty was reflected by the limited nature of the five pledges on the party's membership card. One concerned fast-track punishment for persistent young offenders. Three others addressed core welfare issues:

- cut class sizes to 30 for 5–7-year-olds
- cut waiting lists by treating an extra 100,000 patients
- get 250,000 under 25-year-olds off benefit and into work.

The final one confirmed that, initially at least, any increased financial support for public expenditure would be indirect:

- no rise in income tax rates, cut VAT on heating to 5 per cent and inflation and interest rates as low as possible.

Implementing such a modest programme might have laid the foundation for continuing financial confidence and economic growth. Could it simultaneously retain support within the electorate and enthusiasm within the Party? It appeared not. New Labour's victory, despite its restrained manifesto, had excited popular expectations about improvements in public services. For two years, however, there was no money to realize such expectations. Instead, as has been seen with Brown's presentation of the 1998 comprehensive spending review, ministers resorted to 'spin'. This created a pervasive public disillusion in relation to both the capacity of welfare services to improve and the government's honesty.

Worse still, the Conservatives' long-term spending plans had been deliberately designed to embarrass New Labour. They included cuts which, had they been unexpectedly returned to office, they themselves – on their own admission – would not have implemented.[13] New Labour thus faced a dilemma. Should it break its pledge to stay within the spending plans and risk jeopardizing financial confidence? Alternatively, should it make the cuts and offend its own supporters? It chose to do the latter. Thus in November 1997 the premium paid to lone parents on means-tested benefit was cut; and whilst the

4   Resuscitating the NHS
For its first three years, New Labour based welfare reform on better management not funding. Under-resourcing was not addressed. This frustrated and angered many. Ironically, shortly after this cartoon was published, the NHS received its largest ever injection of money.
Source: © Dave Brown, *The Independent*, 27 January 2000.

Prime Minister hosted a 'cool Brittania' party in Downing Street, 47 Labour MPs duly rebelled against the government in Parliament. The decision was also taken in 1998 to introduce tuition fees and substitute maintenance grants by student loans. Two of New Labour's first welfare decisions, therefore, were not to improve services but to disadvantage a particularly vulnerable group of claimants and to end free higher education.

Despite such decisions, however, some solid foundations were laid for constructive welfare reform in the future. Not all initiatives were successful, particularly in policy areas where there had been insufficient preparation in opposition. One such area was social security, where Frank Field was appointed 'minister for welfare reform' to think the unthinkable. Unfortunately, like John Moore a decade earlier, he only identified the unworkable. Then, when a Cabinet committee was appointed to resolve the difficulties, it found them unresolvable. This was a repetition of Mrs Thatcher's worst working practices, although this time there was the added piquancy of civil servants having to be posted as lookouts within Whitehall to ensure certain ministers never met.[14] Both Field and Harriet Harman, his nominal superior as secretary of state for social security, had to resign rather ignominiously in July 1998.

Nevertheless there was a raft of positive initiatives. Government revenue was surreptitiously boosted by a windfall tax on privatized utilities (which netted £5.2 billion), a tax on private pensions (bringing in £11.7 billion within three years), and the final abolition in 1999 of mortgage interest tax relief. Here were the seeds of redistribution. The increased revenue, moreover, was used to the lay the foundation of an 'active' welfare state which, in accordance with the Third Way and the report of the Social Justice Commission, addressed not just the symptoms but also the causes of need. Thus the windfall tax was earmarked for the 'New Deal'. This was the name given to the expansion of the Conservatives' welfare-to work measures, which encouraged as well as compelled unemployed under-25s back to work. Even more imaginatively, a Social Exclusion Unit was established to identify and combat the multiple causes of deprivation.

In addition, the 1998 comprehensive spending review previewed the wide range of reforms to be implemented immediately the fiscal straitjacket was removed. In particular, to further discourage a dependency culture, work was to be made to pay. Britain's first minimum wage, for instance, was to be introduced in April 1999. It was to be swiftly followed by the first in a long line of tax credits, the working family tax credit (WFTC). Greater self-reliance was also to be encouraged by the launching of a new 'stakeholder' pension, whilst poverty amongst current pensioners was to be relieved by a minimum income guarantee. Not to be outdone by his Chancellor, the Prime Minister also made the dramatic (if not fully considered) pledge in March 1998 to abolish child poverty within 20 years.[15]

Despite rising disillusion amongst the public and party members, therefore, the foundations were laid within the first two years of office not just for financial confidence and economic growth but also for welfare reform. The

New Deal, WFTC and the Social Exclusion Unit in particular promised a distinctive new approach.

These reforms, moreover, were accompanied by a major constitutional development. Following referendums in 1997 and elections in May 1999, the Scottish Parliament and Welsh Assembly were due to hold their first meeting in September 1999. Both, as will be seen, had a measure of devolved power over welfare policy.

A serious loss of faith, however, forestalled a further constitutional innovation. Before the election proportional representation had been advocated within New Labour as a means to 'make the twenty-first century safe for progressive forces'.[16] Once installed, it would prevent– as had been possible for Mrs Thatcher – advantage being take of a split in the anti-Conservative vote to impose deeply divisive policies on a 'mandate' from a minority of the electorate. After New Labour's landslide victory on a 43 per cent vote, reform mysteriously seemed less urgent.

Of all the early innovations, the Social Exclusion Unit (established in December 1997) laid the most distinctive foundation for future reform. As a body consciously seeking 'joined up solutions to joined up problems', it also defies easy categorization.

Social exclusion was a French, rather than an American, concept. In France, however, the term referred to people excluded from the social security system. In Britain it came to refer more broadly to people excluded from normal social life and expectations. It was 'a shorthand term for what can happen when people and areas suffer from a combination of linked problems such as unemployment, poor skills, low incomes, unfair discrimination, poor housing, high crime, bad health and family breakdown'.[17]

The Unit was thus concerned with combating, in the present and for the future, a variety of problems, in a variety of ways, for a variety of reasons. The problems included a lack of individual self-belief and self-reliance. Remedial action included not just employment and educational programmes but also measures to combat racial prejudice and the worst instances of urban degeneration (identified through a ward-by-ward deprivation index). The mix of motives included social justice (ensuring equality of opportunity), economic efficiency (the utilization of all talent) and social cohesion (strengthened communities). Immediate problems, such as rough sleeping and teenage pregnancy, had to be addressed. Most important, however, was the breaking of the cycle of deprivation by which children might be condemned through their parents' circumstances to life-long poverty.

Such a novel, multi-dimensional attack on deprivation required a novel partnership between both government departments and all those involved in policy delivery. Consequently, within minister-led teams, officials worked with representatives of business and the voluntary sector. The design and implementation of specific projects were also agreed with the intended beneficiaries. 'If the answer lay in Whitehall', the Unit's first head was fond of repeating, 'we would have found it long ago.'[18]

→

This attempt to build equal partnerships accorded with the principles of new public management. It contrasted with the simultaneous attempt by the Treasury to encourage joined-up programmes of public expenditure by such centralized mechanism as public service agreements. Freed from many of its former responsibilities for macroeconomic policy, the Treasury lost its traditional negativity towards welfare policy. It did not lose, however, its traditional desire for control (see Section 3.1.2).

14.3.3   Driving through reform

(i)   Increasing funding

Once released from its fiscal straitjacket, New Labour made a serious attempt to reverse the long-term underfunding of the welfare state. The key budgets were those for 2000 and 2002. The former followed an unexpected pledge on television by the Prime Minister to raise spending on the NHS to the European average. This took the Cabinet as much by surprise as Mrs Thatcher's televized commitment to reform the NHS in 1988. The latter followed the Prime Minister's commitment after the 2001 election to deliver improved services.[19]

Both budgets provided sustained increases in the health and education expenditure. In 2000, for instance, NHS spending was increased in real terms by 7.4 per cent for the following fiscal year. In 2002 that same percentage increase was promised for each of the next five years. The 2002 budget also increased educational expenditure in real terms by 6 per cent over each of the following three years. A similar increase was also promised to the personal social services, if only to reduce 'bed blocking' by elderly patients in the NHS.

Such sustained increases were historically unprecedented; but the extent of the largesse should not be exaggerated. After 1997, the percentage of both public and social expenditure as a percentage of GDP *fell* and by 2002 neither had regained the relative position inherited from the Conservatives (see Tables 14.1 and 14.2). There were some positive reasons for this. For instance, economic growth meant that unemployment and thus social security payments were low. Rising GDP also meant that a real increase in government expenditure need not simultaneously be a percentage increase. In addition there was the issue identified earlier that some welfare payments (such as tax credits) were not recorded in the public accounts.

The main explanation for the decreased percentage of GDP consumed, however, was that initial expenditure increases were marginal. This was in part because of the fiscal straitjacket. It was also because New Labour believed that effective reform required not large injections of money but better management. Thus even after the 1998 comprehensive spending review had provided a vision of future reform, the 1999 budget *reduced* the basic rate of income tax by 1p (a reduction that had to be reversed in 2002 by an increase

Table 14.1   Public expenditure, 1996/7–2005/6

Fiscal year	£bn	Percentage of GDP
1996–7	365.8	40.8
1997–8	364.7	39.2
1998–9	365.5	38.3
1999–00	369.3	37.4
2000–1	389.4	38.1
2001–2	403.8	38.9
2002–3	418.9	39.7
2003–4	446.5	41.2
2004–5	463.7	41.5
2005–6	482.7	41.9

Note: £ at 2002–3 prices.
Source: HM Treasury, *Public expenditure* (Cm 6201, 2004) table 3.1.

of 1 per cent in national insurance contributions). Pensions, strictly in line with inflation, were also raised by a derisory 95p.

Such decisions provoked public anger which, together with the perceived overstretching of NHS resources during a flu epidemic in the winter of 1999/2000, convinced ministers that funding had radically to be increased. Ironically the income tax cut simultaneously persuaded the public that such increases did not require tax rises. In 2000, *British Social Attitudes* recorded for the only time since the 1970s a fall in the secular upward trend of respondents favouring increased taxation to fund improved services. The percentage fell to 50 per cent from the peaks of 65 per cent and 63 per cent in 1991 and 1998 respectively.[20] Such opinion poll evidence was given substance by an unprecedented display of civil disobedience in September 2000. Petrol refineries were blockaded in a protest against increased fuel tax.[21] Support for the government fell to 36 per cent, just one point above the Conservatives, although it had quickly reverted by November to a dominant 47 per cent.

Such public reaction clearly required a serious debate. Despite public and media protests against 'stealth' taxes, Britain remained a relatively low-tax country particularly in relation to western Europe (see Table 14.3). 'World class' public services could not be funded adequately on such restricted revenue. The necessary debate appeared impossible, however, even in the 2001 election. This was for two reasons. The first was 'triangulation': the need for New Labour to advance new policies whilst fending off simultaneous attacks from those within the Party who wanted greater intervention (Old Labour) and those outside who wanted less (mainly the Conservatives). The second was continuing 'civic illiteracy' (see Section 2.2.3). At all levels of society, there was gross misapprehension about the extent of welfare spending, particularly on stigmatized groups such as the unemployed and lone parents.

Table 14.2 Social expenditure, 1996/7–2005/6

| | 1996–7 | | 1997–8 | | 1998–9 | | 1999–00 | | 2000–1 | | 2001–2 | | 2005–6 |
	£bn	%	£bn	%	£bn	%	£bn	%	£bn	%	£bn (estimated)	%	% (projected)
Education	40.2	4.7	40.1	4.5	40.7	4.5	41.7	4.5	44.1	4.6	49.4	5.1	5.6
Health	45.0	5.3	45.6	5.2	46.6	5.1	49.6	5.3	52.6	5.5	56.7	5.8	7.2
Personal social services	11.2	1.3	11.5	1.3	11.8	1.4	12.7	1.4	13.4	1.4	13.7	1.4	1.6
Housing	5.1	0.6	4.0	0.5	3.8	0.4	2.9	0.3	3.2	0.3	4.9	0.5	0.6
Social security	106.5	12.5	104.4	11.8	103.6	11.4	105.1	11.3	105.4	11.0	109.1	11.2	–
Social expenditure as % GDP		24.4		23.3		22.8		22.8		22.8		24.0	

Source: See Appendix, Tables A.6 and A.7; H. Glennerster, *Understanding the Finance of Welfare* (Bristol, 2003) table 9.2.

This, as it has been diplomatically expressed, raised 'difficult issues for governments seeking to plan public spending in a way that [would] both meet service goals and obtain an enthusiastic response from the voters'.[22] Open debate might win minds in the long term. In the short term, it risked losing votes.

(ii) Improving delivery

By 2002, the necessary funding for effective welfare reform was in place. The priority was now delivery. This had been made the more urgent by the unprecedented apathy at the general election, in which the turnout collapsed from the traditional 70 per cent to a mere 59 per cent. This was deemed to reflect growing disillusion about not just the government's honesty but also the possibility of public service reform.

Delivery had caused problems earlier. The Prime Minister, for example, had controversially referred in 1999 to 'scars on my back' caused by doctors' opposition to NHS reform.[23] In 2002, however, two fundamental issues which had been raised by the Conservatives' restructuring of the welfare state were translated into two particular controversies. The issues were the extent to which, on the one hand, public services should be contracted out and, on the other hand, power should be decentralized even in publicly provided services. Public Private Partnerships (PPPs) and foundation hospitals provided the particular controversies. Both led to major divisions within the Party (which tested the degree to which it had been modernized) and between the Prime Minister and the Chancellor (when the authority of the former was increasingly weakened by controversy over the 2003 Iraq war).

PPPs were New Labour's variant of the Private Finance Initiative (PFI), which the Conservatives had introduced in 1992. Government had always relied on borrowing from the market to fund capital investment. After 1992, the private sector was encouraged not just to finance but also to construct

---

Table 14.3 Tax as a percentage of GDP, 1985–2000

	1985	1990	1995	2000
Sweden	49	54	48	54
France	44	43	44	45
Germany	37	36	38	38
UK	38	37	35	37
USA	26	27	28	30
Japan	27	30	28	27

Note: Figures are for tax and social security contributions.
Source: H. Glennerster, *Understanding the Finance of Welfare* (Bristol, 2003) table 3.1.

buildings, such as hospitals or prisons, themselves and then to lease them to government. It could also, as in prisons or 'failed' schools, be contracted to run, manage and even staff the service. By 2002 the principle of PPPs should no longer have been controversial. One of Gordon Brown's first actions as chancellor, after all, had been to sanction the building of 12 hospitals negotiated under PFI. However, the issue had flared up in the 2001 election. Public sector unions threatened to withdraw funding from the Labour Party and to use militant action to halt further deals.[24] Why was this?

One basic reason for continuing suspicion was that the greater efficiency of PPPs remained unproven. A succession of reports culminating with one from the Prime Minister's favourite think tank, the Institute for Public Policy Research (IPPR), in June 2001 pointed only to mixed success.[25] Such success, moreover, was often achieved at the expense of future tax-payers (who had to fund the cost of interest repayment and leasing for up to 30 years) or current workers. The unions were particularly apprehensive about the creation of a 'two-tier' workforce, where the pay and conditions for those in the contracted-out sector were inferior to those directly employed by government. A promise was made at the 2001 Party conference that this would not be so, but it was reneged upon before being restored in 2003.[26]

Union opposition may have represented the very assertion of producer over consumer interest which the introduction of market discipline was designed to combat. Good working conditions do not automatically guarantee good standards of service. However, union opposition was grounded in principle because PPPs might legitimately be seen to challenge basic values underpinning state welfare. Private investment in healthcare, for example, was heavily influenced by what local hospital trusts could afford and by which procedures were profitable. This threatened two of the founding principles of the NHS: national planning and the primacy of clinical need.

For government, PPPs were initially (like tax credits) a 'pure accounting trick'.[27] It defrayed the cost of borrowing over a number of years. At a stroke, it thus freed government from a budgetary constraint that had traditionally discouraged capital investment: the need, for the retention of financial confidence, to keep annual borrowing within agreed limits. This meant an immediate start could be made on the urgent task of repairing and replacing the crumbling infrastructure within the public sector. Consequently, in New Labour's pragmatic spirit of 'what counts is what works', greater private involvement was a price well worth paying. 'I don't care who builds them', the Prime Minister asserted as he threw down a challenge to his Party conference in 2002, 'so long as they are on time, on budget, and helping to deliver a better NHS and better state schools'.[28]

There were additional advantages which persuaded the government, against rising Party opposition, to accept PPPs not just as a means of tackling an urgent backlog but as a permanent commitment. They transferred the risks of construction and management from government. Crucially, they also facilitated the introduction of private management techniques into the public sector. As Gordon Brown sought to persuade his Party, lessons had to be learnt from the private sector to 'revitalise our public services from the inside or the opposition will seek to dismantle them from the outside'.

Such an argument, however, had a logical flaw. Its unspoken assumption was that private management was endemically superior to public management. However, the evidence for this – as for the efficiency of PPPs – was lacking. Thus New Labour might legitimately argue that PPPs did not directly erode the principle of the welfare state. Services were still publicly funded and free at the point of access. Nevertheless they implicitly undermined the public service ethos and thus the core values upon which state welfare was based. Such latent contempt might or might not affect the future. In the present, it lowered morale and thus standards within the public services.

An attempt was made to heal the rifts created by PPPs by the offering of greater independence to those service providers, such as GPs and head teachers, who were employed directly by government. New Labour's first period in government had been dominated by typical 'command and control' mechanisms, such as targets, public service agreements and inspection. Their purpose had been to ensure swift results. Their immediate impact, however, had been to frustrate and eventually demoralize the very staff upon whom the achievement of those results depended. To remedy the situation, the Prime Minister (in a typical New Labour gesture) dispatched to 10,000 leading public sector workers in March 2002 a glossy pamphlet, *Reforming our Public Services*, which promised: 'Whitehall is serious about letting go and giving successful front-line professionals the freedom to deliver these standards. I know it has not always seemed like this. I hope we are learning from experience.' A full understanding, however, had been reached with neither public sector unions nor the Chancellor, with whom he sparred at the 2003 Party conference over the respective values of Old and New Labour.

The focus of the dispute was foundation hospitals. These were high-achieving hospital trusts which, in the words of the 2000 NHS Plan, had 'earned' autonomy. They were to gain far greater control over their budgets. This meant *inter alia* that they could vary rates of pay and conditions for their staff and raise loans on the open market. The unions again opposed any variation of nationally negotiated pay and conditions. They also argued that specialist staff would be enticed away from other hospitals, thereby creating a two-tier health service. Autonomous trusts, it was also argued, were also ripe for privatization if only under a future Conservative government. For his part, as has been seen, the Chancellor favoured local autonomy and management initiative. However, consistent with Treasury administrative traditions, this was acceptable only within strict guidelines issued from the centre. Consistent with Treasury financial traditions, he also opposed the independent raising of loans. Were fiscal irresponsibility to lead to a hospital being declared bankrupt, would not the tax-payer be expected to foot the bill?

The Prime Minister had no such doubts, fully ascribing to new public management belief that it was the government's responsibility to 'steer and not to row' (see Section 3.1.2). This meant giving front-line professionals genuine autonomy, subject to broad agreement over targets and inspection. The aim was to revitalize not privatize. Moreover, whatever the aspiration, welfare services had never been equal throughout the country. A key purpose of his reforms indeed was to generate the knowledge and incentives amongst both staff and patients which would lead to standards being levelled up, not down.

Another key purpose was political. By 2003, the Conservative Party was at last developing a coherent policy of patient and schools passports (the latest variant of vouchers) which gave consumers a genuine choice of public or private services. Greater autonomy within public services was designed to provide the additional flexibility to pre-empt the need to use the private sector. Whether, of course, the majority of welfare customers actually wanted increased choice, or just the assurance of a good service, remained a moot point.[29]

Service delivery was the latest of many issues to divide Tony Blair and Gordon Brown since the decision in 1992 to allow the former to succeed John Smith as Party leader. It reflected their contrasting philosophies and political strengths.[30]

As a 'social liberal' and adherent of the Third Way, Blair fundamentally believes in an 'enabling' state. In other words, government should provide a framework in which individuals, by exercising their rights and duties as citizens, can maximize individual and communal welfare. Hence his encouragement of genuine local discretion to permit choice and a person-alized form of welfare. This policy is also designed to reach out beyond Party activists to meet the needs of Middle England ('Blair's Tories'). Its values are very different to those summarized by Donnison (see Section 2.2.2). Its votes, nevertheless, are essential for New Labour's continuing electoral success.

As a 'social democrat', Brown has an inherent belief in the power of government to engineer greater equality. Centralized control also coin-cides, as has been seen, with the traditional view of the Treasury. Hence his desire for national standards and uniform services for all. Genuine consumer choice, in any case, is unrealizable until the capacity of public services is increased. The detailed understanding of welfare policy Brown enjoys provides the ideal foil for Blair's electoral instincts.

By combining complementary philosophies and skills, the partnership between Blair and Brown has been crucial to New Labour's success. A similar partnership could have been forged between Gaitskell and Bevan in the 1950s. It was not and Labour was condemned to electoral defeat (see Section 4.3). The cost of personal tensions might therefore be consid-ered a price well worth paying. They appear, however, to be unnecessar-ily exacerbated by ministers' increased reliance for support since the 1980s on special partisan advisers rather than 'neutral' civil servants.

14.4　DEVOLUTION

One of the 'firm foundations' laid for better government, as has been seen, was the creation by 1999 of a separately elected Scottish Parliament and Welsh Assembly. The Northern Ireland Assembly was also revived in 1998 although it and, more particularly, its power-sharing executive were only able to function intermittently owing to disputes over the peace process. They were finally suspended in 2002.[31] The Scottish Parliament has the right to initiate, and the Welsh Assembly to vary, national welfare legislation except in relation to social security. In Scotland, taxation can also be varied by up to three percentage points (although by 2004 this option has yet to be exercised).

The effectiveness of devolution depends on the resources available to the independent executives. Their *allocation* was determined by the arcane Barnett formula, based on population size and estimated need in 1978. The consequences for the distribution of resources from England to the rest of the UK through welfare expenditure are summarized in Table 14.4. In 2000/1, Scots received 18 per cent per head more than the national average, the Welsh 13 per cent more and the English 4 per cent less.[32] Such variation would be justified were the rest of the UK to have a significantly lower standard of living than England. There is evidence to suggest, however, that this is not the case. Scotland is considerably over-resourced whilst Wales (and much of England outside London) is under-provided.[33]

The *size* of the Barnett allocation is determined by departmental negotiations with the Treasury in England. The devolved executives then receive their proportionate share of the agreed amount. They receive it, however, as a block grant. In other words they can spend it on whatever programmes they choose. This can, and has, led to increasing variation in welfare policy – although national variations, it should be remembered from Section 4.4, existed long before devolution.

The greatest policy variation has been in education where, for example, school league tables have been uniformly abandoned. The greatest national variation has been in Scotland where, for example, there has been in contrast to England:

- a different system of university finance (maintenance grants, a graduation tax and no tuition fees)
- free personal as well as nursing care for the elderly
- no intrusion of the market into the NHS (with no foundation hospitals being established and no formal 'concordat' having been signed with the private sector).

Such variation might be presented as an example of the local diversity for which the Prime Minister was calling at the 2003 Labour Party. Ironically, however, it was achieved by jettisoning the very 'market' mechanisms by which it was supposed to be delivered. This was because, particularly in

Table 14.4   Identifiable public expenditure per head in the UK, 2000/1

	England	Scotland	Wales	N. Ireland
Education	96	124	98	138
Health and personal social services	97	116	112	110
Housing	86	164	142	243
Social security	97	110	116	120
Total public spending	96	118	113	128

Note: UK = 100.
Source: H. Glennerster, *Understanding the Finance of Welfare* (Bristol, 2003) table 9.1; HM Treasury, *Public Expenditure* (Cm 6201, 2004) table 8.2

Scotland, there remains a strong belief in the methods and values of public service which sustained the classic welfare state.[34] Arguably it continues to sustain the Chancellor. Blair could legitimately retort that 'what works is what counts'. Whether such variations in values and resources can continue to work in the long term, however, is a moot point. Will English regions continue to acquiesce in their apparent under-funding? What tensions would arise were a different political party to control government in Westminster and the devolved executives?

14.5   THE NEW LABOUR PROJECT

There were, therefore, few external economic constraints on the realization of the self-proclaimed New Labour 'project' after 1997. Firm foundations for reform were duly laid and sustained increases in funding, at an unprecedentedly high level, provided. Devolution assured a greater sensitivity to different national traditions and culture. However, public disillusion swiftly grew, as demonstrated by the historically low turnout at the 2001 election. So too did discord within both the Party and government. In part this was the consequence of genuine practical difficulties. Public services had for long been chronically underfunded. Vested interests within both public sector unions and professions could still frustrate reform. Whilst appearing to demand change, public opinion (not knowingly enlightened by most of the press) remained determinedly ignorant of the nature of current, and the cost of future, reform. Such difficulties undoubtedly complicated and thereby delayed reform. The government belatedly realized that a thorough modernization of the public services would require far longer than one Parliament to achieve.[35]

These practical difficulties, however, were exacerbated by the underprepared and consequently highly improvised nature of much of the 'project'. Little sustained attempt was then made to raise the level of debate on fundamental issues such as redistribution. 'Little was done' as Toynbee and Walker have bemoaned, 'to change the hearts and minds of Middle England, much to appease it.'[36] The Prime Minister's chosen strategy for dealing with opposition within the Party, over such critical issues as the balance between local discretion and uniform standards, also appeared to be that of confrontation rather than consultation. Collective decision-making, and even the synchronization of policy between the Prime Minister and the Chancellor, was often notable for its absence. This is the broad context within which the evolution of individual polices has to be analysed.

14.6 FURTHER READING

There have been many attempts to make political sense of New Labour. Amongst the better insider accounts are B. Gould, *The Unfinished Revolution* (1998); J. Rentoul, *Tony Blair* (2001); and P. Routledge, *Gordon Brown* (1998). Amongst the better instant commentaries are A. Seldon, *The Blair Effect* (2001); S. White (ed.), *New Labour* (Basingstoke, 2001); and S. Ludlam and M. J. Smith (eds), *Governing as New Labour* (Basingstoke, 2004). The latter has two particularly good chapters on welfare policy and the public services. These accounts can be put into historical perspective by D. Tanner, P. Thane and N. Tiratsoo, *Labour's First Century* (Cambridge, 2000) and into a wider context by a number of excellent politics textbooks, of which I. Budge et al., *The New British Politics* (Harlow, 2004) is always stimulating if not always accurate on historical detail.

On the impact of devolution, J. Stewart, *Scottish Social Welfare after Devolution* (Bristol, 2004) promises to be authoritative. The journal *Scottish Affairs* provides analyses which are not limited to Scotland. The Constitutional Unit at University College, London also has a special programme on devolution and health. Details are provided at www.ucl.ac.uk/constitution-unit

The internet provides instant access to legislative change and its analysis. www.Scotland.gov.uk provides the latest information on Scotland as well as links to parallel information for Wales, Northern Ireland and England. www.statistics.gov.uk provides access to all official statistics including an online edition of *Social Trends*, which offers an annual summary and selective commentary on policy output and outcomes. Two other sites for authoritative and clearly presented research findings are those of the Joseph Rowntree Foundation (www.poverty.org.uk) and the Institute of Fiscal Studies (www.ifs.org.uk). Government departments each naturally have their own websites but also their own distinct message to convey. Given its predominance in domestic policy, the Treasury's is invaluable, not least because much of its research and information (such as the Wanless reports on the NHS) is only provided electronically: www.hm.treasury.gov.uk. Also useful for evidence of joined-up government is www.socialexclusionunit.gov.uk.

The digest of events and analysis formerly provided in the *Journal of Social Policy* is also now available online at http://uk.cambridge.org/journals/jsp. Given its links with the Social Policy Association, the Policy Press of Bristol is fast establishing itself as a specialist publisher of welfare policy texts. A full catalogue is available at www.policypress.org.uk.

chapter

15

The Impact of New Labour

This chapter examines, tentatively and selectively, policy developments in each of the five core areas of welfare. It looks particularly at:

- funding
- conflicts of principle
- tension between the centralization and devolution of power
- continuity from previous Conservative policy.

It will then address the key issues identified at the start of the previous chapter in relation to equality, consensus and international comparisons

15.1 SOCIAL SECURITY

Social security was the policy area which New Labour treated with most disdain, but it was also the one to which it directed its most innovative thinking.

Following American or 'Thatcherite' precedents, disdain was expressed by the pejorative use of the term 'welfare' and even 'welfare state' as a synonym for cash benefits. Such benefits, it was agreed, were at the root of much social and political malaise. They created a dependency culture and encouraged fraud. They exasperated tax-payers and thereby brought government into disrepute. It was vital, the Prime Minister concluded in 1999, to 'restore public trust and confidence in a welfare state that fifty years ago was acclaimed but today has so many people wanting to bury it'.[1] Given such disdain, the formal social security budget was not expanded like the ones for the NHS or education. Between 1997 and 2002, it scarcely increased in real terms and fell significantly as a percentage of GDP (see Table 14.2).

Such a fall, however, could be – and was – presented in a positive light. Soon after becoming Party leader, Tony Blair had defied Old Labour thinking by asserting that a large social security budget was 'not a sign of socialist success' but a sign of failure.[2] Once in office he insisted, in line with the report of the Social Justice Commission and Third Way thinking, that New Labour should create

> a welfare system which is 'active' rather than 'passive', genuinely providing people with a 'hand up' not a 'hand out'. Previous governments were satisfied simply to dole out money . . . That is not our approach. We believe the role of the welfare state is to help people help themselves, to give people the means to be independent.

In the first administration, the favoured means was work. 'Work', it was endlessly repeated, was 'the best form of welfare'. After 2001, the focus changed to 'asset-based welfare', and in particular saving for old age. 'The very act of saving', the Treasury intoned, 'encourages greater self-reliance, forward-planning and an increased willingness to make personal investments.' Social security policy, in short, was fundamentally realigned, as was demonstrated by the 'rebranding' of the responsible government department. In 2001 the Department of Social Security was transformed into the Department of Work and Pensions.

The renewed emphasis on work accorded fully with the spirit of the Beveridge Report. It had championed 'the maintenance of employment' because cash benefits alone were an inadequate 'provision for personal happiness'. It had also recommended that those on benefit had a responsibility, and so could be required, to attend 'a work or training centre'.[3] The new principle on which cash benefits were dispensed, however, would have deeply concerned Beveridge. 'Selective universalism' was to be embraced. This meant continuing universal provision of those services which Middle England was still deemed to value, such as education and the NHS. Cash benefits, however, were to become increasingly means-tested.

It was this change in policy that, in essence, caused the most serious crisis in welfare policy after 1997: the enforced resignation of the social security ministers in 1998. The Treasury, as has been seen, was exercising increasing influence over welfare policy. It was determined to target benefit more directly on those in need. This would minimize cost. Simultaneously it would help to ensure, through closer monitoring, that claimants did not just demand rights but also accepted civic responsibilities.

Frank Field, as minister for welfare reform, in particular objected. Means-testing, as has been seen, had long been recognized as an inefficient means of transferring resources to those in need. This was because of the low take-up of such benefits. More importantly, Field subscribed to Charles Murray's belief that the method of welfare payment affected the claimants' behaviour.[4] With means-tested benefits it was generally for the worse. As he saw in his own deprived constituency, any system in which claimants had no direct stake was one they tried to 'beat'. It thereby encouraged dishonesty and fraud. Worse, it discouraged the very virtues which government was seeking to foster. Motivation to work was undermined by the withdrawal of benefit as income increased (the long-standing 'poverty trap'). Likewise, motivation to save was undermined by the realization that few later benefits would accrue from the forgoing of immediate pleasures. The standard of living assured by safety nets, such as the minimum income guarantee for pensioners, matched that which modest savings from modest incomes could deliver. There was the additional irony that income from such savings would help to disqualify the recipient from such means-tested rights.

Field's solution was to maintain universalism. It was not, however, to be administered by government but within the private market through personal 'stakeholder' accounts, which established an individual's right to a given level of income based on their contribution record. This would both encourage honesty and reward work. The problem, as with all such attempts properly to fund long-term policy whilst financing current policy on a 'pay-as-you-go' basis, was cost. The projected annual cost to government was up to £10 billion. This was unsustainable.

Was, however, the alternative to universal benefits any more sustainable in the long term? A policy based on 'in work' benefits assumed the ready availability of work. Indeed one of the Treasury's essential assumptions was that its policy, by ensuring a flexible workforce, would maximize employment. In the absence of any demand-led management of the economy, however, what would happen if unemployment did actually rise?

There was also, as will be seen, a host of other doubts about the practicality and consequences of Treasury policy. They included the quality of jobs available (which would affect workers' continuing motivation) and the demeaning of unpaid work (which particularly affected the self-esteem of mothers who chose to care full time for their children). Moreover, policy exuded an increasing air of authoritarianism. Benefit, for example, could be withdrawn from those who declined either to work or train. This raised very real fears about the use of the benefit system to discipline others. Those who indeed were threatened included claimants who disregarded court orders (following the 2000 Child Support, Pensions and Social Security Act) and stigmatized groups (such as asylum seekers and other migrants).

The greatest danger of the new emphasis on work and savings, however, was that it led to the neglect and under-funding of older benefits. This could be politically damaging, as the back-bench revolts over cuts to lone parent and disability benefit in 1997 and 1999 demonstrated. It could also be, and was, counter-productive. For example, the final safety net within the welfare state was the Social Fund. It was subject to a damning independent report in 2002. Its budget had fallen in real terms and remained below its 1997 level. Shortage of resources had also impaired the quality of service, thereby condemning very vulnerable claimants to considerable, and unnecessary, hardship.[5] How did this reduce social exclusion and help to break the cycle of deprivation with which the government was reputedly so concerned?

These broad issues will be illuminated by the two major policies designed to make people work and work pay: the New Deal and tax credits. Their impact will then be analysed in relation to two 'legitimately inactive' groups of claimants, children and pensioners. These were the government's most favoured groups. They may therefore have fared better than the other two-fifths of claimants.

The New Deal

The New Deal was the Treasury's first bold move into welfare policy. The scheme, as the name implied, was influenced very much by American experience, and especially the Democrat's significantly entitled 1996 Personal Responsibility and Work Opportunity Reconciliation Act. However, it also built on earlier Conservative initiatives and was influenced by experience in other countries such as Australia.

There were six principal schemes which essentially encouraged, but eventually compelled benefit claimants to accept offers of work, training or education. The first ones concentrated on those who were most 'employable': the under-25s, the long-term unemployed, lone parents and the partners of the unemployed. Attention then turned to those who were less easy to place in work (the 'non-economically active'): claimants over 50 and the disabled.

Typically each client was assigned a personal adviser and called for regular interviews to discuss job prospects and applications. Sanctions, such as a reduction or even a suspension of benefit, could be applied if the offer of either an interview or a job was refused. In 2001 all the schemes were merged in the ONE gateway initiative administered by the new JobCentre Plus agency. This resulted from the amalgamation of local offices of the former Department for Education and Employment (DfEE; the old jobcentres) and Department of Social Security (DSS; paying benefit). There was a fear that claimants would be disadvantaged as the proactive support of the DfEE was diluted by the rather less sympathetic culture of the DSS.

These schemes were supported by a range of job creation initiatives. Employment action zones, for instance, were established to permit a private company in which government had a one-third holding (Working Links) to pilot a range of experimental measures. Public Private

Partnership was similarly encouraged in 2002 when 63 'action teams' were also contracted to help claimants find work in areas where social exclusion was deemed particularly severe. There were also schemes, such as the StepUp programme, under which government subsidized the wages of those with disabilities (such as learning problems) whom employers would otherwise have rejected.

How successful was the New Deal? It certainly decreased fraud, by discouraging those who were working in the 'black economy' from claiming. By 2001, over 32,000 'workshy' claimants had also forfeited benefit for refusing work. More positively, the pre-election pledge to 'get 250,000 under-25-year-olds off benefit and into work' was more than achieved. Success with other groups was more limited. However, the percentage of lone parents in work did rise between 1997 and 2001 from 45 to 51.5; and it was estimated that about a quarter of those entering work would not have done so without help from the New Deal.[6] Nevertheless, the figure fell far short of the target government had set of 70 per cent of all lone parents being in work by 2010.

A major difficulty in estimating success is the counterfactual issue. Given sustained economic growth, how many of those finding work under the New Deal would have done so anyway? Moreover, given that the criterion of success was the retention of an unsubsidized job for only 13 weeks, how many found permanent (not to mention rewarding) work? Was the culture of dependency within individuals and neighbourhoods really transformed?

On balance it would seem unquestionable that the New Deal did increase and accelerate job placements. The major criticism in relation to numbers typically concerned the government's exaggeration of success and the considerable cost of each placement. There were, however, real grounds for reservation. A principal one was the implicit demeaning of *unpaid* caring by the stress on the virtues of *paid* work. Full-time motherhood particularly in a single parent household, for example, appeared to be devalued. The underlying assumption seemed to be that children would gain more, and would break out of the cycle of deprivation, were they to have an example of a working parent rather than the presence of a full-time parent. A range of evidence, including children's examination success, did not unambiguously support this assumption.[7]

A second and equally fundamental reservation was the narrow concentration on individual behaviour. Really effective inducement to undertake paid work, it was frequently pointed out, required much more imagination. For the poor, for example, a cheap and efficient transport system would have removed a major barrier to work. For carers, in addition to affordable childcare, more flexible working conditions and practices would enable them to work and discharge their other responsibilities.[8] Such remedies, however, required a greater regulation of the market rather than of individuals. This, despite its pride in 'joined-up' thinking, the government was reluctant to embrace.

The disabled were one of the government's less favoured group of claimants. Their experience illustrates the benefits and disbenefits of the New Deal.

The principal universal and non-means tested benefit, which over 2.5 million disabled people claimed throughout the period, was incapacity benefit. This benefit was the product of the Conservatives' fundamental review in 1995 and rationalized all previous schemes. The number of claimants had remained high, however, because it was an alternative to the jobseekers' allowance. For government, therefore, it was a means of reducing the official unemployment figures. One medical check typically established a person's disability for the rest of their working life.

This, New Labour adjudged, could encourage fraud and certainly encouraged dependency. Accordingly, in 1999 a more stringent 'all work test' was introduced to determine a person's capacity for, rather than their inability to, work. This was administered in part through the New Deal for Disabled People. Tougher sanctions were mooted immediately after the 2001 election, but were largely defeated by the threat of another backbench rebellion.[9] In 2004, these sanctions – such as a requirement to attend interviews – were reintroduced. They were applied, however, only in pilot areas. They were also matched by incentives, such as 13 weeks' medical therapy and subsidies to both find and hold down a regular job.

Policy was designed simultaneously to increase the independence of those capable of work and to concentrate scarce resources on the *severely* disabled. Both were clearly desirable objectives. However, the constant threat of greater stringency and compulsion reduced the quality of life of many disabled people. It eroded their peace of mind. Ironically, any questioning of their universal right to benefit and, above all, their right to choice also threatened the very sense of independence which the government was seeking to foster.

Tax credits

If the New Deal was the Treasury's principal means for inducing people to work, tax credits were its principal means for ensuring work paid. They represented a belated realization of the 'holy grail' of the 1960s: a unified taxation and benefit system. Beveridge, as seen in Section 6.1, had been retrospectively criticized for failing to anticipate the need for such an initiative.

Tax credits, as explained in Section 14.1, were a means of transferring money through the tax system to meet specific needs. They could either reduce the amount of tax a person had to pay or, if their tax liability was exhausted, increase that person's income through their pay packet. There was a bewildering array of such credits, commencing with the working families tax credit (WFTC) in October 1999. They were rationalized in April 2003 into three main schemes:

- Child tax credit (CTC). This amalgamated all former tax allowances and credits for children, including those for child-care, together with the special allowances for children in such means-tested benefits as Income Support and Jobseekers' Allowance.
- Working tax credit (WTC). This similarly amalgamated most means-tested benefits for single people and childless couples, including the disabled.
- Pension credit (PC). This replaced the minimum income guarantee given to pensioners in 2000.

Each time the Treasury reformed the system it became more generous. For example, where the level of children's benefit had varied by age, standardization was always at the highest rate. To reduce disincentives to work, there was a reduction in the rate at which credits were withdrawn as working income rose (the 'taper'). Similarly to reduce disincentives to save, there was an increase in the amount of unearned income disregarded in the calculation of entitlement to credit. All these changes redistributed a very large sum of money. The cost of CTC and WTC in 2003 was in the region of £1.6 billion. That for PC was £4.4 billion.

Despite such generosity, however, the new system was far from perfect. Many of the practical and principled objections, which had stalled reform in the 1960s, still had considerable force.

First, take-up was far from universal. In 2000/1, for example, over half a million people entitled to WFTC did not claim.[10] One reason for non-take-up was ignorance. Tax credits, unlike other means-tested benefits, did not require multiple and repeated claims. That was one of their major attractions. However, they did require an initial claim. Many failed to make this because they were unaware of their entitlement. There were others, however, who did not claim because of more intrinsic difficulties. Some workers, for instance, were threatened with dismissal. Employers objected to the extra cost of having to make the required adjustment to their employees' pay. Credits were also classified as income. They could therefore disqualify some claimants from mean-tested benefits outside the tax system (such as free school meals).[11]

Second, the Treasury lacked the capacity to administer the credits efficiently. The National Audit Office, the government's chief financial watchdog, used its strongest possible sanction of 'qualifying' the Inland Revenue accounts in 2003 because of a £2 billion overspend on credits over the previous three years. Such an error rate, the House of Commons' own watchdog (the Public Accounts Committee) condemned as wholly unacceptable.[12] Worse, however, followed. The computer system responsible for CTC (the product of a public–private partnership) immediately failed. In consequence the regularity and accuracy of its payment could not be guaranteed until 2005, some two years after its introduction. Many claimants suffered temporarily serious losses of income. No department other than the Treasury, so it was argued, could have escaped so lightly from such a catalogue of maladministration.

Third, the extent of redistribution – although considerable – had its limits. The poorest were not always the greatest beneficiaries. It was they, for example, who were most likely to forfeit other means-tested benefits. In addition, they were unable to claim childcare credit. It could only be spent on registered child minders, not informal ones like the extended family. It also covered only 70 per cent of the cost. Since the annual charge for registered care averaged over £5000 a year, the credit consequently became yet another welfare service enjoyed mainly by the middle class.[13] Finally, there was a gender dimension. WFTC in particular was designed to make work pay (or at least to make more explicit the advantages of work). Benefits accordingly had to be dispensed through the pay packet rather than in cash over a Post Office counter. In two-parent families, this tended to mean a transfer of resources from the mother to the male breadwinner. It was a perverse consequence which later credits, and particularly CTC, sought to rectify.

Fourth and finally, there were all the dangers inherent in means-testing earlier identified by Field. By 2003 up to half the population had been drawn into means-tested benefit, principally as a result of PC and childcare credits. Critics, such as Field, were convinced that eventually all universal benefits, including child benefit, would be withdrawn.[14] This would fundamentally alter the nature of the welfare state and, more generally, the relationship between government and the individual. Beveridge, after all, had based his plan for social security on a system of contributory insurance guaranteeing everyone equal benefits as of right. This was out of respect for people's wish to be independent. They wanted income security 'not as charity but as a right' (see Section 6.1). Now a government professing a desire 'to give people the means to be independent' appeared to be doing the exact opposite. Of even greater sinister potential was the separation of credits for children and adults in 2003. This created the opportunity for the use of the social security system to 'discipline' adults without, as in the past, incurring the political opprobrium of directly disadvantaging children.

Child poverty

Tony Blair's commitment in 1999 to eradicate child poverty within a generation was one of New Labour's most dramatic pledges. As will be seen, it was also – despite considerable opposition – one of its least well defined. It was, nevertheless, extremely astute politics. It established the Prime Minister's reputation for radicalism just before his Chancellor's first major spending budget. By targeting those who would be the future workforce, it was consistent with the supply-side priorities of economic policy. By requiring a significant redistribution of resources to the poor, it also satisfied one of Old Labour's key demands. All this was to be achieved, moreover, without undue controversy. No political opponent seeking re-election could openly oppose measures to help children.

The eradication of child poverty duly became the principal focus of joined-up government. The value of cash benefits and tax credits was consistently and considerably increased. By 2000 alone this had added between £1300 and £3000, or up to a third, to the annual income of poor families.[15] The majority of social exclusion initiatives also addressed the childhood causes of deprivation. Amongst the most successful was Sure Start, another policy borrowed from the USA. It brought together a range of health and social workers in a variety of initiatives, such as toddler groups and toy libraries. The objective was to ensure that, on entering school, children from the most deprived areas were not at a disadvantage. Amongst the most dramatic initiatives was the introduction of a children's trust fund in the 2003 budget. It sought to provide a 'savings gateway' by placing a minimum of £250 in trust for each child born after September 2002. The money could be supplemented by the family on favourable terms, but could not be accessed until the child was eighteen.

What, however, did the original commitment actually mean? How could progress be monitored? In 1998/9, it was agreed, one third of children or some 4.5 million were in poverty. This represented a threefold increase since 1979. The number, it was belatedly agreed, should be reduced by one-quarter by 2004 and one-half by 2010. This provided the means by which progress towards total eradication by 2020 should be monitored.

A major dispute then broke out over definitions. During the 2001 election, Gordon Brown claimed that New Labour had reduced the number of children in poverty by 1.2 million. Immediately afterwards, official statistics revealed the 'true' number was only 500,000. Official figures continued to remain stubbornly high (see Table 15.1).

Accordingly, in 2004 both the definition of poverty and the aspiration were changed. By the new definition, the number of children living in poverty was

Table 15.1   Percentage of individuals in poverty, 1996/7–2001/2

	Total		Children		Pensioners	
	BHC	AHC	BHC	AHC	BHC	AHC
1996–7	18	25	25	34	21	27
1997–8	18	24	25	33	22	27
1998–9	18	24	24	33	23	27
1999–0	18	23	23	32	22	25
2000–1	17	23	21	31	21	24
2001–2	17	22	21	30	22	22

Notes: Poverty defined as individuals living below 60 per cent of the contemporary median income level. BHC: Before housing costs. AHC: After housing costs.

Source: H. Sutherland, T. Sefton and D. Piachaud, *Poverty in Britain* (York, 2003) table 1.

reduced at a stroke by 900,000. The policy goal was also made instantly more achievable. Poverty like unemployment, it was agreed, could never be totally eradicated. The aim should rather be to reduce it to the lowest rate in Europe.

These adjustments were not pure trickery. The aspiration remained a bold one. In 2000 Britain had one of the highest rates of child poverty at 32 per cent. The comparable percentage in Germany was 13 and in France 12. The average in the European Union was 20 per cent. To achieve the lowest rate in Europe required a significant reallocation of resources.

Moreover, as was seen in Section 6.2, there can never be a fully satisfactory or agreed definition of poverty. The generally accepted definition today contains three elements:

- Since 2003, the preferred European Union measure has been the number of people with an income below 60 per cent of the *median* income of the country in which they live.[16]
- The measure is calculated *after housing costs* (AHC) have been deducted from both the individual's and the median income. This AHC calculation is preferred because of the wide variation in housing costs. In an area of high housing costs such as London, for example, a BHC (before housing costs) calculation might underestimate the true extent of poverty. This is because it would exaggerate an individual's ability to meet the cost of needs other than housing.
- The measure is *dynamic*. In other words, like all measures of relative poverty, the poverty line rises in line with median income.

It was the latter element that caused confusion during the 2001 election. Brown was using a static rather than a dynamic measure of poverty. In other words his figure of 1.2 million included 700,000 children who *would* have been living in poverty, as defined in 1997, had there not been the sizeable redistribution of resources in their favour. In contrast, official figures (as in Table 15.1) used a dynamic measure. They recorded the number of children *actually* living in poverty. This number only declined slowly because, whatever the *absolute* increase in income of the poorest households, their increase *relative* to median income was less impressive. This was because, as a result of economic growth, median income was growing fast.

The 2004 change in the definition of child poverty was more contestable. It used a BHC measure and so, for example, reduced the number of children recorded as living in poverty in London. In compensation it also employed three different 'indicators' of poverty, in which greater weight was given to the neediest of children (such as the very young). Poverty will only be deemed to be falling when all three indicators fall.[17]

Despite these changes, the consensus among independent experts is that the government will objectively meet its 2004 target.[18] By their preferred dynamic AHC measure, child poverty had been reduced between 1998/9 and 2003/4 from 4.2 million to 3.6 million. When the full impact is recorded of the changes to tax credits and benefits in the 2003 and 2004 budgets, child poverty should have been cut by more than a quarter. That, however, would leave the most intractable cases of poverty still to be resolved. This, the experts equally agree, will require – as with the most intractable cases of unemployment – measures more radical than the ones already implemented.

Pensions

Existing pensioners were treated by New Labour even more favourably than children. They had four main sources of public income:

- The basic state pension. By 2001 this was equivalent only to 18 per cent of average full-time earnings.
- Automatic additional payments such as the winter fuel allowance, and free television licences for the over-75s.
- A range of means-tested benefits such as council tax benefit.
- The minimum income guarantee (MIG), introduced in 2000 and transformed into the Pension Credit in 2003.

The introduction of the MIG has been described as 'one of the great milestones' in the first New Labour administration.[19] It was prompted by the furore after the unquestionably prudent, statutorily correct, but politically inane decision in 1999 to raise the basic pension in line with inflation by only 95p. Its objective, in conjunction with the other three measures, was to remove all pensioners from poverty. Initially it reflected a restricted definition of poverty. By the time it was transformed into Pension Credit, however, it was being uprated annually in line with earnings. Its relative value was thereby being maintained. Moreover, so as not to penalize past savings, 60 per cent of unearned income was being disregarded in calculations of entitlement.

Pensioner poverty was not eradicated, as demonstrated by Table 15.1. Over one-fifth were still living below the poverty line in 2001/2. The main reason was, as with all means-tested benefits, incomplete take-up. Only 72 per cent of pensioners were estimated to claim their full range of entitlements. The main point, however, was that the extent to which the income of some pensioners still fell below the poverty line (the *intensity* of poverty) was typically very low. Numbers were also falling. Indeed one impartial report concluded in 2004 that 'for the first time in almost twenty years, a pensioner drawn at random from the population is less likely to be in poverty than a non-pensioner'.[20] Given the historic link between poverty and old age this was a notable achievement.

Consequently, where the real problem lay was not with existing pensioners but with the pension entitlement of the existing workforce. By 2050, it was estimated, the basic pension on current trends would have fallen to a mere 9 per cent of average earnings. There were three possible ways of supplementing it. The first was occupational pensions. These were hit, however, first by the pension fund tax New Labour surreptitiously introduced in 1997 and then by the collapse in the stock market after 2001. Having awarded themselves 'holidays' from making contributions when rising share prices swelled the value of these funds, companies did not make compensatory increases (except to senior management pension schemes) when the value contracted. Rather they revised their schemes so that new employees could expect a pension of less certain but definitely smaller value. Government took no action to correct this seeming example of market injustice.

Where the government did take action, but to no greater effect, was in the provision of two types of state regulated earnings-related pension. The first was a 'stakeholder' pension. This was a watered-down version of the compulsory, universal private pension Field had championed.[21] It was made available for employees in companies which did not have their own occupational scheme. Only 90,000 had taken up the offer by 2001. This was partly due to traditional unwillingness to plan for the future. More significantly, it was due to the realization that a lifetime of savings would not ensure a pension any higher than the minimum guaranteed by the state. Here was a perfect example of Field's warning that means-testing discouraged people from saving.

The second state initiative was the 'state second pension' which replaced SERPS in 2002. This too was quickly adjudged a failure because, even when combined with the basic pension, it would provide as of right only a very low income. In consequence, as one commentator lamented, pension reform continued to 'take on the guise of a Heath-Robinson cartoon as the problems of means-testing are addressed by bolting on further mean-testing mechanisms' to produce what could only be called 'a unwieldy and unworkable structure'.[22]

Conclusion

While parts of the social security system atrophied, therefore, others were revolutionized. Did this represent the forging of a new social democratic policy or an evolutionary stage in the fashioning of a new cross-party consensus?

The primacy accorded to the market certainly followed Conservative precedent. The focus, as in the New Deal, was steadfastly on supply-side measures to improve the efficient working of the market. Private agencies were used widely and where – as in the case of the provision of greater work flexibility – changes in market practice were required, these were not insisted upon.

Similarly the primacy placed on individual self-reliance and responsibility accorded with the conservative American thinking which had so influenced the New Right in the 1980s. This enabled New Labour initially to make welfare cuts and to add a punitive dimension to later reforms which was consistent with the 'Thatcherite' nature of the Conservatives' 1993 fundamental review. More significantly, its policy also converged with more traditional forms of Conservatism, which had continued to influence government under Mrs Thatcher's premiership. Key ideological disputes which had characterized the 1960s were resolved – on Conservative terms (see Section 6.3). The ultimate objective of social security, it was agreed, was to achieve equality of opportunity not outcome. The principal means was also to be selectivity not universalism.

New Labour retained some distinctiveness. It placed faith in the power of government – if only to fund and coordinate private initiative. Redistribution, amounting to £11.5 billion during its first administration, was considerable if surreptitious: 70 per cent of the gains went to the poorest half of the population and at least £5 billion to pensioners and to children.[23] This all but ended pensioner poverty and reversed the shameful escalation in child poverty. Was such distinctiveness, however, an alternative to or merely a variant of policies which New Labour had inherited?

15.2 THE PERSONAL SOCIAL SERVICES

After 1997 the personal social services remained a cinderella service. The resources allocated to it continued to be small, rising from only 1.3 per cent to a projected 1.6 per cent of GDP by 2005/6 (see Table 14.2). Politically, it was downgraded in 2003 when ministerial responsibility for children was transferred from the Department of Health to the DfEE. Administratively, local authorities' social service departments also lost staff and responsibilities to NHS Primary Care Trusts. Here, as envisioned by reformers in the 1960s, GPs could become heads of multi-professional teams alive to the social as well as the medical needs of patients (see Section 7.3).

As ever, the professional social workers were dwarfed by informal carers.[24] They were also dwarfed by commercial and not-for-profit (voluntary and community) providers. This was true both in new initiatives, such as those designed to combat social exclusion, and in traditional services such as the provision of residential and domiciliary care.

With regard to the latter, New Labour immediately removed the requirement that 85 per cent of contracted-out services be placed with private providers. The percentage, however, did not fall. Rather, domiciliary care (which local authorities had typically continued to provide directly under the Conservatives) was increasingly privatized. Between 1997 and 2002, for example, the share of contact hours for home care delivered by independent contractors rose from two-thirds to double those provided by local authorities.[25]

- How did New Labour seek to modernize the personal social services?
- How were its principal 'customers', the elderly and the young, affected?

Modernization

A plethora of administrative initiatives followed the publication of the 1998 white paper *Modernising Social Services: promoting independence, improving protection, raising standards* (Cm 4169). They included the creation of:

- The General Social Care Council to design a new social work degree by 2003.
- The Social Care Institute for Excellence, to establish best practice.

- National service frameworks to demonstrate how best practice could be applied in given circumstances.
- Performance assessment frameworks (PSSPAFs) by which to monitor efficiency. Results could be used to identify 'failing' and 'starred' social service departments.
- The National Care Standards Commission, which was swiftly merged with the social service inspectorate in 2003 to form the Commission for Social Care Inspection. Its role, as its name implied, was to provide rigorous outside inspection.

What the regular inspection regularly found was unaccountable variations in practice and a generally low standard of service. The latter could be largely explained by continuing low levels of resources and morale.[26] However, rather than increase resources (and reduce monitoring which itself consumed scarce resources) a new panacea was proposed: the grouping of all 150 English social service departments into ten regional agencies. This was intended to achieve significant economies by streamlining administration and driving down, through concentrated purchasing power, contractors' prices. The panacea was devised by one of New Labour's business advisers, Sir Peter Gershon. It contrasted sharply with the passionate defence of local democracy advanced by Mrs Thatcher's business adviser, Sir Roy Griffiths, in 1987 (see Section 13.2).

The initial modernization programme failed noticeably to raise standards. It did not enjoy much more success in realizing the white paper's two other objectives. 'Promoting independence' presumed some measure of consumer empowerment. 'Improving protection' required more effective *prevention* of problems. In the drive to achieve quick results, however, local authorities were denied the discretion and flexibility needed to achieve such ends. Despite New Labour's rhetoric, the new regulatory framework institutionalized, in the words of one commentator, a 'punitive, top-down, outcome-orientated' approach.[27]

New Labour sought to modernize central government's relationship not just with local authorities but also non-state service providers. Not-for-profit voluntary and community organizations (VCOs) were seen to be not just a cheap alternative to state care but also the embodiment of a strong civil society. It was desirable therefore to strengthen them. A formal compact was duly signed with VCOs in 1998 and various codes of good practice issued. An attempt was then made to 'normalize' voluntary work and charitable giving. The Treasury, for example, issued a target that by 2010 three-quarters of all adults should be spending at least two hours a week as a volunteer. The 2000 budget also introduced tax incentives for donations (Gift Aid). Charitable work and funding did increase, but not noticeably in response to these initiatives. Industry, for example, remained reluctant to release staff for volunteering duties and the cost of corporate sponsorship remained well under 0.5 per cent of pre-tax profits.

New Labour's basic failing, however, was once again its impatience for results. Defying the logic of its rhetoric, it started to dominate VCOs rather than engage them in an equal partnership. Increased regulation increased administrative costs, which government funding continued to overlook. Tighter contracts also provided little room for discretion in either the setting or delivery of targets. Far from strengthening civil society, as one distinguished commentator complained, New Labour was in effect 'nationalizing' VCOs.[28]

New Labour also sought, with rather greater justification, to regulate commercial service providers. Its principal initiative here was the 2000 Care Standards Act. Its raising of minimum standards, as will be seen, had an immediate impact on the private provision of residential care for the elderly.

The elderly

Care for the elderly typically accounts for just under half of public expenditure on the personal social services. It had, as seen in Section 10.1, also been the historic site of internecine warfare between the NHS and local authorities over the issue of 'bed-blocking'. The 'Berlin wall' between the two services was finally dismantled. The 2002 budget allocated responsibility to the personal social services with a corresponding increase in resources. The threat was simultaneously issued of penalties for any local authority which failed to provide the requisite facilities. Such penalties smacked of New Labour's penchant for centralized discipline. They were, however, also standard practice in social democratic Sweden.

However, two other problems arose. The first related to payment for long-term residential care. It was supposed to be resolved by the 1999 Sutherland Royal Commission on Long-Term Care (Cm 4192). It was not, because the commission produced two reports. Both agreed that the government should pay for nursing care. They also agreed that residents, or their families, should pay the cost of food and accommodation on a means-tested basis. That left the issue of 'personal' care, such as dressing and washing. The majority report suggested the government should pay. The minority report demured. Such a policy change would, it argued, be extremely expensive. The majority report had grossly underestimated the extent of demographic change and, above all, the additional cost of a 'free' service which would inevitably raise both expectation and demand.[29] It would also disproportionately benefit the better-off. Why should those who stood to inherit the family home along with other assets be relieved of their traditional family responsibilities?[30]

New Labour sided with the minority report. Its decision was immediately attacked on political and administrative grounds. The Scottish Parliament approved state payment for 'personal' care and won praise for its greater humanity. The Royal College of Nursing, amongst others, also stressed the impracticality of the new regime. There was no clear dividing line between 'nursing' and 'personal' care. A common budget would allow a rationalization of care and save scarce resources. This was re-emphasized by the eventual definition of 'nursing' care as care provided by a registered nurse. This resulted in unnecessary duplication, as unregistered staff were debarred from performing duties they had been competently discharging, under supervision, for a long time.

The second problem arose from the 2000 Care Standards Act. Owners of private residential homes had already been put under pressure by tighter local authority contracts and higher labour costs (as a result of the national minimum wage). An increase in the minimum standards of care, they argued, would drive them out of business. Indeed, the number of private residential homes did fall by 6 per cent in 2002/3. Who in future would provide long-term care?

The extent of both problems, however was not as great as portrayed at the time. The cost to the elderly of 'personal' care, for example, was marginal compared to that for food and accommodation, over which there was no dispute. The 6 per cent fall in the number of residential homes also disguised the fact that the number of places had only fallen by 1.5 per cent. This suggested that it was only the smaller, and arguably the less efficient, homes that were being closed.[31]

What the political furore in fact disguised, and was perhaps meant to disguise, was a commendable government policy of encouraging and enabling the elderly to remain in their homes for as long as possible. Historically this had been accepted as both the most economical and humane option. Money spent in Scotland on 'personal' care, so it could be argued, was better spent on domiciliary care. Private residential homes should concentrate on providing for the specialist needs of those who were too infirm to remain in their own homes. Government policy, however, required an additional positive element. This meant, at minimum, a significant increase in resources for local authorities. It also meant a compact with carers which, whilst not relieving them of their responsibilities, genuinely met their needs. These two long-standing issues were not effectively addressed.

Children

Care for children typically accounts for just under a quarter of public expenditure on the personal social services. From the 1948 Children Act, it had formally been a welfare priority. However the record, if not the prevalence, of child abuse relentlessly rose. New Labour had to deal with the legacy of systematic abuse in residential homes. The comprehensive Utting Report, *People Like Us* was published in 1997 and 98 police investigations were continuing in the early 2000s. Even more serious, however, were the continuing individual instances of child abuse.

Amongst the most distressing were the deaths in 2000 and 2004 respectively of Victoria Climbie and Toni-Ann Byfield.[32] Victoria was starved and beaten by her great-aunt. Toni-Ann was shot dead in a gangland feud involving her putative father who was a convicted drugs dealer. Both cases reflected the complexity of issues with which social workers had to deal with limited resources and conflicting agendas. In the Byfield case, for instance, lack of resources led to unread files, missed visits and inadequate liaison with other relevant authorities. A desire to implement the spirit of the 1989 Children Act, that care within the family should always have precedence, also led to precipitate action in placing the child near her putative father before the requisite checks had been completed. Social workers were clearly at fault.

In the Climbie case so too were a range of other professionals, such as doctors and police. They failed to respond to explicit signs of abuse. In the resulting enquiry the recommendation was made that, in order to eradicate such systemic failure, there should be a clearer identification of ultimate political and administrative responsibility. A minister for children was appointed in 2003, but not (as in Wales) a commissioner for children in England. The ministerial appointment patently had no immediate effect.

Conclusion

By accepting an enlarged role for non-state providers, New Labour drew closer to Conservative policy on the personal social services. It did, however, seek to vary that policy by removing the requirement that contracts should almost exclusively be signed with independent providers and be concerned with economic efficiency. Under 'best value' contracts quality of service could also be considered. This included responsiveness to 'expressed need' and to differences in culture and lifestyle. Non-state provision, however, expanded rather than contracted. The limited resources available to local authorities, and the regulatory regime under which they were placed, also restricted the degree of responsiveness to which they could aspire.

In practice, therefore, New Labour policy differed little from the Conservatives'. As in social security policy, innovation might be encouraged in new initiatives, such as those combating social exclusion. It was not in the more established services. As such their 'customers', such as vulnerable children, suffered. More fundamental issues, such as the potential conflict between uniform national standards and consumer empowerment, were also evaded rather than resolved.

15.3   HEALTHCARE

As seen in Chapter 14, the NHS attracted more resources and more controversy than any other welfare service. Following the two major 'spending' budgets of 2000 and 2002, its share of GDP was scheduled to rise from 5.3 per cent to 9.4 per cent by 2007/8. Controversy within the Party over the delivery of public services also centred on hospitals. Their construction and ownership under Private–Public Finance Partnerships begged fundamental questions about the extent and nature of non-state provision. 'Foundation' hospitals raised equally fundamental questions about the desirable degree of local autonomy.

The NHS attracted a disproportionate amount of resources because it was seen to provide a key electoral test. Could New Labour fulfil its promise to provide 'world-class public services'? Indeed, was government capable of ensuring the delivery of such services? Controversy was intense because the NHS was still revered as the essential embodiment of a welfare state, broadly defined. As Gordon Brown, for example, reassured the 2002 Labour Party conference:

> What we say and do about the NHS is not just about the future of our public services, but about the character of our country. It is an affirmation that duty, oblig-ation, service, and not just markets and self-interest, are at the very heart of our idea of society – at the heart of what it means to be a citizen of Britain.[33]

Before January 2000, when the Prime Minister made his televised promise to raise health spending to the European average, reform within the NHS had concentrated not on increased resources but increased regulation. This led to a torrent of targets. It also led to major administrative changes. These included the creation of:

- The National Institute of Clinical Excellence (NICE). Its role was to estab-lish the clinical and cost effectiveness of specific treatments and drugs. Initial fears that decisions would favour economic rather than clinical crite-ria proved groundless.
- National Service Frameworks (NSFs). These specified the optimal way in which particular diseases should be treated. The first diseases to be covered were cancer, coronary heart disease and diabetes. Various 'tsars' were simul-taneously appointed to coordinate action in key areas, such as mental health.
- The Commission of Health Improvement (CHI). Its duty was to provide regular inspection of hospitals to ensure NICE guidelines and NSFs were being followed. By 2001 hospitals were duly being awarded star ratings, based on some 62 indicators. In 2002, league tables were even published of heart surgeons. In 2004 CHI evolved with an enlarged remit into CHAI, the Commission on Healthcare Audit and Inspection.
- Primary Care Groups. All GP practices in England were grouped into some 480 units, each covering approximately 100,000 patients. After 2000 they could become trusts (PCTs). They had their own budgets – accounting in aggregate for 75 per cent of all NHS spending – and the responsibility of negotiating contracts with service deliverers, which might be public, private or even overseas organizations. They differed little in principle from the Conservatives' system of fund-holding GPs, which had been abolished in 1998. One practical difference, however, was that they covered all GPs so that there was not, as before, the potential inequity of a 'two-tier' system. Another was that they were much larger than fund-holding GP practices and therefore tended to be more bureaucratic and less entrepreneurial.

The 2000 budget, as has been seen, injected an unparalleled amount of new money into the NHS. Two key initiatives followed. An NHS Plan was published, providing details of how the money would be spent. More controversially, a concordat was signed with the Independent Healthcare Association for the greater provision of services by profit and not-for-profit providers. The NHS Plan issued a further rash of targets and threatened to assume control of the personal social services from local authorities. It also made further administrative changes. A Modernization Board and a Modernization Agency were established respectively to oversee and to drive through reform. Their major template was the ten-year Quality Agenda, agreed in 1998.

The NHS Plan could be presented as yet another exercise in overbearing centralization. For all its rhetoric about 'a health service designed around the patient' and devolved power, it famously referred to 'earned autonomy'.[34] Local discretion was apparently to be regarded not as the natural product of civil society but as a concession to be won from government. For all such failings, however, it did genuinely represent a new departure. Unlike so many earlier reforms it promised a real improvement in health standards because, as Toynbee and Walker have written, it was 'designed to spend money not to save it, devoted to outcomes not process, with scores of specific targets to be delivered to patients instead of new management systems'.[35] The NHS in other words was in a 'last-chance saloon'. With an unparalleled guarantee of sustained increases in resources, there was no longer any excuse for failure.

5   *Celebrating fifty years of the NHS*
Tony Blair used the anniversary of Labour's 'greatest achievement' to promise modernization. Others felt, however, that the NHS had been irreparably damaged by Mrs Thatcher.
Source: © Steve Bell, *The Guardian*, 2 July 1998.

Delivery thereafter became the key issue. This was demonstrated by the battles over PPPs and foundation hospitals not just within the Labour Party but also within government between the Treasury and the Ministry of Health (or more particularly their ministers, Gordon Brown and the leading 'Blairite', Alan Milburn, who felt obliged to resign in 2003). Controversy over the role of non-state providers, and the latent threat of privatization, intensified rather than ameliorated. In 2004, for example, seven private organizations were contracted to perform 250,000 operations a year over five years in order to cut NHS waiting lists. Opponents asserted that these, largely overseas, organizations would relieve the NHS of not just its income but also its staff. The NHS would be duly pilloried as being less efficient than its market competitors. In reply, supporters questioned how else, given the immediate lack of capacity in the NHS, the pledge to reduce waiting times for operations to six months could be honoured.

More positively, administrative burdens were eased in 2004 with the reduction of some 700 targets to 24 healthcare standards. The Treasury also published a report, *Securing Good Health for the Whole Population*, which placed renewed emphasis on the need for preventive measures. Since the 1950s, the Treasury had declined such a potentially cost-effective policy (see Section 7.2). Was there, as with the NHS Plan, to be another genuinely new departure? Was the NHS finally to be turned from a national sickness into a national health service?

The report was the second to be written for the Treasury by Sir Derek Wanless, the former chief executive of the NatWest bank. The first, entitled *Securing Our Future Health: taking a long-term view*, had provided the justification for massive investment in the NHS as currently financed. It had strongly advised against the adoption of alternative systems based on either social or private insurance, thereby confirming Nigel Lawson's riposte to Mrs Thatcher some 15 years earlier (see Section 13.3). Most of the shortcomings for which the NHS was criticized, Wanless argued, were common to healthcare systems throughout the world. If they were of greater intensity in the UK, it was because of a cumulative underspend since 1972 in relation to average European health spending of some £268 billion. There was no good reason for a radical change to Britain's virtually unique system of central funding. 'There is no evidence', he concluded:

> that any alternative financing method to the UK's would deliver a given quality of healthcare at a lower cost to the economy. Indeed other systems seem likely to prove more costly. . . . The current method by which healthcare is financed through general taxation is both a fair and efficient one.[36]

Taking into consideration all likely technological, demographic and medical developments, he then identified three speeds at which health policy might develop up to 2020. The three scenarios were entitled 'slow uptake', 'solid progress' and 'fully engaged'.

The second report was commissioned to determine how the 'fully engaged' scenario could be achieved. 'Our health service', it concluded, ' must evolve from dealing with acute problems through more effective control of chronic conditions to promoting the maintenance of good health.'[37] Much depended on changes in individual lifestyle, such as diet, smoking and exercise. The government could not dictate such changes. Through taxes, regulation and advice, however, it could provide a framework within which individual behaviour could be influenced. For example, taxes could be imposed on 'junk' food to combat obesity, and smoking in public places could be banned to reduce lung cancer. There should also be major improvements in the targeting, monitoring and administration of public health. The report, however, was short on specific recommendations. It certainly did not start to address the 'green' agenda (see Section 2.3.5).

Given this exceptional period of change and the increased concentration on service delivery:

- How, if at all, were health standards affected in the short term?
- How, if at all, did New Labour's policy differ in essence from that of the Conservatives?

Improving health standards

The public conviction was that the quality of healthcare fell after 1997. In part this was due to a series of scandals, such as the regular but unauthorized retention of dead patients' organs by hospitals and the revelation that a GP (Harold Shipman) was a mass murderer. Ministers, as in the 1960s with the revelation of abuse in mental hospitals, did not minimize such scandals. This enabled them to maintain pressure on the medical profession to reform. To ministers' discredit, however, public disillusion was also the result of their early and unrealistic inflation of expectations.

Convictions about lowering standards were not typically supported by individual experience. This is well demonstrated by the findings of a major opinion survey in 2002. Of those polled, only 15 per cent rated as 'good' the standard of service provided by the NHS nationally. Yet the percentage rose to 41 in relation to the standard of local services. It rose still further to 75 per cent in relation to most recent visits to the GP or local hospital. This discrepancy was reflected and reinforced by the media. It was typically left unreported that such discrepancies were a worldwide phenomenon. So too was the fact that expressed satisfaction within Britain was relatively high. Another poll organized by the Commonwealth Fund in 2002, for example, recorded that – of the five countries covered (including the USA) – there was least dissatisfaction with healthcare in Britain, popular estimates of declining standards were average and concern about the cost of care was by far the lowest.[38]

There can as yet be no conclusive resolution of the dispute over whether standards of health and of healthcare rose or fell after 1997. This is because there is an inevitable time lag in the collection of data and, more importantly in relation to standards of health, in the actual impact of reform on standards of health. There is also, as all major surveys such as the second Wanless report have bemoaned, a remarkable failure systematically to collect and assimilate what data are available. Nevertheless, there is sufficient evidence to suggest that inputs, outputs and outcomes of healthcare have all significantly improved.

- The NHS, as is well known, is one of the largest organizations in the world. With 1.2 million employees in 2000, its only serious competitors are the Russian army and the Indian state railways. Every day in 2000, one million patients saw a primary care doctor; 1.5 million prescriptions were dispensed; and 25,000 operations were performed.
- *Inputs.*   The capacity of the NHS significantly increased after 1997 to meet growing demand. For example, between 1997 and 2002 the whole-time-equivalent number of doctors rose from just under 83,000 to 95,611. The number of nurses simultaneously rose by 35,000 to 291,285. There were also some imaginative innovations to meet patients' changing expectations. In 1999, for example, the telephone/internet service, NHS Direct, and walk-in centres were established. By 2003, NHS Direct was handling some 6.3 million calls a year.
- *Outputs.*   After a slight lag, increased capacity produced results. A key test is patients' waiting time. Most improved. Between 2000 and 2003, for example, the number of people having to wait over a year for hospital admission fell from 4.7 per cent to zero. Conversely, those waiting for *less* than four hours in Accident and Emergency departments rose in 2002/3 from 77 per cent to 82 per cent. Equally importantly, in the key area of breast cancer 98 per cent of patients in 2003 were seen by a consultant within 14 days of referral and 96 per cent were treated within a month of diagnosis.
- *Outcomes.*   Improved outputs were translated into improvements in individual health. Mortality rates are accepted as providing a reliable measure of changing health standards. They are typically calculated on a three-year rolling average. Between 1995/7 and 1999/2001, the rate for two of the most common causes of death is recorded as having decreased significantly. Out of every 100,000 people, the rate for circulatory disease fell from 142 to 115, and that for cancer from 141 to 129. The infant mortality rate, perhaps the most sensitive indicator reflecting all socio-economic as well as institutional factors affecting health, also fell. In 1996/8 there were 5.7 deaths for every 1000 live births. In 1999/2001 there were 5.3.

Despite popular and press convictions to the contrary, therefore, the available evidence suggests that the reform of the NHS since 1997 has borne results. By international comparison, healthcare in Britain is well planned and increasingly effective. 'England may well be unique', an authoritative Nuffield Trust study has concluded, 'in the nature of its comprehensive conceptualisation and implementation of a systemic quality agenda.' Glennerster has also confirmed the judgement of the first Wanless report that 'the UK has one of the most progressively financed systems of healthcare and one of the most equitably delivered'.[39]

The *achievement* of greater equity of outcome, however, still eluded the NHS. A new funding formula was designed by the Advisory Committee of Resources Allocation to apportion resources to PCTs more sensitively in relation to age, class and ethnic need. Health action zones were also established to target additional resources on deprived areas. Despite the aggregate improvement in infant mortality, however, the differential in the rates between the top and bottom three social groups nevertheless increased between 1996/8 and 1999/2001. Moreover, whilst that for all other groups declined, the rate for the bottom class marginally increased.

Infant mortality is determined in part by the health of mothers, which would be affected by their experience before 1997. It is also too soon to record the impact of increased expenditure after 2000. Such statistics, however, must qualify any positive assessment of improvements to healthcare and health standards after 1997.

Increasing consensus?

In opposition, New Labour had been diametrically opposed to internal markets and the use of private healthcare organizations. Any government, Robin Cook as the Party's health spokesman had proclaimed, would 'get it in the neck'. Similarly, Alan Milburn had sworn that he would 'come down like a ton of bricks' on any health manager dallying with the private sector.[40] However Primary Care Trusts, as has been seen, were little different in principle from the Conservatives' fund-holding GPs. Milburn himself, as secretary of state for health, also signed the concordat with the Independent Healthcare Association in 2000 and actually appointed private sector managers to take over four 'failing' hospitals in 2002.

There was further engagement with the private sector. As has been seen, Private Public Finance Partnerships were crucial from 1997 onwards to the modernization of the NHS's infrastructure. In 2004 private companies also became crucial to the provision of 'fast track' treatment to clear the backlog of operations. Significant elements of healthcare were also effectively privatized. In dentistry, for example, private treatment between 1997 and 2001 increased by 60 per cent. Under a half of adults and two-thirds of children were registered with an NHS dentist.

Under New Labour, therefore, the market both provided services and influenced the nature of management within the NHS. As the Nuffield Trust survey concluded: 'Despite the government's ostensible rejection of the internal market model . . . the direction of initiatives over the past five years has been to develop and foster dynamics commonly associated with a market environment.'[41]

Such a *volte face* and apparent convergence with former Conservative policy could, and was, readily justified on the pragmatic grounds that 'what counts is what works'. Hospitals had to be built and the 'golden rules' disallowed the necessary public borrowing. When fund-holding was disbanded in 1998, productivity within healthcare – which had been annually increasing by

2 per cent – was recorded as decreasing in absolute terms.[42] There was also the crucial need to meet changing patient expectations. At the 2003 Labour Party conference, the new health secretary actually quoted Mrs Thatcher's earlier justification for private healthcare. She wanted, she had said, to go to hospital on the day she wanted at the time she wanted and to be treated by the doctor she wanted. She had been reviled. Now such a wish was to be regarded as everyone's right. That required a mix of provision by public, private and not-for-profit agencies.[43]

Gordon Brown conceded the need for greater pragmatism. The ideological battle over the virtues of services provided exclusively by the market or the state was, he argued, obsolete. The real challenge was to make informed judgements in each area of policy about whether the role of the market should be enhanced, more tightly regulated or rejected as inappropriate. Healthcare, in his judgement, was an area where the market was inappropriate. As he concluded in an important speech to the Social Market Foundation in 2003, even its effective regulation was impractical. In any case public was to be preferred to market provision because it was 'likely to achieve more at less cost to efficiency and without putting at risk the gains from the ethic of public service where, at its best, dedicated public servants put duty, obligation and service before profit or personal reward'.[44]

What then of PPPs and the change of management ethos within the NHS? PPPs were, he claimed, in no sense privatisation. They were wholly shaped by the 'public interest', which he defined as the achievement of 'opportunity and security for all'. In contrast private provision would have been shaped by the maximization of private profit. Accordingly, priority would have been given to the needs of those who could pay the most. Equally, changed management priorities within the NHS were not a capitulation to the market values but a necessary response to the growing variety of consumer need. They were designed to show those 'who assert that whatever the market failure, state failure will always be greater' that 'a publicly funded and provided service can deliver efficiency, equity and be responsive to the consumer'. In short, there was no emerging consensus. New Labour might be adopting some of the Conservatives' means. It was not adopting their ends.

Lack of consensus, however, arguably existed within the Labour Party rather than between New Labour and the Conservatives. To satisfy consumer choice, Brown agreed, there should be a 'maximum amount of diversity consistent with equity'. He was distinctly ambivalent, however, over how that circle could be squared and, in particular, whether diversity should be delivered by non-state providers. How far, therefore, were consumers to be really empowered? Were they to favour non-state provision, was this to be allowed? The Ministry of Health, supported by the Prime Minister, championed – like the Conservatives - the maximum decentralization of both management within the NHS and power to the consumer. Brown appeared willing only to contemplate the former to satisfy the latter.[45] This is where the real fault line lay within government (see also Section 14.3.3).

15.4   EDUCATION

Education was New Labour's declared priority and, together with healthcare, the service which received the greatest budget increase. 'Education, education, education' was the mantra endlessly repeated at the 1997 election when questions were raised about the Party's main aims. In 2004 Tony Blair remained equally committed. 'Education was, is and will be', he reassured head teachers, 'the top priority so long as we are in office.'[46] Accordingly, its percentage of GDP was scheduled to rise from 4.7 in 1996/7 to 5.6 in 2005/6 (see Table 14.2). The reason for such commitment was that education was seen as key to the achievement of both social inclusion and labour market reform. It promised greater equality of opportunity. Equally it promised greater employability.

There were, however, two qualifications to educational advance. First, whatever its relative increase in funding, its share of GDP remained well below the 6.5 per cent it had enjoyed at the end of the classic welfare state in 1975/6. Moreover, until 2001/2 the percentage remained below that attained under the Conservatives in the 1990s.[47] Second, the advance was not smooth. In fact it was so imperfectly planned and implemented that it was the cause of two major political crises and much unnecessary disruption.

Politically, one secretary of state for education felt obliged to resign; and a rebellion within the Party over university tuition fees, as has been seen, temporarily reduced the government's parliamentary majority to five.

The minister who felt obliged to resign in 2002 was Estelle Morris. She was, nominally, the victim of a remarkable success for which the government perversely won little credit. In 1997, education ministers had committed themselves to the raising of the standard of numeracy and literacy amongst children leaving primary school. By 2002, the percentage achieving the target level in mathematics was to be raised from 45 to 75. The parallel rise in English was to be from 49 per cent to 80 per cent. If these targets were not met, the ministers promised, they would resign. After 1997 standards of both numeracy and literacy improved faster than at any time since the 1940s. The precise targets, however, were not met.[48] The minister felt honour bound to resign.

University tuition fees again exposed the fault line within New Labour over the degree of independence service providers (in this case universities) should enjoy and the amount of diversity or choice that should be offered their customers (students). Initially this divided the No 10 Policy Unit (which advised the Prime Minister) and the Treasury. Both agreed that higher education desperately required more money. Both also agreed that, because graduates typically commanded larger salaries than school leavers, they should contribute towards its cost. But how? In 1997, New Labour had abolished maintenance grants and introduced means-tested tuition fees. At a stroke the universal right to free higher education, established under the classic welfare state, had been withdrawn. The required increase in both university income and equality of opportunity, however, had not been attained.

The new compromise policy was that universities should to be permitted to charge annual tuition fees of up to £3000. Their income would thereby be boosted. Student loans to cover both these fees and maintenance were to continue; but no student needed to repay these loans until their graduate income approached three-quarters of the national average. Less advantaged students might be discouraged by the increased cost. Means-tested maintenance grants were therefore reintroduced (for which, it was estimated, the poorer third would qualify). In addition, universities charging the maximum fee were obliged to offer bursaries of £300 p.a. They had also to strive for an optimum social mix, under the watchful eye of the Office of Fair Access.

Potentially this was a highly redistributive package. For students from relatively 'deprived' backgrounds, access was to be more open and the cost low until their graduate income approached the national average. More affluent students would bear more up-front costs. Why, then, did so many Labour MPs rebel? There were three principal reasons. First, there was considerable anger at the breaking of an election commitment not to introduce 'top-up' fees. Second, there was a conviction that the £3000 cap on fees would be raised as soon as was politic. Finally, there was apprehension that a two-tier higher education system would emerge, as poorer students opted for cheaper courses and universities. More considered and open planning could have allayed many of these concerns.

Professional disruption principally centred around examinations and teacher morale. A bold attempt to increase the 'relevance' and broaden the content of education following the 1997 Kennedy report, *Learning Works*. In particular, vocational GCSEs were introduced in England. So too was an A/S level exam, designed to slow the speed at which students had to specialize in order to qualify for university entrance. The precipitate and unpiloted introduction of such initiatives, however, left unclear the requisite standards of attainment. This became transparent when A/S marks were incorporated for the first time into A level grades in 2002. A public outcry ensued over apparent grading errors, which prevented students from entering their university of choice. In the end, after extensive remarking, only 2000 students had their papers regraded. Confidence in the examination system had nevertheless been undermined.

Confidence within the teaching profession, seriously eroded under the Conservatives, continued to decline. This was in part because, as a result of the fiscal straitjacket, pay in England (but not in Scotland) fell in real terms by some 14 per cent. It was also because increased regulation and inspection added to teachers' burdens outside the classroom whilst reducing their professional freedom within.

The government belatedly strove to make amends. Merit pay was introduced, for which 80 per cent of teachers duly qualified. A new contract also limited their administrative responsibilities, in part by the employment of more classroom assistants. These changes were contested. How was merit best judged? Did the employment of untrained assistants threaten the professional status? In any case, their implementation was forestalled by a funding crisis. Given rising national insurance contributions (to help fund the NHS) and decreasing income from a falling number of students (as a result of demographic change), neither merit pay nor an increase of assistants could be fully afforded. Morale, and faith in government, was further shaken.

Given such a catalogue of crises:

- How were general standards maintained and improved?
- How were special needs met?
- How, if at all, did New Labour's policy differ from that which it had inherited?

General standards

As in healthcare, New Labour provided a plethora of targets and prescriptions as well as comprehensive inspection. The abrasive chief inspector of schools, inherited from the Conservatives, was not impressed. In 2001 he concluded that one-tenth of primary schools, one-eighth of secondary schools and one-twentieth of lessons were unsatisfactory.[49] Other more measured judgements have been that standards of *provision* have improved, particularly as the result of the employment of an additional 25,000 teachers and 90,000 support staff between 1997 and 2004. So too has *attainment*. In short, by international standards, the British education system has provided good value for money.[50]

At the nursery level, the 1997 pledges were honoured to provide places for all 4-year-olds and for all 3-years-olds who required one. This denoted a five-fold increase to over one million places. The promise was made in 2002 to extend increased provision to 2-year-olds.

In primary schools, provision was increased by the honouring of the 1997 pledge to reduce class sizes for 5- to 7-year-olds. The number of children in oversized classes fell from 485,000 to virtually nil, before rising slightly in 2003. League tables were also introduced in 1999. This provided a competitive edge for the attainment of higher standards. The means was new daily 'literacy hours' and 'numeracy hours', introduced respectively in 1998 and 1999. This innovation was highly prescriptive. Teachers were being told for the first time not just what to teach but how to teach. As seen from the rising levels of literacy and numeracy, however, it was highly successful.

At the secondary level, examination results similarly improved. For example, the number of children attaining one key goal – five passes at GCSE at A* to C grade – increased by 2 per cent a year to almost 53 per cent in 2004. The pass rate at A level simultaneously increased from 87 per cent to 95 per cent. The percentage of A grades awarded similarly rose from 16 to almost 21.

The inevitable controversy broke out over whether these results represented declining standards or better teaching. What such arguments overlooked was the increased motivation to succeed provided to schools by their greater freedom both to spend their own income and to specialize. In opposition, David Blunkett had been adamant in rejecting Conservative policy.

'Read my lips', he had instructed a Party conference, 'no selection by examination or interview.'[51] The specialization he endorsed, however, permitted just such selection. Some 450 schools were initially involved and a total of 1500 was planned by 2006. The days of the 'bog standard' comprehensive were numbered. So too, indeed, were 'bog standard' buildings. In 2004 a £40 billion plan was launched to rebuild or refurbish all secondary schools within eight years.

Higher education was the area which fared least well in relation to provision. This was demonstrated by the urgency with which increased tuition fees were introduced. Between 1995 and 2000, its share of GDP shrank from 1.2 per cent to 1 per cent. It thereby slipped from tenth to nineteenth in the OECD expenditure rankings. At the same time the number of school leavers entering university had risen to 43 per cent. The graduation rate remained internationally high. Universities did, however, start to subside under a deluge of regulation and inspection.

The introduction of league tables for primary schools illustrated New Labour's willingness to accept, but also to adapt, Conservative innovation. League tables had been ridiculed when introduced. Now their coverage was extended from secondary to primary education. However, an attempt was made to remedy one of their major weaknesses. This was the lack of a 'value added' score. How far did a school counter the effects of social exclusion? How far was the potential of all, not just of the more clever and privileged, children realized? Simple tests on entry and modified tests at 7 provided a benchmark for individual pupil's progress by the age of 11.

Special needs

New Labour's concern was not just to raise general standards, thereby retaining middle-class confidence in state schools. It was also to address social exclusion, thereby achieving greater equality of opportunity. At each level of education, therefore, there were attempts to encourage as well as to compel the education system to address disadvantage.

Since the days of Mrs Thatcher as minister of education in the early 1970s, there had been an aspiration to expand pre-school provision to reduce disadvantage. Aspiration was finally transformed into reality by the expansion of nursery education, noted above, combined with initiatives such as Sure Start (see Section 15.1).

In primary schools, it was later conceded, the targeting of deprivation was not maximized. The resources expended on reducing all class sizes below 30 could arguably have been better spent on achieving even greater reductions in deprived areas. This is an instance of where an over-hasty commitment, made in response to public concern about educational standards in general, deflected concentration from the attack on social exclusion.

At the secondary level, better targeting was attempted through Education Action Zones, in which Private Public Partnerships could be used both to physically develop and manage schools. It was not a great success, and contracts started to be terminated in 2001. In their place City Academies were championed. They were schools with a specialist mission which could also call on a mix of public and private finance. Success, it was thought, would be better assured if attention was concentrated on individual institutions rather than complete neighbourhoods. Competition, in short, was favoured over cooperation.

Compulsion was also largely concentrated at the secondary level. 'Failing' schools were identified and tackled. Most were to be found in deprived areas. Within three weeks, for example, New Labour had 'named and shamed' 18 schools. Then in 2000, schools in which less than 15 per cent of pupils gained five A*–C grades at GCSE were threatened with closure. Typically these schools were given a 'Fresh Start' with a new head teacher, governors and even private management. Closure was rarely enforced, but total success was equally rare.[52] The high profile attack on truancy was equally ineffective. Such failings, however, may have reflected not the inadequacy of schools but wider social forces, such as 'failing' parents.

Considerable effort, as has been seen, was made to broaden access in England to higher education. Its effectiveness can be contrasted to that of alternative policies in Scotland. There tuition fees had been rejected because of the potential disincentive they were seen to represent. Established courses (such as HNDs) at established colleges of education were also used to assist disadvantaged students, rather than untried experiments such as foundation degrees. By 2004, the target had already been attained of having 50 per cent of all 18- to 30-year-olds in higher education. This admittedly may reflect not just more effective policy but a national culture which holds education in high esteem.

Consensus?

New Labour overtly sought to distance itself from the Conservatives by ending assisted places and the nursery voucher scheme. Both were seen to use public money to increase inequality and support private education. Covertly, however, it accepted the bulk of Conservative reforms in relation, for example, to the national curriculum, testing, and increased devolution of power to individual schools and parents. Indeed, in some cases it extended them further than the Conservatives may have dared.

Following on from the national curriculum, for example, prescription was greatly increased by the introduction of the daily literacy and numeracy hour. Selection of pupils by schools was reintroduced under the guise of specialization. The role of Local Education Authorities (LEAs) was also further downgraded, with the requirement under the 'Fair Funding' formula that the percentage of grant they passed directly to schools be increased from 85 to 90. Greater sums of money were also allocated directly from the centre.[53]

Even more remarkable was the accommodation with the market. Private education was not attacked (as it had been in the 1960s) but in some ways treated as a 'beacon' for advancing good practice. Cooperation with, and even the taking over of 'failing' schools within, the state sector was encouraged. Private companies actually did assume control of such schools as well as 'failing' LEAs, such as Bradford, Hackney and Islington. Where standards did not rise, and profits were thereby threatened, contracts were even revised to permit lower standards.[54]

Such a policy could again be justified on pragmatic grounds. All the available evidence showed that both the poorest performing schools and those with the largest number of poor pupils benefited disproportionately from the mixture of competition and compulsion which New Labour embraced. It was, as Glennerster has tactfully concluded, 'difficult not to accept that something significant had occurred'.[55]

New Labour could also argue that, although it was using Conservative means, it was pursuing very different ends. It was actively and not just passively seeking greater equality of opportunity. The success of such a policy is impossible to gauge in the short term. The effectiveness of increased pre-school education, for example, in breaking the cycle of deprivation will take a generation to prove. In the short term, however, there are grounds for concern. As with infant mortality, for instance, improvements in overall standards conceal growing class disparities. This is true, for example, of GCSE results.[56] The plateauing at around 75 per cent of adequacy in numeracy and literacy at the age of 11 also reveals a potential hard core of permanent disadvantage. Existing policy may not be sufficient.

15.5   HOUSING

Housing, together with social security, was the area of welfare of greatest potential importance to New Labour's concept of joined-up government. This was because it affected, and was affected by, all other economic and social policies. Economically, for example, the emphasis placed in 1997 on the control of inflation (and thus interest rates) reflected the voting power of home-owners with mortgages, whom the Conservatives were earlier perceived to have betrayed. Conversely, by 2004 considerable concern was being expressed that escalating house prices, and the level of personal indebtedness they encouraged, could adversely affect economic growth. Socially, improved housing was identified as a key to greater social inclusion. Hence, together with measures to combat crime and to promote education, it had a central place in the major initiatives of the Social Exclusion Unit, such as the New Deal for Communities and the Neighbourhood Renewal Fund.[57]

Given such potential importance, it was all the more surprising that –

particularly in relation to social security and the New Deal – so little attention was paid to housing in opposition. Equally surprising, little legislative time was spent on it after 1997 and little attention was accorded to it during both the 1997 and 2001 elections. In addition the percentage of GDP spent on it actually halved between 1997 and 2000 to the extraordinarily low figure of 0.3 (see Table 14.2). In 1999, an innovatory programme was advanced by an Urban Task Force under the chairmanship of the architect, Lord Rogers.[58] Its more imaginative recommendations were, however, ignored.

Given such neglect, how well – if at all – were the traditional objectives of housing policy, identified in Chapter 9, satisfied? These objectives were the provision of:

- a sufficient quantity of housing in a well-planned environment
- of an acceptable quality
- at an affordable price.

Quantity

In the late 1990s it was officially estimated that there would be an additional 3.8 million households in the UK by 2021. This meant that on average an extra 150,000 homes needed to be built each year; 60 per cent of these, it was hoped, could be built on land that had already been developed but had fallen into disuse ('brown field' sites).

The Urban Task Force provided a vision of how these goals might be achieved through a mixture of incentives and penalties. There should be incentives to attract people to city centres, where some three-quarter of a million properties were lying empty. These included the creation of Home Zones (where the needs of pedestrians took precedence over traffic) and Urban Priority Areas (which would enjoy a number of tax breaks). There should also be an active regional policy, as adopted in the 1940s, to prevent a drift of employment to the south-east of England. The major penalty should be an environmental tax to discourage building on underdeveloped ('green field') sites.

New Labour, however, failed both to safeguard the environment and to build sufficient houses. In the interest of 'market efficiency', no serious attempt was made to minimize the adverse externalities of firms locating themselves in areas where private profit could be maximized (see Section 3.2.1). Consequently, while unused buildings were being demolished in the north of England, a major house-building programme was announced in 2002 for the south-east – regardless of the environmental damage and the over-stretching of the social infrastructure (such as transport networks) which this entailed.

Simultaneously the building of new homes fell to its lowest point since the war, with only 179,160 units completed in 2000/1 (of which a mere 25,527 were publicly built). Given concurrent demolition, this was insufficient to meet long-term need. It was also insufficient in the short term. In the 1997 manifesto, people sleeping rough had been condemned as a 'powerful symbol of Tory neglect of our society'.[59] The cutting of their number by two-thirds by 2001 was much trumpeted. However, the number of rough sleepers had only been 1850 and the consequent reduction a mere 1300. At the very same time, the number of 'statutorily homeless' in England had soared from just under 44,000 in 1997 to 75,000 in 2002. Those living in the most unsatisfactory option of temporary 'bed and breakfast accommodation' more than trebled to over 12,000. This was given rather less publicity.

Quality

After 1997, the principal focus of government policy with regard to quality was the £19 billion backlog of repairs in properties owned by local authorities. A decent home for all was promised and an ever-increasing sum of money allocated to achieve this end.

In a complete reversal of Bevan's postwar drive to municipalize all rented accommodation, however, a condition for the release of the new money was that local authority ownership of social housing should end. The object was to empower and provide diversity of choice for tenants, who had arguably been long neglected by housing managers. There were safeguards. Removal from local government control was only to be possible if the majority of tenants voted in favour. The new owners were also to be mainly not-for-profit housing associations, over which tenants could exercise a greater influence.

What New Labour failed to foresee, however, was that tenants increasingly regarded any transfer from local authority control as 'privatization' and rejected it. Nevertheless the key principle behind the policy was not abandoned, although it had been developed under the Conservatives. The justification was that, in most social democracies within Western Europe, social housing was owned and managed by non-state bodies. Britain's council house programme had been exceptional.

The government's greatest success came in April 2002 when agreement was reached in Glasgow, despite its 'red Clydeside' tradition, that all municipal housing should be transferred to the Glasgow Housing Association. Just over two-thirds of tenants voted, and of them 58 per cent voted in favour. At a stroke the council's housing debt of almost £1 billion was cleared and a further £1.5 billion allocated for renovation. Simultaneously, however, a similar deal was rejected in Birmingham – despite its Chamberlainite Tory Democrat tradition. Policy was duly modified. As well as entering Private Public Finance Partnerships, local authorities were additionally allowed to transfer the management, but not the ownership, of properties to ALMOs (arm-length management organisations). Even this compromise, however, was rejected by voters in the London borough of Camden in 2004. A renovation grant of over £250 million was thereby lost. Camden, by all official criteria, was a highly efficient local authority. Why, in the pragmatic spirit of 'what counts is what works', should access to the grant have been made conditional on the transfer of management to a new and untried body?

As a result of such disruption, the government's renovation programme was placed in jeopardy. By 2004, just under 1.6 million properties had been transferred in equal number to housing associations and ALMOs. Voting was due on a further 300,000 properties. That still left over 1.2 million firmly under local authority management and with insufficient resources for renovation.[60]

Price

Given the shortage of housing in required areas, the problem of price also remained unresolved. The final ending of mortgage interest tax relief in 2000 increased equity, but did not, as expected, reduce the rise in *private* house prices. A Starter Home initiative even had to be introduced to enable key public sector workers to live in high-cost areas. At the same time, the affordability of *social* housing continued to be dogged by the complexity of housing benefit. It was claimed by one-quarter of all households and, as a social security benefit, was applicable in Scotland and Wales. It thereby impeded any devolved remedies.

The complexity of housing benefit and the attendant social inequities actually increased. There were over 90 administrative changes during New Labour's first year in office. Then in 2000 many councils contracted out its administration to a private firm, CSL, which immediately collapsed under the weight. One senior director was aptly named Dick Turpin. In 2003/4 eight pilot schemes were launched to stabilize and make more equitable all support throughout the social housing sector. Inevitably it was predicted that, to attain 'economic' levels of rent throughout the sector, there would have to be sustained rent rises for half a million people over the following ten years.[61]

Conclusion

One verdict on New Labour's housing policy was that it represented an 'insipid attempt to achieve modest objectives'.[62] The objectives were modest because, on issues such as the location of employment and the regeneration of inner cities, policy failed to challenge the 'market logic'. The means chosen – be it 'brown field' development, the ending of mortgage interest tax relief or the transfer of social housing from local authority control – were also strikingly similar to those of preceding Conservative governments. Initially there was an almost exclusive focus on the localized issue of social exclusion. Even here, however, anticipated progress – as with later attempts to transfer social housing – was frustrated by unanticipated public reaction.

15.6   THE COMPARATIVE ACHIEVEMENT

After its 1992 election defeat, the Labour Party fundamentally rethought its political principles and strategy. Hence the attraction of the Third Way and the Party's rebranding as New Labour. The consequence was that, after the landslide victory in 1997, its welfare policy – as has been seen – bore a marked resemblance to that of the preceding Conservative government.

Convergence was comprehensive, covering all major areas of welfare from a basic understanding of human nature to the ultimate objectives of policy and the means of their attainment. In accordance with conservative thinking in the USA, for instance, welfare dependency was abhorred as a reflection of personal weakness. Individual responsibility was as important as individual rights. Personal self-reliance should therefore be encouraged, in particular through paid work and private savings. Likewise, the ultimate goal of policy was perceived to be no longer equality of outcome but equality of opportunity. The principal means for its attainment should be, as favoured by the Conservatives in the 1960s, means-tested and not universal benefits.

The real core of convergence, however, was the pre-eminence accorded to the market. Under the preceding social democratic consensus, the accepted role of government had been to maximize individual welfare through the active management of the economy. This was deemed to have failed. After 1997, therefore, New Labour abandoned Keynesian demand management in favour of monetarism. Moreover, it immediately ceded control over monetary policy to the Bank of England. Consequently it could only advance individual welfare indirectly. The market, it was assumed, could best maximize wealth creation and employment. Government should do all it could to ensure its efficiency. Thus welfare policy, such as the New Deal, was geared to increase the flexibility of the labour market. Moreover, when the needs of individual welfare clashed with those of the market – as over industrial location or the provision of more flexible working conditions – they were disregarded. A subtle shift, in other words, had occurred in the relative importance to government of individual welfare and the market. The market now took precedence.

There was a similarly subtle shift in the relationship between the market and government. Under the classic welfare state, government had actively intervened – most dramatically through nationalization – to correct market failure. Now the market was actively encouraged to intervene to correct perceived government failure. Thus private companies were invited to take over 'failing' schools. They were also encouraged, as in healthcare and the personal social services, to provide core welfare services in competition with the state and voluntary organizations. Even where direct intervention was impossible, surrogate market discipline was introduced in the form of internal or quasi-markets. Moreover, the virtues of private-sector management techniques were lauded over the public service ethic. As with the market, the ultimate purpose was to maximize cost-effectiveness and to respond to changing consumer demand. The producers of welfare remained, as under the Conservatives, discredited.[63]

- Did such convergence signify the creation of a new welfare consensus?
- How – if at all – did the record of New Labour and the Conservatives diverge in traditionally the most contentious area of welfare: the achievement of greater 'equality'?

- Did convergence provide a model for the restructuring of other welfare states? Had Britain once again become a welfare pioneer?

The new consensus

Despite the growing political convergence, tensions remained both between *and* within the two Parties. They had, in essence, a common source. How far could and should the market subsume the former role of government?

Within the Conservative Party, as has been seen, there was a specific battle in the 1980s over the 'privatization' of the NHS. Then, as a result the 1993 fundamental review, there was a more generalized battle over the extent to which the welfare state should be 'dismantled'. Within the Labour movement, and in particular within the trade unions, there were still those who opposed any encroachment by the market. Within government, however, there was ready acknowledgement – as Gordon Brown's speech to the Social Market Foundation in 2003 testified – that there could no longer be a wholesale ideological rejection of the market.[64] The key question was now a pragmatic one. In each specific area of welfare, should the role of the market be enhanced, regulated or acknowledged to be inappropriate? Even this question, however, split the Cabinet. If consumers were fully empowered and could enjoy a personalized form of welfare (as wanted by the Prime Minister) would this not destroy the welfare state as the institutional embodiment of social solidarity?

The existence of such tensions, however, does not invalidate the concept of consensus. They merely represented variation within, not a direct challenge to, the common framework in which individual welfare policies were formulated and implemented by both Parties: the pre-eminence of the market, a mixed economy of welfare and the empowerment of consumers. Similar tensions had existed within the postwar social democratic consensus. They were simply testimony to the fact that the two Parties had converged from very different ideological positions.

The reasons for this 'effective' or 'implicit' consensus were, in addition, identical to those which had fashioned the postwar consensus.[65] *Administratively*, policy had to be practical. New Labour, for example, had initially disbanded the internal market within the NHS. Productivity declined. The internal market, therefore, had to be reintroduced in the form of Primary Care Trusts. Similarly, in the personal social services the requirement to 'privatize' service delivery was dropped. Local authorities, however, chose to continue with it and even proceeded to privatize domiciliary care. *Electorally*, resounding defeat in 1992 convinced Labour leaders that the traditional policy of 'tax and spend' was no longer viable. Even the landslide victory in 1997, in the interpretation of Toynbee and Walker, could be viewed simply as a call for a kinder form of Conservatism.[66]

How could the new consensus be described? It could hardly be called 'Thatcherite'. Mrs Thatcher might have finally destroyed the old social democratic consensus, but her personal mission, as has been seen, was to dismantle not to reform the welfare state. Nor could it be called a 'Washington' consensus. International financiers undoubtedly approved of many of New Labour's initiatives: its fiscal discipline, tax changes to encourage labour market participation (tax credits), and public *investment* in both health and education. However, the *scale* of government intervention remained consonant with British welfare traditions and was thus excessive by their standards.

Rather, the consensus accorded more to the social market advocated by the Social Democratic Party in the 1980s or even the principle of 'reluctant collectivism' advanced by 'One Nation' Conservatives in the 1950s and 1960s (see Section 2.2.1). Both acknowledged the pre-eminence of the market, but insisted upon a judicious degree of state intervention to correct its inherent flaws. Both, it should be noted, were also attacked – like New Labour – for unprincipled opportunism.

Equality

Within the postwar social democratic consensus, the greatest tension between the Parties had concerned equality. To what extent, in rhetoric and substance, did the Conservatives and New Labour continue to diverge?

The Conservatives' principal rhetorical device after 1997 was a Tax Freedom Day. This was the day on which tax-payers 'stopped working for the state and started working for themselves'. By 2003, it was calculated, taxation consumed aggregate earnings for the first 147 days of the year. Tax Freedom Day was therefore May 27. Such a concept was, of course, disingenuous for three main reasons. First, so far as taxation funded welfare policy, it ignored the reality of the welfare state as 'a piggy bank' redistributing resources horizontally as much as vertically (see Chapter 1). The better-off, as has been seen, were consistently among the principal beneficiaries of state welfare. Second, even social security expenditure, as with the New Deal, was increasingly geared to support the market. Finally, whatever political rhetoric and popular conviction, Britain remained – as has been seen in Table 14.3 – a relatively low-taxed country.

On the left, the Fabian Society Commission on Tax and Citizenship in 2000 sought to counter this negative vision of tax. It reasserted Keynes' dictum that taxation was the justifiable subscription to be paid for living in a civilized society. It also recommended ways in which, and purposes for which, it could be justifiably expanded. The New Labour government itself was not quite so bold. Its leaders had been deeply shaken by the rejection of its proposal for tax increases in 1992. They were so again in 2000 by the intensity of popular anger during the fuel tax protest. Consequently, they proceeded by stealth. In both the 1997 and 2001 elections, the pledge was made not to increase rates of income tax or VAT. Instead, extra revenue was amassed from the proceeds of economic growth, increases in indirect taxation (such as the new tax on pension funds), and the withdrawal of tax allowances (such as tax relief on mortgage interest payments). The extra revenue amassed was considerable. As has been seen, some £11 billion was

Table 15.2   Distribution of personal wealth, 1976–2001

% of wealth held by wealthiest	1976	1986	1996	1999	2001
1%	21	18	20	23	23
5%	38	36	40	43	43
10%	50	50	52	55	56
25%	71	73	74	74	75
50%	92	90	93	94	95

Source: Inland Revenue at www.statistics.gov.uk/cci (April 2004)

redistributed between 1997 and 2001, with the main recipients being pensioners and working families.

The remarkable fact, however, was that such redistribution failed to reverse the exceptional increase in inequality that was Mrs Thatcher's legacy.[67] As can be seen from Table 15.2, the distribution of personal *wealth* actually grew more unequal under New Labour. The share of wealth held by the richest half of the population rose from 93 per cent to 95 per cent between 1996 and 2001. The same was true of the distribution of *personal income*. As explained in Section 11.1, the gini coefficient is the conventional measure of income equality. The nearer it is to zero, the greater the equality. Between 1979 and 1997, it had leapt from 0.25 to 0.34. Britain had been transformed from one of the most equal societies in the European Union to the sixth most unequal. Under New Labour, the gini coefficient remained at an historic high. It even rose marginally. Britain by 2001 was the fourth most unequal country in the EU.

The increasing inequality of income over time is represented graphically in Figure 15.2, where the ninetieth percentile represent the top 10 per cent of income earners and the tenth percentile the lowest. Further evidence of escalating inequality under Mrs Thatcher is provided by the bottom graph in Figure 15.1.

Figure 15.1 also confirms the surprising fact that income inequality was reduced under John Major's government whilst, for all its apparent redistribution, there was no such reduction under New Labour before 2003. There were two main reasons for this. First, under New Labour, there *was* some vertical redistribution within the middle 70 per cent of income earners. However, at the two extremes, the incomes of the richest 15 per cent rose disproportionately fast (at 4 per cent a year) whilst those of the poorest 15 per cent rose disproportionately slowly (0.3 per cent). Greater inequality at the extremes outweighed greater equality amongst the majority of the population. The second reason was that the market was generating even greater inequalities. This was because of economic restructuring, which increased the pay differentials between skilled and unskilled work, and the excessive salaries top

Blair: 1996/97–2002/03

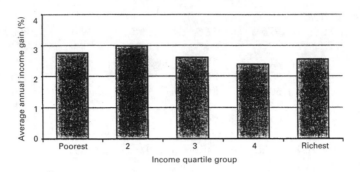

Major 1990–1996/97

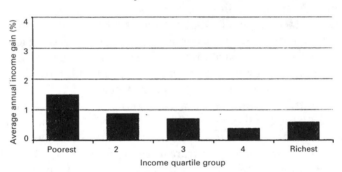

Thatcher: 1979–1990

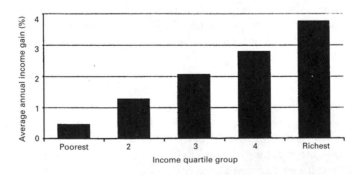

Figure 15.1   Real income growth, 1979–2002/3

Notes: The averages in each quintile group correspond to the mid-points, i.e. the 10th, 30th, 50th, 70th and 90th percentile points of the income distribution. Incomes have been measured before housing costs have been deducted.

Source: M. Brewer, A. Goodman, M. Myck, J. Shaw and A. Shepherd, *Poverty and Inequality in Britain* (2004) fig. 2.3.

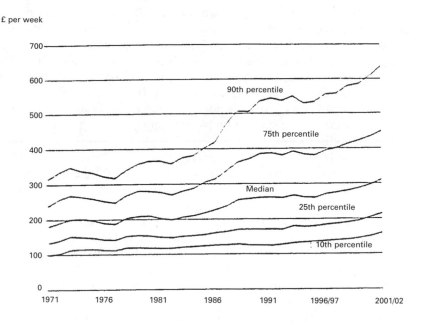

Figure 15.2 Distribution of personal income in the UK, 1971–2001/2

Source: Inland Revenue at www.statistics.gov.uk/cci (April 2004).

management awarded itself. A virtue of New Labour's tax and benefit programme was that it at least halved the impact of the growing inequality in 'primary' income distribution.

Nevertheless rising inequality exposed the limitations of New Labour's redistribution programme. It also demonstrated, by inference, how much more closely the two Parties were aligned than their rhetoric would suggest. This is because the remedy for increasing inequality was, at the same time, easy and difficult to attain. The lowest 15 per cent of income earners were suffering because of the nature of means-tested targeting under the new tax credit system. The top 15 per cent were unduly benefiting because no serious attempt was being made to counteract the *generation* of inequality by the market. The simple answer was, therefore, to modify the nature of means-testing and the pre-eminence of the market. That, however, meant challenging two of the keystones of the new consensus.

Britain as a welfare pioneer?

'The essential question', Paul Pierson has concluded after analysing the future of the welfare state in the new era of austerity, 'is whether an effective centrist "restructuring" coalition can emerge between the alternatives of preserving the status quo and radical neo-liberal reform.'[68] In Britain by the late 1990s, a consensus appeared to have been forged around such a centrist position.

Radical neo-liberal reform had been defeated implicitly during Mrs Thatcher's premiership and, following the Conservatives' fundamental review, explicitly at the 1997 election. Likewise, the political impossibility of preserving the *status quo* had been recognized by Labour's leaders following their devastating electoral defeat in 1992. This consensus supported the restructuring, not the dismantling, of the welfare state. Costs were to be contained, new needs met (through, for example, supply-side reform of the economy) and old ones delivered more efficiently (through, for example, increased market discipline).

As the succession of international conferences on the Third Way illustrated, New Labour was keen to promote its new vision of future welfare policy. As it has been vividly described, it 'picked up the baton from Clinton and handed it on to reforming social democrats in Europe'.[69] Moreover, it could lead by example. This was because, as seen in Section 2.1, British governments have the capacity to act decisively. They are, by international standards, faced with few constitutional constraints. Support for state welfare was also less embedded in British culture and institutions. Thus, as a result of swift labour market reform, Britain could enhance its international competitiveness and enjoy sustained economic growth. By an equally swift injection of market discipline into service delivery it could also ensure greater cost containment *and* responsiveness to consumer needs.

Other welfare states were beset by similar pressures to Britain, including globalization, economic restructuring, the ageing of the population and changes to family structure. Their response was similar: cost containment, labour market reform, greater privatization and more extensive means-testing. It tended, however, to be more protracted and thereby less effective. In consequence there were, for example, continuing high levels of unemployment in the once competitive German economy and the remarkable coincidence of high costs and serious shortages in the once-vaunted French health service.[70] Given such relative international failure, could Britain thus provide a model for viable reform?

The answer is a qualified no. This is not just because, as has been seen, there are many fundamental internal issues still to be resolved. It is also because reform in each country has necessarily to be mediated through distinctive national institutions and cultures. As with the Beveridge Report in the 1940s, Britain might have briefly provided a beacon for reform. Mrs Thatcher first emphatically exposed the imperfections of the *status quo*. The emerging consensus in the 1990s demonstrated how a more constructive accommodation could be reached with both the market and market disciplines. However, the answers to Britain's problems provided by the new centrist 'restructuring' coalition are as unique to Britain as those provided by Churchill's wartime coalition in the 1940s. They will be treated as such by other welfare states.

15.7 FURTHER READING

The sources cited at the end of the previous chapter, and in particular the websites, provide much detailed evidence on individual welfare policies.

Of the books focused more particularly on welfare policy, N. Timmins, *The Five Giants* (2001) and H. Glennerster, *British Social Policy since 1945* (Oxford, 2000) remain invaluable for the period they cover. Inevitably Glennerster has written another model introduction to a central and complex subject, *Understanding the Finance of Welfare* (Bristol, 2003). An insider account is E. Balls and G. O'Donnell, *Reforming Britain's Economic and Social Policy* (Basingstoke, 2002), whilst during the 2001 election the record of Labour's first administration was assessed by two leading journalists, P. Toynbee and D. Walker, in *Did Things Get Any Better?* (Harmondsworth, 2001). A running academic analysis has been marshalled under the editorship of M. Powell: *New Labour, New Welfare State?* (Bristol, 1999) and *Evaluating New Labour's Welfare Reforms* (Bristol, 2002). It may be supplemented by J. Clarke, S. Gewirtz and E. McLaughlin, *New Managerialism, New Welfare?* (2000). P. Alcock, A. Erskine and M. May (eds), *The Student's Companion to Social Policy* (Oxford, 2003) provides the broader context.

For succinct international comparisons, P. Taylor-Gooby, *Welfare States under Pressure* (2001) and M. Ferrera and M. Rhodes (eds), *Recasting European Welfare States* (2000) are in a field of their own.

Appendix: The Cost of Welfare Policy

CONTENTS

To provide a framework within which to study welfare policy, three relatively straightforward questions need to be answered. How much of the total output of the economy is spent by government? How much of government expenditure is consumed by welfare policy as a whole and by individual policies? Finally, how have proportions changed over time?

The answers to these questions were made potentially more easy by the establishment of the Central Statistical Office during the Second World War. It helped to revolutionize the collection of official statistics and, consequently, detailed estimates of national income and expenditure, together with their various components, have been published since 1950 in a standardized form. The answers, nevertheless, remain anything but straightforward. There are practical problems with the collection of relevant data, so that estimates can never be more than informed guesses and are open to constant revision (as anyone seeking to construct a consistent historical series will find). This has the important consequence, for historical analysis, that the statistics used objectively to analyse past policy may not be the same as those to which policy-makers at the time were responding. There are also conceptual problems over the definition of, and the relationship between, the various aggregate figures. For example, the definition of 'public expenditure' used by the CSO in its major publication, *National Income and Expenditure*, differs from that used by the Treasury in white papers on public expenditure. Moreover, in the

'fiscal crisis' of the mid-1970s the Treasury suddenly changed both its definition of public expenditure and the means of expressing it as a percentage of
the total output of the economy. Comparisons over time and between countries – which continue to use different definitions of public expenditure and
economic output, despite the attempts of bodies such as the UN and the
OECD to standardize practice – are, therefore, extremely hazardous.

The following analysis will concentrate on the period of the classic welfare
state but Tables A.6 and A.7 provide details of both overall government
expenditure and the cost of individual welfare services after 1978.

A.1 ESTIMATES OF THE NATIONAL PRODUCT

The aggregate output of the economy can be estimated in one of three ways:
through the *output* of each sector of the economy, such as industry and agriculture; through the *income* accruing to each economic activity, such as
employment and profits; and through categories of *expenditure*, such as that
by consumers and public authorities. There are major practical problems in
collecting the relevant information in each of these three ways and inevitably
the three estimates differ considerably.

There are also three different ways in which the statistics can be presented.
Gross Domestic Product (GDP) includes broadly all the income and wealth
generated within Britain. Gross National Product (GNP) also includes income
from British investment overseas, but excludes the profits of foreign-owned
enterprises in the UK. Net National Product (NNP) excludes capital consumption or depreciation. To complicate matters still further, these three estimates
may be calculated at market prices or at factor cost. The latter excludes taxes
on expenditure (such as VAT) but adds subsidies. In most cases, therefore, it
is lower than the market price.

The choice of which measure to use is not purely academic; it can be of
considerable political and analytical importance. In 1976, for instance, the
respective estimates of the total output of the economy were as follows:

GNP at market prices: £123,891 million
GDP at market prices: £122,576 million
GNP at factor cost: £110,814 million
GDP at factor cost: £109,499 million
NNP at factor cost: £97,370 million

There was thus a £26,521 million or a 21 per cent difference between the
largest and the smallest estimate; and the same measure of public expenditure
could legitimately be presented as consuming 61.4 per cent or 47 per cent of
total output, depending on the estimate used. Those who wish to control or
attack public expenditure naturally contrast it with the lower estimates. Thus
until 1977 the Treasury used estimates of GDP at factor cost and the New
Right have conventionally used NNP. The generally accepted measure now
taken is GDP at market prices.

A.2 DEFINITIONS OF PUBLIC EXPENDITURE

Public expenditure, as the differing practice of the CSO and the Treasury illustrates, is open to as many definitions as national output. At minimum it consists of the *consumption* by central and local government ('general government') of goods and services – the capital costs, for example, of building and equipping hospitals and the current cost of maintaining them and paying the staff. If estimates of public expenditure are to be set against those of national output to determine what percentage of national resources government consumes, this is strictly the only measure that should be used (see Table A.2 and Table A.3, line 10).

Public expenditure, however, has conventionally included *transfer payments*. These are cash payments, such as pensions and supplementary benefit, which redistribute (or transfer) resources between individuals. They do not actually consume any resources – except in their administrative costs – and so are excluded from calculations of national output. Consequently to include them in the estimates of public expenditure and then to contrast those estimates with, for example, GDP will give a very distorted picture of the amount of national resources being 'consumed' by government – especially as between 1957 and 1977 they accounted for approximately 43–45 per cent of public expenditure. They continue to be included, however, because they illustrate the power of government – as opposed to the market – to influence distribution of resources.

Conversely there are certain types of government expenditure which are not included in the conventional calculations. The most important is *tax expenditure*, or the revenue which government forgoes through the granting of tax relief. Tax expenditure is synonymous with transfer payments in that government is, in effect, collecting taxation and then paying it back to the same individual to cover certain types of approved expenditure, such as the payment of mortgage interest. If transfer payments are included in estimates of public expenditure, then so should tax expenditure; but this has rarely been the case. The practical explanation is that the full cost cannot be identified in public accounts (even when the government privately has made such calculations). The cultural one is that individuals' right to retain their own income does not feel like public expenditure. The cost, nevertheless, is considerable. In 1973–4, it has been calculated, the revenue from income tax would have been 40 per cent higher but for tax relief.

A final component to public expenditure is the *cost of public corporations*, and particularly of nationalized industries. Before 1977 Britain was exceptional in that all the costs of nationalized industries were included within estimates of public expenditure. The removal of all such costs (except direct government loans) together with all interest payments on public debts (except those which could not be covered by trading revenue) enabled the government overnight to reduce its calculation of public expenditure for 1975–6 from 58.5 per cent to 51.5 per cent of GDP (see Table A.2).

Such a recalculation underlines the considerable political and analytical importance that the choice of a given definition of public expenditure can have. In Britain the Treasury had traditionally taken the broadest possible definition of public expenditure (bar tax expenditure) together with a narrow definition of the national product. This has given the impression of high public expenditure and served the Treasury well in its battle to control government spending. This was especially true during the 'fiscal crisis' of the mid-1970s, but once the priority had changed to that of convincing international financiers – and in particular the IMF – that the necessary remedial action had been taken, it was to the government's advantage to adopt different definitions. To do so was not necessarily dishonest, because it brought Britain more into line with European practice.

A.3 TRENDS IN WELFARE EXPENDITURE

Welfare policy is also difficult to define. All government policy, including defence expenditure, might be said to enhance individual well-being; and, as argued in Chapter 2, economic policy should certainly be included in any broad definition of welfare policy. Hence the statistics for expenditure on economic services are included in Tables A.1, A.3 and A.5. However, it is conventional to concentrate attention on the five 'core' social services, as in Table A.4, where social spending is divided by services, by economic category (current and capital expenditure) and by spending agency (central and local government, and public corporations). More detailed statistics for individual services have been provided in earlier chapters.

There are many pitfalls in the interpretation of these figures. Over the years many services have changed heads, the most notable being the transfer of local authority health expenditure to the NHS in 1971. Arbitrary decisions have also been taken on where to place other services. Should the training of nurses and doctors, for example, come under health or education expenditure? In a traditional British compromise, nurses have been placed under health and doctors under education – because their essential training is, respectively, in hospitals and universities. Finally, an increase in the relative or absolute size of social expenditure should not automatically be equated with an improved service or a change in the policy. The rate of inflation is likely to be higher than average in the social services because they tend to be labour-intensive. They are therefore less able than other sectors of the economy to benefit from productivity resulting from technological innovation. The phenomenon is called 'the relative price effect' and means that the relative cost of the service often has to increase over the years simply to sustain the same standard. Demographic and economic change (such as an increase in the number of pensioners or a rise in unemployment) can also automatically increase the cost of social expenditure without any change in policy.

As in the rest of the industrialized world, social expenditure has risen dramatically since 1945 so that, by whatever measure taken, it represented over 50 per cent of government spending and 25 per cent of national output by the mid-1970s (Table A.1). By then, expenditure on social security, health and welfare, and education individually exceeded that on the two items that had dominated public expenditure until the 1950s – defence and interest on the national debt (Table A.3). Expenditure on housing would also have done so, had not its true size been disguised by 'tax expenditure'. The relative rise in expenditure was slow in the 1950s and then accelerated in the 1960s. There was no explosion until 1972–5 – and that explosion was the common experience of most industrial nations, not a phenomenon unique to Britain. The dominant trend in welfare expenditure between 1945 and 1975 was, therefore, its steady balanced growth (Table A.5).

A.4 EMPLOYMENT IN THE PUBLIC AND WELFARE SECTORS

An alternative measure of the relative importance of public and welfare expenditure is the amount of human, as opposed to financial, resources they consume. This attracted particular attention in the 1970s when it was widely felt that public employment was adversely affecting the economy by attracting labour away from 'productive' employment and, through the strength of public sector unions, fuelling wage-inflation.

Inevitably the choice of statistics is again controversial. What, for instance, constitutes the 'public sector'? One measure is the 'extended public sector', which includes all institutions which have tax-raising powers, have executives appointed by government (such as nationalized industries), or receive most of their finance from government (like universities). This definition has been simultaneously attacked for being too restrictive and too extensive. On the one hand it excludes all those working in the private sector (such as in the defence and construction industries) whose employment is dependent on government contracts. On the other hand it includes the NHS and nationalized industries, which are usually excluded from other countries' definitions. There is also the recurrent problem of how to count part-time workers, who are increasing steadily in the public sector as in the labour market as a whole. Should they be counted individually or conflated into 'full-time equivalents'? Finally, how should the underlying significance of the figures be assessed? The importance of aggregate public employment, it could be argued, depends not so much on its mere size as on other factors, such as whether it is absorbing skilled manpower in a tight labour market or unskilled workers who would otherwise be unemployed – and who, as in the case of part-time female labour, might not otherwise even be regarded as part of the labour force.

Figures for the 'extended public sector' confirm certain trends apparent in financial expenditure. Employment jumped from 10 per cent of the labour force to 27 per cent between 1938 and 1951, but then slowly declined to 24 per cent by the mid-1960s before accelerating to 30.5 per cent in 1976. During this period labour was shed in the defence and nationalized industries but increased dramatically in the welfare sector – by 166 per cent in education, for example, and 142 per cent in the NHS. By conventional international measures, public employment exceeded most European countries (but not the USA) until the mid-1960s, when it was calculated at approximately 16 per cent of the total labour force. Its rate of growth was then comparatively fast, reaching approximately 21 per cent by 1977.

A.5 FURTHER READING

A full range of expenditure statistics can be found in the *Annual Abstract of Statistics*; the annual white papers on *Public Expenditure* published by the Treasury; and *Social Trends*, first published in 1970. *Social Trends* changed the basis of its tables from the CSO to the Treasury definition of public expenditure in 1976, which accounts for the slight discrepancy for the final date used in certain statistical tables in this appendix and in Part II of this book. Another exhaustive source for both expenditure and manpower statistics is P. Flora, *State, Economy and Society in Western Europe* (1983) from which Table A.1 has been extracted. Its first volume represents a bold attempt to collate, in a standardized form, statistics relevant to the development of welfare policy throughout western Europe over the past century. Inevitably it presents these statistics in a somewhat unconventional form and, in column 2 of Table A.1, Flora's figures of public expenditure as a percentage of GDP are contrasted to the standardized figures of the OECD. The standard work on public expenditure is D. Heald, *Public Expenditure* (1983); on social expenditure, A. Walker (ed.), *Public Expenditure and Social Policy* (1982); and on public employment, R. Parry, *UK Public Employment* (1980).

Table A.1 Government expenditure, central and local, 1945–75

	£(m)	% of GDP	Major categories as % of GDP					Major categories as % of total expenditure					Central government expend. as % of total
			Defence	Admin/ justice	Economic/ environ- ment	Social services	Residual	Defence	Admin/ justice	Economic/ environ- ment	Social services	Residual	
		(2)	(3)	(4)	(5)	(6)	(7)	(8)	(9)	(10)	(11)	(12)	(13)
1945	5779	58.4	–	–	–	–	–	–	–	–	–	–	90.6
1946	4530	45.5	–	–	–	–	–	–	–	–	–	–	84.7
1947	4130	38.8	–	–	–	–	–	–	–	–	–	–	78.0
1948	4215	36.0	–	–	–	–	–	–	–	–	–	–	76.6
1949	4423	35.6	–	–	–	–	–	–	–	–	–	–	77.2
1950	4539	35.1	6.5	2.0	5.2	16.2	5.3	18.4	5.6	14.7	46.1	15.1	76.6
1951	5208	36.1	9.0	1.8	5.5	15.5	4.4	24.8	4.9	15.2	42.9	12.2	77.2
1952	5777	37.0	10.5	1.7	4.8	15.6	4.4	28.4	4.6	13.0	42.2	11.9	76.7
1953	6048	36.2	10.3	1.7	4.5	15.5	4.3	28.5	4.6	12.3	42.8	11.8	75.7
1954	5976	33.8	9.6	1.6	3.7	14.8	4.0	28.5	4.8	11.1	43.7	11.9	74.8
1955	6143	32.1	8.4	1.6	3.7	14.3	4.1	26.1	4.8	11.6	44.6	12.8	75.0
1956	7054	34.3	7.9	1.4	7.5	14.4	5.4	21.6	3.9	20.4	39.3	14.7	75.0
1957	7652	35.3	7.3	1.5	8.1	14.4	5.3	20.0	4.0	22.2	39.4	14.3	75.5
1958	8001	35.4	6.8	1.5	7.9	15.0	5.5	18.6	4.1	21.4	41.0	14.9	75.8
1959	8539	35.8	6.6	1.8	8.0	15.4	5.4	17.7	4.8	21.5	41.3	14.7	75.5
1960	9001	35.3 (32.6)	6.3	1.5	8.3	15.3	5.7	17.0	4.1	22.3	41.3	15.2	75.0
1961	9893	36.4 (33.4)	6.4	1.7	8.9	15.8	5.7	16.6	4.3	23.1	41.1	14.9	73.9
1962	10442	36.7 (34.2)	6.5	1.7	8.9	16.2	5.5	16.7	4.5	23.0	41.6	14.2	72.6
1963	12427	41.0 (35.6)	6.3	1.6	8.7	16.8	5.3	16.3	4.1	22.4	43.5	13.6	74.7
1964	12042	36.4 (33.9)	6.1	1.5	8.9	17.1	5.0	15.7	3.8	22.9	44.4	13.1	69.7
1965	13376	37.7 (36.4)	6.0	1.5	9.1	18.2	5.0	15.0	3.8	22.9	45.7	12.7	69.3
1966	14532	38.4 (35.6)	5.9	1.6	9.5	18.4	5.0	14.5	3.9	23.5	45.6	12.4	69.1
1967	16764	42.0 (38.5)	6.1	1.7	11.3	19.6	5.2	13.9	3.8	25.8	44.7	11.9	69.6
1968	18393	42.6 (39.6)	5.7	1.8	11.5	20.1	5.3	12.8	4.0	26.0	45.3	11.9	70.0

Table A.1 continued

			Major categories as % of GDP					Major categories as % of total expenditure					Central government expend. as % total
	£(m)	% of GDP	Defence	Admin/ justice	Economic/ environ- ment	Social services	Residual	Defence	Admin/ justice	Economic/ environ- ment	Social services	Residual	
	(1)	(2)	(3)	(4)	(5)	(6)	(7)	(8)	(9)	(10)	(11)	(12)	(13)
1969	19083	41.4 (41.5)	5.0	1.8	10.8	20.0	5.3	11.6	4.2	25.1	46.7	12.3	69.1
1970	20857	41.1 (39.3)	4.9	2.0	10.9	20.3	5.1	11.3	4.5	25.3	47.1	11.8	68.1
1971	23358	41.1 (38.4)	4.9	2.1	11.2	20.0	4.8	11.4	4.8	26.0	46.7	11.2	68.7
1972	26571	42.3 (40.0)	4.9	2.3	10.4	21.2	4.7	11.3	5.2	24.0	48.7	10.8	68.2
1973	30491	42.4 (41.1)	4.7	2.1	11.0	21.6	5.2	10.6	4.7	24.7	48.4	11.7	65.9
1974	39108	47.7 (45.2)	5.0	1.9	9.5	24.9	6.4	10.5	4.1	19.9	52.2	13.3	67.4
1975	51495	49.9 (46.9)	5.0	2.1	11.1	25.7	6.0	10.1	4.2	22.3	51.5	11.9	68.0

Notes: Columns 3–12 are calculated on a slightly different basis from columns 1–2.
Administration and Justice: administration, foreign affairs, judiciary, police.
Economic and Environmental: agriculture, industry and commerce, transport and communication.
Social services: social insurance and assistance, other social transfers, health, housing, education and science.
Residual: national debt.

Source: P. Flora, *State, Economy and Society*, vol. 1 (1983) pp. 345–6, 440–2.

Table A.2 Public expenditure by economic category, 1955–76 (percentage of GDP)

	Treasury definition		Public consumption	Public investment	Transfer payments
	Pre-1977	1977			
1955–9	41.1	–	18.9	7.6	14.7
1960–4	42.9	–	19.0	7.9	16.0
1965–9	48.2	40.5	20.2	9.8	18.5
1970–1	50.6	–	21.0	9.7	19.8
1971–2	50.0	–	21.2	9.5	19.2
1972–3	50.1	–	21.5	8.7	19.9
1973–4	51.1	–	21.2	9.2	20.3
1974–5	57.3	–	22.9	10.1	24.3
1975–6	58.5	51.5			–

Source: M. Wright, 'Public expenditure in Britain', *Public Administration*, 55 (1977) 143–69.

Table A.3 Public expenditure, 1951–75, selected services

	1951 £(m)	1951 %	1961 £(m)	1961 %	1966 £(m)	1966 %	1971 £(m)	1971 %	1975 £(m)	1975 %
Social services										
1. Social security	707	12.1	1628	15.8	2577	16.8	4309	17.8	8918	16.4
2. Welfare services	96	1.6	158	1.5	262	1.7 }				
3. NHS	498	8.4	930	9.0	1395	9.1	2784	11.4	6707	12.3
4. Education	398	6.8	1013	9.8	1768	11.6	3023	12.4	6840	12.5
5. Housing	404	6.9	555	5.4	968	6.3	1240	5.2	4291	7.9
6. Other environmental services*	135	2.3	379	3.8	652	4.3	1179	4.8	2405	4.4
Other										
7. Commerce and industry	850	14.6	1203	11.7	1759	11.5	3180	13.1	7825	14.4
8. Defence and external relations	1411	24.2	1859	18.0	2512	16.4	3164	13.0	5876	10.8
9. Debt interest	687	11.8	1261	12.2	1558	10.2	2213	9.1	4513	8.3
10. Government expenditure on goods and services as percentage of GNP (factor cost)		22.8		26.3		29.2		31.0		34.6

*Includes such local services as public health, recreation, water supply, sewerage, etc.
Source: *Social Trends* (1970, 1976).

Table A.4 Social expenditure, 1951–77

	1951–2 £(m)	1951–2 %	1956–7 £(m)	1956–7 %	1961–2 £(m)	1961–2 %	1966–7 £(m)	1966–7 %	1971–2 £(m)	1971–2 %	1976–7 £(m)	1976–7 %
1. Total public expenditure on social services	2135	100.0	3011	100.0	4396	100.0	7198	100.0	11790	100.0	32145	100.0
Individual service												
2. Social security	702	32.8	1068	35.5	1674	38.1	2642	36.7	4578	38.8	11575	36.0
3. Personal social services	33	1.5	44	1.5	67	1.5	123	1.7	324	2.7	1243	3.9
4. School meals, milk and welfare food	73	3.4	99	3.3	102	2.3	148	2.1	149	1.3	470	1.5
5. NHS	494	23.1	639	21.2	928	21.1	1446	20.1	2362	20.0	6249	19.4
6. Education	416	19.5	671	22.3	1057	24.0	1827	25.4	3023	25.6	7438	23.1
7. Housing	417	19.5	490	16.3	567	12.9	1012	14.1	1354	11.5	5170	16.1
8. Current expenditure	1694	79.3	2478	82.3	3714	84.5	5938	82.5	10058	85.3	27652	86.0
9. Capital expenditure	441	21.7	533	17.7	682	15.5	1260	17.5	1732	14.7	4493	14.0
10. Central government*	1309	61.3	1833	60.9	2821	64.2	4423	61.4	7692	65.2	21444	66.7
11. Local government	805	38.7	1146	38.1	1550	35.2	2715	37.7	4098	34.8	10701	33.3
12. Public corporations	21	1.0	32	1.0	25	0.6	60	0.8	–		–	

*Excludes grants to local authorities.
Source: Annual Abstract of Statistics (1964, 1969, 1979).

Table A.5 Social expenditure, annual growth relative to growth of GDP, 1950–77

	1950–60	1960–70	1970–4	1974–7
1. Total social spending	1.10	1.40	1.50	0.98
2. Social security	1.25	1.42	1.17	1.25
3. Personal social services	1.13	2.24	2.20	1.14
4. NHS	0.91	1.21	1.43	1.05
5. Education	1.37	1.46	1.27	0.99
6. Housing	0.58	1.42	2.61	0.37
7. Defence	0.96	0.60	1.07	0.95
8. Industry and trade	3.03	2.40	0.17	–
9. Employment services	0.62	2.11	1.56	2.54

Note: A ratio of increase greater than one signifies that expenditure on a given programme was increasing faster than GDP.
Source: F. Gould and B. Roweth, 'Public spending and social policy: the UK 1950–77', *Journal of Social Policy*, vol. 9 (1980) 349–50.

Table A.6 Total managed expenditure by function in real terms, 1984/5–2001/2 (£ billion)

	1978-9 outturn	1984-5 outturn	1986-7 outturn	1988-9 outturn	1990-1 outturn	1992-3 outturn	1994-5 outturn	1996-7 outturn	1997-8 outturn	1998-9 outturn	1999-00 outturn	2000-1 outturn	2001-2 outturn
Education	27.3	30.2	31.5	33.2	34.6	37.6	39.9	40.2	40.1	40.7	41.7	44.1	49.4
Health and personal social services of	27.6	36.1	37.8	40.8	43.2	48.9	53.1	56.2	57.1	58.4	62.3	66.0	70.4
which: Health	23.5	30.7	32.0	34.4	36.1	41.2	43.3	45.0	45.6	46.6	49.6	52.6	56.7
Transport	9.0	12.4	11.5	10.5	12.7	15.1	13.9	11.1	9.9	9.1	8.8	8.7	9.8
Housing	13.5	8.4	6.9	4.9	6.4	7.5	6.1	5.1	4.0	3.8	2.9	3.2	4.9
Other environmental services	7.9	7.1	7.9	7.4	8.6	9.3	9.4	9.0	9.0	8.7	8.6	10.2	10.5
Law, order and protective services	7.7	11.8	12.2	13.6	15.0	16.9	17.6	17.9	18.1	18.1	19.1	20.1	22.5
Defence	22.7	31.9	31.1	28.9	28.2	27.2	25.8	23.5	22.4	23.6	23.1	24.9	23.6
International development assistance and other international services	3.2	2.7	2.9	3.0	3.1	3.6	3.7	3.3	3.1	3.3	3.5	3.7	4.6
Trade, industry, energy and employment	12.4	14.4	13.6	12.1	11.5	11.6	11.0	9.5	9.0	9.0	9.2	10.0	11.6
Agriculture, fisheries, food and forestry	3.1	4.5	3.8	3.3	3.8	3.8	4.3	6.7	5.5	5.3	4.9	5.1	7.7
Culture, media and sport	2.2	2.9	3.1	3.4	3.7	3.6	3.8	4.1	4.5	5.2	5.7	5.5	5.6
Social security	50.7	73.2	79.0	75.2	77.2	94.8	102.0	106.5	104.4	103.6	105.1	105.4	109.1

Table A.6 continued

	1978–9 outturn	1984–5 outturn	1986–7 outturn	1988–9 outturn	1990–1 outturn	1992–3 outturn	1994–5 outturn	1996–7 outturn	1997–8 outturn	1998–9 outturn	1999–00 outturn	2000–1 outturn	2001–2 outturn
Central administration and associated expenditure	8.3	8.9	9.1	9.3	11.1	9.8	8.5	9.0	9.0	10.9	10.7	12.1	10.4
Total expenditure on services	**195.7**	**244.6**	**250.4**	**245.6**	**259.2**	**289.8**	**298.7**	**302.1**	**295.9**	**299.7**	**305.6**	**319.2**	**340.1**
Public sector debt interest	13.3	32.2	32.6	30.9	26.9	22.9	27.2	31.4	32.6	31.2	26.1	25.9	21.6
Other accounting adjustments	6.6	17.3	9.2	9.3	8.2	12.8	16.0	16.9	18.3	16.7	19.1	22.1	22.7
Allowance for shorfall								0.0	0.0	-0.1	-0.1	0.0	-2.0
Total managed expenditure	**215.7**	**294.2**	**292.2**	**285.9**	**294.3**	**325.4**	**341.9**	**350.4**	**346.8**	**347.5**	**350.7**	**367.2**	**382.5**

Note: The statistics for 1978–9 were calculated on a slightly different basis to those for other years.
Source: HM Treasury, *Public Expenditure* (Cm 3601, 1997) table 3.3; and *Public Expenditure* (Cm 5401, 2002) table 3.4.

Table A.7 Total managed expenditure as a percentage of GDP, 1984/5–2001/2 (%)

	1978–9 outturn	1984–5 outturn	1986–7 outturn	1988–9 outturn	1990–1 outturn	1992–3 outturn	1994–5 outturn	1996–7 outturn	1997–8 outturn	1998–9 outturn	1999–00 outturn	2000–1 outturn	2001–2 estimated outturn
Education	5.4	4.9	4.8	4.6	4.7	5.1	5.0	4.7	4.5	4.5	4.5	4.6	5.1
Health and personal social services	5.4	5.9	5.7	5.6	5.9	6.6	6.7	6.6	6.5	6.5	6.7	6.9	7.2
of which: Health	4.6	5.0	4.8	4.7	4.9	5.6	5.5	5.3	5.2	5.1	5.3	5.5	5.8
Transport	1.8	2.0	1.7	1.5	1.7	2.0	1.8	1.3	1.1	1.0	0.9	0.9	1.0
Housing	2.6	1.4	1.0	0.7	0.9	1.0	0.8	0.6	0.5	0.4	0.3	0.3	0.5
Other environmental services	1.6	1.2	1.2	1.0	1.2	1.3	1.2	1.1	1.0	1.0	0.9	1.1	1.1
Law, order and protective services	1.5	1.9	1.8	1.9	2.0	2.3	2.2	2.1	2.0	2.0	2.1	2.1	2.3
Defence	4.5	5.2	4.7	4.0	3.8	3.7	3.3	2.8	2.5	2.6	2.5	2.6	2.4
International development assistance and other international services	0.6	0.4	0.4	0.4	0.4	0.5	0.5	0.4	0.3	0.4	0.4	0.4	0.5
Trade, industry, energy and employment	2.4	2.3	2.0	1.7	1.6	1.6	1.4	1.1	1.0	1.0	1.0	1.0	1.2
Agriculture, fisheries, food and forestry	0.6	0.7	0.6	0.5	0.5	0.5	0.5	0.8	0.6	0.6	0.5	0.5	0.8
Culture, media and sport	0.4	0.5	0.5	0.5	0.5	0.5	0.5	0.5	0.5	0.6	0.6	0.6	0.6
Social security	9.9	11.9	11.9	10.3	10.5	12.9	12.9	12.5	11.8	11.4	11.3	11.0	11.2

Table A.7 continued

	1978–9 outturn	1984–5 outturn	1986–7 outturn	1988–9 outturn	1990–1 outturn	1992–3 outturn	1994–5 outturn	1996–7 outturn	1997–8 outturn	1998–9 outturn	1999–00 outturn	2000–1 outturn	2001–2 outturn
Central administration and associated expenditure	1.6	1.5	1.4	1.3	1.5	1.3	1.1	1.1	1.0	1.2	1.1	1.3	1.1
Total expenditure on services	**38.3**	**39.9**	**37.8**	**33.8**	**35.1**	**39.4**	**37.8**	**35.4**	**33.5**	**33.1**	**32.8**	**33.4**	**34.8**
Public sector debt interest	2.6	5.3	4.9	4.3	3.6	3.1	3.4	3.7	3.7	3.4	2.8	2.7	2.2
Other accounting adjustments	1.3	2.8	1.4	1.3	1.1	1.7	2.0	2.0	2.1	1.8	2.1	2.3	2.3
Allowance for shortfall								0.0	0.0	0.0	0.0	0.0	-0.2
Total managed expenditure	**42.2**	**48.0**	**44.1**	**39.3**	**39.9**	**44.2**	**43.2**	**41.0**	**39.3**	**38.4**	**37.7**	**38.4**	**39.2**

Note: The statistics for 1978–9 were calculated on a slightly different basis to those for other years.
Source: HM Treasury, *Public Expenditure* (Cm 3601, 1997) table 3.4; and *Public Expenditure* (Cm 5401, 2002) table 3.5.

Notes and
References

Note: The place of publication is London unless otherwise stated.

1 INTRODUCTION

1. Labour Party, *Report of the 75th Annual Conference* (1976) p. 188.
2. Cmd 6404 (1942) para. 440.
3. Cmd 6527 (1944) Foreword.
4. B. Donoughue, *Prime Minister* (1987) p. 187.
5. Speech to the Institute of Economic Studies in New York, 15 September 1975.
6. S. Brittan, 'The economic contradictions of democracy', *British Journal of Political Science*, 5 (1975) 129–59. A succinct summary of the perceived welfare state crisis is provided in C. Pierson, *Beyond the Welfare State* (Cambridge, 1998) ch. 5.
7. This was the classic headline in the *Sun* newspaper of 11 January 1979, apocryphally reporting Callaghan's response to the winter of discontent when he returned suntanned from a summit meeting in Guadeloupe.
8. P. Taylor-Gooby, *The Politics of Welfare* (1985) ch. 5. In the more developed welfare states, high earnings-related benefits maintain the income differentials of the better-off and were deliberately designed to tie them to the support of the welfare state. Hence the seeming anomaly that any 'tax-payers' revolt' against the cost of state welfare developed in these countries later than in those where lower benefits gave the better-off no such advantage.
9. P. Kavanagh, *Thatcherism and British Politics* (Oxford, 1990) p. 311.
10. The terminology is from N. Barr, *The Welfare State as Piggy Bank* (Oxford, 2001) p. 1.
11. Historians nevertheless have a vital role to play in the testing against empirical evidence, and hence the refinement, of abstract theory. Arthur Marwick has reminded me that his *The New Nature of History* (Basingstoke, 2001) remains the most accessible introduction to these issues. The classic refutation of postmodernism, with which this book does not directly grapple, is R. J. Evans, *In Defence of History* (2000).
12. The term 'classic' welfare state was coined in Anne Digby, *British Welfare Policy* (1989).
13. M. Powell and M. Hewitt, *Welfare State and Welfare Change* (Buckingham, 2002) p. 173.
14. P. Baldwin, *The Politics of Social Solidarity* (Cambridge, 1990) p. 1.

2   THE NATURE OF THE WELFARE STATE

1. Cm. 3805, ch. 2. For recent introductions to the issues see C. Pierson, *Beyond the Welfare State?* (Cambridge, 1998), esp. chs. 4–6; and M. Powell and M. Hewitt, *Welfare State and Welfare Change* (Buckingham, 2002), esp. ch. 1.
2. Cm. 3805, pp. iii and 1. In the USA, the term 'welfare state' is rarely used by policy-makers. 'Welfare' traditionally referred almost exclusively to food stamps and cash benefits paid to lone mothers and their children.
3. B. Abel-Smith and K. Titmuss (eds), *The Philosophy of Welfare* (1987) p. 141; and J. Veit-Wilson, 'States of welfare', *Social Policy and Administration*, 34 (2000) 1–25, which notes that politicians tend to resort to high-flown rhetoric about the virtues of welfare states at the very time they cut benefits to those most in need. Even Beveridge disliked the 'Santa Claus', or 'something for nothing' connotations of the term. He preferred 'the social service state' which emphasized individual responsi-bilities as well as rights. See J. Harris, *William Beveridge* (Oxford, 1997) p. 452.
4. P. Flora and A. J. Heidenheimer (eds), *The Development of Welfare States in Europe and America* (1980) p. 19. Many Germans would still prefer the broader and more posi-tive term 'sozialstaat' which defines a nation not as a geographical or military entity but as the guarantor of certain social rights.
5. See H. Pelling, *The Labour Governments, 1945–1951* (1984) pp. 117–18. T. H. Marshall used the phrase in his famous lecture *Citizenship and Social Class*, delivered in February 1949 (Cambridge, 1950) p. 42.
6. P. Addison, *The Road to 1945* (1975) p. 168. See also p. 216 for the popular usage of the term 'social security', which had been incorporated into legislation in several countries such as the USA and New Zealand in the 1930s.
7. P. Baldwin, 'Beveridge in the *Longue Durée*', in J. Hills, J. Ditch and Howard Glennerster (eds), *Beveridge and Social Security* (Oxford, 1994) p. 40.
8. W. Korpi and J. Palme, *Contested Citizenship* (transcript); G. Esping-Andersen, *The Three Worlds of Welfare Capitalism* (Cambridge, 1990) ch. 1; F. Castles and D. Mitchell, 'Identifying Welfare State regimes', *Governance*, 5 (1992) 1–26.
9. P. Pierson, *The New Politics of the Welfare State* (Oxford, 2001) p. 455.
10. J. Harris, 'Society and state in twentieth-century Britain', in F. M. L. Thompson (ed.), *The Cambridge Social History of Britain*, vol. 3 (Cambridge, 1990) pp. 67, 68 and 96.
11. V. George and P. Wilding, *Ideology and Social Welfare* (1985) p. 62. See also N. Whiteside, 'Creating the Welfare State in Britain, 1945–1960', *Journal of Social Policy*, 25 (1996) 83–103.
12. 'The scheme proposed here is in some ways a revolution, but in more important ways it is a natural development from the past. It is a British Revolution' (Cmd 6404, para. 31).
13. T. H. Marshall, *Social Policy* (1975) pp. 99, 84.
14. A. Briggs, 'The Welfare State in historical perspective', *European Journal of Sociology*, 2 (1961) 228.
15. Guillebaud Committee on the Cost of the Health Service, Cmd 9663, paras 94–8.
16. D. Ellwood, *Poor Support* (New York, 1988) p. 6.
17. B. Donoughue, *Prime Minister* (1987) p. 191.
18. P. Pierson, *The New Politics of the Welfare State* (Oxford, 2001) chs 1 and 13.
19. For an historical examination of this issue, see R. Lowe and R. Roberts, 'Sir Horace Wilson, 1900–1935', *Historical Journal*, 30 (1987) esp. p. 655.

20. See M. Thatcher, *The Downing Street Years* (1993) p. 626. The original extract was published in *Woman's Own*, 31 October 1987. The sense of community has also been challenged, as will be seen from Section 2.3.4, from a very different source: multiculturalism.

21. See, in particular, J. Lewis, *The Voluntary Sector, the State and Social Work in Britain* (Aldershot, 1995) ch. 7.

22. R. Lowe, *Adjusting to Democracy* (1986) ch. 1; R. Middleton, *Towards the Managed Economy* (1985) p. 176. It is because of this interpretation of the welfare state as an inevitable feature of advanced capitalism that Flora and Heidenheimer have suggested that Germany (as the institutional innovator) rather than Britain (as the exceptional propagator of the idea) should be taken as a model against which to judge the international development of welfare states. See *The Development of Welfare States in Western Europe*, ch. 1.

23. Wanless Interim Report (Treasury, 2001), paras 1.4, 2.4 and 2.21.

24. R. F. Harrod, *The Life of John Maynard Keynes* (1951) p. 436.

25. W. H. Beveridge, *Why I am a Liberal* (1945) p. 9. Too great a conflation of the views of Beveridge and Keynes is, however, dangerous. See J. Harris, 'Political ideas and the debate on state welfare, 1940–5', in H. L. Smith (ed.), *War and Social Change* (Manchester, 1986) pp. 233–63.

26. Cmd 6404, para. 9.

27. For a contemporary justification, see T. E. Utley, *Not Guilty* (1957); and for a more recent one, D. Willetts, *Modern Conservatism* (1992) ch. 10.

28. One was hesitantly provided by backbenchers, but never officially endorsed, in the pamphlets *One Nation* (1950) and *The Responsible Society* (1959).

29. T. H. Marshall, *Citizenship and Social Class and Other Essays* (1950) pp. 58, 40, 84. For a succinct summary of Marshall's views, see the chapter by R. Pinker in V. George and R. Page (eds), *Modern Thinkers on Welfare* (1995). For an overview of a contested concept, see J. M. Barbalet, *Citizenship* (1988).

30. Abel-Smith and Titmuss (eds), *The Philosophy of Welfare*, p. 14. For a good summary of Titmuss's views, see the chapter by P. Wilding in George and Page (eds), *Modern Thinkers on Welfare*.

31. C. A. R. Crosland, *The Future of Socialism* (1956) pp. 518, 63, 194. The following quotations are from pp. 20–1, 61. Raymond Plant has sought to strengthen Crosland's analysis by arguing that to achieve 'democratic equality' as opposed to 'equality of result', there needs to be a clear presumption of everyone's equal worth (as held by Tawney) combined with an explicit theory of justified inequality (as advanced by Rawls in *A Theory of Justice*, Oxford, 1972). See ch. 5 of D. Lipsey and D. Leonard (eds), *The Socialist Agenda: Crosland's legacy* (1981).

32. D. Donnison, *The Politics of Poverty* (1982) pp. 20–1.

33. The phrase is Hugh Stephenson's. For the early years of the IEA, see R. Cockett, *Thinking the Unthinkable* (1994) chs. 4–5, and for gathering support, see N. Timmins, *The Five Giants* (1995) ch. 13.

34. K. Joseph, *Stranded on the Middle Ground* (1976) p. 57.

35. IEA, *Choice in Welfare* (1965) p. 7. The 'public choice' school, which accredits the expansion of the state to the self-interest of politicians and bureaucrats, is best represented by W. A. Niskanen, *Bureaucracy: servant or master?* (1973). It has been well answered by P. Self, *Government by the Market?* (1993), esp. pp. 33–4.

36. F. A. Hayek, *The Road to Serfdom* (1944) p. 84. The following quotations are from pp. 153, 101, 10.

37. Ibid., p. 90. Desmond King in *The New Right* (1987) was amongst the first to iden-

tify the potential conflict between its liberal strand (favouring individualism, limited government and the market) and its conservative one (concerned to maintain through government traditional order and authority). Government can of course exercise a minimal role strongly. Both strands were united in opposition to the social citizenship rights of which Marshall wrote and of which the welfare state is the 'key institutional expression' (p. 3). By extending the state such rights reduce individual freedom, whilst by empowering previously disadvantaged groups (such as women and ethnic minorities) they threaten the existing hierarchy.

38. IEA, *Choice in Welfare* (1965) p. 58.

39. Giddens, quoted in R. S. Boynton, 'Letter from London', *New Yorker* (6 October 1997) pp. 66 –74. Excellent overviews are provided by S. Driver and L. Martell, 'Left, right and the Third Way', *Policy and Politics*, 28 (2000) 147–61; and D. T. Studlar, 'The Anglo-American origins and international diffusion of the "Third Way"', *Politics and Policy*, 31 (2003) 27–51.

40. A. Giddens, *The Third Way* (Cambridge, 1997) pp. 24, 35. The report of the Commission on Social Justice was published as *Social Justice* in 1994 and the 'tale of three futures' was told in ch. 3. Giddens's analysis and proposed limited role for government was underpinned by the economic theory succinctly termed by Gordon Brown's economic adviser, Ed Balls, as post-neoclassical endogenous growth theory. Hearing the shadow chancellor's reference to this at a Labour Party conference in September 1994, Michael Heseltine's inevitable response was: 'this is not Brown, but Balls.'

41. A. Giddens, *The Third Way*, p. 65. For the succeeding quotes, see ibid., pp. 127, 100, 16, 69; and Driver and Martell, 'Left, right and the Third Way', p. 149. For all Giddens' self-proclaimed 'respect for the past and for history' (p. 68) he does nevertheless provide an ill-informed critique of Beveridge as 'almost entirely negative' and of the classic welfare state as having treated economic and social policy separately (pp. 111–28). Part II of this book will correct such views. It should also be noted that 'civic society' can be as restrictive of individual free-dom as the state – hence the welcome to state welfare given by many after 1900 as they were gradually relieved from the local censoriousness of the Poor Law.

42. The best summary of criticisms of the Third Way, with a riposte, is A. Giddens, *The Third Way and its Critics* (Cambridge, 2000). French social democrats were particularly insistent that greater state power should be used to counteract global capitalism. The succeeding quote is from Tony Blair, *The Third Way* (1998).

43. C. Ham, *Health Policy in Britain* (1982) ch. 7.

44. K. Middlemas, *Power, Competition and the State*, vol. 1 (1986). See also T. Smith, *The Politics of the Corporate Economy* (1979).

45. Crosland, *The Future of Socialism*, chs 1, 3, 8.

46. R. Miliband, *Capitalist Democracy in Britain* (1982).

47. See B. Jessop, *The Capitalist State* (Oxford, 1982).

48. See, for example, S. Hall, *The Hard Road to Renewal* (1988).

49. J. O'Connor, *The Fiscal Crisis of the State* (New York, 1973); I. Gough, *The Political Economy of the Welfare State* (1979). Gough provides a balanced appreciation of O'Connor's work in George and Page (eds), *Modern Thinkers on Welfare*, ch. 12.

50. C. Offe, 'Some contradictions of the modern Welfare State', *Critical Social Policy*, 2 (1982) 11.

51. J. Dearlove and P. Saunders, *Introduction to British Politics* (1984) p. 319.

52. S. Koven and S. Michel, 'Womanly duties: maternalist policies and the origins of welfare states', *American Historical Review*, 95 (1990) 1076–108; J. S. O'Connor, 'Gender, class and citizenship in the comparative analysis of welfare state regimes', *British Journal of Sociology*, 44 (1993) 501–18. For a comprehensive review of feminist critiques, see F. Williams, *Social Policy: a critical introduction* (1989). For contemporary British practice, see C. Hallett (ed.), *Women and Social Policy* (1996); and for a comparative perspective, J. Lewis (ed.), *Women and Social Policies in Europe* (Aldershot, 1993).

53. E. Wilson, *Women and the Welfare State* (1977) p. 148; Cmd 6404 (1942) para. 114. As a pioneering critique of the British welfare state, Wilson's book is itself 'crudely ideological' and therefore eminently quotable. For an antidote, see J. Harris, *William Beveridge* (1977) pp. 402–7; and S. Blackburn, 'How useful are feminist theories of the welfare state?', *Women's History Review*, 4 (1995) 369–94.

54. Abel-Smith and Titmuss (eds), *The Philosophy of Welfare*, p. 92. The emancipatory effect of welfare policy is well expressed by Sally Alexander in M. Wander (ed.), *Once a Feminist* (1990) p. 91: 'a child of the Welfare State, I was born into the right to education, subsistence, housing and health – that birthright gave my generation the confidence to expect more'.

55. The succeeding examples are from R. Broad and J. Fleming (eds), *Nella Last's War* (1981) p. 227; PEP, *Family Needs and the Social Services* (1961) p. 39; M. Young and P. Wilmott, *Family and Kinship in East London* (1957) p. 15.

56. See in particular L. Doyal, *The Political Economy of Health* (1979) ch. 6; and C. Ungerson and M. Kember (eds), *Women and Social Policy* (1996). Poorer jobs and pay also weakened women's right to occupational welfare and their ability to purchase 'private' welfare. Until the late 1980s, fiscal welfare respected the Victorian tenet that 'in marriage men and women are one person, and that person is the man'.

57. See Section 7.3 for a further discussion of this issue.

58. The limited impact on policy and analysis is admitted, for example, by J. Solomos in N. Ellison and C. Pierson (eds), *Developments in British Social Policy* (Basingstoke, 1998) ch. 3.

59. The Parekh report, *The Future of Multi-Ethnic Britain* (2000) p. xv.

60. For the aftermath of the 1958 Rent Act, see J. Davis, 'Rent and race in 1960s London', *Twentieth Century British History*, 12 (2001) 69–92; and for the USA, A. Deacon, *Perspectives on Welfare* (Buckingham, 2002) pp. 26–9. A vivid account of the experience of the first wave of black postwar immigrants is M. and T. Phillips, *Windrush* (1998).

61. *The Future of Multi-Ethnic Britain*, p. xix.

62. Such issues have started to influence academic economists. See, for example, A. Oswald, 'Happiness and economic performance', *Economic Journal*, 103 (1997) 1815–31. For the continuing lack of greater influence, however, see J. Barry in N. Ellison and C. Pierson, *Developments in British Social Policy* (Basingstoke, 1998) ch. 14. A survey of more traditional policy is J. Sheail, *An Environmental History of Twentieth-Century Britain* (Basingstoke, 2002).

63. T. Skocpol, 'Political response to capital crisis', *Politics and Society*, 10 (1980–1) 157.

64. R. Lowe, *Adjusting to Democracy*, pp. 246–7.

65. R. M. Titmuss, *Problems of Social Policy* (1950) p. 434.

3 THE NATURE OF POLICY-MAKING

1. M. J. Smith et al., 'Central government departments', in R. A. W. Rhodes and P. Dunleavy (eds), *Prime Minister, Cabinet and Core Executive* (1995) p. 50.
2. Cmd 9663 (1956) para. 733 (2); C. Webster, *The National Health Service since the War*, vol. 1 (1998) pp. 220–2.
3. R. Harris and A. Seldon, *Choice in Welfare* (1965) p. 58.
4. Bureaucracy has a multitude of meanings from 'rule by officials' in its classical sense to 'inefficiency' in popular usage. A masterly summary of these definitions and the theories relating to bureaucracy is M. Albrow, *Bureaucracy* (1970).
5. M. Powell and M. Hewitt, *Welfare State and Welfare Change* (Buckingham, 2002) p. 119.
6. G. Roth and C. Willich, *Max Weber: economy and society*, vol. 3 (New York, 1968) pp. 983–5.
7. T. E. Borcheding, *Budgets and Bureaucrats* (North Columbia, 1977) p. 61; W. A. Niskanen, *Bureaucracy: servant or master?* (1973) p. 23.
8. Cmnd 3638 (1968); R. H. S. Crossman, *The Diaries of a Cabinet Minister*, vols 1–3 (1975–7).
9. B. Castle, *The Castle Diaries, 1974–6* (1980) p. 170; Crossman, *The Diaries of a Cabinet Minister*, vol. 1 (1975) pp. 21–39, 614–28; R. Lowe, 'Milestone or millstone? The 1959–61 Plowden Committee and its impact on British welfare policy', *Historical Journal*, 40 (1997) 463–91.
10. See Section 9.2 and H. Macmillan, *Tides of Fortune* (1969) ch. 13. Macmillan had to side-step his permanent secretary (Sir Thomas Sheepshanks) who, significantly, had been the official in charge of the detailed, and somewhat dispirited, implementation of the Beveridge Report in 1943.
11. See Section 6.1; and J. Harris, *William Beveridge* (1977) pp. 422–3.
12. M. Kogan, *The Politics of Education* (1971). The ministers were Boyle (1962–4) and Crosland (1965–7).
13. Castle, *The Castle Diaries, 1974–6*, p. 209.
14. The leading proponent of governance is R. A. W. Rhodes, from whose lively *Understanding Governance* (Buckingham, 1997) most of the impenetrable terminology used in this and the succeeding paragraph is taken. See D. Richards and M. J. Smith, *Governance and Public Policy in the UK* (Oxford, 2002) for a recent overview.
15. M. Freeden, 'True blood or false genealogy?', *Political Quarterly*, 70 (1999) 1.
16. C. Campbell and G. Wilson, *The End of Whitehall* (1995) p. 60.
17. C. Ham, *Health Policy in Britain* (1992) p. 34 and N. Timmins, *The Five Giants* (1995) chs. 17–18.
18. See R. Lowe, 'Bureaucracy triumphant or denied? The expansion of the British civil service', *Public Administration*, 62 (1984) 291.
19. M. Hill, *The Sociology of Public Administration* (1972) ch. 4.
20. C. Ham, *Health Policy in Britain*, ch. 5. Such divergences do qualify the common criticism, in for example J. Mohan, *A National Health Service?* (1995), that NHS reforms since 1979 will lead to widely differing standards of healthcare.
21. K. Mannheim, *Freedom, Power and Democratic Planning* (1951) p. xvii.
22. The principal influence of sociology on policy has been through the work of T. H. Marshall and Anthony Giddens.
23. An explicit monetary target (M3), introduced as the cornerstone of policy in 1979,

was rarely met and formally abandoned in 1985. For an insider's confession, see N. Lawson, *The View from No 11* (1992) ch. 36, significantly entitled 'the myth of a monetarist golden age'.

24. Cmnd 1432 (1961) para. 23.
25. S. Charles and A. Webb, *The Economic Approach to Social Policy* (1986) p. 66.
26. See S. Gorovitz, 'John Rawls: a theory of justice', in A. de Crespigny and K. R. Minogue (eds), *Contemporary Political Philosophers* (1975) pp. 272–89. For Rawls's importance to the refinement of social democracy, see Chapter 2, note 31.
27. Sir A. Cairncross, *Essays in Economic Management* (1971) p. 63.
28. N. Barr, *The Economics of the Welfare State* (Oxford, 1993) p. 433.
29. For a full analysis of the relative inefficiency of insurance in relation to health, see ibid., in particular pp. 297–300.
30. J. Le Grand, C. Propper and R. Robinson, *The Economics of Social Problems* (1992) p. 61. See also J. Le Grand and W. Bartlett (eds), *Quasi-Markets and Social Policy* (1993).
31. See A. Maynard and A. Ladbrook, 'Budget allocation in the NHS', *Journal of Social Policy*, 9 (1980) 289–312.

4   THE HISTORICAL CONTEXT

1. D. Donnison, *The Politics of Poverty* (1982) p. 20.
2. C. Feinstein, *National Income, Expenditure and Output of the United Kingdom* (1972), table 58.
3. Sir A. Cairncross, 'The postwar years', in R. Floud and D. McCloskey (eds), *The Economic History of Britain since 1700*, vol. 2 (1981) p. 376. The apparent incompatibility between the overall and the quinquennial rates is explained by the different base years taken.
4. For Beveridge's figures, see Cmd 6404, p. 91. From 1951 to 1971 women increased their relative superiority, with their life expectancy at birth rising from 71.2 to 75.2 years, and at 65 from 79.4 to 81.3. The number of people over 75 (on whom expenditure per head was highest) increased only from 1.8 to 2.6 million.
5. Those over 75 tend to require more care since dementia becomes a more common problem and there is an increasingly disproportionate number of women, who typically have fewer resources. However, the burden of an 'ageing' population was not as great as had been feared before 1939, mainly because the elderly enjoyed better health and greater resources in terms of both national and family support. They even became major providers of care themselves. See P. Thane, 'The debate on the declining birth-rate in Britain: the "menace" of an ageing population, 1920s–1950s', *Continuity and Change*, 5 (1990) 283–305, and 'The growing burden of an ageing population?', *Journal of Public Policy*, 7 (1987) 373–87. See also P Thane, *Old Age in English History* (Oxford, 2000), esp. ch. 24, and Section 6.4.
6. The succeeding figures are largely taken from A. H. Halsey (ed.), *British Social Trends since 1900* (1988) ch. 2.
7. J. F. Ermisch, *The Political Economy of Demographic Change* (1983) p. 45. For a summary of the response, see P. Ely and D. Denney, *Social Work in a Multi-Racial Society* (Aldershot, 1987).
8. In the early 1960s the trade unions insisted on the retention of Clause 4 either in

response to their increasingly militant members or, purely defensively, to retain the historical link between the various factions of the Labour movement. See V. Bogdanor, 'The Labour party in opposition, 1951–1964', in V. Bogdanor and R. Skidelsky (eds), *The Age of Affluence, 1951–64* (1970).

9. The National Archives (TNA): Public Record Office (PRO), CAB 124/1016.

10. K. Morgan, *Labour in Power, 1945–1951* (1984) p. 186. For the most sympathetic account of the Wilson governments, see B. Pimlott, *Harold Wilson* (1992).

11. T. Utley, *Not Guilty* (1957) p. 156. For the early impact on policy of the economic liberals, see H. Jones, 'New tricks for an old dog? The Conservatives' social policy, 1951–5', in A. Gorst, L. Johnman and W. Scott Lucas (eds), *Contemporary British History, 1931–1961* (1991).

12. TNA: PRO, CAB 130/139, GEN 625; *The Right Road for Britain* (1949) p. 14. See also R. Lowe, 'Resignation at the Treasury: the Social Services Committee and the failure to reform the Welfare State, 1955–57', *Journal of Social Policy*, 18 (1989) 505–26; and for a rather broader interpretation, E. E. H. Green, *Ideologies of Conservatism* (Oxford, 2002) ch. 7.

13. The following quotations are from *One Nation* (1950) p. 72 and *The Responsible Society* (1959) p. 41. See also I. Macleod and E. Powell, *The Social Services: needs and means* (1954); and the overviews provided in R. Shepherd, *Iain Macleod* (1994), and *Enoch Powell* (1996). The impact of One-Nationism on welfare policy is examined in R. Lowe, 'The replanning of the welfare state, 1957–64', in M. Francis and I. Zweiniger-Bargielowska (eds), *The Conservatives and British Society, 1890–1990* (Cardiff, 1996) pp. 255–73. Its broader history is surveyed by R. Walsha, 'The One Nation Group, 1950–1955', *Twentieth Century British History*, 11 (2000) 183–214, and 'The One Nation Group, 1950–2002', *Contemporary British History* 17 (2003) 69–120.

14. D. Kavanagh, 'The Heath Government, 1970–1974', in P. Hennessy and A. Seldon (eds), *Ruling Performance* (Oxford, 1987) p. 234. See also S. Ball and A. Seldon (eds), *The Heath Government, 1970–1974: a reappraisal* (1996), which includes a chapter on the planning and implementation of social policy.

15. Estimates for defence expenditure may be underestimates. The initial cost of developing the atom bomb in the 1940s was kept secret from Cabinet and from Parliament through its funding from the Civil Contingencies Fund. Similarly, in the 1970s the cost of the 'Chevaline' updating of the Polaris submarine was presented to Cabinet as £24 million, whereas its full cost was over £1000 million.

16. See especially C. A. R. Crosland, *The Conservative Enemy* (1962) p. 123; also, R. Lowe, 'The Second World War, consensus and the foundation of the Welfare State', *Twentieth Century British History*, 1 (1990) 152–82.

17. Cmnd 3638, Ch. 1, paras 17 and 12. An analysis of its finding is provided in G. K. Fry, *Reforming the Civil Service: the Fulton Committee on the British Home Civil Service, 1966–1968* (Edinburgh, 1993).

18. P. Hennessy, *Whitehall* (1989) pp. 131 and 135.

19. D. Marquand, *The Unprincipled Society* (1988) p. 26; A. Booth, ' "The Keynesian revolution" in economic policy-making', *Economic History Review*, 36 (1983) 118; Hennessy, *Whitehall*, p. 235.

20. Cmnd 1432, *Report on the Control of Public Expenditure*.

21. A major failure of the British Treasury was the refusal to discuss the constructive relationship between social and economic policy and the social consequences of taxation when the opportunity arose between 1955 and 1957. See R. Lowe, 'Resignation at the Treasury', 520–3.

22. K. Newton and T. Karran, *The Politics of Local Expenditure* (1985) p. 52. For local government income, see R. Jackman, 'Local government finance', in M. Loughlin, M. D. Gelfand and K. Young (eds), *Half a Century of Municipal Decline* (1985) ch. 7.

23. A. G. Geen, 'Educational policy-making in Cardiff, 1944–70', *Public Administration*, 59 (1981) 85–104; M. Kogan (ed.), *The Politics of Education* (1971) p. 48.

24. Cmnd 4040, para. 96.

25. Ibid., para. 85. In England and Wales in 1945 there were, in urban areas, 83 county boroughs and, in rural areas, 61 counties with 309 non-county boroughs, 572 urban districts and 475 rural districts. In addition there was the London County Council with 28 boroughs. After 1974 there were six metropolitan authorities divided into 36 districts, and 47 counties divided into 333 districts. In addition there was the Greater London Council (founded in 1964 and disbanded in 1986, both by Conservative governments) with 32 boroughs.

26. Ibid., para 243.

27. See L. Paterson, 'Scottish autonomy and the future of the welfare state', *Scottish Affairs*, 19 (1997) 59. Scottish local government reorganization witnessed parallel political interference with the recommendation of the 1969 Wheatley Royal Commission (Cmnd 4150). It had been its intention to consolidate the existing 4 cities, 33 county councils, 21 large burghs and 176 small burghs into 7 regions and 37 districts. Northern Ireland's complex structure of 2 corporations, 6 county councils and 65 lesser authorities was simplified into 26 district councils, although appointed boards became responsible for welfare policy.

28. D. Birrell and A. Murie, 'Ideology, conflict and social policy', *Journal of Social Policy*, 4 (1975) 251; J. Ditch, *Social Policy in Northern Ireland between 1939–1950* (Avebury, 1988) p. xi.

29. The decision in 1965 to site the province's second university at Coleraine rather than in Derry, Northern Ireland's second – but mainly Catholic – city, was also responsible for convincing 'even moderate nationalists that they need not expect fair play from any Unionist government'. See T. Wilson, *Ulster: conflict and consent* (Oxford, 1989) p. 147.

30. J. G. Kellas, *The Scottish Political System* (Cambridge, 1975) p. 308.

31. I. Levitt, 'The origins of the Scottish Development Bond', *Scottish Affairs* 14 (1996) 55; L. Paterson, *The Autonomy of Scotland* (Edinburgh, 1994) p. 130. For the revolution in the personal social services, see J. Murphy, *British Social Services: the Scottish dimension* (Edinburgh, 1992).

32. A. Gibb, 'Policy and politics in Scottish housing since 1945', in R. Rodger (ed.), *Scottish Housing in the Twentieth Century* (Leicester, 1989) p. 167.

33. See the 'oral history' symposia reported in *Contemporary Record*, 2/2 (1988), 2/6 (1989), and 3/1 (1989).

34. Cmd 6527, foreword; R. M. Titmuss, *Problems of Social Policy* (1950) p. 434.

35. P. Addison, *The Road to 1945* (1975) p. 15.

36. TNA: PRO, CAB 134/459, meeting of the ministerial Information Services Committee, 25 February 1949; PEP, *Family Needs and the Social Services* (1961) p. 33; R. Harris and A. Seldon, *Choice in Welfare* (1965) p. 58. The popular surge for Scottish nationalism should be qualified by the fact that of those polled in 1970, only half had heard of the Scottish Office, see Kellas, *The Scottish Political System*, p. 50.

37. See for instance D. E. Butler and A. King, *The British General Election of 1964* (1965) chs 4–5.

38. D. Butler and D. Stokes, *Political Change in Britain* (1974) p. 297.
39. The surveys are summarized in P. Taylor-Gooby, *Public Opinion, Ideology and State Welfare* (1985) ch. 2, on which the succeeding analysis is based. Rather than encouraging altruism, welfare policy could create resentment, such as that of owner-occupiers against council tenants and of small or childless families against large families in receipt of family allowances.
40. The survey was carried out in 1963/4 and its results published in J. Goldthorpe et al., *The Affluent Worker*, 3 vols (Cambridge, 1968–9). The quotation is from vol. 3, p. 170.
41. In the periods 1960–8 and 1969–73. unofficial strikes accounted respectively for 57 and 50 per cent of all working days lost. That government in 1960 started to collect statistics which distinguished between official and unofficial strikes was a measure of its concern. See J. W. Durcan, W. E. J. McCarthy and G. P. Redman, *Strikes in Post-War Britain* (1983) pp. 110, 149.
42. M. Pinto-Duschinsky, 'Bread and circuses? The Conservatives in office, 1951–1964', in Bogdanor and Skidelsky (eds), *The Age of Affluence*, p. 77.
43. See R. Lowe, 'The Second World War, consensus and the foundation of the Welfare State', 178–9.
44. As reported to Macmillan in TNA: PRO, PREM 11/2421.
45. TNA: PRO, T171/478, memo 25 for the 1957 budget.
46. D. Marquand, *The Unprincipled Society* (1988) p. 224.
47. One attempt to relate the consumer boom to welfare policy is R. Lowe, 'Modernizing Britain's welfare state: the influence of affluence', in L. Black and H. Pemberton (eds), *An Affluent Society? Britain's Post-War 'Golden Age' Revisited* (Aldershot, 2004).

5   EMPLOYMENT POLICY

1. Cmd 6527. The following quotations are from paragraphs 41 and 66.
2. See G. C. Peden, 'Sir Richard Hopkins and the "Keynesian Revolution" in employment policy, 1929–45', *Economic History Review*, 36 (1983) 281–96.
3. It was the Treasury (conscious of interwar hardship) which wished to bring 'work to the workers', whilst the 'progressive' Keynesians (confident that general reflation would soak up local unemployment) insisted on labour mobility regardless of its social cost.
4. One reason for non-implementation was the incompatibility of the economic need to vary contributions with the social and political need to maintain the 'actuarial' relationship between insurance contributions and benefits. Variations in contribution would for example have exploded the reality, or the myth, that increased benefits could only be financed through increased contributions (see Section 6.1). Legislation was passed in 1961 to permit variation but the Minister of Pensions and National Insurance threatened to resign and it was never implemented. TNA: PRO, PREM 11/3762.
5. The 'disinterested' nature of policy-making is well illustrated by a note from the Minister of Reconstruction (Lord Woolton) to Churchill on 16 May 1944: 'Sir William Beveridge has been working for some time on a plan for maintaining employment after the war, and his book on this subject is now with the printer. The Reconstruction Committee are unanimous that we ought not to allow him to

get the credit for being the first to put before the country a policy for full employ-ment; and we have been striving to get ahead of him.' TNA: PRO, PREM 4/96/6.

6. J. Tomlinson, *Employment Policy* (Oxford, 1987) p. 68. The following quotations are from Sir W. Beveridge, *Full Employment in a Free Society* (1944) pp. 261, 273.

7. The comment in 1952 of Churchill's far from moderate adviser, Lord Cherwell, was conclusive: 'it is no good looking back to Victorian times . . . the people will not accept mass unemployment' (TNA: PRO, T236/3242). So was Sir Keith Joseph's confession in *The Times* of 6 September 1974: 'We were dominated by the fear of unemployment. It was this which made us turn back against our own better judgement.' The private papers of reluctant collectivists such as Macmillan are explicit on the moral commitment. See also R. Shepherd, *Iain Macleod* (1994) p. 465.

8. The term was coined in A. Gamble and S. A. Walkland, *The British Party System and Economic Policy, 1945–1983* (Oxford, 1984) and is examined in depth in H. Pemberton, *Policy Learning and British Governance in the 1960s* (Basingstoke, 2004).

9. The examples cited in this paragraph are taken from P. D. Balacs, 'Economic data and economic policy', *Lloyds Bank Review*, 104 (1972) 35–50; S. Brittan, *Steering the Economy* (1971); and C. D. Cohen, *British Economic Policy, 1960–1969* (1971).

10. The calculations are even more complicated in relation to national insurance, where increased benefits are matched by increased contributions – and where the increased employer's contribution will gradually feed through into increased prices. In the 1960s it was calculated that the direct effect on demand would be an increase equivalent to 90 per cent of the increased benefit rate and a decrease equivalent to 85 per cent to 90 per cent respectively of the employee's and employer's increased contribution rate. Hence, if benefits went up by £300 million, financed by a £175 million and £125 million increase respectively in employer's and employee's contributions, the net increase in real demand would be £185 million. See C. D. Cohen, *British Economic Policy, 1960–1969* (1971) p. 57.

11. S. Brittan, *Steering the Economy* (1971) p. 423.

12. The statistics in this paragraph are taken from Sir Alec Cairncross, 'The postwar years, 1945–77', in R. Floud and D. McCloskey (eds), *The Economic History of Britain since 1700*, vol. 2 (Cambridge, 1981) pp. 370–416; and J. F. Wright, *Britain in the Age of Economic Management* (Oxford, 1979).

13. Cmnd 1432, paras 22 and 23.

14. Its early failure can be attributed in part to the Treasury's surreptitious attempt to use PESC to cap or even reduce welfare expenditure, of which many officials still disapproved. See R. Lowe, 'Milestone or millstone? The 1959–61 Plowden Committee and its impact on British welfare policy', *Historical Journal*, 40 (1997) 463–91, and 'The core executive, modernisation and the creation of PESC, 1960–4', *Public Administration*, 75 (1997) 601–15. For a good introduction, see D. Heald, *Public Expenditure* (1983) ch. 8 and C. Thain and M. Wright, *The Treasury and Whitehall* (Oxford, 1995) part 1.

15. N. Rollings, 'British budgetary policy, 1945–54: a "Keynesian revolution?"', *Economic History Review*, 41 (1988) 283–98.

16. *The Economist*, 19 February 1954; R. A. Butler, *The Art of the Possible* (1971) p. 160; TNA: PRO, T230/295; P. M. Williams, *Hugh Gaitskell* (1979) p. 217. See also N. Rollings, 'Poor Mr Butskell', *Twentieth Century British History*, 5 (1994) 183–205 and S. Kelly, *The Myth of Mr Butskell* (Aldershot, 2002).

17. To encourage long-term investment and to combat international competition, industrial concentration was found to be frequently desirable. This legislation

consequently had a greater effect on retailing rather than manufacturing, especially after the outlawing of price fixing by the 1964 Resale Price Maintenance Act – which helped to propel Heath to the leadership of the Conservative Party and, more permanently, encumbered him with the nickname of 'grocer'. On the Monopolies Commission and industrial training respectively, the standard works are H. Mercer, *Constructing the Competitive Order* (Cambridge, 1995) and D. King, *Actively Seeking Work?* (1995).

18. See S. Young and A. V. Lowe, *Intervention in the Mixed Economy* (1974) part 1. For an introduction to developments in Scotland, where the intellectual impetus for regional policy lay in the 1950s, and Northern Ireland, see L. Paterson, *The Autonomy of Scotland* (1994) pp. 117–23 and T. Wilson, *Ulster* (1989) chs 10–11.

19. Cmnd 1337. On steel, see K. Burk, *The First Privatisation* (1988).

20. *European Cooperation. Memoranda Submitted to OEEC relating to Economic Affairs in the period 1949 to 1953* (Cmd 7572, 1948). The document, more conveniently known as the long-term plan, was prepared as a condition of Marshall Aid, which was ironic because earlier plans had been modified for fear that their 'socialist' implications would offend the US government.

21. A. Shonfield, *Modern Capitalism* (1965) p. 88. For an authoritative analysis, see A. Ringe and N. Rollings, 'Responding to relative decline: the creation of the NEDC', *Economic History Review*, 53 (2000) 331–53; and for the views of participants, the transcript of the 'witness' seminar in A. Ringe, 'The NEDC, 1962–1967', *Contemporary British History*, 12 (1998) 82–130.

22. S. Young and A. V. Lowe, *Intervention in the Mixed Economy* (1974) p. 28. The book is a case study of the IRC. See also R. Coopey, 'Industrial policy', in R. Coopey, S. Fielding and N. Tiratsoo (eds), *The Wilson Governments, 1964–1970* (1993) pp. 102–22.

23. A. Shonfield, *Modern Capitalism* (1965) p. 160. Industrial resistance is well documented in A. A. Rogow, *The Labour Government and British Industry, 1945–51* (Oxford, 1955). The only tentative attempt to develop an 'active labour market policy' (whereby, as on the continent, a commitment by government and industry to finance long-term investment was matched by a parallel trade union commitment to wage restraint and occupational mobility) was in the early 1960s. Important legislation on such issues as contracts of employment, industrial training and redundancy pay was then passed, see P. Bridgen and R. Lowe, *Welfare Policy under the Conservatives, 1951–1964* (1998) ch. 1.6 and P. Bridgen, 'The state, redundancy pay and economic policy-making in the early 1960s', *Twentieth Century British History* 3 (2000) 233–58.

24. J. Leruez, *Economic Planning and Politics in Britain* (Oxford, 1975) p. 280; Sir R. Clarke, *Public Expenditure, Management and Control* (1978) pp. 74–5.

25. National Enterprise Board, *Annual Reports and Accounts, 1978* (1979).

26. A. Shonfield, *Modern Capitalism* (1965) p. 94.

27. Sir W. Beveridge, *Full Employment in a Free Society* (1944) p. 182.

28. See, in particular, the 1958 memorandum by senior officials on the 'United Kingdom's interests abroad', in TNA: PRO, PREM 11/2321.

6 SOCIAL SECURITY

1. Cmd 6404, para. 451; F. A. Hayek, *The Road to Serfdom* (1944) pp. 89–90.

2. Cmd 6404, para. 8. The Treasury's desire for secrecy is noted in J. Harris, *Beveridge* (Oxford, 1977) p. 383.

3. Cmd 6404, para. 17. When the principles were described at greater length in paragraphs 303–9, the principle of 'comprehensiveness' was revealed to embrace the controversial assumption of universalism: benefits should be 'comprehensive in respect both of persons covered and of their needs'. They were also to be adequate in amount and 'in time'.

4. Ibid., para. 273. The quotations in the following paragraph are from para. 296.

5. A small part of the cost of the health service was to be financed through insurance contributions (ibid, para. 437). Beveridge himself admitted in para. 415 the self-imposed financial limitation: 'flat insurance contributions are either a poll-tax or a tax on employment, justifiable up to certain limits, but not capable of indefinite expansion'.

6. Ibid., para. 19(v). The 'housewives' charter' is unveiled in paras 107–17 and 339–48.

7. Beveridge made both suggestions to reinforce the work ethic, but the Coalition government rejected them. Simultaneously it rejected the proposal that unemployment benefit should be limitless, thus ending the principle that insurance benefits should be adequate in amount and 'in time'.

8. Ibid., para. 29.

9. Ibid., paras 294, 375–84. Foreign practice is examined in Appendix F and rejected in paras 304–5. One form of voluntary insurance which Beveridge did want to end, because he adjudged it highly inefficient and exploitative, was industrial assurance – essentially the high-pressure door-to-door sale of policies to cover funeral expenses and life assurance by firms such as the Prudential. The insurance scheme was to provide a death grant and his hope was that assurance companies would be nationalized (paras 181–92, Appendix D). They were not but, encouraged by tax exemptions, they turned their attention to occupational pensions and became the major pension funds which have since dominated industrial investment.

10. The most explicit criticism of the Report can be found in the following documents at the TNA: PRO, CAB 87/3, RP(43)5, memorandum by the Chancellor of the Exchequer on 'the financial aspects of the social security plan', 11 January 1943; RP(43)6, report of the Official Committee on the Beveridge Report, chaired by Sir Thomas Phillips, 14 January 1943; and T273/57, the Treasury's major policy file on the draft Report, July–December 1942.

11. TNA: PRO, ED 136/229, observation by R. A. Butler, 14 September 1942, p. 221. Conservative Party opposition mirrored that of the Treasury, as revealed by the report of a secret backbench committee, chaired by Ralph Assheton. See P. Addison, *The Road to 1945* (1975).

12. Cmd 6404, paras 447, 240, 420. The final cost of Beveridge's proposals was only one-fifth of that of his ideal programme – see J. Harris, 'Enterprise and Welfare States', *Transactions of the Royal Historical Society*, 40 (1990) 187. Keynes's comment, and his estimate that the Treasury was already committed to extra annual expenditure of £40–50 million, is in TNA: PRO, T273/57, 9 December 1942.

13. T. Cutler, K. Williams and J. Williams, *Keynes, Beveridge and Beyond* (1986) p. 16; Cmd 6404, para. 459. For the relative cost of the new scheme, see paras 275–99. In 1962, when Britain first applied to join the EEC, the Treasury calculated that

British employers paid some £1000m p.a. less than their continental rivals, given the latter's liability to fund payroll taxes (TNA: PRO, T 320/52).

14. See in particular H. D. Henderson, 'The principles of the Beveridge plan', in TNA: PRO, T273/57, 4 August 1942 and the report of the Phillips Committee, cited in note 10. Beveridge, it should be noted, did not explicitly defend, or indeed use, the term 'universalism'. It was subsumed in the principle of 'comprehensiveness'; see note 3 above.

15. Cmd 6404, para. 196; J. H. Veit-Wilson, 'Condemned to deprivation? Beveridge's responsibility for the invisibility of poverty', in J. Hills, J. Ditch and H. Glennerster (eds), *Beveridge and Social Security* (Oxford, 1994) pp. 97–117. Beveridge's subsistence income was equivalent to only two-thirds of Rowntree's contemporary estimates and the government reduced benefit even further below this 'irreducible minimum'.

16. *Social Insurance, Part I* (Cmd 6550, 1944) para. 13. In 1966 a Ministry of Social Security was belatedly established, but this change in terminology hardly represented a delayed victory for Beveridge. National assistance was simultaneously renamed *supplementary* benefit.

17. See Cmd 6404, para. 27. Beveridge also stated in 1942 that 'the standard of minimum subsistence adopted by Mr Rowntree in 1899 was rejected by him a generation later as too low, and would be rejected decisively by public opinion today'. TNA: PRO, CAB 87/79, SIC (42)3, para. 6.

18. A. Bullock, *The Life and Times of Ernest Bevin*, vol. 2 (1967) p. 242.

19. Cmd 6404, para. 449.

20. P. Baldwin, 'Beveridge in the *Longue Durée*' in Hills et al. (eds), *Beveridge and Social Security*, p. 40.

21. For Beveridge's rejection in Germany see F. Grundger, 'Beveridge meets Bismarck', in Hills et al. (eds), *Beveridge and Social Security*, ch. 9. For a fuller analysis of Beveridge's rejection in Britain, see R. Lowe, 'A prophet dishonoured in his own country?', (ibid., ch. 8). The universality of the British welfare state effectively depended on the availability of means-tested benefits and should therefore be credited less to Beveridge than to the legacy of the much maligned Poor Law.

22. K. G. Banting, *Poverty, Politics and Policy* (1979) p. 68; A. Deacon and J. Bradshaw, *Reserved for the Poor* (1983) p. 61. See also R. Lowe, 'The rediscovery of poverty and the creation of the Child Poverty Action Group', *Contemporary Record*, 9 (1995) 602–37.

23. B. S. Rowntree, *Poverty: a study in town life* (1901) pp. 295–8; P. Townsend, *Poverty in the United Kingdom* (Harmondsworth, 1979) p. 31.

24. P. Townsend, 'The meaning of poverty', *British Journal of Sociology*, 13 (1962) 210–27; G. C. Fiegehen, P. S. Lansley and A. D. Smith, *Poverty and Progress in Britain, 1953–73* (1977) p. 131; J. Veit-Wilson, 'The National Assistance Board and the "Rediscovery of Poverty"', in H. Fawcett and R. Lowe (eds), *British Postwar Welfare Policy: the road from 1945* (1998) ch. 6. Rowntree himself had embraced the 'minimum participatory level' in *The Human Needs of Labour* (1937). The conceptual issue has been summarized thus by I. Gazeley: all 'subsistence definitions of poverty are relative measures ... Exactly when a poverty line stops being a subsistence measure and starts being a social participation measure is unanswerable objectively', *Poverty in Britain, 1900–1925* (Basingstoke, 2003) p. 2.

25. For changing perspectives on the 'problem family' see J. Welshman. 'Evacuation, hygiene and social policy', *Historical Journal*, 42 (1999) 781–807; J. Macnicol, 'From

"problem family" to "underclass", 1945–95' in H. Fawcett and R. Lowe (eds), *Welfare Policy in Britain* (Basingstoke, 1999) pp 69 –93; P Starkey, *Families and Social Workers: the work of Family Service Units, 1940–1985* (Liverpool, 2000), and 'The feckless mother', *Women's History Review*, 9 (2000) 539–57. For two very different analyses of the long-term consequences, see J. Macnicol 'In search of the underclass', *Journal of Social Policy*, 16 (1987) 293–318; and A. Deacon, *Perspectives on Welfare* (Buckingham, 2002).

26. In the 1970s, poverty was defined in this way by the European Union . Any individual whose disposable income fell below 50 per cent of the national average disposable income in the relevant member state was deemed to be in poverty. There were further refinements after 2000 (see p. 408).

27. Townsend, *Poverty in the United Kingdom*, ch. 11.

28. B. Abel-Smith and P. Townsend, *The Poor and the Poorest* (1965) p. 17.

29. A. B. Atkinson, *Poverty in Britain and the Reform of Social Security* (Cambridge, 1969) p. 35. Another source of bias, identified by Abel-Smith and Townsend in 1965, is that reported income tends to be understated by 10 per cent (because irregular earnings, for example, are omitted), whilst expenditure is overstated by 5 per cent (because, for example, respondents want to impress).

30. Fiegehen et al., *Poverty and Progress in Britain*, pp. 36–48. In some respects Rowntree (with his seeming obsession with the value of garden produce) and the assumption underlying the much-hated 'household' means test (that relations would support those in need) provided a more accurate picture of *actual* living conditions than statistics derived from government surveys.

31. B. S. Rowntree and G. R. Lavers, *Poverty and the Welfare State* (1951); A. B. Atkinson et al., 'National Assistance and low incomes in 1950', *Social Policy and Administration*, 15 (1981) 19–31; Abel-Smith and Townsend, *The Poor and the Poorest*; I. Gough and T. Stark, 'Low incomes in the United Kingdom', *Manchester School*, 36 (1968); A. B. Atkinson, *Poverty in Britain and the Reform of Social Security* and 'Poverty and income inequality in Britain', in D. Wedderburn (ed.), *Poverty, Inequality and Class Structure* (Cambridge, 1974); Townsend, *Poverty in the United Kingdom*; Fiegehen et al., *Poverty and Progress in Britain,*; W. Beckerman and S. Clark, *Poverty and Social Security in Britain since 1961* (Oxford, 1982); R. Layard, D. Piachaud and M. Stewart, *The Causes of Poverty* (1978); R. Berthoud and J. Brown, *Poverty and the Development of Anti-Poverty Policy in the UK* (1981).

32. In 'Seebohm Rowntree and the postwar poverty puzzle', *Economic History Review*, 53 (2000) 517–43, T. J. Hatton and R. E. Bailey painstakingly rework Rowntree's figures. They conclude 11.8 per cent rather than 4.6 per cent of working-class households should have been found in poverty and that Rowntree doubled the real reduction in poverty for which welfare measures were responsible. By so obscuring the real level of policy and exaggerating the impact of state welfare, they argue, an effective anti-poverty strategy was delayed for 'nearly two decades'. Whilst useful as a corrective, the analysis suffers from a range of ahistorical assumptions, an occupational hazard not unknown to quantitative historians. For instance, under American influence from the 1980s (and perhaps because it is easily quantifiable) welfare policy is equated to cash benefits (see Section 2.1 above). Rowntree's explicit definition is far wider.

33. Atkinson et al., 'National Assistance and low incomes in 1950', 24. This article provides the best comparison of the surveys of Rowntree and Abel-Smith and Townsend and, in particular, argues that generalization from York is dangerous since it did not have a full range of low-paid industries. On the 'scientific' basis

of the sample, Rowntree and Lavers wrote: 'We took a list of all the streets in York and a man who has lived in the city for more than half a century . . . marked on our list every street where working-class families live' (*Poverty and the Welfare State*, p. 2).

34. The level of insurance contributions had been based on an anticipated rate of 8.5 per cent unemployment, whereas the actual rate was under 3 per cent. The cost of unemployment benefit in 1955, at 1948–9 prices, which had been estimated by Beveridge at £123 million, was only £11.3 million. See A. W. Dilnot, J. Kay and C. N. Morris, *The Reform of Social Security* (Oxford, 1984), pp. 14–15.

35. L. Hannah, *Inventing Retirement* (Cambridge, 1986) p. 53. By 1955 the real cost of retirement pensions was almost 50 per cent higher than Beveridge's prediction and by 1965 it was 100 per cent higher. See Dilnot et al., *The Reform of Social Security*, pp. 14–15.

36. R. Lister, *Social Security: the case for reform* (1975) p. 67.

37. The phrase was coined by D. Piachaud in the *New Statesman*, 3 December 1971. Contemporary estimates are provided in J. C. Kincaid, *Poverty and Equality in Britain* (Harmondsworth, 1973) pp. 118–24.

38. R. Hemming, *Poverty and Incentives* (Oxford, 1984) p. 81.

39. Dilnot et al., *The Reform of Social Security*, p. 28.

40. Ibid., p. 45, and Hemming, *Poverty and Incentives*, p. 81.

41. Ibid., p. 49, and Atkinson, *Poverty in Britain and the Reform of Social Security*, p. 58.

42. D. Donnison, *The Politics of Poverty* (1982) pp. 43–4, 92; A. Deacon and J. Bradshaw, *Reserved for the Poor* (Oxford, 1983) p. 111. The system grew more complicated with a change in clientele. The number of unemployed and one-parent families (who typically left and rejoined the register frequently) increased, whilst the number of pensioners (who tended to stay constantly on the register) declined. Discretionary payments, which had fallen after the 1966 reforms, also accelerated with inflation. In 1976, 49 per cent of claimants were in receipt of regular 'exceptional circumstances' payments, mainly to cover the cost of heating, whilst 27 per cent were in receipt of one-off 'exceptional needs' payments, mainly to cover clothing needs. See S. Macgregor, *The Politics of Poverty* (1981) pp. 39–40.

43. Excited by the potential of computerization, all countries unsuccessfully flirted with such schemes. Two good, critical summaries are Atkinson, *Poverty in Britain and the Reform of Social Security*, ch. 9 and P. Alcock, *Poverty and State Support* (1987) ch. 11. For the particular problems of the Conservatives, see R. Lowe, 'Social policy', in S. Ball and A. Seldon (eds), *The Heath Government* (1996) pp. 201–3.

44. For a succinct summary, see Deacon and Bradshaw, *Reserved for the Poor*, ch. 4.

45. Cmd 6404, paras 258–64, 347.

46. Trade union dissatisfaction with industrial injury benefit had been the pretext for establishing the Beveridge Committee. To the unions' dismay, Beveridge recommended that the benefit should become contributory, but it was administered from a different fund and paid at a higher rate. It was fully amalgamated with national insurance in 1973. Means-tested disability pensions became payable in 1976.

47. The rise of scroungermania is documented in A. Deacon, 'Unemployment and politics in Britain since 1945', in B. Showler and A. Sinfield (eds), *The Workless State* (Oxford, 1981) pp. 59–88.

48. See Section 11.1; and, in particular, J. C. Kincaid, *Poverty and Equality in Britain* (1973) pp. 118–24.

49. Cmd 6404, paras 410–25. The value of total child support, including family and tax allowances, fell between 1946 and 1976 from 27 to 11 per cent of average male earnings. The large cash increases in 1968 only restored family allowances, briefly, to their real value in 1945.

50. Admittedly low-paid families benefited from certain other measures, such as rent and rate rebates, and family income supplement, but the take-up of those benefits was low. See Dilnot et al., *The Reform of Social Security*, p. 51. The unpopularity of family allowances is noted *inter alia* in PEP, *Family Needs and the Social Services* (1961) p. 38 and P. Taylor-Gooby, *Public Opinion, Ideology and State Welfare* (1985) ch. 2.

51. The discrepancy between the two sets of figures illustrates not only the sensitivity of all calculations to marginal changes in the poverty line but also the large number of children living close to the poverty line, however defined.

52. Cmd 6404, para. 236.

53. Cmd 9333, *Report of the Committee on the Economic and Financial Problems of the Provision for Old Age* (1954) para. 214. The committee had the same chairman, Sir Thomas Phillips, as the one in 1943 which had rejected Beveridge's principle of adequacy. It also recommended raising the age of retirement to 68 for men.

54. However, a certain number of non-claimants (from 20 per cent of couples to 38 per cent of single women) insisted that they were 'managing all right', and this may well have been true because, as seen in Section 6.2 above, official figures for entitlement disregarded certain income as well as help in kind from relatives. Atkinson, *Poverty in Britain and the Reform of Social Security*, ch. 3.

55. Hannah, *Inventing Retirement*, ch. 9; S. Harper, 'The impact of the retirement debate on postwar retirement trends', in T. Gorst, L. Johnman and W. Scott Lucas (eds), *Postwar Britain* (1989) pp. 95–108. In the early 1950s the retirement age in Canada and Sweden, for example, was 70 and 67 respectively, but it was soon reduced.

56. TNA: PRO, CAB 129/89/C(57)208, 16 September 1957. The statistics in this paragraph are taken from Hannah, *Inventing Retirement*, ch. 4 and p. 145. The 1959 Act epitomized the dilemmas of those seeking to reduce the welfare role of government (see Section 3.2.1 above). One Nation Conservatives, led by Macleod, wished to restrict it to the regulation rather than the provision of services. The state pension would continue to cover subsistence need, but to maintain accustomed living standards everyone would be required to take out a government-approved private occupational pension. The Treasury's conflicting priority was to limit the state's financial liability. It therefore favoured, rather surprisingly, a state occupational scheme which would maximize revenue (from earnings-related contributions) whilst minimizing outgoings (on tax allowances for private pensions). The resulting compromise created complexities which delayed further reform. See P. Bridgen and R. Lowe, *Welfare Policy under the Conservatives, 1951–1964* (1998) ch. 4.8.

57. TNA: PRO, T227/2216, Sir C. Jarrett, 5 February 1965 and PREM13/2394, R. Crossman to H. Wilson, 11 March 1968. For historical analysis, see J. Macnicol, *The Politics of Retirement in Britain, 1978–1948* (Cambridge, 1998); P. Bridgen, 'The One Nation idea and state welfare: the Conservatives and state pensions in the 1950s', *Contemporary British History*, 14 (2000) 83–104; H. Fawcett, 'The Beveridge straight-jacket', *Contemporary British History*, 10 (1996) 20–42; and 'Jack Jones, the social contract and social policy', in H. Fawcett and R. Lowe (eds), *Welfare Policy in Britain* (Basingstoke, 1999) pp. 158–83. For an international perspective, see P.

Baldwin, *The Politics of Social Solidarity* (Cambridge, 1990) ch. 4; and for 'path dependency' see P. Pierson, 'Increasing returns, path dependence and the study of politics', *American Political Science Review*, 94 (2000) 251–67.

58. PEP, *Family Needs and the Social Services* (1961) p. 192.

7   HEALTHCARE

1. R. J. Wybrow, *Britain Speaks Out, 1937–87* (1989) pp. 25–6; IEA, *Choice in Welfare* (1965) Appendix A; PEP, *Family Needs and the Social Services* (1961). The latter recorded: 'the attitude of mothers towards the social services was enthusiastic rather than critical, but there was not much doubt that this attitude is governed by their enthusiasm for the health services' (p. 39).

2. Beveridge commissioned Nuffield College, Oxford to survey public opinion towards the social services prior to the drafting of his Report. It found that reform of the health services was accorded top priority. See J. Harris, 'Did British workers want the welfare state?', in J. Winter (ed.), *The Working Class in Modern British History* (Cambridge, 1983) pp. 200–14. For an explanation of changing middle-class attitudes, see P. Baldwin, *The Politics of Social Solidarity* (Cambridge 1990) ch. 1.

3. All the general texts cited at the end of this chapter have an introductory chapter on the interwar period. See in particular R. Klein, *The New Politics of the NHS* (1995) ch. 1. ·

4. Not all these doctors would have been practising because, once registered, doctors were removed from the register only on death or evidence of malpractice. Details of salaries are provided in H. Eckstein, *The English Health Service* (Cambridge, MA, 1958) pp. 76–8. See also A. Digby and N. Bosanquet, 'Doctors and patients', *Economic History Review*, 41 (1988) 74–94; and A. Digby, *The Evolution of General Practice, 1850–1948* (Oxford, 1999).

5. For details of dentists and opticians, see C. Webster, *The Health Services since the War*, vol. 1 (1988) ch. 9.

6. Eckstein, *The English Health Service*, p. 75. Knowledge of interwar hospital provision has been revolutionized by the database developed by M. Gorsky and J. Mohan. Their major findings are summarized in M.Gorsky et al., 'The financial health of voluntary hospitals in interwar Britain', *Economic History Review*, 55 (2002) 533–57 and J. Mohan and M. Gorsky, *Don't Look Back* (2001), ch. 3. By 1940, over 10 million manual workers belonged to hospital contributory schemes which ensured access to voluntary hospitals for both them and typically their dependants. Nationally these schemes raised a quarter of voluntary hospitals' income. For individual hospitals and regions the figure could be far higher.

7. Cmd 6502. From the start the white paper was regarded as a consultation document rather than a serious blueprint for the service.

8. The best introduction to the local authority health service is J. Lewis, *What Price Community Medicine?* (Brighton, 1986), although its conclusions should be balanced against a more sympathetic analysis in J. Welshman, *Municipal Medicine* (Oxford, 2000).

9. In addition doctors claimed that salaries would discourage initiative, diminish their sense of responsibility and encourage mediocrity. In contrast Ministry of Health officials claimed commercial competition was 'undignified' for such a profession and that the battle for patients encouraged the overprescribing of

medicine and lax certification (such as sick notes). The Ministry of Health, as the department responsible for local government, had an 'obsessive desire for the municipal control' of the NHS. See F. Honigsbaum, *Health, Happiness and Security: the creation of the National Health Service* (1989) p. 213.

10. Among those dismayed was the former leader of the LCC, Herbert Morrison, who was the Labour Party's deputy leader from 1945 to 1956, and also the royal family, who were the leading patrons of voluntary hospitals. For the latter the nationalization of hospitals was 'an act of vandalism comparable to the dissolution of the monastries'. See F. Prochaska, *Royal Bounty: the making of a welfare monarchy* (New Haven, CT, 1995) p. 234

11. Cmd 6502, p. 20. One of those directly responsible for the Act admitted that it was very difficult to find in the original structure of the NHS 'much evidence of the democratic control and public participation which had been so strongly emphasised as desirable in the early planning'. See J. Pater, *The Making of the National Health Service* (1981) p. 168. By 1952 the percentage of manual workers on RHBs was 3 per cent, HMCs 6 per cent and Boards of Governors 2 per cent.

12. More provocatively, it has been claimed that health centres 'symbolise the distinction between the socialist and non-socialist conception of the health service', although only one was built under the Attlee government. See C. Webster, 'Conflict and consensus', *Twentieth Century British History*, I (1990) 139.

13. For the pre-eminence of hospital consultants in the USA and elsewhere, see D. M. Fox, *Health Policies, Health Politics* (Princeton, NJ, 1986) and N. Ginsburg, *Divisions of Welfare* (1992). For British public opinion, see R. J. Wybrow, *Britain Speaks Out, 1939–87* (1989) p. 25 and PEP, *Family Needs and the Social Services*, p. 113.

14. Even here Bevan would seem to have been overgenerous. Honigsbaum has estimated that fair compensation for the loss of the right to sell practices was £2700, not the average £4700 paid. See *Health, Happiness and Security*, p. 101.

15. Quoted in ibid. p. 146. In 1942 the interim report of the BMA's Medical Planning Commission appeared to support salaries and health centres but this was due, it is now argued, to the temporary influence on the BMA of a group of left-wing doctors, the Socialist Medical Association.

16. Quoted in B. Watkin, *The National Health Service* (1978) p. 21. Pater's succinct comment was that 'a little more statesmanship from *both* sides might have produced better results', see *The Making of the National Health Service* (1981) p. 179.

17. The criticism was Gaitskell's, quoted in P. Williams, *Hugh Gaitskell* (1979) p. 248.

18. The EMS, under which all hospital resources were pooled between 1939 and 1945 (initially in anticipation of heavy air-raid casualties) not only exposed the poor condition of voluntary hospitals but also encouraged the regionalization and rationalization of the whole hospital service. In addition, it accustomed consultants to salaried employment.

19. Klein, *The New Politics of the NHS*, p. 19. The number of beds per 1000 people was 4.9 in South Wales compared to London's average of 10.2.

20. Except when stated, the following account is based on C. Webster, *The Health Services since the War*, vol. 1 (1988) ch. 5; P. M. Williams, *Hugh Gaitskell* (1979) ch. 8 and the records of the Cabinet Committee on the National Health Service preserved in TNA: PRO, CAB 134/518–9. The last provides a good example of the ill-feeling Bevan created. Its meetings consisted, recorded its secretary, 'of a series of episodes in which the Minister of Health says his piece and is then contradicted by the others' (CAB 21/2027).

21. The Guillebaud Report on the NHS (1956), Cmd 9663, paras 544–7. The number

of prescriptions increased from 71.5 million to 227 million and their average cost from 8p to 20p (paras 466–70). Manpower costs were increased, for example, by the 1947 Nurses Act which established national pay scales and qualifications for the first time.

22. Quoted in Webster, *The Health Services since the War*, vol. 1, p.162 and Klein, *The New Politics of the NHS*, p. 31. In 1949 Bevan also proclaimed that prescription charges were 'a very small aspect indeed . . . what we are considering is not a considerable retreat', see Williams, *Hugh Gaitskell*, p. 263.

23. Quoted in Webster, *The Health Services since the War*, vol. 1, p.150.

24. TNA: PRO, CAB 128/17, CM(20)17, 3 April 1950. A brief summary of charges up to 2000, and of their rationale, is provided in J. Eversley, 'The history of NHS charges', *Contemporary British History*, 15 (2001) 53–75

25. The most bitter attack came on 20 April in the left-wing paper, *Tribune*, which – in an unseemly deal – was being subsidized by Lord Beaverbrook (Churchill's right-wing adviser and patron of left-wing MPs, including Bevan). See Williams, *Hugh Gaitskell*, p. 257. Such associations might seem to confirm the widespread view that Bevan was his own worst enemy, to which Ernest Bevin's classic retort was 'not while I'm alive, he ain't'.

26. Gaitskell's concessions included a rise in the cash limits for the NHS and a two-year limit on charges.

27. See Webster, *The Health Services since the War*, vol. 1 p. 392. For Sweden and the 'Seven Crowns' reform of 1970, see N. Ginsburg, *Divisions of Welfare* (1992) pp. 58–64.

28. Webster, *The Health Services since the War*, vol. 1, p. 209. The Conservative Party had voted against the 1946 National Health Service Act in Parliament, but on rather different grounds. The Act, it argued, 'discourages voluntary effort and association; mutilates the structure of local government; dangerously increases ministerial power and patronage; appropriates trust funds and benefactions in contempt of the wishes of donors and subscribers; and undermines the freedom and independence of the medical profession'.

29. Watkin, *The National Health Service*, p. 36; T. E. Chester, 'The Guillebaud Report', *Public Administration*, 34 (1956) 207. For a summary of the committee's research findings, see B. Abel-Smith and R. M. Titmuss, *The Cost of the National Health Service in England and Wales* (Cambridge, 1956).

30. Cmd 9663, para. 733(3). A survey of its recommendations on adequacy and charges are in paras 730(7) and 732(5). For the Treasury's continuing campaign for money-raising expedients rejected by Guillebaud, see P. Bridgen and R. Lowe, *Welfare Policy under the Conservatives, 1951–1964* (1998) ch. 3.

31. For Cabinet discussions and Treasury objections in 1957, see TNA: PRO, CAB 128/30 part 2, CM(57)2 and T227/485. The prescription charge was an alternative means of persuading doctors to prescribe and patients to behave 'responsibly'; and after Guillebaud's rejection of a proscribed list of drugs, the government also persuaded drug companies to obey a voluntary code of practice on pricing to limit NHS costs. A fully insurance-based NHS was again proposed, and quickly dismissed, in 1970 at the 'Selsdon Park' meeting of the Conservatives shadow cabinet and in 1982.

32. This section is heavily dependent on J. Mohan, *Planning, Markets and Hospitals* (2000) chs 6–7. The minister of health was restored to the Cabinet in 1962. The Hospital Plan was Cmnd 1604 (1962), whilst the complementary white papers on the development of community care were Cmnd 1973 (1963) and 3022 (1966).

33. As summarized in Mohan, *Planning, Markets and Hospital,* p.154. His own conclusions are more favourable.

34. TNA: PRO, T227/1313, Robertson to Douglas, 11 December 1961. The polemical nature of the Plan is characterized by the use of the word 'modern' six times in its first page and a half. When Labour revised the Plan in 1966, significantly entitled *The Hospital Building Programme* (Cmnd 3000), the minister of health assured the prime minister that 'I believe my proposals, unlike the original plan, to be realistic' (TNA: PRO, PREM 13/2252, K. Robinson to H. Wilson).

35. Quoted in Watkin, *The National Health Service,* p. 71; and M. Emrys-Roberts, *The Times,* 26 September 1962. For Powell's own later misgivings, see *Medicine and Politics* (1966) ch. 5.

36. TNA: PRO, MH123/278, paper by N. Goodman, 30 June 1960. Changes in the nature of illness and its treatment justified some reduction in the ratio. Less justified, given its key importance, was the lack of agreement over the definition of a 'district general hospital'. It was here that officials felt most let down by 'the medicos', as reported by the Ministry of Health's deputy secretary who also provided the overall condemnation of the Plan (see Churchill College, Cambridge: Russell Smith letters, RUSM 1/21, 13 November 1961and 15 June 1961).

37. H. Glennerster, *British Social Policy since 1945* (1995) p. 130.

38. Cmnd 5055 (1972), *National Health Service Reorganisation: England,* para. 13. To reinforce public accountability, a health service commissioner (ombudsman) was also to be appointed to hear complaints. Scotland and Northern Ireland avoided much of this nonsense, see Section 4.4 above.

39. For a faithful summary, see B. Watkin, *The National Health Service,* chs 3 and 7. How close GPs came to abandoning the NHS is graphically described in N. Timmins, *The Five Giants* (1995) p. 223.

40. A. Bevan, *In Place of Fear* (1961 edn) p. 110. For consultants' rather different view of GPs as the 'waste product of medical schools', see Timmins, *The Five Giants,* p. 218. For the rest of the paragraph, see F. Honigsbaum, *The Division in British Medicine* (1979) part 8.

41. P. Hall, 'The development of health centres', in P. Hall et al., *Change, Choice and Conflict in Social Policy* (1975) pp. 299–310.

42. The history of nursing is in almost as poor a state as the postwar profession itself. This paragraph depends on P. Starns, *March of the Matrons* (Peterborough, 2000). See also R. Dingwall, A. M. Rafferty and C. Webster, *An Introduction to the Social History of Nursing* (1988); R. White, *The Effects of the National Health Service on the Nursing Profession* (1985); and C. Hart, *Behind the Mask* (1993). The important postwar reports were the Salmon *Report on the Structure of Senior Nursing Staff* (1966), and the *Report of the (Briggs) Committee on Nursing* (Cmd 5115, 1972).

43. See A. H. Halsey, *British Social Trends since 1900* (1988) ch. 11; *Inequalities in Health* (Harmondsworth, 1988) which reprints the 1980 Black Report; and H. Jones, *Health and Society in Twentieth-Century Britain* (1994) ch. 8 for a summary of the conflicting evidence.

44. Tobacco-smoking was the largest self-inflicted cause of disease and might have been officially discouraged earlier than 1957 since the link with cancer was first identified in 1950. Delay was occasioned by the lack of conclusive scientific proof and fears about infringing personal liberty. The tobacco companies also contributed generously to Conservative Party funds and the tobacco tax to government revenue. 'We all know', remarked Macleod as minister of health in

1956, 'that the Welfare State and much else is based on tobacco smoking' (TNA: PRO, MH55/1011). A challenging analysis is V. Berridge, 'Post-war smoking policy and the UK and the redefinition of public health', *Twentieth Century British History*, 14 (2003) 61–82.

45. See E. Powell, *Medicine and Politics* (1966) pp. 48–9 and also Timmins, *The Five Giants*, pp. 258–9. For the background to the 1959 Act, see M. Thomson, *The Problem of Mental Deficiency, Eugenics, Democracy and Social Policy, 1870–1959* (Oxford, 1983) and C. Unsworth, *The Politics of Mental Health Legislation* (Oxford, 1987).

46. Bevan, *In Place of Fear*, p. 109.

47. Powell, *Medicine and Politics*, p. 16.

8　EDUCATION

1. TNA: PRO, RG23/71, Social Survey report on public attitudes towards the Education Act, 1945.

2. There was, of course, a wide range of 'educative' influences outside the formal education system. These included reading and television (which increased with affluence); the family and neighbourhood (which educationalists came to accept as more powerful influences on children than schooling); and other institutions (such as the Army Bureau of Current Affairs, which was held to have radicalized conscripts' opinions during the Second World War).

3. B. Simon, 'The Tory government and education, 1951–1960', *History of Education*, 14 (1985) 283.

4. C. A. R. Crosland, *The Future of Socialism* (1956) p. 258; Cmd 9703, *Technical Education* (1956) p. 4.

5. Crosland's views are expressed in *The Future of Socialism*, ch. 12. Eccles's are in a letter to Eden preserved in TNA: PRO, PREM 11/1785 (June 1955). For the 1944 *Employment Policy* white paper, see Section 5.1.

6. H. C. Dent, *The New Education Bill* (1944); B. Simon, 'The 1944 Education Act: a Conservative measure?', *History of Education*, 15 (1986) 41.

7. Cmd 6458, *Educational Reconstruction* (1943) para. 48.

8. The authority of central over local government was made explicit in Section 68 of the second part of the Act. The extent to which this authority was qualified by the requirement that pupils should be 'educated in accordance with the wishes of their parents' (Section 76 of Part 4) was never fully resolved. Policy in Northern Ireland and Scotland was determined by different, albeit broadly parallel legislation and administered by Stormont and the Scottish Office.

9. The requirement was reduced by 25 per cent in 1959 and 20 per cent in 1969. For details of subsidies in Northern Ireland, which underpinned its sectarian system of education, see T. Wilson, *Ulster: conflict and consent* (Oxford, 1989) ch. 14.

10. The one exception in England and Wales was direct-grant schools. Since 1926 certain prestigious schools such as Manchester Grammar School had received subsidies directly from central rather than local government, and against Butler's better judgement they were permitted to continue charging fees. The Attlee government reduced their number from 232 to 164. See Section 8.4 below.

11. This did not signify the administrative unification of the whole formal education system, as later friction was to prove. The Ministry of Labour retained responsibility for industrial training, and the University Grants Committee (answerable to

the Treasury and then, after 1962, to the Ministry of Education) for universities. Greater local democracy was permitted with the devolution of power from county councils and boroughs to 'district committees', but these committees were explicitly the agent of the larger authorities.

12. Cmd 6458 (1943) paras 2 and 47.

13. Cmd 6458 (1943) para. 28. The Spens Committee had been appointed in 1933 to report on 'secondary education with special reference to grammar schools and technical high schools'.

14. C. Barnett, *The Audit of War* (1986) p. 275.

15. TNA: PRO, ED 136/181.

16. Barnett, *The Audit of War*, p. 284; J. Harris, 'Enterprise and Welfare States', *Transactions of the Royal Historical Society*, 40 (1990) 192.

17. Barnett, *The Audit of War*, p. 291.

18. This paragraph is based on P. H. Gosden, *Education in the Second World War* (1976) chs 11 and 14. The quotation is from p. 334.

19. Ibid., pp. 247, 256. The philosophy underlying the tradition of 'education for leadership', and its articulation by Norwood, is best described in G. McCulloch, *Philosophers and Kings* (Cambridge, 1991).

20. A. Howard, *RAB: the life of R. A. Butler* (1987) p. 115.

21. The defeat was made an issue of confidence and reversed the following day. On the issue of equal pay, see P. Thane, 'Towards equal opportunities? Women in Britain since 1945', in T. Gourvish and A. O'Day (eds), *Britain since 1945* (1991) pp. 183–4.

22. C. Knight, *The Making of Tory Education Policy in Postwar Britain, 1950–86* (1990) p. 11.

23. The increased number of children in specialist primary schools also reflected the decrease in children in all-age schools from 1.1 million in 1946 to 636,246 in 1954.

24. In Northern Ireland, the school leaving age was not raised until 1957 and fees remained. The number of school meals rose from under half a million in 1941 to 2.7 million in 1948 (53 per cent of all school children) and, having fluctuated around 50 per cent in the 1950s, peaked at 70 per cent in 1975. It had been promised that they would be free (providing one reason for keeping family allowances below Beveridge's minimum) but there was always a charge, initially to cover the cost of the food but not administration. There was an immediate 90 per cent take-up of free milk. It was withdrawn from secondary schools by Labour in the 1960s and, notoriously, from 8–11-year-olds in 1971 by Margaret 'milk-snatcher' Thatcher.

25. TNA: PRO, ED 136/890, Butler to Horsbrugh, 7 October 1953. The economies are detailed in T227/401. The low priority accorded to education was illustrated by Churchill's offer of the Ministry to the Liberal leader, in the hope of forming a coalition, and its exclusion from Cabinet until 1962.

26. In the Hutting Operation for the Raising of the School Leaving Age, 4162 classrooms, 2195 practical rooms, and a quarter of a million chairs and desks were provided by 1949. Ellen Wilkinson is quoted in P. Gosden, *The Education System since 1944* (1983) p. 5.

27. TNA: PRO, PREM 11/1785, Eccles to Eden, 6 June 1955. The white paper was Cmnd 604. Following the 1961 economic crisis, the cost of this programme was vigorously challenged. Eccles, like his Labour predecessors in 1947, was able to defeat the Treasury – despite a classic query from the head of the civil service on the need so to improve 'the public system of education that we all become middle class' (Brook to Macmillan, 8 January 1962, PREM 11/3757).

28. Roy Lowe, *Education in the Postwar Years* (1988) p. 200. Popular support for the Scottish education system lasted much longer. The succession of critical reports was seen to address essentially English problems, see J. G. Kellas, *The Scottish Political System* (Cambridge, 1975) pp. 197–8.

29. Gosden, *The Education System since 1944*, p. 32. On the Conservative Party, see Simon, 'The Tory government and education, 1951–60', 289. As Sir Edward Boyle somewhat unsubtly made the political case for comprehensives: 'the proportion of Tory voters in the electorate is more than double the proportion of grammar school places, and over ten times the proportion of those who can afford to educate their children privately' (Bodleian, Oxford: Conservative Party Archives, LCC(67) 123.

30. Its report in 1963 was Cmnd 2154. There was, as will be seen, a deluge of reports and white papers on education, details and abstracts from which can most conveniently be found in J. S. Maclure, *Educational Documents* (5th edn, 1986) and R. Rodgers, *Crowther to Warnock* (1980). Reference, where practical, will be made to these sources rather than the originals.

31. Maclure, *Educational Documents*, pp. 302, 333. The Plowden Committee is covered on pp. 308–23.

32. B. Simon, *Education and the Social Order, 1940–90* (1991) p. 262. Robbins is quoted on p. 251.

33. Legal compulsion was adjudged necessary to galvanize 14 LEAs which had declined to respond to Crosland's request and was finally introduced in England and Wales in 1976. For the succeeding figures, see Simon, *Education and the Social Order*, pp. 420–30. Northern Ireland never accepted comprehensive schooling (despite a threat of compulsion in 1977) whilst Scotland openly welcomed it.

34. H. Young, *One of Us* (1989) pp. 69–70. Margaret Thatcher's permanent secretary has argued conversely that the Open University was saved because 'their degrees cost only half of Oxbridge's', see Simon, *Education and the Social Order*, p. 464. Iain Macleod, as chancellor, had expressed his determination to close the Open University, but died within a month of taking office. See also R. Lowe, 'Social policy', in S. Ball and A. Seldon (eds), *The Heath Government* (1996) pp. 210–13.

35. Two contrasting interpretations of the educational backlash can be found in Simon, *Education and the Social Order*, ch. 8 and Knight, *The Making of Tory Education Policy in Postwar Britain*, chs 1–5.

36. The statistics in these bullet points are taken from H. Glennerster and W. Low, 'Education and the Welfare State: does it all add up?', in J. Hills (ed.), *The State of Welfare* (Oxford, 1990) pp. 28–87. In 1947 the number of candidates for School Certificate and Higher School Certificate was 107,000 and 26,000 respectively. By 1975 the number for the equivalent GCE 'O' and 'A' level was 865,000 and 251,000. See Department of Education and Science, *Educational Statistics* (1978) vol. 2, p. 4.

37. C. B. Cox and A. E. Dyson (eds), *Fight for Education: a black paper* (1969) and P. Lewis, *The Fifties* (1978) p. 172.

38. Boyle's view was expressed in the foreword to the Ministry of Education, *Half our Future* (1962) – the Newsom Report. For its time it was radical since it assumed children's intelligence was not genetically determined, as asserted by educational psychologists such as Burt, but could be 'acquired'.

39. See O. Banks, *Parity and Prestige in English Secondary Education* (1975) pp. 135–8.

40. See M. Sanderson, *Educational Opportunity and Social Change in England* (1987) p. 85: 'The 1870s unequal treatment of equals was as unjust as the 1970s equal

treatment of unequals. . . . Anti-egalitarians would regard English education as having swung from one form of injustice to another. They would see the just equilibrium in that arc as the late 1940s and the 1950s.'

41.   Simon, *Education and the Social Order*, p. 215.

42.   *Educational Reconstruction*, for instance, had stated that it would be 'wrong to suppose' that the three types of education would 'necessarily remain separate and apart' (Cmd 6458, para. 31). However, in their general guide to the implementation of the Act, *The Nation's Schools* (1945) and their specific instruction to LEAs, circular 144/1947, officials (with the sanction of the Labour government) made their preference explicit.

43.   Several comments favourable to comprehensive education in the draft of *Secondary Education for All* were, however, censored. See Simon, *Education and the Social Order*, p. 219.

44.   Sanderson, *Educational Opportunity and Social Change in England*, p. 55. All the examples in the following paragraph are taken from Chapter 3 of that book, unless otherwise stated.

45.   A. Yates and D. E. Pidgeon, *Admission to Grammar Schools* (1958); Roy Lowe, *Education in the Postwar Years*, p. 117.

46.   For a summary of this research, particularly that by Floud, Halsey, Martin and Jackson, see H. Silver (ed.), *Equal Opportunity in Education* (1973). The continuing rejection of comprehensive schools in Northern Ireland was explained in part by 25 per cent of children being guaranteed grammar school places.

47.   The early age of selection had also concerned Conservative ministers such as Butler and Eccles, who commented with characteristic bluntness: 'Eleven plus is too early to show your paces if you come from a dumb or a bad home' (TNA: PRO, ED 147/207). Norwood had also favoured a common curriculum for all children between the ages of 11 and 13 to facilitate late transfers.

48.   *Educational Reconstruction* (1943) para. 17; TNA: PRO, ED 12/479, 10th meeting of the Norwood Committee, October 1942.

49.   See P. Gosden and P. R. Sharp, *The Development of an Education Service* (1978) p. 166. It had been a principal objective of the 1938 Spens report to discourage children with high IQs from automatically opting for an academic rather than a practical training.

50.   D. Thom, 'The 1944 Education Act', in H. L. Smith (ed.), *War and Social Change* (1986) p. 108. See also B. Evans and B. Waites, *IQ and Mental Testing* (1981) ch. 3. The irony is all the greater since IQ tests had been used to exclude fee-paying middle-class children from grammar schools, and thereby to raise those schools' academic standards. See Banks, *Parity and Prestige in English Secondary Education*, ch. 5.

51.   Quoted in Simon, *Education and the Social Order*, pp. 235–6. See also P. E. Vernon, *Secondary School Selection* (1957).

52.   The concept of general intelligence, let alone its measurability, is today seriously questioned. There are, some psychologists have argued, many different kinds of intelligence controlled by different parts of the brain. There is now also general agreement that exceptional ability is not usually transferred from one generation to the next ('regression to the mean').

53.   P. Summerfield, *Women Workers in the Second World War* (1984) ch. 4: *Educational Reconstruction* (1943) para. 8. Summerfield sees the history of nursery education as a major failure in 'collective provision for women's benefit' (p. 119).

54.   The 1972 Halsey Report on *Educational Priority*, quoted in R. Rodgers, *From*

Crowther to Warnock (1980) ch. 8. Unfavourable comparison with European practice should be qualified by the fact that in Britain the age of entry into full-time primary education was 5 not 6.

55. Quoted in Simon, *Education and the Social Order*, p. 364. Progressive educational methods were facilitated by a wide range of factors including courses such as 'new maths' pioneered by the Nuffield Foundation, see Roy Lowe, *Schooling and Social Change, 1969–1990* (1997) pp. 47–55.

56. K. G. Banting, *Poverty, Politics and Policy* (1979) ch. 4; Simon, *Education and the Social Order*, p. 346.

57. B. Simon, 'The 1944 Education Act', *History of Education*, 15 (1986) 33.

58. The quotations are successively from T. C. Worsley, *The End of the Old School Tie* (1941) p. 11; C. A. R. Crosland, *The Future of Socialism* (1956) p. 264; Roy Lowe, *Education in the Postwar Years*, p. 121.

59. Tax relief on gifts to minors and on loans was removed in 1962 and 1969 respectively although, crucially, public schools still retained their charitable status. Public schools were also made subject to inspection after 1957.

60. TNA: PRO. ED 147/211. The official view of the virtues of private schooling is documented in Gosden, *Education in the Second World War*, ch. 14.

61. Glennerster and Low, 'Education and the Welfare State', in Hills (ed.), *The State of Welfare*, p. 51. These figures cover children in preparatory as well as public schools.

62. Roy Lowe, *Education in the Postwar Years*, p. 111.

63. H. Glennerster, *British Social Policy since 1945* (1995) p. 139.

64. In Yorkshire, for example, parents were reported to be 'almost frantic' that their children should not be allocated to secondary moderns. See Gosden and Sharp, *The Development of an Education Service*, p. 174.

65. Quoted in Gosden, *The Education System since 1944*, p. 68.

66. For a lively debate on the education record of the 1945 Labour government, see *History Workshop Journal*, vols 9–10 (1980–1).

67. Quoted in Simon, *Education and the Social Order*, p. 281. The essentially negative purpose behind Labour's plans for comprehensives can be caught in Harold Wilson's slogan 'grammar school education for all'. Later he claimed that grammar schools would be abolished only over his dead body – a challenge to which there was surprisingly little response.

68. See especially, A. Kerckhoff et al., *Going Comprehensive in England and Wales: a study of uneven change* (1996) and Gosden and Sharp, *The Development of an Educational Service*, ch. 7. The West Riding pioneered the concept of the 'middle school' which, by dividing children at 13, permitted some rationalization of existing school buildings.

69. For one view on the 'damping down' of curriculum reform by structural reorganization and its consequences, see Roy Lowe, *Schooling and Social Change, 1964–1990* (1997) pp. 35, 55–69.

70. See N. Rao, 'Labour and education: reorganisation and the neighbourhood school', *Contemporary British History*, 16 (2002) 99–120. The Conservative minister was Boyle, and Crosland secretly agreed. As he minuted: 'Neighbourhood one-class school . . . clearly *is* danger on housing estates or in the old slums: therefore *must* try to draw catchment areas to minimise it.'

71. C. Chitty, 'Central control of the school curriculum, 1944–87', *History of Education*, 17 (1988) 324.

72. Quoted in ibid., p. 330. For the establishment and record of the Schools Council,

on whose governing body teacher representatives were in the majority, see Simon, *Education and the Social Order*, pp. 311–14.

73. W. A. C. Stewart, *Higher Education in Postwar Britain* (1989) pp. 74, 132.
74. See Section 8.2 above. The nine CATs, which gained university status in 1965, were Aston, Bath, Bradford, Brunel, City, Heriot-Watt, Loughborough, Salford and Surrey. Higher education was provided by other institutions, but students largely worked for university external degrees.
75. Founded in 1919, the UGC initially represented the views of individual universities to government but was later entrusted with coordination and planning. Until 1962 it reported directly to the Treasury. Universities were also perceived to encourage inequality. Through their control of the GCE examination, for example, they imposed on secondary schools the specialist curricula which discouraged many working-class pupils. The cost of educating undergraduates, who were largely middle class, was equivalent to that of ten years' education in state schools. See B. Abel-Smith 'Whose Welfare State?', in N. Mackenzie (ed.), *Conviction* (1958) p. 57.
76. For a summary of some of the related innovations in the 1960s embracing a broadening of the curriculum (as at Sussex), teaching techniques (such as the introduction of continuous assessment at East Anglia in 1964) and closer links with industry (as at Warwick), see Roy Lowe, *Schooling and Social Change*, pp. 69–79.
77. The true extent and causes of student unrest is examined in N. Thomas, 'Challenging the myths of the 1960s: the case of student protest in Britain', *Twentieth Century British History*, 13 (2002) 277–97.
78, The choice was explicit. When Eccles in the aftermath of Crowther proposed a right to day release for all under 18 years of age it was rejected on the grounds that the funding for the requisite staff and buildings was committed elsewhere, see TNA: PRO, ED 46/1008–9.
79. TNA: PRO, T227/280, draft UGC statement, December 1954. Lord Cherwell did encourage the foundation of Churchill College, Cambridge, in an unsuccessful attempt to create a British MIT.
80. *Technical Education* (Cmd 9703). The Hives Committee later became the Council for National Academic Awards which validated all degrees outside universities.
81. D. Finegold and D. W. Soskice, 'The failure of training in Britain', *Oxford Review of Economic Policy*, 4 (1988) 21–53; D. King, *Actively Seeking Work?* (1995), ch. 4; H. Pemberton, 'Relative decline, industrial training and the problem of 'governance' in the 1960s' (forthcoming).
82. D. H. Aldcroft, *Education, Training and Economic Performance, 1944–1990* (Manchester, 1992) pp. 54–8.
83. S. J. Prais, 'Vocational qualifications of the labour force in Britain and Germany', *National Institute Economic Review* (1982); Sanderson, *Educational Opportunity and Social Change in England*, p. 124. See also M. Sanderson, 'Social equity and industrial need: a dilemma of English education since 1945', in T. Gourvish and A. O'Day (eds), *Britain since 1945* (1991) pp. 159–82.
84. *Educational Reconstruction* (1942) para. 29.
85. Roy Lowe, *Schooling and Social Change*, p. 40; J. Mansell in C. Chitty (ed.), *Post-16 Education* (1991) pp. 113–23.
86. Cmd 9703, Ch. 5. Employers were abetted in their conservatism by trade unions which (out of a historic fear of unemployment) remained suspicious of any attempt to increase the number of, or to modernize, apprenticeships.

9 HOUSING

1. M. Foot, *Aneurin Bevan*, vol. 1 (1962) p. 473. Eden first used the phrase 'property-owning democracy' at the Conservative Party conference in 1946.

2. R. J. Wybrow, *Britain Speaks Out, 1937–87* (1989) p. 17. The other quotations in this paragraph are from PEP, *Family Needs and the Social Services* (1961) p. 37; and *The Economist*, 5 June 1954.

3. Conservative Political Centre, *One Nation* (1950) pp. 30–1.

4. Cmd 6153 (1940) para. 428.

5. Cmd 6378 and 6291 (1942). On account of the detailed legal issues involved, both Scott and Uthwatt were high court judges.

6. As Macmillan was characteristically to remark, current methods were 'more suitable to an oriental bazaar than to the traditions of the British revenue system' (*Tides of Fortune, 1945–1955* (1969) p. 423).

7. Cmd 6537 (1944) p. 2. The white paper used the term 'betterment', as it is used in this chapter, to cover the increase in value of both undeveloped land granted planning permission (strictly its 'development' value) and of developed land resulting from adjacent improvements. A key prewar Party principle, land nationalization, was dropped by Labour under pressure not from its Conservative coalition partners but its own local councillors. See M. Tichelar, 'The conflict over property rights during the Second World War', *Twentieth Century British History*, 14 (2003) 165–88.

8. In 1947 and 1975 the tax was levied on the developer. In 1967 land was purchased from the owner at 60 per cent of its development value and therefore an effective tax of 40 per cent was imposed.

9. This and the succeeding paragraph are based on A. Cox, *Adversary Politics and Land* (Cambridge, 1984).

10. Hence the 100 per cent betterment tax was designed in 1947 not by ministers to achieve socialist ends but by the Treasury to prevent the Land Commission from raising any money. In 1967 it clawed back all – and in 1975 40 per cent of – the revenue from betterment and the sale of land. The constitutional objections also resulted in local government rather than a central Land Commission being responsible for the execution of policy in 1975.

11. S. Merrett, *State Housing in Britain* (1979) p. 81. The property boom drove Edward Heath to coin the phrase 'the unacceptable face of capitalism', whilst the seriousness of the credit crisis was illustrated by the rare collapse of a bank (the 'secondary' bank, London and Home Securities).

12. J. R. Short, *Housing in Britain* (1982) p. 214; Merrett, *State Housing in Britain*, p. 79. An unusually positive account of consumer reaction to New Towns, as well as a useful bibliography, is provided in M. Clapson, *Invincible Green Suburbs, Brave New Towns* (Manchester, 1998) and 'Working-class women's experiences of moving to new housing estates in England since 1919', *Twentieth Century British History*, 10 (1999) 345–65.

13. Short, *Housing in Britain*, p. 87.

14. Except where specified, housing in this section refers not just to houses but also to 'dwellings', that is, parts of buildings (such as flats) which provide structurally separate living quarters.

15. Economic historians have widely criticized the diversion of resources from industry to housing. Correlli Barnett's comment is typical: 'instead of starting with a

new workshop to become rich enough to afford a new family villa, John Bull opted for the villa straightaway – even though he happened to be bankrupt at the time' (*Audit of War* (1986) pp. 246–7).

16. Partly under Churchill's influence, 160,000 prefabs (each of which could be erected in a day) were built between 1946 and 1948. Like the experiment with prefabricated building in the early 1960s, they proved to be more expensive and of lower quality than conventional housing. They were also urged on government by wartime contractors with spare capacity. They were, in short, 'an object lesson in the failure of centralist planning'. See O. Gay, 'Prefabs: a study in policy-making', *Public Administration*, 65 (1987) 407–22.

17. Quoted in M. Foot, *Aneurin Bevan*, vol. 2 (1973) p. 82. For a critique of Bevan's record, and the broader relationship between housing and welfare policy, see P. Malpass, 'The wobbly pillar? Housing and the postwar welfare state', *Journal of Social Policy*, 32 (2003) 589–606.

18. See M. Sissons and P. French (eds), *Age of Austerity, 1945–1951* (Harmondsworth, 1964) pp. 44–8.

19. The 300,000 target was one of the very few policy decisions forced by a Conservative conference on the Party's leaders – surprisingly by the liberal not the One Nation wing of the Party. For the details see A. Seldon, *Churchill's Indian Summer* (1981) p. 248 and H. Jones, 'The Conservative Party and the welfare state, 1942–55' (unpublished PhD, London 1992) p. 140. It had been anticipated, however, in the 1945 Coalition white paper, *Housing* (Cmd 6609).

20. TNA: PRO, HLG 37/83.

21. TNA: PRO, T273/91, Macmillan to Butler, 21 December 1951. For his antics, which the head of the civil service condemned as 'ridiculous and underhand', see H. Macmillan, *Tides of Fortune, 1945–55* (1969) ch. 13. Dalton's reduction of standards is recorded in TNA:PRO: HLG 37/83.

22. There were 2500 housing associations. They attracted criticism because, being small, they could not reap economies of scale and, as non-elected bodies, they consumed much public money. However, for the Conservatives they provided an attractive alternative to a failing market and state monopoly, see P. Weiler, 'The Conservative's search for a middle way in housing, 1951–1964', *Twentieth Century British History*, 14 (2003) 360–91. For an excellent, comprehensive survey, see P. Malpass, *Housing Associations and Housing Policy* (2000). The Housing Corporation established in 1964 was very different from the one proposed by Labour in the 1940s to actually build houses.

23. Cmnd 2838 (1965) p. 8. Bevan had of course opened the way for greater municipalization through the Housing Act of 1949, which empowered local government for the first time to provide accommodation for all members of the community, not just 'the working classes'. However, the example of Glasgow, as recorded in Section 4.4 above, suggests greater municipalization would have been disastrous.

24. Cmnd 3602 (1968).

25. One analyst in 1969 calculated that it would cost annually £600 million to construct 200,000 local authority houses, but only £230 million to improve 230,000 homes. See P. N. Balchin, *Housing Policy: an introduction* (1989) p. 75. This book provides the best brief introduction to rehabilitation.

26. The statistics in this paragraph are taken from Merrett, *State Housing in Britain*, p. 115 and Short, *Housing in Britain*, p. 59.

27. A. Gibb and D. Maclennan, 'Policy and process in Scottish housing', in R. Saville (ed.), *The Economic Development of Modern Scotland* (Edinburgh, 1985) p. 287. The

Labour government did flirt with a few radical alternatives and briefly revived council house building, but after the economic crisis of 1976 it reverted to more traditional policies, as demonstrated by the 1977 consultative document, *Housing Policy* (Cmnd 6851), which reaffirmed that owner-occupation was a 'basic and natural desire' (p. 50).

28. Nevertheless in 1967 the powerful television documentary on homelessness, *Cathy Come Home*, greatly boosted the support of the incipient housing pressure group, Shelter.

29. Ministry of Housing and Local Government, *Homes for Today and Tomorrow* (1961) para. 7. The later quotation is from para. 10.

30. D. Donnison and C. Ungerson, *Housing Policy* (1982) p. 187. The statistics are taken from A. H. Halsey (ed.), *British Social Trends since 1900* (1988) table 10.13 and Balchin, *Housing Policy*, p. 90. The proportion of households in England and Wales lacking a fixed bath and lavatory fell respectively between 1951 and 1971 from 37 per cent to 9 per cent and from 8 per cent to 4 per cent. Conditions had been particularly bad in Scotland where in 1951 63 per cent of dwellings had only three rooms (which included a kitchen) and 42 per cent had no fixed bath.

31. *One Nation* (1950) p. 26. A masterly analysis of high-rise building is provided by P. Dunleavy, *The Politics of Mass Housing in Britain, 1945–75* (Oxford, 1981), upon which this and the succeeding paragraph are based. Its conclusion is that there was a 'sacrifice of previously maintained design and amenity standards to the overriding imperatives of production' (p. 20).

32. Merrett, *State Housing in Britain*, p. 131. Half of all public dwellings constructed between 1962 and 1972 were flats, and at the peak in 1964 half of all flats were in blocks of 15 storeys or more (ibid., p. 128). Their deliberate destruction started, in Birkenhead, as early as 1979. See N. Timmins, *The Five Giants* (1995) p. 235.

33. Central government could also vary the cost of local government borrowing. Thus cheap loans were provided through the Public Works Loan Board until 1955, after which local authorities had to pay the full market rate. In 1967, however, the Labour government sought to combat inflation by agreeing to pay any interest over 4 per cent. This quickly quadrupled the cost of subsidizing a house. See Short, *Housing in Britain*, p. 57.

34. To encourage home ownership by non-tax-payers, who would not benefit from these concessions, the government introduced 'option mortgages' at especially low rates of interest. Local authorities or building societies, which administered the scheme, were reimbursed for any difference in the proceeds from these and ordinary mortgages which enjoyed tax relief. Until inflation brought most people above the tax thresholds, option mortgages accounted for about a fifth of all mortgages (ibid., p. 56). The figures in the following paragraph are taken from pp. 117–18.

35. In addition to these broad objectives, there was the narrower political objective of breaking up heavily subsidized council estates where tenants tended automatically – as well demonstrated in Glasgow – to vote Labour.

36. See M. Daunton, A *Property-Owning Democracy?* (1987) p. x. Policy was regressive because not only did subsidies go exclusively to those who could afford to buy their homes, but also the largest subsidies went to those who took out the highest mortgages and received relief from the highest tax rates.

37. TNA: PRO, T230/312, EC(S)(56)2, Economic Section discussion paper on rent control, 1956.

38. For an analysis of the Milner Holland Report (which found that only 1 per cent of

tenants were abused and, at most, only 5 per cent were 'completely dissatisfied' with their landlords) and the Rachman scandal, see K. G. Banting, *Poverty, Politics and Policy in Britain in the 1960s* (1979) pp. 14–65. Interesting new analysis is provided in J. Davis, 'Rents and race in 1960s London: new light on Rachmanism', *Twentieth Century British History*, 12 (2001) which argues *inter alia* that, because of the nature of house ownership, 'Rachmanism proper was . . . more likely to be black-on-white abuse than a white-on-black one' (p. 82).

39. The criterion for a 'fair rent' was 'the likely market rent assuming no scarcity' – a concept as impossible to measure as the price of land under the Land Commission in the 1940s.

40. Cmnd 2838 (1965) p. 15. The 1972 Act, it should be noted, broke new ground by introducing rent allowances for the poorest tenants in private rented accommodation – the first direct subsidy this sector of the housing market had received, see R. Lowe, 'Social policy', in S. Ball and A. Seldon (eds), *The Heath Government* (1996) pp. 207–10. Labour leaders' hypocrisy is exposed in Timmins, *The Five Giants*, p. 304. Crossman, for example, called the Act in private 'the most socialistic housing measure this century', but in public 'the most reactionary and socially divisive measure'.

41. For an account of popular resistance, see Merrett, *State Housing in Britain*, ch. 7. For the relative costs of rent and mortgages, see A. H. Halsey (ed.), *British Social Trends since 1900* (1988) table 10.33.

42. Quoted in J. Hills (ed.), *The State of Welfare* (Oxford, 1990) p. 137.

43. Enoch Powell, *The Welfare State* (1961) p. 13.

10 THE PERSONAL SOCIAL SERVICES

1. The ultimate objectives of the personal social services have been alternatively defined as social integration (for those who would otherwise be marginalized) and social control. The latter includes the protection of society from the respective danger, embarrassment and distress which might arise, for instance, from juvenile delinquency, the behaviour of the mentally ill or from the knowledge that elderly people were living in squalor. See M. Evandrou et al., 'The personal social services', in J. Hills (ed.), *The State of Welfare* (Oxford, 1990) p. 209.

2. Cmnd 3703. The term 'personal social services' was coined for this committee.

3. Lord Beveridge, *Voluntary Action: a report on methods of social advance* (1948). For a critique, see K. and J. Williams, *A Beveridge Reader* (1989).

4. Battles were also fought with professionals in other services and especially the NHS. Within hospitals, almoners (renamed 'medical social workers' in 1963) long resisted the attempt to transform them into medical auxiliaries helping doctors, among other things, to process more patients by finding alternative sources of care in the community. They preferred the far more challenging role of identifying possible social causes of illness, such as anxiety or family breakdown. Accordingly in 1973 they left the NHS to join the local authority social service departments. GPs unwisely ignored the Seebohm Committee and thus lost the chance to become 'senior social workers' promoting community medicine (see Section 7.3).

5. See E. Younghusband, *Social Work in Britain, 1950–1975*, vol. 1 (1978) p. 39. For the parsimonious and punitive attitudes of the Scots, before their outburst of radical-

ism in the 1960s, see J. Murphy, *British Social Services: the Scottish dimension* (Edinburgh, 1992) p. 5.

6. Quoted in B. Rodgers and J. Dixon, *Portrait of Social Work* (Oxford, 1960) p. 163. The book provides the best survey of social work practice in the 1950s.

7. The best, and extremely influential, account of the remaining Poor Law 'warehouses' is P. Townsend, *The Last Refuge* (1965).

8. The initial objective was that of the 1930 Poor Law Act; the latter was articulated by the report of the Curtis Care of Children Committee (Cmd 6922) and confirmed by the 1948 Act. This Act was also progressive in that it projected a large number of women for the first time into senior positions within local government.

9. J. Parker, *Local Health and Welfare Services* (1965) p. 108. The Act introduced charges, and thus means tests, for services in order to distinguish them from 'free' but stigmatizing Poor Law services.

10. Younghusband, *Social Work in Britain*, vol. 1, p. 35. The Younghusband working party on social workers in local authority health and welfare services lasted from 1955 to 1959.

11. See Murphy, *British Social Services*, chs 7–8. The 1968 Act was more radical than its 1970 counterpart in England because it imposed on local government the 'duty to promote social welfare' and placed the probation service within the social work departments.

12. Cmnd 3703, para. 1.

13. Ibid., para. 32. The Home Office did successfully use its experience to prevent any discussion of the division of administrative responsibility in Whitehall and the inclusion of the probation service within the social services department. It also excluded from the Committee's membership leading academics, field-workers and consumers of the service.

14. The successive quotations are from ibid., paras 111, 478, 516 and 473. A recommendation which split the Committee was that the Secretary of State should personally sanction the appointment of all directors of social services to head the 'unified' departments. Its purpose was essentially to ensure that successful candidates would have social work qualifications and were not, as had happened in certain combined health and welfare committees in London, medical officers of health. In the event, of the 174 appointees in 1971 only five had medical qualifications, whereas 58 were former children's officers and 79 former welfare officers. In a predominantly female profession, only 21 were women. See Younghusband, *Social Work in Britain*, vol. 1 (1978) p. 240. Of the initial 52 chief officers in Scotland, under half had social work qualifications and only four were women. See Murphy, *British Social Services*, p. 173.

15. Cmnd 3703, para. 454. The Report was equally vague about the content and nature of professional training. Crossman, as the responsible minister, dismissed the report as 'boring and unconvincing' and its adoption was only assured once Baroness Serota had become one of his junior ministers. Characteristically Crossman claimed he was unaware she was a member of the Committee whose report he wished to jettison. See P. Hall, *Reforming the Welfare* (1976) p. 92.

16. R. Pinker, 'Social work and social policy in the twentieth century', in M. Bulmer, J. Lewis and D. Piachaud (eds), *The Goals of Social Policy* (1989) p. 98.

17. Cmnd 3703, paras 477–81.

18. Hall notes that specialization was a major subject of disagreement within the Committee, as was the balance between central and local government, and the

relationship with the Ministry of Education over pre-school education: *Reforming the Welfare*, ch. 4. A vigorous debate soon divided departments over whether clients' needs were best served by an all-purpose social worker or all-purpose teams of specialist social workers.

19. See Younghusband, *Social Work in Britain*, vol. 1, p. 30; and Murphy, *British Social Services*, pp. 177–180.

20. Younghusband, *Social Work in Britain*, vol. 1, p. 45. This figure was equivalent to 7.2 per 1000 children under the age of 18; 29,400 were in foster care, 15,600 remained at home and the others were in residential care.

21. Ibid., p. 51. For details of the tragedies, see J. Packman, *The Child's Generation* (1975), esp. pp. 168–76.

22. Hills (ed.), *The State of Welfare*, p. 232.

23. Age Concern, *The Attitudes of the Retired and Elderly* (Mitcham, 1974). In the 1940s local authorities could only provide home helps (a service originally designed for young mothers). It was made mandatory in 1968. Other services were made permissive – such as chiropody in 1959 and meals-on-wheels in 1962 – and became mandatory in 1971 together with additional concessions such as the provision of telephones.

24. For a full analysis of this issue, see P. Bridgen and J. Lewis, *Elderly People and the Boundary between Health and Social Care* (1999). For a survey of the problems facing geriatric medicine, albeit less acutely in Scotland, see P. Thane, *Old Age in English History* (Oxford, 2000) ch. 22.

25. Cmnd 3703, para. 319. In 1944 a much-vaunted Disabled Persons (Employment) Act had been passed which was designed to reserve jobs for the physically disabled. In time it came largely to be ignored. See especially H. Bolderson, 'The origins of the disabled persons employment quota', *Journal of Social Policy*, 9 (1980) 169–86.

26. Both documents were published by the DHSS, not as command papers. The quotation is from p. 14 of the second report.

27. Voluntary provision existed in all the main welfare services (for example, parents' fund-raising for schools and the 'friends' of hospitals), but was particularly prevalent in areas covered by the personal social services, owing to their nature and underdevelopment.

28. See Section 7.1 and Chapter 6, note 9, above. By 1947 it was estimated that 72 per cent and 41 per cent of households respectively subscribed to industrial assurance and private healthcare (PRO, RG23/138).

29. PEP, *Family Needs and the Social Services* (1961) p. 130.

30. The best, if somewhat over-romanticized, accounts of working-class self-sufficiency, forged in poverty and based on a 'reciprocal flow of services' between mothers and daughters, are two books by M. Young and P. Wilmott: *Family and Kinship in East London* (1957) and *Family and Class in a London Suburb* (1960). Redevelopment did not reduce but changed the nature of informal care, to the disadvantage of the elderly. On the continuity and reality of informal care for the elderly, see Thane, *Old Age in English History*, ch. 21.

31. See Section 2.1 above. Esping-Andersen's typologies, it has been argued, overlook gender issues and voluntary provision and therefore need major revision. See A. Orloff, 'Gender and the social rights of citizenship', *American Sociological Review*, 58 (1993) 303–28.

32. Ibid., p. 130; Evandrou et al., 'The personal social services', in Hills (ed.), *The State of Welfare*, pp. 215, 269. For the difficulties in measuring the value of informal

care, see Section 3.2.2. The most thorough review of informal care is G. Parker, 'Who cares? A review of empirical evidence from Britain', in R. E. Pahl (ed.), *On Work* (Oxford, 1988) pp. 496–511.

33. Quoted in B. Watkin, *The National Health Service* (1978) p. 18. For a definition of the political and functional roles of the welfare state, see Sections 2.1 and 3.2.1 above.

34. Quoted in M. Brasnett, *Voluntary Social Action* (1969) p. 170. For an analysis of concepts of 'active citizenship', see G. Finlayson, *Citizen, State and Social Welfare in Britain, 1830–1990* (Oxford, 1994) introduction, and J. Lewis, *The Voluntary Sector, the State and Social Work in Britain* (Cheltenham, 1995) pp. 5–12. The growing consensus is illustrated by the active participation of two leading Conservatives, Keith Joseph and Iain Macleod, in the early development of the CPAG and Crisis at Christmas.

35. The key issue was power, as was demonstrated by radical changes to the concept of 'community action' between the 1930s and the 1960s. In the 1930s middle-class philanthropy had largely sought to re-create a sense of community based on middle-class values. In the 1960s, as the Seebohm Committee explicitly admitted, the object was again 'social control' (Cmnd 3703, para. 477). Control was to be achieved by peer pressure from within a community, however, rather than imposed from outside by another class – although, of course, the role of the social worker, as a professional worker ultimately responsible to government, was highly ambivalent.

36. *The Future of Voluntary Organisations* (1978) p. 26. The terms of reference for the Wolfenden Committee were to examine 'the role and function of voluntary organisations'. It was financed by the Rowntree Memorial and the Carnegie Trusts.

37. *The Future of Voluntary Organisations*, p. 27. The succeeding quotation is from Cmnd 3703, para. 496.

38. G. Finlayson, *Citizen, State and Social Welfare* (Oxford, 1994) p. 292. The Citizens' Advice Bureaux and the Samaritans, which could respectively call on 7000 and 14,600 volunteers in 1971, represented the two extremes of the spectrum. The former were almost wholly financed by government, the latter hardly at all.

39. Cmnd 3703, para. 498. The Aves Report was published under the title *The Voluntary Worker in the Social Services*.

40. Younghusband, *Social Work in Britain*, vol. 1, p. 264. An indication of the extent of local initiatives in the 1970s is provided by J. Hatch, *Outside the State: Voluntary Organisations in three English towns* (1980).

41. See J. Hinton, 'Voluntarism and the welfare/warfare state: the Women's Voluntary Service in the 1940s', *Twentieth Century British History*, 9 (1998) 274–305 and *Women, Social Leadership and the Second World War: continuities of class* (Oxford, 2002). Hinton argues that, although many working-class women joined the WVS, its clear mission in the 1940s at least was to sustain 'traditional social leadership' in the face of increasing egalitarianism.

42. Quoted in Finlayson, *Citizen, State and Social Welfare*, p. 278; J. Lewis, *The Voluntary Sector, the State and Social Work in Britain* (Cheltenham, 1995) ch. 3. Another pioneer of intensive casework was the Family Service Units, which grew out of the concern of a group of conscientious objectors for those left behind in wartime rest centres following bombing raids. For the history of this pioneering charitable organization, see P. Starkey, *Families and Social Workers* (Liverpool, 2000).

43. For a good survey, see R. Means and R. Smith, *The Development of Welfare Services for Elderly People* (1985) ch. 6.
44. *The Future of Voluntary Organisations* (1978) p. 20; M. Brenton, *The Voluntary Sector in British Social Services* (1985) p. 37.
45. This paragraph is based largely on Younghusband, *Social Work in Britain*, vol. 1, ch. 18. NACRO is described as the 'outstanding example of the new voluntary organisations started in the 1960s which could look questioningly at the present and future, unfettered by past assumptions' (p. 263). Much of the most innovative research was also financed by such philanthropic trusts as the Gulbenkian, Leverhulme, Nuffield and Joseph Rowntree Foundations. For the CPAG, see R. Lowe, 'The rediscovery of poverty and the creation of CPAG, 1962–8', *Contemporary Record*, 9 (1995) 602–37 and M. Meyer-Kelly, *The Poor Got Poorer under Labour: the validity and effect of the CPAG's 1970 campaign* (www.icbh.ac.uk./icbh/witness/html.view).
46. For the full statistical details, see A. Webb et al., *Voluntary Social Services: manpower resources* (1976) and J. Unell, *Voluntary Social Services: financial resources* (1979).
47. Younghusband, *Social Work in Britain*, vol. 1, p. 35
48. The description of the DHSS document, *Priorities for Health and Personal Social Services in England*, is in Hills (ed.), *The State of Welfare*, p. 234.

11   THE ACHIEVEMENT

1. V. George and P. Wilding, *Ideology and Social Welfare* (1985) p. 62.
2. P. M. Williams (ed.), *The Diary of Hugh Gaitskell* (1983) p. 542; *One Nation* (1950) p. 75. See also Sections 2.2.1–2.2.3 and 8.2 above.
3. This criterion was supported by the 1951–5 Royal Commission on the Taxation of Profits and Income which observed that 'not merely progressive taxation, but a steep gradient of taxation, is needed in order to conform with the notions of equitable distribution that are widely, almost universally accepted'. See Cmd 9105 (1954) para. 108. The government's chief economic adviser in 1957 also defined 'the foundations of the Welfare State' as 'the provision of social services and . . . progressive direct taxation' (R. Hall in TNA: PRO, T171/478, memo 25).
4. H. Phelps Brown, *Egalitarianism and the Generation of Inequality* (Oxford, 1988) p. 350. Nevertheless the recorded income and wealth of the very rich did decline and, although the benefits accrued largely to those who were already well off, the net results in international terms were progressive. See R. Middleton, *Government versus the Market* (Cheltenham, 1996) p. 599.
5. TNA: PRO, T171/427. Memorandum by A. Cockfield, 4 February 1950, para. 9. In 1942 Keynes had planned a 'social policy budget' designed to redistribute income as well as raise taxation (T171/360) but in 1975 the Central Policy Review Staff was still calling, in *A Joint Framework for Social Policies*, for regular calculations to be made.
6. F. Field, M. Meacher and C. Pond, *To Him Who Hath* (Harmondsworth, 1977) p. 20. Admittedly a corporation and capital gains tax were introduced in 1965 and 1969 but, unlike most Western countries, Britain has never had an annual wealth tax. For developments in the 1960s in particular, see R. Whiting, *The Labour Party and Taxation* (Cambridge, 2000); and H. Pemberton, 'A taxing task: combating

Britain's relative decline in the 1960s', *Twentieth Century British History*, 12 (2001) 354–75. The broader issue of how the British tax system was transformed from a 'source of national pride and social stability' before 1939 into one perceived to cause political unrest and economic decline in the 1960s is the subject of M. Daunton, *Just Taxes* (Cambridge, 2002). The prewar system, which had permitted a highly redistributive form of direct tax in the 1930s, lost its aura of balance and fairness. This was because, *inter alia*, of the postwar need to increase taxation (to fund increased public expenditure); to use it to manage the economy (to ensure full employment); and to accommodate electoral interests which no longer accepted former definitions of equity. 'Pragmatic equality' was substituted for 'principled equality'. This represented another example of political and administrative failure: 'the machinery of government failed to produce coherence and coordination which was crucially important in the case of taxation where technical expertise and consistency over time are crucial' (p. 367).

7. To avoid too great a surge in taxation, 55 per cent of goods had initially to be zero-rated for VAT, a percentage which has steadily shrunk.

8. In 1952, for example, the first £100 of taxable income was taxed at 12 per cent, the next £150 at 22 per cent and a further £150 at 28 per cent. Only when taxable income reached £400 was it taxed at the 'standard' 47.5 per cent. See Field et al., *To Him Who Hath* pp. 38–42.

9. Ibid., pp. 32, 41 and 53. The tax threshold (or, in other words, the personal tax allowance) should in theory have equated to the poverty line because, since Adam Smith's day, government had accepted that the minimum income required to purchase 'necessities' should be free from tax. In practice there was no such collaboration between the tax and benefit systems. See J. Veit-Wilson, 'The tax threshold: policy, principles and poverty', *Twentieth Century British History*, 10 (1999) 218–34.

10. Reprinted in R. M. Titmuss, *Essays on 'The Welfare State'* (1958) ch. 2.

11. A Sinfield, 'Poverty, privilege and welfare', in P. Bean and D. Whynes (eds), *Barbara Wootton* (1966) p. 112.

12. The share of the total tax paid by the top 10 per cent of tax-payers fell between 1959 and 1976–7 from 65 per cent to 40 per cent. See Cmnd 7595, the Royal Commission on the Distribution of Income and Wealth, *Report* no. 7 (1979) para. 7.2.

13. TNA: PRO, CAB 128/29, CM (55) 45, para. 6(2), Cabinet meeting of 6 December 1955. The following quotations are from Phelps Brown, *Egalitarianism and the Generation of Inequality*, pp. 331–2.

14. B. Abel-Smith, 'Whose welfare state?', in N. MacKenzie (ed.), *Conviction* (1958) p. 57. The same charge might be made of any welfare state including Sweden, see G. Esping-Andersen, *The Three Worlds of Welfare Capitalism* (Oxford, 1990) p. 31.

15. J. Le Grand, *The Strategy of Equality* (1982) p. 3.

16. The first analyses were published in *Economic Trends*, vols 109 (1962) and 124 (1964). For later analysis see P. Johnson, 'The welfare state', in R. Floud and D. McCloskey (eds), *The Economic History of Britain since 1700*, vol. 3 (Cambridge, 1994) pp. 302–5.

17. For a full discussion of the problems in calculating and presenting statistics relating to income, see respectively N. Barr, *The Economics of the Welfare State* (Oxford, 1993) ch. 6 and Phelps Brown, *Egalitarianism and the Generation of Inequality*, ch. 9.

18. For a summary of the inadequacy of statistics relating to wealth, see Cmnd 6171, the Royal Commission on the Distribution of Income and Wealth, *Report* no. 1 (1975) paras 324–35.

19. Phelps Brown, *Egalitarianism and the Generation of Inequality*, p. 350.
20. C. A. R. Crosland, *The Future of Socialism* (1956) p. 347. This book provides the most powerful contemporary perspective of the equalization of economic and political power in postwar Britain (part 1) as well as an agenda for further change (part 4).
21. See Section 2.2.2 above. Marshall had of course argued that universal welfare policy was the means by which the capitalist need for incentive (and hence unequal money incomes) could be reconciled with the democratic need for equality.
22. K. and J. Williams, *A Beveridge Reader* (1987) p. 155.
23. W. D. Rubinstein, *Wealth and Inequality in Britain* (1986) p. 54.
24. P. M. Williams (ed.), *The Diary of Hugh Gaitskell* (1983) p. 542. The succeeding quotation is from T. Utley, *Not Guilty* (1957) p. 87.
25. R. H. S. Crossman, *Socialism and Planning* (1967) p. 80.
26. R. Parry, 'UK', in P. Flora (ed.), *Growth to Limits* (Berlin, 1986) p. 204. This article is a leading example of the use of the framework to examine the efficiency of welfare policy after 1945, whilst some of the conceptual issues it raises are discussed in J. Hills (ed.), *The State of Welfare* (Oxford, 1990) ch. 1.
27. P. Johnson, 'The welfare state', in R. Floud and D. McCloskey (eds), *The Economic History of Britain*, vol. 3 (Cambridge, 1994) p. 305. See also J. Harris's riposte to the polemic of Correlli Barnett in 'Enterprise and welfare states', *Transactions of the Royal Historical Society*, 40 (1990) 175–95.
28. Middleton, *Government versus the Market*, pp. 574, 610.
29. Ibid., p. 606. The author's conclusion is that 'the case for a generalised non-market failure before 1979 has no empirical basis' (p. 608).
30. Parry, 'UK', p. 209. The relative cost of the NHS is summarized in R. M. Page, 'Social welfare since the war', in N. F. R. Crafts and N. Woodward (eds), *The British Economy since 1945* (Oxford, 1991) p. 472.
31. N. Barr, *The Economics of the Welfare State* (Oxford, 1993) p. 333.
32. See R. M. Page, 'Social welfare since the war', pp. 446–7 and R. Lowe, *Adjusting to Democracy* (Oxford, 1986) pp. 217–18.
33. E. Powell, *Medicine and Politics* (1966) p. 16.

12 THE RISE OF 'THATCHERISM', 1976–1997

1. See C. Thain and M. Wright, *The Treasury and Whitehall* (Oxford, 1995) for the introduction of cash limits (pp. 47–9) and a full analysis of the planning and control of public expenditure between 1976 and 1993.
2. Crosland was, symbolically, the Labour minister most closely identified with the belief that government should use the increased wealth generated by economic growth to create painlessly a more just and efficient society (see Section 2.2.2 above). His audience was important, since local government was still responsible for one-third of public expenditure.
3. David Owen, quoted in H. Young, *One of Us* (1989) p. 294. See also Section 8.2 above.
4. R. Parry, 'UK', in P. Flora (ed.), *Growth to Limits*, vol. 2 (Berlin, 1986) p. 169. The popular attack against the civil service was spearheaded in two books with self-explanatory titles: R. Bacon and W. Eltis, *Britain's Economic Problem: too few producers* (1976) and R. Chapman, *Your Disobedient Servant* (1978).

5. Quoted in T. Raison, *Tories and the Welfare State* (1990) p. 91.
6. H. Glennerster, *British Social Policy since 1945* (Oxford, 2000) p.191. On the broad moral issue with which this box is concerned, and for an illuminating analysis of the impact of American thought on British policy, see A. Deacon, *Perspectives on Welfare* (Buckingham, 2002). On its impact on Mrs Thatcher, see her conviction in *The Downing Street Years* (1993) p. 8: 'welfare benefits, distributed with little or no consideration of their effects on behaviour, encouraged illegitimacy, facilitated the breakdown of families, and replaced incentives favouring work and self-reliance with perverse encouragement of idleness and cheating'.
7. Neo-Marxists have described the purpose of the 'authoritarian populism' of Thatcherism as being 'to force-march . . . society, vigorously, into the past'. See S. Hall and M. Jacques (eds), *The Politics of Thatcherism* (1983) pp. 10–11.
8. J. Le Grand in J. Hills (ed.), *The State of Welfare* (Oxford, 1990) p. 350.
9. J. Barnett, *Inside the Treasury* (1982) p. 23.
10. The defection of the former Cabinet minister, Reg Prentice, to the Conservatives in October 1977 was symbolic of the attraction Mrs Thatcher's blend of strong leadership and traditional values held for many social democratic academics and politicians with strong local interests.
11. Young, *One of Us*, p. 298. In 1981 Gallup recorded support for Margaret Thatcher amongst only 25 per cent of those polled. Her average rating of 39 per cent between 1979 and 1987 was lower than that for any other prime minister. See D. Kavanagh, *Thatcherism and British Politics* (Oxford, 1990) p. 269.
12. As she confided to a journalist: 'I am in politics because of the conflict between good and evil, and I believe in the end good will triumph' (*Daily Telegraph*, 18 September 1984).
13. *Government Expenditure, 1980–1981* (Cmnd 7746, 1979). For the practical limitations of MTFS, see N. Lawson, *The View from No 11* (1992) ch. 36 which is significantly entitled 'The myth of a monetarist golden age'.
14. See Lawson, *The View from No 11*, pp. 303–4. *The Economist* duly described the report as 'dismantling huge chunks of the welfare state' and the Labour Party used it (incorrectly) as proof that the Conservatives had 'a secret manifesto' to achieve just that.
15. Young, *One of Us*, p. 498. The temporary support for the Social Democratic Party, which polls regularly recorded at over 30 per cent of the electorate, was a major political constraint on radical action.
16. By 1990 the number of private shareholders had risen from 3 to 9 million. There were over one million new home-owners.
17. The official basis for the calculation of unemployment was constantly tightened with, for example, its restriction to those claiming unemployment benefit; stricter qualification rules for benefit; and the creation of various temporary employment and training programmes. By the traditional definition, the figure for 1986 would have been nearer 3.8 million than 3.1 million. See G. D. N. Worswick, *Unemployment* (Cambridge, 1991).
18. Young, *One of Us*, p. 504.
19. The full extent of policy failure is forensically exposed in D. Butler, A. Adonis and T. Travers, *Failure in British Government: the politics of the poll tax* (Oxford, 1994). Mrs Thatcher's retrospective view of the riot illustrated her empathy with conservative American commentators such as Murray: 'a whole class of people – an "underclass" if you will – had been dragged back into the ranks of the responsible

society and asked to become not just dependants but citizens: their reponse was to riot'. See *The Downing Street Years* (1993) p. 661.

20. Thatcher, *The Downing Street Years*, p. 572. Enthoven's 1985 book had the catchy title *Reflections on the Management of the National Health Service*.

21. For this and the previous quote, see N. Timmins, *The Five Giants* (2001) pp. 477, 480.

22. See Figure 15.1 and P. Johnson, 'The assessment: inequality', *Oxford Review of Economic Policy*, 12 (1996) 13.

23. Conservative Party, *You can only be Sure with the Conservatives* (1997) pp. 1–3, 7.

24. Huge salary increases to company executives, especially in recently privatized utilities, led to a public outcry against fat cats (and demonstrated, contrary to New Right assumptions, the earlier restraint of public servants). The cost of resolving the crisis over cattle with BSE was over £3.5 billion.

25. Margaret Thatcher unilaterally vetoed a compromise at GCHQ based on a 'no-strike' agreement. The unions had admittedly provoked such intransigence by selecting this key security installation for strategic strikes, which had resulted in the loss of 10,000 working days between 1979 and 1981. The industrialists' attack was launched, somewhat symbolically, in the House of Lords Select Committee Report on Overseas Trade of October 1985.

26. Young, *One of Us*, p. 231. For a succinct summary of administrative developments, see K. Theakston, *The Civil Service since 1945* (Oxford, 1995) ch. 5.

27. P. Wilding, 'The welfare state and the Conservatives', *Political Studies*, 45 (1997) 718.

28. This box is based on Timmins, *The Five Giants*, pp. 438, 483, 517 and 520–1 (for education) and pp. 464–9 (for the NHS). Interesting light is cast on the changing power balance between the consumers and producers of welfare by a remark of Woodhead's deputy: 'I don't give a monkey's toss for the teachers. It's the children I care about.'

29. See Chapter 1 above. The conclusion of his principal policy adviser was that Callaghan was not 'a doctrinal monetarist, but he was instinctively conservative . . . his basic position being that monetary laxity was nearly always wrong'. The IMF agreement 'formally entrenched monetarism in Labour's economic policy-making although it really only made public what was already happening in Whitehall' (see B. Donoughue, *Prime Minister* (1987) pp. 82, 100).

30. John Major did remark that 'every prime minister wishes to achieve full employment' (*Independent*, 10 March 1993); and the economic recovery after 1994 did reduce unemployment to under 5 per cent, Keynes' definition of 'full' employment. This encouraged New Labour in its 1997 manifesto to reintroduce a commitment to maintain – in the deliberate evasive phrase of 1944 – 'a high and stable level of employment'. However the means, as will be seen, were on the supply not the demand side.

31. See A. Cairncross, *The British Economy since 1945* (Oxford, 1992) p. 276 and OECD, *Revenue Statistics* (Paris, 1994) chart 1.

32. Young, *One of Us*, p. 367.

33. Ibid., p. 521 and Timmins, *The Five Giants*, p. 465.

34. Quoted in ibid., p. 460.

35. Lawson, *The View from No. 11*, ch. 49.

36. D. Willetts, *Modern Conservatism* (1992) pp. 139–42.

37. For a summary of the polls, see D. Kavanagh, *Thatcherism and British Politics* (Oxford, 1990) pp. 244–306; and the annual reports since 1983 in Social and Community Planning Research, *British Social Attitudes* (Aldershot).

38. P. Taylor-Gooby, 'Comfortable, marginal and excluded', in *British Social Attitudes* (1995) p. 17; and L. Brook et al., 'Public spending and taxation', in *British Social Attitudes* (1996) pp. 189–200.
39. Labour Party, *Because Britain Deserves Better* (1997) pp. 11–13.
40. Le Grand in Hills (ed.), *The State of Welfare*, p. 351.

13 THE IMPACT OF 'THATCHERISM', 1976–1997

1. John Moore was the symbolic victim of, and explanation for, the failure to procede beyond managerial reform under Mrs Thatcher. Touted as her successor, he was broken by the post. Quickly becoming a figure of ridicule, he saw his responsibilities halved (to social security) in 1988 and was dismissed in 1989, never to regain office. As a colleague, quoted in N. Timmins, *The Five Giants* (2001) p 444, remarked: 'John Moore went out there to demonstrate what a real man could do if he had right-wing credentials. He was carried off in the wide blue yonder.'
2. HM Treasury, Public Expenditure (Cm 3601, 1997) table 3.3.
3. The earnings-related pension was indexed against price rises, the flat-rate pension against increases in prices or earnings (whichever were the higher).
4. H. Land, 'The child benefit fiasco', in *The Yearbook of Social Policy in Britain* (1979) and F. Field, *Poverty and Politics* (1982), pp 43–50, 108–13.
5. See M. Hill, *Social Security in Britain* (Aldershot, 1990) p. 52.
6. N. Barr and F. Coulter, 'Social security', in J. Hills (ed.), *The State of Welfare* (Oxford, 1990) p. 284.
7. For the relevant figures, see H. Glennerster, *British Social Policy since 1945* (Oxford, 1995) p. 182; and Timmins, *The Five Giants*, pp. 374, 400. Redistribution was particularly decreased by the abolition in 1988 of the Treasury subsidy to the national insurance scheme, which had been equivalent to 18 per cent of total contributions in 1980.
8. Ibid., p. 402.
9. D. Price, *Office of Hope* (2000), pp. 256, 299.
10. Timmins, *The Five Giants*, p. 399.
11. *The Times*, 20 January 1984.
12. Price, *Office of Hope*, p. 306; Glennerster, *British Social Policy since 1945*, p. 199.
13. For a full examination of all the relevant issues, see K. Kiernan, H. Land and J. Lewis, *Lone Motherhood in Twentieth-century Britain* (Oxford, 1998).
14. N. Barr and F. Coulter, 'Social security', in Hills (ed.), *The State of Welfare*, 1990) pp. 288–91. The real value of benefit was calculated in terms of the retail price index, but there is evidence that the price of goods typically bought by the poor rose faster. This would mean their absolute living standards rose more slowly or even fell during the 1980s. Consistent with the policy to encourage the work ethic, the difference between the benefit and former earnings of the average unemployed worker ('the replacement rate') increased at this time. Ibid., pp. 316–17.
15. In 1988, only one person could take out a mortgage on a given house, and in 1993 the allowance could only be set against the lowest rate of tax. The inflation of house prices did erode the real value of the benefit and, in direct contrast to other benefits, Mrs Thatcher sought to index it by raising the ceiling on the amount that could be claimed. She was only successful once, in 1983. After her departure from

office in 1990, the cost of the allowance fell from its peak of £9.2 billion (at 1995–6 prices) to £2.6 billion in 1996–7. This was its lowest since the 1960s. See H. Glennerster and J. Hills (eds), *The State of Welfare* (Oxford, 1988) p. 134.

16. A. Deacon, 'Spending more to achieve less?', in D. Gladstone (ed.), *British Welfare Policy* (1995) p. 91.

17. J. Hills, *The Future of Welfare* (York, 1993) p. 39.

18. Ibid., p. 27; Timmins, *The Five Giants*, p. 399; Barr and Coulter, 'Social security', in Hills (ed.), *The State of Welfare*, p. 329.

19. Some even claimed that, at the cost of £7 billion, one in five claims were frudulent. See Timmins, *The Five Grants*, p. 527. Lilley's broad vision was expressed personally in his 1993 Mais lecture and officially in Department of Social Security, *The Growth of Social Security* (1993).

20. Hills, *The future of Welfare*, p. 37.

21. See Sections 10.1, 10.3 above.

22. Mount was the author of *The Subversive Family* (1983), which argued that the family would function best if not subjected to unwarranted interference from social workers, health visitors and other meddlers drawing salaries from the taxpayer.

23. R. A. Parker, 'Childcare and the personal social services', in D. Gladstone (ed.), *British Social Welfare* (1995) p. 181.

24. H. Hendrick, *Child Welfare: England 1872–1989* (1994) p. 275.

25. Timmins, *The Five Giants*, pp. 414–15.

26. This change in definition was made explicit in *Growing Older*, Cmnd 8173 (1981) para. 1.9. Care *in* the community also meant in practice care by women who were accordingly obliged, in Hilary Land's classic phrase, to practice 'compulsory altruism'. This was despite the fact that they were as likely to be in waged work as their partners – if, of course, with the breakdown of traditional family structure their partners had not left them.

27. Timmins, *The Five Giants*, p. 475. For further details of the 1980s anomalies and the 1990 legislation, see M. Evandrou et al., 'The personal social services', in Hills (ed.), *The State of Welfare*, pp. 206–73.

28. Hills, *The Future of Welfare*, pp. 74–5. See J. Lewis and H. Glennerster, *Implementing the New Community Care* (Milton Keynes, 1996); J. Lewis, 'Developing the mixed economy of care', *Journal of Social Policy*, 22 (1993) 173–92, and 'Voluntary organizations in "new partnerships" with local authorities', *Social Policy and Administration*, 28 (1994) 206–20.

29. Department of Health, *People like Us* (the Utting Report, 1997). See also M. Jones and R. Lowe, *From Beveridge to Blair* (Manchester, 2002) pp 221–3.

30. HM Treasury, *Public Expenditure* (Cm 3601, 1997) tables 3.2 and 3.3; Timmins, *The Five Giaants*, p. 552. The white paper was published by the Department of Health in 1996.

31. Cmnd 7615.

32. DHSS, *Report of the NHS Management Inquiry* (1983) p. 22.

33. Social Services Committee, *First Report* (HC 209, 1984) p. 4. The succeeding account draws heavily on Timmins, *The Five Giants*, pp. 403–15, 451–70.

34. *Independent*, 7 December 1987.

35. Timmins, *The Five Giants*, p. 470.

36. H. Glennerster, *Paying for Welfare* (Hemel Hempstead, 1997) p. 42. Chapter 3 of this book is a succinct analysis of internal markets.

37. William Weldegrave quoted in Timmins, *The Five Giants*, p. 480.

38. Timmins, *The Five Giants*, p. 480.
39. See Hills (ed.), *The State of Welfare*, pp. 103–4.
40. Hills, *The Future of Welfare*, p. 60. The best comparative work on the problems facing all healthcare systems in the late 1980s is C. Ham, R. Robertson and M. Benzeval, *Health Check* (1990).
41. Timmins, *The Five Giants*, p. 503.
42. King Fund Institute, *Health Finance* (1988).
43. Timmins, *The Five Giants*, p. 510.
44. *Working for Patients* (Cm 555).
45. HM Treasury, *Public Expenditure* (Cm 3601, 1997) tables 3.2 and 3.3.
46. Hills, *The Future of Welfare*. See also H. Glennerster and W. Low, 'Education and the welfare state', in Hills (ed.), *The State of Welfare*, pp. 55–75 and Timmins, *The Five Giants*, p. 481.
47. See Sections 8.2 and 8.4 above.
48. An excellent summary is provided by D. King, *Actively Seeking Work?* (Chicago, 1995) ch. 5.
49. A. Green and H. Steedman, *Education Provision, Education Attainment and the Needs of Industry* (1993). See also M. Sanderson, *Education and Economic Decline in Britain, 1870 to the 1990s* (Cambridge, 1999) for a brief summary and full bibliography.
50. The tests revealed as late as 1997 that only half of 11-year-olds attained the expected standard in English and mathematics. This is why the Labour Party in its manifesto branded education the Conservatives' 'biggest failure'. See *Because Britain Deserves Better* (1997) p. 7.
51. D. King and V. Nash, 'Continuity of ideas and the politics of higher education in Britain from Robbins to Dearing', *Twentieth Century British History*, 12 (2001) 201. This article argues that the expansion of universities after 1963 was consistently driven by the belief that it would enhance economic performance. Both the content and balance of degrees was changed to reflect this imperative. Ironically, in a typical confusion of policy aims, it was an imperative that had to be down-played in 1988. In order to cut expenditure, maintenance fees were to be frozen and replaced by loans. Why should students have to start underwriting the cost of something that was beneficial not just to them but to the country as a whole?
52. *Sunday Times*, 12 July 1990; J. Campbell, *Margaret Thatcher* (vol. 2, 2003) pp. 542–3; John Major, *The Autobiography* (1999) p. 394.
53. Conservative Party, *You can only be Sure with the Conservatives* (1997) p. 21.
54. Hills, *The Future of Welfare*, p. 66. Limitations of payments to children attending state schools avoided the problem, as with nursery vouchers in 1995, that they would be used to subsidize private eduaction. For selected pupils, however, the government did buy private education through the 'assisted places scheme'. Their numbers increased from 5300 in 1980 to 34,000 by 1994.
55. Pay was another policy area in which power was centralized after the abolition in 1986 of the semi-autonomous Burnham Committee. It had been one of the welcome innovations of the 1944 Butler Act.
56. Glennerster, *British Social Policy since 1945*, p.181.
57. Glennerster and Hills (eds), *The State of Welfare*, p. 134. The percentage includes the cost of the tax allowance on mortgage interest repayments. John Hills chapter in this book is the source of most of the statistics in this section, including the box.
58. J. Hills, 'Housing', in Hills (ed.), *The State of Welfare*, p. 154.
59. Campbell, *Margaret Thatcher* (vol. 2) p. 234. This paragraph is largely based on Campbell's excellent account.

60. Quoted in Timmins, *The Five Giants*, p. 378.
61. Glennerster, *British Social Policy since 1945*, p. 179.
62. *The Times*, 21 April 1999, the Rab Butler memorial lecture.
63. Glennerster, *British Social Policy since 1945*, p. 227.
64. D. Donnison, *The Politics of Poverty* (Oxford, 1982) p. 132.
65. Quoted in Timmins, *The Five Giants*, p. 510.
66. Hills, *The Future of Welfare*, pp. 38 and 79.
67. *The Week*, 22 June 2002.

14 NEW LABOUR AND WELFARE SINCE 1997

1. The 'exquisite' timing of the 1981 letter, signed by five former chief economic advisers to government, provided Nigel Lawson with a permanent source of amusement, see N. Lawson, *The View from No 11* (1992) p. 98. The second letter was published in the *Financial Times* on 1 October 1997. Its political purpose was made explicit by its timing: the eve of the annual Labour Party conference.
2. The *Independent*, 19 September 2002, speech at Hackney.
3. P. Toynbee and D. Walker, *Did Things Get Better?* (2001) p. 230. Thus reliable evidence is scarce because of the abundance, not absence, of targeted objectives (such as public service agreements between the Treasury and spending departments) and bodies responsible for their monitoring (auditors, regulators and inspectors). The appropriate acronym of PAP has been fashioned from all the government's promises, aspirations and pledges. See M. Powell, *Evaluating New Labour's Welfare Reforms* (Bristol, 2002) chs 1 and 12.
4. H. Glennerster, *Understanding the Finance of Welfare* (Bristol, 2003) p. 137.
5. P. Taylor-Gooby, *Welfare states under Pressure* (2001), table 1.8.
6. The *Independent*, 12 August and 28 September 1999. The validity of the British measure of unemployment was discredited by the 31 changes made to its method of calculation by the Conservatives. Unsurprisingly each led to a decrease in numbers. Equally unsurprisingly New Labour, having condemned these changes, showed little interest in reversing them.
7. Another postwar measure of full employment was an unemployed count of less than one million. This was achieved in March 2001, conveniently close to the general election. The current ILO measure, however, was 1.5 million. It was higher because, following continental European practice, it was based on a sample of all those of working age. This included age groups, such as those between 16 and 18 or 60 and 65, who were ineligible for Jobseekers' Allowance as well as other non-claimants, such as those on sickness benefit.
8. The *Independent*, 13 March 2002, talk at the London School of Economics.
9. *New Statesman*, 15 July 1994.
10. *The Times*, 13 March 2002.
11. Blair drove home the point to his opponents, within and outside the Party, at the 2003 Labour Party conference. The Conservatives, he argued 'hated us even more because by occupying the centre ground, by modernising, by reaching out beyond our activists, we helped to turn the Tories into a replica of what we used to be. A narrow base. Obsessed about the wrong things. Old fashioned. In retreat'. See the *Guardian*, 1 October 2003.
12. The 1992 manifesto promised increases of only £3.3 billion, whereas the manifestos in 1987 and 1983 had respectively promised £6 billion and the earth.
13. N. Timmins, *The Five Giants* (2001) pp. 567–8. That the lone parent cut was a

symbolic rather than necessary economy is demonstrated by the fact the annual saving was £60m. The social security budget as a whole was £2 billion underspent in its first two years alone. The cut was effectively restored in the following budget.

14. Ibid., p. 571.
15. For a transcript of the speech and a commentary upon it by leading academics, see R. Walker (ed.), *Ending Child Poverty* (Bristol, 1999).
16. Toynbee and Walker, *Did Things Get Better?*, p. 238.
17. Social Exclusion Unit, *Tackling Social Exclusion* (2004) p. 2. This report summarizes both past action and 'emerging findings'.
18. Timmins, *The Five Giants*, p. 567.
19. This budget, which significantly followed rather than preceded the 2001 election, was hailed by Peter Riddell as a 'distinctively Labour budget with redistributive tax measures and big increases in public expenditure', *The Times*, 18 April 2002.
20. P. Taylor-Gooby and C. Hastie, 'Support for state spending', in A. Park, *British Social Attitudes* (2002), p. 76. The figure reverted to 59 per cent in 2001 with 34 per cent, as opposed to 40 per cent, favouring the *status quo*. The percentage favouring reduced services and taxation remained between 3 per cent and 5 per cent throughout the 1990s.
21. An automatic mechanism to increase fuel tax above the annual rate of inflation had been introduced by the Conservatives to discourage road use on environmental grounds. New Labour's cancellation of this mechanism did not enhance its 'green' credentials.
22. Taylor-Gooby and Hastie, 'Support for state spending', in Park, *British Social Attitudes*, p. 86. Throughout western Europe, social democratic parties were simultaneously under severe electoral presure to cut taxation.
23. This charge was repeated even more controversially in January and October 2002 when implicitly public sector unions as well as HM Opposition were accused of being 'wreckers' and 'forces of conservatism'.
24. The most militant unions were Unison, which annually contributed £1.4 million to the Labour Party, and the NUT, which was the biggest teachers' union but made no regular contribution. The most outspoken leader was John Edmonds of the GMB, which annually contributed £1.3 million. A dinner was arranged by the TUC on 27 June 2001 so that the Prime Minister could meet the unions. It was not a success. In September 2003, however, a public sector forum was created to regularize such contacts. It was the mildest of revivals for postwar corporatism.
25. IPPR, *Building Better Partnerships* (2001).
26. *The Economist*, 22 February 2003.
27. Glennerster, *Understanding the Finance of Welfare*, p. 193.
28. *The Times*, 2 October 2002. For the succeeding defence by Brown, see *The Times*, 6 July 2001.
29. Doubts about the public's eagerness for choice was specifically raised in 2004 in B. Schwarz, *The Paradox of Choice*.
30. For an expansion of the points in this box, see in particular R. Skidelsky, 'Five years Labour', in *Prospect* (May 2002) pp. 22–6. Gordon Brown was ceded control over domestic policy, in much the same way as Ernest Bevin was put in charge of the home front by Churchill during the Second World War. He was accused of frequently treating his Cabinet colleagues as his junior ministers. His greatest achievement has also been seen by many to be not economic stability but welfare reform. See, for example, Peter Riddell in *The Times*, 5 March 2001.

31. This permitted a member of Sinn Fein, Martin McGuiness, to be minister for education. Northern Ireland's peculiar problems are illustrated by the fact that in 2004 more than 90 per cent of schools and social housing remain religiously segregated.

32. There are large regional variations in England, with the north-west and London typically receiving per head more than 10 per cent of the national average, and the south-east over 15 per cent less. See HM Treasury, *Public Expenditure* (Cm 6201, 2004) table 8.2. For the Barnett formula, see Glennerster, *Understanding the Finance of Welfare*, pp. 190–1.

33. See I. McLean and A. McMillan. 'The fiscal crisis in the UK', Nuffield College Working Papers in Politics, 2002W10 (www.nuff.ox.ac.uk/users/McLean).

34. Significantly only two schools in Scotland opted out of local authority control in the 1990s. The internal market, moreover, was never introduced into the Scottish NHS. One of the first appointments in Edinburgh in 1999 was also a minister of social justice. This was not a portfolio New Labour would have openly endorsed – and admittedly the title was soon dropped. In Wales, there were reforms driven by similar values, such as the reintroduction of free prescriptions for the under 25s and learning grants for those in further education.

35. See, for example, the *Guardian*, 13 February 2004: 'Blair: fixing key services will take 15 years'.

36. Toynbee and Walker, *Did Things Get Better?*, p. 9.

15   THE IMPACT OF NEW LABOUR

1. The Beveridge memorial lecture in R. Walker, *Ending Child Poverty* (Bristol, 1999) ch. 2. In his foreword to the first white paper on welfare reform, Tony Blair did refer to 'those of us who believe the welfare state is not just about cash benefits, but is about services too'. This broader definition was reinforced by the first half of the paper's opening paragraph. The second half, however, then asserted that 'the existing system needs reform. For many people the system is increasing their dependence on benefit, rather than helping them to lead independent and fulfilling lives.' The rest of the foreword also concentrated on the failings of the benefit system. This was not an aberration. The 2001 manifesto had separate chapters on 'world-class public services' and 'the welfare state'. See *A New Contract for Welfare* (Cm 3805, 1998) and *Ambitions for Britain: Labour's manifesto, 2001*. Just like Bevan in 1948, it would seem New Labour did not want services like the NHS tainted by association with social security.

2. Quoted in N. Timmins, *The Five Giants* (2001) p. 540. For the following quotations, see Walker, *Ending Child Poverty*, ch.2; Harriet Harman in the *Financial Times*, 7 May 1997; HM Treasury, *Saving and Assets for All* (2001).

3. See above, Chapter 1; and Cmd 6404 (1942) paras 326 and 440.

4. See above, Section 12.1; and A. Deacon, *Perspectives on Welfare* (Buckingham, 2002) pp. 42–8. For a full exposition and discussion of Field's views, see F. Field, *Stakeholder Welfare* (1996).

5. A. Barton, *Unfair and Underfunded* (National Association of Citizens Advice Bureaux, 2002).

6. J. Millar and T. Ridge, 'Parents, children, families and New Labour', in M. Powell (ed.), *Evaluating New Labour's Welfare Reforms* (Bristol, 2002) p. 95.

7. Formally, lone mothers with children under 5 years of age were treated more sympathetically than in liberal welfare states (such as the USA) and social democratic ones (such as Sweden). There they were required to return to work well within a year of giving birth. The psychological damage caused by the constant extolling of paid work was nevertheless real.

8. For this and related issues, see J. Lewis, 'The decline of the male breadwinner model: implications for work and care', *Social Politics*, 8 (2001) pp. 152–69

9. *The Times*, 7 July 2001.

10. The figures for the take-up of all means-tested benefit (estimated at £5 billion unclaimed) were so bad that the government withdrew a report scheduled for September 2001 and only published it in October 2003, perhaps to 'bury bad news' at the height of controversy over the Iraq war. See the *Independent*, 29 March 2003.

11. National Association of Citizens Advice Bureaux, *Work in Progress* (February 2001). Tax credits were another policy transfer from the USA. There, however, they are administered directly by the tax authorities, not through the medium of employers.

12. The *Guardian*, 20 November 2003 and the *Independent*, 22 April 2004.

13. The cost (£5700 p.a. in 2001) was considerably more than the average annual cost to a two-parent family of housing (£4520) or of food (£4400). See Daycare Trust, *The Price Parents Pay* (2001).

14. See, for example, the *Guardian*, 29 June 2002.

15. For a review of the increases, see Millar and Ridge, 'Parents, children, families and New Labour', in Powell (ed.), *Evaluating New Labour's Welfare Reforms*, pp. 88–93.

16. This measure is equivalent to, but provides better comparisons over time than, the older measure of 50 per cent of the *mean* income. This is because a median discounts extremes of wealth, which are an increased feature of income distribution in Britain.

17. The three indicators are: an absolute low-income indicator, a relative low-income indicator, and an indicator which combines relative low income and material deprivation.

18. See, in particular, the Institute of Fiscal Studies commentary 96 by M. Brewer, A. Goodman, M. Myck, J. Shaw and A. Shepherd, *Poverty and Inequality in Britain* (2004).

19. P. Toynbee and D.Walker, *Did Things Get Better?* (Harmondsworth, 2001) p. 25

20. Brewer et al., *Poverty and Inequality in Britain*, p. 2.

21. The change from Field's original proposals was so precipitous that the civil service drafting nightmare was realized: a reference to the jettisoned 'compulsory funded pension' survived in the published white paper, *Partnership in Pensions* (Cm 4179, 1998). See Timmins, *The Five Giants*, p. 573.

22. M. Hewitt, 'New Labour and the redefinition of social security', in Powell (ed.), *Evaluating New Labour's Welfare Reforms*, p. 206.

23. Timmins, *The Five Giants*, p. 613.

24. Measured by inputs (such as the time and income foregone by carers) the value of informal care was estimated at 2.5 per cent of GDP. Measured by outputs (the cost of providing a market alternative to, for example, parenting) the estimate rose to between 19 per cent and 25 per cent. More prosaically, the 2001 census recorded that one-tenth of the population (5.2 million people) regarded themselves as carers: 68 per cent provided up to 19 hours a week, 21 per cent over 50 hours. See H. Glennerster, *Understanding the Finance of Welfare* (Bristol, 2003) p. 81.

25. *Social Trends*, 34 (2002) table 8.2. By 2002, there had been a 77 per cent increase in hours provided since 1992; 64 per cent, as opposed to 2 per cent, were provided by independent contractors

26. In early 2004, up to half of inner-city social work positions remained unfilled. Even major cities such as Edinburgh had vacancy rates of 30 per cent. The market solution to such labour market imbalance is improved pay and conditions.

27. M. Baldwin, 'New labour and social care', in Powell (ed.), *Evaluating New Labour's Welfare Reforms*, p. 183.

28. Ralf Dahrendorf, quoted in E. Brunsdon and M. May, 'Evaluating New Labour's approach to independent welfare provision' in ibid., p. 70. The possibility was raised in 2003 of VCOs being granted 25-year contracts which would give them the time and assured income to think and invest long term. See the *Guardian*, 10 December 2003.

29. The minority report's concerns were borne out by the Treasury's Supporting People initiative, designed to help vulnerable tenants, such as those with learning difficulties or mental health problems. In 2004 it overran its £0.8 billion budget by more than 100 per cent. This was because of higher expectations generated by a high quality initiative, and the speed with which other carers (such as local authorities) absolved themselves from their earlier responsibilities.

30. It was the fate of the family home which made the issue so political. Because of increasing longevity and rising house prices, homes were increasingly having to be sold to meet means-tested bills. Before the 1997 election Tony Blair had highlighted this as an example of 'Thatcherite' callousness. The minority report 'resolved' the issue by suggesting homes should only have be sold after an elderly person's death. The state in effect would provide a loan which the heirs had to repay.

31. The cause of private owners was vocally championed by new vested groups, such as the English Community Care Association, which were far from disinterested.

32. See the *Independent*, 30 April 2004. Other tragedies were the deaths of Lauren Creed (1997) and Lauren Wright (2000) at the hands of a step-parent and Ainlee Walker (2002) at the hands of her parents. Each enquiry criticized the lack of liaison and delays which characterized the handling of each case by social workers.

33. Reported in *The Times*, 2 October 2002.

34. See the executive summary of *The NHS Plan: a plan for investment, a plan for reform* at www.doh.gov.uk/nhs.htm

35. Toynbee and Walker, *Did Things Get Better?*, p. 83. The reference to a 'last-chance saloon' was made by the secretary of state for health, Alan Milburn. For this and the reaction of consultants, see Timmins, *The Five Giants*, pp. 593, 596.

36. The first Wanless report was divided between an interim and a final report. The figures for underspend and the quotation are taken from the interim report, para. 2.21, 2.24 and 3.20. Both reports were only published electronically and can be located at www.hm-treasury.gov.uk For an excellent review of the competing methods of financing healthcare, see C. Propper, 'Expenditure on healthcare in the UK', *Fiscal Studies*, 22 (2001) pp. 151–83.

37. *Securing Good Health for the Whole Population*, p. 10 (www.hm-treasury.gov.uk).

38. For both polls, see S. Leatherman and K. Sutherland, *The Quest for Quality in the NHS* (2003), pp. 17 and 147. This report, published by the Nuffield Trust, draws together a wide range of independent evidence in a comprehensive evaluation of the government's ten-year Quality Agenda. It is the source for all the succeeding statistics unless otherwise stated.

39. Ibid, p. 11 and Glennerster, *Understanding the Finance of Welfare*, p. 71.

40. Timmins, *The Five Giants*, pp. 463 and 598.

41. Leatherman and Sutherland, *The Quest for Quality in the NHS*, p. 8.

42. Glennerster, *Understanding the Finance of Welfare*, pp. 74–5. For a summary of the impact of the internal market under the Conservatives, see J. Le Grand, N. Mays and J.-A. Mulligan, *Learning from the NHS Internal Market* (1998). Its relative pessimism was later tempered in J. Le Grand, *From Knave to Knights, from Pawn to Queen: agency and public policy* (Oxford, 2003). This reasserted the author's original faith that a mimicking of the market could empower consumers (transforming them from pawns to queens). Simultaneously it would oblige welfare producers to respond to expressed need more efficiently (thereby ensuring they were altruistic knights rather than selfish knaves).

43. Reported in the *Independent*, 2 October 2003.

44. The text of the paper, delivered on 3 February 2003, was available at www.hm-treasury.gov.uk and has been published as G. Brown, *A Modern Agenda for Prosperity and Social Reform* (Social Market Foundation, 2004).

45. The battle was rejoined in the drafting of the manifesto for the 2005 election. Alan Milburn championed the greater devolution of responsibilities to not-for-profit agencies. As reported in the *Independent* for 7 May 2004, he insisted that 'in a world where the consumer is king, public services can no longer be run by diktat from the top down . . . Giving up power is never easy. But it is necessary.' Whether the consumer was actually prepared to play a more constructive active role was, of course, a moot point. When elections were held for the governing bodies of the first ten foundation hospitals, only 1 per cent of a possible 2 million electors voted. See the *Guardian*, 7 April 2004.

46. The *Independent*, 3 May 2004.

47. See Appendix, Table A.7. Spending nevertheless remained comparable with most OECD countries. See Glennerster, *Understanding the Finance of Welfare*, pp. 106–7.

48. By 2004 the percentage of children reaching the required standard appeared to have stabilized at the marginally lower percentages of 73 in maths and 75 in literacy: the *Independent*, 5 January 2004. Media intrusion and latent Party warfare over university tuition fees also played their part in the minister's decision.

49. R. Naidoo and Y. Muschamp, 'A decent education for all?', in Powell (ed.), *Evaluating New Labour's Welfare Reforms*, p. 152.

50. Glennerster, *Understanding the Finance of Welfare*, p. 108.

51. Toynbee and Walker, *Did Things Get Better?*, p. 53. 'Bog standard' was a term coined by the Prime Minister's press spokesman, Alastair Campbell. It wholly discredited Labour's aspirations in the 1960s.

52. Of the 70 schools named in 2000, however, only 23 were still recorded as underperforming in 2004. See the *Independent*, 5 January 2004. Of the original 18 schools 'named and shamed' one-third were primary schools.

53. Glennerster, *Understanding the Finance of Welfare*, pp. 111–2.

54. The *Independent*, 22 March 2004. Gordon Brown even sought to replicate Conservative efforts in the 1980s to have 'enterprise' taught in schools. See Toynbee and Walker, *Did Things Get Better?*, p. 54.

55. Glennerster, *Understanding the Finance of Welfare*, p. 122.

56. 75 per cent of middle-class children reached the five required grades, but only 25 per cent of working-class ones. See the *Independent*, 13 February 2004. One

imaginative attempt to combat continuing deprivation was the £7 million programme to provide all primary school children with free meals in Hull, one of the lowest LEAs in the league tables. See the *Guardian*, 13 February 2004.

57. These initiatives were not particularly successful. Two-thirds of the money allocated to the first year of the New Deal, for example, was not spent. This was in part due to the difficulty of arranging the required level of collaboration with local businesses and community groups. In relation to social exclusion, arrangements were also made to give housing benefit – like other social security benefits – a disciplinary element. Benefit could be denied anti-social tenants.

58. Urban Task Force, *Towards an Urban Renaissance* (1999).

59. *New Labour Because Britain Deserves Better* (1997) p. 27. For figures of the homeless, see *Social Trends*, 34 (2004) fig. 10.14.

60. The *Guardian*, 16 January 2004. For the situation in Glasgow, see M. Jones and R. Lowe, *From Beveridge to Blair* (Manchester, 2002), section 5.3.5; and the *Guardian*, 6 April 2002.

61. B. Lund, 'Safe as houses?', in Powell (ed.), *Evaluating New Labour's Welfare Reforms*, p. 114. For Dick Turpin, see the *Independent*, 22 May 2000. For an excellent introduction to the mysteries of housing benefit, see Glennerster, *Understanding the Finance of Welfare*, pp. 170–2.

62. Lund, 'Safe as houses?', p. 120.

63. As the *Guardian*, for example, reported on 12 October 2002 after the party conferences: 'this new conference season produced a new consensus in politics. The man in Whitehall – the man who used to know best – is now probably the most reviled figure in British politics.'

64. See Section 15.3.

65. See P. Taylor-Gooby (ed.), *Welfare States under Pressure* (2001) pp. 169, 198. Taylor-Gooby agrees that convergence was driven by the commitment of both Parties to maintain economic competitiveness in a global economy and a belief that low taxation was essential for electoral success. Furthermore, 'much of the disagreement' between the Parties was 'on matters of degree rather than principle'.

66. Toynbee and Walker, *Did Things Get Better?*, p. 1.

67. The following analysis is based on the exceptional overview provided for the Institute of Fiscal Studies by Brewer et al., *Poverty and Inequality in Britain* (2004). For an equally good historical study, see P. Johnson, 'Welfare state, income and living standards', in R. Floud and P. Johnson, *The Cambridge Economic History of Modern Britain*, vol. 3 (Cambridge, 2004) ch. 9.

68. P. Pierson, *The New Politics of Welfare* (Oxford, 2001) p. 10.

69. R. Skidelsky, 'Five year's Labour', in *Prospect* (May 2002) 26.

70. For attempts to modernize healthcare internationally, see C. Ham, R. Robinson and M. Benzeval, *Health Check* (1990). In 2000, the World Health Organisation officially proclaimed the French health service as the best in the world. Such an accolade rested uneasily with its condemnation in 2004 by an official committee, the Haut Conseil Pour L'Avenir de L'Assurance-maladie. It detected a wholesale lack of control over both the demand for and supply of medical care. The consequence was a lethal mix of excessive spending, increasing shortages and threatened bankruptcy. See the *Independent*, 2 January 2004.

Glossary of Acronyms

AHA   Area Health Authority
AHC   after housing costs
ALMOs   arm-length management organizations
BHC   before housing costs
BMA   British Medical Council
CAT   College of Advanced Technology
CBI   Confederation of British Industry
CHAI   Commission on Health Care Audit and Inspection
CHI   Commission for Health Improvement
COS   Charity Organisation Society
CPAG   Child Poverty Action Group
CPRS   Central Policy Review Staff
CSA   Child Support Agency
CSO   Central Statistical Office
CTC   child tax credit
DfEE   Department for Education and Employment
DHSS   Department of Health and Social Security
DIG   Disabled Income Group
DSS   Department of Social Security
EEC   European Economic Community
EMS   Emergency Medical Service
EMS   European Monetary System
FIS   family income supplement
GDP   Gross Domestic Product
GLC   Greater London Council
GNP   Gross National Product
HATs   Housing Action Trusts
HMC   Hospital Management Committee
IEA   Institute of Economic Affairs
ILO   International Labour Organization
IMF   International Monetary Fund
IPPR   Institute for Public Policy Research
IRC   Industrial Reorganization Corporation
LCC   London County Council
LMS   local management of schools
MIG   minimum income guarantee
MSC   Manpower Services Commission
MTFS   medium term financial strategy
NACRO   National Association for the Care and Resettlement of Prisoners

NATO	North Atlantic Treaty Organization
NEC	National Executive Committee
NEDC	National Economic Development Council
NEDO	National Economic Development Office
NHS	National Health Service
NICE	National Institute of Clinical Excellence
NSF	national service frameworks
NVQs	National Vocational Qualifications
OECD	Organization for Economic Cooperation and Development
OPEC	Organization of Petroleum-Exporting Countries
PC	pension credit
PCT	Primary Care Trust
PEP	Political and Economic Planning
PESC	Public Expenditure Survey Committee
PFI	Private Finance Initiative
PPPs	Public Private Partnerships
RHA	regional health authority
RHB	Regional Hospital Board
SERPS	State-Earnings-Related Pension Scheme
TECs	Training and Enterprise Councils
TNA	The National Archives
TUC	Trades Union Congress
TVEI	Technical and Vocational Education Initiative
VCOs	voluntary and community organizations
WFTC	working family tax credit
WTC	working tax credit
WVS	Women's Voluntary Service

Index